Congress and Public Policy

A Source Book of Documents and Readings

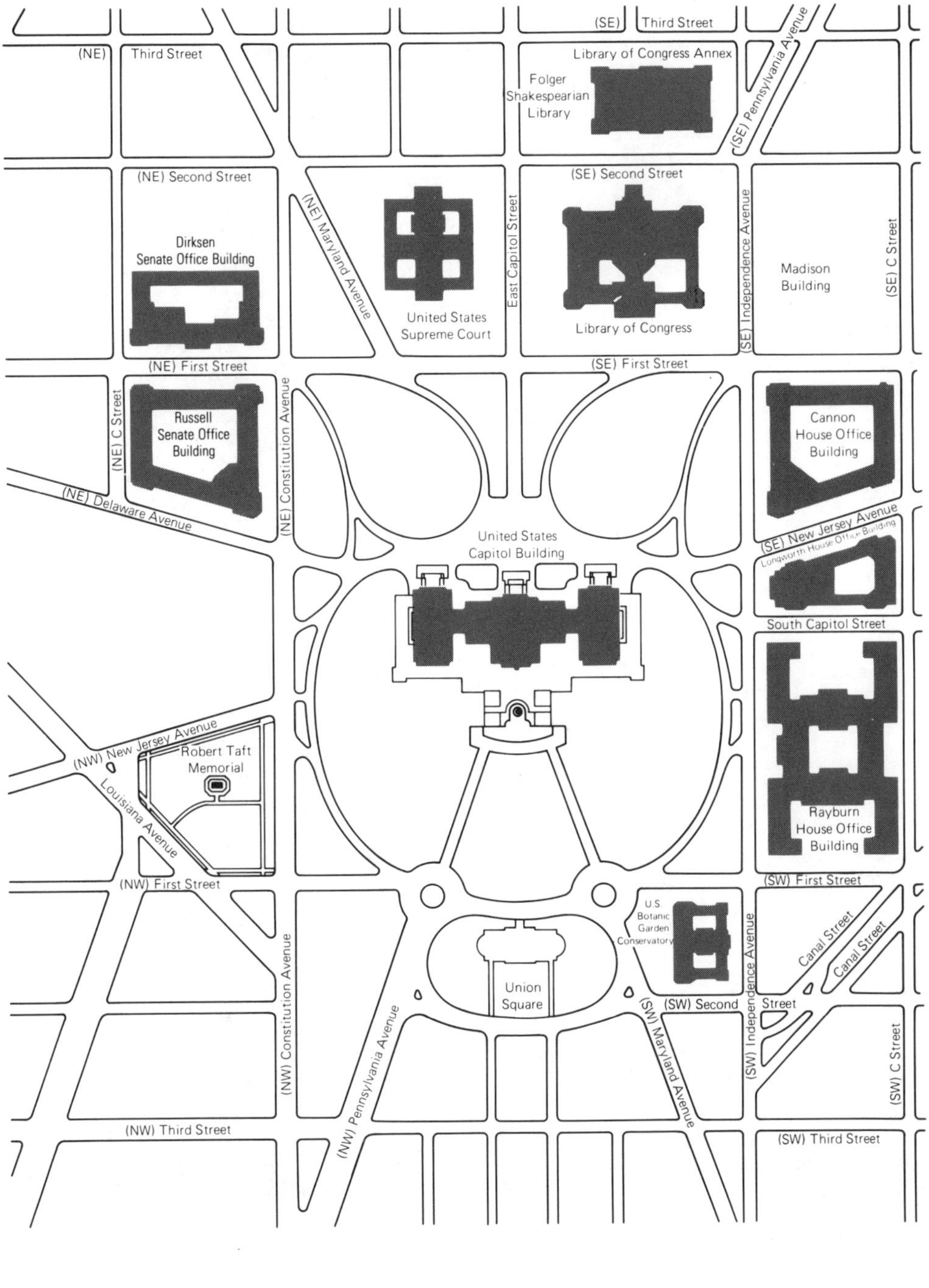

(SE) Third Street
(NE) Third Street
Library of Congress Annex
Folger Shakespearian Library
(SE) Pennsylvania Avenue
(NE) Second Street
(SE) Second Street
(NE) Maryland Avenue
East Capitol Street
(SE) Independence Avenue
(SE) C Street
Dirksen Senate Office Building
United States Supreme Court
Library of Congress
Madison Building
(NE) First Street
(SE) First Street
(NE) C Street
Russell Senate Office Building
(NE) Constitution Avenue
Cannon House Office Building
(NE) Delaware Avenue
(SE) New Jersey Avenue
United States Capitol Building
Longworth House Office Building
South Capitol Street
(NW) New Jersey Avenue
Robert Taft Memorial
Louisiana Avenue
Rayburn House Office Building
(NW) First Street
(SW) First Street
U.S. Botanic Garden Conservatory
Canal Street
Canal Street
(NW) Constitution Avenue
Union Square
(SW) Second Street
(SW) Independence Avenue
(NW) Pennsylvania Avenue
(SW) Maryland Avenue
(SW) C Street
(NW) Third Street
(SW) Third Street

The Dorsey Series in Political Science
Consulting Editor **Samuel C. Patterson** The University of Iowa

Congress and Public Policy

A Source Book of Documents and Readings

Edited by

David C. Kozak, Ph.D.
The National War College Faculty

and

John D. Macartney, Ph.D.
Formerly, United States Air Force Academy Faculty

1982

THE DORSEY PRESS
Homewood, Illinois 60430

ISBN 0-256-02664-5
Library of Congress Catalog Card No. 81–70948

Printed in the United States of America

1 2 3 4 5 6 7 8 9 0 ML 9 8 7 6 5 4 3 2

To our children
Steve Macartney
Jeffrey, Timothy, and Jacqueline Kozak

Foreword

The view of Congress from those who work on Capitol Hill is much different from that of those who have not shared this enriching experience.

Next to a three-month internship during college (most members of Congress offer this experience to bright young applicants) or a two-year stint on a congressperson's staff (these jobs are also available to any bright young college graduate who is willing to brave Washington's notorious weather), this collection edited by Professors Kozak and Macartney is as good a documentation as I have seen of the current workings of Congress.

The discussions of Congress—history, elections, committee procedures, party machinations, floor rules, decision making, policy relationships, and perhaps most of all, change—provide a political science course most universities can never match. Selections from both scholarly and governmental sources reflect the difference between academic and practitioner perspectives. Former members Jim Lloyd and Fred Harris furnish a behind-the-scenes view most college professors without Hill experience can never understand. The precise examples of bills, rules, committee reports, information sources, and the *Congressional Record* are more educational than a thousand newspaper articles describing them.

The editors' work covers ground which has previously gone unreported, partly because congresspersons, like most professionals, are not overly anxious that the public learn the entire truth about their professions. Macartney's study of staff and home districts is illuminating, as is Kozak's huge study of congressional decision making.

To one who has served in the House for 14 years and who views the greatest hope for America as a growing cadre of U.S. citizens who care deeply enough about their country to work with, educate, and bring enlightened pressure upon their elected representatives in Washington, this book is one I would like to see widely circulated and read.

Honorable Paul N. McCloskey, Jr., R., Calif.*

* Editors note: "Pete" McCloskey gained national prominence in 1972 when, as a member of the House, he challenged incumbent Richard Nixon for the Republican presidential nomination. He is leaving the House at the end of the 97th Congress in 1982 to seek a U.S. Senate seat from California.

Preface

This is a unique academic reader as well as a collection of data and documents about the Congress of the United States. While many selections here will be familiar to those who keep up with the literature, much of the material—more than half—comes from a different and heretofore untapped source: congressional documents. That source is a goldmine!

We know of no other institution that has committed so much effort to self-analysis nor produced so many high-quality, readable studies of itself. Over the past decade, Capitol Hill has convened a number of special committees and commissions, each given the task of analyzing the Legislative Branch and producing reform proposals. After the Bolling Committee came the Obey Commission. Meanwhile, over in the Senate, there were the Stevenson Committee and the Hughes Commission, and, back in the House, just last year, the Patterson Committee.* Congressional scholars know only too well the rather meager outcomes of those reform efforts. But of more lasting value are the analytical outputs, the by-products.

Although many of the specific reform recommendations came to naught, their legacy is volume upon volume of high-quality data and analysis written by both reputable scholars and staff members of the Congressional Research Service, selections of which are in this book.

In assembling this reader, we found that the reports of those prominent reform commissions were really only the tip of a documentary iceberg. To begin with, many working papers and preliminary studies were produced that did not make it into the final reports. We've included some of those. Beyond that, we discovered an

* The formal titles of these bodies are: Bolling (House Select Committee on Committees, 1973–74); Obey (Commission on Administrative Review, 1976–77); Hughes (Commission on the Operation of the Senate, 1975–76); Stevenson (Senate Select Committee on Committees, 1976–77); and Patterson (House Select Committee on Committees, 1979–80). The reform efforts are named after their chairmen: Representative Richard Bolling (D–Mo.), Representative David Obey (D–Wis.), Senator Harold Hughes (D–Iowa), Senator Adlai Stevenson, Jr. (D–Ill.), and Representative Jerry M. Patterson (D–Calif.).

incredible array of useful material in such miscellaneous Hill products as a Senate history inserted into the *Congressional Record* by Senator Robert Byrd (D–W. Va.), a handbook for newly hired congressional employees, glossy public information handouts, detailed synopses of legislative procedures, histories provided by various leadership offices, internal publications such as *Staff* magazine, research products, as well as bylaws from various caucuses, and releases from lobbying groups. Generally speaking, this material is well written and very informative.

In addition to the analytical materials described above, we've included a number of exhibit documents, examples of everyday items on the Hill—a bill, a rule, a Whip Notice, a few pages from a calendar, a Dear Colleague letter, and such. The idea here is to give readers, especially undergraduate students, a source book that features an experiential insider's "feel" for the legislative milieu and "blood" of Congress. Undergraduates, especially, should be interested in the example of a report, rule, and bill presented in this book. All pertain to the 1980 draft registration.

The book is not only made up of congressional documents and exhibits, of course. We've supplemented that material with a number of excellent excerpts and articles from academic books and journals, together with original essays by leading authorities. The resulting volume, we believe, will be useful to graduate scholars as well as new staffers and interested observers of Congress and public policy and, in particular, for undergraduate courses focused on the Hill. Our basic intention is to provide a collection that advances an understanding of basic concepts and fundamental points.

The substance and organization reflects the two editors' very different approaches to matters congressional. Both teach and write about Congress, but David Kozak is more apt to focus on the legislative process and the floor votes of members, while John Macartney is fascinated by the organizational/bureaucratic dynamics and the contributions of staff. Those orientations are evident in the table of contents, which also reveals selections on the history of Congress, elective politics, the membership, the committee system, partisan leadership, legislative rules and procedures, and public policy.

As is the case in all major endeavors, this project was not completed alone. The editors received much advice, encouragement, and assistance. Professor Samuel C. Patterson, editorial adviser for the Dorsey series in political science, provided the initial impulse. Walter Oleszek and Roger Davidson of the Congressional Research Service were instrumental in pointing the way to a wealth of documents. Indeed, Oleszek's bookshelves at CRS were an absolutely indispensable source, especially for working papers from now-disbanded committees and commissions. Two former members of Congress, Representative Jim Lloyd and Senator Fred Harris (both political scientists) were especially helpful. Along with encouragement and sage advice came original pieces from each. Also, Jim Lloyd made his Hill office available to us as a base while we were chasing down all those documents in the fall of 1980. In addition, he gave a great deal of useful advice that has found its way into these pages. Much thanks goes to Brigid Davis, formerly of Lloyd's staff and now with Congressman Tom Lantos (D–Calif.).

Overall, the lion's share of kudos and thanks are due to Maryanne M. Kozak. Nominally a part-time secretarial assistant for this project, her contributions greatly exceeded her status. Along with her own busy life as a wife, mother, and English instructor at the University of Colorado, she did everything from typing to proofreading, correspondence, and editing. We simply could not have made it without her. Finally, we should acknowledge the role of the mails and long-distance telephone. After spending a number of years together on the Air Force Academy faculty, both editors were reassigned in the summer of 1981—Dave to Washington and John to Honolulu. Thus the final frenzied months of manuscript preparations were completed while the co-editors were separated by some 5,000 miles.

It goes without saying that we remain fully responsible for the contents, although we'll always be tempted to claim that the inevitable minor discrepancies or omissions were probably the fault of our employer, our publisher, the individual contributors, the other co-editor, or mischievous gremlins.

D.C.K.
J.D.M.

Contributors

Aberbach, Joel D. Professor of Political Science and Public Policy and Research Scientist at the Institute of Public Policy Studies, The University of Michigan.

Abramowitz, Alan I. Assistant Professor of Government at the College of William and Mary.

Bacheller, John M. Research Associate, New York State Senate.

Bullock, Charles S., III. Richard Russell Professor of Political Science, University of Georgia.

Carroll, Holbert N. Professor of Political Science, University of Pittsburgh.

Davidson, Roger H. Government and Public Administration at the Congressional Research Service, U.S. Library of Congress, and Professor of Political Science at the University of California, Santa Barbara.

Fenno, Richard F., Jr. Professor of Political Science at the University of Rochester.

Fisher, Louis. Specialist in American National Government at the Congressional Research Service, Library of Congress.

Franklin, Grace A. Senior Research Associate at the Mershon Center at the Ohio State University.

Getz, Robert S. Professor of Political Science, University of New York, Brockport.

Hammond, Susan Webb. Faculty member of the School of Government and Public Administration, American University.

Harris, Fred R. Professor of Political Science, the University of New Mexico, and a former United States Senator.

Hillier, Carol M. Deputy Director of the Law Library at the General Accounting Office.

Johannes, John R. Associate Professor and Chairman, Department of Political Science, Marquette University, Milwaukee, Wisconsin.

Jones, Charles O. Robert Kent Gooch Professor of Government and Foreign Affairs at the University of Virginia.

Keefe, William J. Professor of Political Science at the University of Pittsburgh.

Kimmet, J. S. Secretary of the United States Senate from 1977–1980.

Lloyd, Jim. Member of Congress (D.–Calif.), 1974–1980 and a college teacher.

Lockwood, Robert S. Permanent Professor of Law & Politics at The National War College in Washington, D.C.

Mayhew, David R. Professor of Political Science, Yale University.

Nelson, Garrison. Associate Professor of Political Science at the University of Vermont.

Oleszek, Walter J. Specialist on Congress, Congressional Research Service, Library of Congress.

Ogul, Morris S. Professor and Chairman of Political Science, University of Pittsburgh.

Ornstein, Norman J. Professor of Political Science at Catholic University, Adjunct Scholar at the American Enterprise Institute, and Political Editor for "The Lawmakers," a weekly TV series on PBS.

Parker, Glenn R. Associate Professor of Political Science at Florida State University.

Patterson, Samuel C. Professor of Political Science at the University of Iowa.

Polsby, Nelson W. Professor of Political Science, University of California, Berkeley.

Riddick, Floyd M. Parliamentarian Emeritus of the United States Senate.

Ripley, Randall B. Professor and Chairperson in the Department of Political Science at the Ohio State University.

Rohde, David. Professor and Chairman of the Department of Political Science at Michigan State University.

Runquist, Barry S. Associate Professor of Political Science at the University of Illinois at Chicago Circle.

Schneider, Jerrold E. Associate Professor of Political Science at the University of Delaware.

Strom, Gerald S. Associate Professor of Political Science at the University of Illinois at Chicago Circle.

Walker, Jack L. Professor of Political Science and Public Policy, Institute of Public Policy Studies, the University of Michigan.

Willett, Edward F., Jr., Esq. The Law Revision Counsel of the United States House of Representatives.

Zeidenstein, Harvey G. Professor of Political Science at Illinois State University.

Zweben, Murray. The Parliamentarian of the U.S. Senate from 1975–1980.

EDITORS

Kozak, David C. BA, Gannon College; MA, Kent State University; advanced work Wichita State University; Ph.D., University of Pittsburgh. Formerly Associate Professor, U.S. Air Force Academy and Adjunct Professor, Graduate School of Public Affairs, University of Colorado. Currently Professor, The National War College and 1981–82 American Political Science Association Congressional Fellow.

Macartney, John D. BS, USAF Academy; MA, Ph.D., University of California, Los Angeles. Career Air Force officer and fighter pilot, currently serving on the staff, Commander-in-Chief Pacific, in Hawaii. Former Associate Professor at both the U.S. Air Force Academy and The National War College.

Contents

CHAPTER 1

The Historical Context

As with any institution, Congress must be viewed in historical context in order to be understood.

A historical review of Congress is most revealing. It shows over time different organizations, different relationships with Presidents, different public expectations and demands. The Congress of the 20th century is a very different animal from the Congress of the 18th and 19th centuries, and there is every reason to believe that the Congress of the 21st century will be strikingly different from its 20th-century predecessor.

The selections in this section will address the historical context of Congress by illustrating different normative perspectives that have evolved over time and by examining recent changes in the modern Congress.

1.1 Theories of Congress*

Roger H. Davidson, David M. Kovenok, and Michael K. O'Leary

Throughout American history several contending theories have emerged concerning the role of Congress in the American polity. In the following selection, Davidson, Kovenok, and O'Leary argue that the three major theories of Congress differ in terms of the functions of the legislature they choose to emphasize. This piece is especially useful for its enumeration of the major functions of Congress.

---

* From *Congress in Crisis,* by Roger H. Davidson, David M. Kovenok, and Michael K. O'Leary, pp. 15–36. Copyright © 1966 by Wadsworth, Inc. Reprinted by permission of the publisher, Brooks/Cole Publishing Company, Monterey, California.

The Congress that emerged from the Philadelphia Convention of 1787 was the outgrowth of a prolonged institutional struggle, which affected both sides of the Atlantic and which produced a rather explicit theory of legislative functions. Though scholars often correctly observe that the Founding Fathers were pragmatic politicians who were loath to bind succeeding generations to excessively rigid formulations, they tend to neglect the fact that the pragmatism of the Framers was conditioned by an accepted body of political thought—a set of explicit beliefs about the nature of man and his institutions that were assumed to be valid. The Framers were not always able to see what they had done, but a serious study of their debates and commentaries indicates that they were intensely aware of what it was they *intended* to do.

Nothing less should be asked of contemporary students of legislative institutions. The advice which Harold D. Smith, then director of the Budget Bureau, gave to the LaFollette–Monroney Committee in 1945 is so relevant that it deserves repeating:

> This is a different sort of world from that which existed when the Constitutional Convention devised the framework of our government. Yet we still lack a penetrating and practical restatement of the role of representative assemblies in light of the changing problems under which they operate. . . . Your own talents and the keenest minds you can command could very well be devoted to rethinking the functions of the Congress under present conditions. A sound reformulation of the role of the representative body is basic to all the work of your committee.[1]

This was and is sound intellectual procedure, quite apart from the question of whether the constitutional formula demands radical revision. More important, Smith's injunction has not always been heeded by the proponents of congressional reform, including the LaFollette–Monroney Committee itself.

In recent years, a number of students have devoted explicit attention to the functions that the contemporary Congress performs in the political system.[2] Sometimes their conclusions have led them to propose or to evaluate remedial steps that would alter the roles of Congress or would assist it in performing its present roles more effectively. But it is fair to conclude that, by and large, students of Congress have not been sufficiently attentive to the theory of Congress. Ralph K. Huitt observed that "there is no 'model' of a proper legislature to which men of good intention can repair."[3]

What should be included in a theory of the legislature? Such a theory would begin with a series of factual generalizations specifying those functions that the legislature does in fact perform in a political system. Within this framework, specific traditions and practices may be accounted for and their consequences (intended or not) for the system may be spelled out. The analyst who chooses not to lay down his tools at this point would then set forth his view of an ideal legislature in an ideal system. He would specify the point of disharmony between this ideal world and the real world. Finally he would propose specific innovations that would bring the ideal world into being.

Hopefully, the theorist would be attentive to the probable and the unintended consequences of these innovations. More attention to objectives and possible consequences would make the proposal of reforms more meaningful than it has been in the past.[4]

Implicit in most of the recent writing on congressional reform are concepts that can be categorized into reasonably distinct theories of the proper functions of a legislative body. These theories are three in number: the "literary" theory, based primarily on a literal reading of the Constitution; the "executive-force" theory, which stresses policy leadership emanating from the President and the bureaucracy; and the "party-government" theory, which emphasizes the legislature's responsibility to the national party constituency. In terms of the weight given Congress in relation to the executive, the literary theory comes closest to legislative supremacy, the executive-force theory stands at the opposite pole, and the party-government theory stands somewhere in between. The overall weight that each theory gives to Congress is less important, however, than the kinds of functions which each assigns to Congress and to the other branches of government.

THE LITERARY THEORY

The literary theory is essentially a restatement of the constitutional formulation of blended and coordinate powers—the "institutionalized mutual responsibility of coequals."[5] Adherence to this position need not imply a naive belief that nothing fundamental in the congressional environment has changed since 1789; it does imply, however, that the constitutional delineation of functions is still valid and that the relative weight assigned to the three branches by the Constitution is essentially correct. Proponents of this point of view maintain that Congress should exercise *at least* its present level of power within the political system.

REVERSING THE FLOW OF EVENTS

Advocates of the literary theory are most commonly obsessed with what they interpret as a severe, and perhaps fatal, erosion of congressional prerogatives. James Burnham, whose book *Congress and the American Tradition* is a fascinating and incisive polemic, sounded the theme when he declared:

> What the American government system now needs is . . . a very considerably strengthened Congress: strengthened in the political sense of gaining (regaining, in historical fact) increased relative weight within the political equilibrium. On this assumption . . . the performance of Congress will be judged much less than stellar.[6]

The decline and fall of Congress, according to this theory, can be attributed to three developments. Most fundamental of these developments is the advent of the sprawling welfare state, which makes the Executive Branch the source of many government services now largely beyond legislative control. Secondly, the compelling public image of the strong President and the academic and journalistic criticisms of legislative institutions reduce public support for Congress. Finally, Congress itself abets its declining influence by "failing to fight back stoutly and intelligently" and by dissipating its resistance to encroachments in "verbal complaints and rhetorical grumblings, which fizzle out in petty amendments of administration projects. Congress has been shadow-boxing, not fighting."[7] This theme is often heard from legislators themselves and is reminiscent of former Congressman Dewey Short's (R–Mo.) indictment of the House of Representatives as "that supine, subservient, soporific, supercilious, pusillanimous body of nitwits." Many literary-theory advocates insist that these trends toward executive empire building and judicial activism could be reversed if Congressmen would only "stiffen their spines" against unconstitutional intrusions upon their legislative powers.

At least one literary theorist does not share this pessimism over legislative decline. In fact, argues Willmoore Kendall, Congress wins more frequently than is generally supposed in its tug-of-war with the executive. For one thing, many congressional victories are hidden from public view: President Franklin D. Roosevelt obtained the highly publicized Tennessee Valley Authority, for example, but what ever happened to proposals for a spate of TVAs in other river basins? Second, no one can ever know how many proposals the executive refrains from making because of expected congressional resistance—"the ten thousand . . . drastic proposals cooking away in ten thousand bureaucratic heads in Washington that the attackers [of tradition] do not dare even to embody in a bill, do not dare even to mention, because the proposals would not stand a Chinaman's chance." Thus, Kendall enjoins the supporters of Congress to keep up their courage "if they are going to keep on winning."[8]

THE "REPUBLICAN FORCE."

Advocates of the literary theory predictably perceive that their values and interests are disadvantaged by the policies of the executive and the judiciary, and they look upon revitalization of Congress as the means of reweighting the balance in their favor. This pro-Congress contingent is a not inconsiderable group, which looks to Capitol Hill for the reversal of the long-term trends of centralism and paternalism. This "republican force," as Alfred de Grazia has termed it, has gathered many recruits during the past generation: economic conservatives, who are hostile to post-New Deal social-welfare legislation; advocates of "states' rights," who find local autonomy threatened on every front by the courts and the executive; fundamentalists, who are confused and dismayed by modernism and secularism; and "the rural folk"—rural and small-town interests who feel themselves being plowed under by the alien trends of urbanism. All of these groups demand that Congress be preserved as a check upon the hostile powers entrenched elsewhere in the government system.

Although the contemporary Supreme Court is consistently criticized for usurping the legislative function, the President and his executive establishment are seen as the greatest enemies of the republican virtues. As the president of the Americans for Constitutional Action told the Joint Committee on the Organization of the Congress in June 1965:

> The President is the head of the party. He exercises vast powers in spending the money appropriated by Congress. He represents the father image in the paternalistic order of government. He represents the dominant political philosophy. All the resources of the political party and of socialist-oriented intellectuals are committed to the increase of his powers and to the destruction of the constitutional restraints.[9]

Such critics insist that supporters of a strong Presidency identify Congress as the "obstacle course" to their goals. "As Congress is the bulwark of that [constitutional] system, the goal of the socialist planners is to be won by rendering Congress ineffectual."[10]

Representatives and Senators have reasons quite apart from ideology for resisting the attrition of their powers and their influence. Many express the understandable frustration of men in high public office who find that their actual influence is not what they expected it would be. Thus, Senator Abraham Ribicoff (D–Conn.), certainly no friend of the policy positions of most literary theorists, complained bitterly in 1964 that Congress has "surrendered its rightful leadership in the lawmaking process to the White House." The Legislative Branch, he wrote, "now merely filters legislative proposals from the President. . . . These days no one expects Congress to devise important bills. Instead, the legislative views of the President dominate the press, the public, the Congress itself."[11] This frustration is not uncommon among legislators, regardless of their political affiliation.

Tenets of the Theory

According to the advocates of the literary theory, Congress must assert its right to exercise "all legislative powers." Policies should be initiated by Congress at least as often as by the executive, for "the primary business of the legislature in a democratic republic is to answer the big questions of policy."[12] Executive Branch officials would be consulted on technical aspects of policymaking, but they should be prohibited from lobbying or pressuring. When the executive, by necessity, initiates legislative proposals, it should do so in an advisory capacity, fully respectful of congressional supremacy in lawmaking. The ultimate authority of elected laymen to set priorities on complicated and technical matters is an indispensible feature of democratic government.

For the defender of the literary theory, the legislator's legitimacy as the ultimate policymaker rests on his near-monopoly of the channels of communication to the sovereign electorate. Since the President also is elected by and responsible to the electorate, this monopoly is not total. But the President is the only elected official in the Executive Branch; his constituency is diffuse, his mandate imprecise. Congressmen, on the other hand, are specific and precise representatives, who "necessarily and properly reflect the attitudes and needs of their individual districts.''[13] The legislative process, therefore, is not a simple ''yes'' or ''no'' vote on policy alternatives but a complex combinatorial process through which numerous and shifting minority claims are acknowledged. One contemporary scholar has defended the particularity of congressional representation in the following manner:

> Congress has the strength of the free enterprise system; it multiplies the decision-makers, the points of access to influence and power, and the creative moving agents. It is hard to believe that a small group of leaders could do better. What would be gained in orderliness might well be lost in vitality and in sensitiveness to the pressures for change. Moreover, Congress resembles the social system it serves; it reflects the diversity of the country. There is much to be said for a system in which almost every interest can find some spokesman, in which every cause can strike a blow, however feeble, in its own behalf.[14]

More often than not, in a government modeled on the literary theory, no legislative decision can be reached on momentous political conflicts: on intensely felt issues at least, a government that acts before a ''concurrent majority'' can be found or constructed is tyrannical.[15] Thorough exploration of the consensus of the society is the high function of the elected policymaker and the essence of the ''legislative way of life.'' Neither speed, efficiency, nor ''passing a lot of laws'' are valid indicators of congressional effectiveness in performing these delicate deliberative tasks. From a conservative vantage point, in fact, the refusal to pass laws is often a blessing.

All advocates of the literary theory view executive power with suspicion, but they differ on the extent to which they think the Executive Branch should be cut down. The theory requires merely a semblance of balance among the branches of government; and constitutional history provides ample precedents for a strong and autonomous Executive Branch, as well as an activist Congress. However, one version of the literary theory—which we call the ''Whig'' variant—would enthrone Congress as *the* dominant institution in the political system. This variant of the theory would reduce Presidents to weaklings, even in foreign and military affairs.[16] The degree to which one wishes to pare down executive power is presumably related to the depth of one's dissatisfaction with contemporary political trends.

On this much the literary theory is clear: what Congress proposes, the executive should dispose. The executive branch should engage in the detailed implementation of laws that are as specific and detailed as possible, leaving bureaucrats little leeway for interpretation. Curiously, one advocate of the literary theory, Burnham, takes an opposite view. The bureaucracy, which conducts the day-to-day operations of government, will always be able to circumvent detailed provisos laid down by Congress. Thus he reasons:

> . . . the only way to control the chief officials of the colossal managerial-bureaucratic state is to give an unambiguous main policy directive, to define clear limits, and then to insist on strict public accountability for satisfactory performance. . . .
>
> If the reins are kept too tight, the horse will get the bit in its teeth. They must normally be loose, if the curbing is to be effective. If Congress tries to watch each million, the billions will get away.[17]

In any event, Congress must exercise extensive supervision (usually termed ''oversight'') of the administration of laws, intervening vigorously and often to ensure compliance. And, if necessary, remedial legislation should be passed.

The courts, in this view, should similarly be prevented from usurping legislative functions. The jurists should recognize that a wide variety of ''political questions'' are the proper sphere of only the elected decision makers. In the opinion of the ''constitutionalists,'' the judicial ''lawmaking'' that most impinges upon legislative autonomy is the apportionment ruling.[18] They argue, first, that electoral laws are by nature political questions which should be determined by the elected bodies themselves. Secondly, the Court's newly enunciated ''one man, one vote'' criterion will clearly dilute the influence of the rural minority, thus rendering the collective congressional constituency more nearly like that of the President. This melding of constituencies, in the judgment of constitutionalists, will reduce the healthy dichotomy of the two branches of government. And in political terms, it will submerge those constituencies that have traditionally been championed by Congress but not by the Executive Branch.[19]

The other major area of judicial impingement upon Congress is the Court's review of alleged violations of civil liberties that result from legislative investigations.[20] While others might argue that the Court's involvement in such questions has been marginal and discontinuous, the constitutionalist interprets such forays as a trespass upon Congress' control over its own rules and procedures.

Reform Propositions

While there may be differences of opinion on precise means-ends relationships, the following list of reform propositions would probably be approved by most advocates of the literary theory:

A. Constituencies and the electoral system
   1. Rather than rigid adherence to the "one man, one vote" principle, legislative apportionment should recognize the validity of other criteria of representation—geographic interests, for example, or political subdivisions—in order to ensure that the greatest possible diversity of interests is embodied in Congress.
   2. Congress itself—probably in concert with state and local authorities—should exercise authority over whatever electoral devices are employed.
   3. The electorate should be educated on congressional government through the initiation of public relations campaigns and the provision of more time for legislators in their districts.

B. Political parties
   1. Innovations that would centralize the party under noncongressional control (for example, through national party councils) should be resisted.
   2. Diversified, rather than "responsible," party structure should be encouraged to stress the party function of building a national consensus.[21]

C. The Presidency
   1. The 22nd Amendment, which limits the President to two terms, should be maintained.
   2. The presidential discretion in implementing policies and in withholding information from Congress should be limited.
   3. Presidential messages should be answered by formal speeches from congressional leaders, both majority and minority.
   4. The proposal that plans initiated by the President become effective unless vetoed by Congress should be opposed.

D. Congressional procedures
   1. Staffs for individual legislators and committees should be moderately increased, with maximum staff assistance for minority members—perhaps even in reverse ratio to the size of the minority representation in Congress.
   2. Attempts to centralize congressional leadership should be resisted in order to maximize the deliberative and even obstructionist tendencies of the individual legislators.[22]
   3. Moderate dilatory devices, such as the Senate filibuster and a strong House Rules Committee, should be sanctioned.
   4. Legislators should continue to help constituents in dealing with the Executive Branch bureaucracy (so-called casework).
   5. Congressional oversight of the executive should be facilitated through increased use of the General Accounting Office, of budgetary controls, of special investigative subcommittees, and

of detailed committee review of legislation, appointments, and appropriations.

6. Congress should resist formal ties to the executive through joint legislative-executive councils and should avoid dependence upon Executive Branch agencies for such commodities as travel or research facilities.

THE EXECUTIVE-FORCE THEORY

In a sense, the executive-force theory reverses the formulation of the literary theory: the executive initiates and implements; the legislature modifies and ratifies.

WHICH WAY IS HISTORY GOING?

The rationales for the executive-force theory illustrate the ambiguities of historical interpretation. Advocates of this theory either (*a*) concur with the constitutionalists' thesis that the balance of power has shifted radically toward the Executive Branch but propose that reforms should be instituted to ensure this new executive hegemony or (*b*) disagree entirely with that assessment and hold that legislative intimidation of executives is now more extreme than ever before. In either case, the conclusion is that the executive establishment ought to be granted wide latitude for decision making and substantial insulation from legislative obstruction.

Adherents of the first rationale—the shift of the balance of power toward the executive—cite historical precedents to show that presidential ascendancy is a fulfillment of original constitutional principles. Indeed, they hold that the ponderous counterbalances devised by the Founding Fathers are viable only when supplemented by an initiator-ratifier relationship between the White House and Capitol Hill.

The architects of the Presidency at the Constitutional Convention—Alexander Hamilton, James Wilson, and Gouverneur Morris—were advocates of strong and vigorous executive responsibility. Hamilton praised "energy" as the outstanding feature of good government and declared that all men of good sense must agree on the necessity of an energetic executive.[23] Federalist political theory showed a decided preference for the executive partly because of its distrust of the people. As Leonard White has characterized the Federalist position, "Decisions on programs thought out by [well-educated and cultivated] national leaders might be subject to the vote of popular assemblies, but the latter . . . had neither the capacity, nor the unity, to work out the plans themselves."[24]

The precedents established by the strong Presidents lend historical weight to this argument. Referring to Thomas Jefferson's active intervention in legislation, Congressman Richard Bolling explains that the early House of Representatives was "the organ of ratification of the decisions presented to it by those members . . . who . . . sat as agents of the President and his advisors."[25] The demands of the national emergency—prompt, concerted action and clarity of policy—have repeatedly strengthened the executive branch. Looking back on the remarkable performance of the first New Deal Congress, Franklin Roosevelt observed: "The letter of the Constitution wisely declared a separation, but the impulse of common purpose declares a union."[26]

The present age of permanent semicrisis has reinforced this historical tendency because every contemporary President is required to be strong. The pull of executive leadership is thus seen as inevitable and irreversible. "The cause of the opponents of a strong Presidency," Rossiter writes with finality, "is ill-starred because they cannot win a war against American history. The strong Presidency is the product of events that cannot be undone and of forces that continue to roll."[27]

The theory of the President-as-chief-legislator would appear to be an abstraction of things as they are. But some critics, not so sanguine about the course of recent events, still see the cards stacked in favor of the legislature; they believe the legislative branch more meddlesome than ever. Columnist Walter Lippmann, often called Washington's "philosopher-in-residence," paints a bleak picture of executives cowering before the rampant power of legislatures. When the New Frontier program ran into legislative deadlock in 1963, he questioned, "What kind of legislative body is it that will not or cannot legislate?" And writing on the Fourth of July that year, he voiced his fears for the future of representative government:

> I find myself thinking how rarely free governments have been overthrown by foreign tyrants, except temporarily in time of war, but how often free governments have fallen because of their own weakness and incapacity. To one thinking such thoughts there is nothing reassuring about the present Congress.[28]

In Lippmann's opinion, "derangement" of powers has occurred at the governmental level because representative assemblies, supported by mass opinion, have acquired "the monopoly of effective powers." The "enfeebled" executive can no longer act decisively or rationally to solve complex public problems.[29]

A somewhat less cataclysmic interpretation of the "deadlock of democracy" is given by James M. Burns in his highly publicized critique of the Madisonian system of mutual distrust and irresponsibility. Entrenched on Capitol Hill by gerrymandered districts and the seniority system, legislators from stagnant, one-party regions are able to thwart liberal, urban majorities that represent the "presidential wings" of the two parties.[30]

From their vantage point at the western reaches of Pennsylvania Avenue, Presidents themselves are fervent believers in the power of Congress to frustrate their programs. In his television report of December 1962, President Kennedy admitted with a note of irony that "the fact is . . . that the Congress looks more powerful sitting here than it did when I was there in the Congress."[31]

The President's Constituency

The legitimacy of executive dominance rests on a concept of representation quite at variance with the Madison–Calhoun pluralism of the literary theorists. As the only official elected by the whole population, the President is considered the embodiment of the nation. Legislators represent partial and minority interests; the President represents the "general will" of the community. Burns has given a more precise definition of this dichotomy:

> The Madisonian system finds its tension in the competition among struggling groups, multiparty factions, and mutually checking branches of government. The Jeffersonian system, a more hierarchical arrangement, finds its tension in the relation of leader and led, with the leader usually pressing his troops, like an army commander, and the troops usually restraining, but sometimes outrunning, their leader.[32]

Thus, Theodore Roosevelt saw the President as a "steward of the people"; and, some years before his own elevation to the office, Woodrow Wilson sensed its representative potentialities. "His is the only national voice in affairs," he declared in his 1907 Columbia University lectures. "He is the representative of no constituency, but of the whole people."[33]

The electoral rationale for Executive Branch dominance has obvious consequences. Because of the pivotal power of large urban states in presidential elections and the importance of urban centers within each state under the winner-take-all electoral-college system, contemporary Presidents have become attuned to the forces of urbanism, minority rights, and the social-welfare state. And because of his unique role as the "nation's sole organ in foreign affairs," the modern President must consider his foreign "constituencies." In contrast, the congressional power system places leadership in the hands of "those members . . . least aware of the problems of industrial society and least equipped to deal with them."[34] The reaction, localism, and delay of Congress acts as a brake on the progressive nationalism of the executive. Congress must be reconstituted if it is to participate in the policies of the President and his partisans "to save ourselves from nuclear destruction, help the world feed its children and protect their lands from totalitarian Communism, put our people to work and make our cities habitable, and realize the fact as well as the name of equality."[35]

Tenets of the Theory

The executive-force theory seeks to mitigate Congress' "historic role of obstructionism."[36] First, Congress must recognize that "the executive is the active power in the state, the asking and the proposing power."[37] As a prominent liberal Democratic Congressman explains, "It is the natural thing for the executive branch to take the initiative, to make proposals, and to present us with programs."[38] Congress is "the consenting power, the petitioning, the approving and the criticizing, the accepting and the refusing power."[39] Second, Congress cannot administer or "manage and meddle" in administrative provinces. As Joseph P. Harris has cautioned:

> It is not the function of the legislature to participate in executive decisions or share responsibility with executive officers, for which it is ill equipped, but rather to check on the administration in order to hold the officers in charge accountable for their decisions and for management and results.[40]

The executive-dominance theory thus emphasizes oversight as in the 1946 Legislative Reorganization Act's injunction that congressional committees exercise "continuous watchfulness" over executive agencies within their jurisdiction. To prevent this watchfulness from degenerating into meddling, however, executive theorists usually specify that congressional review be in terms of generalized policy considerations rather than details.[41]

Executive theorists point out, however, that congressional policy initiation need not be wholly foreclosed. If the President fails to act, or if there are gaps at the fringes of public policy, Congress can and must serve as a "seedbed for the breeding and maturing of new legislative ideas."[42] Senator J. William Fulbright's (D–Ark.) view of the congressional partnership in foreign policy is a notable example of this congressional role. He reasons that, although Congress is poorly equipped to participate in "short-term policies and . . . day-to-day operations," it can cooperate effectively in debating "longer-range, more basic questions" and in initiating ideas "on the periphery."[43] Fulbright's own record of initiating policy alternatives demonstrates that this role need not be a niggardly one.

Reform Propositions

With the usual caveat on the complexity of means-ends relationships in mind, an observer may expect proponents of the executive-force theory to advocate the following reforms of Congress:

A. Parties and the electoral system
   1. Reapportionment on the basis of population should be strongly supported on the assumption that elements of the presidential constituency (for example, urban and suburban areas) would thereby be strengthened in Congress.
   2. National party councils to develop and implement a truly national party program should be strengthened; campaign finances should be centralized in the hands of the national committees.
   3. Four-year terms that would coincide with the presidential terms should be enacted for Representatives. (Similar four-year terms for Senators would probably be desirable.)

B. The Presidency
   1. The 22nd Amendment should be repealed.
   2. Funds for the Executive Branch should be appropriated on a long-term basis—two years or more.
   3. The President should be granted an "item veto"—that is, part of a measure could be vetoed without nullifying the entire bill.

C. Congressional rules and procedures
   1. Congress should be required to act on all executive proposals within a specified period of time (for example, six months).
   2. Strong, centralized congressional parties should be created.

3. The seniority system for selecting committee leaders should be discontinued, and elections by majority and minority caucuses should be substituted.
4. Individual Congressmen and Senators should be relieved of constituent "casework," and an Office of Administrative Counsel, under the general control of Congress, should be created to perform this service.
5. Congress should grant relatively broad mandates to executive agencies and should cease such harassing tactics as one-year authorizations or required committee clearances for certain executive actions.

PARTY-GOVERNMENT THEORY

Party government is the logical extension, and perhaps the end result, of the executive-force theory; but its roots and emphases are sufficiently distinct to warrant separate treatment. Actually, it is not a theory about Congress at all, but rather a proposal to reconstruct the American party system, so that a party would formulate a clear-cut and specific policy (platform) that would be responsibly effectuated when that party enjoyed a national majority. "The party system that is needed must be democratic, responsible, and effective," according to the academic manifesto of party government—the 1950 report of the American Political Science Association's Committee on Political Parties.[44] The basic malady of the American Congress is not myopic legislators or even archaic legislative rules and procedures, but rather the "parochialism of American life and the electoral system that fosters its." Thus, meaningful congressional reorganization can come about only through profound changes in the American party system.[45]

"AN ALMOST IDEAL FORM"

The empirical foundation of party-government theory is the familiar observation that American parties are unwieldy coalitions of parochial interests.[46] The party that is elected to power is incapable of organizing its members in the Legislative and Executive Branches into a coherent, energetic, and effective government. The disorganization and parochialism of the parties debilitates the American political system. First, it renders impossible the "orderly, relevant, and effective politics" necessary in an era of urgent national and international problems.[47] Second, it perverts the concepts of the party platform and the public will. Frequently, a party, once in power, fails to effectuate even those programs which were delineated as electoral issues.

The Jeffersonian notion of popular majorities organized in national blocs or parties is the base of the party-government system. Such a system would have a tidiness unknown to the incoherent parties to which Americans are accustomed. A constant inspiration for many party-government theorists is the British party system, which Woodrow Wilson openly admired and which Burns calls "an almost ideal form of representative government."[48]

Coherent, democratic, and responsible parties would necessarily reflect themselves in strengthened party organizations on Capitol Hill. As the APSA Committee stated:

> A general structure of congressional party organization already exists. It should be tightened up. The party leadership in both houses already has certain functions with respect to the handling of relations with the President and the shaping of the committee structure . . . [and] other functions with respect to the legislative schedule. [These functions] should be strengthened.
>
> If such action were taken, it would not mean that every issue would become a party issue. It would not eliminate the need for or the possibility of nonpartisan and bipartisan policies. But it would result in a more responsible approach to party programs and a more orderly handling of *all* congressional activities.[49]

Such powers as committee appointment and legislative scheduling should therefore be centralized in the elective party leadership. According to Representative Bolling, "there is every reason to justify the right of the majority to have its major proposals voted on by the whole House without undue delay . . ."[50]

The authors of the APSA Committee's report were not optimistic about the prospects of "engineering consent" for such revisions. "It cannot be expected," they wrote, "that all congressional leaders will be sympathetic to the concept of party responsibility."[51] However, the committee hoped that nationally oriented Congressmen and Senators would take the lead in publicizing the cause of strong party organization. This hope is being partially realized in the writings of Senator Clark, Representative Bolling, and others of the "national" wings of both political parties who have worked to strengthen the party caucus and the elective leadership.

Reform Propositions

Advocates of the party-government theory follow the executive-force theory in many respects but place particular emphasis on the following proposals:[52]

1. Control of congressional nominations and elections should be centralized—with national party clearance for candidates.
2. Congressional party leaders should be chosen after wide consultation among the entire "national" party, including the President.
3. Meaningful party policy committees should be created in each house; these committees should be responsible for legislative scheduling and for committee appointments conditioned on party loyalty.
4. Both houses should schedule frequent party caucuses, whose decisions would bind members to vote the party line on important issues.
5. Committee assignments and chairmanships should be recommended by the party policy committee, ratified by the caucus, and subject to periodic review. Ratios of party membership on committees should favor the majority party.
6. Staff assistance should be provided both majority and minority committee members.
7. The House Rules Committee should be an arm of the elective leadership in scheduling measures for floor debate.
8. The present Senate filibuster rule should be altered to allow cloture of debate by a majority vote.

CONCLUSION: THE PARLIAMENTARY CRISIS

Divergent theories of the congressional function are the outgrowth of a complex, contentious society marked by numerous and often conflicting demands upon the institutions of government. Those citizens who urge upon the federal government an interventionist, problem-solving role will conceive of a legislature far differently than will those who see the government's role as a passive consensus-building one. The rules of the political game, as defined by the structure of institutions, cannot be divorced from the stakes for which the game is played. Moreover, these differing stakes are related to divergent intellectual interpretations of the role of institutions in a democratic polity. The theories of Congress should not be characterized merely as rationalizations for one's substantive positions; yet the two levels of debate are closely related. The struggle being waged over the character of Congress is indeed a part of the "war over America's future."

When the three theories are compared, a composite picture of the American Congress emerges—a picture with important convergences and deep differences. In this chapter's discussion, formal "powers" of the legislature were consciously played down, in favor of the broader and more fundamental concept of "function"—those things of major consequence that an institution (in this case, Congress) does for the political system as a whole. Table 1.1.1 presents a rough comparison of the functions specified for Congress by the three theories discussed in this chapter, and the following paragraph defines these functions as they have emerged from the discussion.

TABLE 1.1.1 THREE THEORIES OF CONGRESSIONAL FUNCTIONS

	LITERARY THEORY	EXECUTIVE-FORCE THEORY	PARTY-GOVERNMENT THEORY
PRIMARY FUNCTIONS	Lawmaking Representation Consensus building Oversight	Legitimizing Oversight Representation	Policy clarification Representation
SECONDARY FUNCTIONS	Policy clarification Legitimizing	Consensus building Policy clarification Lawmaking	Lawmaking Legitimizing Consensus building

Lawmaking is the traditional task of deliberating, often at a technical level, the actual content of policies. *Representation* is the process of articulating the demands or interests of geographic, economic, religious, ethnic, and professional constituencies. The legislator may accomplish this through actual contact (residence in a district, membership in a pressure group) or through "virtual" means ("taking into account" a viewpoint, perhaps by anticipating constituent response). *Consensus building* is the traditional bargaining function through which these various constituency demands are combined (or aggregated) in such a way that no significant constituency is severely or permanently disadvantaged. *Legitimizing* is the ratification of a measure or policy in such a way that it seems appropriate, acceptable, and authoritative. The legislature promotes *policy clarification* by providing a public platform where issues may be identified and publicized. *Legislative oversight* is the review of the implementation of policy in order to either alter the fundamental policy or introduce equity into the application of laws. Other functions—for example, *constituent service* and *recruitment of political leadership*—might also be explored, but are omitted here because they are not fundamental to the current debate over Congress.

The functions that theorists choose to emphasize have a profound impact upon the nature of the "model" Congress, not to mention the relationship of Congress with other elements in the political system. The most ambitious mandate is offered by the literary theory, which would involve the legislature at almost every step in the policymaking process—from initial conception to detailed review of implementation. In addition, this theory views the legislature as the prime representational and consensus-building institution in the political system. The executive-force theory, on the other hand, sees the legislature as ancillary to the executive establishment, which by the nature of things must assume the lead in both policy initiation and implementation. Like the board of directors of a corporation, Congress would have certain review powers but few operating powers; the legislature would find itself in most cases ratifying decisions of the executive "managers." According to the party-government conception, Congress (as well as the executive) would be set in motion by a strong and lucid party structure, serving chiefly as a forum for the staged confrontation of party ideologies.

No matter how far-reaching the consequences of accepting one theory over another, the differences in the concepts of the normative functions of Congress are differences of emphasis. Few observers would deny that Congress should, at one time or another, perform all the roles that have been discussed. Even the most dedicated advocate of executive dominance, for example, would undoubtedly concede that certain occasions may demand legislative initiative in policymaking. Most theories of congressional functioning therefore admit to what might be called the "multifunctionality" of the institution. The priority assigned to these various functions then becomes the all-important question.

1.2 Overview of Principal Legislative Developments of the 1970s*

Select Committee on Committees, U.S. House of Representatives

It has been argued that the 20th century Congress is strikingly different from the Congress of the 18th and 19th centuries. The differences are said to lie in increased institutionalization: careerism, seniority, membership stability, leadership by inside party stalwarts, developed committee and party infrastructure, provincialism, differentiation from the Executive Branch, coherent norms, and professional staff.

These differences stem not only from changes in American society and politics in general, but from a spate of both leadership excesses and reactions to them in the period surrounding the turn of the century.

In the 1970s, a number of major changes and reforms occurred that significantly altered the 20th-century Congress. Some say that because of those changes, the Congress of the 1980s is as different from the Congress of the 1960s as the 1960s Congress was from its 19th-century forerunner. The following report details the major legislative changes of the 1970s, especially as they pertain to the House.

SECTIONS I—OVERVIEW OF PRINCIPAL LEGISLATIVE DEVELOPMENTS OF THE 1970s

The 1970s have been a period of fundamental change in the House of Representatives. Not since the congressional revolution of 1910 and the accompanying progressive era has there been a comparable overhaul of House procedures and practices. These modern changes have been influenced by the steady influx of new members who differ in their attitudes and experiences from an earlier generation of Representatives. Changes have also occurred through reform in the procedures and norms of the House.

Government at all levels has been the target of public criticism during the past decade. Public confidence in governmental institutions and elected leaders has declined to unprecedented levels. The number and complexity of public policy issues seem immune to remedial action by government at both the federal and local levels. Rivalry and conflict between the branches of the federal government have increased, and seem likely to continue.

In response to these pressures, the Congress generally, and the House in particular, has made a number of significant changes in its organization and procedure. The goals of these reforms were (1) to increase the public accountability of the Congress; (2) to strengthen the legislative branch to maintain its constitutional role as a "co-equal" partner in the federal system; and (3) to make the House a more democratic institution, while, at the same time, making the congressional leadership more effective.

The issues delineated below have contributed significantly to a number of key legislative developments during the 1970s:

---

* From "Overview of Principal Legislative Developments of the 1970s," *Final Report of the Select Committee on Committees, U.S. House of Representatives,* 1980, House Report No. 96–866, reprinted as part of the public domain.

1. More openness.
2. The expanding workload of Congress.
3. Growth in the number of ad hoc groups.
4. Larger membership turnover.
5. Greater dispersal of power of subcommittees.
6. Some steps toward a stronger Speakership.
7. New multiple referral process.
8. Increase in staff.
9. Resurgence of the party caucus.
10. Decline of informal membership norms.

Openness

During the 1970s, the Congress responded to demands for greater public accountability. One manifestation of this spirit was in opening many congressional activities which previously had been closed to the public and the press.

Although congressional committees had, on rare occasions, permitted live coverage of their proceedings, provisions were included in the 1970 Legislative Reorganization Act establishing standard committee guidelines for broadcast media coverage of their hearings. In 1974, House Rules were amended to additionally permit broadcast coverage of committee markup sessions.

Prior to 1970, no public accounting of members' votes in Committee of the Whole was possible. The Reorganization Act of that year established procedures for a "recorded teller vote" through which members votes in Committee of the Whole could be published in the Congressional Record. Subsequently, the House installed an electronic voting system with which to expedite the conduct of all of its votes and quorum calls. Some observers have claimed the installation of the electronic voting system, by reducing the time required for the House vote, has, in fact, contributed to the overall frequency with which recorded votes are demanded.

The 1970 Reorganization Act also dealt with voting in committee. Previously, no written public record of votes in committee was maintained. The Reorganization Act required that the results of each rollcall vote in committee, and each member's vote, be recorded, and made available for public inspection. Committees were also required to include in their reports on bills the results of the vote by which the committee approved the measure.

In 1973, the House adopted rules changes requiring that most committee meetings be open to the public. In prior years, approximately 30 percent of all committee meetings were held in executive, or closed, session. Some committees held upwards of 90 percent of their meetings in closed session. Now, virtually all committee meetings, hearings, and markup sessions are open to the public.

Increasingly, opposition to committee openness has been voiced: Open meetings unnecessarily slow the legislative process; open sessions are inherently formal sessions, and thus, require more time to achieve the same decisions that could have been reached more informally. Open sessions may inhibit the range of discussion in committee meetings as members are mindful of press coverage and hesitant to publicly explore controversial issues. Open sessions make it more difficult for members to change their positions once they have been publicly announced. Open sessions generally assure the presence of lobbyists and representatives of special interest organizations at committee meetings. Their presence may put undue pressure on members. Some observers also charge that open sessions inhibit the discussions and compromises which are an essential part of House-Senate conference committee meetings; increasingly, conferees meet informally to agree upon a position which will then be offered *pro forma* at an open session.

Expanding Workload of Congress

Between the 92d and the 95th Congress, the number of days in session has increased, but not markedly, from 295 to 323. During the same period, there has been a decline in the number of bills enacted, from 265 to 250. The increase in the number of congressional committee and subcommittee meetings is even more significant. Between the 91st and the 95th Congresses, the number of committee meetings increased by over 30 percent, from 5,066 to 6,771. Moreover, the number of record votes has increased from 193 in the 92d Congress to 505 in the 95th Congress.

Other indexes of congressional workload have increased as well. The House Post Office has steadily increased the amount of mail processed. It is estimated to have tripled in volume from 1972 to 1979. More specifically, the volume of mail has increased over 300 percent during the past six years.

Changes in the volume of congressional workload seem to have been accompanied by an increase in its complexity, as well.

Growth in Number of Ad Hoc Groups

Within recent Congresses, there has been an unprecedented growth in both the number, and organizational complexity of informal member associations which seek to influence the policymaking process. Prior to 1970, only three informal congressional groups were organized: DSG (1959), the House (Republican) Wednesday Group (1964), and the bicameral, bipartisan members of Congress for Peace Through Law (1966). As of May 1979, the number of member groups has risen more than three dozen.

In recent years, the major emphasis among new informal groups has been a bipartisan orientation which underscores economic and regional shared interests over partisan considerations. Since the 91st Congress, 19 bipartisan groups have been formally organized, only three new partisan groups have emerged.

Along with this bipartisan orientation has been an informal group orientation toward single issue concentration and regional organizations. During the 94th and 95th Congresses, informal groups organized with a concentration on Vietnam-era veterans affairs, problems affecting seaports, textiles, the steel industry, oceans policy, the Washington metropolitan area, suburban areas, the "Sunbelt," the "Frostbelt," blue-collar workers, congressional employees, and alternative energy resources, among others.

Three new bipartisan groups supplemented earlier groups organized to examine policy issues relating to the New England States, The Great Lakes Region, rural areas, and black Americans.

Large Membership Turnover

In recent years, the House has undergone significant membership turnoer, especially considering that at the beginning of the 92d Congress, 20 percent of its membership had been elected to at least 10 terms. However, at the beginning of the second session of the 94th Congress in 1976, only 14 percent of House members met the 10-term criterion (the lowest since 1955).

Over one third of House members at the beginning of the 94th Congress were beginning their first or second term, and the middle House members, in terms of seniority, were beginning their fourth term. By the start of the 96th Congress, 54 percent of House members had served three terms or less.

There are changes in the membership of the House. The average age of House members has dropped. The average age, at the beginning of the 94th Congress of a House member was less than 50 for the first time since World War II, and 87 of the members were 40 years old or under, a 50 percent increase over the 93rd Congress.

There have also been changes in the racial and sexual composition of the House. Although the number of black House members has not changed dramatically during the 70s, a larger number of black members hold committee and subcommittee leadership positions than ever before. The first black member has been elected to the Rules Committee during this decade, as were the first black whips.

Relative to the increased activity of women in politics, there has also been an increase in the number of women elected to the House. In 1974, all 12 women incumbents (10 Democrats and 2 Republicans) who sought reelection to the House were successful, and six other women won seats for the first time. The election of 18 women to the House set a record.

Greater Dispersal of Power to Subcommittees

The period of the 1970s has seen increasing restraint on the power of committee chairmen, and an increasing shift of power to subcommittee chairmen. Beginning in the 92d Congress, members could chair only one legislative subcommittee. The immediate effect was to increase the total number of members who held subcommittee chairmanships, and to place relatively junior members in positions of subcommittee leadership. In 1975, committees were required to establish a minimum number of subcommittees. With the increasingly large membership turnover of recent Congresses, coupled with the larger number of subcommittees, it is not uncommon for members in their second or third terms to rise to the chairmanship of a subcommittee.

The absolute power of committee chairmen has also been weakened by reforms in the seniority system. In 1975, three committee chairmen were deposed by the House Democratic Caucus, and more junior members chosen as chairmen to replace them.

The relative influence of subcommittees on legislation is shown by committee meeting statistics. In the 95th Congress, roughly 80 percent of all committee meetings were subcommittee meetings. Action, either markups or hearings, taken by the full committees normally was done merely to ratify previous action taken by a subcommittee. Increasingly, subcommittees have also become the focus of oversight activity in the House.

Steps Toward Stronger Speakership

Today, the floor leadership of the Democratic Party in the House has more potential instruments of power, according to some authorities, than has been the case in recent years. Recent actions by the House Democratic Caucus have strengthened the floor leadership. In 1973, the Caucus established the Democratic Steering and Policy Committee. (The Speaker serves as Chairman, the majority leader as Vice Chairman, and the caucus chairman as Second Vice Chairman.) The Speaker has the authority to appoint up to eight (8) of the total 23 members. Moreover, the stated functions of the Committee are vague and as a result, the Speaker is given discretionary power in defining the stated functions.

At the beginning of the 94th Congress, the function of serving as the party "Committee on Committees" was included in the mandate of the Steering and Policy Committee. Consequently, the Speaker is the leader of a committee that can greatly affect the members' careers.

Finally, the Speaker now has the prerogative to choose Democratic nominees to the Committee on Rules, subject to their approval by the Caucus. Additionally, the Speaker is given broad discretion in the reference of bills to committees, especially in the case of multiple referrals. The net effect has been to increase the theoretic power of the Speaker, but to limit it in practice by the continuing need to seek a majority party consensus on major issues.

The Multiple Referral Process

Prior to the 94th Congress, bills were required to be referred to the single committee which had the predominant legislative jurisdiction over the subject of a bill. Beginning with the 94th Congress, the Speaker was given the authority to refer bills (or parts of bills) to more than one committee. The general process is called a "multiple referral," although it refers to three different procedures: joint referrals, sequential referrals, and split referrals. A joint referral occurs when a measure is referred to two or more committees simultaneously. In a sequential referral, a bill is referred to one committee with the understanding that after the first committee acts, the bill will be referred to the second, or next, committee in the sequence. In a split referral, a portion (title or section) of a bill is referred to one committee, while other committees are referred other sections of the bill. Various permutations and combinations of these procedures are possible, and the Speaker is permitted under the rule to establish whatever conditions to the referral (for example, time limits) he may think necessary. The various referrals (joint, sequential, and split) have many advantages. They serve as avenues for flexibility, as facilitators of intercommittee cooperation and allow for the input, wisdom, and differing points of view to be considered on a measure.

During the 94th Congress, there were 1,161 bills multiply referred. Of that number, 38 were reported. During the 95th Congress, 1,855 bills were multiply referred. Of that number, 84 were reported. Given the complexity of much legislation and the overlapping jurisdiction characteristic of the congressional committee system, the Bolling Commission, as a result of its works, found it desirable that various bills, or titles thereof, be capable of referral to two or more House Committees.

Recently, opposition to the large number of multiple referrals has been voiced. Critics charge that the process is unnecessarily complex, and causes substantial delays in the legislative process.

Growth of Committee Staff

The Legislative Reorganization Act of 1970 provided for six professional and six clerical staff persons. H. Res. 988, effective in January 1975, set staff size at 18 professional staff members and 12 clerical persons except for two House committees—Appropriations and Budget. From 1973 to 1978, committee staffs increased from 878 to 1,844 with the largest increase occurring between 1974 and 1975 (326).

All House committees except Appropriations and Budget are authorized to employ up to 30 statutory staff (18 professional and 12 clerical).

The Appropriations and Budget Committees are permitted by House rules to establish their own staff levels, and their own required amount of funding.

There are two categories of committee staff in the House, statutory and investigative. Statutory employees are hired solely on the basis of their ability to perform required duties and are prohibited from performing work other than committee business during their hours of employment. Statutory committee staff may receive higher salaries than their investigative staff counterparts. Investigative personnel are hired pursuant to annual "studies and investigations" funding resolutions. Investigative staff are not covered by the legal protections and prohibitions under which statutory staff functions.

Resurgence of Party Caucuses

The revival of the party caucuses has been one of the most significant developments in the Congress over the last decade. Since 1969, the following developments have occurred:

1. Debates have been held on legislative policy, and party rules and procedures at regular monthly meetings of the House Democratic Caucus.
2. The caucus has adopted party positions on certain issues and has accomplished significant changes in party rules and procedures (i.e., means of selecting committee chairmen).

Use of the Conference of policy discussions by House Republicans predates the revitalization of the Democratic Party Caucus.

Since the institution of monthly caucus meetings, House Democrats have significantly reduced the powers of their committee chairmen. Specifically, they have empowered caucuses of Democrats on each standing committee with the authority to adopt rules which:

1. Establish powers and duties of subcommittees.
2. Fix subcommittee jurisdictions and provide for referral of legislation.
3. Permit subcommittee chairmen to select

staff, subject to budgetary limits and the control of Democratic Committee Caucus.
4. Set party ratios on subcommittees at least as favorable to Democrats as the full committee ratio.
5. Limit the chairman's power to assign members to vacant subcommittee seats.
6. Thoroughly revised the procedure by which subcommittee chairmen are selected.

House Republicans like their Democratic colleagues have also provided for secret ballot votes on nominees for party leadership positions on committees.

Decline of Informal Norms Particularly Apprenticeship

Several significant and unusual developments have occurred in the last three Congresses:

1. Junior members have been appointed to the very powerful ''exclusive'' committees shortly after entering the House.
2. A large number have been appointed to the exclusive committees.
3. The participation of junior members in floor debates and sponsoring floor amendments.
4. The development of new freshmen member organizations.

There have been a number of junior members assigned to the very powerful ''exclusive committees'' (Appropriations, Ways and Means, and Budget). Half of the Democratic members on the Rules Committee have been elected to the House since 1975. Fourteen members of the 24 Democratic members of the House Ways and Means Committee have served for three or fewer consecutive terms. On the Appropriations Committee, there are three—first-term Democratic members.

The development of new freshmen member organizations is another significant development which occurred during the 1970s. During the 94th Congress, when the ''New Members' Caucus'' was virtually unheard of, the group requested nominees for committee chairmanships to present themselves for interviews. It is generally agreed that the votes of the ''New Members' Caucus'' were instrumental in removing three incumbent chairmen from their posts in 1975.

SECTION II—RELEVANCE OF 1970S LEGISLATIVE CHANGES TO CONTEMPORARY COMMITTEE REORGANIZATION

The transformation of the House brought about by the 1970s changes will clearly affect 1979–1980 committee reorganization efforts. It is not possible to identify every direct or indirect consequence of the 1970s changes for committee reorganization. However, the task force believes there are seven particularly noteworthy developments of the 1970s that will likely affect the work of the Select Committee on Committees. These include:

1. Shift from Committee Government to Subcommittee Government

Policymaking authority in the House has significantly devolved upon subcommittees. Changes adopted by the Democratic Caucus during the 1970s (and several House rule changes) granted subcommittees new authority and independence from full committee control. No longer do full committee chairmen control the internal organizational structure of their committee. Under the Subcommittee Bill of Rights adopted in 1973 by the Democratic Caucus, the Democratic members of each standing committee—subject to regulations established by the Caucus—determine such matters as the size, jurisdiction, and budget of their subcommittees. Heretofore, these matters were the prerogatives of the committee chairman.

The Democratic Caucus also made other changes during the 1970s that opened subcommittee chairmanships to numerous members, including junior legislators. Today, many more members have subcommittees to nurture and protect. They have a stake in subcommittee government, and are likely to oppose any proposal that significantly reduces the number of subcommittees standing committees may have. Contemporary committee reorganization, in short, must consider how any proposed changes affect committees and subcommittees.

2. More Difficult for House to Formulate Coherent Public Policies Given So Many Participants in Policymaking

Committees, subcommittees, and the Caucus play significant roles in the legislative process. Despite its assets, committee government does have serious liabilities. There are flaws that undermine the ability of Congress to fulfill its constitutional responsibilities, to make legislative policy, and oversee the implementation of that policy. The view is that internally, Congress needs central leadership because most major questions of public policy (such as economic or the energy issues) cut across individual committee jurisdictions. Since each committee and subcommittee may differ in its policy orientation, and since the support of all relevant committees will be essential to an overall program, it is difficult to enact a coherent general approach to broad policy questions.

A central party leader or central congressional steering committee with extensive control over the standing committees could provide the leadership necessary to assist the development and passage of a coherent policy across the various committees. However, committee government resists the centralization of power in a single person or unit.

Centralized leadership requires a willingness of members to cede their smaller grants of authority. However, members are likely to do this only if general agreement exists regarding the policies a stronger leadership would follow. On most current issues, no coherent party policy exists which has the general support of all party members. Hence, it is unlikely that the dispersed legislative authority in the House soon will be centralized. Too much effort has been expended in the last decade dispersing leadership authority for this tendency to be easily or quickly reversed.

3. Staffing and Space Needs

During the 1970s, the Congress generally, and the House in particular, made concerted efforts to expand its staff. The Congress in 1970 was incapable of countering the massive information and analytic resources available to the Executive Branch. The Congress, in many instances, was forced to rely upon information provided by the agencies and departments. Lacking adequate staff resources in many areas, the Congress was not always able to exercise independent judgment on Executive Branch proposals. The expansion of staff for members, for committees, and for the Congress generally, was caused by this need for independent analysis.

The growth in staff, however, has placed unforeseen strains on congressional facilities. Space in the principal House office buildings was rapidly filled, and more space in two annex office buildings was required. The growth in high technology office equipment has also contributed to space shortages, while enabling staff to handle an ever increasing volume of work. Inadequate space for staff and equipment limits the ability of the Congress to perform its duties efficiently.

In recent years, there has been concern voiced over the growth of congressional staff. Some observers, both inside and outside of Congress, believe that staff growth should be slowed, if not halted outright. In a period of fiscal restraint, it is claimed that the public will oppose continuing growth of the congressional establishment. As staff grows, the administrative duties of members increase commensurately, restricting time available to members to consider policy issues. Fiscal constraints additionally may make it impossible for the Congress to increase its office space further, thereby implicitly limiting future staff growth.

This combination of factors must be considered by the select committee in any action it takes regarding staffing and facilities of House committees.

4. Numerous Committee Scheduling Conflicts

The efficacious handling of the nation's business through the committee process cannot proceed orderly and properly if House members are not at committee meetings because of conflicting committee meeting scheduling. Conflict problems have increased in severity as the number of committee and subcommittee meetings continue to rise (from 5,066 in the 91st Congress to 6,771 in the 95th Congress).

An equitable and logical procedure for scheduling committee meetings remains an urgent priority for the House leadership and members. The ingenuity and resources of the House members must be collectively brought to bear on a resolution of conflicting meeting scheduling. Failure to address this critical matter may result in an erosion of the efficiency and productivity of the House in working its will in the legislative process.

5. Jurisdictional Overlaps

In a simpler age, it was not considered necessary to enumerate House committees' subject jurisdiction in House Rules. Since 1947, however, fairly detailed subject guidelines have been a part of House Rule X. Several previous attempts at codifying these jurisdictions, and eliminating subject overlaps and archaic language have failed. Concurrently, the complexity of policy issues facing the Congress has increased enormously. Often, new policy issues do not accommodate themselves to the committee jurisdictions enumerated in the House Rules.

As part of the Bolling reforms, House Rules were amended to permit the referral of bills (or parts of bills) to more than one committee. To a degree, this minimized jurisdictional conflicts among committees sharing partial responsibility for a major policy issue. However, the experience of four years of multiple referrals casts doubt on its legislative effectiveness. Each year, more and more bills are being referred to several committees. In the 95th Congress, more than 3,000 bills (or one out of every five House bills) was referred to more than one committee. While multiple referrals assure that divergent committee viewpoints are reflected, they also appear to delay committee and full House action on bills.

Jurisdictional fragmentation and the rise of multiple committee consideration of bills are issues which will influence the work of the select committee. Currently, no standard procedures exist for the referral of legislation to more than one committee. If the number of multiple referrals continues to rise, the establishment of such mechanisms may be considered essential. The Bolling Committee believed that multiple referrals would be required in only a few instances each year because that committee also strove to restructure existing committee jurisdictions. In failing to consolidate major policy issues in a single committee, the House was forced into greater reliance upon multiple referrals. If the House were to adopt restrictive guidelines on the use of multiple referrals, the conflicting jurisdictional claims of House committees may increase in severity. Conversely, if the House acted to reduce jurisdictional overlap among its committees, the need for bills to be referred to more than one committee might be reduced.

6. Concern About Committee Capacity to Conduct Oversight

The factor of promise and fulfillment has become a pivotal and critical element in the oversight function in recent times. Congressional leadership and House members have been enormously concerned that the plethora of legislation enacted by the Congress accomplishes what it was intended to achieve and is carefully monitored and evaluated. There is a "chasm" that continues in regard to the enactment of legislation in determining its efficacy and impact on the citizenry. The effectiveness in the last analysis in oversight responsibilities may well be determined, in large measure, by the extent of the members, their intent and commitment, particularly as it serves their constituents and their own political careers. This factor suggests that the House leadership may wish to give greater care to the assignment of members to committees based upon their interests.

7. Leadership Has Harder Time Governing the House

Vigorous congressional leadership is inhibited, not only by the decentralized power centers in the House but also by the lack of a firm base upon which to build leadership power. The political parties are shaky foundations on which to erect a viable system of legislative leadership. The party has rarely, in modern times, been a dominant force in the national legislature. The Democratic Caucus reforms of the past decade have yet to prove themselves as something more than the instruments of factional advance by the liberal bloc. Moreover, as other entities have assumed functions which historically were the responsibility of parties, formal party organizations have lost much of their influence. Weakened party loyalties have further reduced the influence of the congressional leadership.

Changed member attitudes have reinforced the decline of congressional leadership. Members frequently are elected without the aid of a strong, local party organization. Relying on their own electoral skills, new members are acutely sensitive to constituent opinion, and will normally support constituency attitudes, even if they must, therefore, oppose their party's congressional leadership. Many new members do not see House service as the high point of their political career. Consequently, they are not content to serve a lengthy apprenticeship before taking a visible part in the legislative process. Junior member activism has further contributed to the weakening of House leadership.

CHAPTER 2

The Congressional Election Process

Congressional elections provide a major link between governed and governors. The electoral process strongly affects what happens in the Congress by channeling mass demands and opinion and ultimately by deciding who will serve as members and, thus, who will make decisions and whose views and preferences will prevail.

The congressional election process is a long gauntlet, invoking in all districts and states the drama of high theater. The writings offered in this chapter address the major aspects of elections and how the ensuing incentive system affects member behavior.

Political scientists have developed three different theories of congressional elections. One theory is a ''surge and decline'' interpretation that emphasizes straight-ticket voting and coattail effects during congressional elections coinciding with presidential elections (or in what are referred to as ''in'' years). According to this theory, the historic pattern of losses during the midterm or ''off-year'' elections for the party controlling the presidency can be explained by a surge of support by marginal voters for the winning presidential candidate's party during the in year and then an eventual decline of support during the ''off'' year. In other words, in-year and off-year congressional elections reflect very different electoral dynamics. The in-year elections are heavily influenced by short-term factors, such as issues and presidential candidate appeal. An expanded, surging electorate of both marginal voters and strong partisans carry the day in marginal or competitive districts in what is generally a ''high-stimulus,'' politically charged atmosphere. In contrast, in off years, politics returns to normal; strong partisans and a sense of partisanship are the determining factors; and coattail-related gains of the President's party are pruned by the normal vote.

A second theory that has emerged is one of ''incumbency retention.'' Congressional elections are viewed as heavily determined by incumbency. Attention is called to a high rate of careerism in Congress among many members and, the 1980 elections aside, their relatively high survival rate when challenged. An election is conceptualized as a ratification of an incumbent member's district-serving ability. Incumbency survival is tied to incumbent savvy in the performance of casework and errand-boy functions and the adroit political use of the resources of incumbency.

The third theory might best be called "presidential referendum." Many now view congressional elections, especially the midterm ones, as a referendum on the President's leadership accomplishments and programs. From this perspective, it is argued that congressional elections are influenced strongly by presidential popularity and the state of the economy, with the President's party doing well when things are well and doing poorly when things are perceived to be poor.

In concluding a consideration of congressional elections, three thoughts should be kept in mind. First, the electoral process involves more than just nomination, campaign, and general election melodrama. It also includes debates and decisions concerning reapportionment, districting, and gerrymandering that occur in state capitals at the outset of each decade following the federal census. Decisions concerning the configuration, contours, and character of House districts strongly color election outcomes in these districts.

Second, congressional nominations are an important but not well studied aspect of congressional recruitment. Through an infinite variety of different nominating systems, prospective legislative elites are winnowed in and out of the election contest.

Third, elections are not the only mechanism of leader/follower linkages in Congress. There are other avenues—group lobbying, parochial contracts (one-on-one lobbying), media crusades—through which popular demands can be forwarded to legislative elites. These channels differ in terms of the pressure they exert, the specifics of their communications, and their representativeness. Elections are the most representative but exert only diffuse pressure and communicate only the most general preferences.

2.1 A Comparison of Voting for U.S. Senator and Representative in 1978*

Alan I. Abramowitz

Abramowitz demonstrates that there is a big difference between House and Senate elections in terms of mass voting behavior. Thus, when discussing congressional elections, we must differentiate not only between in and off-year (midterm) elections, filled and unfilled (vacant) seats, and safe and competitive districts, but between House and Senate elections.

This article compares voting for U.S. Senator and Representative in 1978. Analysis of data from the Center for Political Studies 1978 Election Study reveals that incumbents were better known and more positively evaluated than challengers, but House incumbents enjoyed a much greater advantage than Senate incumbents. The invisibility of most House challengers was a serious obstacle to accountability in House elections. Senate challengers were much more visible to the electorate. In addition, ideology and party identification had a greater impact on evaluations of Senate candidates than on evaluations of House candidates. Evaluations of House incumbents appear to have been based largely on frequent positive contacts between voters and their representative. As a result, ideological voting was more prevalent in Senate elections than in House elections.

Recent elections have produced a wide disparity between the outcomes of House and Senate races involving incumbents. While House incumbents have continued to enjoy overwhelming success, incumbent Senators have been highly vulnerable. In both 1976 and 1978, less than 5 percent of incumbents seeking reelection to the House were defeated while close to a third of the incumbent Senators seeking reelection lost their races. Despite having only a third of its seats at stake, the Senate actually had proportionately greater turnover in its membership than the House in the past two elections.

Several factors may help to explain the difference between House and Senate elections. A House district is more likely to be dominated by one party than a state. In addition, Senate challengers generally appear to wage more visible and effective campaigns than House challengers. Electoral accountability requires effective competition. Even if the voters are less than completely satisfied with an incumbent's performance, they may be reluctant to vote for a challenger who is an unknown quantity. Finally, voters may use different criteria to evaluate the performance of Senators and Representatives. Senators appear to be associated more often with controversial national issues than Representatives, whose positions on such issues do not generally receive as much public-

---

* From Alan I. Abramowitz, "A Comparison of Voting for U.S. Senator and Representative in 1978," *American Political Science Review* 74 (1980): 633–40.

The data used in this study were made available by the Inter-University Consortium for Political and Social Research. The author accepts all responsibility for the analyses and interpretations included in this article. He would like to thank John McGlennon and Ronald Rapoport for their comments on an earlier draft of this paper. Support for the research on which this article is based was provided by a Summer Research Grant from the College of William and Mary.

ity. Their greater prominence in the media may result in Senators having less control than Representatives over the information which voters receive about their performance. Thus voters may receive more objective, or even critical information about individual Senators than about individual Representatives. Most of the information which voters receive about their Representatives in the House probably comes from Representatives themselves.

DATA

The data used in this study come from the Center for Political Studies 1978 National Election Study. Post-election interviews were conducted with 2,304 eligible voters in 108 congressional districts throughout the United States. For the first time since 1958, the survey instrument was designed explicitly for the purpose of analyzing voting in congressional elections. Many questions concerning perceptions and evaluations of individual House and Senate candidates were included in addition to more traditional items concerning the parties, issues, and national political figures. Therefore the 1978 election study is particularly well suited to our purpose.[1]

FINDINGS

As might be expected, incumbents were generally better known and more positively evaluated than challengers. There was, however, a substantial difference between House and Senate races. Table 2.1.1 shows that incumbency had a much greater impact on candidate evaluations and voting decisions in House races than in Senate races. In House races, incumbents were evaluated more favorably than challengers by all groups of voters, including those who identified with the challenger's party, and almost half of the supporters of the challenger's party voted for the incumbent. Senate

Table 2.1.1 Incumbency, Candidate Evaluation, and Voting for House and Senate in 1978

	Democratic Incumbent	Open Seat	Republican Incumbent	Tau	(Sig.)
House:					
Candidate evaluation*					
Democrats	+56	+29	−37	.45	(.001)
Independents	+41	− 6	−41	.44	(.001)
Republicans	+14	−34	−65	.43	(.001)
Vote†					
Democrats	95	81	53	.35	(.001)
Independents	79	38	18	.60	(.001)
Republicans	45	16	3	.41	(.001)
Senate:					
Candidate evaluation:					
Democrats	+37	+38	+ 9	.15	(.001)
Independents	+ 4	+ 4	−25	.16	(.001)
Republicans	−18	−23	−48	.16	(.01)
Vote:					
Democrats	85	81	74	.10	(.05)
Independents	64	47	30	.27	(.001)
Republicans	35	22	10	.20	(.01)

* Percentage more favorable toward Democratic candidate minus percentage more favorable toward Republican candidate on feeling thermometer.

† Percentage voting Democratic.

Source: 1978 Election Study, Center for Political Studies, University of Michigan.

challengers generally fared much better than their House counterparts, especially among their own party's voters and among independents. Altogether, 78 percent of the votes in contested House races favored the incumbent while only 60 percent of the votes in contested Senate races favored the incumbent.

Why did House incumbents do so much better than Senate incumbents? There appear to be two answers to this question. First, House incumbents are evaluated more positively than Senate incumbents. Among all respondents, 56 percent gave their House incumbent a positive rating on the feeling thermometer while only 8 percent gave the incumbent a negative rating. Among respondents in states with Senate races, 53 percent gave the Senate incumbent a positive rating while 16 percent gave the incumbent a negative rating. Even more striking, however, is the difference between House and Senate challengers. Only 14 percent of respondents gave a positive rating to the House challenger while 7 percent gave the challenger a negative rating. The vast majority of respondents (79 percent) had no opinion about the House challenger. In contrast, 40 percent of respondents gave the Senate challenger a positive rating while 16 percent gave the challenger a negative rating and 44 percent had no opinion. Thus, House incumbents are doubly advantaged. Not only do they receive overwhelmingly positive evaluations from their constituents, but also their opponents are almost invisible. In contrast, Senate incumbents face a larger group of dissatisfied voters and much more vigorous opposition.

Mayhew (1974) has argued that the popularity of House incumbents is a function of their ability to control the information which constituents receive about their performance through such activities as advertising, credit-claiming, and position-taking. If this is the case, we would expect voters' evaluations of House incumbents to be based largely on contact with their representative, rather than ideology or party affiliation. The more contact voters have with their representative, the more positive their evaluation should be. If, as hypothesized, Senators have less control over information voters receive about their performance than Representatives, contact may not have as positive an impact on evaluations of Senate incumbents.

The 1978 election study included questions about various types of contact with candidates

TABLE 2.1.2 CONTACT WITH INCUMBENTS AND CHALLENGERS (PERCENT)

TYPE OF CONTACT	HOUSE INCUMBENT	HOUSE CHALLENGER	SENATE INCUMBENT	SENATE CHALLENGER
Personal meeting	14	3	7	4
Group meeting	12	2	8	3
Staff	8	2	5	3
Mailing	52	13	41	22
Radio	27	11	40	30
Television	43	20	72	61
Newspaper	52	24	60	49
Indirect[a]	28	8	b	b
Self-initiated	15	c	b	c
Other-initiated[d]	19	c	b	c
Total reporting any contact	77	37	84	70

NOTE: Percentages based on all respondents.

[a] Does respondent know of anyone else who has had contact with candidate?

[b] Not asked about Senate candidates.

[c] Not relevant for challenger.

[d] Does respondent know of anyone else who has initiated contact with candidate?

SOURCE: 1978 Election Study, Center for Political Studies, University of Michigan.

for the House and Senate. Table 2.1.2 shows high levels of contact between respondents and House incumbents. High levels of contact were also reported with Senate incumbents, although these contacts followed a somewhat different pattern, with more media contact and less personal contact. Once again, there was a large discrepancy between House and Senate challengers. Largely because of the influence of the mass media, respondents reported fairly high levels of exposure to Senate challengers. In contrast, the large majority of respondents reported having had no contact with the House challenger in their district.

In order to assess the relative impact of party identification, ideology, and contact on evaluations of House and Senate candidates, a path analysis was conducted, using relative ratings of incumbents and challengers on the feeling thermometer as the dependent variable. The independent variables were overall incumbent contact, overall challenger contact, party identification, and a measure of ideological proximity to the incumbent based on the respondent's self-classification on a seven-point liberal-conservative scale and the incumbent's ADA rating (see Appendix). The results shown in Figure 2.1.1 indicate that evaluations of House and Senate candidates were based on somewhat different criteria. Contact with the incumbent was by far the most important influence on evaluations of House candidates. The more respondents had seen or heard about the incumbent, the more highly they tended to evaluate the incumbent relative to the challenger on the feeling thermometer. Ideology had no discernible impact on evaluations of House candidates. In contrast, contact with the incumbent had a somewhat weaker impact on evaluations of Senate candidates, while party identification and ideology were more important.

FIGURE 2.1.1 PATH ANALYSIS OF CANDIDATE EVALUATION IN HOUSE AND SENATE CONTESTS INVOLVING INCUMBENTS

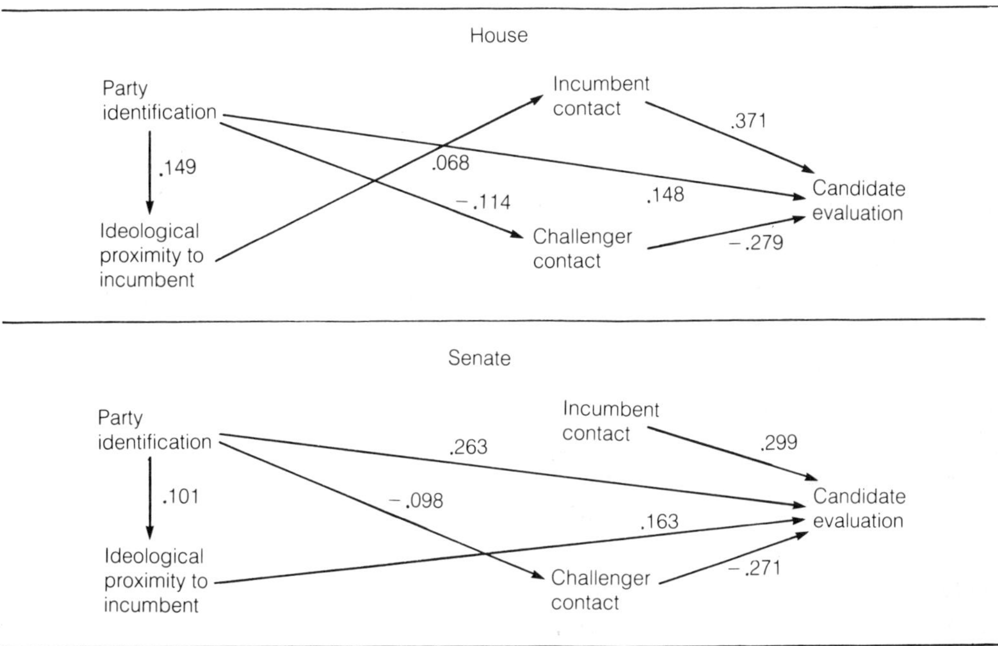

NOTE: All nonsignificant paths omitted. Weights shown are standardized regression coefficients. Analysis assumes no causal connection between incumbent and challenger contact.

SOURCE: 1978 Election Study, Center for Political Studies, University of Michigan.

TABLE 2.1.3 THE IMPACT OF CONTACT ON EVALUATIONS OF HOUSE AND SENATE CANDIDATES

TYPE OF CONTACT	B	(S.E.)	FREQUENCY	NET EFFECT
House incumbents:				
Personal meeting	+5.3	(1.4)	.14	+0.74
Group meeting	+4.2	(1.5)	.12	+0.50
Staff	+2.9	(1.7)	.08	+0.23
Mailing	+5.2	(0.9)	.52	+2.70
Radio	+0.9	(1.0)	.27	+0.24
Television	+3.6	(0.9)	.43	+1.55
Newspaper	+3.2	(1.0)	.52	+1.66
Indirect	+3.5	(1.1)	.28	+0.98
Self-initiated	+3.5	(1.3)	.15	+0.52
Other-initiated	+3.1	(1.2)	.19	+0.59
Intercept (54.00) + Total effect (+ 9.71) = Average rating (63.71)				
House challenges:				
Personal meeting	+9.5	(1.9)	.03	+0.23
Group meeting	−2.4	(2.5)	.02	−0.05
Staff	+7.1	(2.7)	.02	+0.14
Mailing	+2.6	(0.9)	.13	+0.34
Radio	+1.6	(1.0)	.11	+0.18
Television	+1.8	(0.8)	.20	+0.36
Newspaper	−0.6	(0.8)	.24	−0.14
Indirect	+0.3	(1.2)	.08	+0.02
Intercept (50.05) + Total effect (+ 1.13) = Average rating (51.18)				
Senate Incumbents:				
Personal meeting	+7.7	(3.4)	.07	+0.54
Group meeting	+5.0	(3.2)	.08	+0.40
Staff	+5.7	(3.7)	.05	+0.28
Mailing	+1.8	(1.7)	.41	+0.74
Radio	+2.4	(1.8)	.40	+0.96
Television	+3.7	(1.9)	.72	+2.66
Newspaper	−1.4	(1.8)	.60	−0.84
Intercept (55.42) + Total effect (+ 4.74) = Average rating (60.16)				
Senate challengers:				
Personal meeting	+16.4	(3.8)	.04	+0.66
Group meeting	+8.7	(4.1)	.03	+0.26
Staff	+7.2	(4.2)	.03	+0.22
Mailing	+0.8	(1.7)	.22	+0.18
Radio	+2.8	(1.6)	.30	+0.84
Television	+6.5	(1.6)	.61	+3.96
Newspaper	−3.3	(1.6)	.49	−1.62
Intercept (51.30) + Total effect (+4.50) = Average rating (55.80)				

SOURCE: 1978 Election Study, Center for Political Studies, University of Michigan.

Different types of contact may have different effects on voters' evaluations of candidates. Table 2.1.3 presents the results of a multiple regression analysis of the effects of contact on evaluations of incumbents and challengers. Since the dependent variable is the rating of the incumbent or challenger on the feeling thermometer, each unstandardized regression coefficient (B) can be interpreted as the average change in degrees on the feeling thermometer produced by each type of contact, controlling for all other types of contact. Multiplying this figure by the frequency of each type of contact indicates the net effect of each type of contact on the average evaluation of each type of candidate. These effects can then be summed to estimate the overall impact of contact for each type of candidate.

The results presented in Table 2.1.3 indicate that House incumbents derived considerably greater benefit from contact (a net gain of almost 10 degrees on the feeling thermometer) than any other type of candidate. Mailings (presumably newsletters and questionnaires as well as campaign literature) had the largest positive effect, followed by television and newspaper coverage. It is striking that every type of contact had a positive effect on evaluations of House incumbents, even after controlling for all other types of contact. In contrast, the impact of contact on evaluations of House challengers was negligible (a gain of only one degree on the feeling thermometer). The effects of contact on evaluations of Senate incumbents and challengers were almost identical, with television coverage having by far the largest positive impact on both. Presumably much of this television coverage consisted of paid advertising which has become a major factor in most Senate campaigns. If we remove the effects of contact, the advantage of incumbency in House elections was almost identical to the advantage of incumbency in Senate elections. More than two thirds of the difference between ratings of House incumbents and challengers can be attributed to the effects of contact.

The fact that House incumbents enjoyed a much greater advantage than Senate incumbents over their challengers in 1978 was due in large part to the much lower visibility of House challengers. A much larger proportion of respondents reported having had some contact with, and having an opinion about, Senate challengers than House challengers. Unless they are aware of the challenger, voters who are dissatisfied with the incumbent may be reluctant to replace a known quantity with an unknown quantity. Table 2.1.4 lends support to this hypothesis. The relationship between evaluation of the incumbent and candidate choice in House and Senate elections was much stronger among voters who were exposed to the challenger than among those who were not. Among voters with a favorable opinion of the incumbent, contact with the challenger made little or no difference. However, among voters who had an unfavorable opinion or were undecided about the incumbent, contact with the challenger greatly increased the likelihood of voting against the incumbent.

The findings presented in Table 2.1.4 underline the crucial role that the challenger plays in the process of electoral accountability. Among voters in Senate races involving an incumbent, 83 percent reported having had some contact with the challenger. In contrast, only 44 percent of the voters in House races involving an incumbent reported having had some contact with the challenger.

The greater visibility of Senate challengers is

TABLE 2.1.4 PERCENTAGE VOTING FOR INCUMBENT IN HOUSE AND SENATE CONTESTS BY EVALUATION OF INCUMBENT AND EXPOSURE TO CHALLENGER

EXPOSURE TO CHALLENGER	EVALUATION OF INCUMBENT: POSITIVE	EVALUATION OF INCUMBENT: NEUTRAL OR NEGATIVE	TAU	(SIG.)
House:				
Yes	84	29	.43	(.001)
No	93	65	.24	(.001)
Senate				
Yes	78	22	.59	(.001)
No	83	72	.15	(N.S.)

SOURCE: 1978 Election Study, Center for Political Studies, University of Michigan.

not, however, the only difference between House and Senate elections. In addition, House and Senate candidates seem to be evaluated according to different criteria. Evaluations of House candidates were based largely on contacts between constituents and their Representatives, which were overwhelmingly positive in nature. Contacts with Senators did not have as large a net positive impact, suggesting that voters were less dependent on these contacts for information about the incumbent. Party affiliation and ideology had a greater impact on evaluations of Senate candidates than on evaluations of House candidates. The result of this is shown in Table 2.1.5. While ideological proximity to the incumbent had a negligible impact on candidate choice in House elections, it had a substantial impact on candidate choice in Senate elections among two groups of voters: independents and supporters of the challenger's party. The ability of Senate incumbents to draw support from independents and voters of the opposing party depended largely on their ideological position. Whereas House incumbents were favored by an overwhelming 66 percent of voters whose ideology was opposite to their own, Senate incumbents received only 30 percent of the vote among this group.

DISCUSSION

The evidence available from the 1978 election study does not allow us to answer the question of why Senators were more likely to be held accountable on the basis of their overall voting record than Representatives. It does appear that constituents were more likely to know something about their Senator's voting record than about their Representative's voting record. Whereas 51 percent of respondents were able to place their Senate incumbent on a seven-point liberal-conservative scale, only 37 percent were able to place their House incumbent on the same scale. In addition, perceptions of Senators' positions appear to have been somewhat more accurate than perceptions of Representatives' positions.[2] We can only speculate that this may be a function of the information available to constituents about their Senators and Representatives. With greater control over the information constituents receive about themselves, House members may stress noncontroversial activities such as casework and constituency service, rather than positions on controversial national issues. These findings may also reflect greater involvement of ideological or single-issue interest groups in Senate campaigns. Whatever the explanation, the result is a significant difference in the extent of ideological voting in Senate and House elections.

Even if House challengers were provided with resources which would enable them to reach many more voters with their message, most House incumbents would probably remain secure in their positions because the large majority of their constituents are very satisfied

TABLE 2.1.5 PERCENTAGE VOTING FOR INCUMBENT IN HOUSE AND SENATE CONTESTS BY PARTY IDENTIFICATION AND IDEOLOGY

PARTY IDENTIFICATION	IDEOLOGICAL PROXIMITY TO INCUMBENT				
	CLOSEST	MEDIUM	FARTHEST	TAU	(SIG.)
House:					
Same party	96	94	100	−.00	(N.S.)
Independent	87	81	69	.13	(.05)
Other party	52	46	40	.11	(N.S.)
Senate:					
Same party	87	90	*	−.02	(N.S.)
Independent	83	62	39	.33	(.001)
Other party	39	15	7	.30	(.01)

*Fewer than 10 cases.

SOURCE: 1978 Election Study, Center for Political Studies, University of Michigan.

with their performance.[3] When asked to rate the job performance of their own Representative, 72 percent of respondents expressed an opinion, and 65 percent of those with an opinion gave a rating of "very good" or "good," while 31 percent gave a rating of "fair" and only 5 percent gave a rating of "poor" or "very poor." In sharp contrast, among the 80 percent of respondents expressing an opinion about the performance of Congress, only 20 percent gave a rating of "very good" or "good," while 52 percent gave Congress a "fair" rating and 28 percent rated its performance as "poor" or "very poor." These findings lend strong quantitative backing to Fenno's conclusion (1975), based on his observation of 10 House members in their districts, that voters love their Congressmen but dislike Congress. Although the job performance question was not asked about Senate incumbents, comparison of the feeling thermometer ratings of Senators and Representatives indicates that voters do not love their Senator quite as much as they love their Representative.

It is often suggested that members of Congress can use noncontroversial activities such as casework and constituency service to earn political support from the voters and thereby gain freedom of action on important national issues as long as they answer their mail, act as ombudsmen, and bring federal projects into the district. The findings reported here suggest, however, that voters are more tolerant about their Representative's voting record than about their Senator's voting record. After the 1976 and 1978 elections, many Senators are probably looking over their shoulders as they cast their votes.

APPENDIX

The measure of ideological proximity was constructed by comparing Senators' and Representatives' ADA ratings with respondents' positions on the seven-point liberal-conservative scale (1 = most liberal, 7 = most conservative). ADA ratings were used because of the well-established liberal identification of this organization and because of the wide variety of issues on which the rating was based. ADA ratings also correlate very highly with ratings of other ideological groups. Ideological proximity to the incumbent was calculated as follows (1 = closest to incumbent, 3 = farthest from incumbent):

ADA RATING	RESPONDENT'S POSITION	PROXIMITY SCORE
Senate:		
0–19	1–3	3
0–19	4	2
0–19	5–7	1
20–39	1–3	2
20–39	4–7	1
50–59	1–4	1
50–59	5–7	2
60+	1–3	1
60+	4	2
60+	5–7	3
House:		
0–39	1–3	3
0–39	4	2
0–39	5–7	1
40–59	1–3	2
40–59	4	1
40–59	5–7	2
60+	1–3	1
60+	4	2
60+	5–7	3

NOTE: No running Senate incumbent had an ADA rating between 40 and 49.

2.2 The Electoral Incentive*

David R. Mayhew

In a classic statement, David R. Mayhew, in *Congress: The Electoral Connection,* argues that members of Congress are driven by a desire to be reelected. As such, there is a sense of "shared fates" among incumbents and an effort by them collectively to enhance the prospects for their return. We include two excerpts from Mayhew's work. One, addressing the characteristics of policymaking, is presented in Chapter 9. The selection at hand emphasizes the behavior of legislators as they vie for reelection. Here, Mayhew's argument is that, because of the "electoral incentive," Congressmen behave in a certain way in dealing with their constituents.

Whether they are safe or marginal, cautious or audacious, Congressmen must constantly engage in activities related to reelection. There will be differences in emphasis, but all members share the root need to do things—indeed, to do things day in and day out during their terms. The next step here is to present a typology, a short list of the *kinds* of activities Congressmen find it electorally useful to engage in. The case will be that there are three basic kinds of activities.

One activity is *advertising,* defined here as any effort to disseminate one's name among constituents in such a fashion as to create a favorable image but in messages having little or no issue content. A successful Congressman builds what amounts to a brand name, which may have a generalized electoral value for other politicians in the same family. The personal qualities to emphasize are experience, knowledge, responsiveness, concern, sincerity, independence, and the like. Just getting one's name across is difficult enough; only about half the electorate, if asked, can supply their House members' names. It helps a Congressman to be known. "In the main, recognition carries a positive valence; to be perceived at all is to be perceived favorably."[1] A vital advantage enjoyed by House incumbents is that they are much better known among voters than their November challengers.[2] They are better known because they spend a great deal of time, energy, and money trying to make themselves better known.[3] There are standard routines—frequent visits to the constituency, nonpolitical speeches to home audiences,[4] the sending out of infant-care booklets and letters of condolence and congratulation. Of 158 House members questioned in the mid-1960s, 121 said that they regularly sent newsletters to their constituents,[5] 48 wrote separate news or opinion columns for newspapers; 82 regularly reported to their constituencies by radio or television;[6] 89 regularly sent out mail questionnaires.[7] Some routines are less standard. Congressman George E. Shipley (D–Ill.) claims to have met personally about half his constituents (i.e. some 200,000 people).[8] For over 20 years Congressman Charles C. Diggs, Jr. (D–Mich.) has run a radio program featuring himself as a "combination disc jockey–commentator and minister."[9] Congressman Daniel J. Flood (D–Pa.) is "famous for appearing unannounced and often uninvited at wedding anniversaries and other events."[10] Anniversaries and other events aside, congressional advertising is done largely at public expense. Use of the franking privilege has mushroomed in recent years; in early 1973

---

* From David R. Mayhew, *Congress: The Electoral Connection* (New Haven, Conn.: Yale University Press, 1974), pp. 49–77.

one estimate predicted that House and Senate members would send out about 476 million pieces of mail in the year 1974, at a public cost of $38.1 million—or about 900,000 pieces per member with a subsidy of $70,000 per member.[11] By far the heaviest mailroom traffic comes in Octobers of even-numbered years.[12] There are some differences between House and Senate members in the ways they go about getting their names across. House members are free to blanket their constituencies with mailings for all boxholders; Senators are not. But Senators find it easier to appear on national television—for example, in short reaction statements on the nightly news shows. Advertising is a staple congressional activity, and there is no end to it. For each member there are always new voters to be apprised of his worthiness and old voters to be reminded of it.[13]

A second activity may be called *credit claiming,* defined here as acting so as to generate a belief in a relevant political actor (or actors) that one is personally responsible for causing the government, or some unit thereof, to do something that the actor (or actors) considers desirable. The political logic of this, from the Congressman's point of view, is that an actor who believes that a member can make pleasing things happen will no doubt wish to keep him in office so that he can make pleasing things happen in the future. The emphasis here is on individual accomplishment (rather than, say, party or governmental accomplishment) and on the Congressman as doer (rather than as, say, expounder of constituency views). Credit claiming is highly important to Congressmen, with the consequence that much of congressional life is a relentless search for opportunities to engage in it.

Where can credit be found? If there were only one Congressman rather than 535, the answer would in principle be simple enough.[14] Credit (or blame) would attach in Downsian fashion to the doings of the government as a whole. But there are 535. Hence it becomes necessary for each Congressman to try to peel off pieces of governmental accomplishment for which he can believably generate a sense of responsibility. For the average Congressman the staple way of doing this is to traffic in what may be called "particularized benefits."[15] Particularized governmental benefits, as the term will be used here, have two properties: (1) each benefit is given out to a specific individual, group, or geographical constituency, the recipient unit being of a scale that allows a single Congressman to be recognized (by relevant political actors and other Congressmen) as the claimant for the benefit (other Congressmen being perceived as indifferent or hostile); (2) each benefit is given out in apparently ad hoc fashion (unlike, say, social security checks) with a Congressman apparently having a hand in the allocation. A particularized benefit can normally be regarded as a member of a class. That is, a benefit given out to an individual, group, or constituency can normally be looked upon by Congressmen as one of a class of similar benefits given out to sizable numbers of individuals, groups, or constituencies. Hence the impression can arise that a Congressman is getting "his share" of whatever it is the government is offering. (The classes may be vaguely defined. Some state legislatures deal in what their members call "local legislation.")

In sheer volume the bulk of particularized benefits come under the heading of "casework"—the thousands of favors congressional offices perform for supplicants in ways that normally do not require legislative action. High school students ask for essay materials, soldiers for emergency leaves, pensioners for location of missing checks, local governments for grant information, and on and on. Each office has skilled professionals who can play the bureaucracy like an organ—pushing the right pedals to produce the desired effects.[16] But many benefits require new legislation, or at least they require important allocative decisions on matters covered by existent legislation. Here the Congressman fills the traditional role of supplier of goods to the home district. It is a believable role; when a member claims credit for a benefit on the order of a dam, he may well receive it.[17] Shiny construction projects seem especially useful.[18] In the decades before 1934, tariff duties for local industries were a major commodity.[19] In recent years awards given under grant-in-aid programs have become more useful as they have become more numerous. Some quests for credit are ingenious; in 1971 the story broke that Congressmen had been earmarking foreign aid money for specific projects in Israel in order to win favor with home constituents.[20] It should be said of constituency benefits that Congressmen are quite capable of taking the initiative in drumming them up; that is, there can be no automatic assumption that a Congressman's activity is the result of pressures brought to bear by organized interests. Fenno shows the importance of member initiative in his discussion of the House Interior Committee.[21]

A final point here has to do with geography. The examples given so far are all of benefits conferred upon home constituencies or recipients therein (the latter including the home residents who applauded the Israeli projects). But the properties of particularized benefits were carefully specified so as not to exclude the possibility that some benefits may be given to recipients outside the home constituencies. Some probably are. Narrowly drawn tax loopholes qualify as particularized benefits, and some of them are probably conferred upon recipients outside the home districts.[22] (It is difficult to find solid evidence on the point.) Campaign contributions flow into districts from the outside, so it would not be surprising to find that benefits go where the resources are.[23]

How much particularized benefits count for at the polls is extraordinarily difficult to say. But it would be hard to find a Congressman who thinks he can afford to wait around until precise information is available. The lore is that they count—furthermore, given home expectations, that they must be supplied in regular quantities for a member to stay electorally even with the board. Awareness of favors may spread beyond their recipients,[24] building for a member a general reputation as a good provider. "Rivers Delivers." "He Can Do More For Massachusetts."[25] A good example of Capitol Hill lore on electoral impact is given in this account of the activities of Congressman Frank Thompson, Jr. (D–N.J., 4th district):

> In 1966, the fourth was altered drastically by redistricting; it lost Burlington County and gained Hunterdon, Warren, and Sussex. Thompson's performance at the polls since 1966 is a case study of how an incumbent Congressman, out of line with his district's ideological persuasions, can become unbeatable. In 1966, Thompson carried Mercer by 23,000 votes and lost the three new counties by 4,600, winning reelection with 56 percent of the votes. He then survived a districtwide drop in his vote two years later. In 1970, the Congressman carried Mercer County by 20,000 votes and the rest of the district by 6,000, finishing with 58 percent. The drop in Mercer resulted from the attempt of his hard-line conservative opponent to exploit the racial unrest which had developed in Trenton. But for four years Thompson had been making friends in Hunterdon, Warren, and Sussex, busy doing the kind of chores that Congressmen do. In this case, Thompson concerned himself with the interests of dairy farmers at the Department of Agriculture. The results of his efforts were clear when the results came in from the fourth's northern counties.[26]

So much for particularized benefits. But is credit available elsewhere? For government accomplishments beyond the scale of those already discussed? The general answer is that the prime mover role is a hard one to play on larger matters—at least before broad electorates. A claim, after all, has to be credible. If a Congressman goes before an audience and says, "I am responsible for passing a bill to curb inflation," or "I am responsible for the highway program," hardly anyone will believe him. There are two reasons why people may be skeptical of such claims. First, there is a numbers problem. On an accomplishment of a sort that probably engaged the supportive interest of more than one member it is reasonable to suppose that credit should be apportioned among them. But second, there is an overwhelming problem of information costs. For typical voters Capitol Hill is a distant and mysterious place; few have anything like a working knowledge of its maneuverings. Hence there is no easy way of knowing whether a Congressman is staking a valid claim or not. The odds are that the information problem cuts in different ways on different kinds of issues. On particularized benefits it may work in a Congressman's favor; he may get credit for the dam he had nothing to do with building. Sprinkling a district with dams, after all, is something a Congressman is supposed to be able to do. But on larger matters it may work against him. For a voter lacking an easy way to sort out valid from invalid claims the sensible recourse is skepticism. Hence it is unlikely that Congressmen get much mileage out of credit claiming on larger matters before broad electorates.[27]

Yet there is an obvious and important qualification here. For many Congressmen credit claiming on nonparticularized matters is possible in specialized subject areas because of the congressional division of labor. The term *governmental unit* in the original definition of credit claiming is broad enough to include committees, subcommittees, and the two houses of Congress itself. Thus many Congressmen can believably claim credit for blocking bills in subcommittee, adding on amendments in committee, and so on. The audience for transactions of this sort is usually small. But it may include important political actors (e.g. an interest group, the President, The *New York Times,* Ralph Nader) who are capable of both paying Capitol Hill information costs and deploying electoral resources. There is a well-documented example of this in Fenno's treatment of Post Office politics in the 1960s. The postal employee unions used to watch very closely the activities of the House and Senate Post Office Committees and supply valuable electoral resources (money, volunteer work) to members who did their bidding on salary bills.[28]

The third activity Congressmen engage in may be called *position taking,* defined here as the public enunciation of a judgmental statement on anything likely to be of interest to political actors. The statement may take the form of a roll-call vote. The most important classes of judgmental statements are those prescribing American governmental ends (a vote cast against the war; a statement that "the war should be ended immediately") or governmental means (a statement that "the way to end the war is to take it to the United Nations"). The judgments may be implicit rather than explicit, as in: "I will support the President on this matter." But judgments may range far beyond these classes to take in implicit or explicit statements on what almost anybody should do or how he should do it: "The great Polish scientist Copernicus has been unjustly neglected"; "The way for Israel to achieve peace is to give up the Sinai."[29] The Congressman as position taker is a speaker rather than a doer. The electoral requirement is not that he make pleasing things happen but that he make pleasing judgmental statements. The position itself is the political commodity. Especially on matters where governmental responsibility is widely diffused, it is not surprising that political actors should fall back on positions as tests of incumbent virtue. For voters ignorant of congressional processes the recourse is an easy one. The following comment by one of Clapp's House interviewees is highly revealing: "Recently, I went home and began to talk about the ——— Act. I was pleased to have sponsored that bill, but it soon dawned on me that the point wasn't getting through at all. What was getting through was that the act might be a help to people. I changed the emphasis: I didn't mention my role particularly, but stressed my support of the legislation."[30]

The ways in which positions can be registered are numerous and often imaginative. There are floor addresses ranging from weighty orations to mass-produced "nationality day statements."[31] There are speeches before home groups, television appearances, letters, newsletters, press releases, ghostwritten books, *Playboy* articles, even interviews with political scientists. On occasion Congressmen generate what amount to petitions; whether or not to sign the 1956 Southern Manifesto defying school desegregation rulings was an important decision for southern members.[32] Outside the roll-call process the Congressman is usually able to tailor his positions to suit his audiences. A solid consensus in the constituency calls for ringing declarations; for years the late Senator James K. Vardaman (D–Miss.) campaigned on a proposal to repeal the 15th Amendment.[33] Division or uncertainty in the constituency calls for waffling; in the late 1960s a Congressman had to be a poor politician indeed not to be able to come up with an inoffensive statement on Vietnam. ("We must have peace with honor at the earliest possible moment consistent with the national interest.") On a controversial issue a Capitol Hill office normally prepares two form letters to send out to constituent letter writers—one for the pros and one (not directly contradictory) for the antis.[34] Handling discrete audiences in person requires simple agility, a talent well demonstrated in this selection from a Nader profile:

> "You may find this difficult to understand," said Democrat Edward R. Roybal, the Mexican-American representative from California's 30th district, "but sometimes I wind up making a patriotic speech one afternoon and later on that same day an antiwar speech. In the patriotic speech I speak of past wars but I also speak of the need to prevent more wars. My positions are not inconsistent; I just approach different people differently." Roybal went on to depict the diversity of crowds he speaks to: One afternoon he is surrounded by balding men wearing Veterans' caps and holding American flags; a few hours later he speaks to a crowd of Chicano youths, angry over American involvement in Vietnam. Such a diverse constituency, Roybal believes, calls for different methods of expressing one's convictions.[35]

Indeed it does. Versatility of this sort is occasionally possible in roll-call voting. For example a Congressman may vote one way on recommittal and the other on final passage, leaving it unclear just how he stands on a bill.[36] Members who cast identical votes on a measure may give different reasons for having done so. Yet it is on roll calls that the crunch comes; there is no way for a member to avoid making a record on hundreds of issues, some of which are controversial in the home constituencies. Of course, most roll-call positions considered in isolation are not likely to cause much of a ripple at home. But broad voting patterns can and do; member "ratings" calculated by the Americans for Democratic Action, Americans for Constitutional Action, and other outfits are used as guidelines in the deploying of electoral resources. And particular issues often have their alert publics. Some national interest groups watch the votes of all Congressmen on single issues and ostentatiously try to reward or punish members for their positions; over the years some notable examples of such interest groups have been the Anti-Saloon League,[37] the early Farm Bureau,[38] The American Legion,[39] the American Medical Association,[40] and the National Rifle Association.[41] On rare occasions single roll calls achieve a rather high salience among the public generally. This seems especially true of the Senate, which every now and then winds up for what might be called a "showdown vote," with pressures on all sides, presidential involvement, media attention given to individual Senators' positions, and suspense about the outcome. Examples are the votes on the nuclear test-ban treaty in 1963, civil rights cloture in 1964, civil rights cloture again in 1965, the Haynsworth appointment in 1969, the Carswell appointment in 1970, and the ABM in 1970. Controversies on roll calls like these are often relived in subsequent campaigns, the southern Senate elections of 1970 with their Haynsworth and Carswell issues being cases in point.

Probably the best position-taking strategy for most Congressmen at most times is to be conservative—to cling to their own positions of the past where possible and to reach for new ones with great caution where necessary. Yet in an earlier discussion of strategy the suggestion was made that it might be rational for members in electoral danger to resort to innovation. The form of innovation available is entrepreneurial position taking, its logic being that for a member facing defeat with his old array of positions it makes good sense to gamble on some new ones. It may be that congressional marginals fulfill an important function here as issue pioneers—experimenters who test out new issues and thereby show other politicians which ones are usable.[42] An example of such a pioneer is Senator Warren Magnuson (D–Wash.), who responded to a surprisingly narrow victory in 1962 by reaching for a reputation in the area of consumer affairs.[43] Another example is Senator Ernest Hollings (D–S.C.), a servant of a shaky and racially heterogeneous southern constituency who launched "hunger" as an issue in 1969—at once pointing to a problem and giving it a useful nonracial definition.[44] One of the most successful issue entrepreneurs of recent decades was the late Senator Joseph McCarthy (R–Wis.); it was all there—the close primary in 1946, the fear of defeat in 1952, the desperate casting about for an issue, the famous 1950 dinner at the Colony Restaurant where suggestions were tendered, the decision that "communism" might just do the trick.[45]

The effect of position taking on electoral behavior is about as hard to measure as the effect of credit claiming. Once again there is a variance problem; Congressmen do not differ very much among themselves in the methods they use or the skills they display in attuning themselves to their diverse constituencies. All of them, after all, are professional politicians. There is intriguing hard evidence on some matters where variance can be captured. Schoenberger has found that House Republicans who signed an early pro-Goldwater petition plummeted significantly farther in their 1964 percentages than their colleagues who did not sign.[46] (The signers appeared genuinely to believe that identification with Goldwater was an electoral plus.) Erikson has found that roll-call records are interestingly related to election percentages: "[A] reasonable estimate is that an unusually liberal Republican Representative gets at least 6 percent more of the two-party vote . . . than his extreme conservative counterpart would in the same district."[47] In other words, taking some roll-call positions that please voters of the opposite party can be electorally helpful. (More specifically, it can help in November; some primary electorates will be more tolerant of it than others.) Sometimes an inspection of deviant cases offers clues. There is the ideological odyssey of former Congressman Walter Baring (D–Nev.), who entered Congress as a more or less regular Democrat in the mid-1950s but who moved over to a point where he was the most conservative House Democrat outside the South by the late 1960s. The Nevada electorate reacted predictably; Baring's November percentages rose astoundingly high (82.5 percent in 1970), but he encountered guerrilla warfare in the primaries which finally cost him his nomination in 1972—whereupon the seat turned Republican.

There can be no doubt that Congressmen believe positions make a difference. An important consequence of this belief is their custom of watching each other's elections to try to figure out what positions are salable. Nothing is more important in Capitol Hill politics than the shared conviction that election returns have proven a point. Thus the 1950 returns were read not only as a rejection of health insurance but as a ratification of McCarthyism.[48] When two North Carolina nonsigners of the 1956 Southern Manifesto immediately lost their primaries, the message was clear to southern members that there could be no straying from a hard line on the school desegregation issue. Any breath of life left in the cause of school busing was squeezed out by House returns from the Detroit area in 1972. Senator Douglas gives an interesting report on the passage on the first minimum wage bill in the 75th Congress. In 1937 the bill was tied up in the House Rules Committee, and there was an effort to get it to the floor through use of a discharge petition. Then two primary elections broke the jam. Claude Pepper (D–Fla.) and Lister Hill (D–Ala.) won nominations to fill vacant Senate seats. "Both campaigned on behalf of the Wages and Hours bill, and both won smashing victories. . . . Immediately after the results of the Florida and Alabama primaries became known, there was a stampede to sign the petition, and the necessary 218 signatures were quickly obtained."[49] The bill later passed. It may be useful to close this section on position taking with a piece of political lore on electoral impact that can stand beside the piece on the impact of credit claiming offered earlier. The discussion is of the pre-1972 sixth California House district:

> Since 1952 the district's Congressman has been Republican William S. Mailliard, a wealthy member of an old California family. For many years Mailliard had a generally liberal voting record. He had no trouble at the polls, winning elections by large majorities in what is, by a small margin at least, a Democratic district. More recently, Mailliard seems caught between the increasing conservatism of the state's Republican party and the increasing liberalism of his constituency.
>
> After [Governor Ronald] Reagan's victory [in 1966], Mailliard's voting record became noticeably more conservative. Because of this, he has been spared the tough conservative primary opposition that Paul McCloskey has confronted in the 11th. But Mailliard's move to the right has not gone unnoticed in the sixth district. In 1968 he received 73 percent of the vote, but in 1970 he won only 53 percent—a highly unusual drop for an incumbent of such long standing. Much of the difference must be attributed to the war issue. San Francisco and Marin are both antiwar strongholds; but Mailliard, who is the ranking Republican on the House Foreign Affairs Committee, has supported the Nixon Administration's war policy. In the sixth district, at least, that position is a sure vote-loser.[50]

These, then are the three kinds of electorally oriented activities Congressmen engage in—advertising, credit claiming, and position taking. It remains only to offer some brief comments on the emphases different members give to the different activities. No deterministic statements can be made; within limits each member has freedom to build his own electoral coalition and hence freedom to choose the means of doing is.[51] Yet there are broad patterns. For one thing Senators, with their access to the media, seem to put more emphasis on position taking than House members; probably House members rely more heavily on particularized benefits. But there are important differences among House members. Congressmen from the traditional parts of old machine cities rarely advertise and seldom take positions on anything (except on roll calls), but devote a great deal of time and energy to the distribution of benefits. In fact, they use their office resources to plug themselves into their local party organizations. Congressman William A. Barrett (D–downtown Philadelphia), chairman of the Housing Subcommittee of the House Banking and Currency Committee, claimed in 1971 to have spent only three nights in Washington in the preceding six years. He meets constituents each night from 9:00 P.M. to 1:00 A.M. in the home district: "Folks line up to tell Bill Barrett their problems."[52] On the other hand Congressmen with upper-middle-class bases (suburban, city reform, or academic) tend to deal in positions. In New York City the switch from regular to reform Democrats is a switch from members who emphasize benefits to members who emphasize positions; it reflects a shift in consumer taste.[53] The same difference appears geographically rather than temporally as one goes from the inner wards to the outer suburbs of Chicago.[54]

Another kind of difference appears if the initial assumption of a reelection quest is relaxed to take into account the "progressive" ambitions of some members—the aspirations of some to move up to higher electoral offices rather than keep the ones they have.[55] There are two important subsets of climbers in the Congress—House members who would like to be Senators (over the years about a quarter of the Senators have come up directly from the House),[56] and Senators who would like to be Presidents or Vice Presidents (in the 93d Congress about a quarter of the Senators had at one time or another run for these offices or been seriously "mentioned" for them). In both cases higher aspirations seem to produce the same distinctive mix of activities. For one thing credit claiming is all but useless. It does little good to talk about the bacon you have brought back to a district you are trying to abandon. And, as Lyndon Johnson found in 1960, claiming credit on legislative maneuvers is no way to reach a new mass audience; it baffles rather than persuades.

Office advancement seems to require a judicious mixture of advertising and position taking. Thus a House member aiming for the Senate heralds his quest with press releases; there must be a new "image," sometimes an ideological overhaul to make ready for the new constituency.[57] Senators aiming for the White House do more or less the same thing—advertising to get the name across, position taking ("We can do better"). In recent years presidential aspirants have sought Foreign Relations Committee membership as a platform for making statements on foreign policy.[58]

There are these distinctions, but it would be a mistake to elevate them over the commonalities. For most Congressmen most of the time all three activities are essential. This closing vignette of Senator Strom Thurmond (R–S.C.) making his peace with universal suffrage is a good picture of what the electoral side of American legislative politics is all about. The Senator was reacting in 1971 to a 1970 Democratic gubernatorial victory in his state in which black turnout was high:

> Since then, the Republican Senator has done the following things:
>
> —Hired Thomas Moss, a black political organizer who directed Negro voter registration efforts for the South Carolina Voter Education Project, for his staff in South Carolina, and a black secretary for his Washington office.
>
> —Announced federal grants for projects in black areas, including at least one occasion when he addressed a predominantly black audience to announce a rural water project and remained afterwards to shake hands.
>
> —Issued moderate statements on racial issues.
>
> In a statement to Ebony magazine that aides say Thurmond wrote himself, he said, "In most instances I am confident that we have more in common as southerners than we have reason to oppose each other because of race. Equality of opportunity for all is a goal upon which blacks and southern whites can agree."[59]

CHAPTER

3 The Congress: Who Is It?

In addition to being a political institution and instrument of government, Congress is a human organization, replete with its interpersonal relations, cliques, norms and folkways, and dynamics of power, authority, and formal and informal leadership.

The readings in this section aim to define Congress as a human organization. To do this, selections are included on the legislator as actor, the House versus the Senate, staff growth, staff in the district, office dynamics, and congressional agencies, together with the views of two former, prominent insiders concerning the sociology of Congress.

A major issue to be aware of concerning the social and human side of Congress pertains to the enormous proliferation of congressional staff. According to some, burgeoning staffs have led to a system of "unelected representatives" that pose the danger of overwhelming members with analytical studies and self-serving and self-justifying make-work. For others less concerned, staff recruitment places boundaries on staff behavior, requiring staffers to anticipate member positions and to work within "parameters" of acceptability established by members. From this perspective, staff growth is a boon, not a bane, assisting Congress in its oversight responsibilities and strengthening the Congress's hand vis-à-vis the Executive Branch.

Illustration 3A Organizational Charts of House and Senate

The following are organizational schematics of both houses of Congress. These charts graphically illustrate that the Congress is more than just 435 House members, 100 Senators, and their staffs. Congress is comprised of numerous support organizations and offices. These charts show the many offices established to support each house.

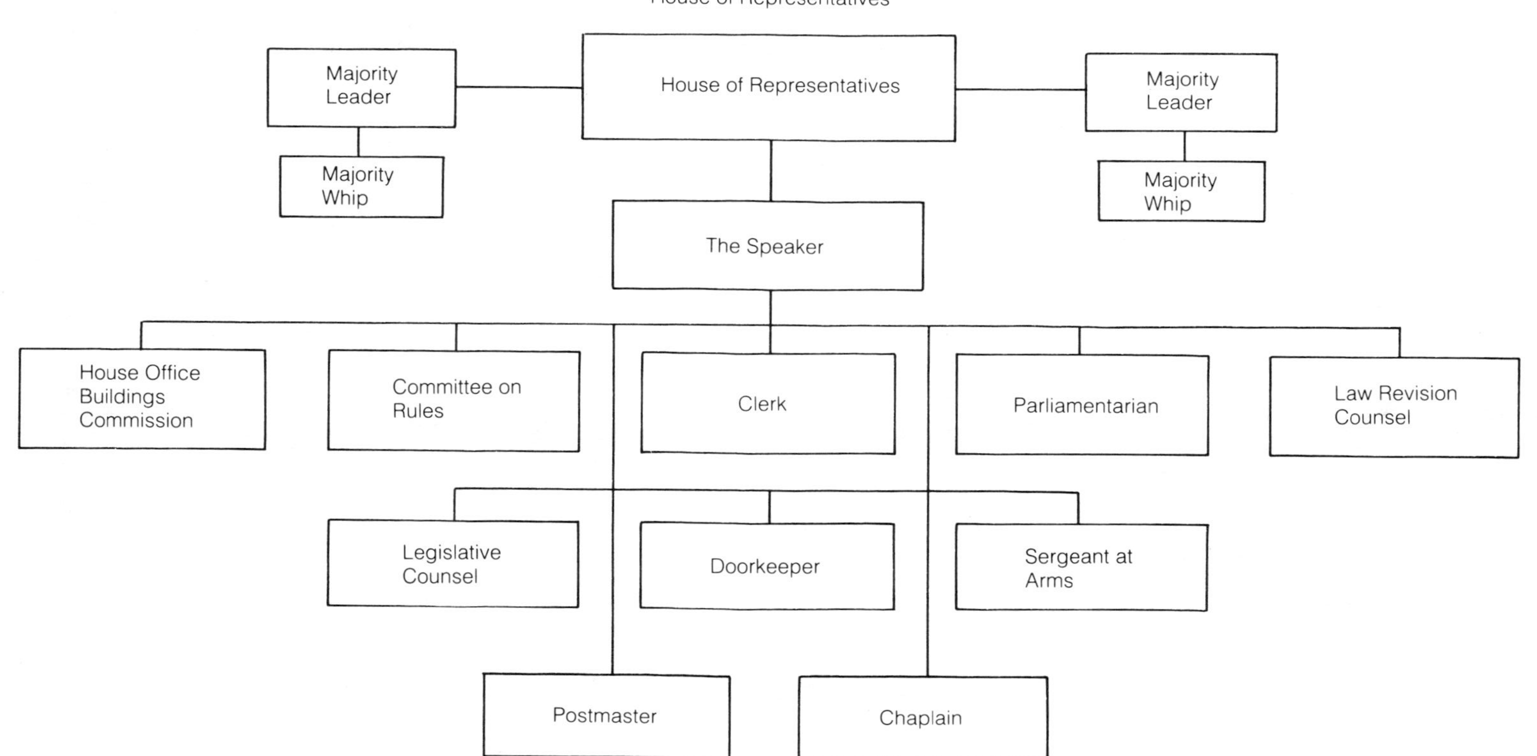

SOURCE: From United States Government Manual, 1980–81, pp. 35–38. Reprinted from the public domain.

ILLUSTRATION 3A (*continued*)

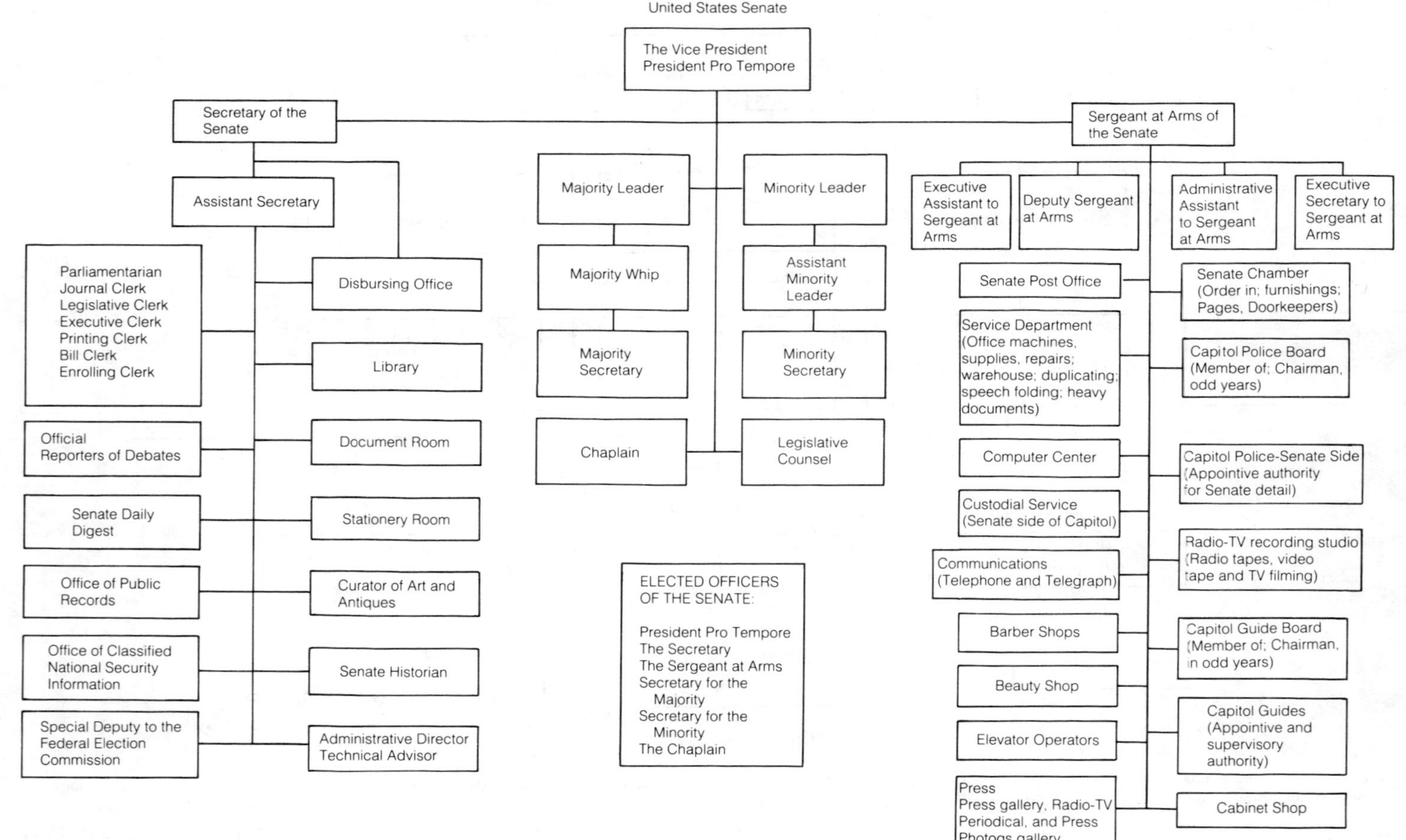

3.1 Congressional versus Bureaucratic Policy Actors *

Randall B. Ripley and Grace A. Franklin

Congressmen and their staffs are major actors in policymaking. The following selection from a widely used text illustrates the distinctive personal and institutional characteristics of members of Congress and congressional staffers in comparison to political executives and bureaucrats.

Table 3.1.1 summarizes the personal characteristics of major congressional and bureaucratic policy actors. When added to the information in the following section, a composite picture of the various groups of policy actors begins to emerge that shows that these characteristics can have some impact on the nature of relations between the groups as they labor on public policy.

THE INSTITUTIONAL SETTING

The institutional setting in which congressional and bureaucratic actors function is simply the general work environment that serves as a framework for any person in a particular job. A member of Congress operates in a different job environment from an agency head, as does a staff member for a congressional committee from a Secretary of a Department. The literature suggests a number of factors important in the institutional setting or job environment for each of the four groups of actors being examined. These include method of selection, job tenure and orientation, principal loyalties and representativeness, substantive specialization, professionalism, political expertise, and anonymity. In general, these factors are relatively unchanging over time, regardless of the individuals holding the positions.

Method of selection means simply how actors achieve the positions they hold. The principal options are election, political appointment, or merit advancement. *Job tenure and orientation* is related to the means of selection and involves the length of service and careerist aspirations associated with different actors. *Principal loyalties* involve the actors' perceptions of the entity to which they feel they owe primary service. *Representativeness* of various actors varies both according to the geographic area represented (national versus local) and the breadth of interests represented (broad-gauged interests versus narrow, special interests). Do actors tend to become expert in a few issues (specialists) or do they tend to have a general understanding of many issues (generalists)? The notion of *degrees of substantive specialization* addresses these questions. An actor's identification with a profession, in addition to identification as a government employee, is the focus of the discussion of *degree of professionalism*. The *degree of political expertise* inherent in different actors' jobs involves how political those jobs are and how much political skill is necessary for successfully holding them—skills in bargaining, negotiations, and competing for limited amounts of power and resources. The final factor presented to describe the institutional setting is the *degree of*

* From Randall B. Ripley and Grace A. Franklin, *Congress, the Bureaucracy, and Public Policy*, rev. ed. (Homewood, Ill: Dorsey Press, 1976). Copyright © The Dorsey Press, 1976. Reprinted by permission.

TABLE 3.1.1 PERSONAL CHARACTERISTICS OF MAJOR CONGRESSIONAL AND BUREAUCRATIC POLICY ACTORS

CHARACTERISTICS	SENATORS AND REPRESENTATIVES	CONGRESSIONAL STAFF MEMBERS	HIGHER CAREER CIVIL SERVANTS	FEDERAL POLITICAL EXECUTIVES
Geographical representativeness	Broadly representative geographically; overrepresentative of small towns	Broadly representative geographically	Broadly representative	Broadly representative geographically; overrepresentative of large cities (especially New York and Washington)
Education	Highly educated	Highly educated	Highly educated	Highly educated
Occupation	Heavily in law and business; some educators; many professional politicians	Occupational speciality tied to job; many professional public servants; some generalists	Occupational speciality tied to job; many professional public servants; many with business background; some educators	Heavily in business and law; some educators
Age	Median: late 40s (Senators slightly older)	Median: about 40	Median: late 40s	Median: late 40s
Sex and race	Mostly white males	Mostly white males	Mostly white males	Mostly white males
Previous governmental and political experience	High experience in both government and politics	Limited government experience; more political experience	High government experience through civil service career	Moderately high experience in federal service
Beliefs	Believes in subgovernments and interest-group access; ideology shifts with election results	Believes in subgovernments and interest-group access; ideology reflects that of congressional employer	Believes in subgovernments and interest-group access; ideology reflects that of agency	Believes in subgovernments and interest-group access; ideology reflects that of agency

anonymity (or conversely, visibility) associated with the actors—how publicly visible are different groups as they perform their daily routines?

Method of Selection

Of the four groups, only one—members of the House and Senate—is elected. This simple fact makes an enormous difference in the kinds of considerations that are most salient to members as they deal with policy. Concern for job security nurtures a predisposition for Congressmen to provide the voters back home with sufficient tangible benefits that they will reelect the providers. Congressmen usually evaluate their behavior, either consciously or unconsciously, in terms of the impact it will have on the electoral constituency and the constituency's reaction to it (Mayhew, 1974).*

Once in Congress, members seek appointment to specific committees and subcommittees for a variety of reasons (see Fenno, 1973). A number of members consciously seek positions because of the electoral advantage it can bring them. Even those who pursue memberships primarily because of their policy interests and because of their interest in increasing their influence within their chamber are mindful of opportunities a given assignment might afford them to serve their constituents. As members become more senior, they are generally less vulnerable at election time and can afford to pursue policy views that are particularly congenial to them as they work in committee and subcommittee settings.

The congressional staff is appointed by members of Congress and so reflect some of the members' concern with reelection and constituents. But, given the fact that an experienced staff member with an individual Senator or Representative can probably find another such job with a different member if his employer should lose an election, his or her personal stake is not nearly as strong as the member's own stake.

———

* Reference list in Endnotes.

Political appointments in the Executive Branch are made by the President. At least in theory, he is responsible for selecting the appointees, but in practice many appointees are chosen by other high-ranking officials in his adminstration, either because they know and want a particular individual or because he or she comes highly recommended by an important party figure—such as a major contributor of funds or an important Senator or Representative.

Civil servants and their military and foreign service equivalents are appointed on the basis of competitive examinations in the first instance and they advance on the basis of merit after that.

Job Tenure and Orientation

Not surprisingly, job tenure and orientation are related to the way an actor acquires his office. Personnel turnover in positions dependent on electoral results in greater than in nonelective positions among civil servants. The shortest length of service occurs among political appointees in the Executive Branch. Median tenure in the mid-1960s was only 28 months in a position and 31 months in an agency (Stanley, Mann, and Doig, 1967: 57; see also Heclo, 1977: 104). Because of their short tenure, political appointees generally have their careers in some field other than government service.

Tenure for individual Congressmen will always be uncertain because these are elective positions, but overall length of service in Congress has increased over time (not always steadily, depending on election results). The average number of years of service for members of both houses has dropped a bit in the 1970s but is still high; in 1977 it stood at almost 10 years for a Senator and over eight years for a Representative. Careerist aspirations are now well entrenched among most members of Congress. (See Huntington, 1973; Polsby, 1968; Price, 1971; and Witmer, 1964 on the development of a congressional career.)

Although data are relatively scarce, it seems that many congressional staff members have become oriented toward a career in legislative staff work and are able to realize their ambitions, in many cases, for two reasons. First, the long service of the members (the appointing authorities) helps them stay in their positions for a long time. Second, even if their original patron is unseated they are often sought out by new members of the House and Senate and offered jobs because of the high value placed on their experience. (On the development of a congressional staff career see Fox and Hammond, 1977: 62–65.) The size of congressional staff has expanded dramatically in recent years—between 1967 and 1976, for example, Senate personal staff increased by 86 percent, House personal staff increased by 71 percent, Senate committee staff increased by 147 percent, and House committee staff increased by 163 percent. Thus it is not surprising that a number of staff members are still both relatively young and relatively junior in service. Some years from now we will be better able to tell how many of them are making their careers on the Hill.

Careerism among bureaucrats at the policy-making levels is characterized by long service but low mobility in terms of shifting occupational specialties, shifting between agencies, and shifting between Washington and federal field installations (see Corson and Paul, 1966: 22, 175, 176, and Stanley, 1964: 27, 32–34, 102–103). In the early 1960s, for example, the higher civil servants had an average length of service of 23 years. Almost three quarters of these individuals had served for more than 20 years. Over 86 percent of them had spent their entire careers in no more than two Departments (almost 56 percent had been in only one Department), and over 68 percent had served in no more than two bureaus (over 37 percent had only been in one bureau). Movement between Washington headquarters and field offices was very low. (Almost 90 percent had never left headquarters to go into the field.) Recent figures published by the Civil Service Commission (1976) show the same lack of mobility in the 1970s.

Corson and Paul's figures on supergrades in the civil service in 1963 show the same pattern: Two thirds had worked in no more than two bureaus and about 40 percent in only one. About half had worked in the same agency or Department for their entire careers. Only 15 percent had ever worked outside the federal government once they had begun service and over three fourths had held all of their federal jobs in the same occupational field.

The civil servants are the most career-oriented of all the four groups and are also most likely to serve a full career wholly within a single institutional location. For example, a sample of federal civil servants interviewed in 1960 and 1961 showed that most were highly intent on staying in federal service; 88 percent of the general employees were very sure or fairly sure they wanted to stay in federal service, and only 7 percent planned to leave. Among executives in the civil service 94 percent were very sure or fairly sure they wanted to stay and only 3 percent planned to leave. Even among professionals (natural scientists, social scientists, and engineers whose major loyalties might be to their professions and not to the government organization with which they were employed) there was a high propensity to stay with federal service. Between 69 and 82 percent of these three professional groups were either sure or fairly sure they wanted to stay in federal service, and only between 10 and 18 percent planned to leave (Kilpatrick, Cummings, and Jennings, 1963: 188). Predictably, civil servants who were older and had more service were the most wedded to remaining.

Principal Loyalties and Representativeness

The principal loyalties of members of the House and Senate are generally split between loyalty to their constituencies (or, more accurately, to their perceptions of various constituencies—see Fenno, 1978) and loyalty to their congressional parties. In general, congressional life is structured so that the two loyalties do not compete in head-on fashion a great deal of the time. When they do compete directly, a member will ordinarily stick with his perceptions of the constituency's interest.

Congressional staff members are primarily loyal to their appointing authority—that is, to the individual Senator or Representative responsible for having put them in their present jobs. Thus if a staff member's "sponsor" is highly oriented toward constituency interests the staff member is also likely to reflect that concern. If a sponsor is more oriented toward maintaining a given programmatic or ideological stance then the staff member is more likely to take that tack too.

In theory, executive political appointees are primarily loyal to the President, the President's program, and the Administration as a collectivity. In practice, political appointees are also at least partially loyal to the organization to which they are appointed. Thus a Secretary of Agriculture will try to be responsive to the President who appointed him, but if career bureaucrats within the Department perceive their interests to be at odds with the President's policy initiatives, the Secretary will find himself cross-pressured. Ordinarily he will try to find some compromise that will allow him not to disagree with the President, at least publicly, while still not "selling out" the Department.

Civil servants are primarily loyal to the organizations in which they work and in which they are likely to make their career. They are perhaps less cross-pressured than the other major actors. Those in agencies who are also professionals (lawyers, engineers, scientists, etc.) may also feel considerable loyalty to the standards of their profession and may be cross-pressured by the perceived competing demands of profession and agency at times (see Wilensky, 1967).

Members of the House and Senate are concerned with representing their geographical areas—their districts or states—and are usually also concerned with representing a variety of interests they perceive to be important. While the notion of representation may be interpreted differently by different Senators and Representatives, they are virtually all genuinely concerned with being representative. For some this may mean focusing mostly on tangible benefits for the district and for the most important organized groups in the district. For others this may mean thinking about the broader needs of the district and of national interests and groups—both organized and unorganized. For most members representation probably involves a range of activities—from seeking a new post office for some town in the district or state to worrying about the welfare of all poor people or all cotton farmers or all black people or whatever group seems to the member to be important.

Congressional staff members are also interested in representation in the same several senses in which members are interested. Their interest is largely a reflection of the interests of their sponsors, although some individuals personally may also feel strongly about their representative capacities serving in a staff role.

Executive Branch officials are also concerned with representation, but they are not concerned with a specific constituency in the same sense as individuals on Capitol Hill. The geographical ties to a local constituency of both political appointees and civil servants stationed in Washington are weaker than those of members of Congress and usually weaker than those of congressional staff members. They may retain some ties to the region in which they grew up, or more likely, their program may have a particular regional focus. (An Agriculture Department official working with cotton price supports is, of course, going to be concerned mostly with the cotton growing regions of the South, and an official in the Bureau of Reclamation is going to be concerned mainly with the arid lands of the West.) But many Washington officials are involved with programs that have a national scope and they are therefore likely to think about the program in national terms.

But 87 percent of bureaucrats in the United States are not located in the metropolitan Washington, D.C., area. These individuals (over 2.35 million of them in 1976) are scattered throughout the country in a variety of federal field installations such as state, regional, and local offices. The bureaucrats who populate these field installations outside Washington have regional and local geographic loyalties tied to their agencies' programs, and they undertake their work in such a way as to maximize the size of their particular operation in their region, state, or locality.

In addition to geographic interests, bureaucrats—both political appointees and civil servants—are also typically concerned with representing interests they perceive to be important to their programs and worthy of their attention. In general, political appointees are expected to be supportive of and sympathetic to the programmatic interests of the President and to represent those interests to Congress. They also may be concerned with representing the interests thought to be important to their political party, and thus their concern with specific representation may not be very well-developed, although it seems reasonable to argue that a Republican Secretary of Labor, for example, will concern himself with representing managerial interests at least some of the time and that a Democratic Secretary of Labor will concern himself with representing organized labor's interests most of the time. To survive politically, appointees in departments and agencies are most likely to be representative of many interests involved with their agencies rather than representing only one or two interests. An appointee who principally advocates a single, narrow interest is apt to be a controversial figure and a political liability for the President's program and in the national electorate.

Political appointees can be representative in the critical sense of allowing competing points of view to be heard in the Executive Branch on controversial matters before final action is taken. Sometimes policy debates take place almost wholly within the Executive Branch and the major decisions are made and the major compromises are struck before the matter even becomes an important item on the congressional agenda. This was the case, for example, with the bargaining and arguments that led up to the passage of the Communications Satellite Act of 1962 and the Economic Opportunity Act of 1964 (Davidson, 1967: 390–393).

Civil servants often become very concerned with representing interests and organized groups they conceive to be important in the substantive fields in which they are working. Sometimes this representational activity simply takes the form of advocacy by strategically placed civil servants on behalf of interests and groups. In other cases the advocacy of specific interests by a bureaucracy becomes more institutionalized. For example, some agencies use a variety of advisory committees to make and enforce decisions at the local level. These committees operate in several policy areas, including agriculture and land use (see Foss, 1960; Lowi, 1973). A potential problem with advisory committees is that they may become captives of some segment of the served clientele, and bureaucrats, in heeding their advice, are thus responding to only a narrow interest group. This was the case with federal lands grazing policy (see Foss, 1960: chapter 6).

Degree of Substantive Specialization

Members of the House and Senate are both subject matter specialists and generalists. They are generalists because they are given the constitutional power—which they exercise with considerable, even if uneven, vigor—to oversee the entire range of federal government activities. They must consider and vote on literally everything the federal government does, at least in broad outline. Naturally, any individual is going to have a number of substantive areas in which his or her knowledge is minimal, but most Senators and Representatives who serve for more than a short time begin to develop familiarity with and some competence in a wide variety of subject matter areas.

At the same time members have also become specialists through their service on the standing committees and subcommittees of the two chambers. The committee system emerged in large part as the congressional response to a bureaucracy constantly growing in size, specialization, and expertise. Especially in the House—where in the 93d Congress (1973–1974) the average member had assignments to only 1.6 standing committees and 3.5 subcommittees (Asher, 1974: 68)—members who serve for more than a short period become genuine experts in some piece of the policy world. In the Senate the members are spread more thinly because each Senator has more assignments—an average of 2.6 standing committees and 9.7 subcommittees in 1973–1974 (Asher, 1974: 68).

The congressional urge to specialize in order to compete with the bureaucrats is reinforced by the staff on the Hill. In both houses staff members have become genuinely expert in some bounded portion of the policy universe although staff members working in the offices of individual Senators and Representatives have much less time for work on substantive legislative matters than staff working for committees. Senate staff members—both those on committees and a few working in individual Senators' offices—are particularly important as specialists because of the limited time and attention the typical Senator can give to his committee and subcommittee assignments. Senators often rely principally on a staff member to do most of the substantive work in some subcommittees to which the Senator is formally assigned (Ripley, 1969: chapter 8). Many staff members, including those on committees, are also expected to attend to political matters and to deal with constituents in a variety of ways.

In the bureaucracy the degree of substantive specialization in the civil service is very high. The main reason for the emergence of a large bureaucracy is, after all, to facilitate dealing with technical and complex topics. On the other hand, the degree of specialization among political appointees is typically very low—much lower than for a member of the House or Senate with even a few years of service. The typical political appointee in the Executive Branch has little experience in the subject matter with which he or she is expected to deal and usually does not stay in office long enough to develop much expertise through on-the-job training.

DEGREE OF PROFESSIONALISM

''Professionalism'' is used to denote allegiance on the part of individuals to a profession other than that of government employee. For example, if a chemist is employed by the Food and Drug Administration he or she may well remain loyal to the norms of the chemistry profession, attend meetings of the American Chemical Society, and subscribe to a variety of professional journals. Such an individual is likely to be equally concerned with national professional standards and judgments as with the narrower interests of the Food and Drug Administration as an agency.

Most professionalism in this sense resides in the civil service. Scattered throughout the bureaucracy are social scientists, natural scientists, engineers, dentists, physicians, and others whose professional identification is very high.

In the rest of the government—the appointed parts of the Executive Branch and both the elected and appointed parts of the Legislative Branch—the degree of professionalism is much lower. There are many lawyers, particularly in Congress, but they seem to retain little identification with abstract norms of the profession. For many, law was both a form of academic training and a natural entry into public service but not a profession actively practiced, at least for very long.

DEGREE OF POLITICAL EXPERTISE

By definition Senators and Representatives are and must be politicians. A few may not be, but they are likely to be very transient residents of the congressional institution. Members need the political skill of assessing the mood of their constituency and the amount of latitude they have within that mood. They also are likely to develop considerable bargaining skills as they pursue their daily tasks in Congress. Staff members typically possess a number of the same kinds of political skills. Some are hired expressly for their political skills that can be used to help the member gain reelection and/or have the maximum impact on substantive policy questions.

In the Executive Branch, political appointees presumably possess considerable political skills—both in advancing the interests of the

Administration and the party of the President and in bargaining. Some political appointees are very adroit politically. In fact, some are so skillful that they develop their own constituency and support apart from the President who is presumably their sponsor. A classic case is that of Jesse Jones, Secretary of Commerce under President Franklin Roosevelt (Fenno, 1959: 234–247). His ties with powerful business interests and his excellent relations with Congress allowed him to take policy stands contrary to those desired by Roosevelt. Yet the President tolerated his behavior for over four years because, on balance, he thought his independent strength helped the Administration more than it hurt it.

Some political appointees turn out to be quite inept politically. President Eisenhower's Secretary of Defense, Charles Wilson of General Motors, was usually in hot water with some congressional committee for his seemingly thoughtless remarks (''What's good for the country is good for General Motors, and vice versa.'') and behavior. In speaking of the Cabinet specifically, Fenno (1959: 207–208) concluded that politically a skillful Secretary ''maintains legislative-executive relations in an equilibrium and prevents them from deteriorating to the point where they hurt the President. What the ordinary Cabinet member supplies is a kind of *preventive assistance*. . . . The best that he can ordinarily do is to help the President in small amounts—probably disproportionate to the time he consumes doing it.'' The same generalization probably applies to the whole range of political appointees in the Executive Branch.

In theory, civil servants are supposed to be apolitical. They are barred from overt partisan activity by federal statute. The textbooks proclaim them to be ''above politics'' and concerned only with rational, economical, and efficient implementation of public policy objectives determined by their political superiors.

In the United States, however, the textbook model does not apply in large part. Senior civil servants are fully political actors and in many respects the governmental system in which they work expects that they will be if they are to be successful (see Heclo, 1977).

The political stance of the bureaucracy is the result of several factors—grants of administrative discretion, congressional reliance on the bureaucracy, and competition in advancing the agencies' perceived interests. Broad administrative discretion to fill in the gaps of basic legislation does not promote ''neutral'' administration. Bureaucrats' decisions have political impact and repercussions, and bureaucrats experience pressure for and against their administrative decisions. Congress relies on the bureaucracy as a primary source of policy ideas and initiatives, and policy is rarely neutral—it almost always conveys benefits to some and deprives others. Who wins and who loses is, after all, what politics is all about. The continuous maneuvering by senior agency officials to maximize the interests of their agencies and programs, especially at budget time, but also throughout daily routines, requires a high degree of political skill. Agency officials cannot afford to be neutral if their agency's interests are to be advanced.

Richard Neustadt has convincingly explained the basic reason for the political nature of our top civil servants: The governmental system puts them in direct competition with other actors and thereby breeds the necessity of developing political skills in order to gain or preserve the resources to perform programmatic tasks effectively. The following excerpt elaborates the idea (Neustadt, 1973: 132):

> . . . we maximize the insecurities of men and agencies alike. Careerists jostle in-and-outers (from the law firms, business, academic life) for the positions of effective influence; their agencies contend with the committees on the Hill, the Office of Management and Budget, other agencies for the prerequisites of institutional survival, *year by year*. Pursuit of programs authorized in law can be a constant struggle to maintain and hold support of influential clients, or the press. And seeking new authority to innovate a program can be very much like coalition warfare. Accordingly, most agencies have need for men of passion and conviction—or at least enormous powers of re-

Table 3.1.2 The General Institutional Setting for Congressional and Bureaucratic Policy Actors

Characteristic	Members of House and Senate	Congressional Staff Members	Executive Branch Political Appointees	Civil Servants and Equivalents
Method of selection	Election	Appointment by Senators and Representatives	Appointment by President	Competition and merit
Job tenure and orientation	Relatively long service; careerist orientation	Relatively long service; relatively careerist orientation	Short service; noncareer orientation	Long service; career orientation
Principal loyalties	Constituencies and congressional parties	Sponsors (appointing members)	President and agency to which appointed	Agency
Degree of concern with representation	High for geographical constituencies and special interests	Moderately high for geographical constituencies and interests	Low for geographical units; moderately low for special interests	High for special interests; moderate for geographical units among non-Washington-based civil servants; low for geographical units among Washington-based civil servants
Degree of substantive specialization	Moderately high (especially in House)	Moderately high	Low	High
Degree of professionalism	Low	Generally low	Low	High for major subgroups of employees
Degree of political expertise	High	Moderately high	Moderately high	Moderately high (for highest grades)
Degree of anonymity	Low	High	Moderately low	High

sistance—near the top. American officialdom may generate no more of these than other systems do, but it rewards them well: they rise toward the top.

DEGREE OF ANONYMITY

Anonymity is, of course, relative, and it may vary from observer to observer. To even an interested part of the general public, for example, virtually all of the actors being discussed here except some Senators and Representatives are anonymous. To most journalists covering Washington only Senators and Representatives and a few political appointees in the Executive Branch are consistently visible. A really skillful reporter will also come to know important congressional staff members and, occasionally, even a civil servant or two. Skillful lobbyists will tend to know individuals in all of the major clusters of actors. In general it would be most accurate to say that Senators and Representatives and the major political appointees in the Executive Branch, such as the President's Cabinet, tend to be the most visible to most observers. Congressional staff members and civil servants tend to be relatively unknown to a large number of observers.

Table 3.1.2 summarizes the discussion of the institutional work setting for the four major clusters of actors.

3.2 House versus Senate*

Nelson W. Polsby

Firsthand experience on Capitol Hill quickly teaches that there is not a "Congress" per se. "Congress" as an institution more often than not is a media fixation. In reality, there are two separate legislative institutions: House and Senate. It has been said—not with tongue in cheek—that the two houses have only three things in common: their members are elected, they both pass legislation, and they share the same building. Each has a distinctive time frame, constituency, structure, way of doing business, and policy role. The House, because it is larger, is more formal, rigid, and hierarchical. The Senate, because it is smaller, is more informal, flexible, and nonhierarchical. In the following selection, Nelson Polsby specifies the unique policy roles of each house.

As institutions, the House and the Senate differ markedly in their essential character. The House is a highly specialized instrument for processing legislation. Its great strength lies in its firmly structured division of labor. This division of labor provides the House with a toehold in the policymaking process by virtue of its capacity to farm out and hence, in some collective sense, to master technical details. House members are frequently better prepared than Senators in conferences,[1] and usually have the better grasp of the peculiarities of the executive agencies they supervise. This is an artifact of the strong division of labor that the House maintains: Members are generally assigned to

* From Nelson W. Polsby, "Policy Analysis and Congress," *Public Policy* 17 (1969): 62–64. Copyright © by John Wiley & Sons, 1969. Reprinted by permission.

one or two committees only; and floor debate is generally limited to participation by committee members. There is an expectation that members will concentrate their energies, rather than range widely over the full spectrum of public policy. Patterns of news coverage encourage specialization; general pronouncements by House members are normally not widely reported. Senators, because they are fewer, more socially prominent, and serve longer terms (hence are around long enough for newsmen to cultivate), and allegedly serve "larger" districts, can draw attention to themselves by well-timed press releases almost regardless of their content.

The coordination of an organism like the House is difficult because it cannot entail excessive centralization of power. Decentralization is necessary for the House to maintain its capacity to cope with the outside world (that is, through its complex and specialized division of labor). And this in turn produces the House's major career incentive—namely, the opportunity accorded a tenth to a fifth of its members to possess the substance of power in the form of a committee or subcommittee chairmanship or membership on a key committee. At present seniority acts as a bulwark of this incentive system, by guaranteeing a form of job security at least within the division of labor of the organization.[2]

Thus, as I once observed in another connection:

> To that large fraction of members for whom the House is a career and a vocation, the longevity of members above them in the many hierarchies of the House—not the entirely predictable congressional election returns in their home districts—is the key to the political future.[3]

The essence of the Senate is that it is a great forum, an echo chamber, a publicity machine.[4] Thus "passing bills," which is central to the life of the House, is peripheral to the Senate. In the Senate the three central activities are (1) the cultivation of national constituencies (that is, beyond state lines) by political leaders; (2) the formulation of questions for debate and discussion on a national scale (especially in opposition to the President); and (3) the incubation of new policy proposals that may at some future time find their way into legislation.

This conception of the Senate is, in some respects, novel, since it focuses on an aspect of Senate life that is much deplored by aficionados of the "inner club" conception of the institution, who often defend the curious thesis that the persons anointed by the mysterious chemistry of Senate popularity are the very elite that keeps this nation from the mob scene in *The Day of the Locust*.

I think, however, that there is considerable use in a democratic republic for an organization that encourages—as the Senate currently does—the generation of publicity on issues of public importance. One must grant there have been abuses in the pursuit of publicity by Senators; but Senate "great debates," investigations, and hearings have also performed considerable public service.

Where the House of Representatives is a large, impersonal, and highly specialized machine for processing bills and overseeing the Executive Branch, the Senate is, in a way, a theater where dramas—comedies and tragedies, soap operas and horse operas—are staged to enhance the careers of its members and to influence public policy by means of debate and public investigation.

In both the House and the Senate the first commandment to newcomers is "Specialize." But this means vastly different things in the two houses.[5] "Specialize" to a Representative means "tend to your knitting": Work hard on the committee to which you are assigned, pursue the interests of your state and region. In the Senate everyone has several committee assignments. Boundaries between committees are not strictly observed. Occasionally a Senator who is not a committee member will sit in on a hearing if a subject interests him. On the floor, quite unlike the House, virtually any Senator may speak for any length of time about anything. Thus the institution itself gives few cues and no compulsions to new Senators wondering what they should specialize in. For the Senate, specialization seems to mean finding a subject matter and a nationwide constituency interested in the subject that have not already been preempted by some more senior Senator.

It is a cliché of academic political science that in legislative matters, it is the President who initiates policy and Congress which responds, amplifying and modifying and rearranging elements which are essentially originated in the Executive Branch. Not much work has been done, however, on following this river of bills-becoming-and-not-becoming-laws back to its sources. Where do innovations in policy come from *before* the President "initiates" them?

Old Washington hands know the answer. There is very little new under the sun. A great many newly enacted policies have "been around," "in the air" for quite a while. In the heat of a presidential campaign or when a newly inaugurated President wants a "new" program, desk drawers fly open all over Washington. Pet schemes are fished out, dusted off, and tried out on the new political leaders.

There is often a hiatus of years—sometimes decades—between the first proposal of a policy innovation and its appearance as a presidential "initiative"—much less as a law. Commentators have greatly underestimated the role of the Senate in gestating these ideas, by providing a forum for speeches, hearings, and the introduction of bills going nowhere for the moment. This process of gestation accomplishes a number of things. It maintains a sense of community among far-flung interest groups that favor the innovation, by giving them occasional opportunities to come in and testify. It provides an incentive for persons favoring the innovation to keep up to date information on its prospective benefits and technical feasibility. And it accustoms the uncommitted to a new idea.

Thus the Senate is in some respects at a crucial nerve-end of the polity. It articulates, formulates, shapes, and publicizes demands, and can serve as a hothouse for significant policy innovation.

3.3 The Growth of Staff*

The fastest-growing bureaucracy in Washington, D.C. is not, as some would think, the institutionalized Presidency in the Executive Office of the President; it is congressional staffs. The following excerpt from a congressional study of staff details the expansion of staff at both the personal office and committee levels.

EARLY STAFFING PRACTICES

Staffing began in both the House of Representatives and the Senate as clerical assistance. Before the middle of the 19th century, clerks were provided to congressional committees on a temporary basis by special resolutions adopted by each House every session. In 1856, the House Ways and Means Committee and the Senate Finance Committee received regular appropriations for full-time clerks. Rather slowly at first, but at an accelerating pace, other committees followed suit until by 1900 the Legislative Branch appropriations acts were carrying funds for the employment of clerical staff for the standing committees in both chambers.

* From *Final Report of the Select Committee on Committees, U.S. House of Representatives,* 1980, pp. 531–41. House Report No. 96–866, Reprinted from the public domain.

Senators were first authorized to employ personal clerks in 1885; the House passed similar authorizations eight years later, in 1893. In 1896, clerk hire was authorized on a year-round basis for Representatives who were not committee chairmen, and in 1898 committee chairmen were authorized year-round clerk hire allowances.

COMMITTEE STAFFING: LEGISLATIVE REORGANIZATION ACT OF 1946

Committee staffing underwent substantial change after passage of the Legislative Reorganization Act of 1946. Under the legislation, committees were allowed to hire four professional staff members and up to six clerical workers each. The Appropriations Committees were allowed to determine the number of their employees by a majority vote of the Committee. Thus, the total number of staff allowed for committees under the 1946 act was 340, plus the additional numbers employed by the Appropriations Committees.

COMMITTEE STAFFING: LEGISLATIVE REORGANIZATION ACT OF 1970

Passage of the Legislative Reorganization Act of 1970 brought significant change in committee staffing procedures. As enacted, the law had five major provisions relating to committee staff:

The act increased to six from four the number of permanent professional staff members for each standing committee. Two members of the professional staff, in addition to one of the six permanent clerical staff members, might be selected by a majority of the committee's minority party members. This provision did not apply to the House and Senate Appropriations Committees or to the House Committee on Standards of Official Conduct.

The act authorized standing committees—with approval of the Senate Rules Committee or the Committee on House Administration—to hire temporary consultants.

The act authorized standing committees—with approval of the Senate Rules Committee or the Committee on House Administration—to provide staff members with specialized training.

The act authorized salaries of Senate committee staff personnel comparable to House committee staff personnel.

The act required that no less than one third of a House committee's funds be used for minority staff. (The House voted in 1971 to disregard this provision. It was revived in 1974 but killed in 1975.)

HOUSE SELECT COMMITTEE ON COMMITTEES (BOLLING/HANSEN PROVISIONS)

The House Select Committee on Committees (Bolling Committee) proposed revisions in many House procedures. The proposals, as revised by the Democratic Caucus, Committee on Organization, Study and Review, were adopted as H. Res. 988. H. Res. 988 increased the number of professional staff members from 6 to 18 and of clerical employees from 6 to 12 for each House standing committee, except Appropriations and Budget. If they desired, a majority of the minority party members on a standing committee (except for the Committee on Standards of Official Conduct) might select six of the professional and four of the clerical staff persons for appointment by a majority of the committee. If the committee should reject any of these minority party choices, a majority of the minority might select others until the appointments were made. Minority staff would work on committee business as assigned by the minority party members. The remainder of the staff would be appointed solely on their ability to perform requisite tasks, and any staff members could be dismissed by a majority vote of the committee.

H. Res. 988 retained the language of the existing House rule that professional staff members should be appointed on a permanent and merit basis and should not be assigned any work other than committee business. It deleted the requirement that they be appointed without regard to political affiliation. However, H. Res.

988 did permit a committee to employ nonpartisan staff, in lieu of or in addition to staff designated exclusively for the majority or minority party, if a majority of the members of each party on that committee voted to do so.

H. Res. 988 granted the minority party members on each standing committee, upon request by a majority of them, one third of the funds for specially authorized staff. From these funds for the minority, the ranking minority member of the full committee could provide the ranking minority member of each subcommittee with money to hire at least one professional staff person. All specially authorized staff selected for appointment by the minority party had to be acceptable to a majority of the committee. If the committee disapproved any of the minority party choices, a majority of the minority party members might select others until the appointments were made. However, this provision never went into effect. On January 13, 1975, the House Democratic Caucus rescinded the allocation of one third of the specially authorized staff funds to the minority party members. It incorporated in H. Res. 5 an amendment to the House rules, substituting for this arrangement. On each standing committee, from the funds provided for specially authorized staff, the chairman and ranking member of each standing subcommittee (up to a maximum of six, except for Appropriations) were authorized to appoint one staff person apiece who would serve at their pleasure. These staff positions would be taken from the quota of permanent professional staff for the committee if specially authorized funds were not made available for them.

SENATE RESOLUTION 60

The members' need for personal assistance on committee work has been an issue for many years. In early 1975, Sen. Mike Gravel introduced a resolution, S. Res. 60, which would institute this idea through the concept of associate committee staff. S. Res. 60 was approved on June 12, 1975. As passed, S. Res. 60, in effect, allowed every Senator to hire a maximum of three committee assistants at near the top professional staff salary. It entitled each Senator to a staff allowance of $33,975 apiece for up to two major committee assignments and another $33,975 for one minor, select to joint committee assignment. If a Senator were not on a minor select or joint committee but served on more than two major committees, he or she could receive $33,975 for a third major committee. However, this staff allowance would be reduced by an amount equal to the total annual basic pay of committee employees whose appointments were made, recommended, or approved by a Senator if they were assigned to assist with duties on a committee for which an allowance was received.

In other words, a Senator with no committee staff could receive as much as $101,925; but a Senator with control over at least one staff member each on two major and one minor or three major committees could receive nothing. Any employee hired under this provision was to be certified, by the Senator who made the appointment, to the chairman and ranking minority member of the committee with which he or she was designated to work, and was to be accorded all privileges of a professional staff member of that committee. In short, under the prescribed conditions, a Senator could appoint several personal legislative assistants who would have all the privileges of professional staff members of the committee with which they worked.

CURRENT STAFF PRACTICES

Since 1971, the Committee on House Administration has had authority to approve additional personal staffing allowances, with no House vote required. Senate personal staffing formulas are determined by the Legislative Branch subcommittee of the Senate Appropriations Committee. In both houses, committee "investigative" staffing budgets must be approved by the full chamber after consideration by the Committee on House Administration or the Senate Rules and Administration Committee.

HOUSE COMMITTEE STAFF

Committee staff in the House are divided into two categories: statutory and investigative. Statutory employees are hired without regard to political affiliation, solely on the basis of their ability to perform required duties, and are prohibited from performing work other than committee business during their hours of employment. Statutory staff are augmented by "investigative" personnel, hired pursuant to annual "studies and investigations" funding resolutions. Investigative staff are not covered by the legal protections and prohibitions under which statutory staff function.

All House committees except Appropriations and Budget are authorized to employ up to 30 statutory staff (18 professional and 12 clerical). The Appropriations and Budget Committees are permitted by House Rule XI to determine the appropriate level of staff they require. Neither committee is required to submit a funding resolution for employment of investigative staff.

The 1946 Legislative Reorganization Act, which established the statutory committee staff positions, also required semiannual reports from House committees showing the numbers of employees, dates of employment, titles, and salaries. Since 1970, the Report of the Clerk of the House has provided a compilation of these data.

The committee staff employee report formats have not always been uniform. These variances often make employee status difficult to determine. For example, until 1957 the semiannual reports did not consistently distinguish between statutory and investigative staff.

Statutory and investigative staff data are presented in Tables 3.3.1 and 3.3.2. Each table contains data from 1957–1978. In Table 3.3.3 are the combined totals for statutory and investigative staff since 1947.

The staff levels in all tables are those as of June 30 of each year, except for 1977 and 1978. In 1977 the publication date of the Clerk's Report was changed to conform to the new fiscal year. The levels for 1977 and 1978 are those as of September 30.

TABLE 3.3.1 HOUSE STANDING COMMITTEE STATUTORY STAFF, 1957–1978

COMMITTEE	1957	1958	1959	1960	1961	1962	1963	1964	1965	1966	1967
Agriculture	9	10	10	10	10	10	10	10	10	10	9
Appropriations*	55	57	53	52	60	57	50	48	60	54	62
Armed Services	10	10	10	10	10	10	10	12	14	19	21
Banking	6	7	8	9	9	9	9	10	10	10	10
Budget*	(†)	(†)	(†)	(†)	(†)	(†)	(†)	(†)	(†)	(†)	(†)
District of Columbia	6	9	8	8	10	9	10	9	10	10	10
Education and Labor	12	12	10	11	10	10	13	10	10	10	9
Government Operations	8	11	10	10	10	10	10	10	10	9	10
House Administration	4	4	5	4	4	3	3	4	6	8	8
Interior	10	10	10	10	10	10	10	10	10	10	10
Internal Security	10	10	10	10	10	10	10	10	10	10	10
International Relations	12	12	12	14	12	15	16	17	17	17	18
Interstate and Foreign Commerce	10	10	12	12	12	12	14	14	14	14	13
Judiciary	13	13	13	11	13	13	13	13	12	10	13
Merchant Marine and Fisheries	9	9	9	9	9	9	9	9	9	10	10
Post Office and Civil Service	10	10	10	9	10	10	10	10	10	10	10
Public Works	10	10	10	10	10	10	10	9	10	9	8
Rules	3	3	3	2	3	3	4	4	3	5	5
Science and Technology	(†)	(†)	10	10	10	10	9	10	10	10	10
Small Business	(†)	(†)	(†)	(†)	(†)	(†)	(†)	(†)	(†)	(†)	(†)
Standards of Official Conduct	(†)	(†)	(†)	(†)	(†)	(†)	(†)	(†)	(†)	(†)	(†)
Veterans Affairs	10	10	10	10	10	10	9	9	9	10	10
Ways and Means	14	18	16	15	19	22	22	23	23	19	23
	1968	1969	1970	1971	1972	1973	1974	1975	1976	1977	1978
Agriculture	10	10	10	11	11	11	10	26	29	29	31
Appropriations*	64	70	66	65	68	69	78	91	111	125	129
Armed Services	22	23	24	22	24	23	25	29	27	30	29
Banking	10	10	8	9	9	9	9	17	26	24	29
Budget*	(†)	(†)	(†)	(†)	(†)	(†)	(†)	67	65	56	77
District of Columbia	10	10	10	10	9	13	12	28	30	24	24
Education and Labor	10	10	9	12	12	12	12	26	25	23	22
Government Operations	9	10	10	12	12	11	12	20	17	15	19
House Administration	9	23‡	25‡	12	12	12	12	26	30	28	35
Interior	10	10	10	12	10	12	10	30	30	28	29
Internal Security	10	10	10	10	12	12	11	(†)	(†)	(†)	(†)
International Relations	20	20	21	14	14	11	10	28	24	26	26
Interstate and Foreign Commerce	14	14	14	15	15	16	16	29	25	27	28
Judiciary	13	35‡	13	15	14	15	15	23	22	28	29
Merchant Marine and Fisheries	10	11	10	12	12	10	10	20	24	30	29
Post Office and Civil Service	10	10	10	11	11	11	9	23	27	28	30
Public Works	9	9	8	11	12	12	12	22	25	25	27
Rules	6	6	7	6	6	7	9	18	26	24	25
Science and Technology	10	28‡	10	11	12	12	12	28	28	28	33
Small Business	(†)	(†)	(†)	(†)	(†)	(†)	(†)	13	10	11	9
Standards of Official Conduct	5	5	5	5	6	5	6	5	14	26	28
Veterans Affairs	10	10	9	11	11	10	12	20	22	19	22
Ways and Means	22	22	24	23	27	27	28	26	30	26	29

* Appropriations and Budget Committees are permitted to establish their own staff levels. Staff figures for the Appropriations Committee may include "investigative" staff as a result of the format of the Report of the Clerk of the House.

† Not a standing committee for the year in question.

‡ Figures include investigative as well as statutory staff; the report format did not make itemization of statutory staff possible.

SOURCE: Committee employment reports for the period ending June 30 of each year, printed in *Congressional Record* for 1947–70. For 1971–76, the Report of the Clerk of the House for the period ending June 30 of each year. For 1977 and 1978, the report for the period ending September 30 was used.

TABLE 3.3.2 HOUSE STANDING COMMITTEE INVESTIGATIVE STAFFS, 1957–78

COMMITTEE	1957	1958	1959	1960	1961	1962	1963	1964	1965	1966	1967
Agriculture	(*)	(*)	(*)	(*)	3	1	3	4	8	6	5
Appropriations	14	7	7	5	5	6	5	5	5	5	5
Armed Services	10	10	6	5	5	6	5	5	6	8	9
Banking	7	5	4	5	6	7	27	32	25	31	39
Budget	(†)	(†)	(†)	(†)	(†)	(†)	(†)	(†)	(*)	(*)	(†)
District of Columbia	(*)	(*)	(†)	(†)	(†)	(†)	(†)	(†)	(†)	(†)	(†)
Education and Labor	(*)	7	10	14	33	37	31	32	47	71	47
Government Operations	53	57	41	44	40	41	43	44	51	46	51
House Administration	6	10	(†)	(†)	(†)	(†)	(†)	(†)	(†)	(†)	(†)
Interior	(*)	(*)	(†)	(†)	(†)	(†)	(†)	(†)	3	4	4
Internal Security	35	40	37	36	42	47	42	45	47	42	41
International Relations	(*)	(*)	(*)	(*)	(*)	(*)	(*)	(*)	(*)	(*)	(*)
Interstate and Foreign Commerce	8	27	20	33	10	15	15	23	17	18	23
Judiciary	16	16	22	17	23	31	35	33	25	24	17
Merchant Marine and Fisheries	(*)	(*)	(*)	(*)	(*)	(*)	(*)	(*)	(*)	(*)	9
Post Office and Civil Service	(*)	(*)	(*)	(*)	(*)	(*)	(*)	(*)	22	25	24
Public Works	(*)	8	7	22	26	39	45	45	29	27	29
Rules	(*)	(*)	(*)	(*)	(*)	(*)	(*)	(*)	(*)	(*)	(*)
Science and Technology	(†)	(†)	6	7	8	7	7	10	10	11	13
Small Business	(†)	(†)	(†)	(†)	(†)	(†)	(†)	(†)	(†)	(†)	(†)
Standards of Official Conduct	(†)	(†)	(†)	(†)	(†)	(†)	(†)	(†)	(†)	(†)	(*)
Veterans Affairs	7	6	10	8	8	7	6	8	9	12	7
Ways and Means	7	6	5	7	(†)	(†)	(†)	(†)	(†)	(†)	(†)

COMMITTEE	1968	1969	1970	1971	1972	1973	1974	1975	1976	1977	1978
Agriculture	5	6	7	7	6	9	12	22	29	27	27
Appropriations	6	5	5	6	7	8	7	7	7	(‡)	(‡)
Armed Services	9	11	13	11	9	6	5	9	12	18	16
Banking	37	37	42	40	39	42	50	68	86	83	81
Budget	(†)	(†)	(†)	(†)	(†)	(†)	(†)	0	0	20	20
District of Columbia	8	4	5	5	11	21	25	15	24	14	11
Education and Labor	61	64	68	70	82	83	96	88	104	79	81
Government Operations	46	48	50	45	43	47	52	48	56	65	63
House Administration (§)	(†)	(‡)	(‡)	19	58	110	151	191	218	240	234
Interior	4	4	4	7	16	26	31	27	28	36	39
Internal Security	38	39	41	45	39	30	31	27	(†)	(†)	(†)
International Relations	(*)	(*)	(*)	18	21	25	31	26	40	67	75
Interstate and Foreign Commerce	18	25	28	31	39	40	42	83	113	103	121
Judiciary	14	(‡)	22	24	22	29	157	46	62	56	53
Merchant Marine and Fisheries	9	11	11	11	15	12	12	8	10	32	50
Post Office and Civil Service	27	35	36	33	37	33	34	38	37	33	35
Public Works	26	27	32	36	42	52	60	66	76	63	56
Rules	(*)	(*)	(*)	(*)	(*)	(*)	(*)	(*)	(*)	(*)	(*)
Science and Technology	14	(‡)	16	14	14	15	17	19	25	49	47
Small Business	(†)	(†)	(†)	(†)	†)	(†)	(†)	14	21	28	31
Standards of Official Conduct	(*)	(*)	(*)	(*)	(*)	(*)	(*)	(*)	(*)	5	9
Veterans Affairs	6	9	9	8	7	8	6	6	9	12	12
Ways and Means	(†)	(†)	(†)	(†)	1	4	4	37	56	66	64

* Indicates committee did not employ investigative staff.

† Not a standing committee for year in question.

‡ Staff report formats make it impossible to determine which staff held statutory positions and which held investigative positions. In such instances, combined staff figures are included in statutory staff table.

§ For 1972 to present, figure includes employees of House Information Systems, the House of Representatives central computer facility.

SOURCE: Committee employment reports for the period ending June 30 of each year, printed in *Congressional Record* for 1947–70. For 1971–76, the Report of the Clerk of the House for the period ending June 30 of each year. For 1977 and 1978 the report for the period ending September 30 was used.

TABLE 3.3.3 HOUSE COMMITTEE STAFF TOTALS, 1947–77 (COMBINED STATUTORY AND INVESTIGATIVE STAFF)

COMMITTEE	1947	1948	1949	1950	1951	1952	1953	1954	1955	1956	1957	1958
Agriculture	9	11	11	7	8	7	10	8	9	9	9	10
Appropriations	29	33	45	39	45	53	96	80	75	69	69	64
Armed Services	10	11	10	11	13	16	15	18	19	18	20	20
Banking	4	5	6	6	6	11	6	6	6	12	13	12
Budget	(*)	(*)	(*)	(*)	(*)	(*)	(*)	(*)	(*)	(*)	(*)	(*)
District of Columbia	7	6	7	6	5	5	5	5	6	6	6	9
Education and Labor	10	14	10	10	10	10	10	11	11	10	12	19
Government Operations	9	19	34	28	21	28	37	38	45	62	61	68
House Administration†	7	7	9	6	7	5	7	4	6	10	10	14†
Interior	4	7	9	9	10	10	7	10	10	10	10	10
Internal Security	10	34	33	35	42	42	39	41	38	42	45	50
International Relations	10	9	8	9	10	9	9	9	10	11	12	12
Interstate and Foreign Commerce	10	12	11	11	11	14	10	10	12	12	18	37
Judiciary	7	7	11	13	21	40	23	13	27	27	29	29
Merchant Marine and Fisheries	6	3	10	11	8	8	9	7	9	10	9	9
Post Office and Civil Service	6	11	7	11	7	7	8	8	8	9	10	10
Public Works	6	20	20	7	14	17	10	7	9	10	10	18
Rules	4	5	5	5	5	6	4	3	3	4	3	3
Science and Technology	(*)	(*)	(*)	(*)	(*)	(*)	(*)	(*)	(*)	(*)	(*)	(*)
Small Business	(*)	(*)	(*)	(*)	(*)	(*)	(*)	(*)	(*)	(*)	(*)	(*)
Standards of Official Conduct	(*)	(*)	(*)	(*)	(*)	(*)	(*)	(*)	(*)	(*)	(*)	(*)
Veterans Affairs	7	9	10	9	9	9	11	11	13	14	17	16
Ways and Means	12	13	13	13	24	36	30	14	13	16	21	24
Total, standing committees	167	236	269	246	276	333	346	303	329	361	384	434

COMMITTEE	1959	1960	1961	1962	1963	1964	1965	1966	1967	1968	1969	1970
Agriculture	10	10	13	11	13	14	18	16	14	15	16	11
Appropriations	60	59	65	63	55	53	65	59	67	70	75	77
Armed Services	16	15	15	16	15	17	20	27	30	31	34	37
Banking	12	14	15	16	36	42	35	41	49	47	47	50
Budget	(*)	(*)	(*)	(*)	(*)	(*)	(*)	(*)	(*)	(*)	(*)	(*)
District of Columbia	8	8	10	9	10	11	10	10	16	18	14	15
Education and Labor	20	25	43	47	44	42	57	81	56	71	74	77
Government Operations	51	54	51	51	53	54	61	55	61	55	58	60
House Administration†	5	4	4	3	3	4	6	8	8	9	23	25
Interior	10	10	10	10	10	10	13	14	14	14	14	14
Internal Security	47	46	52	57	52	55	57	52	51	48	49	51
International Relations	12	14	12	15	16	17	17	17	18	20	20	21
Interstate and Foreign Commerce	32	45	22	27	29	37	31	32	36	32	39	42
Judiciary	35	27	36	44	48	46	37	34	30	27	35	35
Merchant Marine and Fisheries	9	9	9	9	9	9	9	10	19	19	22	21
Post Office and Civil Service	10	9	10	10	10	10	32	35	34	37	45	46
Public Works	17	32	36	49	55	54	39	36	37	35	36	40
Rules	3	2	3	3	4	4	3	5	5	6	6	7
Science and Technology	(*)	17	18	17	16	20	20	21	23	24	28	26
Small Business	(*)	(*)	(*)	(*)	(*)	(*)	(*)	(*)	(*)	(*)	(*)	(*)
Standards of Official Conduct	(*)	(*)	(*)	(*)	(*)	(*)	(*)	(*)	(*)	5	5	5
Veterans Affairs	20	18	18	17	15	17	18	22	17	16	19	18
Ways and Means	21	22	19	22	22	23	23	19	23	22	22	24
Total, standing committees	398	440	461	496	515	539	571	594	608	621	681	702

TABLE 3.3.3 *(continued)*

	1971	1972	1973	1974	1975	1976	1977	1978
Agriculture	18	17	20	22	48	58	56	59
Appropriations	61	75	75	85	98	188	125	128
Armed Services	33	33	29	30	38	39	48	45
Banking	49	48	51	59	85	112	107	110
Budget	(*)	(*)	(*)	(*)	67	65	76	77
District of Columbia	15	20	34	37	43	54	38	35
Education & Labor	82	94	95	108	114	129	102	103
Government Operations	57	55	58	64	68	73	80	82
House Administration†	31	70	122	163	217	248	268	269
Interior	19	26	38	31	57	58	64	68
Internal Security	55	51	42	42	27	(*)	(*)	(*)
International Relations	32	35	36	41	54	64	93	101
Interstate and Foreign Commerce	46	44	56	58	112	138	130	149
Judiciary	39	36	44	172	69	84	84	82
Merchant Marine and Fisheries	23	27	22	22	28	34	62	79
Post Office and Civil Service	44	48	44	43	61	64	61	65
Public Works	47	54	64	72	88	101	88	83
Rules	6	6	7	9	18	26	24	25
Science and Technology	25	26	27	29	47	53	77	80
Small Business	(*)	(*)	(*)	(*)	27	31	39	40
Standards of Official Conduct	5	6	5	6	5	14	31	37
Veterans Affairs	19	18	18	18	26	31	31	34
Ways and Means	23	28	31	32	63	86	92	93
Total, standing committees	729	817	918	1,143	1,460	1,680	1,776	1,844

* Not a standing committee for year in question.
† For 1972 to present, figure includes employees of House Information Systems, the House of Representatives central computer facility.

SOURCE: Committee employment reports for the period ending June 30 of each year, printed in *Congressional Record* for 1947–70. For 1971–76, the Report of the Clerk of the House for the period ending June 30 of each year. For 1977 and 1978, the report for the period ending September 30 was used.

SENATE COMMITTEE STAFF

Table 3.3.4 shows Senate committee staff numbers for selected years between 1947 and 1978. The Reports of the Secretary of the Senate are the source for the staff data. The staffing levels for the years 1947–1975 are as of June 30 while September 30 reports are the source for 1976, 1977, and 1978 data.

Committees are listed under their current name; parenthetical references cite previous names.

TABLE 3.3.4 SENATE COMMITTEE STAFF (SELECTED YEARS)

COMMITTEE	YEARS						
	1947	1950	1955	1960	1965	1970	1971
Aeronautics and Space Sciences	(*)	(*)	(*)	10	14	12	13
Agriculture, Nutrition, and Forestry	3	8	7	10	7	7	13
Appropriations	23	18	36	31	38	42	41
Armed Services	10	19	23	23	18	19	25
Banking, Housing, and Urban Affairs	9	28	23	22	20	23	25
Budget	(*)	(*)	(*)	(*)	(*)	(*)	(*)
Commerce, Science, and Transportation	8	31	32	52	35	53	55
District of Columbia	4	10	5	7	9	18	27
Energy and Natural Resources (Interior)	7	13	30	26	18	22	24
Environment (Public Works)	10	11	11	11	15	34	35
Finance	6	8	6	6	6	16	17
Foreign Relations	8	16	17	25	21	31	34
Governmental Affairs	29	30	27	47	64	55	76
Judiciary	19	42	190	137	162	190	194
Labor and Human Resources	9	38	33	28	40	69	82
Post Office and Civil Service	46	10	33	20	20	31	23
Rules and Administration	41	18	13	15	22	13	15
Veterans Affairs	(*)	(*)	(*)	(*)	(*)	(*)	12
Total, standing committees	232	300	386	470	509	635	711
	1972	1973	1974	1975	1976	1977	1978
Aeronautics and Space Sciences	10	15	16	22	14	(*)	(*)
Agriculture, Nutrition, and Forestry	16	18	21	22	36	27	34
Appropriations	38	47	58	72	72	71	78
Armed Services	29	29	25	30	34	30	30
Banking, Housing, and Urban Affairs	36	40	41	55	48	41	48
Budget	(*)	(*)	(*)	90	91	78	93
Commerce, Science and Transportation	76	72	83	111	103	91	96
District of Columbia	25	29	25	33	31	(*)	(*)
Energy and Natural Resources (Interior)	29	42	45	53	53	54	49
Environment (Public Works)	35	43	54	70	62	52	62
Finance	20	21	25	26	39	35	45
Foreign Relations	38	46	50	62	63	62	61
Governmental Affairs	90	90	104	144	172	154	178
Judiciary	202	209	221	251	200	170	200
Labor and Human Resources	105	110	112	150	110	112	123
Post Office and Civil Service	32	19	23	25	25	(*)	(*)
Rules and Administration	48	21	20	29	27	28	30
Veterans Affairs	15	22	25	32	21	23	24
Total, standing committees	844	873	948	1,277	1,201	1,028	1,151

* Committee not in existence.

SOURCE: Report of the Secretary of the Senate. For 1976, 1977, and 1978 staff levels are as of September 30; for all other years levels are as of June 30.

TABLE 3.3.5 NUMBER OF COMMITTEE STAFF, 1947–78 (SELECTED YEARS)

YEAR	HOUSE OF REPRESENTATIVES	SENATE
1947......	167	232
1950......	246	300
1955......	329	386
1960......	440	470
1965......	571	509
1970......	702	635
1971......	729	711
1972......	817	844
1973......	878	873
1974......	1,107	948
1975......	1,433	1,277
1976......	1,680	1,201
1977......	1,776	1,028
1978......	1,844	1,151

SOURCE: Report of the Clerk of the House and Report of the Secretary of the Senate. For 1977 and 1978 for period ending September 30; all other years as of June 30.

TABLE 3.3.6 PERSONAL STAFF NUMBERS, 1946–78 (SELECTED YEARS)

YEAR	HOUSE OF REPRESENTATIVES (EXCLUDING DISTRICT STAFF)	SENATE
1946......	(*)	751
1950......	(*)	950
1955......	(*)	1,044
1960......	(*)	1,399
1965......	(*)	2,029
1970......	(*)	2,428
1971......	5,381	2,456
1972......	5,827	2,683
1973......	5,994	2,747
1974......	6,120	3,096
1975......	6,615	3,188
1976......	6,828	3,099
1977......	6,315	3,554
1978......	6,295	3,268

*Information not available.

SOURCE: Report of the Clerk of the House and Report of the Secretary of the Senate. For 1977 and 1978 for period ending September 30; all other years as of June 30.

PERSONAL STAFF

After 1946, the increase in authorizations for personal staff on members accelerated. Between 1893, when clerks were first approved for members other than committee chairmen in the House, and 1946, personal staff levels increased from one or two to a maximum of five for each Representative. Since 1946, the number of personal staff has increased fairly regularly: to eight by 1955, to 10 by 1965, to 18 in March 1975, and 22 in July 1979.

Senate personal staff were first authorized in 1885, eight years earlier than in the House. Annual allowances for staff are based on state populations. Senators use of these allowances vary. It is up to the individual member to determine how to apportion these funds. While some use these allowances in their entirety, others return a percentage. In addition, salary levels are flexible and Senators can use discretion in defining number of staff and corresponding salary.

Table 3.3.8 provides staff data for leadership positions in both chambers; Tables 3.3.9 and 3.3.10 provide levels of staff for congressional officers. As with previous tables, the levels for 1977 and 1978 are as of September 30 while all other levels are as of June 30.

TABLE 3.3.7 DISTRICT EMPLOYEES OF HOUSE MEMBERS, 1970–1978

YEAR	NUMBER OF EMPLOYEES
1970	1,035
1971	1,121
1972	1,189
1973	1,347
1974	1,519
1975	1,732
1976	1,943
1977	2,058
1978	2,137

SOURCE: Charles B. Brownson, *Congressional Staff Directory*, Mt. Vernon, Va., the years 1970–1978.

TABLE 3.3.8 NUMBER OF LEADERSHIP EMPLOYEES, 1946–78 (SELECTED YEARS)

	SPEAKER/VICE PRESIDENT		MAJORITY LEADER		MINORITY LEADER		MAJORITY WHIP		MINORITY WHIP		LEGISLATIVE COUNSEL	
YEAR	HOUSE	SENATE	HOUSE	SENATE	HOUSE	SENATE	HOUSE	SENATE	HOUSE	SENATE	HOUSE	SENATE
1946......	(*)	(*)	(*)	(*)	(*)	(*)	(*)	(*)	(*)	(*)	(*)	(*)
1950......	(*)	10	(*)	(*)	(*)	(*)	(*)	(*)	(*)	(*)	(*)	15
1955......	(*)	9	(*)	(*)	(*)	(*)	(*)	(*)	(*)	(*)	(*)	15
1960......	(*)	15	(*)	(*)	(*)	(*)	(*)	(*)	(*)	(*)	(*)	15
1965......	(*)	18	(*)	(*)	(*)	(*)	(*)	1	(*)	1	(*)	16
1970......	(*)	30	(*)	2	(*)	4	(*)	2	(*)	2	(*)	16
1971......	15	27	8	1	5	4	9	2	9	2	26	17
1972......	17	25	9	1	6	4	10	2	8	2	30	18
1973......	20	22	20	(*)	7	(*)	12	(*)	8	(*)	32	18
1974......	22	25	43	3	13	4	14	2	9	2	36	19
1975......	17	37	29	2	16	4	9	2	12	2	30	20
1976......	18	31	20	2	15	3	12	3	13	3	38	22
1977......	18	33	10	5	13	6	13	3	11	9	47	22
1978	19	36	11	5	14	8	9	4	13	5	47	22

* Information not available.

SOURCES: Report of the Clerk of the House and Report of the Secretary of the Senate. For 1977 and 1978 for period ending September 30; all other years as of June 30.

TABLE 3.3.9 EMPLOYEES OF OFFICERS OF THE HOUSE OF REPRESENTATIVES, 1946–78 (SELECTED YEARS)

OFFICE	1946	1950	1955	1960	1965	1970	1971	1972	1973	1974	1975	1976	1977	1978
Sergeant at Arms	(*)	(*)	(*)	(*)	(*)	(*)	372	609	608	582	636	657	624	627
Clerk	(*)	(*)	(*)	(*)	(*)	(*)	255	319	331	330	329	348	326	394
Doorkeeper	(*)	(*)	(*)	(*)	(*)	(*)	347	425	417	353	344	343	321	340
Parliamentarian	(*)	(*)	(*)	(*)	(*)	(*)	5	5	6	5	6	5	5	6
Postmaster	(*)	(*)	(*)	(*)	(*)	(*)	86	120	143	92	99	99	87	95

* For the years 1946–70, the listing of employees and their salaries is presented in alphabetical form under e general category of "House of Representatives." Therefore, staffing data for particular officers of the House of Representatives is unavailable for these years.

SOURCE: U.S. Congress. House. Report of the Clerk of the House. Washington, U.S. Government Printing Office. Years 1971–78. Data for 1977 and 1978 are as of September 30; all other years are as of June 30.

TABLE 3.3.10 EMPLOYEES OF OFFICERS OF THE U.S. SENATE, 1946–78 (SELECTED YEARS)

OFFICE	1946*	1950*	1955*	1960	1965	1970	1971	1972	1973	1974	1975	1976	1977	1978
Secretary of the Senate	(†)	(†)	(†)	(†)	98	118	123	131	160	176	139	156	151	157
Sergeant at Arms and Doorkeeper	(†)	(†)	(†)	(†)	400	555	587	740	769	1,035	887	1,005	998	1,066
Secretary for the majority	(†)	(†)	(†)	(†)	6	5	6	6	NA	5	7	6	7	7
Secretary for the minority	(†)	(†)	(†)	(†)	6	6	6	6	NA	6	6	6	6	7
Postmaster	(†)	(†)	(†)	(†)	62	68	65	69	71	102	75	88	82	80
Parliamentarian‡	(†)	(†)	(†)	(†)	NA	NA	NA	NA	NA	NA	NA	NA	NA	NA

* For the years 1946, 1950, and 1965, information regarding the salaries of officers, clerks and employees of the Senate is presented under the single category of "officers, clerks and employees of the Senate." Therefore, a determination of the number of employees on the payroll of each officer is not possible.

† Information not available.

‡ For the listed years, payroll information for the Parliamentarian and his staff is included with that for the Secretary of the Senate. It is therefore not possible to identify staff members on the payroll of the Parliamentarian.

SOURCE: U.S. Congress. Senate. Report of the Secretary of the Senate. Washington, U.S. Government Printing Office. Data for 1977 and 1978 are as of September 30; data for all other years are as of June 30.

Table 3.3.11 contains staff levels for the congressional support agencies. The numbers are as of October 31 of each year. The employees for each agency do not include outside consultants.

TABLE 3.3.11 CONGRESSIONAL SUPPORT AGENCIES

YEAR	LIBRARY OF CONGRESS	GENERAL ACCOUNTING OFFICE	CONGRESSIONAL BUDGET OFFICE	OFFICE OF TECHNOLOGY ASSESSMENT
1946	(*)	(*)	(†)	(†)
1950	(*)	(*)	(†)	(†)
1955	(*)	(*)	(†)	(†)
1960	(*)	(*)	(†)	(†)
1965	(*)	(*)	(†)	(†)
1970	3,863	4,704	(†)	(*)
1971	3,948	4,718	(†)	(*)
1972	4,174	4,742	(†)	(*)
1973	4,320	4,908	(†)	(*)
1974	4,448	5,270	(†)	(*)
1975	4,715	4,905	(*)	(*)
1976	4,896	5,391	203	(*)
1977	5,086	5,315	201	139
1978	5,199	5,476	203	164

* Information not available.

† Agency not in existence.

SOURCE: Bureau of Manpower Information Systems. U.S. Civil Service Commission. Federal Civilian Workforce Statistics, Monthly Release. (As of October 31 for each year.)

3.4 Congressional Staff: The View from the District*

John Macartney

Congressional staffs on the Capitol grounds are only part of the picture. Huge congressional bureaucracies have been established "back home" in states and congressional districts to assist members in the performance of congressional functions. This original essay by John Macartney presents data on the operation of district staff offices. These data are based on the author's extensive field study of legislature offices in southern California.[1]

The theme of this article is simple: Only part of the U.S. Congress is to be found on Capitol Hill. Much of it is located in storefront offices, professional, and federal buildings across America.[2] A look at the phone book—any American phone book—tells the tale. Virtually everyone in this country resides within 25 miles of Congress.

Civics texts and news accounts notwithstanding, most "lawmakers," especially their staffs, spend the lion's share of their time and effort on a variety of nonlawmaking functions, most of which relate to the constituents back home. Increasingly, the bulk of those operations are being carried out from district offices, and that is the stuff of this essay. What is the 97th Congress accomplishing? Only part of the answer is recorded in roll-call votes, committee hearings, and legislation, while much of the remainder concerns what's going on back in 435 districts and 50 states. In many respects, the district is where Congress is at.

Consider the case of an imaginary but typical office of a member of the House of Representatives. It is divided into two distinct operations—one on Capitol Hill and another back in the district. Both offices—the one in Washington and the one in the district—share the member's various tasks, but legislation receives much more attention in Washington, while constituents and local matters dominate the district office. The Congressman shuttles between the two offices, spending almost two thirds of his or her time at the Capitol. The Washington office, of course, deals with the more weighty, national issues, while the district office concerns itself with minor, local matters. But four things stand out: (1) The Congressman does not share influence with so many powerful rivals at home; the district is a smaller pond. (2) The kinds of tasks and projects undertaken at the district office are such that they usually are pursued to completion—instead of dying in the hopper, the fate of 96 percent of the proposed legislation with which Washington busies itself. (3) The staff at the district office enjoys more autonomy than their counterparts in Washington simply because the boss is away. Most of the time the top field aide is the acting congressman. (4) Issues and projects that may seem minor on the national scale are crucial on individual and local scales.

The variety of issues and projects undertaken at the field office is endless. For example, there is the widow who gets a bureaucratic run-around instead of a social security check; a call from the district office cuts red tape. There is also the businessman looking for a government contract, the school district that wants a federal grant, and the GI seeking an early discharge.

* Prepared especially for this volume from an unpublished Ph.D. dissertation by John D. Macartney, UCLA, 1975.

Multiply those cases by 6,653* and it adds up to "who gets what, when, and how" in our imaginary district. And there are a great many undertakings that seemingly have nothing at all to do with Congress or the federal government. Some are private matters; others involve state or local government. Maybe the issue is a municipal park—or parking lot—putting the schools on double sessions, a local election, attracting industry and jobs to the community, promoting a charity drive, organizing a Little League program, encouraging local merchants to hire teenagers, or changing zoning laws. Whatever the issue, if it is important to the community, the congressional district office is likely to become involved.

Additionally, there often is the direct delivery of public services. Consider, for example, just one project undertaken over the last several years by the district office of Los Angeles Congressman Barry Goldwater, Jr. Goldwater's constituency is predominately suburban and is located about 20 miles from the coast, across the Santa Monica mountains. The problem was finding transportation to the beach—primarily for youngsters, but also to reduce fuel consumption, pollution, and parking problems. (Los Angeles has no public mass transit worthy of the name.) Goldwater's field representative organized the Recreation Transit System (RTS), a massive program involving hundreds of leased school buses, a nonprofit corporation, and a huge fund-raising and publicity campaign. Result: Several hundred thousand San Fernando Valley residents, mostly young people, have been transported to the beach over the past few summers. No legislation and no federal funds are involved in this operation, yet it is part of what the Congress is doing (a part not acknowledged in lists of congressional functions found in political science texts). For many youngsters and their grateful parents in California's 27th District, the RTS is probably more important and certainly has more visibility than all the committee work, all the bills introduced, and all the floor votes cast by Mr. Goldwater (of which they know little). And Goldwater's direct delivery of public services is not at all unique. To cite one more example, Denver Congresswoman Pat Schroeder's large district operation (a three-story suburban house with 10 employees plus 20 eager volunteers) sponsors a low-income housing project, plus a grocery store on wheels for shut-ins, among other direct services.

Today, virtually every Senator and Representative maintains one or more full-time offices back in his/her state or district. That is a relatively new development in the 200-year history of the U.S. Congress. Little is recorded about the development of district offices.[3] However, one woman interviewed for this study had been working in Chet Holifield's California district office since it was established in 1942, when, she believes, it was the only one in the country. Decentralization, the deployment of office resources to states and districts, accelerated during the 1960s, and by the late 70s no member was without such an operation.

Decentralization has several roots. An obvious one is the electoral advantage of a strong district office. Another is simply staff growth. Until staffs were large enough to have two complete operations, there was an either-or dilemma. Today, the average House member uses about one third to one half of 22 staff positions (18 full-time, 4 part-time) to operate one or more offices back home. Senators usually keep a fifth to a third of their much larger staffs in the state. Since each member decides for his or herself how office resources will be deployed, the variations are great. Such decisions depend upon what Dick Fenno calls "home style," but by and large, the more extensive field operations can be expected in urban areas, particularly if the incumbent is recently elected or anticipates stiff electoral competition. Many southern and most rural legislators maintain relatively small field offices.

* The average number of constituent cases handled by each House district office in Los Angeles County during the 1973–74 congressional term. Another 2,851 cases, on the average, were handled at the respective Washington offices. The volumes would be considerably higher today. Success rate—resolving a case in the constituent's favor—is better than 80 percent.

Decentralization is also encouraged by the lack of office space in Washington and the avalanche of constituent business that threatens to overwhelm lawmaking efforts. Deploying part of the congressional office organization to the district serves both purposes. Hundreds of square feet of additional space becomes available, while the efforts of staffers remaining on the Hill can be focused on legislation.

DISTRICT OFFICE FUNCTIONS

What do district offices do? What goes on there? The short answer would be constituent service and promotion. In order to tell the story in more detail, this paper will discuss 13 separate functions carried out by congressional field offices.

1. Office management.
2. Communications and public relations.
3. Casework.
4. Political organizing.
5. Surveillance.
6. Alter ego.
7. Group liaison.
8. Representation.
9. Scheduling and advancing.
10. Community organizer/direct action.
11. Oversight.
12. Legislative support.
13. Personal errands.

1. Office and Staff Management

Although the incumbent is ultimately the director of his own staff, the burdens of that task usually fall on a chief of staff. The job includes training and supervision of other staff employees and volunteers and, in 71 percent of these offices, the hiring and firing of other staffers. There are funds and budgets to handle as well. This can be a major task because of the separate office accounts, private funds, campaign contributions, and (sometimes) the incumbent's personal accounts. The practice in some offices of switching staffers on and off the payroll (in order to circumvent the maximum employee limit) further complicates the manager's task.[4] Many offices have bookkeepers who handle office accounts as well as campaign finances.

2. Communications and Public Relations

Words and symbols are the ammunition of politics; no politician can endure without attending to his public image. In many respects the incumbent's staff is a communications machine, a public relations organization.

The communications effort generally has two goals: *promotion* of the incumbent's political fortunes; and *education* of the citizenry, to inform and persuade about policy alternatives. These two goals are difficult to separate; all communications, simply by naming the incumbent, result in promotion. Most communications involve education as well. Research on Congress has indicated promotion, rather than education, is usually the central concern.[5] That conclusion seems to hold for most of the offices studied in Los Angeles, but there were exceptions. A few offices devoted their communications efforts primarily to education on specific issues or causes. Some legislators, just like some candidates, use the bulk of their office resources not for the apparent purpose but to espouse some cherished cause or idea. The prestige and office resources of an individual legislator, especially a Congressman (because of the frank) can be an excellent vehicle for advocacy that goes far beyond district boundaries. In practice, such educational efforts take the form of nationally syndicated newspaper columns and broadcast messages, pamphlets, books and articles, and statewide or national mailings (to selected subscribers) of ideological newsletters—all prepared and distributed, at least in part, by staff. Four of the 19 Representatives' offices were engaging in major educational efforts on a statewide or national basis, as were four offices of state legislators. In these cases the incumbent was either a doctrinaire conservative with an ideological message or a spokesman for some minority group.

In order to communicate, staffs make use of five basic mediums: direct mail, telephone, face-to-face, news media, and publications.

Table 3.4.1 Newsletter and Questionnaire Use by Los Angeles-Based Political Offices

	Percent Sending Newsletters	Opinion Polls	Average Number of Newsletter Issues per Year/per Office
U.S. Senator	100%	50%	Unknown
Representative	94	83	4.4
State Senator	93	89	2.8
Assemblyman	100	87	3.6
Supervisor	20	60	3.0
City Councilman	87	60	2.2

Note: In most cases the newsletters/polls emanate from the central offices. The U.S. Senators do not send a statewide newsletter, but they do send newsletters periodically to selected sub-areas (usually congressional districts). The Senator's goal is to have covered most of the state, at least the more politically crucial districts, once per six-year term.

Communications are received and sent from both central and district offices. Generally speaking, the Washington office communicates with constituents by mail while the district office relies on the telephone. Constituents, as will be shown, prefer the phone—at least in Los Angeles.

MAIL

The mails carry the bulk of the outgoing (office-to-constituent) messages. Although district offices handle considerable mail, the Washington offices are likely to handle even more.

Mass Mailings. Nearly all of the offices in this study send out *newsletters* on a regular basis. Most include *questionnaires* that poll constituents about various issue questions and legislative proposals. Table 3.4.1 indicates newsletter and poll use. The average number of newsletters per year is fairly representative, but there are offices that send many more. One L.A. congressman has sent as many as 24 newsletters in a single year; one Assemblyman sends 15. Such efforts, of course, depend upon private contributions.*

* At the time this research was conducted, Congressmen received no funds for the printing and preparation of newsletters and all congressional newsletters were dependent upon "slush funds." At present, allowances are provided, numbers of mailing are limited, and slush funds are prohibited.

Newsletters keep the incumbent's name, picture,* and accomplishments before his constituents. Questionnaires are primarily a promotional device, "a placebo for constituents," as one aide put it. When sent in bulk mailings, addressed to "occupant," the questionnaire's purpose is to stimulate contacts and supplement mailing lists. Questionnaires tend to flatter voters because they indicate the incumbent's concern for their opinions. Results are tabulated (a time-consuming staff chore) and reflected in subsequent newsletters. Sometimes congressional staffs will insert the results into the *Congressional Record* and then mass mail reprints of the *Record* back to the district.

Most offices break down mailing lists into categories of constituents to allow for *specialized mass mail appeals* to, for example, newspaper editors, union members, businessmen, policemen, teachers, physicians, etc. These mailing lists are computerized, and a few offices go to the trouble and expense to prepare their newsletter in multiple editions, specialized for different categories or neighborhoods of constituents.

Congratulations and Condolences. A member of the PR staff (often an intern or volunteer) usually monitors newspapers and other sources to find names for "congrat" and

* The California Legislature allows only two photographs of the incumbent per newsletter. Most newsletters have a sketch of the incumbent on the masthead—to squeeze in a third picture.

TABLE 3.4.2 SPECIALIZED MAIL APPEALS—PERCENT OF L.A.-BASED OFFICES THAT SEND SPECIALIZED MASS MAILINGS TO SUBGROUPS OF CONSTITUENTS

U.S. Senators	50%
Representatives	65
State Senators	62
Assemblymen	93
Supervisors	100
City Councilmen	87

condolence mailings. Major accomplishments—election to the school board, winning a special honor—rate a personal letter, a phone call, or a presentation. More mundane achievements—graduating from high school, Eagle Scout awards, bar mitzvahs, marriages, anniversaries, births, business promotions, even birthdays—result in cards. Similarly, deaths or illnesses are occasions for condolence cards, telegrams, or flowers. Congressmen are provided with materials besides greeting cards—baby books (2,500 per year), bride kits, flags, etc.—that they can send. Names may be gathered from institutional sources—schools, churches, hospitals, marriage license offices, or wherever—as well as from local newspapers.

Some offices send congratulatory mailings to as many constituents as possible, while other offices honor only those who are identified supporters or limit their effort to really significant achievements. The volume of this activity is related to security and seniority in office as well as higher ambitions.

> We did more of those PR-type things years ago, but it's not necessary anymore.
>
> CONGRESSIONAL AIDE

> We used to do that, but casework takes all our time these days. A new Congressman should do it. Once you're entrenched, you can let it go.
>
> CONGRESSIONAL AIDE

The volume can be substantial—running to 30,000 honored constituents per year. Usually there is a choice of honors, ranging from a greeting card through letters and wall plaques or mention in the *Congressional Record,* plus flags or legislative resolutions. The more substantial honors are usually presented rather than mailed.

During one interview, a State Assemblyman's administrative aide received a call from a city recreation department requesting a legislative resolution for a winning Little League coach. Negotiations ensued. Resolutions cost the state $600 each, the administrative aide explained, and frankly, his boss wanted to maximize their political effect. If the recipient coach was going to keep the award at home, he'd have to settle for a letter of congratulations, but if, on the other hand, the award could be permanently displayed in a public place, perhaps at the recreation department, a resolution would be possible. (A resolution was the final decision.)

A related activity is the sending of Christmas and Hanukkah cards to favored constituents. These mailings may go just to close friends and supporters or to all constituents who have ever come into contact with the office. One congressional aide said that volunteers begin in July of each year to prepare their Christmas card mailing of 10,000.

GENERAL CORRESPONDENCE. Political staffs, of course, handle a great deal of general correspondence. Letters from constituents are answered promptly. If a great many are received on the same issue, a form response is prepared for the robo-typewriters. Inquiries usually result in copies of bills or committee reports along with letters. This is one reason such an incredible number of bills with absolutely no hope of passage are introduced each year—members can demonstrate their concern for the issue raised by the constituent by sending along a bill they have introduced, no matter what the issue. While district offices send and receive large volumes of such correspondence, much more is handled in Washington.

TELEPHONE

Frustrated citizens are advised to "write their Congressman," and studies of legislative bod-

TABLE 3.4.3 VOLUME OF CONGRAT ACTIVITY BY OFFICE TYPE

	AVERAGE VOLUME PER YEAR	TOP VOLUME	LOWEST VOLUME
Representatives	5,877	30,000	0
State Senators	1,220	5,300	48
Assemblymen	2,326	7,500	140
Supervisors	5,588	7,900	2,000
City Councilmen	1,908	13,000	40

NOTE: Includes all types—letters, plaques, telegrams, flowers, etc. Based on estimates supplied by top aides. A very few offices had actual counts; these tended to be higher than the estimates received elsewhere. Both U.S. Senators perform this function, but from Washington; no estimates on volume were available.

ies never fail to mention the large and increasing volumes of incoming mail. The importance of Alexander Graham Bell's invention should not be overlooked. While Washington offices rely primarily on the mails, the field office communicates by phone. The recent growth of field office operations is changing the means of communication between constituents and Congress; more and more southern California citizens telephone the local number rather than write to the Washington address.

Although conventional wisdom holds that letters are *the* means of citizen-legislator communication, that is reasonably valid only for the two U.S. Senators among Los Angeles-based officials. Generally speaking, the Washington office takes in most of the mail while the field office gets some mail plus most of the calls and visits. For Los Angeles-based Congressmen it is actually the field office that is the primary point of incoming contacts. Less than two decades ago, field offices were rare; now they are common. One result is that citizens are dropping by or telephoning more often than they write those letters so prominent in the literature.

TABLE 3.4.4 MEDIUM OF COMMUNICATION—PERCENTAGE OF CONSTITUENT-INITIATED COMMUNICATIONS BY MEDIUM OF COMMUNICATION (LOS ANGELES-BASED)

	MAIL	PHONE	DROP–IN VISITORS	(*n* =)
U.S. Senators	80%	19%	1%	(2)
Representatives	52	39	9	(18)
State Senators	41	49	10	(13)
Assemblymen	39	51	10	(31)
Supervisors	50	46	4	(4)
City Councilmen	38	50	12	(14)

NOTE: Estimates by top aides. Covers commumications received by entire office organization—field *and central*. One Council office maintained actual records on this: 16 percent by mail; 65 percent by phone; and 20 percent drop-ins.

FACE-TO-FACE COMMUNICATIONS

District offices receive a steady stream of drop-in visitors, while field aides spend much of their time (about 25 percent) out in the community meeting with constituents. This takes the form of attendance by staffers at countless local meetings and what aides refer to as "town halls." Town halls are previously announced open-house meetings where the incumbent and his staff meet with all comers at the district office, a school, or other convenient location. Use of this technique, incidentally, has in-

TABLE 3.4.5 CONSTITUENT-INITIATED COMMUNICATIONS—PERCENTAGE OF OFFICES REPORTING HALF OR MORE OF COMMUNICATIONS:

	BY PHONE	THROUGH FIELD OFFICE
U.S. Senators	0%	0%
Representatives	31	63
State Senators	62	85
Assemblymen	69	79
Supervisors	50	25
City Councilmen	80	29

NOTE: Number of cases (n) same as for Table 3.4.4.

creased dramatically since data for this study were gathered in 1974. Even President Carter did it.

More and more incumbents have "mobile field offices" in vans or campers that crisscross the district to take advantage of large public gatherings such as athletic events, street fairs, carnivals, etc. Colorado Senator Gary Hart keeps a large van crisscrossing his state.

While the vast majority of communications are handled by mail or phone, face-to-face contacts are important, especially from a political standpoint. Political aides are personable people; when they can talk to a constituent they usually secure a friend, and a voter, for their patron.

> I tell each of my staff that they are responsible for making five friends a day—friends for me, for the office. If they do that we don't have to worry very much about reelection.
>
> SOUTHERN CALIFORNIA CONGRESSMAN

NEWS MEDIA: THE PRESS AIDE'S BAILIWICK

Press aides usually have been working journalists or public relations specialists.

> First I was a newspaper reporter, then a TV newsman. Then I was editor of a magazine line. After that I worked in public relations for an aerospace corporation, and next I opened my own PR firm. This job is part of the same line.
>
> SUPERVISOR'S DEPUTY

They are responsible for preparing press releases, organizing news conferences, monitoring the local media, and, usually, overseeing the other communications/PR activities discussed here. They are often recruited from the ranks of local media people, and their friendships and contacts with their former colleagues constitute one of the office's more valuable resources. Part of the job is media liaison—keeping on good terms with the local newspapers and TV/radio stations. Whenever possible, the press aide seeks to maximize favorable media coverage and minimize unfavorable exposure—old friends help. One state legislator's administrative aide (known as an AA) told of using news tips to cultivate reporters. She kept a record of "scoops" handed out—to insure the largess was evenly distributed—and she attempted to reward more favorable coverage with better tips.

WRITING

A major staff activity in all offices is writing—speeches, press releases, newsletters, legislation, correspondence, and so on. Usually it is the press aide who doubles as a professional writer and whose products may include ghost-written articles and books published under the incumbent's name.

3. CASEWORK

The core of constituent service is casework—the troubleshooting of constituent requests for assistance. Case variations are infinite. They include requests for jobs, government publications, expediting or overturning bureaucratic decisions, helping constituents to get out of the Army or to secure a better assignment, sightseeing tours around the Capitol, etc. The matters may seem trivial, except to aggrieved or hopeful citizens and their families.

In theory (and in the literature) casework means assistance in dealings with *government* agencies applicable to the incumbent's *level* of government. Practice does not follow theory in Los Angeles. Casework problems, as often as not, cross jurisdictional lines, while a large number of cases do not involve government at all.

Consider the following case handled by a Los Angeles congressional office. A shipyard worker had been severely crippled in an on-the-job accident. Because of technicalities in his former employment status, he had been three times ruled ineligible for disability compensation. A "catch-22" interpretation also made welfare unavailable. By the time the constituent sought help at his Congressman's field office the situation was desperate. He had been unable to work for several years, medical and other bills had piled up, the family budget was in shambles, home utilities were about to be cut off, the family car had been repossessed, and a bank was about to foreclose on the home mortgage.

Resolving this one case required several months and more than a hundred caseworker hours. Eventually the shipyard (federal agency) was persuaded to reclassify the former employee. That enabled the constituent to qualify (following more appeals by the caseworker) for disability compensation (state agency) as well as for welfare (county agency—more appeals). Meanwhile, the caseworker and the AA used their patron's good offices to persuade the constituent's banker (private), automobile credit agency (private), hospital (county), and utility company (city) to accept delayed debt-repayment schedules. Finally, the caseworker went to the constituent's home to give advice and instruction on home economics and family budgeting.

While this case is unusual in its complexity, cases similar to this are taken on every day in Los Angeles. Note that this case involved several different agencies at three levels of government as well as the private sector and the family unit itself. The constituent received no more than his legal due—but would in all likelihood have received nothing without the intervention of this Congressman's staff.

> He was merely a statistic in some bureaucrat's in-basket without our help. Once we started making inquiries he became a 'problem' for the agencies. By the time we were through he had become an individual person—instead of a statistic or problem.
>
> CONGRESSIONAL AIDE

Although cases come in all varieties, most offices—at all levels—report that miscellaneous welfare and income maintenance cases are the largest category. These include county welfare, social security, unemployment, disability, Medicare and medical, and old-age security. While the most frequent case types handled by any given office usually fall within their own government jurisdiction, the host of other miscellaneous cases they also handle may well constitute the bulk of their workload and may often take them across jurisdictional boundaries. Furthermore, many cases, like the one with the shipyard worker, involve multiple problems, agencies, and government levels. Political offices tend to categorize such cases according to their own level of government. Thus that particular case was regarded as a shipyard (federal) case by the congressional office involved; a state legislator's aide, had he handled it, would probably have considered it a workers' disability (state) problem.

Different offices define casework differently. In some offices it is a "case" only if correspondence and/or fieldwork are involved; problems handled by a phone call or two aren't counted. But other offices handle everything by phone. Sometimes, especially in congressional offices, a distinction is made between "projects" and casework. Projects (or "major casework") involve institutional clients, such as labor unions, corporations, school districts, or city governments seeking assistance, usually with government contracts or grants. But many offices recognize no such distinctions; they count almost all constituent contacts as casework, whether the constituent is Widow Jones asking for the dogcatcher's phone number or the University of California seeking a multimillion-dollar grant.

Attempts to tally the volume of casework have foundered on these definitional problems and on the fact that most studies have excluded field offices—and hence the major portion of the casework load. Data on volume for this study are derived from staff estimates—aides were asked to count only those cases that resulted in an entry in their files (thus excluding requests for phone numbers, routine advice, and information).

As Table 3.4.6 reveals, a great many Los Angeles citizens receive "service," and the bulk of the casework load is handled by the field staff rather than Washington employees. Some offices handle casework at the point of contact—and keep caseworkers busy in both Washington and field offices. More typical in Los Angeles is the practice of concentrating most of the workload in the field office—cases received in Washington are passed on to the district.

TABLE 3.4.6 CASEWORK VOLUME (PER OFFICE)

	AVERAGE ANNUAL VOLUME	AVERAGE PERCENT HANDLED BY FIELD OFFICE	LOWEST VOLUME REPORTED	HIGHEST VOLUME REPORTED	(*n* =)
U.S. Senators	29,520	73%	14,400	42,640	2
Representatives	4,752	70	650	10,500	17
State Senators	1,775	78	120	4,500	13
Assemblymen	1,623	89	180	7,800	29
Supervisors	4,800	na	3,600	5,200	3
City Councilmen	6,025	36	2,000	12,000	13

NOTE: Includes "projects" as well as casework. Based primarily on aides' estimates, but in a few offices actual counts rather than estimates were available. All U.S. Senate data above are from 1973 records. One Representative *counted* 1,040 cases in 1969 (volume much higher now). One Assembly aide estimated 20,000 annually (this was discounted as too high); two Assembly offices had *counted* 800 and 6,000 cases, respectively. A Supervisor's office *counted* 3,600 cases (1972), and three Council offices had counts: 2,800, 4,000, and 5,000.

Some well-managed field offices are organized and deployed to dispense constituent favors on a assembly-line bases. Somebody handles correspondence on the matter, others specialize in certain types of cases—military personnel problems, social security, veterans' benefits, and immigration are the big four at the federal level. When a particularly touching case is favorably resolved, it is turned over to the press aide for media exposure (which stimulates still more requests).

Saloma's data on House offices show that the staff is the principal instrument for casework,[6] while this study reveals (see Table 3.4.6) that it is the field staff that handles three fourths of the workload. And they handle a great deal. The offices of the 85 Los Angeles federal, state, and local legislators, taken together, were working some 340,641 cases in 1974, and the volume has been rising. Since most cases involve a family unit and some involve groups of constituents, a significant portion of the southern California citizenry receive annual "service" from their representatives.

What all this casework activity means for public policy—who gets what—is a matter that needs investigation. Essentially two things can happen when a political office goes to bat for a constituent: The issue can be resolved in the constituent's favor (about 80 percent); or the constituent can "lose" anyway. If the constituent does "win," several explanations are possible:

The constituent gets exactly what he or she would have gotten anyway. The representative's intervention has no real effect, except to bring credit upon the incumbent.

The constituent gets what he or she would have eventually gotten without the intercession of the representative but gets it sooner. Thus the incumbent gets credit, while citizens who are competing for the agency's attention (without political benefactors) are elbowed to the rear of the line or bottom of the in-basket.

The constituent gets what he or she deserves but would not have gotten at all (because of red-tape snarls) without the intercession of the political representative. (This is how casework is supposed to function.)

The constituent gets something he or she would not normally qualify for, but the representative's clout tips the scales in the constituent's favor. (The system is subverted.)

Judging from information gleaned during this study, plus conversations with bureaucrats who handle "congressionals" for Social Security and for the Veterans Administration, as well as my own experience in handling congressional inquiries for the Air Force Office of Legislative Liaison, it would seem that the second option is most frequent.[7] Since public resources—time, money, food stamps, government contracts, etc.—are always limited, the growing volume of political casework efforts may have important ramifications. Citizens who take advantage of these "services" get more of what there is to get, and get it sooner, than citizens who do not. Thus these extensive service operations by political staffs increase political representation for some constituents at the expense of others.

4. POLITICAL ORGANIZING

Political offices are just that—political; staffers are, for the most part, political animals. Scratch an incumbent's top aide, especially his top field aide, and you'll often find his campaign manager.

Campaign management is only one political activity at the field office. Another is the continuous care and upkeep of political supporter lists. Names are added daily, 10 or 20 or more per week, and the lists are kept for campaign purposes—to mobilize volunteers, solicit funds, turn out voters.[8]

> Your list is one of your main assets. Politics is people—without a list you can't even get started. You don't just appear on a street corner and start campaigning, you know.
>
> ASSEMBLYMAN'S AIDE (FORMER PARTY PROFESSIONAL, CANDIDATE FOR CONGRESS)

Besides management and the building of lists—both of which go on year in and year out—there is also staff participation in the actual campaign effort. This is a sensitive subject because so many challengers try to make a campaign issue of it. Some aides were more frank than others is discussing this subject, but most denied any staff campaign work whatsoever on government time.* Denials to the contrary, campaign activities were actually observed in 54 percent of the offices visited during this study. While all types of activity were in evidence at one office or another, the most common (and the hardest to conceal from an interviewer) were interrupting phone calls concerning fund raisers, campaign strategy, rallies, volunteers, and endorsements.

Political fund raising was not a subject many aides were willing to discuss. That some government-paid staffers work as fund raisers is certain—two aides were especially frank.

> You might say that I'm a professional fund raiser—that's where my expertise lies, that's why I'm here. I've been running charity drives in [the Los Angeles area] for over 20 years. I do all of [the incumbent's] fund raising.
>
> CONGRESSMAN'S FIELD REPRESENTATIVE

> My biggest job is fund raising. And I'm damn good at it. I've raised almost $200,000 this year for our office. And that doesn't count money I've raised for other candidates—here in California, in Michigan, in New Mexico, Arizona, all over. We're not going to be an Assemblyman forever.
>
> AIDE

One final point about political activity should be stressed. Political staffs are politically active, but not only and not necessarily in their patron's behalf. Many aides run for office themselves, and many participate in campaigns other than those of their employer, including issue campaigns (ballot propositions, stop oil drilling, outlaw abortion, etc.).

> You can bet your ass I'm working on the campaign—about 15 hours a day worth. But I'm not working for [aide's employer], he's a shoo-in; we don't need to campaign. I'm working for Jerry Brown.
>
> ASSEMBLY AIDE

Many of the observed incidents of outright campaigning took place in offices where the incumbent was not running in 1974 and/or involved candidates other than the boss.

5. SURVEILLANCE

The surveillance function is often overlooked. The national media, for example, made

* After-hours campaigning is perfectly legal. Political aides—at all levels of government—are specifically exempted from Hatch Act provisions.

TABLE 3.4.7 STAFF POLITICAL ACTIVITIES (PERCENTAGE OF OCCURRENCES BY OFFICE TYPE)

	TOP AIDE ACTIVE IN PATRON'S CAMPAIGN	POLITICAL LISTS MAINTAINED BY STAFF	STAFF MEMBER HAD RUN FOR OFFICE*	STAFF CAMPAIGNING OBSERVED
U.S. Senator	100%	100%	50%	100%
Representative	90	100	61	53
State Senator	86	100	43	50
Assemblyman	94	100	42	68
Supervisor	100	100	90	20
City Councilmen	100	100	33	33
All Offices	93%	100%	47%	54%
Number of Offices	79	78	40	46

* Percentage of offices where a member or former member of the staff had ever run for public office. Five aides interviewed were candidates in 1974.

a great to-do of Congressmen using the 1981 July 4 recess to personally "take the pulse" of their constituents on the economy issue. But pulse taking is continuous and institutionalized; the field staff is always performing this function. The field staff are political antennae—monitoring local newspapers and broadcast media, listening to talk shows, conversing with newsmen, citizens, community leaders, and activists, attending countless meetings and functions, cross-checking findings with other aides, and relaying all this information to the incumbent. When elected officials return to their districts (as in the 1981 recess) their time is carefully programmed by field aides who squire them about, partly to hear opinions, but primarily to maximize media exposure—hence those stories about "pulse taking."

Some offices systematize their surveillance efforts. Staff members are actually assigned to read certain newspapers and journals, monitor designated news broadcasts, and keep track of what goes on in specific organizations, businesses, and institutions. Efforts are also made to cultivate contacts throughout the district.

> I've developed a network of neighborhood contacts—friends of the office. They keep me posted. So I always know who is supporting whom, and who is doing what to whom, politically. I also hear who has lost their job, gone to the hospital, been arrested, opened a business, had a baby, or whatever.
>
> ASSEMBLY AIDE

6. ALTER EGO

In many respects, top aides are assistant incumbents, not merely assistants *to* the incumbent. They share their patron's office. In his absence, they speak for him, deal with lobbyists and other legislators, make decisions—the line between top aide and employer can be a hazy one.

Four out of five top aides interviewed for this study used a collective "we" when discussing the incumbent: "We decided to duck that whole issue"; "We hope to be a Senator, someday"; "We got our committee chairmanship because we backed the right guy for Speaker." In a very few cases the operative pronoun was "I": "I decided against [his] running for the Senate this year."

7. GROUP LIAISON

Some offices assign staffers to join certain community organizations. Others seek to develop a contact—a friend of the office—who is already a group member. The number of group contacts a new employee can bring into the office is sometimes a criterion for hiring new staffers. Group leaders are cultivated with care by aggressive offices. This is one place the letters and resolutions of congratulations come in.

> We have a part-time college student—the guy who stepped in a minute ago. He's been politically active since he was about 12, and he runs

errands and does legwork for us. He's just compiled dossiers on all the community and organization leaders in our new district. We're using them to cultivate those people and groups.

CONGRESSMAN'S FIELD REPRESENTATIVE

What groups? The list is endless and depends on the district and the incumbent. Frequently mentioned in Los Angeles:

Chamber of Commerce	League of Women Voters
Service clubs	School teachers
Senior citizens groups	Public employees
Student groups	Labor unions
Political party clubs	City governments

8. REPRESENTING THE INCUMBENT

Incumbents are deluged with invitations to be at ceremonies, give speeches, and attend luncheons and dinners. More invitations are received than the incumbent himself can possibly fulfill. When possible, the Congressman attends, but more often he sends one of his assistants. As a group, district political aides must attend more retirement ceremonies, award presentations, ribbon cuttings, luncheons, meetings, etc., than any other group alive. And they actually deliver more formal speeches than their patrons do—before district audiences.* Representing the incumbent takes a great deal of field staff time—including evenings and weekends. This function, more than any other, made interview appointments for this research difficult.

9. SCHEDULING AND ADVANCING

While staffers attend many meetings and functions, the incumbent is busy, too, especially on his visits back to the district. Seeing to the incumbent's public appearances is essentially the same function described by Bruno and Greenfield in their book, *The Advance Man* (Bantam, 1971).

Scheduling is a major task. It is also a professional one involving decisions—how many appearances, where and where not. The object is to maximize the incumbent's time and exposure.

When there is a choice—and there usually is—I always schedule him to meet with groups that don't agree with him—businessmen, conservatives, you know. They need to listen to what he's got to say, and he ought to hear them, too. His supporters all agree with him, and they'll vote for him anyway. It's the others that count. He gets pretty tired of it [unfriendly audiences], but he goes where I tell him.

CONGRESSMAN'S AIDE

The scheduler (usually the top aide, assisted by the incumbent's private secretary) decides which invitations are answered with regrets, with an aide representative, or by the incumbent. In most offices, scheduling goes beyond deciding where to go—it becomes advancing.

Let me tell you something about advancing. I try to have ______ make two or three functions per evening when he's in town. That means he'll pop in and out—arriving late and leaving early. The trick is to get the group to appreciate his being there without being 'pissed off' because he ducks out before the chicken is served. The MC has to handle this just right, and one of my biggest jobs is seeing to it that he does.

CONGRESSMAN'S FIELD REPRESENTATIVE

Staffers sometimes arrange their employer's public appearance with meticulous detail. The schedule becomes an operations plan that may include recommendations for attire (incumbent and wife), transportation arrangements, information on podium lighting, a pocket diagram of seating arrangements with names, recommendations on who to talk to and who to avoid, what to say and not say, entrance and exit plans, and so on.

10. COMMUNITY ORGANIZER/DIRECT ACTION

In some respects political field offices are like agencies. They go beyond the legislative function and do things directly. Often they are the organizational catalyst behind local movements (''save the pier,'' ''stop oil drilling,'' ''stop the freeway'').

* One state Senator does not make speeches at all. His speaking engagements (even when he is in attendance himself) are all handled by aides.

When such issues develop, local activists will take their case to the nearest political field office. The object, of course, is to get the incumbent's endorsement for "their side." But another goal is to enlist the office's resources—staff, expertise, mailing lists, contacts, prestige, duplicating machines, telephones—into the battle.

The direct delivery of services by congressional district offices is not unusual. Congressman Goldwater's operation of a mass transit system was mentioned earlier, as were the housing project and the grocery store on wheels operated by Pat Schroeder's office. Congressman Hawkins' top field aide is president of the South Central Improvement Action Council and also director of Ujima Village. The former has secured $10 million in SBA loans for minority businessmen and has a $275,000-a-year operating budget; the latter is a subsidized, 300-unit, low-income housing project and shopping center. Another office was using volunteer law professors to operate a public service law office.

11. Oversight[9]

While oversight is a traditional legislative role, it does not concern many field staffers. Washington aides are much more likely to be involved in this.

Nevertheless, because casework inquiries serve to keep agencies and bureaucrats on their toes, oversight is a by-product, albeit a generally unintended one, of the massive constituent service load carried by Los Angeles field offices. Occasionally a local issue campaign will also involve field staffers in oversight.

12. Legislative Support

Field staffs, for the most part, play a minor role in legislation; it's not within their task environment. District offices relay ideas from constituents and local groups, act as "thermometers"—gauging the temperature of the district in regard to major vote decisions—and are sometimes the focus of lobbying efforts. Thus the field staff normally enters the law-making process only as a communications relay.

Legislative committee hearings held back in the home state or district are becoming commonplace. The responsibility for arranging such hearings often falls on personal field staff. Indeed, for some Los Angeles aides this is their principal function. Whether or not this is a legislative support function is another matter. In most cases the goal is local media exposure—promotion of the incumbent or of an idea. During interviews several congressional aides cited these hearings as examples of how they carried out their PR responsibilities. Not one mentioned them as part of the legislative process.

13. Personal Errands

Personal assistants are often "coat holders"; they are frequently called upon to perform private and personal chores for their employers. Tasks such as looking after the incumbent's house or aging mother while he is away in Washington, delivering clothes to the cleaner, and driving the incumbent or a member of his family to or from the airport are not uncommon. While many observers criticize such use of government-paid staff, staffers see this as a legitimate function.

> We think of his time as a valuable commodity, something to be protected. He only gets to spend a few days here a month, and they should be spent seeing people and doing useful things—not running little errands or waiting for taxis.
>
> Congressman's Aide

Many aides pointed out that their performance of personal favors stemmed more from their private relationship with their boss than their employee–employer relationship.

> We're like a family. When he's here for a visit, I pick him up at the airport, he uses my car and stays at my house. When I go to Washington, he meets me and I stay at his house.
>
> Congressman's Field Rrepresentative

SUMMARY: PUBLIC SERVICE AND PROMOTION

Thirteen distinct functions were discussed. These include some functions traditionally associated with Congress—citizen education and communication, legislative support, casework information gathering, representation, oversight. Also included were functions not usually acknowledged as things the Congress does: surveillance, group liaison, community organizing, direct action, nongovernment projects.

Fundamental to office functions is the combination of public service and political promotion. Good deeds are done, but each one has the incumbent's label firmly attached. Several offices in Los Angeles, for example, have mass mailed telephone adhesives to their constituents. These stickers are to be placed on the citizen's phone where they conveniently display emergency fire and police numbers (a public service) along with the incumbent's name and local phone number (promotion). Similarly, there are field offices that regularly hold showings for local artists. Every month or so a different artist is invited to show his work at the field office; the artist's friends are invited to an opening reception, as are friends of the office and the general public. Result: The arts and aspiring artists are encouraged (public service); the artist and his friends are grateful (promotion); the incumbent increases his visibility and public contact (promotion); and office decor is enhanced.

THE ELECTORAL CONNECTION

A simple yet profound approach to understanding Congress is set forth by David Mayhew. In Mayhew's scheme, electioneering and legislative behavior emerge as one and the same. He offers "a vision of United States congressmen as single-minded seekers of reelection."[11] Although conceding the simplicity of this unidimensional viewpoint, he goes on to argue rather convincingly that virtually all aspects of legislative behavior can be usefully explained or predicted from that one premise.

Mayhew also notes that personal organizations, rather than political parties, are the key to the reelection goal and that incumbency is the foundation of the personal followings. He finds that all Congressmen feel politically insecure, all of the time, even those who in reality are quite "safe." He goes on to show that campaigning is endless, and that besides keeping supporters in line and insuring that necessary contributions and other vote-getting resources will accrue to him, an incumbent seeks to minimize the probability he will face a serious, well-financed challenger.

Once the "electoral connection" is perceived, according to Mayhew, it is also easy to see why the chief activities of "lawmakers" consist of "advertising," "credit claiming," and "position taking." Mayhew's work is especially relevant to this study. While Mayhew barely mentions staff, much if not most of the activity he attributes to Congressmen (casework, newsletters, public relations, etc.) are actually staff functions. Furthermore, the single-minded devotion to reelection Mayhew attributes to incumbents extends to their aides as well. The Mayhew approach, in short, can be used to explain why staffs, especially field staffs, do what they do.

DOES CONSTITUENT SERVICE PAY OFF?

The late Vice President Alben Barkley's favorite story was about Farmer Jones. Over a period of 33 years Barkley had done favors for Mr. Jones—visited him at an Army hospital in France, interceded with General Pershing to get him shipped home early, got the VA to speed up his disability compensation, assisted in getting federal loans to start his farm and later to rebuild it after a flood. On top of all this, he got Mrs. Jones an appointment as postmistress. Then, in 1938, Barkley was flabbergasted to learn Mr. Jones was supporting his opponent in a close primary battle. "Surely," Barkley said, "you remember all these things I have done for you?" "Yeah," said Farmer Jones sullenly, "but what in hell have you done for me lately?"

The moral of the story is clear, and politicians are fond of repeating it. Nevertheless, there is ample evidence to show they don't accept its message. Incumbents seem to believe the key to reelection lies in what they do for their constituents.[11]

> The best way to get reelected is to spend a great majority of your time on casework.
>
> REPRESENTATIVE KEN HECHLER[12]

> You take care of your constituents and they'll take care of you.
>
> PRESIDENT GERALD FORD

> The goodwill from casework comes back in a thousand ways—in the voting booth, volunteer workers, good publicity, useful contacts, even campaign contributions.
>
> CONGRESSMAN'S AIDE

Ninety-eight percent of the Los Angeles aides agreed that casework is an important electoral asset; one out of five believe it is *the* most effective electioneering technique of all. Satisfied constituents, it is hoped, will not only vote for their benefactor themselves, but will also influence their families and friends to do the same. A number of the Los Angeles aides mentioned a rule-of-thumb figure of six to eight votes influenced by every well-handled case. Morris Fiorina argues that constituency service is the key to reelection. Furthermore, he implies that Congress creates, or at least acquiesces to, red tape because of the credit incumbents can reap from cutting through it for their constituents.[13]

Over 90 percent reported that they had received campaign contributions or volunteer help from persons who had been "serviced." In some offices this source of contributions or workers was substantial. One aide told how a single afternoon he'd spent on a case years ago—steering a business license application through the bureaucratic maze—continued to pay off. The grateful businessman had afterwards volunteered to help raise funds and to have his employees design, prepare, and install all the signs and posters for the upcoming campaign—services he has continued to supply for every subsequent election, for the city council, later the state senate and, recently, the U.S. Congress.

While most aides spoke of generating goodwill and influencing votes through casework, there was a different and perhaps more insightful view expressed by some. These aides saw the reelection problem primarily as a matter of avoiding strong challengers rather than of securing votes.

CONCLUSION

A Congressman is a "big man" among the people who elected him, and his district office can become a real force in the community—directly involving itself in anything that concerns the constituency. Besides significantly altering the distribution of public goods through their casework efforts, field staffs were found to be organizing charity drives, managing nonprofit corporations, campaigning for or against ballot propositions and local candidates, running public service law firms, changing the routes of planned freeways, mounting state and even nationwide propaganda campaigns in behalf of some cherished idea, lobbying other levels of government, creating and running mass transit systems, producing regular radio programs and ghost-writing syndicated newspaper columns, establishing bird sanctuaries and parks, and so on. Many of the constituent service cases, as well as a number of the direct-action efforts, exceed the jurisdictional boundaries of the applicable government. Congressional offices lead campaign efforts for or against state ballot propositions, state legislative offices lobby local city councils, and all offices seem to be in continuous contact with the county welfare department. Such nongovernment matters as attracting industry to the community, finding jobs for teenagers, organizing senior citizen activities, planning civic celebrations, sponsoring art shows, and promoting home vegetable gardens are commonplace in all types of "legislative" district offices. In short, much of Congress' impact on "who gets what" takes place far from Washington and bears little resemblance to what we read in the papers and are taught in civics courses.

3.5 The Operation of a Senator's Office*

Susan Webb Hammond

Each of the 535 offices of members of Congress constitute a very different organization both reflecting and extending the personality and style of "the boss." The following article examines office mechanics, dynamics, variation, and support in the U.S. Senate.

The personal offices of the 100 Senators in the Senate are important parts of the institution's operations. Within these offices personal staff aides perform a variety of activities to help Senators carry out their responsibilities. Yet the offices, as they exist and operate today, are a comparatively recent development.

Two major factors have governed the changes in Senators' personal offices over the years: incrementalism and individualism. Gradual increases in the number of aides, and slow changes in office practices, have been the norm. This incrementalism has occurred in an environment whose predominant ethos emphasizes senatorial equality and the authority of each Senator to manage his own time, activities, and perquisites. The organizational structure of the Senate, which is flat rather than hierarchical, is a significant determinant. This is true even though seniority, leadership, party affiliation, and other coordinative mechanisms have an impact on senatorial decision-making. Nowhere else in the national government are decisions made in an arena with the Senate's organizational pattern; even the House of Representatives is more structured.

The result of these factors is that the Senate has 100 different bureaucracies at the personal office level. Managing a small bureaucracy thus becomes an important aspect of each Senator's job.

---

* From Susan Webb Hammond, "The Operation of a Senator's Office," *Senators: Offices, Ethics, and Pressures, A Compilation of Papers Prepared for the Commission on the Operation of the Senate,* 1977, pp. 4–18. Printed from public domain.

FOCUS AND PURPOSE OF THIS STUDY

Personal staffs in the Senate range in size from 13 to 71, with an average staff of about 31. A majority of these are on the office staffs in Washington, D.C., rather than in state offices, although some decentralization of office staffs is presently underway.[1]

As of January 1976, personal staff aides in the Senate totaled approximately 3,100. In addition, by December 1975, 187 aides had been appointed by 75 Senators to assist with committee work pursuant to the authority of S. Res. 60 (see also Sec. 108, P.L. 94–54). When Senators also control committee staff, and when (as in some cases) that staff operates as part of a coordinated personal office/committee legislative department, the number of employees a Senator supervises is roughly equivalent to some divisional sections in Executive Branch Departments.

This study focuses on three aspects of Senate office operations: how office staffs assist a Senator in performing his work; how offices could be managed for more effective support to Senators; and the relationship of Senate offices to Senate-wide administrative support services.

By describing in some detail how Senators' personal offices presently operate, the study serves an informational function. Identification of problem areas in office operations is one result. Another is the identification of specific methods which have worked particularly well in one or more offices and which might be adopted by others. Finally, an assessment of personal office operations in the broader context of the role and responsibility of the Senate is possible. Recommendations to improve working conditions and office operations should, if implemented, enhance the efficiency and effectiveness of the Senate as an institution.

THE SENATOR'S JOB AND OFFICE OPERATIONS

The way a Senator defines his or her job shapes personal office operations. Representation, lawmaking, and oversight are commonly accepted Senate responsibilities. The emphasis on these components varies among Senators; they also have different views as to what constitutes effective supporting activities. A fourth function, the strengthening and maintenance of the Senate as in institution, is also emphasized in some offices.

Although each office is unique, every office engages in similar activities in support of the commonly accepted Senate functions. Although it would be a mistake to search for one optimum way in which a Senator's office "should" be run, the organizational similarities and the common problems experienced by Senate offices suggest that several models of operation can be identified. This section focuses on (1) the activities of personal office aides; (2) changes in staff organization in recent years; and (3) organization and management style of the offices, including matters delegated by Senators to staff, the extent to which and how responsibilities are divided within offices, and the question of access to the Senator by staff.

PERSONAL AIDES

Personal aides perform a variety of activities in support of the Senator. It is often suggested that constituent service activities, which support the representation obligations of the Senator, occupy much staff time. In fact, however, personal aides provide support across a broad range of areas, which relate not only to representation but also to lawmaking and policy formulation, oversight, and institutional maintenance. Aides oversee office operations, handle mail and other communications with constituents, do casework, assist on federal projects, and are involved in various stages of legislative decisionmaking. The organization of Senate offices reflects these varied duties. Analysis of the type of personnel increased during the past 15 years supports these observations.

The number of aides on Senate personal staffs has more than doubled in the last 15 years. In December 1960, the members of the Senate employed 1,418 persons, an average of 14 aides per office. On December 31, 1975, 3,122 aides were on Senate office payrolls (approximately 31 per office), an increase of 1,704 aides, or 120 percent. Much of the increase has come in the last few years, as the Table 3.5.1 indicates.

In addition, there were 187 S. Res. 60 aides employed by December 31, 1975, making a total of 3,309 aides on Senate personal staffs.

This increase in staff numbers has meant increasing staff specialization. In a number of offices, staff have been added in all areas of office operations: constituent service, including casework; legislative; administrative; and secretarial.

Since 1960, the number of aides designated by title on payroll records as having responsibilities involving legislation (legislative assistant, legislative aide, legislative correspondent, legislative clerk, etc.) has risen considerably. There were 73 in 53 offices in 1960, and 345 in 91 offices (531 in 95 offices when S. Res. 60 aides are included, a 600 percent increase) in 1975. Some of this increase was in the number of secretarial and clerical aides assigned to legislative matters. The figures also reflect the departmentalization of larger staffs and the increased use of specialized titles (rather than simply "staff assistant" or "clerk"). The number of aides who work on legislation may be understated by this data, however, because administrative assistants, special assistants, and other aides often carry substantial legislative duties. Table 3.5.2 summarizes these data.

TABLE 3.5.1 NUMBER OF EMPLOYEES ON SENATE OFFICE STAFFS, 1960–1975

	1960*	1970*	1972*	1975*
Total number of aides	1,418	2,299	2,515	3,122
Smallest office staff	7	6	8	13
Largest office staff	29	42	53	71
Average staff size	14	23	25	31

* As of December 31.

SOURCE: Reports of the Secretary of the Senate.

TABLE 3.5.2 LEGISLATIVE* AIDES ON PERSONAL STAFFS, 1960–1975

	1960	1970	1972	1974	1975
Number of aides	73	203	239	344	531
Senate Resolution 60 aides					187
Number of offices	53	78	86	91	95
Largest legislative staff	4	9	14	17	
Average legislative staff	1.4	2.6	2.8	3.8	5.6
Average legislative staff per 100 offices	0.7	2.0	2.4	3.4	5.3

* As determined by relevant titles.

SOURCE: Reports of the Secretary of the Senate.

Staff designated by title as press aides also increased from 17 in 17 offices in 1960 to 123 in 78 offices in 1975, a percentage increase similar to that for legislative aides.

It is difficult to document the increase in caseworkers. Few caseworkers were so designated in 1960, and this situation had changed little by 1975. But there are now a number of aides specifically designated as executive assistants or office managers, another reflection of larger staffs and increased managerial needs. In short, the personal office staffs of Senators have increased significantly in a relatively short time, and the increase has been accompanied by job differentiation.

DEPARTMENTALIZATION

Management needs and problems necessarily differ in offices of such varying size as presently exist in the Senate. The larger staffs may require different coordination techniques and a greater degree of structure. Most offices are departmentalized, to some degree. A typical division is by function—administrative, press, legislative, constituent service, or state (federal projects and casework) and field (state) offices—although the number of departments may vary. Administration, for example, may be divided into administration and personnel or into office management and mail. Many offices specialize further within these departments, assigning (for example) teams composed of a legislative assistant, legislative correspondent, and secretary to different issue areas. In a number of offices a secretarial pool is no longer used, since it has been found more effective to assign secretaries to each department; in this way more staff develop expertise. However, others find a secretarial pool an effective organizational unit because secretaries can be shifted to handle peak workloads.

Routine mail is often handled by a separate mail department, particularly in offices with a heavy load. Although some offices separate legislative mail duties from legislative assistant responsibilities, legislative assistants continue to answer legislative mail in a majority of offices, either by supervising a legislative secretary or drafting letters themselves. Constituent ideas about legislation are usually considered important, and having legislative assistants handle legislative mail is one way to assure that citizens' views reach the Senator. Some legislative assistants, for similar reasons, also handle federal projects. It is possible, however, that lower-level aides could satisfactorily handle some matters now included in the responsibilities of top-level legislative assistants.

Departmentalizing in Senators' offices is not easy, however, as divisions are rarely clearcut. Federal projects work, for example, is a constituent service, but it may involve legislative issues as well. One office reorganized its rigidly separated federal projects and legislative departments when federal projects aides became more and more involved in legislative work. Senate offices often reorganize; if one system doesn't work, another is tried. A number of offices have obtained assistance from management consulting firms in an attempt to improve their office organization, space use, and office management procedures. Most offices report that such assistance has been valuable. In some few instances, however, recommendations could not be implemented because of lack of space or other constraints. On occasion the suggestions seemed more applicable to business organizations than to congressional offices. Although office management assistance is particularly critical for newly elected Senators, the need is felt by Senators at all levels of seniority.

SPACE

Space is at a premium in the Senate. A major concern of staff members is the lack of space in Senate offices. It is not uncommon to have four or five desks and typewriters in one room. Noise levels are high; there is no privacy and no space for conferences; and there is little provision for storage of current files. Commission staff members on occasion had to interview secretarial staff aides in the Senate cafeterias; offices report that constituent groups are often met in the hall. Space utilization in the Senate is the subject of a separate commission study. Here it should simply be noted that lack of space has a significant impact on the efficient and effective operation of personal offices.

STAFF ACCESS TO SENATORS

Meetings between Senators and aides are often highly informal, a typical Senate trademark for many years. Senatorial staff members often have direct and unrestricted access to their Senators. Most Senators work with their top professional aides, including most legislative assistants, on an as-needed basis, although direct access may be coordinated by the administrative assistant, a department head, or a personal secretary. In a few offices scheduling aides attempt—not always successfully—to "schedule" staff appointments with the Senator just as the rest of his meetings are scheduled.

IMPROVING OFFICE MANAGEMENT

The personal styles of a Senator and his top aide, as well as political priorities and previous experience in or outside of politics, shape both office organization and communication with the Senator. A Senator's experience as a governor with a personalized staff style, or in a voluntary and informal party organization where high motivation is assumed and little effort is devoted to creating either psychological or financial rewards, or in a business organization with its emphasis on cost effectiveness, all have their impact. It is clear that no single management style would be appropriate for every Senate office. But knowledge of the specific experiences and procedures of other offices would give Senators a range of possibilities which is not now available. Few personal aides have management training or experience. Personnel competent in office organization and management and familiar with procedures both within and outside the Senate should be available for consultation. It seems clear that Senators want, and need, assistance in managing office operations.

Thus, there should be a special office within the Senate to assist Senators in office organization and management. Staffed by professionals who understand the different aspects of office operations (accounting, personnel management, workflow, etc.), such an office could (1) offer direct and confidential assistance on request; (2) serve as a resource on Senate operations and procedures through surveys and data on the various Senate offices, compilation of sample manuals, and description of different models; and (3) maintain a list of competent management consulting firms for the use of Senators who wish to retain an outside firm. The retention of outside consultants may require modifications in the regulations governing consolidated allowances, since such assistance must now be paid for from separate accounts or by Senators personally. If office allowance funds are used to retain consulting firms, copies of any reports should be made available to the Senate management-assistance office.

COORDINATION

Coordination of units within personal offices and coordination between the personal offices of Senators are, and should be, major concerns of the Senate today. Increases in staff size, departmentalization of tasks, the need to oversee one or more State offices, to coordinate a staff divided among two or more buildings on Capitol Hill, and (for many Senators) to supervise the staff on one or more subcommittees all make increased coordination a necessity. Regular coordination mechanisms do exist. A number of administrative assistants supervise Washington, field office, and committee staffs. They are responsible for dividing workloads, overseeing recruitment, and determining pay and leave policies. Most are not involved in supervising the substantive legislative work of committee staff members, although some are kept apprised of it and some in their own work supplement it. Although subcommittee staffing practices vary (a major factor being the role of the committee chairman and the autonomy of the subcommittee) some personal Senate offices operate "integrated" legislative departments. Legislative staff are shifted between personal and committee payrolls; salary of subcommittees are integrated with legislative departments of personal offices, and leave policies are the same for both staffs.[2]

In offices with these arrangements, much of the managerial responsibility for a large number of Senate staff members rests with the Senator's personal office. And Senate personal office bureaucracies are in fact augmented, often considerably, so that personal office payrolls understate the magnitude of the managerial job.

Various methods of coordination exist in different offices. They include:

1. Regular and frequent departmental meetings, called by the administrative assistant or the department head.
2. Regular and frequent meetings of department heads with the administrative assistant.
3. Coordination of committee and office staff at weekly breakfasts with the Senator.
4. Previous experience between committee staff and personal staff, which enhances coordinating.
5. Regular (weekly or monthly) meetings, usually at breakfast, of all staff with the Senator (described as "mostly window dressing" but nevertheless useful).
6. Weekly reports from field office heads (some Senators have four or more field offices), and frequent travel to the State by top aides.

What seems clear is that within personal offices some formal, institutionalized mechanism is helpful, both for coordination and morale purposes, and that direct access to the administrative assistant (or a top-level coordinator) is also important.

Contacts between Senate offices, including coordination and exchange of information, is less regularized and more difficult to design. Nevertheless, it is necessary and enhances the effectiveness of Senators and the Senate. At present, the system is essentially an ad hoc one that depends on office proximity, friendships, political relationships, and previous practices. There are some formal arrangements, however. Administrative assistants to Republican Senators meet regularly; early in the 94th Congress, administrative assistants to newly elected Senators met; and the staff of some subgroups (the Republican Steering Committee, for example) met regularly.

Regular meetings of staff in the different Senate offices are a useful device for coordination and the exchange of information and should be institutionalized. The responsibility for calling bipartisan meetings should rest initially with the appropriate Senate officer; thereafter, the group could designate one or more members to take responsibility for arranging meetings. The meetings need not be frequent, but should be regularly scheduled at the start of a Congress. They may be less necessary later in a session.

Party groups (administrative or legislative assistants to majority and minority members, for example) could operate similarly, with responsibility initially resting with the leadership but thereafter with group members. Such meetings could be arranged for various categories—administrative assistants, legislative assistants, office managers, caseworkers, press aides. The topics to be discussed should be both substantive and procedural. (A number of administrative assistants endorse the notion of occasional meetings to discuss management issues.) Ad hoc staff group meetings could continue to supplement regular meetings.

There is an information vacuum among Senate offices regarding organization, and services. Too often, offices are afraid to share problems with each other, out of concern that an admission of difficulty will have unpleasant repercussions. Yet common interests and activities as well as common problems are present. The creation of regular and institutionalized opportunities for objective discussion and exchange of information would increase the effectiveness of each office and of the Senate as a whole.

LEGISLATIVE SUPPORT

Obtaining accurate and current information on the status of bills, committee actions, and floor proceedings, is of major concern to legislative staffs. Some offices regularly assign an aide to sit in the Senate gallery and monitor floor proceedings. Offices may designate one aide to review the *Congressional Record* and Whip Notices, and to compile a daily memo of legislative actions, which is sent to legislative staff members and to the Senator. Other offices, having been caught unaware in the past, coordinate the monitoring of all bills reported by committees in order to be able to inform their Senators during floor debate.

Better information to enable monitoring of committee activity and floor proceedings is needed, however, and legislative operating information is the subject of a separate Commission study. In any case, assignment of a staff to monitor all floor proceedings from the gallery would not appear to be an effective use of staff time, although at present it may be necessary.

For legislative staff, whether personal or committee, the majority and minority leadership might hold seminars with experts on particular substantive topics, followed by briefings by committee and/or subcommittee staff. These would supplement briefings presently conducted by the Congressional Research Service (CRS), The Brookings Institution, and others. A standardized format for reports on bills would also be helpful.

Although information for, and analysis of, legislative decision making are covered by other Commission studies, several considerations relevant to personal staffs should be mentioned here:

1. Some Senators are adding legislative aides with technical expertise to their personal staffs. Similarly, Senators are hiring experts, often from the Executive Branch, in areas such as foreign policy and health, for both personal and committee staff positions. A discussion of the demographics of staff is beyond the scope of this study, but this diversification of Senate staff adds a useful dimension to policy decisions.

2. Some Senators have experimented in using staff aides on a temporary task basis rather than for long-term legislative assignments. If clerk-hire amounts permit flexibility, this appears to be a useful method of bringing expertise to specific areas of concern.

3. A few Senators have formalized a system for obtaining the advice of outside experts

through the use of task forces. Although arrangements of this kind present additional coordination problems, they can also add a significant dimension to the refining of policy options. Some consideration should be given to paying the travel expenses of outside experts from Senators' office allowances.

OVERSIGHT

Most personal offices are not organized to carry out oversight activities, although at times significant oversight has been performed by personal staff. Managers of Senate offices might give consideration to arranging office procedures so that casework and federal project matters can be monitored for possible oversight implications (that is, moving the remedy beyond the individual case or project to a broader administrative or legislative remedy). They might also consider transferring such matters from constituent services to legislative departments, and to committees, if deemed appropriate. Legislative staff may also be involved in oversight activities resulting from individual concerns of the Senator or staff, or from committee work. Separate Commission studies on oversight relate to these issues.

THE QUESTION OF STAFF SIZE

Much of the foregoing has dealt with management of staff at its present size. But must the Senate concur in present trends, or is it possible to reduce the size of personal staffs?

It has been suggested that centralization of some activities presently performed by separate staffs could result in reduction in staff size. The possibility of a Senate-wide secretarial pool was discussed with a number of Senate staffers. There was little support for establishing a pool. Instead, staff members emphasized such considerations as differing office procedures, dissimilar peak load periods, and the need for staff loyal to one office.

Nevertheless, some centralization of mail operations by central support offices might be explored; it may be that routine typing, such as envelope addressing, could be performed more efficiently by a central office. Draft language for stating bill status (for use in legislative mail) has been suggested by some offices. Use of improved technology (computers, CMS systems) might also occur as part of a central service. And the possibility of centralizing constituent services such as casework, to some degree is discussed in the Commission study, "Constituent Services."

Alternatively, some functions might be removed from Senators' offices. It has been suggested that casework, for example, might be performed by an ombudsman. The arguments against this, however, seem persuasive.

Another possibility might be to assign the legislative function to committee staffs or the staffs of support agencies instead of to personal staffs. Such a change presumably would require increased staff size for these groups. The consequences of such a shift would be varied kinds of citizen input, and at different points; possibly a somewhat different control of resources than at present; and different coordination needs and structures, to list a few. All in all, such a change does not seem either feasible or warranted, barring a major restructuring of Senate roles and organization. What seems clear is that Senators both want and need trusted personal staff to assess and advise, and in some instances to coordinate action, on various policy matters. Most Senators share the concern that increased staff size may result in less responsiveness to citizen concerns and further bureaucratization. On the other hand, however, demands and workload appear to have increased and become more complex, and Senators need assistance.

Some Senators have managed to reduce the size of their staffs, primarily through implementing management studies of their offices. By reorganizing, by changing equipment, and in some instances by using different office procedures, increased efficiency and the elimination of several positions (usually by attrition and usually at lower staff levels) have resulted.

Any major reduction in personal office operations would result in a major shift in Senate organization, resources, priorities, and hence an assessment of the consequences of any specific proposals should be carefully made. But reduced staff through increased efficiency seems possible, given the present functions and activities of personal offices.

MANAGEMENT OF OFFICES

Managing Senate offices, including recruitment, pay, and leave policies, monitoring of workloads and workflow, and acquisition of office equipment and supplies, is an important aspect of Senate office operations. In most offices, Senators delegate specific decisions and day-to-day monitoring to aides, although many oversee decisions at various levels and may monitor in detail. The degree of involvement is a personal decision for each Senator.

A number of offices now employ an office manager or administrative director, a relatively new position. Duties vary from ordering supplies and equipment and keeping office accounts to monitoring vacation and other leave for both personal and committee staff and assisting in recruitment of personnel. Offices with such a position find that the arrangement works well. Some office managers also oversee the mail department, or the production of communications to constituents; others also advise on, or administer, separate office accounts.

Many offices have regularized work-hour and leave policies. Both vacation and sick leave are often based on years of work for the Senators (10 to 12 days vacation the first year, 15 the second year, 20 to 26 thereafter). Senate offices have drawn on Executive Branch practices as well as the experiences of business firms and state and local governments in establishing their policies. In some offices all staff get the same amount of vacation, regardless of length of employment; in most offices, leave is noncumulative after January; some offices require a three-month employment period before leave is earned.

Office hours also vary. Some offices remain open on Saturdays and holidays, others operate during the normal business hours of their home state, some want employees to take many brief vacations or to vacation during recess.

Although there will be differing office requirements, each Senator should develop a written statement of policy on hours of work; vacation, sick, and administrative leave; termination (both voluntary and involuntary) policies; and applicability of such policies to personal office staff, Senate Resolution 60 aides, and majority or minority committee employees under his jurisdiction. Leave records should be kept by a designated employee. Assistance in establishing such policies, including general information based on policies and experience in other offices, and samples (with identification removed) should be available from the management-assistance office.

SALARIES

The salaries of personal staff members tend to remain personalized, negotiable, and, at times, inequitable within and between offices. Salary information is available in the report of the Secretary of the Senate, but it is fragmented and often unclear. Some offices do not automatically give their employees government cost-of-living increases but give all raises on merit; other offices, because of limited clerk-hire funds, give raises primarily through promotion or year-end bonuses. Some Senate offices are presently working to establish clear pay structures that categorize jobs by grades and set upper and lower limits for salaries within those grades. State field offices and subcommittee staff salary structure are coordinated with Washington offices. In some instances, formal and systematic evaluations of personnel are a part of the procedure.

Nonetheless, most Senators need assistance in determining equitable salary structures. At present, information is obtained ad hoc through telephone calls to other offices, random perusal of the Secretary's report, or occasional inquiries to management consulting firms. Establishment of a pay structure and personnel evaluation system in Senators' offices would result in improved management. Assistance should be offered on request by the management-assistance office.[3]

Some Senators' offices are concerned that staff allowances are not adequate. Partially due to differences in funding procedure, committees may have higher-level salary structures; on occasion, this results in different pay for similar work performed by committee and personal staff members supervised by the same Senator. Annual allowances for staff salaries are based on state population and vary from a minimum of $413,082 for Senators from states of less than 2 million to $844,608 for Senators from the most populous states (more than 21 million).[4] A number of Senators return a portion of their clerk-hire allowances each year; other Senators use virtually all of it.

As Table 3.5.3 indicates, many of the increments for staff allowances vary nonsystematically. As the table shows, wide variations in population are ignored. For example, Alaska's population in 1974 was approximately 337,000, while Rhode Island's population was 937,000. Yet Senators from both states receive the same office staff allowance because they both have less than 2 million inhabitants.

There are also variations on the per capita basis. States with larger populations have larger staffs, but it appears that the large states have more difficulty working within the allotted amounts.

It is difficult, admittedly, to devise a formula for clerk-hire which is clearly equitable. It is also difficult to isolate functions which are similar for all offices, or to assess quantitatively the factors which result in variable workloads. Legislative functions, which are common to all Senators, might be funded similarly, with other functions (such as constituent service) funded on the basis of population. But staff aides from larger states often argue that federal legislation has a greater impact on states with larger populations and that therefore those Senators need a larger legislative staff. Mail loads vary with populations to some extent, but not in a systematic manner. Casework loads appear to be similar. Do some Senators have heavier workloads because they represent a "national" constituency? And if so, should this in some way be recognized in an increased staff allowance?

It may be that certain jobs should be designated as common to all offices and paid for by a standard staff allowance, with other jobs funded according to a population formula. The Legislative Appropriations Subcommittee has wrestled with this problem and has made significant changes in the allowance base. However, larger states do appear to have substantially greater difficulty than smaller states staying within their clerk-hire allowance. It may be that the problem is unsolvable but there should be further examination of the basis for setting staff allowance amounts.

Greater flexibility in the way allowances are used is supported by a number of Senate offices. The approach of the Legislative Appropriations Subcommittee seems useful here. There should be increased flexibility in regulations governing allowances, in conjunction with disclosure in order to prevent abuses. One specific action would be removal of the statutory limitations on

TABLE 3.5.3 STAFF ALLOWANCES

STATE POPULATION		TOTAL	
AT LEAST	AND LESS THAN	ALLOWANCE	INCREMENT
—	2,000,000	$413,082.00	—
2,000,000	3,000,000	425,484.00	12,402
3,000,000	4,000,000	455,376.00	29,892
4,000,000	5,000,000	493,854.00	38,478
5,000,000	7,000,000	525,336.00	31,482
7,000,000	9,000,000	558,408.00	33,072
9,000,000	10,000,000	504,342.00	35,934
10,000,000	11,000,000	622,008.00	27,666
11,000,000	12,000,000	658,260.00	36,252
12,000,000	13,000,000	685,926.00	27,666
13,000,000	15,000,000	721,224.00	35,298
15,000,000	17,000,000	756,522.00	35,298
17,000,000	19,000,000	791,820.00	35,298
19,000,000	21,000,000	818,214.00	26,394
21,000,000	—	844,608.00	26,394

TABLE 3.5.4 OFFICE STAFF ALLOWANCE, SELECTED STATES, PER CAPITA

Alaska	$1.22
Rhode Island	0.44
West Virginia	0.23
Iowa	0.11
Wisconsin	0.11
Virginia	0.10
Michigan	0.06
Texas	0.05
New York	0.04
California	0.03

personal staff salaries, except for the existing upper limit. In conjunction with the establishment of a formal pay structure for offices, this action would eliminate the need to raise salaries through committee personnel shuffles or other means.

S. RES. 60 ASSISTANCE

S. Res. 60 was passed in an effort to redress what some Senators perceived as an imbalance in access to substantive staffing. By December 31, 1975, 75 Senators employed aides hired under the resolution. As expected, a higher percentage of middle-level and junior Senators than of senior Senators have appointed such aides. (See Table 3.5.5.)

TABLE 3.5.5 APPOINTMENT OF AIDES UNDER S. RES. 60

SENIORITY	PERCENT APPOINTING AIDES
Senior	40
Middle senior	97
Junior	88

However, some committee chairmen and ranking minority members have also appointed similar S. Res. 60 personnel, and the resolution appears to offer resources in an area which Senators consider important.

OFFICE OPERATION ALLOWANCES

Allowances for office operations are of two kinds: dollar allowances to cover some office expenses, such as telephone, travel, and postage, and in-kind allowances to cover others, such as equipment, envelopes, and paper. Representatives of virtually all offices agree that establishment of a consolidated allowance for office expenses several years ago was an improvement and greatly simplified office operations. There is also a widespread appreciation for recent and continuing changes in items managed by the Sergeant at Arms, and for notification efforts by that office and by minority staff of the Rules Committee.

Problems remain, however. Too often, offices ''discover'' unexpectedly that new equipment is available. The regulations governing replacement of equipment, ordering of equipment, and amounts and type of equipment seem unduly rigid. Although it is clear that there must be controls, it should be possible to use full disclosure rather than detailed rules as the major form of control. As it is, staff members often are forced to work through a labyrinth, seeking help from one office after another in the hope that eventually someone will suggest new equipment or approve an expenditure.

Greater flexibility in office operations allowances, and incresed efforts to disseminate information regarding allowances and the items available under them, would be helpful to all offices. Offices also need authoritative guidance on the appropriate use of office allowances.

General policy on office allowances should be set by some central authority. The basis for allocations should be equitable and clearly understood. Implementation of the policies, including dissemination of lists and types of equipment, should be handled by the appropriate Senate officer. Full information regarding allowances and equipment should be sent regularly to all offices. The following kinds of information would be useful:

- A detailed manual on allowances, including, for example, regulations governing the use of allowances, the printing of newsletters, etc.
- Lists of available equipment (including catalogs, and equipment available to field offices).
- Regular notification about new equipment and services.
- Regular notification of any actions by the Rules Committee, Appropriations Committee, or Senate officers, which change allowances in any way.
- Occasional briefing on new equipment or services.

Several other changes in regard to equipment and supplies can also be suggested.

The Senate office with responsibility for furnishing equipment to Senators' personal offices should evaluate new equipment and office systems and these evaluations should be made available to Senators as rapidly as feasible. To many, present equipment lists often seem outdated.

Flexibility in the type and amount of office equipment, and in interpreting regulations regarding equipment ordering and use, should be increased. Allowing equipment to be used only for a specific length of time may hinder office efficiency; on the other hand, ordering several items of one kind may improve efficiency.

Authorizing lease or purchase of office machines from an increased consolidated office account might also be explored.

Consolidation of all paper and envelope allowances would increase flexibility. In addition, these allowances in-kind might be converted to dollars and combined with the consolidated office allowance.

TRANSITION PERIOD

Newly elected Senators face the problems of setting up an office, hiring staff, establishing office procedures, and obtaining equipment. A number of new Senators reported taking office in 1975 with a backlog of several thousand letters to answer. Some administrative assistants have paid their own expenses during December while they assisted in hiring staff and making other office arrangements; others have been able to work on the staff of a retiring Senator to learn Senate practices and procedures prior to the start of the session. Earlier assistance to newly elected Senators would improve the efficiency and effectiveness of office operations.

A small staff assistance allowance for newly elected Senators, to permit employment of perhaps one senior aide and one secretary from December 1 following the election until the Senator takes office, would be helpful in solving these problems, as would an arrangement for minimal office space.

Establishing an office checking account during the transition period to cover vouchered items payable from the funds of the consolidated office allowance is also difficult for many Senators. The present system results in Senators often being out-of-pocket as much as $1,000 or in the vouchers submitted in anticipation of expenditures. Newly elected Senators should be able to establish an office checking account from their authorized office funds prior to the start of a new session. Detailed orientation briefings for newly elected Senators and their aides should also be available.

Additional complexity arises from the separate office accounts that can be established under Senate Rule 42. Some offices do not establish such accounts; others are closing them out; still others find them necessary in order to meet office expenses. Present regulations require full disclosure of both contributions and expenditures. The Senate should address the question of whether allowances should be increased to meet some expenses now covered by Rule 42 office accounts. The Senate should also give further guidance to Senators on their use, and examine the impact of any Federal Election Commission regulations.

CENTRAL SUPPORT SERVICES

Senators' offices perceive the delivery of central support services as fragmented, personalized, and nonsystematic. Although most offices have learned to live with the situation, there remains a rather high level of frustration due to the time-consuming delays involved in making the requisite number of telephone calls or written requests to obtain needed services. Lack of information is a major concern. It is difficult for staff to know which office handles a particular service, and several telephone calls may be necessary to discover which employee is in charge of a particular service.

Furthermore, the system is sometimes illogical. One office handles the moving of furniture, while another handles the moving of office equipment; bell lights on office wall clocks are repaired by one office, the works of the clock by another. This fragmentation also wastes time, as when staff members wait for different groups to move equipment and furniture, for example.

The organization of Senate-wide administrative support services is the subject of a separate study by the Commission. As far as the operations of Senators' offices are concerned, however, it seems clear that some changes in organization which would minimize fragmentation are needed. An arrangement which would require one telephone call or letter would assist in streamlining the work of Senate offices. In addition, complete and detailed information on the services available, and on the offices to contact for these services, is essential. Many offices now prepare their own lists of whom to contact for what, based on their own experience. Although these are undoubtedly useful—and necessary, given the present system—it appears to be unnecessary duplication to have each office doing this. As a supplement to the Handbook of the Joint Committee on Congressional Operations, the preparation of a detailed handbook on Senate-wide services listing (1) services and goods provided, and (2) the office, telephone number, and, if possible, the staff aide to contact for each of the services listed, would be helpful. The handbook should include details on how to order goods and services, and it should be updated regularly as new services and equipment become available. A series of informational pamphlets on different offices and/or services might also be issued.

The handbook could be supplemented by (1) regular notices to Senate offices summarizing services, equipment, or personnel changes, and (2) occasional briefing sessions at which the personnel of Senate-wide services offices could discuss services available and obtain systematic feedback on the concerns and needs of individual Senators' offices.

CONCLUSION

The personal offices of Senators are an important part of the Senate system. These offices not only support and assist Senators in carrying out their various activities and functions, but in doing so interact with, and in many cases give guidance to, other groups in the Senate. Increased efficiency and effectiveness in office operations will, in turn, enhance the operations of the Senate as a whole.

Each Senator has chief authority and responsibility for his office personnel and operations, and therefore each senatorial office is unique. Office operations are based on the Senator's view of his various responsibilities, on his seniority and committee or subcommittee chairmanships, on Senate procedures and operations, and on such external factors as state population, mail, and caseloads.

Staff activity is shaped by a Senator's style. Does he want alternatives presented to him for a judgelike decision, or positions presented for him to question, or a position based on objective, "scientific," factual data? Does he emphasize writing, legislative arguments, or businesslike efficiency? These are not necessarily mutually exclusive predilections, but a Senator's style is an important determinant of office emphasis and priorities.

Each Senator's perception of the Senate as an institution and his role within it also shape staff operations. Senators who view as important maintenance of the Senate as an institution and who see themselves as mediators of differing points of view will encourage their staffs to establish wide-ranging contacts among different groups and to devise legislation on which there can be cooperation with Senators of different views. Other Senators, also concerned with the Senate as an institution, may emphasize and encourage staff to structure opportunities for impact on the external political system through, for example, major debates and televised proceedings.

Senate offices today require improved managerial and administrative skills. Senators face problems of staff morale. For some, coordination of both Hill and home state staff, or a move from the House to the Senate offer special circumstances. Many offices promote from within; in doing so, some face problems as co-workers continue to view the promoted employee from the initial job level. Some offices have effectively consulted communications and interpersonal relations specialists on office management. In some offices every effort is made to give middle-level employees responsibilities commensurate with their abilities. New Senators, and their staffs, need an orderly introduction to Senate procedures and facilities. New staff may need specific training. Overall, effective management of staff is important to Senate operations. As the Senate moves toward the 1980s with heavy responsibilities and an apparently increasing workload, Senators' offices can effectively assist and support Senators in the performance of their many responsibilities.

3.6 Legislative Support Agencies*

In addition to staff in personal offices, district offices, and committees, congressional bureaucracy extends to major congressional support agencies: CRS, GAO, OTA, and CBO. The following excerpt from a congressional manual, intended for staff, specifies the roles of each of these support agencies and the kinds of services they offer.

Most of the assistance to the Congress in carrying out its oversight responsibilities is provided by legislative support agencies: the Congressional Research Service, the General Accounting Office, the Office of Technology Assessment, and the Congressional Budget Office.

A. *Congressional Research Service* (CRS)

1. *Capabilities*

The Congressional Research Service of the Library of Congress works exclusively for members and committees of Congress and their staffs to assist them in carrying out their responsibilities. CRS has nine divisions: American Law, Economics, Foreign Affairs and National Defense, Government, Education and Public Welfare, Environment and Natural Resources Policy, Science Policy Research, Congressional Reference, and Library Services. In addition, there is the Office of Senior Specialists, which is composed of nationally recognized policy experts.

* From "Legislative Support Agencies," *Congressional Oversight Manual*, 1979, pp. 46–60. Reprinted from the public domain.

Through its staff of about *550 subject specialists,* supported by professional information and editorial personnel, CRS assists congressional offices by providing the following types of services:

a. Analysis of issues facing Congress. Preparation of analytical studies, general background reports, pro and con arguments, and evaluation of alternative proposals.

b. Legal research and analysis. Examination of the *constitutionality* or interpretation of existing or proposed legislation; summaries and analyses of *court decisions;* surveys of federal or state legislation on given subjects; *legislative histories;* and legal research on related topics.

c. Consultation with members and their staffs. Subject *specialists* are available for consultation on legislative issues and proposals.

d. General reference assistance. Searches of the *Congressional*

Record, books, newspapers, periodicals, etc.; bibliographical and biographical information, addresses, quotations, etc.; preparation of materials for use in the Congressional Reading Room.

e. Assistance to committees. The Legislative Reorganization Act of 1970 required CRS to provide the following services:

(1) *Emerging issues:* Provide each committee, at the opening of each Congress, with a *list of subjects and policy areas* the committee might profitably analyze in depth. Some committees work closely with the CRS in jointly developing such lists and description of emerging issues.

(2) *Terminating programs.* Provide each committee, at the opening of each new Congress, with a *list of programs and activities* under the committee's jurisdiction *scheduled* to expire during that Congress. These are, in essence, programs which are already subject to "sunset" provisions. Also included in such listings are the reports required to be submitted to the Congress and to the appropriate committees during a particular Congress.

(3) *Advise and assist committees.* Upon request, assist in the analysis and evaluation of legislative proposals, in determining the advisability of enacting such proposals, in estimating the probable results of such proposals, and in evaluating alternative methods.

(4) *Liaison.* Maintain continuous liaison with all committees.

f. *Oversight hearings assistance.* CRS can also assist committees in their planning and conduct of oversight hearings by preparing background and policy studies; suggesting outside specialists as possible hearing witnesses; preparing questions which might be appropriate to ask witnesses; supplying information on program accomplishments, interest-group positions, and relevant major studies; analyzing testimony; helping draft the committee report; and making follow-up studies.

g. Special publications and services. CRS provides a number of special services and aids for Congress. Principal among these are:

(1) *The Congressional Research Review.* This monthly publication provides the Congress with highlights of topics of immediate concern to the Congress based upon recent CRS analyses, with citations to relevant literature from the congressional community. Seminars and workshops for Congress are also announced.

(2) *The Digest of Public General Bills and Resolutions.* The Bill Digest furnishes brief synopses of all public bills and resolutions introduced in the current session.

(3) *Major Legislation of the . . . Congress.* MCL, published monthly, selects the 600 to 700 most important bills, arranges them

into subject groupings, and tells what they will do and where they stand at the moment.

(4) *Issues briefs*. These are summarized major issues of concern to Congress available in *print* or by *videoscreen*. Each of the more than *300 briefs* in the computerized data base at any given time contains a definition of the issue, background and policy analysis, legislative highlights, etc. (Also in the computer are a legislative and a bibliographic data base.)

(5) *On-demand bibiliographies and SDI services*. Members and committees of Congress may be provided with printouts from the CRS automated bibliographic data base. These printouts contain citations of congressional and other official documents and of selected items from professional journals, other current public affairs articles, and selected monographs. A Selective Dissemination of Information (SDI) service (now available to all Senate offices and currently being extended to House offices) provides weekly computer printouts of citations to the most recent writings in the fields of interest specified by individual members.

(6) *Reports*. Each year the service prepares several thousand analytical and background reports and duplicates those reports which seem to be of general interest.

(7) *Translation services*. CRS can assist in translating official correspondence to or from any of the major foreign languages.

h. *Computer services*.

(1) *Capitol Hill Network*. The Automated Systems Office of the Library and CRS are working with the computer centers of the Senate and the House of Representatives in development of the Capitol Hill Network. This network will enable computer users on the Hill to interact more effectively in *common information retrieval and data transfer activities*. Staffs of the three provide technical expertise, consultation, programming, and systems analysis services to congressional and committee offices at their request.

(2) *Access to automated data bases*. Four automated data bases are maintained by CRS: *legislative* (bill digest for the 94th, 95th, and 96th Congresses), *major issues* (issue briefs), *bibliographic,* and an *index to the daily Congressional Record*. These files are constantly updated and, through the use of *SCORPIO,* an interactive, question-answer retrieval system which CRS will teach people, can be "accessed" or searched by computer terminals located in terminal-equipped congressional offices, CRS Reference Centers, and

throughout CRS itself. In addition, the Service makes various private or executive branch data bases available, including the *New York Times Information Bank,* the *Department of Justice legal information system* (JURIS), and many others.

2. *Limitations*

   Although CRS attempts to provide any information or analysis that may help committees or members with their oversight functions, CRS *cannot do the following:*

   a. Draft bills. (This is a function of the office of the legislative counsel.) CRS does assist with preparing legislative proposals but cannot draft legislation.

   b. Meet unreasonable deadlines or excessive demands, which CRS may be able to comply with only by dropping or jeopardizing the quality of responses to urgent legislative requests related to the public policy work of the Congress.

   c. Provide personal information relating to individual members or former members of Congress, except at the specified request or with permission of the member concerned.

   d. Prepare reports or speech drafts which are of a partisan nature or which deal with individual members or parties.

   e. Conduct field investigations.

B. *General Accounting Office* (GAO)

1. *Capabilities*

   The General Accounting Office (GAO), headed by the Comptroller General of the United States, was created by the Budget and Accounting Act in 1921, "independent of the executive department," to assist the Congress in its oversight of the Executive Branch in carrying out programs enacted by Congress. GAO's basic resonsibilities have been modified by numerous statutes since 1921. The most recent revision was the Congressional Budget and Impoundment Control Act of 1974.

   While GAO is required by statute to assist committee chairmen on request, most of its work is self-initiated under its responsibility for reviewing the operations of the Executive Branch. The Comptroller General has discretion as to the subject matter to be reviewed, the timing of these reviews, and the conclusions and recommendations in individual audits and evaluations. Thus GAO serves a dual role of directly assisting the Congress and of independently auditing, investigating, and evaluating—all in the interest of improved congressional oversight.

   In initiating work, GAO seeks congressional views so that it can produce information that will be timely and useful to committees and members. Reports are normally sent to Congress and its Committees. They are available to the public.

   The following services are performed under GAO's continuing responsibility to assist the Congress or at the request of committees or individual members.

   a. "On-board" staffing. GAO staff is multidisciplinary. It includes accountants and auditors, attorneys, actuaries, and other mathematical scientists, claims adjudicators and examiners, engineers, computer and information specialists, economists and other social scientists, personnel management specialists, as well as members of a variety of other disciplines.

   b. Consultants. As extensive as GAO's regular staff capabilities are, they are supplemented, as needed, by consultants and experts. Consultants from all academic and professional disciplines are utilized to meet any request for which "on-board" staff are insufficient.

c. *Proximity to places where programs are carried out.* GAO staff is permanently located in 15 regional offices and 21 suboffices throughout the continental United States and in 4 offices around the world. In Washington, D.C., auditors and evaluators are stationed at over 70 agency locations. These staffing arrangements promote travel economy and facilitate the GAO role of on-site verification, validation, and evaluation.

d. *Information sources, models, and data bases.* Primarily to support the performance of its audits and evaluations, GAO has contracted for access to a variety of computerized data bases which include published information in a wide range of subject areas, including physical sciences and technology, business, social sciences, and the arts and humanities. GAO also has access to various econometric and other "manipulative" models, which help GAO staff forecast the impact of program alternatives. GAO staff also uses libraries and reference facilities in the agencies of which they are performing work.

2. *GAO services*

a. *Audits and evaluations of programs, activities, and financial operations of federal departments and agencies and their contractors and grantees.* Far and away GAO's biggest "product," audits and evaluations answer questions on how federal resources are managed, controlled, and accounted for; how economically programs are carried out; and whether they are meeting intended objectives. Audits and evaluations are performed—on a self-initiated basis—to fulfill GAO's continuing responsibility to provide adequate coverage of federal agencies and programs.

Views of interested committees and members are an important input to GAO in programming its self-initiated overall audit coverage of federal agencies and programs. Frequently, in addition to using reports on GAO's self-initiated work, committees and members request special audits to assist them in their oversight and legislative roles and in dealing with constituent concerns.

b. *Substantive support to appropriation, authorization, and oversight hearings.* On request, GAO will review the results of its work and provide relevant questions or otherwise help committees probe areas of concern.

c. *Comments on legislative proposals.* GAO reviews and evaluates proposed legislation or proposed changes in legislation when asked. By reviewing agency programs and activities firsthand, GAO can objectively advise how a program can be expected to work out or whether a better alternative exists. Such advice may be oral or written.

d. *Assistance in developing statements of legislative objectives and goals.* Knowledge gained by GAO in auditing and evaluating programs is available, on request, when goals and objectives are being considered for inclusion in legislative proposals. Advice may be oral or in writing.

e. *Assessing federal agency program reviews and recommending methods for evaluating federal programs.* GAO assists committees in analyzing and assessing program reviews or evaluations prepared by or for any federal agency. GAO also develops and recommends to the Congress methods for reviewing and evaluating government programs and activities carried on under existing law.

f. *Legislative recommendations.* At times, GAO audit and evaluation work—either requested or self-initiated—indicates that program economy, efficiency, or effectiveness would be improved by changes to legislation. GAO reports include recommendations for such corrective legislation.

g. *Legal opinions.* GAO issues opinions on the authority of departments and agencies and the circumstances under which public funds may be spent. This differs from legal advice from other legislative support agencies in that GAO opinions on the use of public funds are binding on the Executive Branch. GAO also issues advisory opinions to committees and members of Congress on a wide variety of issues to assist Congress in its legislative and oversight functions.

h. *Testimony at committee hearings.* GAO representatives are available to testify on reports and other office issuances and to give views on pending legislation.

i. *Briefing committees on GAO findings and recommendations.* GAO officials brief committee staff on GAO work of interest to them. These briefings include the results of completed or ongoing work which has progressed far enough to provide meaningful information.

j. *Review of rescissions and deferrals.* The Budget and Impoundment Control Act of 1974 requires the Comptroller General to review and report to the Congress the facts surrounding rescissions or deferrals of budget authority by Executive Branch agencies. As part of this function, GAO reports impoundments which Executive Branch agencies fail to submit to the Congress or submit with an incorrect classification.

k. *Identifying and helping to meet information needs.* GAO works with committees and members of Congress to identify their needs for fiscal, budgetary, and program-related information. In doing so, GAO works closely with the Congressional Budget Office, the Treasury, and the Office of Management and Budget. By law, these agencies standardize the terminology, definitions, and classifications so that Executive Branch agency information systems will more directly support Congress' information needs. GAO also maintains directories of federal information sources, of program evaluations commissioned by Executive Branch agencies, and of recurring reports required by the Congress and its committees.

l. *Approving agency accounting systems.* GAO approves agencies' principles and standards and accounting system designs when they are determined to be adequate.

m. *Claims settlement and debt collection.* Claims are settled by GAO when the departments and agencies have not been given specific authority to handle their own claims, and when they involve (1) doubtful questions of law or fact, (2) appeals of agency actions, (3) certain debts which agencies are unable to collect, and (4) waivers of certain erroneous payments for pay, etc.

n. *Legislative digest information and library services.* Complete legislative history files are maintained on all public and private bills. The GAO library has legal and technical sections designed to support GAO staff need. These facilities are available to respond to committee and member questions. They are not, however, as extensive as those of the Library of Congress which are available to committees and members through the Congressional Research Service.

o. *Auditing services for the Legislative Branch.* GAO has a small professional staff located in the Capitol complex. This staff performs work required by various statutes in auditing private organizations and other commercial types of activities performing services at the Capitol complex. It assists in House and Senate financial and administrative operations and provides advisory services.

p. *Staff assignments to committees.* In special cases—and on a very limited basis—when committees need audit and evaluation skills rather than particular "products," staff assignments of up to a year to committees can be arranged. In the Senate, GAO is required to be reimbursed for the salary of staff members loaned to committees.

3. *Limitations*

At times, a committee may ask GAO to assist it by performing work which is the primary responsibility of another congressional support agency. When this happens, GAO informs the committee of its reluctance to work in such areas. If GAO is unable to get the request reassigned, it will work closely with the other agency to avoid duplication or overlap. Areas not in the primary responsibility of GAO include:

a. Literature or bibliographical research.

b. Logistical arrangements in connection with hearings.

c. Studies concentrating on early warning of the long-range impact of new or evolving technology.

d. Studies involving impacts of alternative budget levels.

e. Multiyear cost and outlay estimates of carrying out newly authorized public bills.

f. Forecasts of aggregate economic trends or analyses directed solely or primarily to aggregate impacts of alternative spending and revenue levels, aggregate levels of tax expenditures under existing law, or alternative allocations among federal programs or budget functional categories.

g. Policy analysis based only or predominately on information available in the literature or from expert or informed opinion.

C. *Office of Technology Assessment* (OTA)

1. *Capabilities*

a. OTA provides Congress with comprehensive, even-handed assessments of the likely impacts—beneficial and adverse, expected and unanticipated—of the applications of scientific and technological knowledge. OTA operates with a relatively small *in-house staff of about 130 persons,* of whom about half are professionals working on assessments. In addition, *OTA hires contractors and consultants,* who bring specific expertise or talents to bear on particular studies. Also, advisory committees made up of experts and representatives of affected groups are appointed to assist with the study. "Technology assessment" is the thorough and balanced analysis of all significant primary, secondary, indirect, and delayed consequences or impacts, present and foreseen, of a technological innovation on society, the environment, or the economy.

b. OTA assessments typically take from six months to two years to complete. In response to specific requests, OTA can and has undertaken studies in which information is supplied to Congress on a shorter time frame. The length of an assessment depends on the issues being studied, the resources available to OTA, and the time frame in which the requesting committees need the information.

c. Its current priority areas of assessment include: *energy, food, genetics and population, health, materials, national security, oceans, R&D policies and priorities, technology and world trade, telecommunications and information systems,* and *transportation.*

d. *In studying the likely impacts of technological change, OTA assesses the social, environmental, economic, political,* and *physical changes that new or emerging technologies, or technological programs, may bring about.*

e. OTA also identifies policy options that Congress and the Executive Branch might select from in addressing these impacts. The benefits and risks of each option are analyzed.

f. The Technology Assessment Board (TAB), the governing body of OTA, is assisted by a Technology Assessment Advisory Council, comprised of 10 public members eminent in scientific, technological, or educational fields, plus the Comptroller General of the United States and the Director of the Congressional Research Service of the Library of Congress. The Advisory Council advises the Board on matters relating to science, technology, and technology assessment.

2. *Limitations*

OTA has limited financial and personnel resources. All technology assessment requests from committees must be approved by the Board.

3. *Procedures to Use in Requesting OTA Assistance*

a. Requests for OTA studies may originate with the chairman of any congressional committee, a member of the OTA Board, or the OTA Director. In the past, most studies were requested by a committee chairman or Board member. However, OTA has now established procedures for identifying and initiating studies of priority issues facing the United States. To become official studies, all requests must be approved by the Board.

b. OTA is governed by a congressional Board consisting of six Senators and six Representatives evenly divided by party. The chairmanship and vice chairmanship rotate between House and Senate in alternate Congresses. The members of each house select their officers. By precedent, the chairman is from the majority party and the vice chairman from the minority.

D. *Congressional Budget Office* (CBO)

1. *Capabilities*

The CBO assists the Congress in carrying out its responsibilities under the Congressional Budget and Impoundment Control Act (P.L. 93–344). This act strengthens congressional control over the budgetary process. The CBO provides budget-related information and analyses of alternative fiscal, budgetary, and programmatic policies. The office does not make recommendations on matters of policy; its principal missions are to present the Congress with options for consideration and to study the possible budgetary ramifications of those options.

CBO's specific responsibilities include: estimates of the five-year budgetary costs of proposed legislation; analyses of the inflationary impact of proposed legislation; tracking of Congressional budgetary actions against budget targets and limits established in the annual concurrent resolutions (scorekeeping); periodic forecasts of economic trends and analyses of alternative fiscal policies; studies of programmatic or policy issues that affect the federal budget; and an annual report on major budgetary options.

a. *Cost estimates.* The Budget Act requires CBO to provide cost estimates on proposed legislation. CBO prepares, to the extent practicable, a five-year estimate of what it would cost the federal government to carry out any public bill or resolution reported by congressional committees. These estimates include projections of new or increased tax expenditures and new budget authority when applicable. CBO shows a comparison of these cost estimates with any estimates available from congressional committees or federal agencies. As soon as practicable after the beginning of each fiscal year, CBO prepares a report that projects federal revenues and spending for the next five years if current policies were continued unchanged. The purpose of these projections is to provide a neutral baseline against which the Congress can consider potential changes as it examines the budget for the upcoming fiscal years.

b. *Inflation analysis.* CBO prepares estimates of the inflationary effect of major legislative proposals. The estimates are intended to provide the Congress with guidelines about the cost in terms of inflation that new programs might entail. More generally, the office is charged with identifying and analyzing the cause of inflation.

c. *Scorekeeping.* CBO keeps track, or score, of congressional action on individual appropriation and revenue bills against the targets or ceilings in the concurrent resolutions. The office issues periodic reports showing the status of congressional actions.

d. *Fiscal policy and the economy.* Since the federal budget both affects and is affected by the national economy, the Congress must consider the federal budget in the context of the current and projected state of the economy. To provide a framework for such consideration, CBO prepares periodic analyses and forecasts of economic trends. It also prepares analyses of alternative fiscal policies.

e. Program analysis and policy analysis. CBO undertakes analyses of programmatic issues that affect the federal budget. These reports include an examination of alternative approaches to current policy; all reports are nonpartisan in nature. Major studies have been completed in such diverse areas as agriculture, energy, housing, hospital and medical costs, defense, state and local government, employment programs, transportation, education, and budget procedures.

f. Annual report on budget options. By April 1 of each year, CBO furnishes to the House and Senate Committees on the Budget a report that combines many aspects of the functions outlined above. The annual report presents a discussion of alternative spending and revenue levels, levels of tax expenditure under existing law, and alternative allocations among major programs and functional categories.

2. *Limitations*

   CBO prepares its studies and cost estimates at the request of the chairman or ranking minority member of a full committee of jurisdiction or the chairman of a subcommittee of jurisdiction. The Budget Act establishes the following priority for these services: first, the Senate and House Budget Committees; second, the Senate and House Appropriations Committees and the House Ways and Means Committee and Senate Finance Committee; third, all other congressional committees; finally, any member of the House or Senate.

3. *Procedures for requesting CBO assistance*

   a. Chairmen or ranking minority members (as outlined in 2, above) requesting CBO assistance should contact the Director of the Congressional Budget Office, House Annex 2, Second and D Streets, S.W., Washington, D.C. 20515.

   b. Copies of CBO analyses are made available to all members of Congress upon publication. For additional copies or assistance concerning these studies, contact the Office of Intergovernmental Relations, (202) 225–4416.

ILLUSTRATION 3B A REPRESENTATIVE'S WORKDAY

A major development in the modern Congress is the increased busyness of the institutions and its members. The heavy workloads of members are best dramatized by these two illustrations. The table shows the portrait of an average day as revealed by a survey and statistical study of House members. The example of Congressman Lantos' day is a fairly typical day faced by most members.

A REPRESENTATIVE'S "AVERAGE DAY"

ACTIVITY		AVERAGE TIME
In the House chamber		2:53 hours
In committee/subcommittee work		1:24 hours
Hearings	26 minutes	
Business	9 minutes	
Markups	42 minutes	
Other	5 minutes	
In his/her office		3:19 hours
With constituents	17 minutes	
With organized groups	9 minutes	
With others	20 minutes	
With staff aides	53 minutes	
With other representatives	5 minutes	
Answering mail	46 minutes	
Preparing legislation, speeches	12 minutes	
Reading	11 minutes	
On telephone	26 minutes	
In other Washington locations		2:02 hours
With constituents at Capitol	9 minutes	
At events	33 minutes	
With leadership	3 minutes	
With other representatives	11 minutes	
With informal groups	8 minutes	
In party meetings	5 minutes	
Personal time	28 minutes	
Other	25 minutes	
Other		1:40 hours
Total average Representative's day		11:18 hours

SOURCE: From Samuel C. Patterson and Roger H. Davidson, *A More Perfect Union* (Homewood, Ill.: Dorsey Press, 1979, p. 453. Copyright © 1979, Dorsey. Reprinted with permission.

ACTUAL DAILY SCHEDULE OF CONGRESSMAN TOM LANTOS (D–CALIF.), TUESDAY, MARCH 24, 1981

8:30 AM	Demo. Rsrch. Org. (TL is on Exec. Brd.) re/tax & ec. measures; Rm. 210 CHOB.
9:00 AM	Eur. & ME Sub: re/NATO reps. on situation in Persian Gulf; Rm. 2200 RHOB
10:00 AM	Burton Wood, Mortgage Bankers Assn.
10–4	Communications Technology Fair, B-352 RHOB
10:15 AM	Rich Trachtman, Amer. Soc. of Internal Medic.
11:45 AM	Rich Altman, AIPAC (lunch)
12:00 PM	HOUSE IN PRO FORMA SESSION
1:30 PM	Fred Perkins, Machinists Union
2:00 PM	John Parkhurst, VP Pacific Telephone
2:00 PM	Asian Sub.; re/aid to Thailand; 2255
2:45 PM	Bernard Imming, Rbt. Kerney, United Fruit & Veg. Assn.
3:00 PM	Closed Briefing re/negotiations w/Egypt, US & Israel w/Michael Sterner, Dep. Asst. Sec. Bur. of Near East & S. Asia (per Lee Hamilton) Room H-236, the Capitol
3:00 PM	Natl. Assn. of Realtors (7 people) Fran Pres (Art Pollock says it's important to see them)
3–5 PM	Meeting w/physicians from France, USSR, US, England, Japan re/nuclear war; 116 Annex I
3:30 PM	Tracy Foster (S.M. Co.) Wash. Workshop-Coll. S.
4:00 PM	Lynn Keeys (intern, 2 minutes) re/For. Affrs.
4:00 PM	Tea/For. Affrs. Minister of Japan, His Excell. Masayoshi; 2172
5–7 PM	Amer. Dietetic Assn. Recep. Capitol Hill Club
5:30–7:30	Soc. of Amer. Florists Recep. 1202 Dirksen
6–8 PM	I'Natl. Assn. of Machinists & Aerospace Workers Recep./Sheraton Ballroom
6–8 PM	Natl. Assn. of Realtors Recep; I'Natl. Ballroom Washingtom Hilton
6–9 PM	Natl. Council of Sr. Cits. Recep.; Machinists Bldg., 1300 Connecticut Ave., NW
6:30 PM	Procter & Gamble Proprietary Assn. Recep/Dinner Capitol Hilton (take parking permit)
7:00 PM	CA Del. Dinner per/David Roberti & Willie Brown Jr., Mt. Vernon Rm., Madison Hotel

3.7 So You Want to Go to Congress: A Political Scientist Looks Back on the House*

Honorable Jim Lloyd, Former U.S. Representative (D–Calif.)

In the following essay written especially for this volume, Jim Lloyd gives some insights and impressions gleaned from six years of service in the U.S. House of Representatives.

There is an all-American myth harbored in the heart of every mother that her son or daughter may some day go to Congress. In the history of our nation, some 11,509 sons and 100 daughters have fulfilled this great hope. Some bright offspring have gone even further and proved they can become President of the United States. However, Congress is the subject of this book, so let's take a look at what it takes to become a part of this incredible American institution.

Obviously, the first thing that needs to be done to achieve in this arena is to be successful in running for congressional office. The variables that have propelled, shoved, provided an opportunity, or whatever might be the methodology of winning an election are the subject of another discussion. Suffice it to say, you have obtained more votes than your opponent and have been declared the official winner of the congressional seat in the ——— district of the great state of——— (you fill in the blanks).

Having won the election, you are now ready to make your triumphant entry into the mecca of democracy—namely, Washington, D.C.—and the hallowed halls of the House of Representatives. The first glimpse of the Capitol after you have been elected takes on a new euphoric meaning; the perspective you now have is entirely different from that which is projected in the average political science textbook. You arrive in Camelot . . . the Capitol dome shining in the bright blue sky and the whiteness of that awesome great building beckoning you as no powerful magnet ever attracted a metal object. As you walk up the steps of the Capitol and inform the doorman or policeman that you are the new Congressman/woman from whatever that district of that great state is, the magic occurs. Recognizing you immediately, the policeman or doorman is all too eager to help. You must remember, however, that he has a list indicating who all the new members of Congress are, and he will immediately check out who you are and from where as he welcomes you to the environs of this historical legislative body—so don't fake it! You will find that your wish is his command, because, in the final analysis, the business of the Capitol is indeed you, the representative. Everything turns on what you will do in the ensuing two years—longer if you are lucky enough, agile enough, quick enough, smart enough, and there are even those who say dumb enough, to be reelected.

The first thing you must do is establish yourself with the Clerk of the House, and probably more important, the Sergeant at Arms (which in reality is a complete misnomer because he is your banker). It is always good to remember that the Clerk of the House, the Sergeant at Arms, the Postmaster, the Doorkeeper, the Chaplain, and a lot of other folks who are there to do your bidding are functionaries of the party of the majority. Simply stated, if the House is Democratic, then all of these jobs will be filled with those who are Democrats; and if the House is Republican, the job holders will be, too. It

* Prepared especially for this volume.

makes no difference whether you are with the majority or the minority party insofar as your pay, selection of an office, acquisition of staff, or the normal operations of the day are concerned. It does make a difference, however, when it comes to getting on the committee of your choice, having access to your chairman, or scheduling legislation (remember those political promises). The majority party, indeed a majority of its members, governs; while it can be a benevolent ruler, the majority party, nonetheless, is in the driver's seat and very conscious of its position. Fortunately, the "ins" realize they can be the "outs" in the next term, and conduct themselves accordingly.

Having basked in the reflections of your newfound glory (even though there was no brass band waiting to meet you, the President of the United States did not instantly call you to the White House for consultation, and sadly enough not even the Speaker of the House or the Majority or Minority Leader immediately called you into session to seek your sage political advice), you are there, and you are one of 535 people in the nation's Capital who will vote on the critical (and not-so-critical) issues that will affect our nation for the next two years.

One of the most important facts that suddenly will dawn on you is that having won an election does not necessarily prepare you for putting together the administrative forces that will turn your election victory into substantial performance. Simply stated, now that you have won, you must get to work, and with very little fanfare at that. And you thought *campaigning* was stressful!

We shall now test your mettle in ability to do administratively, legislatively, and politically what you promised all those good folks back home you would do.

Let's take a look at your task of selecting a staff. Surely you were careful not to make any commitments to hire anyone if you won, because if you did, you have violated the law, and you wouldn't want to break those laws before you start making them, would you? In all probability you have at least "thought" about bringing some of the campaign staff along with you; if so, you are in good company. There probably isn't a Congressman who, upon arrival in Washington, hasn't had strong feelings about wanting his dedicated and loyal workers to continue right along with him.

But first things first. You can hire 18 full-time and 4 part-time workers. You must pay a minimum of $100 and no more than $52,000. Now comes the kicker—you are restricted to a total of $300,000. It won't take you very long to figure out that $52,000 goes into $300,000 less that six times. And since it seems easier to ask all those good friends who worked so hard to get you elected (and who worked for little or nothing) to continue their loyalty, it's difficult not to try to hire them. They, too, know how much you can pay. Will the new member of Congress from (that state and district again) show proper gratitude?

You will probably decide that you want a Washington/Capitol Hill pro to head up the staff. He or she will henceforward be known as "my AA" (administrative aide). This is a very "in" term; it shows you to be a real member of "The Hill." And as you already know, "The Hill" is Capitol Hill. (And yes, its altitude, low though it may be, does qualify it to be a hill!)

By this time you have hired legislative aides, clerks, et al. for Washington, and have selected a "field rep" (representative), caseworkers, secretaries, etc., in the home district.

Now you discover you don't yet have an office in either Washington or the district. If there is a federal office building in your district, you will automatically get an office there. If not, you've got to come up with one in a hurry, and that means locate it, contract for it, and equip it, but probably not before you are sworn in office in January. And by the way, from the moment you were elected in November, many of the folks assume you are already the Congressman/woman, and as such you are ready to handle casework, get flags, respond to their various requests, arrange White House tours, etc.

However, the person you defeated or otherwise succeeded is still in the seat until early January. You guessed it—this is a transition period where he holds all the cards. The smoothness and efficiency with which you take over depends on the rapport you can establish with the outgoing member. On my! Remember all those cute little zingers in the campaign? Fortunately, it is at least the Christmas and New Year's season with joyful tidings and goodwill to all (you hope)!

January swearing-in day arrives, and you say "I do." And if you had any doubts about it, you now find you really *do* work a 15-hour day every day.

By now you have acquired your new office in Washington through the perilous process of a drawing. If you are lucky, great! If not, it will be a miserable two years with regard to space, because obviously the least desirable offices are left for the new members. The rooms you draw may not even be together and possibly may be on different floors. Incidentally, if you split a full staff of 18 with half in the district and half in Washington, you will have at least 10 people (counting yourself and probably an intern) in an incredibly small (just over 1000-square-foot) Washington office. OSHA would not tolerate industry having the same space on a per-person basis.

Congress has convened and is sorting out what it wants to do for the coming two years. If the Senate is of one party and the House another (as in 1981–82), you will find some heavy pushing and shoving, both politically and legislatively—and you, dear new Congressman/woman, are caught in the middle. Also, just before all of this is underway, you will have been subjected already to some personal pushing and shoving as your own political party is "getting organized." *Getting organized* is a term meaning political mayhem wherein the decisions as to who is going to be boss take place.

Remember that $1,000 that showed up for the last mailer from good ol' (Congressman) Harry, who was sure you'd win and wanted to help? Well, good ol' Harry is a candidate for the Majority Leader race; he's now ready to collect some of his political IOUs (from you). And you were going to rise above such questionable political dealings. But this push and shove goes all the way to who serves on what committee and can greatly affect your future in the House for years to come. Your desire to be on Appropriations or Ways and Means may now go down the drain as you find senior members have first choice on these committees. You do remember that seniority system you were going to change, don't you? You, sir or madam, will have to wait your turn. You might jump the traces if you have the votes on the Committee on Committees, but review that decision carefully because, even if you win (few rarely do), you still have to negotiate your legislative and committee access with your leadership, which tends to tenaciously support the system that brought it to power. This is a very difficult position, if not impossible, and not easily handled. No, you will fall into line with the rest.

The month of January is now well underway. If it is a presidential election year, you will of course have invited some of your good supporters to attend inauguration festivities. Even if you are not a member of the President's party, still you will have had supporters who were willing to cross the party lines to help you. They expect (sometimes demand) that you deliver the appropriate tickets to the presidential balls, and of course you will take care of Mr. and Mrs. Smith, who expect to have good seats at the swearing-in. If the President is of your party, the requests are tenfold—and I would remind you, no matter how it works, you only get so many tickets. Remember that letter the new President, who was then a candidate, sent to all the constituents in your district saying that he could not go to Washington without you and urging them to vote for you? Now you find that the help he was talking about was more legislative than political. As such, you may have slipped his mind a bit during this crucial period while you are trying to get hotel reservations, tickets, and maybe even enough money to take everybody out to dinner.

You are in what can be referred to as the social phase, not only because of the inauguration, but also because of all of the other routine invitations that deluge your office for this organization's party or that group's soiree. All of them just can't have a successful event without your presence, even if there are 382 people in a room big enough for 200. At first you will try to do it all. But as time goes by, you will begin to be more selective, simply because you do not have adequate time to meet all the requests. The fact remains, however, that it is all very heady wine to be in social demand in Washington, D.C.

Social involvement notwithstanding, you are now shifting gears to get on with the legislative program. You do want to make a favorable impression on the media, your friends at home, and certainly the leadership with your legislative prowess, don't you? The committee chairmen begin the organization of the legislative committees. In all probability you will be on two committees, one major and one minor. You will find your major committee will have anywhere from 35 to 47 members, depending on the percentages agreed to by the leadership. You personally will be number 30 or above; if luck is really against you, you could be number 47 on your major committee. This means that during the questioning period (which allows each member five minutes) you will have to wait for your chance to ask those brilliant questions that will so impress the media and the folks at home. But don't be undaunted; you will have an opportunity to ask your questions and to participate at the subcommittee level. But it doesn't take long for you to realize that there is no possible way to meet the demands of both full committees, your subcommittees, and the action of the floor, all of which are going on simultaneously.

Another problem that will present itself is that the full committee staff and the subcommittee staff serve at the pleasure of the chairmen of those bodies. I need not remind you that you are not the chairman. Therefore the legislative direction will be somewhat dependent upon the chairman's desires, not yours. Don't despair, however, for you do have a say. First of all, your subcommittee chairman wants your goodwill and, more important, your vote, in order to accomplish the programs he wishes. The same is true of the chairman of the full committee; if it ever comes down to it, and it often does, your vote could be the decisive one. The chairman will also need your vote and support for the committee's bills as they go to the House floor. I would remind you, too, that, as a member of the committee, your right to speak on the floor takes precedence over the right of other members of other committees, including those who are in the leadership. In addition, at every level (subcommittee, committee, and committee of the whole) you have the right, and I might point out sometimes the obligation, to submit or support amendments to which your committee chairman does not necessarily agree. Through this process, for all of the frustrations, you will be able to exert a little bit of your will on the legislative action.

In order to make your legislative will more effective, it is imperative that you select those staff members who are legislative pros, who not only agree with you philosophically, but who can also help you project that philosophy effectively in your role as a member of Congress. These selections must be made giving full consideration to all of the variables that present themselves administratively, legislatively, and politically.

Another facet that is like a mantle over all of the areas of your congressional involvement is your political posture vis-à-vis the leadership, your staff, friends, etc. Your participation in this highly structured but not-so-visible arena is very important for you as a member of your party, with its goals and aspirations.

It is possible that, as a new member, you may be elected to the Steering and Policy Committee, or you could serve as a member of the Whip's organization. You might even be asked to serve on an ad hoc committee by your state or regional party organization in some specific area, such as the steel caucus, the women's caucus, the black caucus, or many other involvements. As with all decision-making processes, you must weigh these commitments against what you are already doing, comparing them to the goals that you either articulated in the campaign or have now defined for yourself. Time is of the essence, and you can't do everything.

I have saved what I consider the most difficult task of all for last—that is, your ethical involvement, both in your district and in Washington, D.C. In the light of the Watergate era, which initiated "investigative reporting," and the scandals that have beset Congress à la Elizabeth Ray, Fanny Fox, Rita Jenrette, and Paula Parkinson, not to mention Koreagate and Abscam, you and you alone will have to determine whether you possess the necessary moral fiber and personal integrity, based on all the religious, educational, and moral training you bring with you, to negotiate these political jungles. As you move further into your congressional career and correspondingly rise in importance and visibility, you can rest assured there will be somebody who is willing to misuse your position of power for his or her own gain. You must also remember that there are misguided members of the press, who will be unscrupulous enough, through innuendo and omission in the text of their stories, to taint your personal integrity. Along with this fact of life, a genuine antagonism exists in the political arena because some candidate in the other party can't wait to whisper out-and-out lies about you in order to weaken your political position and thereby eventually defeat you.

Perceived power, or better yet the image of power, brings forth those misguided and foolish people who will encourage you in acts of moral indiscretion. It's not because they wish to damage you personally (although there are those who have that clearly in mind—remember Abscam). It's because they wish only to be on the inner circle of power, with you as their vehicle. Remember, you have the ability to affect literally billions of the taxpayers' dollars, to say nothing of the direction and thrust of the United States for the next 5, 10, or 20 years.

Those "single issues" that were so important while you were running can clearly come back to haunt you, whether they be handguns, food stamps, abortion, or what-have-you. Such issues can greatly cloud an infinitely more important issue, whether it be national defense, foreign policy, or domestic policy. In the final analysis, while there is no question that you must answer to your constituency, you must answer to your own conscience. This, my new congressional friend, can be an awesome responsibility.

This paper has in no way presented all the problems of administering to the needs of your staff, constituents, and family. (We haven't even touched upon the aspects of congressional family life.) Nor has it addressed how to respond to the political realities commensurate with the desired legislative goals. But it is hoped that this paper has shed some light on what it is to be a Congressman in this day and age, with all the problems that beset "your" district, state, nation, and, finally, the world itself. You are, indeed, as a member of Congress, a very important person. Good luck and God bless you!

3.8 An Insider's Impressions of the U.S. Senate*

Honorable Fred Harris, Former U.S. Senator (D–Okla.)

In this essay, original to this collection, Fred Harris gives his perspectives on the U.S. Senate, comparing his service there with his experience in the Oklahoma State Senate.

I used to say that I came to the U.S. Senate (in 1964) with all the expertise in national and international affairs that eight years in the Oklahoma State Senate affords. I was not entirely joking. One thing I thought I did know from my previous experience, though, was how a legislative body functions. But the U.S. Senate was (and is) unlike the Oklahoma State Senate in a number of ways.

I already knew from an earlier visit to Washington that few members were ever on the floor of the U.S. Senate while it was in session, except when it came time to vote; Oklahoma's State Senators *were* on the floor during sessions. Debate counts for little in the national body; only once during my eight years there did it make a major difference on a measure—the final speech of Edmund Muskie (D–Maine) in favor of model cities legislation.

What I did not know at first was that, besides these facts, there were some others that also made the U.S. Senate different from the Oklahoma Senate. First, the U.S. Senate is not only a deliberative body but a deliberate one as well. Major issues that come to floor vote have generally been around awhile; most Senators already know how they are going to vote on them, without waiting for the debate. Second, the committees (and subcommittees) of the U.S. Senate are almost always allowed to meet during the Senate session—causing Senators to spend most afternoons hurrying back and forth between a meeting of their committee (and, often, more than one) and a roll call on the floor. Third, U.S. Senators lead harried lives, a typical day beginning with a breakfast with constituents and ending with a dinner with interest-group representatives. Sandwiched in between are interviews, committee meetings, votes, staff meetings, mail, phone calls, working lunches, and "walking" conferences. Senators feel that they cannot afford the time to sit and listen to floor debate.

The U.S. Senate was different from the Oklahoma Senate in other ways. Since committee assignments are relatively permanent in the national body, the norm of "specialization" is stronger in the U.S. Senate (although not as strong as in the U.S. House, where members have fewer assignments and less power to amend on the floor). Nevertheless, it is expected of both Oklahoma Senators and U.S. Senators that they will not "dance every set" (speak out on every issue); those who do are generally less influential than those who do not.

The number of staff members who assist U.S. Senators is lavish compared to the staff available to Oklahoma State Senators. A member of the British House of Commons once asked me, "Whatever do they all do?" I answered that they handled constituent casework and other matters, did research, typed, filed, and wrote speeches. "Write speeches?" he questioned, incredulously. "In the Commons, it is assumed that members can rise and make their own speeches." Some U.S. Senators do

* Prepared especially for this volume.

worry that having so many staff members insulates them somewhat from the real work, the issues, and the real world. But still, no Senator ever feels that he or she has enough staff. That is one of the several reasons Senators desire to become chairpersons of committees and subcommittees. (Added visibility, prestige, and ability to affect policy are among the other reasons.)

It is harder for U.S. Senators to stay in touch with their constituents than it is for Oklahoma State Senators. Of course, there is the problem of the great diversity in the numbers of people involved. Distances are not so great at the state level, either, and state legislators can go home every weekend. Also, state legislative sessions are usually much shorter. Then, it's home for the rest of the year. More than that, for a state senator, ''home'' really is home, where the senator actually lives. Not so for U.S. Senators. For them, ''home'' is where they are *from*. Washington or one of its suburbs is where they live. In this regard, Senators sometimes envy governors (and a number are former governors). Governors stay in their home states to do their jobs. Senators must leave their home states to do theirs. Senators, then, must work at staying in touch. And they must work, too, at *appearing* to stay in touch. Nothing is worse politically for a U.S. Senator than a growing feeling among the people of the home state that the Senator has ''gone Washington'' and has ''forgotten us.''

The importance of *appearing* to stay in touch with the home folks is illustrated by the home-state images of two U.S. Senators from Oklahoma—the late Robert S. Kerr, my predecessor, and A. S. Mike Monroney, with whom I served. Kerr, who was recognized at his death as the ''uncrowned king of the Senate,'' never spoke on a national issue without tying it into Oklahoma's interests. He took President Truman's side, for example, when the Missourian fired General Douglas MacArthur during the Korean War. But Kerr emphasized that a principal reason for his doing so was that the members of Oklahoma's 45th Division of the National Guard would have been put in greater jeopardy by MacArthur's policies, which might have brought the Chinese into the war. Also, when Kerr went back to Oklahoma, he made a special point with his appearances. For example, I remember a headline about his commencement speech at a little Oklahoma school that only had *seven* graduating seniors.

Monroney, on the other hand, did not always try to find an Oklahoma ''angle'' for his actions. He was a noted liberal leader on national and international matters. He authored legislation that created an international development bank. He co-authored major congressional reform. I am confident that Monroney spent *more* time in Oklahoma than Kerr did, but Monroney's home-state appearances did not especially call attention to the fact that he was still ''one of us.'' The result was, as one of Kerr's sons once told me, ''My dad could spend all of his time in Washington, and people would think he was in Oklahoma, while Mike could spend all his time in Oklahoma, and people would think he was in Washington.'' Staying in touch requires more than appearances, of ourse; but an image of *not* staying in touch was one factor that eventually defeated Monroney. It was a big problem for me, too, when I simultaneously served in the Senate and as Chairman of the Democratic National Committee (1969, 1970), even though during that time I purposely went home more often than before.

In both the Oklahoma State Senate and the U.S. Senate, a number of the norms are much alike. In both there is a weak norm of ''apprenticeship.'' (In earlier times in the U.S. Senate, first-year members were expected to be ''seen and not heard,'' and there was a lot of fanfare at the time of a Senator's first major speech on the floor.) Other norms are stronger in both bodies. A member's word must be good. The norm of ''courtesy''—being ''able to disagree without being disagreeable''—is also valued. So is ''institutional loyalty.'' Former U.S. Senator Joseph Clark (D–Pa.) found this out when he ran for, and lost, a Senate leadership post after having written *The Sapless Branch,* a book critical of the Congress and the U.S. Senate. The ''legislative work'' norm is important in both bodies. To have influence, members must be earnest about the body's work. It is still true, as in Lyndon Johnson's Senate time, that U.S. Senators are graded somewhat by their colleagues on the basis of whether they are "show horses" or "work horses." Those elevated to internal, legislative office are generally of the show-horse, inward-looking variety—one reason Chief Executives are better at affecting public opinion than are legislative leaders. Still, a number of the members of both the Oklahoma State Senate and the U.S. Senate at any one time entertain thoughts of running for higher office. They may seek notice outside the legislative body (and outside their constituency) for this reason. They may seek wider notice, too, because they feel, as the late Hubert H. Humphrey told me he did (and as I did): If a Senator is to be effective in the Senate, he or she must not only work earnestly in that body, but must also seek to influence public opinion generally and to bring it to bear on the Senate.

In neither the Oklahoma State Senate nor the U.S. Senate can a member know all there is to know about any one issue. When it comes time to vote, then, members often rely on "cues"—most of all cues from trusted fellow members. As U.S. Senators rush to the floor for a roll call, they often ask other Senators, "Whose amendment is this?" An answer such as "It's Miller's education amendment" may be about all a Senator needs to know in order to decide to vote for or against the amendment. On the floor, Senators may ask a seatmate, a Senator who usually votes the way they do, the manager of the bill, or some other member they respect or trust, "What are *you* going to do on this?" The answer can be influential.

Most of the time, U.S. Senators (as well as Oklahoma State Senators) are "delegates"—doing what they think a majority of their constituents want. This usually causes no strain, because most Senators probably agree on most matters with their constituents, at least the active ones. Sometimes, Senators act as "trustees"—knowingly taking a different view from their constituents, perhaps hoping to change public opinion. As one Oklahoma State Senator once jokingly put it to me (when he decided to reverse a long-standing position and vote to repeal prohibition, despite the trouble that his vote would cause him back home), "Every now and then, you have to rise above principle and do what's right." Hubert Humphrey told me that a Senator should be willing to compromise on nonfundamental matters, but should be willing to die politically on issues of basic importance (such as civil rights). But he said the trouble is that "you may like it here so much that you begin to decide which is which on that basis." Whether a Senator acts like a delegate or a trustee may depend upon how long it is until he or she must face reelection. The late Senator Richard Russell (D–Ga.) told me that he could watch a Senator walk down the hall and tell what period of the six-year senatorial term the Senator was in. Those with six years ahead of them walk along looking up and thinking lofty thoughts. Those in the middle of their terms walk along looking straight ahead. But those who are nearing reelection time, he said, walk along looking down, watching where they step. There is something to that.

Service in the U.S. Senate can be frustrating. It often seems impossible to move things very much at any one time. Former Senator Edmund Muskie (D–Maine) once told me that after a year of hard senatorial work, he often looked back and felt that, during the year, he had only been able to do something like "change Section 22(*d*) slightly." For many Senators, certain issues may be uncompromisable. (I felt this way about civil rights issues and, later on, about ending the Vietnam War.) That makes legislative work—where often the essence of the job is compromise—difficult, to say the least. But the U.S. Senate is a great platform. It is probably still the "world's greatest deliberative body," as Senators like to call it. For a time at least, it is a great place for those who want to serve the country—and speak to it.

CHAPTER

4 Structural Characteristics I: The Committee System

In this and the next two chapters, selections will be presented concerning the structural characteristics of Congress: committees, political party organizations, and legislative procedures. As is the case with any organization, structural aspects strongly affect the way business is done and the nature of decision outcomes. This is especially true with regard to Congress. Although elections, politics, bargaining, debate, and floor voting are intrinsically more glamorous and interesting than structural characteristics, an appreciation of organizational structure is vital for an understanding of Congress. One cannot overemphasize the importance of the organizational features of Congress in explaining congressional output. Quite simply, our argument is that the decentralization of the committee system, the nonhierarchical and undisciplined nature of the congressional party system, and the multiple decision points and stages of the legislative process make inevitable particularized and incremental policy that usually involves a compromise among contending interests.

Committees are the ''work horses'' of Congress. As political scientist Woodrow Wilson argued at the turn of the century, prior to his debut in politics, congressional government is committee government. Most of the important decisions of government are thrashed out in these ''little legislatures.''

Committees decide which of the many proposed bills will be seriously considered. It is in those panels that proposed legislation is studied and scrutinized. For bills under consideration, committees hold hearings and call various witnesses to give testimony. Before a bill goes to the floor of the House or Senate, its exact wording is hammered out in a ''markup'' session of the committee, and the committee issues a report on the legislation to its parent house.

Readings in this chapter address the different kinds of committees, committee jurisdictions, committee assignments and leadership selection, committee decision making, and an actual committee report.

It should be emphasized that the major trends in committee government over the past decade have been (1) the proliferation of subcommittees and, especially in the House, their growing autonomy, and (2) the curtailment of the autocratic powers of committee chairmen, making their accession to power less dependent on automatic seniority and more dependent upon party caucus approval. A major issue pertaining to congressional committees is their lack of representativeness. Some contend that, because of the committee appointment process, committees are less microcosms of their parent houses and more reelection vehicles for members with constituencies affected by a committee's jurisdiction.

ILLUSTRATION 4A FOUR DIFFERENT KINDS OF COMMITTEES

A variety of committees are used in congressional work. The following excerpt from a government publication details the four types of committees and their major purposes.

Congress in its committee rooms is Congress at work, wrote Woodrow Wilson. It is in the committees of Congress that bills undergo their closest scrutiny, that investigations—including oversight of the Executive Branch—are conducted, and that the differences in bills passed by each House are reconciled into one version acceptable to both.

Congress uses four different types of committees to perform these different functions: standing committees, select or special committees, joint committees, and conference committees.

Committees that continue from Congress to Congress are called *standing committees*. The subject jurisdictions of these permanent committees are set forth in the rules of each house, and virtually every introduced bill is referred to one or more of them according to the subjects involved. These are the committees that actually review proposed legislation and determine which bills shall be reported to each house.

In the 96th Congress, there are 22 standing committees in the House and 15 in the Senate. Most have several subcommittees with specific jurisdictions. Usually a standing committee sends a bill to one of its subcommittees for hearings, review, and recommendations. The bill is then reported to the full committee for consideration. Finally, if approved by the full committee, the bill is reported to the full House or Senate.

Standing committees are also responsible for overseeing the operations of the Executive Branch departments and agencies under their respective jurisdictions. They usually perform this function by studies which provide Congress with the facts necessary to determine whether the agencies are administering legislation as intended. Congressional studies also help committees identify areas in which legislative action might be needed and the form that action might take.

Other congressional studies are performed by *select* or *special committees*. Usually established for a limited period of time, these groups ordinarily deal with more specific subjects and issues than do the standing committees. For example, in recent years each house has established a select committee on aging to study the multitude of problems that affect senior citizens. Select committees in one house or the other have also studied population problems, narcotics, and Indian affairs. During the past decade, each house has used a select committee to study its own committee system and to recommend improvements. Most select committees may investigate, study, and make recommendations but may not report legislation. But both houses have created a few permanent select committees in recent years and authorized them to report legislation.

Congress uses *joint committees* for investigatory and housekeeping purposes. These are usually permanent bodies composed of an equal number of House and Senate members. Although in the past certain joint committees had the authority to consider and report legislation, no joint committee had that power in the 96th Congress. Usually joint committees are used to study broad and complex areas over a long period of time, an example being the Joint Economic Committee. Other joint committees, such as the Joint Committee on Printing, oversee functions connected with the operation of the Legislative Branch.

The last category of committee is the *confer-*

ILLUSTRATION 4A *(continued)*

ence committee. These are formed to reconcile the differences between the House and Senate when each passes a different version of the same bill. Conference committees are ad hoc joint committees, temporary panels appointed to deal with a single piece of legislation, dissolving upon the completion of that task. Members of both Houses serve on each conference committee, and the number of members from each house may be the same. This is not as inequitable as it might seem because the voting in conference committees is by house; its decisions must be approved by a majority of the Representatives and a majority of the Senators on the committee.

Every member of the House must serve on at least one standing committee except the Sepaker and Minority Leader, who, by tradition, serve on none. Senators *must* serve on at least two standing committees. Counting standing, select, and joint committee assignments, some Senators sit on as many as five or six. In the House approximately 90 Representatives have only one committee assignment, usually because they sit on a particularly busy panel, such as Appropriations. All other House members sit on two or three committees. In one way or another, both houses limit the number of chairmanships any single member may hold.

Committee sizes vary considerably and sometimes change from Congress to Congress. Because the House has more than four times as many members as the Senate, its committees are generally larger. In the 96th Congress, the largest House committee—Appropriations—had 54 members; the largest Senate committee—also Appropriations—had 28. Most Senate standing committees have from 14 to 20 members; most House committees have from 30 to 45. Traditionally, party ratios on committees correspond roughly to the party ratio in the full chamber.

Committee and subcommittee service encourages members to specialize in the subject areas of the panels on which they sit. Thus, the committee system continually builds up a reservoir of expertise to guide Congress as it attempts to deal with the nation's problems.

SOURCE: From *The Capitol: A Pictoral History of the Capitol and of the Congress*, 7th ed. (Washington, D.C.: U.S. Government Printing Office, 1979), pp. 136–39. Reprinted from the public domain.

ILLUSTRATION 4B JURISDICTION OF HOUSE AND SENATE STANDING COMMITTEES

The areas of responsibility for each of the standing committees is most complex and far-reaching. In the following abbreviated description of jurisdiction, it should be noted that Senate and House committees are not always coterminous. For example, although the House and Senate Armed Services Committees roughly have identical jurisdictional concerns, space exploration is handled in the House by Science and Technology and in the Senate by Commerce, Science, and Transportation, two very different committees with very different considerations and internal dynamics. It should also be emphasized that each house has a scheme for classifying its standing committees. For example, the Senate distinguishes between "major" and "minor" committees, the importance being that all Senators serve on at least one major committee. The House classifies its standing committees as exclusive, semiexclusive, and nonexclusive. Members on exclusive committees—Appropriations, Rules, and Ways and Means—may serve only on that committee.

HOUSE COMMITTEE	RESPONSIBILITY
Agriculture	Agriculture and forestry in general; farms credit and security, crop insurance, soil conservation, rural electrification, and rural development.
Appropriations	Appropriations of government revenues.
Armed Services	All matters related to the national military establishment; conservation, development, and use of naval petroleum and oil shale reserves; strategic and critical materials; scientific research and development in support of the armed services.
Banking, Finance, and Urban Affairs	Banks and banking, including deposit insurance and federal monetary policy; money and credit, including currency; gold and silver, including coinage; valuation and revaluation of the dollar; urban development; housing, generally economic stabilization; control of prices; international finance; financial aid to commerce and industry.

ILLUSTRATION 4B *(continued)*

HOUSE COMMITTEE	RESPONSIBILITY
Budget	Federal budget generally; Congressional Budget Office.
District of Columbia	All measures relating to municipal affairs of the District of Columbia except its appropriations.
Education and Labor	Education, labor, and welfare matters.
Foreign Affairs	Relations of the United States with other nations and international organizations and movements.
Government Operations	Budget and accounting measures; overall economy and efficiency of government, including federal procurement; reorganization in the Executive Branch; intergovernmental relations; general revenue sharing; National Archives.
House Administration	House administration generally; printing and correction of the *Congressional Record;* federal elections generally; management of the Library of Congress; supervision of the Smithsonian Institution.
Interior and Insular Affairs	Public lands, parks, natural resources, territorial possession of the United States, Indian affairs.
Interstate and Foreign Commerce	Regulation of interstate and foreign commerce and communications; regulation of interstate transmission of power (except between government projects); inland waterways; railroads, railroad labor; securities and exchanges; interstate oil compacts; natural gas; health matters generally (except health care supported by payroll deductions); consumer affairs and consumer protection; travel and tourism; biomedical research and development.
Judiciary	Courts and judicial proceedings generally; constitutional amendments; civil rights; civil liberities; interstate compacts; immigration and naturalization; apportionment of representatives; meetings of Congress and attendance of members; presidential succession; national penitentiaries; patents; copyrights; trademarks; protection of trade and commerce against unlawful restraints and monopolies.
Merchant Marine and Fisheries	Merchant marine generally; Coast Guard; oceanography and marine affairs; maintenance and operation of the Panama Canal and administration of the Canal Zone; fisheries and wildlife.
Post Office	Postal and federal civil services; census and the collection of statistics generally; Hatch Act; holidays and celebrations.
Public Works and Transportation	Public buildings and roads; flood control; improvement of rivers and harbors; water power; pollution of navigable waters; transportation (except railroads).
Rules	Rules and orders of business of the House.
Science and Technology	Scientific and astronautical research and development generally; National Aeronautics and Space Administration; National Aeronautics and Space Council; National Science Foundation; outer space; science scholarships; Bureau of Standards; National Weather Service; civil aviation research and development; environmental research and development; energy research and development (except nuclear research and development).
Small Business	Assistance to and protection of small business, including financial aid; participation of small business enterprises in federal procurement and government contracts.
Standards of Official Conduct	Studies and investigates standards of conduct of House members and employees and may recommend remedial action.
Veterans' Affairs	Veterans' measures generally; pensions; armed forces insurance; rehabilitation, education, medical care, and treatment of veterans; veterans' hospitals and housing.
Ways and Means	Revenue measures generally; tariffs and trade agreements; social security.

ILLUSTRATION 4B *(continued)*

SENATE COMMITTEE	RESPONSIBILITY
Agriculture, Nutrition and Forestry	Agriculture in general, including farm credit and security, crop insurance, soil conservation, and rural electrification; forestry in general; human nutrition; school nutrition programs; and matters relating to food, nutrition, and hunger.
Appropriations	Appropriations of government revenues.
Armed Services	Military affairs; Panama Canal and Canal Zone; strategic and critical materials; aeronautical and space activities peculiar to or primarily associated with development of weapons systems or military operations.
Banking, Housing, and Urban Affairs	Banking and currency generally; financial matters other than taxes and appropriations; public and private housing; economic controls; urban affairs.
Budget	Federal budget generally; Congressional Budget Office.
Commerce, Science, and Transportation	Interstate commerce in general; transportation; merchant marine and navigation; safety and transportation; Coast Guard; inland waterways except construction; communications; regulation of consumer products and services; standards and measurement; highway safety; science, engineering, and technology research, development, and policy; nonmilitary aeronautical and space sciences; marine fisheries; coastal zone management; oceans; weather and atmospheric activities.
Energy and Natural Resources	Energy policy generally; energy regulation and conservation; research and development; solar energy systems; naval petroleum; oil and gas; hydroelectric power; coal; mining; public parks and recreation areas.
Environment and Public Works	Environmental policy, research, and development; ocean dumping; fisheries and wildlife; outer Continental Shelf; solid-waste disposal and recycling; toxic substances and other pesticides; public works, bridges, and dams; water, air, and noise pollution; federal buildings and grounds.
Finance	Taxes, tariffs, foreign trade, import quotas, social security.
Foreign Relations	Relations of the United States with foreign nations generally; treaties; International Red Cross; diplomatic service; United Nations; foreign loans.
Governmental Offices	Budget and accounting measures; reorganization of the Executive Branch; general government and administrative problems; intergovernmental relationship between the federal government and the states and municipalities, and between the United States and international organizations of which the United States is a member.
Judiciary	Federal courts and judges; penitentiaries; civil rights; civil liberties; constitutional amendments; monopolies and unlawful restraints of trade; interstate compacts; immigration and naturalization; apportionment of representatives; meetings of Congress and attendance of members; claims against the United States.
Labor and Human Resources	Education; labor; health and public welfare generally.
Rules and Administration	Senate administration generally; contested elections; presidential succession; management of the Library of Congress and the Smithsonian Institution.
Veterans' Affairs	Veterans' measures generally; pensions; armed forces life insurance; rehabilitation, education, medical treatment of veterans; veterans' hospitals.

SOURCE: Summarized from Rules of the House and Rules of the Senate. Reprinted from the public domain.

4.1 The Selection of Committee Members and Leaders*

Charles S. Bullock, III

In the following article, written expressly for this work, Charles Bullock, a noted authority on the assignment of members to committees, gives an overview of the selection of both committee members and leaders. This piece emphasizes the distinctive machinery used by each congressional party organization (House Democrats and Republicans; Senate Democrats and Republicans) for selecting members for committee service and leadership. The work also emphasizes the declining importance of seniority in committee leadership selection.

The most important event of most freshman legislators' first term occurs before they have been sworn in as members. Success in the committee assignment process, which is completed a month before a new Congress convenes, may determine the substantive orientation of a legislator's career, the legislator's job satisfaction, and conceivably even the newcomer's electoral success. Nonfreshmen can seek to improve their assignments when committee rosters are filled out before each Congress.

Each party in each chamber determines which of its members will serve on the 22 standing committees in the House and the 16 in the Senate. The first step in the assignment process is to determine the distribution of committee seats between parties. This is done through negotiations between party leaders. On most committees the distribution of Democrats to Republicans approximates the partisan composition of the chamber. Thus, during the 94th and 95th Congresses, when House Democrats outnumbered Republicans by two to one, Democrats held just over two thirds of the seats on each committee. In the 97th Congress, in which Democrats constitute 56 percent of the House, their share of the seats on 16 committees is between 55 and 60 percent. The primary exceptions to the norm of proportionate representation are the House's most powerful and prestigious committees, on which the majority party traditionally has held an extraordinary majority regardless of the partisan division in the House,[1] and the ethics committee, on which the parties have equal representation. Little variation exists in Senate committee party ratios, with all committees in the 97th Senate having a one- or two-vote Republican majority.

ASSIGNMENT MACHINERY

House Democrats have given their Steering and Policy Committee responsibility for making committee assignments.[2] The makeup of the Steering Committee insures that all major groups can participate in filling committee vacancies. The committee is chaired by the party's leader (the Speaker when Democrats control the House, the Minority Leader if they are the minority party). Also on the committee are the Majority Leader (unless Democrats are in the minority), the chief party whip and the chair of the Democratic Caucus. Speaker Tip O'Neill (D–Mass.) has also included a Representative from the Black Caucus, the Women's Caucus, the freshman class, and several deputy Whips. In 1980, the chair of Rules and the chairs of the

---

* Prepared especially for this volume. The author wishes to express his appreciation of the helpful comments of James Campbell and Loch Johnson on an earlier draft of this paper.

three committees having the greatest impact on the budget were added to the Steering Committee. States having a Democratic representative are divided into 12 regions, and each region selects a Representative to the Steering Committee. After the 1980 election, the Steering Committee was enlarged from 24 to 30 members, with several of the new seats going to conservative southerners who hold the balance of power between liberal northern Democrats and Republicans.

Committee assignments for *House Republicans* are handled by a separate Committee on Committees, which consists of one person from each state having a Republican in the House. The real decision making is done, however, by a subgroup known as the Executive Committee. The Representatives of the states with the largest Republican delegations serve on the Executive Committee. The party leader, who chairs the committee, also appoints a Representative for the freshman and sophomore classes as well as one person to represent the delegations of sets of states with fewer Republicans—i.e., states with one, two, and three Republicans in the House.

Senate Democrats use the Steering Committee, chaired by the party leader, to make assignments. *Republican Senators* receive their assignments from their Committee on Committees.

PROCEDURES

The seniority norm assures that incumbents can retain their previous assignments. While there are always some members who wish to transfer from one committee to another or to add an assignment to what they already hold, the bulk of the work of those responsible for making assignments involves placing freshmen in committee vacancies.

Freshmen are invited to submit their rank-ordered preferences. House Democrats have classified committees as major and nonmajor; they ask newcomers for their preferences in each group. Some freshmen submit a single request, a few voice none, and occasionally someone will rank as many as 10 preferences. The most common practice, however, it to rank one's top three preferences.

Applicants for appointments to popular committees may follow up their written requests with personal appeals to party leaders, members of the Committee on Committees, and the chair of the committee they seek. The dean of their delegation may endorse their request in a letter to the Committee on Committee members.

Candidates for each committee's vacancies are voted on separately. House Republicans conduct this process using a unique weighted voting procedure. Members on the Executive Committee have as many votes as there are Republicans in their state party delegation or the delegations they represent. Thus, in the 97th Congress, the vote of New York's Frank Horton was worth 17, that of Michigan's William Broomfield was worth 6, and William Dickinson of Alabama, who represented five states with three Republicans each, had 15 votes. On the other committees responsible for making committee assignments, each member casts a single vote.

Applicants for seats on many committees outnumber the available slots; for a few committees, volunteers are rare. A generation ago senior members cornered the desirable positions, while the newly elected were often relegated to the committees that no one wanted. Now there is greater equity in the distribution of seats. No member gets seats on two highly desirable committees until every member of the party has at least one good assignment.

When matching applicants with vacancies, a number of factors are considered. Foremost are the preferences expressed by committee applicants. Most House freshmen are now appointed to one of the committees they have requested (Bullock, 1973; Shepsle, 1978).* This has been made easier by a gradual enlargement of the more desirable committees. Those who are disappointed and do not receive their first choice initially are frequently allowed to transfer to a more desirable committee within a few years (Shepsle, 1978). In addition to considering member preferences, those responsible for

* Reference list in Endnotes.

making assignments also attempt to (1) promote regional representation on most committees, (2) match up applicants' occupational backgrounds with vacancies, (3) accord an advantage to seniority when filling slots on the most prestigious committees, (4) see that women and blacks are distributed across a wide range of committees, and (5) allow state party delegations to maintain seats on committees whose responsibilities are of great concern to the state (Bullock, 1979).

The committee rosters developed by a party's Committee on Committees are presented to the full membership of the party.[3] Occasionally, a disgruntled member will mount a successful challenge and get the party to award him the slot he wanted and overturn the Committee on Committees.

House members are generally limited to two standing committee assignments, of which one can be a major committee. Members of Appropriations, Rules, and Ways and Means usually have a single assignment. Those who are tapped to serve on the Standards of Official Conduct (Ethics) Committee or to take a rotating seat on the Budget Committee hold these seats in addition to their other assignments. In recent years Democrats have had to temporarily relax the two-assigment rule in order to find takers for seats on Judiciary. Senators are limited to three committees and eight subcommittees.

COMMITTEE LEADERSHIP

The seniority norm, which protects the right of members to retain committee seats, is also the single most important determinant for leadership selection. Beginning with the Wilson Presidency and continuing until the mid-1970s, the member of the majority party who had the longest continuous tenure on a committee chaired it. The only exception was that no one could chair more than one committee. Therefore, if an individual was the most senior member of more than one committee, the second most senior member chaired the committee not preferred by the most senior member.

The selection of committee chairs has become less automatic. House and Senate Democrats now provide that each person nominated by the Steering Committee to chair a committee or serve as ranking minority member be approved by secret ballot. Except in 1974, when the chairmen of Armed Services, Banking, and Agriculture were defeated, the seniority norm has continued to guide the selection of House chairs. Senate Democrats and Republicans in both houses have never rejected the person in line, based on seniority, to chair a committee or serve as its ranking minority member. Nonetheless, the defeats of the three House chairs in 1974 has resulted in greater responsiveness to party leaders and to rank-and-file committee members by other chairs.

Seniority has also played a large role in the choice of subcommittee chairs, at least since World War II (Wolanin, 1974). Subcommittee leaders used to be named by the chair of the full committee. But beginning in the 1970s, House Democrats authorized committee members to elect the chairs of their subcommittees.[4] While House subcommittee chairs are now elected, a constraint limits individual Democrats to chairing one subcommittee. Since there are approximately 140 subcommittees, more than half the members of the majority party chair a committee or subcommittee. Because of this limitation, it is often necessary to go far down a committee's seniority roster to find a subcommittee chair.

Reliance on seniority has been rejected several times in recent years. In 1979, three aspirants for subcommittee chairmanships were defeated by more liberal, less senior opponents. Two years earlier, the Caucus stripped Bob Sikes (D–Fla.) of his long-held chairmanship of the Appropriations Military Construction Subcommittee following his reprimand for conflict of interest. In 1981 a subcommittee chair was replaced when his colleagues became critical of his performance.

In the House, seniority, although not inviolable, plays a major role in the choice of committee and subcommittee leaders. It is even more important in the Senate, where no chair has been rejected by the rank and file and where an individual can chair a full committee and up to two subcommittees.

Illustration 4c Assignment of Members to Committee and Procedures for Electing Committee Chairman: The Applicability of Party Rules

As Charles Bullock emphasized, party rules govern the assignment of members to committees and the selection of committee leaders. The following excerpts from House Democratic and Republican rules detail the mechanics.

HOUSE DEMOCRATS

M I. Standing Committee Memberships

A. *Committee Ratios.* Committee ratios should be established to create firm working majorities on each committee. In determining the ratio on the respective standing committees, the Speaker should provide for a *minimum* of three Democrats for each two Republicans.

B. *Seniority.* The Committee on Committees shall recommend to the Caucus nominees for chairman and membership of each committee other than the Committee on Rules for which the Democratic nominee for Speaker or Speaker as the case may be shall have exclusive nominating authority. Recommendations for committee posts need not necessarily follow seniority.

C. *Nominations for Committee Membership.* Upon a letter from a Member, signed by 50 percent or more of said Member's State Democratic Delegation, including said Member, said Member shall automatically be considered for nomination by the Committee on Committees for the committee membership position to which said Member aspires. The Chairman of the Committee on Committees shall see that such Member's name is placed in nomination. The provisions of this paragraph shall not apply with respect to nominations for the Committee on Rules.

D. *Procedures for Electing Committee Chairmen and Members.* The Democratic nominee for Speaker or Speaker as the case may be shall recommend to the Caucus nominees for chairman and membership of the Committee on Rules. Debate and balloting on any such nomination shall be subject to the same provisions as apply to the nominations of chairmen or Members of other committees. If a majority of those present and voting reject any nominee for chairman or membership of the Committee on Rules, the Democratic nominee for Speaker or Speaker as the case may be shall be entitled to submit new nominations until any such positions are filled. Chairmen: The Committee on Committees shall nominate one Member of each standing committee, other than the Committee on Rules and the Budget Committee, for the position of chairman and such nominations need not necessarily follow seniority. If the Member nominated by the Committee on Committees is other than the immediately preceding chairman, or the ranking majority member, additional nominations shall be in order from the floor of the Caucus and election shall be in accord with the provisions of Caucus rule R 7. If a nominee was chairman of the committee in question at the close of the preceding Congress, no other nominations shall be allowed and the Caucus shall vote by secret ballot to approve or disapprove that nominee alone. No debate shall be allowed unless requested by the nominee or a Member who wishes to speak in opposition to a nomination provided that the request to speak in opposition is supported by three or more Members. Debate on any nomination shall be limited to 30 minutes equally divided between proponents and opponents of that nominee, such time to be further extended only by majority vote of the Caucus. If a majority of those present and voting reject its nominee for chairman, the Committee on Committees shall make a new nomination within 5 days. Five to ten days after the Committee on Committees reports such new nominations, the Caucus shall meet to consider the new nominee of the Committee on Committees and any additional nominations offered from the floor. Only Members who have been recommended for membership on the committee shall be eligible for nomination as chairman. Should additional nominations be made from the floor, the election shall be conducted in accord with Caucus rule R 7.

The Committee on Committees shall make recommendations to the Caucus regarding the assignment of Members to each committee other than the Committee on Rules, one committee at a time. Upon a demand supported by 10 or more Members, a separate vote shall be had on any member of the committee. If any such motion prevails, the committee list of that particular committee shall be considered recommitted to the Committee on Committees for the sole purpose of implementing the direction of the Caucus. Also such demand, if made and properly supported, shall be debated for no more than 30 minutes with the time equally divided between proponents and opponents. If the Caucus and the Committee on Committees be in disagreement after completion of the procedure herein provided, the Caucus may make final and complete disposition of the matter.

In making nominations for committee assignments, the Committee on Committees shall not discriminate on the basis of prior occupation or profession in making such nominations.

E. *Rules for Making Committee Assignments.* For the purposes of this section the following committee designations shall apply:

(1) Appropriations; Ways and Means; and Rules Committee shall be "exclusive" committees.

(2) Agriculture; Armed Services; Banking, Finance and Urban Affairs; Education and Labor; Foreign Affairs; Energy and Commerce; the Judiciary; and Public Works and Transportation shall be considered "major" committees.

(3) Budget; District of Columbia; Government Operations; House Administration; Interior and Insular Affairs; Merchant Marine and Fisheries; Post Office and Civil Service; Science and Technology; Small Business; and Veterans' Affairs shall be considered "nonmajor" committees.

(a) No Democratic Member of an exclusive committee shall also serve on another exclusive, major, or nonmajor committee.

(b) Each Democratic Member shall be entitled to serve on one but only one exclusive or one major committee.

(c) No Democratic Member shall serve on more than one major and one nonmajor committee or two nonmajor committees.

(d) No chairman of an exclusive or major committee may serve on another exclusive, major or nonmajor committee.

M XI. Election Procedure for Ways and Means and the Appropriations Committee Vacancies

The Democratic Caucus shall elect Democratic Members to fill vacancies on the Ways and Means Committee and the Appropriations Committee in accord with the following procedure:

(1) *Nominations.* The Democratic Committee on Committees shall nominate one Member for each Democratic vacancy to be filled on the Ways and Means Committee and the Appropriations Committee and shall distribute the name(s) of such nominee(s) to all Members of the Democratic Caucus at least 4 days prior to the election meeting. Members shall then have 2 days to nominate additional candidates by written notice signed by 5 Democratic Members other than the nominee. Written nominations must be delivered to the offices of the Caucus Chairman and the Caucus Secretary not later than noon at the second day immediately preceding the election meeting, and the Caucus Chairman or Secretary shall mail a list of all nominees to Members of the Caucus that same day.

(2) *Election Procedure.* Election shall be by ballot which lists all candidates in the order they were nominated, and a majority shall be required to elect; *Provided, however,* That any ballot which contains votes for more or fewer candidates than there are vacancies to be filled shall not be counted.

(3) *Previous Members.* The nomination of any Member who served on the committee in the preceding Congress shall be reported by the Committee on Committees for action by the Caucus in the same manner as is provided for nomination of Members to other standing committees.

HOUSE REPUBLICANS

COMMITTEE ON COMMITTEES:

RESOLVED, That there is hereby created a House Republican Committee on Committees to be composed of members selected by the Republican delegations from the several states.

RESOLVED FURTHER, That the voting strength of each member shall be equal to the number of Republican members of the House of Representatives elected to the 97th Congress from his state.

RESOLVED FURTHER, That the duties of the House Republican Committee on Committees shall be to:

1. Recommend the Republican members of the standing committees of the House of Representatives.
2. Recommend the Republican members who shall serve as ranking minority members of said standing committees.
3. Recommend directly to the House of Representatives the Republican members to fill vacancies on standing committees which occur following the initial organization of the 97th Congress.

RESOLVED FURTHER, That the member recommended by the House Republican Committee on Committees for ranking minority member need not be the member with the longest consecutive service on that committee.

RESOLVED FURTHER, That nomination for such positions shall be out of order except as contained in the report of the committee.

RESOLVED FURTHER, That the Conference shall vote by secret ballot on each recommendation of the House Republican Committee on Committees for the position of ranking minority member. The call of the Conference at which such balloting will take place shall name and list the individuals recommended by the Committee.

RESOLVED FURTHER, That if the Republican Conference fails to approve a recommendation of the House Republican Committee on Committees the matter shall be automatically recommitted without instructions to that committee.

RESOLVED FURTHER, That the House Republican Leader shall serve as *ex officio* chairman of the Committee on Committees; and

RESOLVED FURTHER, That three members elected by the 97th Club should be included in the structure of the Committee on Committees.

RESOLVED FURTHER, That the voting strength of each member of the Executive Committee of the Committee on Committees shall be equal to the total number of Republican members that member represents on the Executive Committee, excluding the class representative who shall continue to have one vote.

RESOLVED FURTHER, That members of the Executive Committee on the Committee on Committees who are chosen to represent individual multistate groups shall be chosen by a caucus of each individual multistate group.

SOURCE: From *Preamble and Rules Adopted by the Democratic Caucus, 1981;* and *Highlights of the Rules of the Conference, 97th Congress.* Reprinted from the public domain.

4.2 The Anatomy of a Committee*

Holbert N. Carroll

Each congressional committee, like its parent house, is a little society. In this selection, Carroll stresses this point and illustrates the division of labor and specialization that exist within congressional committees.

FORMAL AND EFFICIENT PARTS

Writers of books on American government generally appreciate the role of committees in the legislative process. The half dozen or so committee decisions required, the resulting decentralization and, in many instances, disintegration of leadership and power, the curious but often tragic consequences of the seniority system, the powerful influence of the committee chairmen, government by a multitude of little governments as Wilson so interestingly described it in 1885—all of these features have been properly stressed.

The tendency in following this textbook analysis, however, is to look upon committees primarily as institutions, as monolithic bodies of 30 or so men, bodies roughly equal in power and respect in the eyes of the House and men equally attentive to their duties. A committee, to use a distinction made famous by Bagehot in another situation, has its dignified, ornamental, or formal parts and its efficient parts.[1] An appreciation of this distinction, as well as certain other features of congressional committees, is essential for an understanding of the role of these little legislatures in foreign affairs.

The formal part of a committee consists of the chairman and the party majority, a part of the committee which usually sticks together on procedural matters. In short, the formal part of a committee consists of those who in theory supply the initiative and leadership. They may formally approve legislation in the committee and support it with their votes on the floor, but they do little of the real work. On occasion, though, the formal part of a committee may be the efficient part.

The efficient part of a committee consists of a core of members, usually only a handful of men representing both political parties. These men actively participate in the hearings, propose the amendments that are accepted, and shape the legislation. They write parts of the committee's report, or at least take the time to slant it to their satisfaction. The efficient element then takes the bill to the floor and fights for it. Their knowledge of the subjects within the committee's jurisdiction may be more specialized than that of the witnesses from the Executive Branch who appear before them. Department and agency heads and their top assistants are viewed as mere transitory figures by Representatives whose service extends over more than one Administration. More than one witness has been confounded by questions and observations drawn from the vast reservoir of knowledge gained by individual Congressmen over decades.

The efficient element of a committee is rarely composed of a majority of the members even though it must carry a majority with it. Probably less than 10 members of the 32-member Committee on Foreign Affairs, for example, persistently and actively participate in the deliberations of the group. Indeed, in some instances the efficient element may be just one person. This monologic situation is not unknown in

---

* From Holbert N. Carroll, *The House of Representatives and Foreign Affairs,* rev. ed. (Boston: Little, Brown, 1966), pp. 27–28, 36–37. Copyright © by the author and the University of Pittsburgh Press. Reprinted by permission.

subcommittees of the Appropriations Committee, where occasionally just one member has been present to take important testimony to overwhelm his less attentive colleagues.

The efficient part of a committee, moreover, may change from one piece of legislation to another as the interests of the members wax and wane. Each piece of legislation is in a class by itself. The efficient part of a committee, in sum, is the part which wields influence and power. The fruit of its efforts is embodied in statutes and not merely in bills. The men who compose it are the leaders who determine whether the House will play a responsible role in foreign affairs in its committee rooms, on the floor, and in conference committees.

SUMMARY

Ordinarily, a committee is regarded as an institution, as a corporate body with a unitary voice or, at most, majority and minority voices. A committee is in a sense an institution. The continuity provided by senior members who pass the biennial political tests, staff people who survive periodic turnovers of personnel, committee tradition, history, and prerogative—all these serve to bind human beings into a collective body. But beneath the surface, a committee is but a few men who make decisions, men who are blessed with no unique capacities beyond those given to other mortals, who deliberate in a very human but intensely political environment, and who, like other men, are sometimes lazy and indifferent, overwhelmed with other business, or devoted to duty.

These committees work in jealous isolation from one another and complete for the foreign policy business of the House. Commonly, the scheme of the separation of powers maintained by checks and balances is discussed in terms of the judiciary, the President, and the Senate and the House. But the House of Representatives is afraid of its own power. A scheme of checks and balances has evolved throughout the House, and especially at the committee level. This scheme is not embodied in a clear theory but is nevertheless part of the fabric of the lower chamber. It aims at preventing the massive accumulation of power and decision anywhere in the House. Facets of the scheme include the weak position of party leaders in dealing with committees, the allotment of business among several committees, many of which work simultaneously and at cross-purposes in the same general area of foreign affairs, and the inheritance of committee leadership according to seniority.

Many other facets mark the scheme. Its ramifications penetrate to the Executive Branch. It is not uncommon for a congressional committee to develop intimate relations with leading pressure groups and with the agencies of the Executive Branch in which it has a special interest. The attachment may be sufficiently powerful to defy the best efforts of the President to coordinate and control the Executive Branch. The Committee on Foreign Affairs, for instance, enjoys a clientele relationship with the Department of State, but the foreign policy viewpoint they support may vary quite sharply from that emerging from another committee in deliberations with its clientele. The combination in foreign affairs may be quite weak in bucking the combination of the Department of Agriculture, farm groups, and the Committee on Agriculture or the combination of the shipping interests, the Maritime Administration, and the Committee on Merchant Marine and Fisheries.

4.3 Committee Decision-Making Processes*

Richard F. Fenno, Jr.

Each congressional committee is a unique organism. This has been emphasized by Richard Fenno in *Congressmen in Committees.* The following excerpts from that book capsulize Fenno's listing of variables that affect committee decision making and present his argument that different configurations of these variables lend to very different committee decision processes.

Generalizations about congressional committees are numerous and familiar. The oldest and most familiar is Woodrow Wilson's book-length assertion that committees dominate congressional decision making. A corollary states that committees are autonomous units, which operate quite independently of such external influences as legislative party leaders, chamber majorities, and the President of the United States. Other staples of committee commentary hold: that members specialize in their committee's subject matter, and hence that each committee is the repository of legislative expertise within its jurisdiction; that committee decisions are usually accepted and ratified by the other members of the chamber; that committee chairmen can (and usually do) wield a great deal of influence over their committees. A broader generalization holds that Congress, and by extension its committees, is gradually losing policymaking influence to the Executive Branch.

Most of our empirical generalizations are of the same order. Each one is uttered as if it were equally applicable to all committees. And taken together, they convey the message that committees are similar. Our recent studies of individual committees have taught us, to the contrary, however, that committees are markedly different from one another. Indeed, as we shall show, committees differ in all the respects previously mentioned—their influence in congressional decision making, their autonomy, their success on the chamber floor, their expertise, the control exercised by their chairmen, and their domination by the Executive Branch. If such is—even partially—the case, the need for a new set of generalizations is obvious. One immediate temptation, of course, is to scrap all our familiar generalizations in favor of a single statement asserting the uniqueness of each committee. But that is a counsel of despair; political scientists ought not to eschew the possibility of making limited comparisons before they have tried. This book should be read as one such effort—to describe and generalize about committee similarities and differences at a level somewhere between that which assumes committee uniformity and that which assumes committee uniqueness.

The need for a middle range of generalizations is not purely academic. Reform-minded members of Congress and citizen groups have also viewed committee operations from the perspectives of uniformity and/or uniqueness, and they have been as ill served by this outlook as the scholar. Every Congressman knows that committees are dissimilar. Assertions to that effect are hard currency on Capitol Hill.

---

* From Richard F. Fenno, Jr., *Congressmen in Committees* (Boston: Little, Brown, 1973), pp. xiii–xv, 1, 2, 15, 46, 47, 81.

"Committee behavior all depends on the chairman and every chairman, of course, is different." Or, "Committee behavior all depends on the subject matter, and every committee, of course, handles a different policy area." Why, then, when they prescribe committee reform, do Congressmen abandon their own wisdom and insist on applying every reform in equal dosages to every committee? The answer may be partly intellectual in nature—that they cannot conceive of committee similarities and differences in such a way as to formulate a mixed strategy of reform. It is as if the practitioner were waiting for the student to equip him with a middle range of categories in which to think and make his prescriptions. Thus, the political scientist's search for explanation may be related to the reformer's search for change.

Our theme is, then, that committees differ from one another. And, we shall argue, they differ systematically. We shall examine their similarities and differences with respect to five variables—*member goals, environmental constraints, strategic premises, decision-making processes,* and *decisions.* We shall pursue the following line of argument. The members of each congressional committee have certain goals that they want to achieve through membership on a committee. If there is a high level of consensus on goals, they will organize their committee internally in ways that seem likely to aid them in achieving these individual goals. However, each committee operates within a distinctive set of environmental constraints—most particularly the expectations of influential external groups. Committee members will, therefore, also organize their committee internally in ways that seem likely to satisfy the expectations of these groups that make up their environment. The members of each committee will develop strategies for accommodating the achievement of their individual goals to the satisfaction of key environmental expectations. These strategies become the proximate premises on which each committee's internal decision-making processes are based. From these strategies, operationalized as decision rules, flow committee decisions. In our explanatory scheme, then, member goals and environmental constraints are the independent variables, strategic premises (or, decision rules) are an intervening variable; and decision-making processes and decisions are dependent variables.

FIGURE 4.3.1 ANALYTIC SCHEME FOR COMPARING COMMITTEES

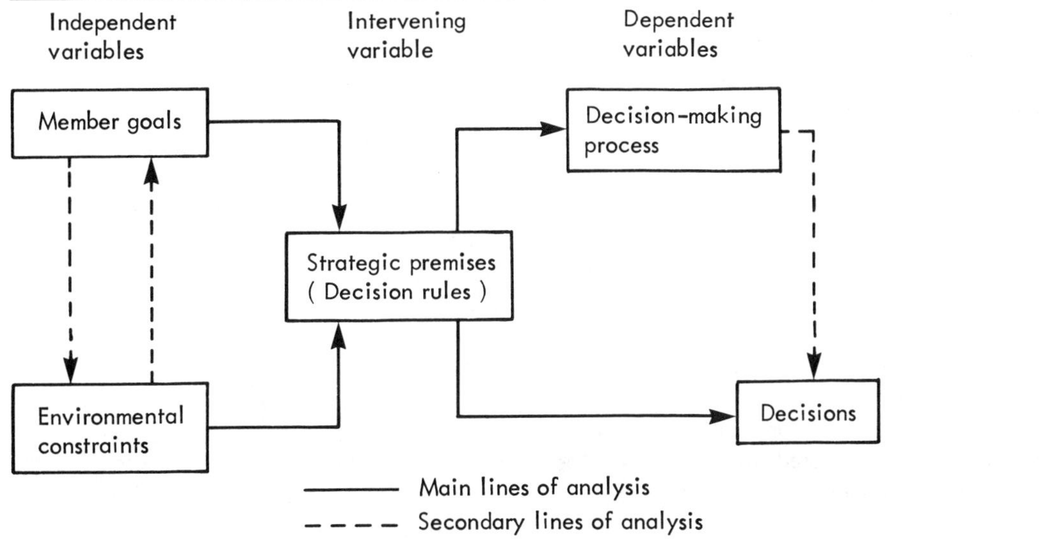

MEMBER GOALS

A member of the House is a Congressman first and a committee member second. As a Congressman he holds certain personal political goals. As a committee member he will work to further these same goals through committee activity. Committee membership, in other words, is not an end in itself for the individuals. Each member of each committee wants his committee service to bring him some benefit in terms of goals he holds as an individual Congressman. And he will act on his committee in ways calculated to achieve such goals. We think it useful to begin our comparative analysis of committees here, by asking each member of each committee what it is he wants committee activity to do for him as a Congressman.

Of all the goals espoused by members of the House, three are basic. They are: *reelection, influence within the House,* and *good public policy*. There are others. A fourth one, *a career beyond the House,* will be treated peripherally. (A fifth one, *private gain,* will not be treated at all.) The first three are the most widely held and the most consequential for committee activity. All Congressmen probably hold all three goals. But each Congressman has his own mix of priorities and intensities—a mix which may, of course, change over time. If every House committee provided an equal opportunity to pursue reelection, influence, and policy, Congressmen holding various mixes would appear randomly distributed across all committees. Such is definitely not the case. The opportunity to achieve the three goals varies widely among committees. House members, therefore, match their individual patterns of aspiration to the diverse patterns of opportunity presented by House committees. The matching process usually takes place as a Congressman seeks an original assignment or a transfer to a committee he believes well suited to his goals. But it may occur when a Congressman adjusts his personal aspirations, temporarily or permanently, to fit the opportunities offered by the committee where he happens to be. By a combination of processes, then, House committees come to be characterized, at any point in time, by distinctive, nonrandom distributions of individual member goals.

ENVIRONMENTAL CONSTRAINTS

Every House committee inhabits an environment in which committee nonmembers seek to persuade committee members to act in ways the nonmembers deem necessary or desirable. Of the various clusters of outsiders, the four most prominent are: members of the *parent House,* members of the *Executive Branch,* members of *clientele groups,* and members of the two major *political parties*—or, more operationally, the leaders of each. These four elements make up the environment of every House committee. Each has an interest in committee behavior coupled with a capacity to influence such behavior. But their interests and their capacities are not the same for all committees; all committees are not, therefore, affected by the same outside influences in the same degree. From the viewpoint of the committee member, the likelihood is that not all the elements of his environment will have an equal effect on his ability to achieve his personal goals. And he will be constrained to take into greater account those outsiders who are more likely to affect his goals than those who are less likely to do so.

STRATEGIC PREMISES

Once we know something about committee members' aspirations and something about the environment in which they must pursue these aspirations, we are almost ready to describe committee decision making. Almost, but not quite. It will help, we think, to understand the processes of decision making and the decisions themselves if we take an intermediary step and ask whether the members of each committee share any underlying guidelines for their decision making. Are there, in each committee, any agreed prescriptions for decision making—particularly any substantive decision rules—which might help us as we move to view the committee less as an aggregate of individuals and more as a working group?

Each member of each committee faces this strategic problem: How shall I proceed in the committee to achieve my personal goals, given the environmental context in which my committee operates? It is a problem very difficult to solve on a individualistic, every-man-for-himself basis. For the solution, we can now see, necessitates some fairly complicated accommodations between the desires of individual committee members on the one hand and the desires of the interested and influential groups that comprise the environment on the other. These accommodations require a degree of collective action, action which takes the form, mainly, of committee decision making. Our concern is to describe members' agreements on strategy that help to promote collective action and that, therefore, underlie the pattern of committee decisions. We call these agreements—designed to implement, through committee action, a given set of member goals in a given context of environmental constraints—the *strategic premises* of decision making.

Agreements on strategic premises take operational form as agreements on rules for making substantive decisions. In this chapter, we shall try to explicate these *decision rules* for each committee. The evidence may not always be persuasive. Committee members do not readily or easily articulate such agreements. They come closest when they discuss "the job of the committee," but Congressmen are notoriously formalistic and tongue-tied on that topic. Some decision rules are easier to discover than others; the wider the agreement and the more operationalized the rule, the easier to find. Every committee formulates—explicitly or implicitly—a few such rules. Indeed, it must. If a committee is to make hundreds of substantive decisions, it will need to simplify the task by developing standardized decision contexts and standardized responses to them.[1] As simplifying devices, a committee's decision rules will obviously influence its decision-making processes and its substantive decisions. Precisely what that influence will be depends on the strategic context in which a committee's rules get formulated.

DECISION-MAKING PROCESSES

Within certain constraining norms established by the House—norms which act as homogenizing influences—the members of each committee are free to devise whatever internal structure they wish. Accordingly they search for a structure that will help them implement their decision rules—especially as those rules reflect a strategy for achieving their personal goals. A committee will alter its internal structure when a solid majority of members feel that it no longer serves their objectives, provided only that they can agree on an alternative. No decision-making structure will completely satisfy all interested parties. At any point in time, therefore, a committee's structure is only an approximation of an arrangement that would give everyone everything he wants. So long as the members regard it as "good enough" or "satisfactory" or "better than any other practicable possibility," the internal structure displays a certain degree of stability. While the structure is stabilized, we can generalize about it and describe the committee's *normal decision-making process*. We can also describe incremental changes in that process. That is what we shall be doing in this chapter. Our description will focus on three important aspects of committee decision making. They are: *partisanship, participation-specialization,* and *leadership*.

As a prefatory note, however, we should remember that every committee's internal structure is bounded by certain formal and informal norms of the parent chamber. One homogenizing constraint comes indirectly from the congressional electorate, which decides at the polls which party shall control all House committees. Other constraints come directly from House rules. Some internal committee procedures—concerning meeting days, parliamentary practice, record keeping, and reporting, for example—are fixed by the House. Committee size and party ratios are set by the House and altered through time by amicable bargaining among the leaders of the two parties.

Illustration 4d Factors Related to Policy Decisions for Six House Committees

In this table, Randall B. Ripley, utilizing the preceding Fenno framework, attempts to summarize the operation of six committees.

	Appropriations	Ways and Means	Foreign Affairs	Education and Labor	Post Office and Civil Service	Interior and Insular Affairs
Members' goals	Maximize influence in the House.	Maximize influence in the House.	Maximize influence in a given policy area.	Maximize influence in a given policy area.	Maximize chances of reelection to the House.	Maximize chances of reelection to the House
Environmental constraints	Parent chamber coalitions led by Executive Branch agencies.	Parent chamber coalitions led by partisan clusters in the House and by Executive Branch agencies.	Coalitions led by Executive Branch agencies (mainly State Department and AID).	Coalitions led by partisan groups in and out of the House.	Coalitions led by clients (civil service unions; and 2d and 3d class mailers).	Coalitions led by clients (many and diverse).
Basic decision rules	1. Reduce executive budget requests. 2. Provide adequate funding for executive programs.	1. Write bills that will pass the House. 2. Allocate credit to majority party for policies adopted.	1. Approve and help pass the foreign aid bill.	1. Allocate credit to parties for policies adopted. 2. Pursue individual policy preferences regardless of partisan implications.	1. Support maximum pay increases and benefits for civil servants; and oppose all postal rate increases. 2. Accede to Executive Branch wishes if necessary to assure some pay and benefits increases.	1. Secure House passage of all constituency-supported, member-sponsored bills. 2. Balance the competing demands of conservationists and private users of land and water resources so as to give special benefits to users.

SOURCE: Randall B. Ripley, *Congress: Process and Policy* (New York: W. W. Norton, 1978), p. 187. © 1978, W.W. Norton. Reprinted by permission. Adapted from Richard F. Fenno, Jr., *Congressmen in Committees* (Boston: Little, Brown, 1973).

ILLUSTRATION 4E A COMMITTEE REPORT

Reprinted here from public domain are excerpts from a report to accompany S. 109, requiring reinstitution of registration for certain persons under the military Selective Services Act, and for other purposes. They illustrate the form and content of a committee report. Pages 129–30 contain a summary of the committee's recommendation and action, together with a precis of the bill; pp. 131–136 contain testimony and hearings; pp. 137–38 present the required information on budgetary impact; pp. 139–40 are the minority, dissenting views of a committee member; and p. 141 discusses changes in existing law.

Calendar No. 240

96TH CONGRESS *1st Session*	SENATE	REPORT No. 96–226

REQUIRING REINSTITUTION OF REGISTRATION FOR CERTAIN PERSONS UNDER THE MILITARY SELECTIVE SERVICE ACT, AND FOR OTHER PURPOSES

JUNE 19 (legislative day, MAY 21), 1979.—Ordered to be printed

---

MR. NUNN, from the Committee on Armed Services, submitted the following

REPORT

together with

ADDITIONAL AND MINORITY VIEWS

[To accompany S. 109]

The Committee on Armed Services, to which was referred the bill (S. 109) to require the reinstitution of procedures for the registration of certain persons under the Military Selective Service Act, and for other purposes, having considered the same, reports favorably thereon with an amendment in the nature of a substitute to the text of the bill and an amendment to the title of the bill and recommends that the bill as amended do pass.

COMMITTEE AMENDMENT IN THE FORM OF A SUBSTITUTE

The committee amended S. 109 by striking all after the enacting clause and substituting a new bill reflecting changes as recommended by the committee.

PURPOSE OF THE BILL

The bill reported by the committee would require the President to commence registration of male persons by January 2, 1980. After registration procedures have been reinstituted the President may suspend registration for the purpose of revising existing procedures or instituting new procedures, but only for a period of 90 days or less and no more than once in any one-year period.

The bill provides only for simple registration. All classification procedures would be suspended until January 1, 1981, unless the Pres-

ILLUSTRATION 4E (*continued*)

ident determines it is in the national interest to conduct classification before that date.

The bill also requires the President to report, by July 1, 1980, to the Congress on categories for deferment and exemption, procedures to be followed for registration and classification, and any other proposed changes in the act. This report is to contain a certification that the Selective Service Act, including any proposed changes, is equitable and can meet military manpower needs.

The bill would also assign the supervision of manpower mobilization planning in the Department of Defense to the Undersecretary of Defense for Policy and require an assessment of manpower mobilization capabilities in the annual Manpower Requirements Report.

COMMITTEE CONSIDERATION

The Subcommittee on Manpower and Personnel held specific hearings on S. 109 and a similar bill (S. 226) on March 13 and May 21, 1979 and included testimony on the need for registration during hearings on overall manpower requirements on February 22, March 20 and 27, April 4, 9 and 10, 1979. It heard from a variety of witnesses representing the military and civilian leadership of the Armed Forces, a cross-section of representatives of military associations and from other individuals and organizations. In addition, the subcommittee as well as the full Armed Services Committee, has reviewed the issue of registration in other hearings this year and in the past. A summary of this testimony appears later in this report.

BASIS FOR COMMITTEE ACTION

MOBILIZATION PROBLEMS

Testimony presented to the committee indicates that manpower problems in the event of mobilization are so severe that the Military Services are not now capable of meeting our national emergency requirements in terms of manpower. The Military Services are encountering increasing difficulty in recruiting sufficient manpower to meet active duty levels. The Selective Reserve—the units that would augment active military forces in a mobilization—are over 30,000 below authorized strength. According to testimony, the Individual Ready Reserve, the primary force of trained individuals for replacement and augmentation in emergencies, is 500,000 below mobilization levels for the Army alone. There are critical shortages of doctors and certain other skilled personnel in both active and reserve components.

If an emergency occurred, the Army indicates it would not have sufficient combat manpower in combat units. It would pull people out of units scheduled to deploy at later dates and use those people for individual augmentation and replacement earlier. Even so, according to Army Chief of Staff General Rogers: "We only have sufficient in there for a very small percentage of combat arms requirement. They would only last for "X" days but "X" is not a very large number of days." The Army would also plan to use personnel who were in inactive status but who had not yet completed their 6 years military obligation.

ILLUSTRATION 4E (*continued*) TESTIMONY

> is certainly not required and, indeed, would be quite counterproductive. On the other hand, to be reasonably prepared and to have an adequate assessment of the availability of people, if indeed an emergency situation were to arise, it seems to me that a limited registration would be in order so that the availability of people would be in front of us. Time could be saved and it would not be necessary to find out while the emergency was going on, what the availability of the people that you wanted would be.
>
> So it is my personal assessment that it would be sensible for us to consider and discuss a limited registration, not classification, but limited to registration only.

Asked to define what he meant by "limited registration", Secretary Alexander responded:

> It would specifically mean accumulating information without a mass of details and without any significant inconvenience to the individuals who would be providing the information.

In answer to a question supplied for the record, Secretary Alexander explained why he felt registration is necessary:

> Peacetime registration will permit the Army to meet its wartime manpower requirements much sooner than is possible with the current capability of the Selective Service System. The inadequate enlisted strength of the Individual Ready Reserve (IRR) places increased importance on the responsiveness of Selective Service to meet Army wartime manpower needs. The Selective Service System was phased to its current "deep standby" mode in FY 1977 and has the ability of delivering the first registrants for induction at M+110 days and 100,000 by M+150. The DOD stated requirement for all Services is delivery of the first inductees at M+30, 100,000 by M+60 and 650,000 by M+180. Recent analyses of the Army training establishment indicates that under future emergency conditions the Army could be able to accept 184,000 new trainees by M+60 and 568,000 by M+180. Peacetime registration will assume the availability of the first inductees by M+15, more than 100,000 by M+60 and 650,000 before M+180 days. Although establishing peacetime Selective Service registration will not eliminate the Army's total mobilization manpower deficit or even influence the manpower shortfall in the first 90 days, it will shorten the time of availability to the deployed units of the first newly trained inductees from M+210 to M+110 days.

General Alexander M. Haig, Jr., Supreme Allied Commander, Europe, Commander-in-Chief, U.S. European Command

General Haig, in testimony before the Manpower and Personnel Subcommittee on February 22, 1979, expressed his concerns with the current All-Volunteer Force and possible remedies and stated,

Today I think we need a system of registration, and I would support also, given what we know already, a classification system. Beyond that, we have to look immediately to what is necessary to remedy our shortfalls in the Reserve structure, especially in the Individual Ready Reserve.

As we proceed along those lines, we will require additional empirical data, which should be shared with the American people and the American Congress. If that data shows, as I suspect it will, that early in the eighties we will have to go beyond reserve remedies and into actual structure itself, we will have already developed the consensus that can be supported enthusiastically by the American people or at least without active opposition.

Addressing the subject of national service, General Haig said, his personal feeling is,

* * * that a young citizen of our Nation should be raised and nurtured in the context of some obligation of service to his Nation in either the military service or some form of Federal service for a brief period of time. It would be hard to judge what impact the all volunteer structure has had on our citizens' sense of obligation, but I think it could be ascertained there must be some.

Admiral Harry D. Train, Commander-in-Chief, Atlantic

Admiral Train, appearing before the Manpower and Personnel Subcommittee on February 22, 1979, was asked whether registration and classification would have an impact on the Navy's manpower problems. He responded:

I agree with General Haig that it is important that, if we have to resort to this device to man our ships, to fill out our fighting structure, that we at least know where the people are that we would call into the service.

In the past, the impact of the draft, as people were being drafted into the Army, had a beneficial impact on the Navy, people would enlist in the Navy rather than be drafted into the Army. Whether that would prevail today or not, I don't know.

General Bernard W. Rogers, Chief of Staff, U.S. Army
Admiral Thomas B. Hayward, Chief of Naval Operations
General Lew Allen, Jr., Chief of Staff, U.S. Air Force
General Louis H. Wilson, Commandant, U.S. Marine Corps

The four chiefs of the military Services appeared together at a hearing of the Manpower and Personnel Subcommittee on March 13, 1979, and testified on the need for the reinstitution of registration procedures.

The witnesses all acknowledged that the Nifty Nugget mobilization exercise indicated that the Services are not now capable of meeting U.S. national emergency requirements.

ILLUSTRATION 4E (*continued*) TESTIMONY

Asked if it is now necessary to reinstitute registration the replies were as follows:

> General ROGERS. As a minimum, we should to go registration just as soon as we can.
>
> General ALLEN. Yes sir . . . the act of registration, while not needed for us in the same way that it is for the Army, would doubtless benefit the ability to recruit. I support registration and limited classification.
>
> Admiral HAYWARD. I am convinced that registration is a logical and sensible thing to do.
>
> General WILSON. I believe that registration is absolutely necessary.

Generals Wilson and Allen and Admiral Hayward were also asked whether they favored classification. Their responses were as follows:

> General WILSON. Yes, sir, I think classification is a follow-on to registration, and should also include examination. I think examination should probably come first—medical examination, and full classification in that order. Registration, examination, and classification in that order, depending again on the administrative difficulties involved. It is going to be difficult to start up again.
>
> General ALLEN. There are certain steps of classification that can be done with very little cost or administrative difficulty associated with registration. The first big charge, as I understand it, comes up with respect to physical examination. I believe that limited classification should certainly be done as part of registration. And I am, frankly, unsure in the matter of weighing expense against benefit as we get into the physical examination question.
>
> Admiral HAYWARD. I believe that if your legislation were to call for registration that the time required to get the mechanism moving and to be effective in registering would allow us more time in determining whether the next step ought to be medical and classification. There is a cost to that and one ought to do it, in my opinion, in conjunction with a decision to go to the draft for the IRR. If a decision is not to go in that direction, then I am not so sure that I can say now that we ought to make that investment in classification.

Asked if reinstitution of registration should include women, the witnesses stated:

> General ROGERS. Women should be required to register in order for us to have an inventory of what the available strength is within the military qualified pool in this country.
>
> General ALLEN. My personal opinion is yes, sir. I think that the importance, with regard to the inventory, is not nearly the same for women as it is for men. Therefore, I would not believe that registration for women is essential. However, if there were feelings of equal treatment that would make the act of registration more acceptable, if it were done the same for men and women, then I would have no objection to the registration of women.

ILLUSTRATION 4E (*continued*) TESTIMONY

> Admiral HAYWARD. I concur almost exactly with what General Allen has said. In my judgment, the requirement for large numbers of women for mobilization purposes, hence registration, is not there. If it were intended to accelerate our ability to mobilize, I would not support a requirement for registration of women nearly to the degree that I could male registration. It seems to me the issue really is a political decision more than a military requirement decision.
>
> General WILSON. Yes. I believe they should be registered. I think from a pure equitable point of view, women in the Marine Corps are doing very well.

Asked whether the witnesses would be in favor of women being drafted for the purposes for which women are used today, they responded:

> General ROGERS. I am not prepared to agree that they should be drafted as of today, even for those skills for which they are today being utilized. But if they are to be drafted, they should only be drafted for those skills for which they are being utilized today.
>
> General ALLEN. As far as the Air Force is concerned, the argument as to whether women should or should not be included in the draft is a deferral to the Army, which has a different kind of problem, or is a question of equity, on which I am really not prepared to voice an opinion. It would not have any unfavorable effect on the Air Force. We would have no objection to such a draft.
>
> Admiral HAYWARD. From a military point of view, there is no need for drafting women into the U.S. Navy. From the standpoint of equity, it seems to me as though that really is a political decision rather than a military decision.
>
> General WILSON. I believe that we can meet our goal satisfactorily. From an equitable point of view, or perhaps as a result of the inevitable court contest which will come up if, in fact, men and not women are drafted, we would be perfectly happy to have women drafted. That is, up to the 5 percent goal which I believe we can handle in the Marine Corps.

The witnesses were asked if they would be in favor of this session of Congress reinstituting the draft and they replied:

> General WILSON. I believe the draft is necessary. I believe it will be necessary in the decade of the 1980's. At the moment I believe registration should come first.
>
> Admiral HAYWARD. I am not in favor of this session of Congress reinstituting the draft.
>
> General ALLEN. I am not in favor of this session of Congress reinstituting the draft.
>
> General ROGERS. If this session of Congress could reinstitute the draft, I would be in favor of it. I believe that we already are behind the timetable that I would like to have seen to reinstitute registration. I personally believe, that there is nothing that we have underway now or anything on the horizon which will solve the problem of the Individual Ready Reserve, ex-

ILLUSTRATION 4E (*continued*) TESTIMONY

Asked if the ACLU would endorse the computerization and use of Internal Revenue Service and Social Security names in order to avoid going to a registration, Mr. Landau answered:

> If we are in an emergency, if we were in a declared war situation like World War II, we would not object to the use of data matching IRS and Social Security files. We do object to the use of it in peacetime. We think that would be a gross abuse of personal privacy.

Reverend Milton Zimmerman, Hutterian Society of Brothers

The Hutterian Society of Brothers requests that any change to the Military Selective Service Act provide for continuation of the conscientious objector status, reviewed by civilian authorities, in return for civilian service, and exclude registration and drafting of women.

Ms. Melva Mueller, Executive Director,
Women's International League for Peace and Freedom

The Women's International League for Peace and Freedom objects to registration or conscription of either men or women. They see conscription "as incompatible with fundamental American values negating as it does freedom of choice for the draftees, interrupting his or her work, education or family life." They believe peacetime conscription is unconstitutional and object to the use of Social Security, school records and Internal Revenue Service records to facilitate registration on the grounds it threatens the right of privacy. They advocate a full examination of our military manpower requirements before any action on registration or conscription takes place.

C. A. (Mack) McKinney, Staff
Director, Non-Commissioned Officers Association

"The Non-Commissioned Officers Association believes there is a necessity not only to register our young men, but to induct them into the reserve and guard in order that this Nation, as well as they, are prepared for any wartime emergency." They suggest that women not be included in a draft proposal because of the need for trained combat soldiers.

James E. Bristol, Staff Member,
Friends Committee on National Legislation

The Friends Committee on National Legislation "opposes draft registration as unnecessary and as a first step toward reactivation of the military draft in the United States." They oppose conscription "because it is an integral part of the war system, whose ultimate intent is the destruction of human life. This is deeply abhorrent to our religious values."

ILLUSTRATION 4E (*continued*)

Lieutenant General Edward C. Meyer, Nominated to be Chief of Staff of the Army

Lieutenant General Meyer, during his nomination hearing to be Chief of Staff of the Army on June 7, 1979, expressed his views on registration as follows:

> I support registration and believe there is some work that has to be done on the Selective Service Act to insure that when we register young people we know what we are registering them for.

Asked how long it would take today, in the event of a national emergency, to process personnel and provide people in new units to bolster our forces, General Meyer responded:

> It would take a minimum of 210 days to get manned, started and turning out the first trained draftees with the current system.

Asked whether he believed there was any military or national security reason to register women General Meyer said:

> It would seem to me that from a purely military point of view, a cataloguing of assets, which is what registration is, is helpful, and therefore, a cataloguing of male and female assets, with a clear understanding that they need never be called, would be useful.

General Meyer was then asked his feelings on calling women in a draft situation and he replied:

> I think that would be a last resort issue involving the survival of this Nation. As you are focusing on the survival of the Nation, knowing where all the available assets are and having them registered makes sense. But calling them up is something that I think you would have to have a national consensus on. That is beyond my military ken.

General Meyer next was asked if he could foresee any scenario under which women would need to be called in a draft situation. He responded, "I cannot, sir.". He was then asked if that were the case, if he did not consider it to be a waste to go through the process of registering and classifying women if there is no intention to use them in a draft situation. He responded, "There is some waste. You said, can I visualize a reasonable scenario? No! Are there scenarios that are unreasonable, but possible? Perhaps—if you had an all-out nuclear exchange, where you really had to know, as best you could, what was left and where people were."

COMMITTEE ACTION

In accordance with the Legislative Reorganization Act of 1946, as amended by the Legislative Reorganization Act of 1970, there is set forth below the committee vote to favorably report this bill, S. 109, as amended.

In favor: Senators Stennis, Jackson, Cannon, Byrd of Virginia, Nunn, Morgan, Tower, Thurmond, Goldwater, Warner, Humphrey, and Jepsen.

Opposed: Senators Culver, Hart, Exon, Levin and Cohen.

Vote: 12–5.

ILLUSTRATION 4E (*continued*)

REGULATORY IMPACT

Paragraph 5 of rule XXIX of the Standing Rules of the Senate requires that a report on the regulatory impact of a bill be included in the report on such bill. S. 109 as amended requires the registration of 18–26 year old men commencing January 2, 1980, in the manner prescribed by the President. Evaluation of the regulatory impact of the bill is not possible at this time, since the bill requires a complete reexamination of classification and examination, as well as other procedures under the Military Selective Service Act.

CONGRESSIONAL BUDGET OFFICE COST ESTIMATE

CONGRESSIONAL BUDGET OFFICE,
U.S. CONGRESS,
Washington, D.C., June 14, 1979.

HON. JOHN C. STENNIS,
Chairman, Committee on Armed Services,
U.S. Senate, Washington, D.C.

DEAR MR. CHAIRMAN: Pursuant to section 403 of the Congressional Budget Act of 1974, the Congressional Budget Office has prepared the attached cost estimate for S. 109, a bill to require the reinstitution of registration of certain persons under the Military Selective Service Act.

Should the committee so desire, we would be pleased to provide further details on this cost estimate.

Sincerely,

JAMES BLUM
(For Alice M. Rivlin, Director).

CONGRESSIONAL BUDGET OFFICE COST ESTIMATE

1. Bill number: S. 109.
2. Bill title: A bill to require the reinstitution of registration of certain persons under the Military Selective Service Act, and for other purposes.
3. Bill status: As ordered reported by the Senate Committee on Armed Services on June 11, 1979.
4. Bill purpose: The bill requires the President to commence registration of citizens and other persons in accordance with the provisions of the Military Selective Service Act on January 2, 1980. It limits the authority of the President to suspend registration and prohibits, prior to January 1, 1981, the classification and examination of persons pursuant to the Act. The bill has other provisions that do not have a cost impact.
5. Cost estimate:

Estimated authorization amounts and estimated outlays:

Fiscal year:	*Millions*
1980	$6
1981	7
1982	7
1983	8
1984	8

ILLUSTRATION 4E (*continued*)

The costs of this bill fall within function 050.

6. Basis of estimate: The estimate is based on implementation plans of the administration and assumes that it registers individuals as required by the bill but does not conduct classification or examination procedures even after the date permitted in the bill. This assumption is made because it is neither the intent of the bill nor the policy of the administration to classify or examine individuals under the act.

7. Estimate comparison: The administration has estimated the costs of "nonemergency" registration to be $6 to $8 million annually for ongoing operations but not including start-up costs.

8. Previous CBO estimate: The cost of this bill could be about $4 million in 1980 increasing to about $5 million in 1984 if another implementation plan were used. For example, the bill could be implemented using existing field structures such as the Federal Postal System and computerized files of the Internal Revenue Service or Social Security Administration instead of expanding or creating new structures to gather data and administer the program. The CBO budget issue paper entitled "The Selective Service System: Mobilization Capabilities and Options for Improvement" contains further discussion of this issue.

9. Estimate prepared by: Michael A. Miller (225–4844).

10. Estimate approved by:

JAMES BLUM,
Assistant Director for Budget Analysis.

ILLUSTRATION 4E (*continued*)

MINORITY VIEWS OF MR. LEVIN

I oppose the bill to re-institute registration under the Military Selective Service Act because the measure is unnecessary, premature and inequitable to both men and women. It also rests on insufficient examination of our mobilization and Selective Service requirements.

While many people, including myself, believe that we would have a mobilization problem in an emergency, the case has not been made out for *registration* as the only or best way of solving that problem.

For instance, the Secretary of Defense has written in a letter dated June 8, 1979, to Senator Cohen that "We are concerned that the Selective Service System cannot now meet the thirty-day requirement."

But that same Secretary of Defense, in that same letter, clearly opposes registration in the following words: "That circumstance does not, however, lead to the conclusion that peacetime registration is necessary. In the near term, we think that the proper course of action is to enhance the standby ability of the Selective Service System, including its computer resources, its staffing and its planning."

The Secretary of Defense noted in that same letter that Acting Selective Service Director Robert E. Shuck "is confident that, if adequate funds are provided by the Congress, the Selective Service System will be able to develop the capability to meet our requirements."

While the Armed Services Committee and its Manpower and Personnel Subcommittee, in split votes, voted for registration, their actions were flawed by a failure to call as witnesses Secretary Brown or Acting Director Shuck to testify relative to the Administration's conclusion that our mobilization problem can be solved by enhanced computer capability.

Nor did the Manpower and Personnel Subcommittee or the Armed Services Committee make a specific analysis of the costs of enhanced computer capability, staffing and planning, as compared to the costs of a registration system. It is also significant that the Committee failed to make a specific analysis of the relative advantages and disadvantages of the different mobilization times under the two approaches. In this regard, the Secretary of Defense said in that same letter that the need is to "begin receiving inductees . . . beginning thirty days after a decision to mobilize" and that "the Selective Service System will be able to develop the capability to meet our requirements" according to Acting Director Shuck "if adequate funds are provided by the Congress."

The registration bill would remove from the President the option and the power he now has to institute registration. This bill would, instead, mandate the President to do so.

Thus the bill would undertake the major step of mandatory registration, without giving the President the chance to prove that his alternative approach would work.

ILLUSTRATION 4E (*continued*)

The President has asked for this chance in the Fiscal 1979 and 1980 budgets. To require registration before giving the President the tools which he believes would work adequately to avoid it is a mistake this Senate need not, and should not, make.

Congress should promptly provide the funding needed by the President so that he can fully explore the alternative which the Secretary of Defense and the Acting Director of Selective Service say will work to avoid a registration system.

Also, before considering the reinstitution of registration under a standby draft system characterized by unfairness to the less-affluent and less educated segments of our citizenry, we should close the "loopholes" in the system which have permitted these inequities.

We should no longer allow a standby draft system which permits the rich and well-educated of our country to avoid military service through deferments and exemptions and which forces, thereby, the brunt of the nation's defense to be borne by the disadvantaged.

The Committee, in its own report on this legislation, recognizes the problems of unfairness inherent in the present law by stating:

"However, the committee believes that the categories and standards for exemption and deferment and the procedures under current law must be completely reviewed. The Selective Service System should be equitable and fair and the committee feels that deferment and exemption categories should be limited to conscientious objectors, those morally, mentally and physically unfit and only such other categories that the President believes are necessary in the national interest."

Indeed, this is why, in part, the Committee bill suspends classification for one year after registration is re-instituted and requires the President to recommend any changes to the registration/classification procedures and to certify that the act is equitable by July 1, 1980.

The Selective Service System should be revamped during which time the enhanced data processing option can be fully tested. In the meantime, we should avoid the spectre of the outdated and unfair draft system which is one reason registration is so disturbing to people across this land.

Finally, in focusing their attention on the mobilization dilemma, and in suggesting registration as the solution to it, the Committee has attempted to address certain manpower problems which affect our armed forces, such as the shortages in selected critical skills areas and shortfalls in the reserves.

Yet even proponents of the bill concede that there is no factual basis for a claim that re-instituting registration will help eliminate these shortages and shortfalls.

Thus, the Committee's recommendation to re-institute registration is inappropriate on these grounds, also.

CARL LEVIN.

Ilustration 4e (*concluded*)

Changes in Existing Law

In compliance with paragraph 4 of rule XXIX of the Standing Rules of the Senate, changes in existing law proposed to be made by the bill are shown as follows: Existing law to be omitted is enclosed in black brackets, new matter is printed in italic, and existing law in which no change is proposed is shown in roman.

TITLE 10, UNITED STATES CODE—ARMED SERVICES

* * * * * * *

Subtitle A—General Military Law

* * * * * * *

CHAPTER 4.—DEPARTMENT OF DEFENSE

* * * * * * *

§ 135. Under Secretaries of Defense: appointment; powers and duties; precedence

(a) There are two Under Secretaries of Defense, one of whom shall be the Under Secretary of Defense for Policy and one of whom shall be the Under Secretary of Defense for Research and Engineering. The Under Secretaries of Defense shall be appointed from civilian life by the President, by and with the advice and consent of the Senate. A person may not be appointed Under Secretary of Defense for Policy within ten years after relief from active duty as a commissioned officer of a regular component of an armed force.

(b) [The Under Secretary of Defense for Policy shall perform such duties and exercise such powers as the Secretary of Defense may prescribe.] *The Under Secretary of Defense for Policy shall supervise manpower mobilization planning in the Department of Defense and shall perform such other duties and exercise such other powers as the Secretary of Defense may prescribe.* The Under Secretary of Defense for Research and Engineering shall perform such duties relating to research and engineering as the Secretary of Defense may prescribe, including—

(1) being the principal adviser to the Secretary on scientific and technical matters;

(2) supervising all research and engineering activities in the Department of Defense; and

(3) directing, controlling, assigning, and reassigning research and engineering activities that the Secretary considers need centralized management.

(c) The Under Secretary of Defense for Policy takes precedence in the Department of Defense after the Secretary of Defense, the Deputy Secretary of Defense, and the Secretaries of the military departments. The Under Secretary of Defense for Research and Engineering takes precedence in the Department of Defense immediately after the Under Secretary of Defense for Policy.

* * * * * * *

CHAPTER

5 Structural Characteristics II: Political Party Leadership and Party Organizations

Party organizations are vital to Congress. In fact, several political scientists, representing a "strong parties" school of thought, have contended that "Congress is as parties are," meaning that healthy, dynamic parties tend to invigorate the Congress, while weak parties lead to an atrophied Congress.

The importance of congressional political parties stems from their being the one, true centripetal force in congressional organization. The four congressional parties—House Democrats, House Republicans, Senate Democrats, and Senate Republicans—are the only real forums in the Congress with the potential to prioritize and coordinate among individual and committee actors.

The centralizing potential of the political parties is seriously circumscribed, however, by their patently nonhierarchical structure. Unlike the organizations with which we are most familiar—businesses, universities, military units—Congress lacks a hierarchy. Those at the top of the congressional pyramid—the congressional party leaders—lack the authority to control member entrance to and exit from the institution. Moreover, the norms of Congress place a premium not on party loyalty but on constituency representation. Thus, deviation from party positions for reasons of constituency are not only tolerated but frequently encouraged by Congress' unwritten rules. Filling the void are a plethora of informal and ad hoc group caucuses that have sprung up in the last several decades, providing competing pressures for members' loyalty.

Despite the weak, fragmented, and undisciplined nature of the congressional parties, the talk of party decline, disaggregation, and deterioration, and the relatively small percentage of party votes (i.e., votes where 90 percent unanimity in one party votes in opposition to 90 percent in the other party), party leaders perform important functions in Congress. The writings in this chapter detail these functions.

Essays also discuss leadership positions, roles, constraints, relationships, and change.

In addressing political parties in Congress, one should be alert to the fact that each of the four parties is a unique organization. Each has its own distinctive structure and information apparatus.

5.1 The Speaker of the House/House Leadership*

This selection gives an overview of party leaders in the House with emphasis on the House's most powerful figure, the Speaker.

THE SPEAKER

It would do no violence to the truth to call the Speaker of the House the second most powerful office holder in the U.S. government, surpassed only by the President. In fact, the Presidential Succession Act of 1947 places the Speaker second in line in succession to the Presidency, behind only the Vice President, whose assumption to that office is required by the Constitution.

SELECTING A SPEAKER

In the early days the Speaker was elected by ballot, but since 1839 all have been chosen by roll call or voice vote. The election of the Speaker is traditionally the first order of business upon the convening of a new Congress.

The choosing of the Speaker has undergone a few significant changes over the past 190 years. Only relatively senior members with 20-plus years of experience have been elected Speaker in this century. From 1789 to 1896, each new Speaker averaged only seven years of experience in Congress. Once elected, a Speaker is customarily reelected as long as his party remains in the majority and he retains his congressional seat.

Although the election officially occurs on the floor of the House, modern-day Speakers are actually decided upon when the majority party meets in caucus on the eve of a new Congress. Despite the foregone conclusion of the contest, the minority party also nominates its candidate, who, upon losing, becomes Minority Leader. Since the 1930s, service in the lesser party leadership posts, such as Majority and Minority Whip, Majority and Minority Leader, have become stepping stones to the Speakership.

The stability of the two-party system in the modern era has led to a period of unbroken lines of succession in the leadership tracks of both parties. This has not always been the case, however. In 1855, more than 130 separate votes were required over a period of two months before a Speaker was finally chosen. In 1859, only four years later, the House balloted 44 times before choosing a first-term New Jersey Congressman for the Speakership—and he was defeated for reelection *to the House* after that one term!

POWERS AND DUTIES

The Constitution makes but scant reference to the office, prescribing in Article I, Section 2

* From *The Capitol: A Pictorial History of the Capitol and of the Congress,* 1980, pp. 78–79, 90–91. Reprinted from the public domain.

that "the House of Representatives shall chuse [sic] their speaker." While the powers and duties of the Speaker are spelled out to some degree in the Rules of the House, the effectiveness of any particular Speaker has depended upon a great many intangibles: the Speaker's own personal dynamism, the size of his majority in the House, his relationship with the Executive Branch, his ability to "get things done." Men of greatly differing styles and temperaments have served as Speaker. Freshmen, septuagenarians, dictators, tyrants, moderates, southerners, northerners, former Presidents, Vice Presidents (and would-be Presidents) have all, at one time or another, served in the Speaker's chair.

In the modern era, the many duties of the Speaker include presiding at the sessions of the House, announcing the order of business, putting questions to a vote, reporting the vote and deciding points of order. He appoints the chairmen of the Committee of the Whole and members of select and conference committees. He chooses Speakers pro tem and refers bills and reports to the appropriate committees and calendars. Although he is not constitutionally required to be an elected member of the House, this *de facto* requirement assures that the Speaker also enjoys the privileges of ordinary House members. He may, therefore, after stepping down from the chair, vote and participate in debate on the floor.

Perhaps the duties of the Speaker were put most idealistically by the first "great" Speaker, Henry Clay, back in 1823. It was up to the Speaker to be prompt and impartial in deciding questions of order, to display "patience, good temper, and courtesy" to every member, and to make "the best arrangement and distribution of the talent of the House," in carrying out the country's business. Finally, Clay noted, the Speaker must "remain cool and unshaken amidst all the storms of debate, carefully guarding the preservation of the permanent laws and rules of the House from being sacrificed to temporary passions, prejudices or interests." But in fact the Speakership today is a partisan office. As Floyd Riddick, parliamentarian emeritus of the U.S. Senate, has commented, "tradition and unwritten law require that the Speaker apply the rules of the House consistently, yet in the twilight zone a large area exists where he may exercise great discrimination and where he has many opportunities to apply the rules to his party's advantage."

Triple Personality

The Speaker of the House is a triple personality, being a member of the House, its presiding officer, and leader of the majority party in the chamber. As a member of the House he has the right to cast his vote on all questions, unlike the President of the Senate (the Vice President of the United States), who has no vote except in the case of a tie. Usually, however, the Speaker does not exercise his right to vote except to break a tie or when he desires to make his position known on a measure before the House. As a member, he also has the right to leave the chair and participate in debate on the House floor as the elected Representative of his district.

As presiding officer of the House, the Speaker interprets the rules that the House has adopted for guidance. In this matter he is customarily bound by precedents, created by prior decisions of the chair. Appeals are usually in order from decisions of the chair, but seldom occur. When they are taken, the chair is usually sustained. The Speaker's power of recognition is partially limited by House rules and conventions that fix the time for considerations of various classes of bills.

He has discretion in choosing the members he will recognize to make motions to suspend the rules on days when such motions are in order. The rules of the House may be suspended by two-thirds vote on the first and third Mondays of the month, the Tuesdays immediately following those days, and the last six days of the session.

As a party leader, the Speaker had certain additional powers prior to 1910: to appoint all standing committees and to name their chairmen; to select members of the Rules Committee; and from 1858 to serve as it chairman. His political power evolved gradually during the 19th century and peaked under the leadership of former Speaker Joseph Cannon.

In 1910, the House cut back some of the Speaker's power. They removed him from the Rules Committee, stripped him of his power to appoint the standing House committees and their chairmen, and restricted his former right of recognition. These actions were not directed so much against the principle of leadership as against the concentration of power in the hands of a single individual.

HOUSE LEADERSHIP

At the beginning of each Congress, the leadership of the House of Representatives is elected. The Constitution authorizes the House to elect a Speaker. Each party caucus also elects its party leader. Under the tradition of the two-party system in this country, the leader of the party with the largest number of members becomes the Majority Leader. The Minority Leader is invariably the member nominated by the minority party for the Speakership.

The Majority Leader works very closely with the Speaker in developing the party's position on major policy issues. He almost always has represented a different geographic area of the country from the Speaker. He consults with committee chairmen and urges them to move legislation which the party considers important.

Each party also appoints a Whip and assistant whips to assist the floor leader in execution of the party's legislative program. The main job of the Whips is to canvas party members on a pending issue and give the floor leader an accurate estimate of the support or opposition expected on a bill. The term *Whip* refers to the responsibility of these members to pressure the other members of their party to the floor for key votes.

In recent years the majority party has revitalized the caucus of its members and the chairman of the caucus, elected by his party colleagues, has become an important part of the leadership structure.

Usually considered as part of the "leadership" are the chairmen of the 22 committees of the House. Until the congressional reforms in 1975, the chairmen achieved their status solely by virtue of their seniority. Currently, chairmen are elected by the majority party caucus, by secret ballot. Committee chairmen are nominated by the Steering and Policy Committee, composed of House leaders, their nominees, and members elected by the caucus on a regional basis.

5.2 | The House Majority Whip*

One of the first things an observer in Congress learns is that "party Whips don't whip." Rather than being the control mechanisms of leadership, Whips serve as an information conduit, forwarding communications from leaders to members, and vice versa. The following details this information system as it exists in the House when the Democrats are in the majority.

The House Majority Whip has served as an arm of the leadership for more than 70 years. Defined by precedent, modified by practice and varying with the business at hand, the job of the Whip remains essentially unchanged—to assist the Speaker and Majority Leader who appoint him. The Whip organization, therefore, is at the core of Democratic Party unity in the House of Representatives.

It is the Majority Whip, the Chief Deputy Whip, three Deputy Whips, and 24 Assistant or Zone Whips—bridging the gap between the Speaker and the membership at large—who are charged by the leadership with the twofold task of informing the majority party members of the program of the Speaker and the Majority Leader, and, at the same time, keeping the leadership apprised of the views and attitudes of the members. The Whip and his organization accomplish this goal by publishing and making available to the membership much informational material, and always maintaining close personal ties with the majority members of the House.

The function of "whip" dates to 1769, when the great British Parliamentarian Edmund Burke during a historic debate in the House of Commons, used the term *whip* to describe the ministers who had sent for their friends as "whipping them in," derived from the term *whipper-in,* the man who kept the hounds from leaving the pack. The document "whip" or notice of legislative activity, was in use as early as 1621 in the House of Commons. In this tradition, the functions of the Majority Whip are to advise party members of legislative activities, and to encourage them to vote the leadership position.

HISTORY OF THE HOUSE MAJORITY WHIP

The position of Majority Whip in the House of Representatives was not established until the end of the 19th century. Prior to that time, individual members occasionally acted as unofficial Whips on specific issues, but because of the smaller size of the House (186 members in 1810, 391 in 1900, 435 today) and the absence of highly organized parties, a formal Whip's office was not needed.

In 1897, Speaker Thomas B. Reed appointed Rep. James A. Tawney (R–Minn.) as the first Majority Whip, and in the early years of the office, the Majority Whip was very often a confidant of the Speaker, appointed by him and acting primarily as an assitant to him.

The first Majority Whip to appoint other Congressmen as his assistants was Rep. John W. Dwight (R–N.Y.) in 1909. Dwight, an appointee of Speaker Joseph Cannon, was also the first Whip to poll members prior to an important vote.

The office of Whip was upgraded and enlarged in 1933, as then Whip Rep. Arthur H.

* From "The House Majority Whip," *The History and Operation of the House Majority Whip Organization* (Washington, D.C.: U.S. Government Printing Office, 1973, House Document No. 94–162), pp. 1–3. Reprinted from the public domain.

Greenwood (D–Ind.) established a system of 15 Assistant Whips, each representing a specific geographic zone, this being the forerunner of the present organizational structure, which has been expanded to 20 zones. The Zone Whips were then, and still are, either elected by the members in their region or selected by the most senior member of the geographic area they represent.

The House Majority Whip himself and his four deputies are chosen by the Speaker and Majority Leader when the Democrats control the House and by the Republican Caucus when the GOP is the majority party.

In 1955, when Rep. Carl Albert (D–Okla.) was Majority Whip, the leadership appointed a Deputy Whip to assist the Whip in his duties; in 1971, during the tenure of Rep. Thomas P. O'Neill (D–Mass.) as Whip, a second Deputy Whip was added. The substructure of the Whip's office was reorganized further in 1973, as Rep. John J. McFall (D–Calif.) assumed the Whip's position with the assignment of a Chief Deputy Whip and three Deputy Whips, in addition to the 20 Zone Whips. In 1975 three at-large Whips were named—representing women, black, and freshman members of the House.

SERVICES AND RESPONSIBILITIES OF THE WHIP

One of the Whip organization's key functions is to poll his party's members prior to consideration of important legislative matters. These polls, or "Whip counts," are undertaken at the request of the Speaker or Majority Leader and include specific questions on the bill or bills to be considered on the floor. These "Whip counts" provide a picture of the attendance and probable outcome of an upcoming vote. Obviously, this information is valuable to the leadership. If party members seem dissatisfied, or if attendance will be low, the party leaders can reschedule or delay consideration of a particular measure or send it back to its sponsoring committee for rewriting. These polls also identify to the Whips members who are uncertain about the legislation in question. Whips can then attempt to persuade the undecided to vote with the leadership.

Another important function of the Whip's office is the distribution at the end of every legislative week of the "Whip Notice," listing all bills to be considered on the floor the following week, and the "Whip Pack," containing a copy of all bills and reports on the Whip Notice. The Speaker may make changes in the legislative program based on a poll of the membership, action by the Rules Committee in clearing a measure for consideration, or for other valid reasons.

The Majority Whip initiated an expanded informational role for the Whip's office in the 93d Congress. "Whip Advisories," a memorandum summarizing the major provisions of a bill and possible amendments to be offered on the floor, are now distributed to all members of the majority party a few days before the legislation is considered by the House. The Advisories, which strive for objectivity rather than espousing a party position, are prepared by the Whip organization with the assistance of the committee which handled the legislation.

With the added resources of a Chief Deputy Whip—who in the 93d Congress for the first time had an office in the Capitol and a staff allowance—the Whip's office now prepares and distributes much additional information for the use of the membership: speeches, testimony for committee hearings, and, perhaps most important, periodic reviews of the legislation passed by the House. These are issued to the members in the form of "speech cards."

The Whip also initiated an improved telephone system in the 93d Congress, which allows the Whip to transmit the schedule of the House to the offices of majority party members on a daily basis shortly after noon, as soon as the Speaker has confirmed the afternoon schedule. The offices are also alerted of important impending votes and other legislative changes via this telephone operation. In addition, members of Congress and their staffs call the Whip's office for information about scheduling and other matters.

THE OPERATION OF THE WHIP'S OFFICE

Because the Whip serves as a conduit of information between the leadership and the members of the majority party, he and his Assistant Whips must spend much more time on the floor than the average Congressman. Moreover, although the Speaker and Majority Leader are relieved of any committee assignments, the Whip and his assistants continue to sit on their regular committees.

The Majority Whip, therefore, serves not only his congressional district and in committee, but also the leadership and all members of his party. He joins the Speaker for a daily strategy session and press conference, and he and all Deputy Whips serve on the Democratic Steering and Policy Committee. In addition, the Whip accompanies the leadership to the White House for meetings with the President and joins the leadership for meetings with their Senate counterparts.

A weekly meeting of the Speaker, Majority Leader, caucus chairman, and all whips is held each Thursday morning in the Whip's office. It is in these sessions that the legislative program for the following week is discussed and eventually decided upon. These sessions are noted for their free-flow, frank discussions about programs and policies.

During the week, it is the job of the Whip and his deputies to see that his party's members are informed of the leadership's program. In doing so, it is also his role to help implement the plans of the Speaker and Majority Leader, and together with his assistants, the Whip is continually contacting members of the party to acquaint them with the wishes of the leadership. The Deputy and Zone Whips work the floor during debate and often play a pivotal role on closely contested legislation.

These contacts are also the source of much of the Whip's contribution to the formulation of party policy and strategy, as he, his assistants, and the Zone Whips represent each of the 42 states with a Democratic member. The Zone Whips especially must bring the views of all party members to the attention of the leadership.

In addition, the Whip acts as Speaker or floor leader when the Speaker or Majority Leader is absent.

ILLUSTRATION 5A WHIP CARDS

The following are reproductions of actual cards provided to Democratic House members by the office of the Majority Whip. These cards illustrate the promotional role of the Whip's office.

THE HOUSE RECORD IN THE 95th CONGRESS

JOHN BRADEMAS
MAJORITY WHIP
H-107 — U.S. Capitol
225-5604

No. 5 May 20, 1977

CONGRESS DELIVERS

Congress and the President, working closely together during the first four months of the Carter Administration, have delivered on four priority goals they promised the nation in January. Most were accomplished well ahead of the July target set by Speaker O'Neill.

* Most of a major economic stimulus package has been enacted into law;
* Strong new financial ethics rules have been adopted as rules of the House and are being drafted for enactment into permanent law;
* Government reorganization authority for the President is now law; and
* Energy legislation is receiving priority consideration and is scheduled for House action within two months.

No President has seen so many major laws enacted at the start of his term, except President Roosevelt in 1933.

* JOBS AND THE ECONOMY *

BUDGET RESOLUTION: In the First Budget Resolution for fiscal 1978, Congress set a goal of creating at least 1.3 million jobs in 1978. (S.Con.Res.19)

JOBS: More than a million jobs are expected to be created by two new laws, and bills with at least 300,000 more jobs are in progress:

		Jobs
Local Public Works	(law)	600,000
New CETA jobs	(law)	415,000
Older Americans	(law)	14,800
Tax Cut		100,000+
Youth jobs, training		203,000

LOCAL PUBLIC WORKS: A new law authorizes $4 billion for local public works through calendar 1978, creating 600,000 construction and related jobs. (PL95-28)

APPROPRIATIONS: A $20-billion Economic Stimulus Appropriations law includes: $7.9 billion to increase CETA public service jobs to 725,000 from 310,000 in fiscal 1978; $59 million for 14,800 jobs for older Americans; and $100 million for railroad rehabilitation. (PL 95-29)

TAX STIMULUS, JOBS CREDIT: A bill cleared for the President would cut taxes by $34 billion over three years and give businesses a tax credit for new employees they hire in 1977 and 1978. Consumer demand alone would create an estimated 100,000 to 200,000 jobs; additional jobs are expected to be created by the jobs credit. (HR 3477)

YOUTH JOBS: The House passed a $1.2-billion three-year Youth Employment bill authorizing a Young Adult Conservation Corps and pilot training programs that would create 203,000 jobs and training positions for disadvantaged youth in fiscal 1978. (HR 6138)

ANTI-RECESSION ASSISTANCE: A bill cleared for the President authorizes $2.25 billion for counter-cyclical assistance to states and localities through fiscal 1978. The funds would preserve or create thousands of jobs. (HR 3477)

FUEL BILL ASSISTANCE: A new law appropriates $200 million to help middle- and low-income persons pay last winter's high fuel bills. (PL 95-26)

* ETHICS *

New financial ethics rules of the House require broad financial disclosure; limit Members' outside earned income, honoraria and gifts; prohibit personal use of campaign funds and abolish unofficial office accounts. (HRes287)

* REORGANIZATION *

A new law gives the President authority to submit government reorganization plans to Congress for three years. Plans take effect unless either house disapproves within 60 days. (PL 95-17)

* ENERGY *

The House in early June will consider President Carter's proprosal to consolidate 50 energy-related agencies into a Cabinet-level Department of Energy. The Senate has already passed such a bill. (HR 6804) Also, the President's energy package, consisting of more than 100 sections, has been referred to five House committees which are required to report by July 13. An Ad Hoc Committee on Energy appointed by Speaker O'Neill and headed by Congressman Thomas L. Ashley will facilitate passage of the legislation, tentatively by early August. (HR 6831)

5/20/77

ILLUSTRATION 5A (*continued*)

THE HOUSE RECORD
IN THE
95th CONGRESS

JOHN BRADEMAS
MAJORITY WHIP
H-107 — U.S. Capitol
225-5604

No. 4 May 20, 1977

ACHIEVEMENTS CHECKLIST

Congress and the President worked hard together to deliver on their promise of major legislation to benefit the American people.

VITAL STATISTICS: Vital statistics show that the hard-working House this year is well ahead of the 94th Congress two years ago.

May 20 1977		May 31 1975
73	House meetings	74
298	hours in session	281
246	roll call votes	180
22	quorums	66
302	measures passed	235
29	enacted into law	27

Following are highlights of major legislative accomplishments:

TAX CUT: A bill cleared for the President would cut taxes by $34 billion over three years and create jobs.

BUDGET: The First Budget Resolution for fiscal 1978 sets a goal of creating at least 1.3 million new jobs in 1978.

PUBLIC WORKS JOBS: A law authorizes $4 billion for local public works that would create 600,000 jobs.

ANTIRECESSION ASSISTANCE: Congress cleared a bill authorizing $2.25 billion to assist states and localities.

YOUTH JOBS: A House-passed bill would create 203,000 jobs and training positions for disadvantaged young people.

APPROPRIATIONS: A $20-billion economic stimulus law funds 415,000 new CETA public service jobs and other jobs.

FUEL BILL ASSISTANCE: A new law appropriates $200 million to help middle and lower income families pay fuel bills.

FINANCIAL ETHICS: A strong new code of financial ethics, including broad disclosure, was adopted as House rules.

SELECT COMMITTEE ON ETHICS: A House committee was created to write Congress' ethics rules into permanent law.

PAY: A new law requires recorded votes by House and Senate on future quadrennial pay raises for Members of Congress

ENERGY POLICY: The President's energy package is being given priority consideration by House committees.

ENERGY COMMITTEE: An ad hoc House committee was created to coordinate consideration of the President's energy bills.

REORGANIZATION: A new law gives the President government reorganization authority for three years.

RHODESIAN CHROME: A law authorizes a renewed ban on Rhodesian chrome as a sanction against minority rule.

NATURAL GAS: A law gave the President authority to deal with the natural gas shortage during January's cold spell.

UNEMPLOYMENT COMPENSATION: A new law extends the 52-week unemployment benefits program through November 1, 1977.

STRIP MINING: A House-passed bill would regulate surface mining of coal and provide for reclamation of mines.

HOUSING AND COMMUNITY DEVELOPMENT: The House passed a 3-year bill to authorize $14 billion for housing programs.

MILITARY PROCUREMENT: Both Houses passed in differing forms a $35.9-billion military procurement bill.

DROUGHT; DISASTER: Congress provided $475 million in several measures for drought and other disaster assistance.

EXPORT ADMINISTRATION: Conferees agreed on a bill to prohibit American firms from supporting Arab boycotts of Israel.

KOREAN INQUIRY: A House inquiry was authorized into South Korean government activities concerning House Members.

U.S.-KOREAN RELATIONS: Another House inquiry was authorized into Korean CIA activities in the United States.

5/20/77

ILLUSTRATION 5A (*continued*)

THE HOUSE RECORD
IN THE
95th CONGRESS

JOHN BRADEMAS
MAJORITY WHIP
H-107 — U.S. Capitol
225-5604

No. 8 May 20, 1977

FUTURE BUSINESS

Not content with an outstanding record of achievement which rivals that for any new Congress and President, the House is looking forward to a heavy workload of major legislation in June and July.

The schedule of upcoming legislative business includes such major initiatives of the President as --

HR 5400 - Universal Voter Registration,

HR 6803 - Consumer Protection Agency,

HR 6804 - Department of Energy, and

HR 10 - Hatch Act Amendments.

Other major legislation for which rules have been requested includes --

HR 6566 - ERDA Security Programs,

HR 6990 - Military Construction,

HR 4544 - Black Lung Benefits Reform,

HR 5959 - Renegotiation Reform Act,

HR 7010 - Victims of Crime Compensation,

HR 3361 - Public Service Attorneys Fees,

HR 2777 - Consumer Cooperative Bank,

HR 6951 - Wage and Price Stability,

HR 6967 - Peace Corps Authorization,

HR 4287 - Mining Health and Safety,

HR 6761 - Youth Camp Safety, and

HR 6666 - Legal Services Corporation.

APPROPRIATIONS

The period from June 8 through 24 will be reserved for the consideration of the regular appropriations bills for fiscal 1978. It is expected that a dozen or more appropriating an estimated $300 billion will come to the floor during June.

ENERGY POLICY

The President's energy policy legislation, now being given priority consideration by five standing House committees and an Ad Hoc Committee on Energy, is expected to be marked up and reported for floor action by late July or early August.

BILLS REPORTED

At least 30 additional bills have been reported from committee, including such important measures as HR 7171 Agricultural Act, HR 75 Soil and Water Conservation, HR 6796 ERDA Non-Nuclear Authorization, HR 6827 Safe Drinking Water Amendments, HR 7073 FIFRA Amendments, and HR 6135 Grain Standards Amendments.

OTHER MAJOR ISSUES

Meanwhile, committees are hard at work on other legislation, including congressional campaign financing, lobbying disclosure, ethics in the executive branch, hospital cost limitation, Social Security revisions, mass transit, congressional ethics act, full employment and minimum wage.

5/20/77

ILLUSTRATION 5A (*concluded*)

THE HOUSE RECORD IN THE 95th CONGRESS

JOHN BRADEMAS
MAJORITY WHIP
H-107 — U.S. Capitol
225-5604

No. 6 May 20, 1977

* L A N D M A R K L A W *

TAX REDUCTION AND SIMPLIFICATION ACT OF 1977
(PL 95-)

Congress passed and the President said he will sign a $34-billion tax cut, tax simplification bill intended to stimulate the economy, boost consumer purchasing power, and encourage businesses to hire new workers.

JOBS: Stimulus from the tax cut alone is expected to produce 100,000 to 200,000 jobs; many additional jobs are expected to be generated by the jobs tax credit.

TAX REDUCTIONS: The act permanently changes the standard deduction to a flat $2200 for single persons and $3200 for joint returns (instead of the previous range of $1700 to $2400 for single persons and $2100 to $2800 for joint returns). The cut is retroactive to January 1, 1977, and will be reflected in reduced withholding beginning June 1. The net $5.1 billion reduction means cuts averaging $111 a year for 46 million taxpayers and increases averaging $52 a year for 2.1 million taxpayers. The bill extends 1977 reductions, including the $35 general tax credit, earned income credit for low-income workers and corporate rate cuts, through 1978. Without the extension, 70 million individuals would pay $12 billion ($170 per person) more and corporations $2.3 billion more in taxes in 1978.

SOME TAX CUTS:

INCOME		single	married	two dependents	four dependents
$ 5,000	-	$ 85	$130	$ 0	$ 0
$ 8,000	-	$ 95	$177	$174	$ 0
$10,000	-	$110	$187	$205	$180
$12,500	-	$ 19	$209	$197	$204
$15,000	-	$ 0	$143	$139	$124

SIMPLIFICATION: The act simplifies tax computation for 95 percent of all taxpayers (those taking the standard deduction) by creating new tax tables incorporating the standard deduction, the $750 personal exemption and the general tax credit.

JOBS CREDIT: The act permits employers to take a tax credit equal to 50 percent of the first $4200 annual wages (i.e., $2100) paid to new employees hired after employment achieves a normal growth of two percent. The credit applies to 1977 and 1978. Credits are limited to $100,000 per year.
Firms hiring the handicapped get an extra 10 percent credit.

SICK PAY EXCLUSION: The act gives taxpayers the choice of filing amended returns to claim the old sick pay exclusion for 1976, if it would benefit them more than the new maximum disability exclusion. The provision will save taxpayers $327 million.

RETIREMENT INCOME CREDIT: The act gives taxpayers the choice of filing amended returns to claim the old retirement income credit for 1976, if it would benefit them more than the new credit for the elderly. The provision is expected to save taxpayers $30 million.

INCOME EARNED ABROAD: The act delays for one year until 1977 the new restrictions on the exclusion for income earned abroad. This would save Americans employed overseas $38 million.

INTANGIBLE DRILLING COSTS: The act relieves oil and gas producers of certain minimum tax obligations in 1977. This would save independents $28 million.

WORK INCENTIVE: The act authorizes $435 million in each fiscal 1978 and 1979 for the Work Incentive Program which sponsors private sector work and training for welfare recipients.

OTHER: Other provisions extend for 1976 the deduction for state legislators' away-from-home living expenses pending further consideration of this issue; provide an exception to the "exclusive use" test for residences providing care for children, elderly or handicapped persons; revise the withholding requirement for gambling winnings from horse, dog, and jai alai parimutuel pools. 5/20/77

ILLUSTRATION 5B WHIP ADVISORY

This advisory shows the form of Whip communications to members. They are usually in the form of basic summaries of the proposed legislation. Notice the lack of endorsement and pressure. Explicit party endorsement is usually conveyed in a communique from party policy committees.

WHIP ADVISORY

THOMAS S. FOLEY
MAJORITY WHIP
The Capitol
225 5604

Number Ninety-two July 27, 1981

TAX INCENTIVE ACT OF 1981
(H.R. 4242)

The House on Wednesday, July 29, is scheduled to consider legislation to provide significant tax relief to individuals and restructure the tax treatment of business income to encourage increased savings, investment and productivity growth.

ACTION BY THE 97TH CONGRESS

-Ordered reported by the Committee on Ways and Means July 23 (voice)
-Reported July 24 (H. Rpt. 97-201)
-Rules Committee meets July 28; modified closed rule, two hours of debate requested.
Floor Manager: Chairman Rostenkowski

BILL SUMMARY

The Ways and Means Committee bill will provide significant and equitable tax relief through a combination of reductions in marginal tax rates targeted at those with incomes of $50,000 or less, increases in the zero bracket amount (standard deduction), the refundable earned income credit, and the child care credit, and a special deduction for working couples to substantially reduce the marriage tax penalty. The bill would provide even-handed tax relief for all businesses by replacing the complex depreciation system in present law with a new "expensing" system and by reducing the top corporate rate. Special provisions are included to target tax relief at small businesses. A summary of the bill by title follows:

TITLE I: INDIVIDUAL TAX CUTS

- Rate Cuts 1981-1983 - Marginal tax rates in all income brackets would be reduced over the period of 1981 through 1983, but the cuts would be targeted at those with incomes below $50,000. In 1982, the rate cuts alone would average 10 percent and by 1983 they would average 16 percent.

- Top Rate - The top marginal tax rate which applies to "unearned" income from interest, dividends and other investments would be reduced from the present 70 percent to 60 percent in 1982 and 50 percent in 1983. Accordingly, the maximum tax on capital gains would be phased down from 28 percent to 24 percent in 1982 and 20 percent in 1983.

- Zero Bracket Amount (Standard Deduction) - The ZBA would be increased by $200 for single persons (to $2,500) and $400 for joint returns (to $3,800) for 1982. As part of the 1981 tax cut for individuals, the ZBA would be increased for 1981 returns by $50 for singles (to $2,350) and $100 for joint returns (to $3,500). This change is particularly important to low-income and elderly taxpayers as it raises the tax entry point.

- Earned Income Credit - The refundable EITC would be increased from 10 percent to 11 percent on the first $5,000 of earnings and the phase-out liberalized. This is designed to assist working families with children in making the transition off of public assistance programs, and would also raise the tax entry point for families with children.

- Marriage Penalty Relief - The bill would provide a 10 percent deduction for two-earner couples based on the earnings of the lesser earning spouse. The maximum deduction would be $5,000 and fully effective in 1982.

ILLUSTRATION 5C LEGISLATIVE DIGEST

House Republicans convey information through their Conference rather than the Whip network. The following is an example of their format.

LEGISLATIVE DIGEST

House Republican Conference

322 House Office Building Annex #1, Washington, D.C. 20515 202/225-3396

JAN OLSON
EXECUTIVE DIRECTOR

KARL T. PFLOCK
PUBLICATIONS DIRECTOR

JACK F. KEMP, M.C.
CHAIRMAN

July 31, 1981
Vol. X, #19, Pt. IV

ADDITIONAL ISSUE FOR THE WEEK OF JULY 27, 1981

H.R. 3982--Omnibus Reconciliation Act of 1981
CONFERENCE REPORT

ILLUSTRATION 5C (*continued*)

LEGISLATIVE DIGEST
House Republican Conference

322 House Office Building Annex #1, Washington, D.C. 20515 202/225-3396

JACK F. KEMP, M.C.
CHAIRMAN

JAN OLSON
EXECUTIVE DIRECTOR

KARL T. PFLOCK
PUBLICATIONS DIRECTOR

August 3, 1981
Vol. X, #20

WEEK OF AUGUST 3, 1981

TUESDAY AND BALANCE

H.R. 4169--Commerce/Justice/State/The Judiciary/Related Agencies Appropriations, FY 1982
(see *Digest*, Vol. X, #19, Pt. III)

H.R. 4242--Tax Incentive Act of 1981
CONFERENCE REPORT.................................. p. 1

ILLUSTRATION 5D THE HOUSE DEMOCRATIC STEERING AND POLICY COMMITTEE

An important organ of the House Democratic machinery is the Steering and Policy Committee. The following excerpt from the *Preamble and Rules of the Democratic Caucus* gives an overview of this body.

M VII. House Democratic Steering and Policy Committee

There shall be a House Democratic Steering and Policy Committee constituted as follows:

A. *Membership.* The Democratic Steering and Policy Committee shall consist of the Democratic leadership (The Speaker, Majority Leader, Caucus Chairman, Caucus Secretary and Whip), 12 Members who shall be elected from 12 equal regions as set forth below, not to exceed 8 Members who shall be appointed by the Speaker, the Chairman of the Committee on Appropriations, the Chairman of the Committee on the Budget, the Chairman of the Committee on Rules, and the Chairman of the Committee on Ways and Means.

B. *Organization and Procedure.* The Speaker shall serve as Chairman of the committee, the Majority Leader as Vice Chairman, and the Caucus Chairman as Second Vice Chairman. The committee shall adopt its own rules which shall be in writing; shall keep a journal of its proceedings; and shall meet at least once each month while the House is in session and upon the call of the Chairman or whenever requested in writing by four of its Members. In addition, the committee may authorize the Chairman to appoint ad hoc committees from among the entire membership of the Caucus to conduct special studies or investigations whenever necessary.

C. *Functions.* The Democratic Steering and Policy Committee shall serve as the Democratic Committee on Committees in the 97th Congress and is herewith vested with authority to report resolutions regarding party policy, legislative priorities, scheduling of matters for House or Caucus action, and other matters as appropriate to further Democratic programs and policies.

D. *Regions.* The 50 States (and other areas represented in the House) shall be divided into 12 compact and contiguous regions, each containing approximately one-twelfth of the Members of the Democratic Caucus. Following each election, the Chairman of the Steering and Policy Committee shall review the number of Members in each region, and if necessary, shall submit to the Caucus for its approval changes necessary to maintain, as near as practicable, an equal number of Members in each region. The proposed changes and a list of Members in each region indicating the total years of service for each as of the start of the new Congress shall be made available to Members of the Caucus at least 7 days before a Caucus which shall meet to approve or amend the regions.

E. *Regional Elections.* Each region shall meet to elect its representatives to the committee at a time determined by the Chairman of the Steering and Policy Committee and announced by written notice at least 7 days in advance. The Chairman shall also designate a Member from each region to call that region's election meeting to order and to preside until a permanent presiding officer is elected, which shall be the first order of business. If at such meeting, the election of a Member to the Steering and Policy Committee does not take place due to lack of a quorum, the Chairman shall reschedule the meeting as soon as practicable, provided Members are given at least 48 hours notice in writing of when and where the rescheduled meeting will be held. Nominations may be made from the floor or in advance of the election meeting by written notice signed by two Members from the region other than the nominee. Written nominations must be delivered to the Steering and Policy Committee office not later than 5 p.m. on the second day immediately preceding the day of the election meeting and mailed to all Members of the Caucus in that region not later than midnight of the second day immediately preceding the day of the election meeting. Following the close of advance nominations, a ballot shall be prepared for each region containing the names of candidates nominated in advance for election from the region. Candidates shall be listed in alphabetical order and all ballots shall contain space to write in the names of Members nominated from the floor. One-half of the Members of a region shall constitute a quorum for an election and a majority of those present and voting for a nominated candidate shall be required to elect. If more than one ballot be required, the candidate receiving the fewest votes on each ballot shall be eliminated from all succeeding votes until one candidate receives a majority of the votes cast. If a region's representative in the preceding Congress had completed 12 or more years service at the start of said Congress, he or she shall be succeeded by a Member who has less than 12 years service. This provision shall not apply to the re-election of an incumbent Member of the committee who is entitled to seek another term.

F. *Terms of Service.* Terms of service for Members of the Steering and Policy Committee shall expire when a successor is elected or appointed. In the event of a regional vacancy the region shall elect a successor to fill the unexpired term. No Member shall be elected or appointed to more than two consecutive full terms, and no regionally elected Member shall serve concurrently as a regional whip.

SOURCE: "The House Democratic Steering and Policy Committee," *Preamble and Rules Adopted by the Democratic Caucus,* 1981, p. 3. Reprinted from the public domain.

ILLUSTRATION 5E HOUSE POLICY COMMITTEE ENDORSEMENTS

The following illustrate endorsements sent to Congressmen by their party's policy committee.

House Democratic Steering and Policy Committee: 225–7187

The House Democratic Steering and Policy Committee today recommended passage of H.R. 4250, a bill to provide Equal Treatment of Craft and Industrial Unions, often referred to as the "situs picketing" bill.

H.R. 4250 would permit a union having a dispute with one of the contractors on a construction job to direct its picketing at all of the contractors engaged on the project. The bill also aims at stabilizing collective bargaining in the construction industry and putting an end to local wildcat strikes through creation of a new Construction Industry Collective Bargaining Committee with broad responsibilities, including helping to resolve labor disputes.

Announcing Steering Committee endorsement of H.R. 4250, Speaker of the House Thomas P. O'Neill, Jr., said, "This is a good bill, good for the construction industry and good for the country. I am sure the House is going to pass it, and we expect the Senate will do likewise. President Carter will keep his word and will sign it."

ILLUSTRATION 5E (*continued*)

THE HOUSE REPUBLICAN POLICY COMMITTEE

DICK CHENEY, CHAIRMAN

Statement No. 7
July 23, 1981

TIM WYNGAARD, Executive Director
1620 Longworth House Office Building
Washington, D.C. 20515, (202) 225-6168

No amount of financial juggling by the House Democratic leadership can make 15 cents seem like more than 25 cents in the pockets of American workers and taxpayers. And no amount of fiscal juggling by those Democratic leaders can make their 15 percent tax cut amount to greater savings for Americans than President Reagan's proposed 25 percent tax reduction.

Even the "new math" of the House Democratic leadership cannot make true the misstatements and deceptions it has voiced throughout the tax cut debate.

Until the November 4 election, the House Democratic leadership denounced every proposal made to help a staggering economy through substantial tax cuts. Faced with crushing defeat in those elections, however, the House Democratic leadership evenutually changed its tune and agreed with Republicans that a tax cut is needed. But only the tax cuts suggested by the House Democratic leadership will help the economy, they argue.

That is the same House Democratic leadership that raised the taxes on the average American by 249 percent during the past decade. Clearly the American people did not believe those Democratic leaders last election day, and they do not believe the House Democratic leadership now. The American people know that the Democratic leadership bill will actually raise taxes, while the Republican plan will lower them.

The American people support President Reagan's tax proposals by an overwhelming margin.

The House Republican Policy Committee agrees. We support a federal tax cut that will benefit all Americans, one that will lead to the investment of billions of dollars previously consumed by government. The result will be an expanded economy which will provide millions of new jobs by restoring incentives for both labor and capital.

The House Republican Policy Committee welcomes the emerging economic optimism of the American people. But we know that much remains to be done before this country returns to full economic growth and health. The fiscal 1982 federal spending cutback mandated by the budget reconciliation bill now in conference is a long first step along that path.

But the reconciliation process is only a part of the package needed to restore economic well-being.

President Reagan fully recognized that fact when he presented Congress with his economic recovery program. One key part of that package included those federal spending cuts. An equally important part of the program calls for across-the-board, three year tax cuts that will spread the incentives of an eased federal tax burden to all American workers, resulting in increased savings, lowered interest rates, and boosted investment.

(more)

ILLUSTRATION 5E (*concluded*)

-2-

Faced with the prospect of across-the-board federal tax reductions sorely needed and strongly supported by the American wage earner, the House Democratic leadership has chosen instead -- by the admission of its own House Budget Committee chairman -- to "play politics" with the program.

Confronted by an intransigent House Democratic leadership, President Reagan showed his willingness to compromise by reducing his three year, 30 percent tax cut plan to a three year, 25 percent reduction. To date, the reaction from the Democratic leadership has been purely rhetorical, and purely political.

The Democratic leadership is buttonholing House Democrats, and flooding the nation's media, with pleas for support. Now the House Democratic leadership contends its plan will provide added tax savings for "low and middle income" Americans.

That claim is patently false, and the Democratic leadership knows that it is.

The Democratic proposal calls for a five percent tax cut in the first year and a 10 percent tax cut in the second year. Only if inflation falls below a 5.7 percent level in the third year and the 1983 deficit is less than $22.9 billion would another 10 percent tax decrease be ordered, under the Democratic leadership plan.

What the Democratic leadership does not tell the American people is that the economic damage done by their tax proposals -- including new loopholes for special interests -- will make it impossible to reach those levels. No third year tax cut would come for average working Americans under the Democratic leadership plan, while those special interests would continue to collect their new tax breaks.

The Republican tax proposal would guarantee those five and 10 percent tax cuts in the first two years of the program, and give all working Americans another 10 percent tax decrease in the third year. Under the Republican proposal all Americans would be assured of a 25 percent tax reduction. Under the Democratic plan, working Americans would get only a 15 percent tax over two years.

The Democratic leadership continues to play a shell game as well on the economic impact of its own past tax increases during the next two years. The Social Security tax increases voted by the Democratic Congress under former President Carter and expected bracket creep in tax rates will increase working people's taxes by 22 percent during the next two years. The Democratic leadership tax proposal will not even cover those increases.

The Republican tax proposal will result in real -- not pretend -- savings for American workers. The House Democratic leadership would do well to remember Mr. Lincoln's warning about trying to "fool all the people all of the time." Clearly, it is the Republican tax cut plan that helps American working men and women the most -- by far.

House Republicans stand willing to work with responsible House Democrats on passing a tax reduction program that will meet the goals of providing across-the-board relief from the crushing tax burdens facing all Americans, and providing a long term base needed for sound growth and investment planning by American industry.

The House Democratic leadership repeatedly has assured the nation that action on a tax cut bill will be completed by August 1. The House Republican Policy Committee calls on the Democratic leadership to honor that commitment, and work in good faith with House Republicans and responsible Democrats for a tax reduction package that will benefit all Americans, across-the-board.

###

5.3 The Senate Majority Leader/Senate Leadership*

The following pieces give an overview of the major senate leaders, officials and organizations.

THE MAJORITY LEADER

The Majority Leader of the Senate is the closest counterpart of the Speaker of the House, although the Framers of the Constitution apparently did not foresee such a development.

The Constitution's only references to leadership posts in the Senate are contained in two passages of Article I, Section 3. One passage provides that the Vice President "shall be President of the Senate, but shall have no vote, unless they be equally divided" (Clause 4). The other passage provides that the "Senate shall choose . . . a President pro tempore, in the absence of the Vice President, or when he shall exercise the office of the President of the United States" (Clause 5). With few exceptions, the Senate has been reluctant to place substantial political power in these offices. It has instead entrusted power to the Majority and Minority Leaders.

Historical studies attempting to explain the Senate's attitude toward these top offices have stressed the unwillingness of Senators to delegate power either to a nonmember (the Vice President), or to a member (the President pro tempore) who may preside only at times of the Vice President's absence. If the Vice President and President pro tempore are of different political parties, which has often been the case, the Vice President is able to neutralize the authority of the President pro tempore by merely assuming the chair. Consequently the Senate has vested the real leadership in its party floor leaders.

* From *The Capitol: A Pictorial History of The Capitol and of the Congress,* 1980, pp. 102–103, 108–109. Reprinted from the public domain.

Selection

Emergence of readily recognizable floor leaders in the Senate did not occur until 1911–13. Designation of these positions was the culmination of an increasing party influence in the chamber which began around 1890. Before that time, leadership in the Senate was usually vested in powerful individuals or small factions of Senators.

In the early years of the 20th century each party elected its own chairman for the party caucus, but no Senator was elected to be the Majority or Minority Leader as we know these offices today. The "caucus" was in charge of putting through the legislative program.

The Majority and Minority Leaders today are elected by a majority vote of all the Senators in their respective parties. The practice has been to choose the leaders for a two-year term at the beginning of each Congress. After the parties have held their elections, the selection is made known through the press or by announcement to the Senate.

Powers and Duties

The Majority Leader is the elected spokesman on the Senate floor for the majority party. The office is a political one, and was not created by the rules of the Senate even though the rules do confer certain powers on the Majority Leader.

The Legislative Reorganization Acts of 1946 and 1970, and more recent amendments to the Senate rules, have given certain unique authorities to the Majority Leader.

The Majority Leader is responsible for the enactment of his party's legislative program.

His role is an integral part of the effective functioning of the machinery of the Senate. The Majority Leader must keep himself informed on national and international problems in addition to pending legislative matters. On the floor of the Senate he is charged by his party members to deal with all procedural questions in consultation with them and his party's policymaking bodies. In turn, he must keep his party colleagues informed as to proposed action on pending measures. In more recent years, the Majority Leader also has been responsible for the scheduling of legislation.

The Majority Leader acts as a clearinghouse for his party as to the status of pending legislation. He works with party members to secure cooperation and unity in carrying out the party's program. The leader or his designee remains on the floor at all times while the Senate is in session to see that the program is carried out to the party's satisfaction.

When the Majority Leader is Democratic, he is also ex-officio chairman of all the party's policymaking and organizational bodies—that is, the Democratic Conference, the Democratic Policy Committee, and the Democratic Steering Committee.

The Majority Leader almost invariably: (*a*) offers motions to recess or adjourn from day to day; (*b*) calls up the *sine die* adjournment resolution and other resolutions relating to adjournment, including resolutions and motions to adjourn for periods of several days; (*c*) makes motions to proceed to the consideration of all proposed legislation (bills and resolutions); and (*d*) proffers routine requests to accommodate the Senate, including orders to permit standing committees to meet while the Senate is in session, notwithstanding the provisions of the rule. These are the parliamentary means which enable the Senate to conduct its day-to-day business.

Through the years, the Majority Leader has made the motions to recess or adjourn from day to day, until it is now assumed to be virtually his prerogative.

The Majority Leader keeps in close touch with the Minority Leader as to proposed legislation to be brought up, the procedure to be followed, and the legislative contests to be staged.

In earlier years, even in the 20th century, chairmen of committees usually submitted motions to proceed to the consideration of bills reported by their own committees. At the present time, however, nearly all such motions are made by the Majority Leader himself.

In summary, the Senate floor leader performs six basic functions of leadership. He is, or has the potential for being, the principal force in organizing the party, scheduling business for the Senate, promoting attendance on the floor, collecting and distributing information, persuading other Senators to unite on policy questions, and providing liaison with the White House.

SENATE LEADERSHIP

The Constitution requires that the Vice President is the President of the Senate. Since the Vice President is frequently not present in the Senate, except in the case of a close vote which may end in a tie, the Senate elects a President pro tempore, by custom, in recent decades, the most senior majority member of the Senate. The President pro tempore is a key member of his party's policymaking body. He usually designates a more junior Senator to preside over daily sessions in his place. The President pro tempore also has the responsibility for the Legislative Counsel, a group of legal specialists who assist Senators in drafting bills.

Since the early days of the 20th century, the Senate has, by custom, developed the position of Majority Leader as a parallel in power to the Speaker of the House.

The real leader of the Senate is the Majority Leader. He is the legislative strategist and exercises considerable influence on committee assignments.

The Majority Leader is elected by the Senators who are members of the political party to which more than 50 percent of the Senators belong. The Senators of the party with the lesser number elect a Minority Leader.

In cooperation with their party organization, each Leader is responsible for the achievement of the legislative program. They manage the order in which legislation moves to passage and expedite noncontroversial legislation. They keep members of their party informed regarding pending business. Each Leader is an ex officio member of his party's policymaking and organizing body. Each is aided by an assistant leader, called the Whip, as in the House, and by the Majority or Minority Secretary, who are professional staff administrators, but not members of the Senate.

Each of the two major parties in the Senate is organized differently. The Democrats have a caucus which nominates the leaders, elects the Steering Committee, and approves Steering Committee nominations for committee chairmen. The Steering Committee nominates committee chairmen and assigns party members to committees. The Democratic Policy Committee develops legislative policy and positions.

The Republican Senators comprise the Republican Conference, which elects their leaders and deals with procedural matters. The Conference Committees assign party members to committees. They also elect the Republican Policy Committee, which handles the research and policy determination function of the party.

5.4 | The Role of Floor Leaders in the Senate*

Floyd M. Riddick

The floor leaders—especially the Majority Leader—are the main power brokers in the Senate. Although the Majority Leader lacks the presiding responsibilities of the Speaker of the House, the Senate nonetheless gravitates around the Majority Leader much in the same way as the House does around the Speaker. The following addresses both floor leader positions in the Senate: Majority and Minority Leader.

The floor leaders, once elected, are confronted with the task of directing to enactment a legislative program. No two leaders approach the problem identically alike. A new Majority Leader more than likely will have certain new ideas as to how he can best conduct the Senate's business and will accordingly try out some new approaches to such an end. For example, when Mr. Byrd of West Virginia became the new Majority Leader, at the beginning of the 95th Congress (1977), he pursued some new procedures (1) to get the legislative program underway, and (2) to expedite the passage of noncontroversial legislation.

In an effort to get the legislative program for the first session of the 95th Congress underway, following the adoption by the Senate of a resolution to reorganize the Senate committee system, he directed the Senate to a schedule of not meeting any more often than was necessary to conduct its business. Likewise the hour of convening the Senate was changed from time to time. In the first four months of Mr. Byrd's leadership, the Senate was convened less than one third of the time before the noon hour—the

---

* From Floyd M. Riddick, *Majority and Minority Leaders of the Senate: History and Development of the Offices of the Floor Leaders* (Washington, D.C.: U.S. Government Printing Office, 1977, Senate Document 95–24), pp. 16–20, 23–24. Reprinted from the public domain.

regular meeting hour—and more than two thirds of the time, the Senate met at noon or later; on several occasions, the Senate was convened as late as 4 P.M. During that period, the Leader had the Senate to recess or to adjourn over approximately one fourth of its working days. This changing of the time for the convening hour and recessing or adjourning over working days was implemented in an effort to allow the committees as much time as possible to consider proposed legislation pending before them, since the standing committees require permission to meet while the Senate is in session after a specified time each day following the convening of a daily session of the Senate. This plan was conceived to assure committees sufficient time to study and prepare reports on measures and get them placed on the Calendar of Business ready for Senate consideration.

The Majority Leader, regardless of the time of day the Senate convened, managed successfully to schedule most roll call votes at an hour in the afternoon so as not to interrupt meetings of committees which had been authorized to meet during the time the Senate was sitting. To save the time of the Senate he has also been able to reduce the number of roll call votes as compared to the number during recent prior Congresses. Mr. Byrd introduced another innovation in Senate operations—namely, at least on two occasions during the first few months of the first session of the 95th Congress, he called together the chief counsels and staff directors of all the committees to work out schedules of committee meetings and markup sessions in an effort to avoid conflicts of such meetings as well as to expedite the preparation the proposed legislation. To save the time of the Senate when it does meet, the Majority Leader has been frequently recessing from day to day instead of adjourning during the first session of the 95th Congress; this eliminates the routine morning business and the business of the morning hour after an adjournment which runs for two hours, except to the extent that time is granted by the consent of the Senate for the transaction of such business.

To expedite the passage of noncontroversial legislation after an orderly fashion, Mr. Byrd requested and the Senate adopted an order on March 10, 1977, to create for the duration of the first session of the 95th Congress a "Unanimous Consent Calendar" on which would be placed "Measures Cleared to be Considered by Unanimous Consent." The order was obtained only for one session to give this procedure a test run.

Instead of calling up and passing noncontroversial bills and resolutions on the first day after they have been reported and placed on the Senate calendar—a common practice of previous years—this new procedure permits bills and resolutions as soon as they have been reported and cleared on both sides for passage by unanimous consent, to be transferred for at least another day to the "Unanimous Consent Calendar," found at another page of the Calendar of Business. All Senators are then able to see at one place, all measures proposed to be passed by unanimous consent procedure.

This allows every member a chance to examine all such measures and to be aware of the fact that those particular measures had been cleared for passage by unanimous consent. This alerts every Senator to make a special effort to be present when any such measure in which he has an interest is called up under this procedure. Having been thus notified, each member can be prepared to offer any amendments that he might care to, to request a roll call vote on one or all of them, or to ask any questions about the proposed legislation he might see fit. At least, it gives every member a day's notice to prepare himself for the consideration of all such bills by unanimous consent.

The bills on this calendar are to be considered "subject to Rules VII and VIII in every respect."

The position of the floor leader is not that of an army general over a multitude of soldiers. Unlike army officers, the floor leaders must maintain continued support. They are subject to periodic reelection by the same persons they have been leading.

The role of the respective party leaders is an integral part of the effective functioning of the machinery of the Senate. The Leader must keep himself briefed and informed on national and international problems in addition to pending legislative matters. On the floor of the Senate he is charged by his party members to deal with all procedural questions in consultation with them and his party's policymaking bodies. In turn, he must keep his membership currently advised as to proposed action on pending measures.

The leaders are in positions to act as clearing houses for their respective party memberships as to the status of pending legislation; the majority leader commonly posts the Senate on such matters. They work with the agents of their party to secure cooperation and unity in carrying out the party's legislative program. The majority leader remains in constant touch with the chairmen of the various standing committees to keep posted on the progress of legislation.

The Majority and Minority leaders, in cooperation with their respective party organizations, manage the legislative program. After informal consultation with Senators concerned, the majority leader proceeds to dispose of nearly all noncontroversial business under unanimous consent procedure. Many controversial measures at the request of the Majority Leader are also called up for consideration under unanimous consent procedure even though such measures after being brought up are subject to entail a great deal of debate as well as action on many amendments thereto before they are finally passed.[1]

All bills and resolutions, under the Call of the Calendar procedure, managed and directed by the Majority Leader, are disposed of after little or no debate and "without objection." While any Senator, independent of party organization, is free to prevent passage of bills under this procedure, objection is seldom heard. Members recognize that the leadership watches this type of legislation very closely in order to protect each individual Senator's concerns even in his absence from the floor.

Not infrequently, agreements between the two Leaders as to the disposition of business or particular procedure act to bar action on specific bills on a certain day. While the Leaders do not in any sense rule by arbitrary edicts the membership usually gives them deference in these instances.

The Majority Leader, or someone designated by him, remains continuously on the floor during each day of the session of the Senate to see that the program is carried out to the party's satisfaction. The Minority Leader or someone designated by him is always present on the floor to protect the rights of the minority. If, at any time, it appears necessary to take some unexpected noncontroversial action, the Majority Leader, or someone acting for him, with the approval of other "key" Senators, in the absence of opposition, will quickly alter his planned program and act on other business.

In more recent years the Leader, in consultation with the policy committee, has had preponderant responsibility regarding the scheduling of legislation. Rarely is a conference of the whole party membership called for the determination of a detailed program. In earlier years, even in the 20th century, chairmen of committees usually submitted motions to proceed to the consideration of bills reported by their own committee. At the present time, however, nearly all such motions are made by the Leader himself or someone designated by him. This includes requests for orders for the call of the calendar. The floor Leaders work with the chairmen of the standing committees in order to keep legislation before the Senate as it is needed, and in order to expedite the legislative program for the year.

The Leaders' part in debate is often designed to bring about passage or defeat of a legislative proposal according to party positions. Their speeches, therefore, recommending the passage or defeat of a measure are not necessarily confined to the substance of a bill. There are included, on occasions, reminders of the needs of the party and of party loyalty.[2]

The position the Leaders take on pending legislation to carry out the will of their party may work adversely for them as individual Senators. The Leaders are Senators of states and the latters' interests may not always coincide with the position of the national political party. Leaders vary in the way they reconcile this conflict. Nevertheless, there is inevitably some constraint to accommodate the President and Administration, particularly when they are of his party.

Senate Leaders seek the highest possible degree of unified party action. The approach of each Leader to this basic objective varies, however, with his personal characteristics and his political approach. Effective Leaders can never lose sight of each Senator's claim to recognition in his own right, because he is not only a member of a party, he is also and foremost an "independent," constitutional entity whose authority is derived from his constituency.

The Leaders, since the creation of the position, have always offered at least one of various technical motions relative to the organization of the Senate at the beginning of a new Congress. These motions include (*a*) informing the House of Representatives that the Senate is in session and ready to do business; (*b*) informing the President of the United States that the Senate is in session with a quorum and ready to transact business; (*c*) setting the usual hour of daily meeting of the Senate; and (*d*) the election of the President pro tempore when such an official has to be elected or reelected.

In addition to the above organizational motions offered at the beginning of a new Congress, the responsibility for making motions essential to the day-to-day operation of the Senate has devolved upon the leadership. For example, the majority leader or someone acting for him almost invariably (*a*) offers motions to recess or adjourn from day to day; (*b*) calls up the *sine die* adjournment resolution and other resolutions relating to adjournment including resolutions and motions to adjourn for periods of several days; (*c*) makes motions to proceed to the consideration of all proposed legislation (bills and resolutions); and (*d*) proffers routine requests to accommodate the Senate, including orders to permit standing committees to meet while the Senate is in session, notwithstanding the provisions of the rule. While under the rules a quorum call is always in order at the suggestion of any Senator, the Majority and Minority Leaders acting together exercise influence in determining when such calls are to be requested as well as when issues will be voted on by yea and nay vote.

Through the years the Majority Leader has made the motions to recess or adjourn from day to day until it is now assumed to be virtually his prerogative. In recent years either the Majority Leader or somebody designated by him almost without exception has made such motions. That does not mean, however, that the Majority Leader does not frequently consult with the Minority Leader. On the contrary, they are invariably in daily consultation about various and sundry matters.

The decision as to when a *sine die* adjournment resolution shall be submitted is dependent upon many factors. The Senate leadership always consults with the President of the United States to see if he has further legislative requests to be considered. The leadership must work closely with the committee chairmen in their efforts to bring a session to a close and with the House of Representatives to determine the day for *sine die* adjournment. In short, the joint leadership plays a very significant role in determining the duration of a session, and, in the end, it is always left to the Majority Leader, or someone designated by him, to submit and call up the resolution for *sine die* adjournment.[3]

In recent years there has been a close personal working relationship between the two leaders. The Majority Leader keeps in close touch with the Minority Leader as to proposed legislation to be brought up, the procedure to be followed, and the legislative contests to be staged. By so doing the programming of legislation has become known to all concerned and the overall operation of the Senate has become a responsibility shared, in part, by the Minority Leader. This constant consultation between the respective leaders on all matters pertaining to Senate business has prevented misunderstandings, conserved the time of individual Senators, and minimized procedural snags and wrangling.

Certain situations require special cooperation between the two leaders. For example, the beginning of a new Congress usually brings some shift of power, which must be reflected in personnel changes in committees, and in new committee ratios. Guided by requests for membership by their respective colleagues, the leaders may reach an agreement to recommend to their respective conferences and ultimately to the Senate a decrease or increase in the total size of a committee, or simply to change the party ratio.

Since the 1940s, the President has been holding special or weekly conferences with the Leaders of both parties. When the Leaders and the President are of the same political party, the former inevitably serve as leading legislative spokesmen for the Administration. Under recent practices, the President meets regularly with the floor leaders and others of the leadership of both Houses to sound them out and to get information on the possibilities of a legislative program. This procedure is used on occasion even when the President and the majority of Congress are of a different political inclination.

The President may follow such White House conferences with legislative recommendations in a message to the Congress. When such proposals are made, he depends on the support of the Leaders at least to insure their full consideration.

Contacts and approaches between the President and the leadership are not limited to such formal conferences; they also include use of a body of full-time personal emissaries of the White House, which is headed by the Assistant to the President for Congressional Relations.

The Leaders invariably are designated to receive and escort the President when he visits the Capitol—whether it be at a formal joint session for a State of the Union address or an informal reception. On state occasions and matters of national importance the Majority and Minority Leaders perform comparable duties in unison.

5.5 Duty of Senate Whips*

Walter J. Oleszek

Here, Oleszek gives a summary of the functions of Senate party Whips.

The duties of the Whip are formally spelled out only in the Republican Conference rules: "The assistant floor leader shall assist in securing the attendance of members at party conferences and upon the floor of the Senate when their presence is considered necessary by the chairman or the floor leader, and shall perform such other duties as the chairman or floor leaders may require."[1] This description, general as it is, underscores the chief duty of Whips—that of assisting the party's floor leaders.[2] In addition, the Republican Whip is given responsibility of conducting, either directly or with the help of the minority secretary, a whip check to determine how Republicans will vote on a particular issue.[3]

It was once the chief duty of a Whip to arrange pairs and know the whereabouts of Senate colleagues, but in recent years this task has been occasionally handled not by the Whip's office,

* From Walter J. Oleszek, *Majority and Minority Whips of the Senate, The History and Development of the Party Whip System in the U.S. Senate* (Washington, D.C.: U.S. Government Printing Office, 1979, Senate Document No. 96–23), pp. 15–18. Reprinted from the public domain.

but by the floor leader's staff, or more often, by the secretaries of the majority and minority parties. For example, in 1949 Senator Ralph E. Flanders (R–Vt.) delivered a note to his party's Whip, Kenneth S. Wherry, stating:

> Instead of arranging for a general pair as I told you on the floor, we have agreed to leave the pairing on specific questions up to Mark Trice (secretary to the minority) and his opposite number. I have left my instructions with him.[4]

Because of the absence of any official formulation, the Whip's duties have been defined by precedent, with some variation developing from the different interpretations of the Whip's role by those who have held the position as well as from the feelings and attitudes toward the Whip's role held by whoever is Majority (Minority) Leader. For example, Republican Whip Thomas Kuchel stated that he learned the duties of his job from several sources: (1) the activities of previous party Whips; (2) the writings of former Senator Hiram Johnson (Calif.); (3) the advice given him by certain Senators; (4) suggestions offered by his party leader; and (5) his personal definition of what a Whip should do.[5] In the case of Senator Robert Griffin, his conception of a Whip's role developed from: (1) his previous service in the House, (2) his personal determination of what the Whip's duties should be, such as preparation of a whip notice, and (3) the need he felt as a junior Senator to be more fully informed on what to expect in the way of Senate actions.[6]

Views concerning the work of a Whip by several Senators who have held this post help to illuminate the assistant floor leader's task. The first Democratic Whip, J. Hamilton Lewis (Ill.), wrote:

> The duties of the Senate whip demand his presence on the floor as constantly as possible. Sometimes the long hours test his physical capacity, but generally he is devoted to "watchful waiting." His is ex officio assistant floor leader, and in the absence of the floor leader, and other assistants, may be called upon to represent his party. At roll calls he reports absentees and pairs which have been brought to his attention. He is not supposed to introduce bills lest they may divert his attention from his floor duties. While the parliamentary whip is not supposed to engage in debate, there is no such restriction on the congressional whips. In fact, as assistant floor leader it often becomes necessary for them to do so.[7]

The biographer of the Republican party Whip from 1944 to 1949 wrote:

> Senator Kenneth S. Wherry saw himself as an official who was chosen by his party to assist in maintaining party discipline and united action in the day-to-day deliberations of the U.S. Senate. He viewed his position as being responsible for the attendance of party members and for the arranging and controlling of the "pairing" process. He reported the absentees, pairs, and voting attitudes of the members on roll calls. He consulted with and worked under the party floor leader in arranging the order of business of the Senate; and he handled the details of the weekly and day-to-day legislative programs, consulting with the floor secretary of his own party and with the whip of the Democratic party.[8]

Senator Leverett Saltonstall, Republican Whip from 1949 to 1957, stated that the Whip's chief responsibility was to do the "dirty work" as assistant floor leader—i.e., being on the Senate floor or ensuring that, in the Whip's absence, someone designated by him would be there to protect the party and national interest.[9]

In addition to his Senate leadership functions, a party Whip sometimes acts as Senate spokesman for major White House policies when his party controls the Presidency.[10] Senator J. Hamilton Lewis gave his view of the Whip's relationship to the White House:

> I particularly desire to stress that it is not sufficient as a justification for our opposition that we ourselves individually may feel that the President is wrong. The President of the United States, coming directly from the people has the right to be wrong. He may be wrong according to the estimate of some other man; he may be wrong according to the measure of some other community; but if he is fulfilling the directions of the people who placed him in office, at the same time giving him instructions as to the methods of relief they seek, however wrong it may appear to the indi-

vidual here and there, that cannot be a justification for opposition to the measure.[11]

A Senate Whip may support a particular measure because his leadership position "requires" him to support his President, particularly on matters involving national security. On occasion, however, party Whips have taken positions opposed to those of their President, as witness the opposition of Minority Whip Robert Griffin (R–Mich.) to President Nixon's nomination of Clement F. Haynsworth to the Supreme Court. Former Minority Whip Griffin stated that, on those issues where the policy position of the White House differed from his own, a Republican leader who supported Administration views defended them on the floor of the Senate.[12]

Finally, party Whips have underscored their responsibility to make the Senate work as efficiently and effectively as possible. "My most important responsibility," Majority Whip Alan Cranston said, "is to try to make the Senate work well, to make it strong and to preserve its independence."[13] In a similar vein, Minority Whip Ted Stevens stated his intention to seek improvements in the management of the Senate and to cooperate with the majority party in strengthening the Senate as an institution.[14]

The relation between the floor leader and his assistant parallels, in some ways, that between the President and Vice President of the United States. Both the Whip and Vice President depend to a great extent, though not completely, of course, upon the directions and duties given them by their party's leader; both have ill-defined responsibilities; and, at times, Whips and Vice Presidents have been selected more for political balance than for ideological compatibility.[15]

Just as a Vice President can be more effective in national affairs if he is close, personally and/or ideologically, to the President, the Whip can be more effective if he is close to the floor leader.

ILLUSTRATION 5F SENATE WHIP NOTICE

The following give an example of Whip Notices in the Senate and the kind of information they provide.

TED STEVENS
ALASKA

Whip Notice

United States Senate
OFFICE OF
THE ASSISTANT MAJORITY LEADER
WASHINGTON, D.C. 20510

October 20, 1981

Dear Colleague:

The Leadership has outlined the plan for taking up Appropriations bills. The dates are for planning purposes and serve to place Senators on notice that the Leadership intends to make every effort to complete this process in a timely fashion.

October 23 and 26	- H.R. 4035, Interior Appropriations
October 27	- H.R. 4119, Agriculture Appropriations
October 29	- H.R. 4121, Treasury-Postal Appropriations
October 30	- H.R. 4209, Transportation Appropriations H.R. 4522, District of Columbia Appropriations
November 2	- H.R. 4522, District of Columbia Appropriations
November 3 and 4	- H.R. 4144, Energy and Water Appropriations
November 5, 6 & 9	- H.R. 4560, Labor/HHS/Education Appropriations
November 10	- H.R. 4169, State, Justice and Commerce Appropriations
November 12	- H.R. 4241, Military Construction Appropriations
Week of November 16	H.R. , Defense Appropriations H.R. , Continuing Resolution

The legislative program for the remainder of the week is as follows:

<u>WEDNESDAY, OCTOBER 21</u>

- Senate expects to complete consideration of S. 1196, the foreign assistance bill.

<u>THURSDAY, OCTOBER 22</u>

- Senate may begin consideration of S. 1503, a bill to authorize the President to allocate supplies of crude oil and petroleum products during a severe petroleum supply shortage.

<u>FRIDAY, OCTOBER 23</u>

- Senate will begin consideration of H.R. 4035, the Interior Appropriations bill.

<u>VOTES EXPECTED THROUGHOUT THE WEEK</u>

<u>AWACS</u>

- The Senate leadership has set October 28th aside for debate on the AWACS issue. Debate will begin no later than 9:00 a.m. with a roll call vote to occur at 5:00 p.m.

Please contact 4-8601 for details on the daily program. My office is available at 4-2708 to answer questions relative to the legislative schedule.

TED STEVENS
4-2708

ILLUSTRATION 5F (*concluded*)

ALAN CRANSTON
CALIFORNIA

Whip Notice

United States Senate

OFFICE OF
THE DEMOCRATIC WHIP
WASHINGTON, D.C. 20510

Friday
October 16, 1981

Dear Colleague,

Monday, October 19

Senate convenes: 12 Noon

Following the usual preliminary activities, the Senate will resume debate on the motion to proceed to consideration of H.R. 4612, the milk price support bill.

Roll Calls: Should be expected

Tuesday, October 20

The Majority Leader has indicated that on Tuesday, October 20, he hopes to be able to return to consideration of the foreign assistance authorization bill, S. 1196.

Democratic Conference: Meets at 12 Noon in S-211 (Capitol)

The Week

It is unclear at this point what the legislative schedule for the remainder of the week will be. Possibilities include the following items:

S. 881, the Small Business Innovation and Research Act
S. 1549, Department of Energy authorization for national security programs
S. 1205, authorization for environmental research, development and demonstrations for FY 1982
S. 1503. Standby Petroleum Allocation Act
S. 391, relating to identification of U.S. intelligence agents
S. 1408, military construction authorization for FY 1982

Alan Cranston

5.6 The Context for a Leadership Role in Policy Analysis*

Randall B. Ripley

Ripley addresses the many constraints that inhibit the influence of congressional party leaders.

THE NATURE OF CONGRESS AND ITS MEMBERS

Several facets of Congress as an institution are particularly relevant to the role of the party leaders in policy leadership.

First, Congress is, by design, pluralistic. In order to provide access for the many interests in a large and diverse society like ours and to cope with a mammoth agenda, responsibility for action (or inaction) and influence over outcomes is diffused throughout Congress to a variety of individuals and groups (especially the standing committees and subcommittees). But the exact form of the pluralism at any given time is not fixed. It can take, and has taken, many different shapes.

Second, Congress is a partisan body. Despite blurring of party lines on most votes, despite the lack of party positions on many issues, and despite the functioning of many committees and subcommittees with a minimum of partisanship, there are still many times when the simple fact of formal party identification is critical in determining both a final legislative decision and its details. Partisanship is even more important on procedural matters.

Third, Congress is capable of conscious, self-directed change. Like any institution it changes in part in response to outside forces. But it also has a demonstrated capacity for considering internal insititutional change in a rather orderly way and acting—sometimes effectively, sometimes not—to bring it about.

Fourth, Congress is powerful and important in terms of the substantive agenda it handles. It considers virtually everything in which the federal government is involved. More important, it need not be a rubber stamp on any issue for any other person or institution in the policymaking process if it does not want to be.

Several characteristics of the individual members of the Senate and House are also particularly relevant to the position of party leaders as potential policymaking leaders.

First, members are election-oriented. Most of them want to retain their seats, and a great deal of their activity is aimed at achieving that result. Most of the choices that confront members are looked at in part from the standpoint of their potential impact on the next election.

Second, members have created and sustained a set of norms for decision making founded on bargaining and compromise as the normal and preferred way of doing business. Bargaining and compromise takes place not only between members as individuals but also between members in special roles (committee chairmen, subcommittee chairmen, Whip, Majority Leader, delegation dean, and so on), and also between members and persons from outside Congress (bureaucrats, interest-group representatives, the President, home-state newspaper editor, home-state party leader or public official, and so on).

Third, members do care about policy. This concern may come from a variety of motiva-

* From Randall B. Ripley, "Party Leaders Policy Committees, and Policy Analysis in the United States Senate," in *Policymaking Role of Leadership in the Senate: A Compilation of Papers Prepared from the Commission of the Operation of the Senate* (Washington, D.C.: U.S. Government Printing Office, 1976), pp. 18–27. Reprinted from the public domain.

tions. (Fenno, 1973, suggests, for example, that committee assignments may be sought to maximize reelection chances or to influence substantive policy, presumably because of personal interest in the subject matter.) But in some ways the motivations do not matter. What matters is that members care about substantive outcomes. These outcomes are far from being their exclusive concerns, but they are often important concerns and rarely totally absent.

Fourth, members care about their standing in their parties. This concern varies over time and is stronger among Representatives than among Senators, but it is rarely absent altogether for any member of either house.

Fifth, despite some grumbling and discontent, most members are or want to be proud of Congress as an institution. They develop a personal stake in having an institution to which they can be loyal.

Many observers of Congress look at the above factors (and others) and conclude that there are inevitable patterns of behavior in Congress that cannot be overcome. These patterns are often alleged to prevent party leadership from playing much of a substantive role. They are also alleged to lead virtually all members of the Senate and House to reject serious policy analysis as a meaningful input to their decision making. Oddly enough, what is proclaimed to be "inevitable" also turns out to be identical with whatever exists at any given time; earlier patterns of behavior and institutional arrangements are usually ignored.

To be sure, some of the above characteristics do limit policy analysis and substantive policy leadership by party leaders, but they do not absolutely prevent either from occurring. The characteristics produce tendencies and create a context. What is often forgotten is that tendencies are not inevitabilities and that any context offers opportunities as well as constraints.

THE NATURE OF PARTY LEADERSHIP

Throughout virtually all of the 20th century there has been a constant tension between those wanting a more important role for the party leadership and those wanting more autonomy for standing committees. On balance, more committee autonomy has been achieved, often at the expense of the influence of the leaders.

However, the situation is more complicated than a simple zero-sum balance between leaders and committees. There have also been demands for more influence for individual members of the Senate and the House and, at the same time, there have been demands for more aggressive and active leaders (often by members other than the leaders themselves). In some ways the demands for more autonomy for individual members and more influence for party leaders are not contradictory. Much as those thinkers attempting to weaken feudal controls in 17th- and 18th-century France linked the cause of individual freedom to a powerful monarchy acting against the nobility, so a number of persons in Congress have linked an increase in the importance of individual members to a simultaneous increase in the importance of the leadership. Those from whom power is to be taken are the committee chairmen, the counterparts of the nobles.

There are problems in maximizing the influence of individual members and party leaders at the same time, but there are also ways in which the two goals can be pursued simultaneously and serve to support each other. Strong leaders are needed if individual autonomy is to be aggregated into important impact on policy. If members are content with limited influence over relatively small aspects of policy, strong leaders may become irrelevant and perhaps threatening. What is critical is the degree to which large numbers of members seek to influence policy. Individuals by themselves cannot have much impact on policy. Those who want broader impact must find some method of aggregating their concern while not negating their individual importance. On balance, strong committee chairmen have not proved helpful to this goal.

The other option that some have taken is to look to aggregation through a strong caucus. But a caucus probably cannot operate with much impact without strong leadership of its own. In short, members of the House and Senate desiring enhanced individual influence on policy are likely to face the necessity of worrying about institutional influence over policy for the Senate or the House, or Congress as a whole. One major option for providing that institutionalized influence resides with the party leadership.

Many changes in recent years have created a situation in which individual members of the Senate and House can, in fact, pursue their own policy ends without being hostile to strong leaders. Indeed, in part they look to strong and active leaders for help (see Stewart, 1975, and Jones, 1976).

Strong leadership, however, has yet to emerge. Jones (1976:263) sums up the situation succinctly: "Whereas recent reforms have provided a greater potential for strong party leadership in Congress than at any time since 1910, seldom have leaders been as unassertive as Speaker Carl Albert and Senate Majority Leader Mike Mansfield." For those who think that party leaders have some potential role in policy leadership, Davidson (1976:305) puts the problem very well: "Party leaders, although stronger on paper than in the Rayburn–Johnson days, lack the political resources to induce coordination among the work groups, much less the analytical resources to foster coordination of policies." The question that remains is whether the political and analytical resources that are available can be used to their full potential to change this situation.

5.7 Senate Party Leadership in Public Policy*

Charles O. Jones

In this selection, Jones addresses the roles and functions of Senate party leaders and concludes with an evaluation of Senate party policy committees.

Analysis of the policy role of Senate party leaders must begin with a consideration of the nature and limits of leadership in a democracy. Every tenet and reasonable definition of democracy complicates the task of leadership. Liberty encourages assertiveness on the part of the citizenry. Equality forces recognition of all legitimate groups in the society. Fraternity asks for a reaching out even to those whom one opposes. Majority rule has been developed as a means to overcome these complexities of democratic government. The Founders of this republic also feared the tyranny of the majority, however, and incorporated in the government structure many checks against it.

John Dewey expressed the democratic idea as that of "community life itself."

> Wherever there is conjoint activity whose consequences are appreciated as good by all singular persons who take part in it, and where the realization of the good is such as to effect an energetic

* From Charles O. Jones, "Senate Party Leadership in Public Policy" in *Policymaking Role of Leadership in the Senate: A Compilation of Papers Prepared For the Commission of the Operation of the Senate* (Washington, D.C.: U.S. Government Printing Office, 1976), pp. 18–27. Reprinted from the public domain.

> desire and effort to sustain it in being just because it is a good shared by all, there is in so far a community. The clear consciousness of a communal life, in all its implications, constitutes the idea of democracy.[1]

To project the notion of community—with its emphasis on awareness, knowledge, communication, understanding, justice—on a national scale over a large land mass is indeed a noble experiment. However worthy the effort might be judged, it must be acknowledged that it creates very special leadership problems. How simple by comparison is the challenge facing leaders in authoritarian political systems. Alexis de Tocqueville drew an interesting comparison during his visits in the 1830s that remains valid today (and particularly in this bicentennial year of high politics):

> On passing from a free country into one which is not free the traveler is struck by the change; in the former all is bustle and activity; in the latter everything seems calm and motionless. . . .
>
> It is not impossible to conceive the surprising liberty that Americans enjoy; some idea may likewise be formed of their extreme equality; but the political activity that pervades the United States must be seen in order to be understood. No sooner do you set foot upon American ground than you are stunned by a kind of tumult; a confused clamor is heard on every side, and a thousand simultaneous voices demand the satisfaction of their social wants.[2]

Seeking to create a national community is obviously neither a calm nor a tidy adventure.

Clearly, leadership under these circumstances must be justified on grounds other than divine right, aristocratic heritage, or some other concept. By definition, leadership in this communal setting of free political activity is highly dependent on what goes on within, not outside, the community. In his brilliant essay on democratic leadership, T.V. Smith observed that, among other things, science went on inside the American democratic community. (John Dewey would have said that it must for a community to exist.) And science prevented a cult of leadership from emerging.

> Science has discredited this type of [absolute] leadership by the simple process of revealing that nature is too tough to be subdued by phraseology and of showing that it is impossible for any one man to know as much about the natural conditions of human welfare as these spectacular leaders of the past ought to have known in order to fulfill their promises.[3]

How fitting for democracy as community. As Smith concluded, "the crucial test of democracy is the health of science under its patronage. . . ."[4] But science also suggests a different style of democratic leadership—"a leadership of knowledge based on facts."

> It is of the specialistic piecemeal type. In order to know enough to lead here, I must choose to be relatively ignorant there. That means that the choice that makes me a leader here requires me to be a follower there. But I must demand of him whom I follow, even as he demands of me, that he shall not put either his prestige or his interests between me and the facts. This clearly means that in a civilized society, every man must be a follower in many fields. For he who today thinks to speak with authority upon things in general remains a fool at home.[5]

One may justifiably ask why a paper for a commission with very practical goals should begin with a theoretical discussion of democratic leadership. The answer is simply that too many prescriptions for legislative reform are based on inaccurate assumptions about what can be achieved. Having initially outlined certain fundamental characteristics of the democratic order, we can now state a number of limiting conditions which are likely to influence any reforms which are enacted.

1. Democracy as community does not countenance absolutist leadership.
2. Democratic leadership is, and must remain, pluralistic.
3. Democratic leadership must facilitate those processes likely to complicate decisionmaking—e.g., public education, growth of expertise, group access to government.

As a consequence of these conditions, one expects democratic political leaders to be oriented more to such process functions as creating organizations and procedures, facilitating communication, supporting research and inquiry, scheduling work, estimating majorities, determining when conclusions have been reached. Accepting this proposition confines this discussion—particularly in terms of the recommendations likely to emerge. So let me say right now: I conclude that strong substance-oriented policy leadership by party leaders is neither possible nor desirable in the U.S. Senate.

THE U.S. SENATE AS A LEGISLATURE

First one must observe that the U.S. Senate is an extraordinary legislative body. Nothing quite like it exists anywhere in the world. Along with the Presidency, this powerful upper chamber represents a unique American contribution to the art of self-government.

However, one cannot really analyze the functions of the Senate apart from those of the House of Representatives. However different the two chambers, they form one Congress and function in response to, and in anticipation of, each other. If we think of Congress overall as the institutionalized community—i.e., the citizenry in state, so to speak, then it serves to inventory problems, discover acceptable solutions, and monitor their effective implementation.

As a practical matter there must be some means by which those with problems can be heard, proposals can be developed, the alternatives debated, conclusions reached, and oversight achieved. As it happens, both chambers have established procedures for accomplishing these ends but they differ in style and emphasis. In general, the Senate tends toward a more integrative, less parochial perspective. Debate and oversight are stressed somewhat more than in the House. But, of course, it is because of the specialized nature of House representation, policy development, and limited debate that the Senate is free to take the broader view. As Lindsay Rogers pointed out many years ago:

> The undemocratic, usurping Senate is the indispensable check and balance in the American system, and only complete freedom of debate permits it to play this role. Its power comes, in large part, from the guillotine to which the House of Representatives submits.[6]

But there is more to consider. The less well-defined channels and debate closures in the Senate encourage a special creativity which contributes mightily to American democracy. Nelson W. Polsby describes it thus:

> The essence of the Senate is that it is a great forum, an echo chamber, a publicity machine. Thus "passing bills," which is central to the life of the House, is peripheral to the Senate. In the Senate the three central activities are (1) cultivating national constituencies; (2) formulating questions for debate and discussion on a national scale (especially in opposition to the President); and (3) incubating new policy proposals that may at some future time find their way into legislation.[7]

Clearly these functions must be preserved. They are presently nutured in the Senate by norms which are seemingly undemocratic in character and thus tempting targets. T.V. Smith argues persuasively in *The Legislative Way of Life* that a major obstacle to be surmounted in legislatures is "the self with its natural egoism and its utopia-building reveries." The legislature must rise "as a triumph over selfishness." "It exists to serve selves, to be sure, but by their own enlargement."[8] The United States Senate has overcome this obstacle by subsuming it. Elsewhere I have described the Senate as "an institution based on 'functional self-indulgence'—a sort of adult Summerhill" characterized by self-promotion and permissive egocentrism. I concluded that such characteristics encourage imaginative policy searches and random innovation, and create a potential for intellectual debate of a high order.[9] Apparently little has changed over the years, for Lindsay Rogers in 1926 concluded that:

> A member of the House of Representatives is a private in the ranks . . . Each Senator, on the other hand, is a staff officer—even a prima donna. He looks upon himself not as *primus inter pares* but as *inter stellas luna minores*.[10]

And very much as I judged the results as worth the peacockery involved, Rogers determined that, "Senators, perhaps, should not be taken too seriously, but the importance of the Senate must not be underestimated."[11]

The creation of an institution which capitalizes on egoism to serve the people was, in its own right, a most fascinating development in democratic government. But our interest here is in its effect on leadership. And it does not take much imagination to see that Senators are unlikely to accept strong leadership. Writing in the 1880s, Woodrow Wilson observed that political life in Congress lacked a "prize at its end" in the form of party leadership. The Speakership developed into such a prize with the Reed Rules, only to be cut in authority with the 1910–1911 rules changes. Recent reforms have restored much of the earlier authority and the office has once more become more of a prize "to attract great competitors." But there is no direct counterpart to the Speaker in the Senate. With a few exceptions (discussed below), Wilson's comments on the Senate remain descriptive today:

> Some Senators are, indeed, seen to be of larger mental stature and built of stauncher moral stuff than their fellow members, and it is not uncommon for individual members to become conspicuous figures in every great event in the Senate's deliberations. The public now and again picks out here and there a Senator who seems to act and to speak with true instinct of statesmanship and who unmistakably merits the confidence of colleagues and of people. But such a man, however eminent, is never more than *a* Senator. No one is the Senator. No one may speak for his party as well as for himself; no one exercises the special trust of acknowledged leadership. The Senate is merely a body of individual critics, representing most of the not very diversified types of society substantially homogeneous; and the weight of every criticism uttered in its chamber depends upon the weight of the critic who utters it, deriving little if any attention to its specific gravity from connection with the designs of a purposeful party organization.[12]

Reforms directed to a stronger policy role for Senate party leaders must accommodate these conditions or fail.

SENATE PARTY LEADERS

Formal party leadership in the Senate is a relatively recent phenomenon—essentially a 20th-century development—and thus is still being institutionalized. The most important position is, of course, the floor leadership post, though there are conditions under which the assistant leader or Whip may also have significant influence. The potential for centralized party leadership is somewhat greater in the Democratic party, given the fact that the Democratic floor leader chairs the major party committees and the caucus. Different individuals serve as heads of the various party units for the Republicans.

Prof. Randall B. Ripley lists the following six major functions for Senate party leaders.

1. Help organize the party.
2. Schedule the business.
3. Get Senators on the floor for voting.
4. Distribute information.
5. Persuade Senators to follow their lead.
6. Maintain liaison with the White House.[13]

He properly observes that party leaders vary in how aggressive and consistent they are in performing these functions. Thus, for example, they may view these functions as primarily procedural in nature; i.e., the leader does little more than permit the party majority to realize itself. By this view, the party is organized to facilitate individual member expression, business is scheduled as the members want, Senators are kept informed of what others think, persuasion follows the emergence of a majority, the White House is kept informed of all these developments.

A more aggressive view would also be more programmatic or substantive in purpose. In this stance, these various functions are exercised toward accomplishing goals set by the leadership. The party is organized to suit their policy preferences, business is scheduled to facilitate movement of preferred legislation, information is developed and distributed to support leadership positions, persuasion is very purposive, etc. We have already discussed whether the political and institutional context in the Senate would permit this more aggressive approach to prevail very often.

It might be helpful in thinking about the boundaries of Senate leadership to illustrate with cases from both ends of the spectrum just introduced. I emphasize that this spectrum does not necessarily represent degrees of strength and weakness in leadership. To speak of strong and weak leaders requires criteria for effectiveness in achieving some political or policy goals and I am not prepared to offer any such criteria here. Rather I am proposing to identify differences in style which are characteristic of specific leaders.

Among the Democrats, the spectrum is most dramatically illustrated by the last two floor leaders—Lyndon B. Johnson (1953–1961) as the more aggressive; Mike Mansfield (1961–1977) as the more quiescent. Of others, John Kern (1913–1917) and Joseph Robinson (1923–1937) tended to be more Johnsonian in approach (with emphasis on the "tended") and Thomas Martin (1911–1913; 1917–1919), Scott Lucas (1949–1951), and Ernest McFarland (1951–1953) more like Mansfield in style, with Oscar Underwood (1919–1923) and Alban Barkley (1937–1949) somewhere in between.

On the Republican side, the Mansfield side of the scale is overloaded. Only Robert Taft (1953) and Everett M. Dirksen (1959–1969) begin to approach the middle of the scale. The other 10 who have held the formal post of floor leader in this century fall on the less active side. One really has to go back to Nelson W. Aldrich to find a Republican Senator as impressively active as Lyndon B. Johnson. However, Aldrich led the Senate from his position as Chairman of the Committee of Finance, not as floor leader.

Thus, it would appear that, in Johnson and Mansfield, we have represented the opposite extremes in floor leadership styles. What are the differences? How did the two leaders function? In comparing them, Robert L. Peabody begins by observing that "the primary role of the majority leader remains similar to that at its inception—namely, to program and to expedite the flow of his party's legislation."[14] So, in Peabody's judgment, the principal functions are procedural in nature—i.e., to keep business moving. But as was emphasized earlier, one may come at these tasks with programmatic purposes—and these may be derived from a number of sources—e.g., the standing committees, the President, the floor leader's own preferences, or possibly some party committee.

One major difference between Johnson and Mansfield was that the former aggressively pursued programmatic purposes. They were not necessarily his own, but at some strategic point he would make it clear where he thought the Senate should be moving on an issue. Peabody identifies several other specific differences in approach between the two men, as summarized below.

These observations characterize how the two men carried out many of the functions listed by Ripley. However, it is difficult to develop a meaningful comparison on one very important

	JOHNSON	MANSFIELD
Policy Committee operations	Actively controlled	Expanded and democratized.
Committee assignments	Involved and influential	Involved but permissive.
Leadership selection	Involved and influential	Neutral.
Staff	Expanded	Limited—a "tight staff."
Relations with Senators	Aggressive—the "Johnson treatment."	Permissive.

function—that of maintaining liaison with the White House. Johnson did not serve with a Democratic President and Mansfield did—indeed, with the forceful Johnson for five years. It has always been interesting to speculate as to how Johnson would have acted under an aggressive Democratic president.

What can be concluded from this brief review? First, party leadership can perform its traditional procedural functions in such a way that it has considerable impact on the substance of legislation. This suggests that there are openings for leadership to initiate, encourage, and facilitate more systematic policy analysis and evaluation. Second, historical evidence on Senate party leaders suggests that a Lyndon B. Johnson and a Nelson W. Aldrich are clearly exceptional. Put another way, it may be dangerous to draw too many conclusions about what is possible or likely from a study of the leadership style of Majority Leader Johnson. We may never see his like again. And that calls to mind the earlier discussion of the nature of the Senate and its constraining influences on independently active leadership.

Finally, as a concluding exercise, it might be useful to think of legislative party leaders in two dimensions: (1) the extent to which they depend on the party or president for determining programmatic initiatives and proposals—dependent, independent; and (2) the extent to which they attempt to pressure legislators into supporting proposals which emerge—aggressive, permissive. Four types would then emerge:

1. *Independent, aggressive.* The Leader independently forms his own programs and aggressively pursues support within the Senate. As noted, one would seldom expect such a Leader to emerge in the Senate. (Nelson W. Aldrich may have fit this pattern.)
2. *Independent, permissive.* While independently forming his own preferences and proposals, this type of Leader permits a consensus or majority to emerge on its own (e.g., Mike Mansfield on many foreign policy issues).
3. *Dependent, aggressive.* While dependent on what the system produces, this leader is aggressive in pressing it into action and insuring output. (Lyndon B. Johnson is the classic case.)
4. *Dependent, permissive.* Again dependent on the system, this leader is permissive as to whether, when, and how the Senate acts (e.g., Mike Mansfield, on many issues, and most other Senate floor leaders in history).

SENATE PARTY ORGANIZATION

On paper, party organizational units of the Senate would appear to offer potential for policy direction and coordination. Each party has a policy committee, a committee on committees, and a caucus or conference. If we didn't know better, we could conceive of the party actually directing policy activities rather than awaiting the initiative of the standing committees and their chairmen. In this model, the policy committees would develop a specific program, the caucus would modify and endorse it, and the committee on committees (perhaps even the campaign committees) would be used as an effective force to punish recalcitrant standing committee members and chairmen. Standing committees would serve party purposes.

The Democrats appear to have moved in this direction by having the floor leader serve as chairman of these various party units (except for the campaign committee). The Republicans, on the other hand, distribute these posts among different Senators. In fact, however, Democratic centralization versus Republican collegiality in leadership posts has not resulted in any great differences in policy direction and coordination. Neither set of units has been used frequently for developing programmatic initiatives or conducting cross-cutting policy analysis.

If the Policy Committees don't make policy, and the Steering Committees don't steer, and the conferences don't confer and consult, what do they do? Can they ever do these things? Are there conditions under which they are more likely to do them? It may be useful to consider each of the units in turn.

The Democratic Policy Committee has a membership of 10, including the Leader, the Whip, the President pro tempore, secretary of the conference, and six members appointed by the Leader. The Committee itself serves in an advisory capacity to the Leader for scheduling legislation. The Committee does not block bills from going to the floor, only advises on scheduling. The final decision rests with the Leader in consultation with his counterpart in the minority. Quite naturally, then, the small Policy Committee staff serves primarily to keep track of legislation and develop the schedules. Scheduling is unquestionably a significant leadership function and can be used by an aggressive party leader for specific policy purposes. But at present scheduling is designed primarily to accommodate the needs of the standing committees, and is not employed as a means for achieving comprehensive policy review. It is questionable whether any such review is even possible to arrange at such a late point in the legislative process. If little or no direction is offered at earlier stages, then legislation arrives at the scheduling point as it will, not necessarily in a sequence facilitating cross-policy analysis or integrated policy development.

What if the Policy Committee were to influence when and what the standing committees take up? The seemingly simple task of scheduling business so as to facilitate floor consideration of related legislation is, in fact, highly complex and demanding. And if the Committee were to assume the even more challenging responsibility of developing a Democratic party program, its staff would have to be enlarged exponentially. Given the fact that the Committee would then be assuming functions presently exercised by the standing committees, perhaps portions of their staffs could be transferred. The Policy Committee would be performing possibly the most important functions of any unit in the Senate and would require a highly specialized staff.

Are there any conditions under which either of these impressive functions (i.e., scheduling for committee consideration and coordinated floor debate and developing a party program) is likely to be realized? The most likely political conditions would seem to be (1) an aggressive Republican President challenging a Democratic majority in the Senate, or (2) an extraordinary crisis to which the President is judged unable or incapable of responding (possibly because he is a Republican!). In fact, the Democratic Policy Committee and conference have played a more important policy role under Presidents Nixon and Ford than previously. For example, an ad hoc committee led by Sen. John Pastore was set up in 1975 to develop an alternative economic and energy plan to present to the Democratic Policy Committee and conference. The Pastore Committee was served by the Policy Committee staff. While this was an interesting development, the work of this unit did not result in anything like party-directed policy development. The committee's recommendations were accepted by the relevant standing committees as input, not policy direction.

The Republican Policy Committee has demonstrated a slightly more substantive policy role than its Democratic counterpart. Members meet every Tuesday for lunch, with all Republican Senators invited. They do not issue policy statements, however, nor make specific attempts to develop Republican positions on issues. Staff is used for tracking legislation, providing research and reports at the request of individual Senators, and speech-writing or other political work. While these are policy-related activities, they do not represent anything close to the functions discussed above. Nor is the potential presently there, either in leadership or in staff experience and capabilities.

Little need be said about the committees on committees. While they theoretically offer considerable potential for building support for an integrated party program, (particularly for the chairman of the Democratic committee), in fact there is little practical possibility that they will be used in this way. Such measures as the Johnson Rule, while laudable on other grounds, have made it even more difficult in recent years to employ the committee assignment process for party policy purposes. All Senators are guaranteed major committee assignments regardless of their policy stands.

What of the recent changes in committee chairmanships in the House? Might these not presage a move toward establishing policy criteria for chairmanships in the Senate? First, one must note that the shifts in the House did not seem to be primarily related to policy. Chairmen were ousted more for reasons of age, personality, or indiscretion.

Second, given the staggered terms in the Senate, the body is unlikely to encounter the kind of ''freshman fervor'' that dominated the House Democratic organizational caucuses of the 94th Congress. The point is that the leadership must rely on resources other than the Committees on Committees if it is to attempt any very imaginative and comprehensive policy drives.

What then of the conferences? Functioning as the debating and legitimating body for a truly policy-oriented Policy Committee, the conference could play a major role. It has not done so in either party since the binding caucuses of the first Woodrow Wilson Administration, however. The Democratic conference was somewhat more active in regard to energy policy in 1975, but it remains an essentially unused resource for policy development. Not even the important 1976 Budget Committee report was debated there.

In summary, one finds little in the existing party apparatus which might serve the leadership in developing cross-cutting policy analysis and/or an integrated policy program. The Policy Committee has some potential for service in this direction because of its critical work on scheduling. This task could logically be extended to other important functions associated with the development of an integrated policy program. But any such move would require support within the party and an enlarged staff.

5.8 Congressional Party Leaders and Standing Committees*

Randall B. Ripley

There is a multiplicity of formal and informal congressional leaders. In addition to the floor leaders and Whips previously discussed, one must count committee leaders as formal party leaders. Committee chairmen and ranking minority members hold enormous sway over legislation emanating from their committees. The interaction between floor and committee leaders dramatizes the fragmentation of party authority, for these leaders are not always lined up in a monolithic way. Frequently, they are at loggerheads. Ripley investigates these interactions, the various kinds of relationships, and the factors affecting the relationships.

Within Congress there are a number of forces that push toward decentralization of influence over the substantive legislative product and lack of coordination of the various legislative enterprises that are being conducted simultaneously. Chief among these forces most of the time are the standing committees of the two houses. There are also a few centralizing forces. Chief among these most of the time are the formal party leaders in the House and Senate, especially those of the President's party if the President views himself as a major figure in the legislative process and behaves aggressively in attempting to implement that self-image.

Party leaders and standing committees must necessarily interact constantly in conducting the business of the two chambers. The exact nature of the interactions, however, varies, as does the relative importance of leaders and committees on critical items of substance. This paper explores those interactions. What follows will focus on (1) the general nature of leader–committee interactions, (2) the principal factors affecting the quality of specific interactions, (3) the basic patterns of interactions, and (4) the impact of the patterns on the way in which Congress performs its major functions.

THE NATURE OF LEADER–COMMITTEE INTERACTIONS

In many ways leaders and committees are interdependent. As party leaders seek specific legislative ends they must rely on the standing committees for a number of things: the detailed substance of bills, the timetable within which bills are ready for floor consideration, the transmission of leaders' legislative preferences to the members of the committee during committee deliberations, and aid in the transmission of those preferences to all party members during floor consideration. Committee leaders must rely on the party leaders for scheduling business for the floor and helping work for its passage or defeat, for communicating important information about members' preferences to the committee, and for helping distribute committee opinions to noncommittee members.

There are three particularly important points of interaction between committee leaders and party leaders. The first involves assignments to

* From Randall B. Ripley, "Congressional Party Leaders and Standing Committees," *Review of Politics,* 1974, pp. 394–409. Copyright © 1974 by *Review of Politics.* Reprinted by permission. The author is grateful to his colleagues, Grace A. Franklin and William B. Moreland, for their aid in the preparation of this paper.

committees. Who sits on a committee may, in many instances, determine what emerges from that committee. As with most facets of congressional life, change has occurred; the relative influence of party leaders has varied considerably through time. At present the leaders of both parties seem disposed to limit their interference to special occasions. The custom of seniority limits leaders' potential impact on committee assignments to sitting members who desire to change assignments or to new members. And in the case of freshman members and new assignments the leaders of both parties are generally disposed to exercise only minimal influence unless vital issues are at stake.[1]

In many ways the most important assignments are, of course, committee chairmen and ranking minority members. After seniority hardened in both the House and Senate as the sole way for members to advance toward these posts, party leaders have had virtually no leverage in making these choices. They have instead been automatic and dependent only on longevity and electoral fortunes.

In changes made in 1971 and 1973, however, the House party leaders have moved into a position to develop some potential for heading movements to prevent individuals from becoming chairmen or ranking minority members if they can persuade a majority of the party that such individuals are undesirable in those positions. In 1971 the Republican Conference agreed to allow the conference to vote by secret ballot and one at a time on the individuals nominated by the Committee on Committees to be ranking minority members. If the Republicans should again become the majority party in the House, the same procedure would presumably apply to chairmanships. No successful challenges to seniority appointments have been made under the new procedure.

In 1971 the Democratic Caucus made a similar change. Committee on Committees' recommendations come to the Caucus one committee at a time and, if 10 members request it, nominations can be debated and voted on—not just for chairmanships but for any position on any committee. If a nomination is rejected then the Committee on Committees will submit another nomination. In 1971 an unsuccessful challenge was mounted against reappointment of the chairman of the Committee on the District of Columbia.

In 1973 the Democrats extended their procedure by making it necessary for chairmen to obtain a majority vote in the caucus. Twenty percent of the members can demand a secret ballot. In 1973 all 21 chairmen (all of whom had advanced to that position by virtue of seniority) were voted on by secret ballot and all won by very large margins.

In short, despite the lack of real change in personnel thus far, both parties in the House have the machinery for rejecting an unacceptable product of the seniority system in the top spot in any standing committee. The Republican Conference members and Democratic Caucus members could, of course, ignore the preferences of the formal party leaders either to retain or reject a chairman or ranking minority member. But it seems likely that members who have come to those positions through seniority will not be deposed if they have the support of the party leaders. And, if the party leaders should ever agree on the necessity of rejecting a nomination for a top position based on seniority, they would probably stand a reasonably good chance of carrying either the Caucus or the Conference with them.

A second major point of interaction between party leaders and the committee system involves the scheduling of floor activity that, of necessity, has implications for the scheduling of committee business. If the party leaders of the majority party have an overall program in mind (and this is particularly likely to be the case if their party also controls the White House), they are going to have some need to spread the program out over a Congress. They cannot afford to have all the important legislation come to the floor of the House in the last two months of a session or, worse yet, the last two months of a Congress. Thus the leaders are going to be consulting with chairmen about major items on the agenda both to get some reading on when reports might be expected and to make some requests either to speed up or, less frequently, slow down committee consideration and action.

Similarly, committee chairmen have their own agenda to consider. Therefore, they will make timing requests of the leaders for floor consideration on specific dates.

A third point of interaction between party leaders and committees involves the substance of legislative proposals. Party leaders may well be too busy with scheduling matters for the floor and working for their passage (or defeat) to have preferences on the substantive details of legislation. They do, however, have general preferences and, particularly if they are working supportively with representatives of the White House or individual Executive Branch departments or agencies, they may have detailed requests on some matters.

In general, leaders in the last few decades have kept their intervention in the substantive work of standing committees to a minimum. They have been much more likely to allow the committee to produce its substantive product by whatever natural processes exist in the committee and then work with the senior members of the committee for the passage (or defeat or amendment) of the committee's handiwork.

A rule adopted in 1973 by the House Democratic Caucus increases the likelihood of more substantive input by the leaders into the work of committees. This rule allows 50 or more members of the party to bring to the Caucus any amendment proposed to a committee-reported bill if the Rules Committee is requesting a closed rule. If the proposed amendment is supported by a majority of the Caucus, then the Rules Committee Democrats will be instructed to write the rule for floor consideration so that specific amendment could be considered on the floor. In effect, this will prevent closed rules on bills if a majority present at a Democratic Caucus opposes such a rule. The leeway for leadership intervention is again present here if the Speaker and/or Majority Leader and/or Majority Whip should decide to side with the members who want to force floor consideration of a specific amendment not favored by the committee (including at least some of the Democrats on the committee).

FACTORS AFFECTING LEADER–COMMITTEE INTERACTIONS

There are at least four principal factors that influence the nature of the relationships between any specific party leaders and any specific committee delegation. These factors include the personalities of the individual actors, the policy stances or ideologies of the actors, the relationship between the partisan nature of the committee and the willingness of the committee to accede to partisan requests made by committee leaders and, finally, the majority or minority party status of the leaders and committees.

First, the personalities of the individuals involved in the relationships are important. Some leaders and senior committee personnel just happen to like one another and get along very well; others are at swords' points on a very personal basis. In any organization such harmonies and disharmonies are inevitable. They are not predictable, but they are important.

Second, the basic policy stances or ideologies of the party leaders and the committee leaders help set the framework for more or less cooperation between the two sets of individuals. These policy stances are, of course, going to vary through time, with individuals, and between committees.

Table 5.8.1 summarizes party loyalty in voting on the floor of the House and Senate for all members of each party, for the chairmen or ranking minority members of each party, and for the floor leader of each party for the period between 1935 and 1970. As can be seen, the party leaders are considerably more loyal in both parties in both houses compared either to all members or to the committee chairmen and ranking minority members as a group. These figures suggest that there will inevitably be some disagreements over policy between party

TABLE 5.8.1 PARTY LOYALTY IN FLOOR VOTING, 1935–1970

GROUP	MEAN PERCENTAGE OF VOTES WITH MAJORITY OF OWN PARTY			
	HOUSE DEMOCRATS	HOUSE REPUBLICANS	SENATE DEMOCRATS	SENATE REPUBLICANS
All party members	82	84	77	80
Chairmen and ranking minority members of standing committees	81	84	74	80
Floor leaders	92	90	89	88

leaders and committee chairmen and ranking minority members. It should also be noted that the gap between leaders on the one hand and all members and committee chairmen and ranking minority members on the other is considerably greater in both houses for the Democrats than for the Republicans. This suggests that Democratic leaders must be more innovative than Republican leaders in finding ways of traversing the ideological distance between themselves and committee leaders in dealing with the various standing committees. This is hardly surprising, given the large group of conservative southerners imbedded in the House and Senate Democratic parties during this period.

The amount of ideological distance to be overcome varies greatly from committee to committee. For example, when the party contingents on the six most important Senate committees between 1947 and 1967 were examined, it was found that conservative Democrats were dominant on Finance, Appropriations, Judiciary, and Armed Services; the Commerce Committee was not consistently under the control of any ideological group; and the liberals (that is, those more in accord with the views of the party leaders on a range of issues) tended to control the Foreign Relations Committee. On the other hand, the Republican contingents on these committees were more balanced and, therefore, closer to the moderately conservative views of the leaders during much of the period. The Finance Committee contingent was regularly controlled by conservatives. Appropriations Committee Republicans were more liberal than most Republicans (and perhaps presented a problem for the leaders). The other four Republican contingents (Armed Services, Commerce, Foreign Relations, and Judiciary) tended to overrepresent neither liberals nor conservatives, thus making them relatively accessible to the leaders, at least in ideological terms. In short, this one example suggests that the Democratic leaders faced an uphill ideological path in at least four out of the six most important Senate Committees during these 20 years, whereas the Republican leaders faced a similar problem in only one case.[2]

Third, the relative degree of partisanship acceptable within various committees is related to the willingness of the committee members to entertain specific partisan requests that may be made by the party leaders. Committees vary a great deal in their partisanship.[3] Some, like House Education and Labor, are unabashedly partisan. Others, like House Ways and Means, exhibit "restrained partisanship," this is, partisan issues are dealt with and final decisions may have a partisan ring but the detailed work of fashioning legislation is handled largely on a nonpartisan basis. Still others, like House Appropriations, are virtually nonpartisan even in terms of final outcomes. The more highly partisan committees are more open to the influence of leaders on substantive matters than the less partisan committees.

Fourth, majority or minority status may make a difference.[4] Majority status, particularly when coupled with control of the White House, means that both the party leaders and the committee leaders have a great deal at stake in what the committees produce because what comes out of the committees is likely to pass on the floor. Minority parties are much less likely to prevail on the floor, particularly if the Presidency is also controlled by the majority party. Therefore, there is less pressure on the leaders of the minority party to seek to influence their standing-committee delegations. They are more likely simply to follow the lead of those delegations on substance and perhaps on other matters as well. The leaders of the majority party, however, are under pressure to seek specific outcomes either because they know they are responsible in some general sense for what Congress produces legislatively or because the White House is stressing to them the necessity for actions of a particular kind.

PATTERNS OF INTERACTION

There are five basic patterns of interaction between party leaders and standing committees. These patterns are characterized by the degree of the leaders' intervention in various aspects of committee functioning, and range along a spectrum from leader activism at one end to committee autonomy at the other end. Table 5.8.2 summarizes the characteristics of the five patterns of interaction.

Specific conditions enhance the emergence of patterns of behavior near the leader-activism end of the interaction spectrum:

1. When the personalities involved (of the party leaders and committee leaders of the same party) are congenial and the party leaders are the more aggressive individuals.
2. When there are relatively few serious policy or ideological disagreements between the party leaders and committee leaders.
3. When committee traditions permit (or even demand) a relatively large degree of partisanship.
4. When the majority party is involved—particularly a new majority that has just come to power in Congress and is full of programmatic zeal.

Other specific conditions can be identified as facilitating the emergence of patterns of behavior near the committee-autonomy end of the spectrum:

1. When there are personal strains between the party leaders and committee leaders and/or when the committee leaders possess the more forceful and aggressive personalities.
2. When a large number of fundamental policy and ideological disagreements divide the party leaders and the committee leaders.
3. When the committees put a high value on nonpartisanship in committee deliberations.
4. When the minority party is involved—particularly a long-standing minority that is accustomed to having only a small percentage of its initiatives pass, at least in recognizable form for which the minority is given credit.

TABLE 5.8.2 PATTERNS OF PARTY LEADER–STANDING COMMITTEE INTERACTION

	DEGREE OF PARTY LEADERS' INTERVENTION IN:		
TYPE OF PATTERN	COMMITTEE ASSIGNMENTS	COMMITTEE SCHEDULING	SUBSTANTIVE QUESTIONS BEFORE THE COMMITTEE
Leader activism	High	High	High
Mixed mode: Personnel and scheduling focus	High	High	Low
Mixed mode: Personnel focus	High	Low	Low
Mixed mode: Scheduling focus	Low	High	Low
Committee autonomy	Low	Low	Low

All of these patterns are drawn from the real world in the sense that they can be illustrated by experience in the House and Senate in the 20th century. Different patterns obviously have prevailed over time. Within a single Congress different patterns may apply to the relations between the leaders and different individual committees. Differences between the two parties are also likely to occur. In general, however, the trend of the last 50 years or so has been toward committee autonomy and against leader activism, but there is nothing inevitable about the continuation of that trend.

THE IMPACT ON THE PATTERNS ON CONGRESSIONAL PERFORMANCE

A logical question now arises: So what? There are different patterns of leader–committee interactions, but why is that important?

The short answer to this question is that the patterns of leader–committee interactions are important because they have differing consequences for the way in which Congress performs its principal functions. And the performance of those functions affects both society and the standing of Congress itself in the governing apparatus.

Congress performs four major functions that collectively determine its impact on society. First, Congress engages in the classic activity of lawmaking—that is, sifting through the myriads of proposals that are introduced and producing roughly 700 to 900 public laws every two years (with, of course, presidential concurrence). This is an activity in which both the formal party leaders and the committees are involved. As indicated, the relative influence of the two groups of individuals (party leaders and committee leaders) can vary significantly. In general it would be accurate to portray the committees' main contribution to lawmaking as consisting of the crafting of specific substantive provisions (often, but not exclusively, in response to an agenda presented by the president or an Executive Branch agency). It would also be accurate to portray the party leaders' main contribution to lawmaking as consisting of managing the products emerging from committee on the floor of the two chambers so as to either facilitate or impede their passage (depending on which set of leaders is involved and their views on any given matter).

Second, Congress is responsible for the oversight of administration—that is, keeping tabs on the implementation of its statutes by bureaucrats. This job is carried out almost entirely by the committees and subcommittees of the House and Senate.

Third, Congress is involved in the education of the public. Every member of Congress can get involved in this information-providing enterprise in interacting with his constituents. Any centralized education stemming from Congress is, however, almost surely going to come from the leaders of one or both parties.

Fourth, Congress performs the function of representation. Congress is representative in many senses and it has many interests it can represent—including those expressed by organized interest groups, but also including interests of constituencies of such territorial units as cities, districts, states or regions, of classes or races, and of the nation as a whole. Most of the specific representative activities are undertaken by individual members, often working within the framework of their committee and subcommittee assignments. The leaders act to represent their own constituents and, at least some of the time, attempt explicitly to represent the "national good."

The patterns of interaction as described are particularly relevant to the lawmaking function but they also have consequences for the performance of the oversight, administration, and representation functions.

The Impact of Leader–Committee Interaction on the Lawmaking Function

There are a number of participants in the legislative process who seek access to critical points in the process in order to maximize their substantive influence. The main participants are the President and individuals in the institutional Presidency, bureaucrats in all parts of the executive branch, interest-group representatives, individual members of Congress, members of specific committees, and the party leaders. The nature of leader–committee interactions affects the relative standing that these participants possess in the lawmaking process.

The President and individuals in the institutional Presidency (principally the White House and the Office of Management and Budget) are dependent in part on their relations with the party leaders for their access to Congress. The leader-activism pattern of leader–committee interaction can serve the President quite well if the leaders of his party are in tune with his policy preferences (as they generally are). Naturally, the President's access can also be limited if the leaders of the party other than his are involved and if they are working against his policy preferences. The President may be particularly severely limited if the opposition party also controls Congress. In the three mixed-mode patterns the President may be afforded access if the leaders use their influence to put individuals in sympathy with presidential legislative objectives on key committees and if his programs are pushed by the leaders as they attempt to help set committee schedules for action. In the committee autonomy pattern, presidential access is probably limited. In this pattern he cannot use the normally close relations with the leaders of his own party to facilitate access to committees but is instead forced to seek direct access. Necessarily, he is likely to have good personal relations with only a few committees. Even top officials in the White House and OMB will only have limited contacts and access if essentially deprived of the good offices of the party leaders.

The access of bureaucrats, interest-group representatives, and committee leaders typically varies. In the leader-activism pattern, constraints are placed on the functioning of *subgovernments* or *whirlpools* that sometimes dominate policymaking in individual subject matter areas.[5] These subgovernments are ordinarily composed of a few key bureaucrats, a few key interest-group representatives, and a few key committee members (typically, subcommittee chairmen and ranking minority members). Critical decisions are made at the subcommittee level and routinely ratified in full committee and on the floor. Thus the few individuals in the subgovernment essentially make policy, particularly on matters that are seemingly routine. The leader-activism pattern does not eliminate the functioning of subgovernments, but it may impinge on it as leaders intervene in some specific policy decisions and use influence over assignment to alter the ideology or policy stance of a committee. The mixed-mode patterns place successively fewer constraints on the functioning of the subgovernments (and the access of the bureaucrats, lobbyists, and key committee members). And the committee-autonomy pattern leaves the subgovernments relatively unfettered, unless a given matter becomes highly visible to a wider public.

The access of the party leaders is, of course, a mirror image of the access of the subgovernment participants. The potential for maximum impact by the leaders on public policy is present in a leader-activism pattern, diminishing potential is present in the three mixed-mode patterns, and very limited potential is present in the committee-autonomy pattern.

The access of individual members of Congress not on a given committee to the work of that committee is relatively low in all five patterns. There are some points of access at the leader-activism end of the spectrum, however. In the leader-activism pattern itself individual members can maximize their impact on the business of committees other than their own through an active party caucus or conference. For example, if the party leaders side with those pushing for the admissibility of an amendment on the floor under the new rule adopted by the House Democrats in 1973, this enhances the potential access of the rank-and-file members. Under the leader-activism pattern and the mixed-mode patterns in which the leaders' impact on committee assignments is high, individual members can, in effect, gain access to committees not their own by persuading the leaders—if they have good relations with them—to help obtain seats for them on the committees in which they are particularly interested. But this is a very limited kind of potential and, given limits on committee memberships, an act that also has costs—an assignment probably has to be surrendered in order to get a different one.

The judgments about relative access that are discussed in the preceding paragraphs are summarized impressionistically in Table 5.8.3. The leader-activism pattern is the only one with even moderate restrictions on the issue-area subgovernments. Those subgovernments may or may not produce "good" or reasonable policy, but, in any event, they cannot be expected to consult more than a narrow range of interests in making their decisions. The access that is opened in the leader-activism pattern to the leaders, the President, and the rank-and-file members of Congress allows for a broader range of interests to be articulated and consulted as the lawmaking function is performed.

Another value in the lawmaking function that can best be served by the leadership-activism pattern is coherence of legislative program. This simply means that some order is apparent in the welter of proposals that are presented to Congress—both in terms of substance and in terms of timing. Necessarily, greater centralization of influence is more likely to result in increased coherence than greater decentralization of influence. The leadership-activism pattern leaves room for an activist President but in no way places Congress in a subordinate position to the President. It simultaneously affords maximum influence for the party leaders and also all members. In addition it puts some restrictions on the influence of the members of the issue-specific subgovernments. If the program is set—both in substance and in timing—by these subgovernments, then little relationship will be seen between programs that are in fact competing for scarce resources. In the leader-activism pattern the centralizing forces can spell out those relationships so that the decisions can be made on the basis of more information rather than less and there is a chance for greater coherence of all legislative results considered together.

TABLE 5.8.3 PATTERNS OF LEADER–COMMITTEE INTERACTIONS AND PARTICIPANTS' POTENTIAL FOR INFLUENCE IN THE LAWMAKING FUNCTION

PARTICIPANT	LEADER ACTIVISM	MIXED MODE: PERSONNEL AND SCHEDULING FOCUS	MIXED MODE: PERSONNEL FOCUS	MIXED MODE: SCHEDULING FOCUS	COMMITTEE AUTONOMY
President and institutional Presidency	High influence	Moderate to high influence	Moderate influence	Moderate to low influence	Low influence
Subgovernments (key committee members, bureaucrats, lobbyists)	Moderate influence	Moderate to high influence	Moderate to high influence	High influence	High influence
Party leaders	High influence	Moderate to high influence	Moderate influence	Moderate to low influence	Low influence
Individual members	Moderate influence	Moderate to low influence	Moderate to low influence	Low influence	Low influence

The Impact of Leader-Committee Interaction on Other Congressional Functions

The leader-activism pattern contributes more to the potential for congressional oversight than the committee-autonomy pattern. Since the latter leaves the subgovernments largely undisturbed to pursue their own rather narrow policy ends and conceptions of policy, oversight much of the time is a moot point. On the other hand, if the subgovernments face some constraints the committee members become more independent of their bureaucratic counterparts and are more willing to ask hard questions of them.

There is the danger, of course, that if activist leaders are simply the handmaidens of the President that they will not themselves encourage vigorous overseeing for fear of embarrassing that President's Administration. Thus, in order for the leader-activism model to promote vigorous overseeing, the leaders, even those of the President's party, also have to be independent of the President, although not necessarily hostile to him and his policies.

The mixed-mode patterns, particularly those in which committee assignments are open to a relatively large degree of leader influence, offer some potential support for vigorous oversight. Focus on scheduling alone is not very likely to help promote oversight.

Effective and meaningful public education by the leaders is most likely to be promoted by the leader-activism pattern of interaction. In this pattern the leaders will, perforce, know more about substance than in the other patterns. Therefore, in their press conferences and other public statements they will be better informed and better able to highlight the most important matters for public attention and consideration.

The broader kinds of representation (less immediately and exclusively constituency-oriented) are promoted by the leader-activism pattern of interaction in that committees have some limits, at least potentially, placed on their natural tendency to respond mainly to constituency interests or the pleas of interest groups. Likewise, since the leaders are better informed about substance than in the other patterns they might well become more effective representatives of some conception of the "national good." This is not to suggest that they will suddenly become omniscient and unerring interpreters of the "national good" but that at least they will think in broader terms more of the time.

This essay began with a number of descriptive points; obviously it has also made a number of judgments. By asserting the virtues of the leader-activism pattern of interaction I hardly mean to claim cure-all qualities for it. Nor do I imply that Congress should somehow move toward a situation of complete party regularity with unimportant standing committees. But it should be noted that if the values promoted by the leader-activism pattern are valued then it is quite feasible for the House and Senate to move toward that end of the spectrum. Such a pattern is fully within the traditions of Congress and has existed at a number of points throughout the history of that body. Neither should it be thought that this pattern simply promotes the interests of the President at the expense of Congress. In fact, in many ways this pattern promotes the possibility of a more genuinely independent stance for Congress *on a range of important issues* than do the other patterns. The committee-autonomy pattern may seem to promote independence—when each issue area is considered separately—but in fact it leaves Congess divided into isolated little units that may, in many instances, simply be subservient to the policy wishes of bureaucrats and interest-group representatives. There is no magic formula for producing a Congress that is both genuinely independent and genuinely influential over a range of policy but the leader-activism pattern, if pursued aggressively, will contribute to those goals.

Some change is, in fact, already apparent. This is especially true in the House, where considerable restlessness over at least some aspects of decentralization is apparent. As already indicated, the Democratic Caucus action on closed rules could represent a modest step toward leader activism. In a more indirect way the House action, restricting closed committee meetings, points in the same direction. In terms of aspiration, the creation of the Democratic Steering and Policy Committee in 1973 also contributes incrementally to the potential for increased influence on the part of the leaders. The Republican Policy Committee in the House has also functioned at times to open up the possibility of a leader-activism pattern of interaction between the leaders of that party and the minority delegations on the committees.[6] The final outcomes of the attempts to revise the budget process in both houses and the committee structure in the House—both still in process in early 1974—may evidence additional movement toward a leader-activism pattern of interaction.

Senators still seem quite content with an extremely decentralized pattern of influence over substantive legislative matters.[7] But, like the House, the Senate has experienced more centralized patterns at different times in its past. Thus it is certainly reasonable to assert that there is nothing immutable about the present situation.

A variety of procedural innovations could support the existence of a leader-activism pattern, but such innovations are not sufficient to create it. What would be needed to create and sustain such a development is will on the part of the party leaders themselves to be aggressive in seeking increased influence within the committees and willingness on the part of a majority of each of the parties to support the leaders in that quest. Such will and willingness cannot be created by machinery and procedures, but the history of Congress has shown that when the will and willingness are present appropriate machinery and procedures can always be invented.

5.9 Partisan Patterns of House Leadership Change, 1789–1977*

Garrison Nelson

Leadership change is an important topic to consider when studying congressional political parties. Nelson demonstrates how each House party is a very different organization in terms of leadership change. His article is a good example of historical based research.

ABSTRACT

This study of 364 leadership selections in the U.S. House from 1789 through 1977 discovered that Democrats have a higher proportion of appointed leaders than Republicans; their leaders move between posts in an ordered succession; their appointed leaders are often "removed

* From "Partisan Patterns of House Leadership Change, 1789–1977," Garrison Nelson, *American Political Science Review* 71 (1977): 918–39.

The author would like to extend his appreciation to Jerome Clubb, Samuel Patterson, James Sundquist, and David Vogler for their thoughtful critiques of earlier incarnations of this manuscript and to W. Ross Brewer, Kathleen Frankovic, Barbara Hinckley, Norman Ornstein, Robert Peabody, and John Wahlke for their helpful comments. An earlier version of this paper was presented to the 70th annual meeting of the American Political Science Association, Chicago, August 29–September 2, 1974.

from above" by their elected ones; and their leaders are subjected to infrequent and unsuccessful caucus challenges. Republicans rely upon election to choose their leaders; their leaders' rate of interpositional mobility is very low; their appointed leaders were never removed by their elected ones; and their leaders face the contests at the same rate as the Democrats do, but the incidence of successful challenges is much greater. They are "removed from below."

Majority versus minority status had little statistically significant impact upon leadership contests and what variation appeared indicated that challenges were more frequent in the majority party where the stakes are higher and the rewards are greater than in the minority. Regardless of electoral consequences, however, Republican leaders are more vulnerable to caucus defeat than Democratic ones, which lends further support to the contention that party identity is more important than party status.

> Of all these Formes of Government, the matter being mortall, so that not onely Monarchs, but also whole Assemblies dy, it is necessary for the conservation of the peace of men, that as there was order taken for an Artificiall Man [the state], so there be order also taken for an Artificiall Eternity of life. . . . This Artificiall Eternity is that which men call the Right of Succession.
>
> THOMAS HOBBES, *LEVIATHAN*

INTRODUCTION

Few of the world's legislative institutions have remained as unchanged over as long a period of time as the U.S. House of Representatives. Unlike the assemblies of France, Germany, and Italy, it has not had to contend with a number of regime changes and functional redefinitions. Unlike the British House of Commons, it has maintained its basic form of representation for almost two centuries. Extending the suffrage to the landless, the blacks, and women has not significantly changed the white, male middle-class character of its membership. The two-party system which exists within it today is very similar to the one which it spawned early in its existence.

The House has enjoyed the luxury of stability and continuity. When the few successful challenges to this continuity have occurred, they have become almost legendary. The "revolt" against Speaker Cannon in 1910–1911 occurred six decades ago, but so little has happened in the House since then, that this incident has taken on grandiose proportions. It has been recounted by congressional analysts in a dozen books and articles.[1] Yet it rates only a paragraph in most of the widely read American history textbooks.

Perhaps the real story of the House is its continuity and not its changes. This may account for the popularity and widespread acceptance of Nelson Polsby's "institutionalization" thesis.[2] The "institutionalized House" which Polsby describes has become much like the "Artificiall Man" of the Hobbes quotation opening this paper. The House now appears to have a life of its own, separated from the parties, committees, and leaders who occupy space within it. The accummulated momentum of almost two centuries has left the House's legislative parties usually more in agreement than disagreement, most of its bipartisan legislative committees with institutional and not partisan loyalties, and a leadership shaped by the House not the shapers of it. The portrait of the House drawn by Polsby, Peabody, Huntington, Hinckley, Jones, Ripley, and others is that of a legislative assembly characterized by internal bureaucratization, electoral insulation, and institutional autonomy marching most often to the regular beat of its own well-worn drum.[3]

The "Artificiall Eternity" which Hobbes bestows upon legislative assemblies manifests itself in the floor leadership succession system of the House. Analysts of congressional leadership have detected signs of institutional routinization in succession patterns which appear to transcend political, partisan, and personality considerations. One attains a post because one occupies the penultimate position which leads to it. Barbara Hinckley's statement addresses this phenomenon directly:

> Although formally elective, the actual selection bears all the marks of a much more automatic

> procedure. Leaders stay in their posts for a number of Congresses. New leaders are recruited from apprenticeship posts. Whip leads to floor leader. Floor leader to Speaker.[4]

Hinckley goes on to suggest that both parties in both houses operate this way in the selection and retention of their leaders. Exceptions have occurred and are duly noted. The thrust of Hinckley's analysis, however, is toward the identification of institutionalized leadership selection norms which seem to triumph over party-related and chamber-related ones.

Hinckley relies upon Robert Peabody's 1967 analysis of leadership change to account for the "violations" of these congressional norms that occur. Peabody contended that change often represents the internal consequences of the external factor of election results: majority or minority status, and the aggregate size of the net gain or loss of seats. As explained by Peabody:

> Strong victories promote good will and generally reflect to the benefit of party leaders. Conversely, defeat results in pessimism, hostility and a search for scapegoats. If the net losses are particularly severe, as many as thirty to fifty seats, then the possibilities of minority leadership change through revolt are greatly enhanced.[5]

Combining the Hinckley and Peabody analyses, two propositions emerge. Since House leadership succession patterns have been institutionalized for both parties, the only violations of these patterns will occur during periods of party frustration. The inference encompasses all of the House changes in the six Democratic Congresses which Peabody observed in his initial study (1955–1966) and all but three of the changes in the 10 postwar Congresses which Hinckley examined (1947–1966). While this proposition may illuminate change in the contemporary House, it is less useful in explaining leadership change in previous Congresses for the simple reason that the present era in the House is very atypical. Democratic dominance of the House in 22 of the 24 Congresses since 1931 has produced an even more persistent era of one-party control than that of the Democratic-Republicans in the first 12 Congresses of the 19th century. Assertions about the impact of majority or minority status on party leadership in the contemporary House may mask genuine differences between the Democrats and Republicans.

Peabody's latest study, *Leadership in Congress,* recognizes the fact that the present-day uniqueness, "makes it impossible to prove or disprove any hypotheses relating leadership change to majority-minority status as over and against party differences, Democrat and Republican. For such interpretations longer range historical refinement will be required."[6]

It is in the spirit of providing the historical dimension that this study was undertaken; for it is my belief that the contemporary quest for both institutional norms of leadership succession and electoral system predictors of leadership change has led to an undervaluation of the impact of political party identity upon the selection of House leaders.

Party factors persist. For years, legislative analysts have contended that party identity is the single best predictor of congressional voting.[7] David Mayhew, for example, has pointed out that the House Democrats have become an "inclusive" party, attentive to the demands of many interests, while the House Republicans have become an "exclusive" party limited to a smaller range of interests.[8] Regarding the recruitment of House members, Joseph Schlesinger has observed that both parties are "office-based" but that the Democrats appear to be recruited in a more "open" system, while the Republican system appears to be more "hierarchic."[9]

Since party members in the House have been recruited differently and seem to vote differently, these differences should also manifest themselves in each party's leadership selection system. In order to test this party-related proposition, the analysis was extended back to the First Congress. In this way, changes over time could be identified and periods could be analyzed in which a number of parties—not just the contemporary Democrats—held majority status.

For this analysis the voting records on the floor during Speakership contests, votes in the various party caucuses, retention rates of House leaders in their positions, and the reasons for the leadership departing were examined. These four sets of data make it possible to discern both party-related and time-related impacts upon the leadership selection process in the House.

HOUSE LEADERS: POSITIONS AND PERIODS

Of all the approaches to leadership identification, the simplest to understand is the "positional" or "formal-leadership" approach which selects as leaders the occupants of key posts.[10] Within the House of Representatives, the most important organizational positions are those of Speaker, floor leader, and Whip. Not all holders of these posts have been prominent members of the House, nor have they even enjoyed the full confidence of the legislative parties which selected them, but there is no question that these offices are crucial, regardless of their occupants. For this reason, any member who held the office of Speaker, floor leader, or party Whip must be categorized as a leader of the House.

POSITIONS

Apart from the Speakership, no leadership position can be consistently defined over the entire course of House history. Different positions during different eras fulfilled the functions of floor leadership. The floor leadership of the majority party was first associated with the appointed chairmanship of the Ways and Means Committee shortly after its creation as a standing committee in 1794.[11] When the Appropriations Committee came into existence in 1865, the floor leadership was often shared by both chairmen. Movement between these two committees was not infrequent and their chairmen and ranking members often served with the Speaker on the Rules Committee during the peak of its influence as a vehicle for the House majority.[12] The most fundamental change in the majority leadership occurred in 1911 when the Democratic caucus asserted its authority and made the post elective.[13] Since then all Majority Leaders have been elected.

Minority leadership prior to 1863 was blurred by the multiplicity of parties in the House and the frequent manifestation of intraparty conflict on the floor during the balloting for Speaker.[14] After 1863 all but one of the 61 Speakership contests were settled on the first ballot, with the minority nominee receiving virtually all of the votes cast by his party.[15] Deciding to use this designation for the Minority Leadership represents a variation on the positional approach for the simple reason that the position did not exist until 1883 and did not receive official recognition until 1911.[16] For practical purposes I am willing to regard the minority's nominee for Speaker as the person to whom they would have entrusted the most important office in the House, hence their Leader.

Party Whips emerged first among the Republicans with Speaker Reed's designation of James A. Tawney in 1897.[17] The Republican leadership held the power of appointment of Whips until 1919, when the caucus took control of the post.[18] In 1921 the Republican Committee on Committees elected the Whip and held this responsibility until 1965 when the Republican membership reasserted its authority and made the post fully elective again.

The position of Democratic Whip had a sporadic history following Oscar Underwood's initial appointment to the post in 1900.[19] Not until 1921 did the post develop clear continuity. It has been an appointive post since its inception. Both the reform-minded 94th and the newly elected 95th Congresses defeated efforts to make the Democratic Whip post elective.[20]

To summarize, the positions and relevant years used to identity the House leadership population are (1) the Speakers of the House (1789–1977); (2) the appointed chairmen of the Ways and Means Committee from its inception in the Fourth Congress to its separation from Speaker selection in the 62nd Congress (1794–1911); (3) the appointed chairmen of the Appropriations Committee from the 39th Congress through the 55th Congress, when only the Ways and Means chairman was designated as Majority Leader (1865–1899), plus one six-year stint when James A. Tawney was its chairman (1905–1911).[21] (4) the caucus-elected Majority Leaders from the 62nd Congress to the present (1911–1977); (5) the minority's nominees for the Speakership (1863–1911); (6) the caucus-elected and *Congressional Director*-designated Minority Leaders (1911–1977); (7) the Republican Whips (1897–1977); and (8) the Democratic Whips (1899–1909, 1913–1915, and 1921–1977).

The positional approach identifies 128 men as holders of leadership posts in the House from 1789 through 1977.[22] These posts have been held by 71 members identified with the Democratic party or its predecessor, the Democratic-Republicans, and by 54 members associated with the major opponents of the Democrats. This latter figure includes six Federalists, five Whigs, one American and 45 Republicans. Three leaders held their positions under different party labels.[23]

In Table 5.9.1, the positions are identified by relevant time frame and the number of selections and occupants for each post are enumerated. The figure of 364 selections constitutes the population of cases examined in this study.

Periods

The House's 189-year history can be divided into three eras based upon the elective-appointive dimension for the leadership posts. The first era, *1789–1863,* contains the Congresses in which only two leadership posts can be readily identified: the elected Speaker and the appointed Chairman of the Ways and Means Committee. The second era, *1863–1911,* be-

Table 5.9.1 House Leadership Positions and Selection Methods: Number of Selections and Occupants by Party, 1789–1977

	Number of					
	Selections			Occupants		
	Dem.	Non-Dem.	N	Dem.	Non-Dem.	N
Elective Posts:						
Speaker of the House, 1789–1977	66	36	102	28	20	46*
Minority Leader, 1863–1977	25	36	61	17	10	27
Majority Leader, 1911–1977	28	8	36	11	4	15
Republican Whip, 1919, 1965–1977	0	8	8	0	3	3
Semi-elective post:						
Republican Whip, 1921–1965	—	23	23	—	5	5
Appointive Post:						
Chairman, Ways & Means, 1795–1911	36	27	63	23	16	38*
Chairman, Appropriations, 1865–1899, 1905–1911	9	13	22	4	7	11
Republican Whip, 1897–1919	—	11	11	—	5	5
Democratic Whip, 1900–1908, 1913, 1921–1977	38	—	38	16	—	16
Totals:						
Elective posts	119	88	207	56	37	91*
Semi-elective posts	0	23	23	0	5	5
Appointive posts	83	51	134	43	28	70*
Total	202	162	364	99	70	166*†

* Two speakers (Muhlenberg and Taylor) and one chairman of Ways and Means (McLane) held their posts during changes in party control.

† Also, two Republican Whips (Knutson and Arends) were selected by two differing methods. This further reduces the number of post occupants to 164.

gins with the 38th Congress, where an organized minority floor vote for Speaker can be detected. This era also includes the addition of the Appropriations Committee chairman as majority co-floor leader and the initial appearances of appointed party Whips. It ends in 1911 with the first election of a majority floor leader by the caucus. The present era, *1911–1977,* is marked by an increase in the number of House party floor leaders directly elected by the membership.

Reducing the House's history to three time periods makes it more manageable but it does reduce the number of temporal observation points. Consequently, time-related changes can only be noted in broad outline and not as a steady progression towards some ultimate destination.

CONTINUITY AND CHANGE IN LEADERSHIP POSITION-HOLDING

In examining leadership change and continuity, one must differentiate between changes in leadership post and changes in leadership rank. The distinction is important because a leader may change his post, but not his rank. For example, leaving the Speakership to become Minority Leader represents a change of institutional posts, but a continuity in party rank. Similarly, a leader may maintain his post but change ranks (e.g., a leader who remained in the post of Whip when his party gained control of the House would be "moved" from the second-ranking post to the third-ranking one).

This particular distinction has increased in importance because of the high degree of interpositional mobility which has occurred since 1863. During the first period, only three leaders (6 percent) moved between posts. Following 1863, mobility has increased with 28 of the 82 leaders (34 percent) having held at least two posts. The reason for this increase is that three more leadership posts were added as the minority became more recognizable and the Whip system was formalized.

Both parties have moved leaders between positions in the last two eras. Since 1863, 17 of the 44 Democratic leaders (39 percent) and 11 of the 38 Republican leaders (29 percent) held more than one post. One major difference occurs in recent years. The rate of interpositional mobility among Democratic leaders since 1931 is 50 percent (9/18), while the Republican figure in the same era is only 22 percent (2/9). There are two reasons for this party differential. First, the Democrats have become a semipermanent majority since 1931 and they have had continually one more leadership post to disburse at the opening of each Congress—namely, the Speakership. Second, the emergence of the "leadership ladder"—the Whip to Leader to Speaker succession—has made holding the upper-level offices contingent upon holding the lower ones.

Interpositional mobility as manifested in the "leadership ladder" is deceptive as a guide to House leadership change. The first post in the sequence, that of Whip, is a much more integral part of the House Democratic leadership structure than it is of the Republican one. Four Democratic Majority Leaders began their ascents as party Whips: Oscar Underwood, Carl Albert, Hale Boggs, and Thomas P. O'Neill. In the cases of the latter three, their service as Whip was a crucial element in their elections for the higher post.[24] Also, the Democrats have used the whip position as their second-ranking post in the last two Congresses in which they served in the minority. Sam Rayburn placed ex-Majority Leader John McCormack in that slot when he assumed the Minority Leadership in both 1947 and 1953.[25] This is not true of the Republicans. Only the first Republican Whip, Tawney, moved into either of the two top leadership positions and that occurred when the floor leadership was also an appointive post. No Republican Whip has been displaced by the former Majority Leader when the party lost control of the House.

The two parties have treated the position differently. For the House Democrats, the position of Whip has become a "penultimate" one, a step away from Majority Leader; but for the Republicans, it is a "career office," to be surrendered only upon departure from the House.[26]

Eight of the 10 Republican Whips had no House career following their last term in that post, and one other served less than six months after relinquishing it. Leslie Arends of Illinois, who held the post from 1943 through 1974, is the latest to follow in that pattern.

This difference between the parties has been overlooked by some House analysts and has led them to conclude that the Republicans are violating a House "norm" when their Whip retains his post regardless of the majority or minority status of the party.[27] Unlike the Democratic Whip, the Republican Whip is not part of the rank structure.

One curious feature of this party differential is that it appears to contradict some of the assumptions of Joseph Schlesinger's "ambition theory." Republican Whips with constituencies almost congruent (and identical since 1965) with the floor leaders should be expected to move up when the floor leadership falls vacant; and the Democratic Whips, the appointees of the incumbent leadership, should be expected to return to the ranks of the ordinary members once their patrons had left their positions of influence. This has not occurred. For this reason it is important to maintain the party variable in discussions of "ambition theory" as well as "institutionalization."

The leadership contests of 1976 reaffirmed in part the continued reliance of the Democrats upon the "leadership ladder" to control the succession process and limit internecine warfare among the members. Majority Leader O'Neill was nominated for Speaker without a dissenting vote and Majority Whip John McFall felt obliged to move up as well.[28] McFall's failure to gain the floor leadership is an indication that the Democratic membership's tolerance for automatic elevations had declined. It is important to note, however, that McFall was O'Neill's personal choice to succeed him in the post and had McFall not been so badly tarnished by the "Korean payoff" scandal, then the "ladder" may have made him the fourth consecutive Democratic Whip to become Majority Leader. O'Neill seems to recognize that the heterogeneity of the party's membership would spawn a number of bitter leadership contests if the succession were less tightly controlled. While he may have been unable to help McFall, the Speaker was able to defeat the man he least wanted in the position, Rep. Philip Burton, and also to retain the power of appointment over the party Whip.

The Republicans, with their more homogeneous composition seem to have no need for a routinized succession system. Leadership changes in that party, particularly in more recent years, appear to have more to do with style than substance.[29]

LEADERSHIP SELECTIONS

All of the 364 selections since 1789 have been classified. Operationally, leadership continuity in any given Congress occurs when the leader remains in the same post as in the previous Congress. Change, therefore, occurs when a leader vacates his post.

Defined in this manner, change and continuity appear to occur at an identical rate. Of the 364 selections, 177 represented post continuations, while 181 represented post changes. There were six cases which involved the first selections in new posts. Focusing solely upon the 358 selections which involved post continuations or post changes, Table 5.9.2 presents the number of instances which occurred in each party by period.

The least surprising aspect of Table 5.9.2 is the steady increase in the proportions of post continuations relative to changes over the three periods. One reason for the increase is the stabilization of the leadership posts. A second reason relates to institutionalization; as more leaders choose to remain in the House, they receive more selections, as may be seen in Table 5.9.3.

The only period in which the Democratic leadership received more selections and experienced fewer post changes than their opponents was in the first one. This was due largely to the fact that the Democrats (and Democratic-Re-

TABLE 5.9.2 POST CONTINUATIONS AND CHANGES BY PARTY AND PERIOD

	CONTINUATION		CHANGE		TOTALS	
ERA AND PARTY	N	PERCENT	N	PERCENT	N	PERCENT
1789–1863						
Democratic	20	36.4	35	63.6	55	100.0
Opponents	4	17.4	19	82.6	23	100.0
	24	30.8	54	69.2	78	100.0
χ^2 = 2.7398, Insignificant; *gamma* = +.462						
1863–1911						
Democratic	16	34.8	30	65.2	46	100.0
Republican	31	52.5	28	47.5	59	100.0
	47	44.8	58	55.2	105	100.0
χ^2 = 3.3109, Insignificant; *gamma* = −.350						
1911–1977						
Democratic	53	54.6	44	45.4	97	100.0
Republican	53	67.9	25	32.1	78	100.0
	106	60.6	69	39.4	175	100.0
χ^2 = 3.2021, Insignificant; *gamma* = −.275						
1789–1977						
Democratic	89	44.9	109	55.1	198	100.0
Opponents	88	55.0	72	45.0	160	100.0
	177	49.4	181	50.6	358	100.0
χ^2 = 3.5809, Insignificant; *gamma* = −.199						

TABLE 5.9.3 PARTY DIFFERENCES IN MEAN SELECTION FREQUENCIES

	DEMOCRATIC		NON–DEMOCRATIC		DEM. OPP.	ALL LEADERS	
PERIODS	MEAN	N	MEAN	N	DIFFERENCES	MEAN	N
I, 1789–1863	1.87	30	1.15	20	+.72	1.68	47
II, 1863–1911	2.18	22	3.05	20	−.87	2.59	42
III, 1911–1977	4.08	24	4.11	19	−.03	4.09	43
Totals	2.73	74*	2.84	57*	−.11	2.87	128*

* Adjusted for period overlapping and party switching.

publicans) organized 26 of the period's 37 Congresses and held this control for lengthy spans of time.

The House Democrats had more leadership changes than the Republicans did in both the second period (in which they organized only eight of the 24 Congresses) and the third period (in which they organized 26 of 34). Despite the consistency of the interparty differences in Table 5.9.2, the reasons for the higher rates of Democratic change vary. In the second period, the major problem was the inability of the Democrats to organize themselves effectively as waves of new southern congressmen rejoined their ranks. As a result, 10 of the 16 caucus nominations for the Democratic Speakership candidate were contested in the years between 1871 and 1899.[30] Only four Republican caucuses in the same period showed dissension.[31] Not until 1899 under the successive leadership stints of James Richardson, John Sharp Williams, and Champ Clark did the Democrats manifest any significant degree of leadership continuity.

Period III's interparty difference indicates more post changes for the Democrats, but with a higher number of selections per leader. The "leadership ladder" accounts for this anomaly as Democratic leaders move between posts but not out of the leadership. Republicans in this era appear to be more conscious of post continuity and leave their leaders in place until either the leader's career ends or the caucus arises and removes him from office.

This variety in reasons for leadership change needs more refinement. In the next section, types of leadership change will be examined for each period.

TYPES OF LEADERSHIP CHANGE

In the most thorough study of leadership in the contemporary Congress, Robert Peabody identified three forms of change in the House: interparty turnover, intraparty change, and institutional reform.[32] The last appears in the redefinition of leadership posts, such as a change from an appointive to an elective Majority Leader or the emergence of a new post among the leadership hierarchy. Comparatively speaking, institutional reform has not been an important agent of leadership change. Interparty and intraparty factors have had a far greater impact upon the identity of the House leadership.

Peabody's identification of change agents allows for but does not deal with the disappearance of leaders because of resignation, death, or electoral defeat. So few leaders have resigned from either the leadership or the House itself in recent times that this factor may not seem relevant to analysts of the contemporary Congress. Similarly, recent House leaders, like the vast majority of the members, have become so immune from the vicissitudes of the American electorate that it is difficult to believe that leadership careers have ended because the leader failed to obtain renomination or reelection in his own district. As presently interpreted by students on Congress, the electorate's impact upon the House leaders is indirect. Party failure at the polls presumably angers the House caucus which thereupon garrots its leaders.

In Table 5.9.4, the various reasons for changes in House posts are catalogued by period. This table includes Peabody's three types of leadership change and adds another category which I call "career-related changes."

CAREER-RELATED CHANGES

Included in this category are events which affect the leader's own career regardless of what happens to his party at the polls or to his position within it. This category has two subdivisions: personal and political. Personal career-related events which affect change include retirement from the House, death in office, or resignation from a leadership post. Retirement refers to a leader's leaving the House and not directly occupying another political office. A number of the retirees in early periods returned to public life after an absence of a year or more. Retirees in this present era are often too old to do much more than contemplate their past achievements. This age factor is reflected in the sizeable number of deaths among House leaders in this century. For example, between 1789 and 1931, only one of 36 Speakers died in office, but since then, five of the last nine Speakers to leave the office died holding the chair.

Comparing the two career-related subdivisions in the present period with the two previous ones indicates that personal factors now outweigh political ones in causing leadership change. Thus, Period III's retirements and deaths easily outnumber leadership departures arising from electoral defeats. Only two of Period III's 43 leaders were defeated in reelection bids: Champ Clark in 1920 and Carl Bachmann in 1932. Prior to 1911, reelection defeats ended 18 leadership careers. The party identity of the leader had no bearing on the rates of reelection defeat; all parties suffered equally.

Leaving the House in quest of other political offices was a very common occurrence in the first period, but less so in the later ones. Most

TABLE 5.9.4 REASONS FOR HOUSE LEADERSHIP CHANGES BY PERIOD

	1789–1863			1863–1911			1911–1977			1789–1977		
TYPES OF CHANGES	DEM.	OPP.	TOTAL	DEM.	REP.	TOTAL	DEM.	REP.	TOTAL	DEM.	OPP.	TOTAL
Career-related changes	51%	42%	48%	40%	57%	48%	36%	52%	42%	42%	51%	46%
Personal	14%	0%	9%	10%	14%	12%	25%	32%	28%	17%	17%	17%
Retired from House	14	0	9	3	7	5	7	16	10	8	8	8
Died in office	0	0	0	3	7	5	18	8	15	8	6	7
Resigned post	0	0	0	3	0	2	0	8	3	1	3	2
Political	37%	42%	39%	30%	43%	36%	11%	20%	14%	25%	35%	29%
Not reelected	11	16	13	20	18	19	2	4	3	10	12	11
Elected: Other office	11	11	11	20	18	14	7	4	6	9	11	10
Appointed: Other office	11	11	11	0	4	2	0	4	1	4	6	4
Defeated: Other office	3	5	4	0	4	2	2	8	4	2	6	3
Interparty turnover	17%	47%	28%	27%	29%	28%	32%	24%	29%	26%	32%	28%
Loses elective post	6	32	15	0	0	0	2	8	4	3	11	6
Loses appointive post	11	16	13	17	11	14	5	0	3	10	8	9
Keeps rank; new post	0	0	0	10	18	14	25	16	22	13	21	13
Intraparty change	31%	11%	24%	30%	11%	21%	30%	24%	28%	30%	15%	24%
Changes post and rank	6	0	4	3	11	7	23	4	16	12	6	9
Defeated on floor	6	0	4	0	0	0	0	0	0	2	0	1
Defeated in caucus	0	0	0	3	0	2	0	16	6	1	6	3
Replaced as elected leader	3	5	4	10	0	5	0	4	1	4	3	3
Replaced as appointed leader	17	5	13	13	0	7	7	0	4	12	1	8
Institutional reform	0%	0%	0%	3%	4%	3%	2%	0%	1%	2%	1%	2%
Post eliminated	0	0	0	3	4	3	2	0	1	2	1	2
Totals												
Percentages	99%	100%	100%	100%	101%	100%	100%	100%	100%	100%	99%	100%
Number of cases	35	19	54	30	28	58	44	25	69	109	72	181

often it was the lure of the Senate which took leaders out of the House. Seventeen of the 24 leaders who left the House for other elective offices contested for Senate seats. Thirteen were successful. The last one was John Sparkman of Alabama who relinquished the whip post in 1947. Two were elected governor (two were defeated), two were elected Vice President (Colfax in 1868 and Garner in 1932), and one, James A. Garfield, left the House to become President. Two leaders became Secretary of State (Henry Clay and Elihu Washburne). Since 1869, only one leader has left the House directly for an appointive post: Gerald Ford in October 1973.

Polsby's contention that the House has developed ''boundaries'' from the other branches and levels of government is supported by the decline in the number and proportion of House leadership changes due to career-related political events.[33] The leadership appears insulated from both their constituents and from whatever ''progressive ambitions'' they may have once had.

Interparty Turnover

This has been a constant factor in House leadership change. The mean deviation from the 29 percent recorded for all three eras is a meager 1 percent. However, the number of leaders who lose their party ranks during changes in party control of the House has dwindled greatly, from 28 percent in the 1789–1863 era to 7 percent in the post-1911 one. There are two major reasons for this change. First, the inability of the opponents of the Democrats to maintain control of the House during Period I insured a high turnover of their elective and appointive leaders as a result of election defeats. The second reason involves the development of a coherent minority following 1863. Leaders whose parties had lost control of the House now had a place to relocate their influence. In the present era, only two elected floor leaders (Kitchin in 1919 and Halleck in 1949 and 1955) lost their posts when loss of House control resulted in a constriction of the number of leadership positions available to their parties. The two appointed leaders in this era to lost their posts because of interparty turnover were Sereno Payne in 1911 and J. Percy Priest in 1953. Priest was removed from the whip post by Minority Leader Rayburn to make room for ex-Majority Leader McCormack. This move preserved McCormack's second-place ranking. One advantage of having appointed whips is that they cannot loudly protest such moves.

Institutional Reform

Concentrating the Majority Leadership in Ways and Means, Chairman Sereno Payne in 1899 eliminated Joe Cannon and the Appropriations Committee from the leadership for a short time. The other two instances involved the Democratic Whip post which disappeared as a leadership position in 1909 and 1913. Since both disappearances of this post were accompanied by changes in the elective leadership of the Democratic party, it would not be unreasonable to consider these to be intraparty changes.

Intraparty Changes

Of the various types of leadership change, none is more fascinating than intraparty change when a leader remains in the House and is moved within or removed from the hierarchy by the members of his own party. Often filled with intrigue and interpersonal machinations, these intraparty changes provide insight into the factions which exist within legislative parties. Changes within this context have shaped much of the writing about the House.

This category has five different manifestations: (1) interpositional mobility when a leader holding one post moves to another within the hierarchy; (2) defeat on the floor for the Speakership when disaffected members of the leader's own party join with the opposition to deny a reelection; (3) a defeat in the caucus for any of the party's elective leaders; (4) replacement of an elective leader as a nominee without a formal denial of support; and (5) demotion to the ranks of the ordinary members of an appointed leader by an elected one. To these might be added the elimination by one leader of a post held by another, such as happened twice to Democratic Whips.

Of the 43 intraparty changes in these top posts, 17 were interpositional moves. The six pre-1911 changes included the moving of three Democratic appointed leaders into the Speakership and of three Republican appointed leaders into other appointive posts.

The 11 interpositional cases in the present era involved one move by a Republican and 10 by Democrats. The lone Republican to move was Majority Leader Nicholas Longworth who became Speaker in 1925. His succession was bitterly contested in the caucus, but he won on the first ballot with 62 percent of the votes.[34] John Rhodes' uncontested elevation to the Minority leadership in 1973 from the chairmanships of the Republican Policy Committee may portend a new development in the Republican patterns of leadership succession.[35] From the historical standpoint of this study, however, the chairmanship of the Republican Policy Committee and Conference as well as their counterparts in the Democratic Caucus and Steering Committees have not been clearly identified as leadership posts for a sufficient length of time to warrant their inclusion here.[36] At some future time they may well qualify for this category.

Interpositional mobility in the highest posts generally meets with less opposition in Democratic caucuses. Only four of these moves were greeted with caucus opposition. Henry Rainey captured 60 percent of the vote in his successful move from the floor leadership to the chair in 1933,[37] and in 1971 Carl Albert received 92 percent of the vote in his identical move.[38] The most serious challenge to an interpositional move was that faced by Hale Boggs in his successful contest to move from Whip to floor leader in 1971. He won 57 percent of the votes on the second ballot.[39] Although challenges were hurled at Byrns's 1934 succession to the speakership,[40] and Albert's and O'Neill's successions to the floor leadership in 1962 and 1973, respectively, they were withdrawn before the caucus vote. Four Democratic interpositional moves between the floor leadership and the chair were uncontested and unchallenged: Bankhead in 1936, Rayburn in 1940, McCormack in 1962, and O'Neill in 1976. The ''leadership ladder'' as it pertains to the floor leader–Speaker rung has enormous legitimacy in the Democratic caucus.

John McFall's fourth place showing in the 1976 floor leadership contest indicates that the Whip–floor leader rung has less legitimacy. McFall's Korean troubles aside, a countertrend has emerged among a segment of the Democratic membership which opposes the ladder concept. If caucus opposition to the ''ladder'' continues to grow, it is quite possible that interpositional mobility may decline as a major form of intraparty change.

VOTED FLOOR DEFEATS

The most dramatic cases of intraparty leadership change occur when the sitting Speaker of the incumbent party is defeated in an open floor fight. Both cases occurred in the first period.[41] Since 1835 only Speaker Frederick Gillett faced defeat on the floor from fellow Republicans. It took nine ballots in 1923 to overcome this challenge.[42]

Intraparty floor contests for the Speakership disappeared with the institutionalization of party caucuses for both majorities and minorities following the Civil War.[43] Conflict was moved from the floor into the confines of the caucus room. Here conflict could be contained and a party which had arrived in Washington with a majority of the seats would not have to face the prospect of seeing its victory snatched away by renegades on the floor.

VOTED CAUCUS DEFEATS

Newspaper accounts of party caucuses from 1863 to 1977 revealed that the 60 Republican caucuses held 77 elections for these major posts, of which 16 (21 percent) were contested.[44] The Democrats in the same period held 61 caucuses with 91 elections. Twenty were contested (22 percent).

Only one Democratic floor leader was defeated in the caucus: Samuel Randall, the minority nominee in the 47th Congress, was defeated on the first ballot by John Carlisle in his bid to become Speaker of the 48th Congress in 1883.[45] As a conciliatory gesture, Carlisle appointed Randall to chair the Appropriations Committee. Ironically, it was this Congress that Woodrow Wilson used to illustrate his observation that "all [House chairmen] are subordinate to the Chairman on Appropriations."[46] So even the lone case of direct removal of a Democratic leader by the caucus had little discernible impact upon the party's power relationships.

Since then the only challenges to incumbent Democratic floor leaders occurred in 1969 and 1973. Speaker McCormack beat back Morris Udall's frontal assault 178 to 58 in the 91st Congress[47] and Speaker Albert thwarted a challenge from John Conyers and the Black Caucus in the 93d.[48]

Leadership challenges in the Republican caucuses are more successful. In 1919 Minority Leader Mann's bid for the Speakership was stopped by Frederick Gillett who received twice as many votes from his fellow partisans (138–69).[49] Twelve years later following another change in House party control, John Q. Tilson, who had been elected three times to be the party's Majority Leader, had his floor leadership endorsement revoked by the caucus when the party organized itself as a minority rather than as the majority which it had anticipated earlier. Eight ballots transpired before Bertrand Snell of New York was victorious.[50]

The two best-known recent cases of leadership change in the Republican caucus were the defeats of Joe Martin by Charles Halleck in 1959 and of Halleck by Gerald Ford in 1965.[51] Both contests were close, but both were decided early: two ballots in 1959 and one in 1965.

Nonvoted Removals

Similar to defeat in the caucus is removal as the nominee in the subsequent Congress. The leader is back in the House, but his party has nominated someone else to lead it without a formal vote on the floor or in a party caucus. A case in point is the replacement of Speaker Nathaniel Macon by Joseph Varnum, a fellow Democratic-Republican, in 1807. Macon had fallen out with President Jefferson over Macon's continuance of John Randolph as Chairman of the Ways and Means Committee during his three terms as Speaker. Students of the period suggest that Macon stayed away from the balloting on the opening day of the 10th Congress to avoid an outright rebuff on the floor.[52] A less clear example of this bypassing occurred in 1791 when Speaker Frederick Muhlenberg was not in contention to succeed himself.[53] However, he was elected in the subsequent Congress to preside over the first Democratic-Republican majority. The other three cases involve Democratic minority nominees who were not renominated by the party caucus in the following Congress (Marshall in 1869, Kerr in 1871, and Wood in 1875). Wood wanted to be renominated, but he withdrew when he saw that his strength in the caucus was slim.[54] Kerr handled credentials contests in the 1871 caucus, but his name was never offered for a formal vote.[55] Marshall's leadership career disappeared without a trace.

The lone post-1911 case of an elected leader being replaced without a vote involved a Republican leader, Harold Knutson. He had been elected Whip in 1919 by the caucus and in 1921 by the Committee on Committees, but he had broken with the leadership and voted for the insurgent Speakership candidate in the 1923 floor fight.[56] Needless to say, he was replaced as an elected leader. Including this nonvoted defeat with the voted ones of Mann, Tilson, Martin, and Halleck brings to five the number of "removals from below" of leaders by members of the Republican caucus in the 1911–1977 era. No such removals occurred in the Democratic caucus.

DEMOTIONS

Demotion of appointed leaders represents "removal from above." In these cases, the top-ranking party leader simply replaces an appointive leader. There generally is little fanfare surrounding these post departures because the power to hire (i.e., appoint) carries with it the inherent power to fire. The first demotion occurred in 1800 when Federalist Speaker Theodore Sedgwick removed Robert Goodlow Harper from the Ways and Means chairmanship. Harper had been initially appointed by Speaker Dayton and had been continued by Sedgwick, but before the end of the session, Sedgwick concluded that he was a man "whom no one can control," and removed him.[57] This is the only case of a non-Democratic leader being demoted.

In the 1789–1863 era, Democratic Speakers demoted six chairmen of Ways and Means.[58] In the next era, 1863–1911, four Democratic appointed leaders were removed by elected ones.[59]

The pattern of Democratic demotion has continued into this present period. Speaker Rainey demoted John McDuffie from the Whip post after the latter had failed in his bid to defeat Rainey for the Speakership nomination in 1933.[60] Two years later, Speaker Byrns removed Rainey's Whip, Arthur Greenwood, and replaced him with Patrick Boland of Pennsylvania. Boland held his office during two Speakership changes, Bankhead's succession in 1936 and Rayburn's in 1940. He was the last Democratic Whip to remain in his post when the elected leaders above him changed.

If one includes the cases of the two Democratic Whips whose posts disappeared in 1909 and 1913, and of J. Percy Priest who was not reappointed Whip by Speaker Rayburn when the Democrats regained control of the House in 1955,[61] as well as O'Neill's nonreappointment of John McFall, then there is a total of 16 demotions of appointed Democratic leaders by the party's elected leaders.

Clearly, this is a power which Republican leaders do not possess. The independently elected Republican Whips may lack opportunities to gain the top slot, but they have been protected from those "above" them. A ready example of this appeared in 1965 when Gerald Ford, then a newly elected Minority Leader, backed Peter Frelinghuysen as his candidate for Whip against Leslie Arends, who had held the post for 22 years. Frelinghuysen was soundly defeated in the caucus, and Minority Leader Ford quickly became aware of the limits of power in the Republican leadership.[62]

Even when the elected Republican leaders had appointive posts under their control (1859–1917) they were reluctant to exercise their authority. None of the 18 appointed Republican floor leaders was removed. This reluctance extended to other appointed officials as well. In the years from 1881 through 1911, the Republican Speakers "violated" seniority in chairmanship selections much less often than the Democratic Speakers did (43 percent to 60 percent).[63] Greater unity and organization combined to minimize the number of rolling heads following each change in the elected officers of the Republican party.

SUMMARY

The patterns of leadership change and continuity reveal little variation over time in the proportions of House leaders leaving their posts under the three broad categories of: career-related departures, interparty turnovers, and intraparty changes. Within these categories, however, there are important trends toward institutionalization as personal career-related departures have increased and politically related departures have decreased. The House leadership career is now an entity unto itself and has declined as a springboard to other offices. In addition, House leaders have more to fear from illness and old age than they do from their constituents. The ratio of electoral defeats to deaths in the pre-1911 periods was 6:1, but the ratio has been reversed since then with a 1:5 relationship between defeats and deaths.

Post continuations in the years since 1911 outnumber post changes for both parties, another indication of institutionalization. Also the development of the Minority Leadership and Whip positions has made it possible for leaders to retain their party ranks regardless of their party's success (or lack of it) at the polls. This has led to greater professionalization within these posts.

As important as the time-related institutionalizing trends may be, there appear to be more important interparty differences in the patterns of leadership change and continuity. Three of these relate directly to intraparty change. Democratic leaders change posts more frequently and do so with little opposition from the caucus. Republican leaders change posts infrequently and the only interpositional move by a Republican in this century was met with caucus opposition. Democratic leaders face infrequent and impotent opposition in their caucuses, while Republicans face similarly infrequent, but highly potent opposition in theirs. And finally, because Democratic leaders retain the power to appoint leaders under them, they can also remove them with relative impunity. Elected Republican leaders did not remove appointive leaders when they possessed the authority to do so and now they possess neither the power of appointment nor the power of removal. They must content themselves with whomever the caucus chooses to assist them in the leadership.

The House parties do differ in their patterns of intraparty leadership change. Combining their separate patterns to generate a picture of House "norms" in the furtherance of the institutionalization thesis may lead to valuable conclusions but it may also lead one to overlook party differences.

Establishing these important party differences indicates that institutionalization theories should maintain the party variable in future explorations of leadership change, but it does not bear on the important contemporary statement regarding the impact of majority or minority statuses upon leadership change. In the next section of this paper, these variables will be directly examined.

THE IMPACT OF MAJORITY AND MINORITY STATUSES UPON LEADERSHIP CONTESTS

In focusing wholly upon majority versus minority statuses, it becomes necessary to confine the analysis to the later two periods. No discernible minority exists before 1863, and since 13 of the 40 reported Speakership contests went beyond a single ballot, it is also hard to discern a majority. In many of the Speakership contests in that era the major opponent to the eventual victor was a fellow member of his own party. Consequently, the terms *majority* and *minority* do not have as much meaning as they do in the two most recent ones.

The literature on leadership change suggests that there should be greater turnover among Minority Leaders because the frustration of losing often takes the form of "scapegoating" the leadership.[64] Regardless of the leaders' inability to affect the outcome of congressional elections throughout the nation, it is presumed in the literature that the leaders must face the consequences of an electorate dissatisfied with the party's House candidates. This contention is examined in Table 5.9.5 for Periods II and III.

Note that the mean frequencies in Table 5.9.5 are generally lower by period than those in Table 5.9.3, which dealt with frequencies by party. The reason is that Majority or Minority Leadership is not the mutually exclusive phenemonon which party leadership has been since 1827. Eighteen of the 82 post-1863 leaders (22 percent) served their parties under both conditions.

The general expectation that leadership selection frequencies would be lower for minorities than for majorities is borne out, but the sizes of the differences are similar to those presented in the interparty comparisons. The lack of mutual exclusivity is one reason, but not the sole reason for this similarity.

The greatest difference in this table appears among the leaders during Period II. A closer examination of this difference reveals an important party factor. None of the 10 Democratic minority nominees from 1863 through 1901 was renominated. This contrasts directly with the nine minority nominations made by the Republican party in this same span. The Republican minority caucuses nominated Reed four times and Garfield three times. The other two Republican nominees, Blaine and Keifer, left the House after their single selections in the minor-

TABLE 5.9.5 MAJORITY–MINORITY DIFFERENCES IN MEAN SELECTION FREQUENCIES

	MAJORITY		MINORITY		MAJ.–MIN.	ALL LEADERS	
PERIODS	MEAN	N	MEAN	N	DIFFERENCES	MEAN	N
II, 1863–1911	2.44	32	1.63	19	+81	2.59	42
III, 1911–1977	3.45	31	3.29	21	+.16	4.09	43
Totals	22.98	62*	2.56	39*	+.42	3.48	82*

* Adjusted for overlapping periods.

ity. This strengthens the assertion that the Republican party had an effective House organization before the post-Civil War Democrats did. Even when they were in the minority, the Republicans had a clearer sense of which of their members they wished to nominate as Speaker. Only two of their nine minority nominations for Speaker in Period II were contested in the caucus.[65] Once again a party contrast emerges. The Democrats had caucus contests for four of their seven minority nominations from 1871 through 1901, one of which took six ballots to decide.[66]

Focusing only upon the elective leaders reveals a sizeable difference in Period II's majorities and minorities (2.50 − 1.53 = +0.97), but an inconsequential one between Period III's elective leaders (3.68 − 3.86 = + 0.18). The lack of any meaningful difference in this category represents a serious challenge to much of the contemporary wisdom concerning the impact of party status upon leadership change. It is possible, however, that the use of averages to examine this proposition may be insufficient.

A more direct test of the minority frustration hypothesis would be to examine only the leadership selections voted on by the membership and to see if caucus dissension appears more often among minorities than among majorities. The first step in this test involves eliminating 95 appointive and 23 semielective selections from the total of 285 recorded in the two later periods. This leaves 167 leadership selections made by the party membership. To this may be added the second Majority Leadership election in the 1919 Republican caucus.[67] Ninety-one of these elections involved Democrats, and 77 involved Republicans; 100 occurred when a party was in the majority and 68 when the party was not. This set of data seems sufficiently large to test the impact of party status upon the House leadership.

The dependent variable to be used in this analysis will be the frequency of caucus contests as reported in contemporaneous newspaper accounts. The newspapers report contests in 36 of the 168 elections (21 percent). Often the news account the following day makes no mention of either a contest or a nomination by acclamation. Since every contest referred to in the House literature may be found in the news accounts plus a number which have eluded previous analysis, I am willing to assume that the absence of a reported contest means that none occurred. The precaucus barrage of news stories surrounding genuine contests makes it seem unlikely that an account would overlook any manifestation of conflict.

In three cases, selections were made without caucuses. Two occurred at the opening of the 40th Congress, which convened a day after the 39th adjourned. Each party rallied around a candidate, and the two men received every vote cast in the House for Speaker between them.[68] The other case occurred in 1863 when the Democrats held a caucus, but made no nominations because of their internal divisions over the Civil War. Samuel Cox, the leading Democrat in the Speakership balloting on the floor, received 42 votes from the 75 Democrats who had been elected to that Congress.[69] This degree of obvious dissension within the party justifies adding this event to the caucus contests, bringing the total to 37.

The 168 intraparty elections are compared in Table 5.9.6 by party and era for the relative

TABLE 5.9.6 FREQUENCY OF INTRAPARTY CONTESTS FOR HOUSE ELECTIVE POSTS BY PERIOD AND PARTY STATUS, 1863–1977

	1863–1911		1911–1977		1863–1977	
PARTY AND STATUS	CONTESTS/ CAUCUSES	PERCENT	CONTESTS/ CAUCUSES	PERCENT	CONTESTS/ CAUCUSES	PERCENT
Democratic majority	6/9	67	10/57	18	16/66	24
Democratic minority	5/17	29	0/8	0	5/25	20
Democratic totals	11/26	42	10/65	15	21/91	23
Gamma	−.655*		−1.000		−.123	
Republican majority	3/16	19	6/18	33	9/34	26
Republican minority	2/9	22	5/34	15	7/43	16
Republican totals	5/25	20	11/52	21	16/77	21
Gamma	+1.06		−.487		−.299	
All majorities	9/25	36	16/75	21	25/100	25
All minorities	7/26	27	5/42	12	12/68	18
Totals	16/51	31	21/117	18	37/168	22
Gamma	−.208		−.335		−.217	

NOTE: In none of the comparisons does statistical significance emerge at the .05 level.

* The direction of the signs tests the proposition that contests will be less frequent in majority-status situations.

frequency of contests within differing party statuses. Correlations are also presented to determine if the generally accepted proposition concerning the greater frequency of leadership contests in the minority is borne out.

In every case but one in Table 5.9.6, the data disconfirm the proposition that minority status engenders leadership contests. In three of the four period and party comparisons, contests are more prevalent in the majority party. The only case which supports the proposition—i.e., the case of the Republicans from 1863 to 1911—represents the smallest percentage differential in the table. And when all majorities are compared to all minorities, regardless of party, the incidence of majority contests is higher in each period.

One explanation for this finding is that the stakes are higher in the majority party than in the minority. As Peabody describes the difference:

> There are more committee assignments and appointments to prestige boards and commissions to be distributed. It is the majority which receives most of the credit when legislation is passed. Their projects receive higher priority. Majority members chair the committees and subcommittees. With position comes staff, superior access to executive officialdom and greater influence on legislative outcomes.[70]

Also in Table 5.9.6, an intriguing interparty difference appears with regard to the incidence of these contests over time. Republican caucuses had a slight increase in dissension in Period III, while the Democratic caucuses have shown a marked decrease between the two eras. This decline in contested Democratic leadership elections is most likely due to the conscious efforts of the leadership itself to minimize conflict and to institutionalize the party's succession system. It appears as if the initial selections for the Democratic leadership ladder are designed to appeal to the widest possible group of members.[71]

There is support for this inference in the congressional voting literature. David Truman's study of the 81st Congress (1949–1951) indicated that the floor leaders in both House parties tended to be ideological "middlemen."[72] But Barbara Hinckley's analysis of more recent Congresses reveals that only the Democratic leaders continue to occupy this location.[73] In these Congresses, the Democratic leadership stood astride the gulf between a liberal-moderate membership and a brace of conservative committee chairmen, while the Republican leadership was more conservative than its membership and ranking committeemen. Whether this was true in the pre-World War II Congresses is an important question beyond the scope of this study.

LEADERSHIP CHANGE TYPOLOGY

In order to add the dimension of incumbency to the study, the data have been placed into Robert Peabody's typology of "intraparty leadership change."[74] Peabody's typology identifies six possible change situations: (1) status quo; (2) routine advancement; (3) appointment or emergence of a consensus choice; (4) open competition; (5) challenge to an heir apparent; and (6) revolt or its aftermath. Two of Peabody's situations—(2) and (5)—depend upon the existence of established succession patterns for their meaning. Since the Democrats appear to have an orderly succession system and the Republicans do not, these two situations lack interparty comparability and will not be included in this analysis.

Using Peabody's other two criteria—vacancy or no vacancy in the leadership post, and a contest or no contest in the caucus—a simple fourfold typology can be created from Peabody's original one. This typology is used in Table 5.9.7 to classify the 168 floor leadership elections in the House since 1863.

Operationally, *status quo* refers to the unopposed continuance of a leader in his party leadership rank, regardless of party control changes. A Speaker becoming Minority Leader after his party has lost the House represents a continuation of his party's leadership status quo. *Consensus* choices represent new moves into ranks which are unopposed by the caucus. Also included in this category are unopposed moves by appointed Democratic whips into the elected Majority Leadership post following changes in party control (e.g., McCormack in 1949 and 1955). The rank remains the same, but dependence upon caucus approval has increased.

Contests occur in two cases: *competition* when there is a vacancy in the leadership rankings, and *revolt* when there is no vacancy and when opposition to the incumbent leader manifests itself in actual caucus votes against him.

The three instances in Period II in which Democratic minority Speakership candidates remained in the House but were replaced as nominees without voted defeats have been classified on the basis of each leader's caucus activity. Since neither Marshall in the 41st Congress nor Kerr in the 42d Congress figured in the leadership contests, these cases were treated as vacancies. In the 44th Congress (1875–1877), however, Fernando Wood, the previous Speakership nominee, contended until his support evaporated in the final week before the vote, that election is considered a revolt.

Focusing first upon the 1863–1911 data in Table 5.9.7 we see that contests occurred at a higher rate in Democratic caucuses regardless of the status of the party or the incumbency of its leaders. Democratic disarray was very pronounced throughout most of this era, particularly during the party's majorities from 1875 through 1885. All four majorities in that period opened with leadership revolts. Two were successful—the replacement of Wood in 1875 and the voted defeat of Randall in 1883; two were unsuccessful—Randall's two first-ballot victories in 1877 and 1879.[75] This contrasts with the failures of the three Republican revolts against Keifer in 1883, Reed in 1889, and Cannon in 1909.[76]

In both parties, contests for occupied offices were more frequent in majority situations. Six of the seven revolts occurred during majorities. This lends further support to the contention that when the stakes are higher competition will be intensified. Such a finding is not unexpected in an era when the Speaker of the House had sole control over the naming of 60-plus committee chairmen.[77] Many House careers prior to 1911 were affected by members' decisions about which Speakership candidate to back.

Regarding minorities, Republican ones were slightly less competitive than Democratic ones (22 percent to 29 percent). As mentioned earlier, however, stability in the Democratic minority was an outgrowth of the consolidation of

TABLE 5.9.7 FREQUENCIES OF INTRAPARTY LEADERSHIP SITUATIONS BY PERIOD, PARTY STATUS, AND POST OCCUPANCY, 1863–1977

	OCCUPIED POST		VACANT POST		TOTALS	
	STATUS QUO	REVOLT	CONSENSUS	COMPETITION	N	PERCENT
1863–1911:						
Democratic majority . . .	33%	44%	0%	22%	9	99%
Democratic minority . . .	41	0	20	29	17	100
Democratic totals .	38	15	19	27	26	99
Republican majority . . .	56	12	25	6	16	99
Republican minority . . .	67	11	11	11	9	100
Republican totals . .	60	12	20	8	25	100
Both majority	48	24	16	12	25	100
Both minority	50	4	23	23	26	100
Both totals	49	14	20	18	51	101
1911–1977:						
Democratic majority . . .	61%	4%	21%	14%	57	100%
Democratic minority . . .	62	0	38	0	8	100
Democratic totals .	62	3	23	12	65	100
Republican majority . . .	44	17	22	17	18	100
Republican minority . . .	76	9	9	6	34	100
Republican totals . .	65	12	13	10	52	100
Both majority	57	7	21	15	75	100
Both minority	74	7	14	5	42	100
Both totals	63	7	19	11	117	100
1863–1977:						
Democratic majority . . .	58%	9%	18%	15%	66	100%
Democratic minority . . .	48	0	32	20	25	100
Democratic totals .	55	7	22	16	91	100
Republican majority . . .	50	15	24	12	34	101
Republican minority . . .	74	9	9	7	43	99
Republican totals . .	64	12	16	9	77	101
All majority	55	11	20	14	100	100
All minority	65	6	18	12	68	101
All totals	59	9	19	13	168	100

the post-1899 leadership of Richardson, Williams, and Clark. These three leaders accounted for six of the 12 uncontested minority nominations in this era. Prior to that time, Democratic minority contests were almost as frequent as majority ones.

The post-1911 data indicate a marked decline in the frequency of Democratic contests regardless once again of the party's status or its leaders' incumbency. Only two revolts occurred during 42 incumbency situations (5 percent): Udall's in 1969 and Conyers's in 1973. No contests occurred during Democratic minorities in this era. Even the three successions of Claude Kitchin in 1921, Finis Garrett in 1923, and John Garner in 1929 were uncontested.

Of the eight instances of competition in the Democratic caucus for open posts, all occurred during majorities, and five were decided on the first ballot. The 1935 Bankhead–O'Connor and 1971 Boggs–Udall contests went to a second ballot, while the Wright–Burton election of 1976 had three ballots. Competition within Democratic caucuses in this era has not been protracted.

Among the post-1911 Republicans, revolts occurred more frequently and were more potent. Three of the six resulted in leadership overthrows—Mann in 1919, Martin in 1959, and Halleck in 1965; while two of the others shortened leadership careers. Mann refused the Majority Leadership after another contest in 1919 and Gillett left the House upon completing his third (and vigorously contested) Speakership in 1925. Only Leslie Arends withstood the revolt against him in the caucus and remained in office during subsequent Congresses. Republican leaders apparently heed the messages of their caucuses.

In cases of vacancy, Republicans are more willing to have a contest than are Democrats (42 percent to 35 percent). As in the case of the Democrats, however, most open Republican contests were settled on the first ballot, with only the eight-ballot Snell–Tilson fight an exception.

Contests have declined in the most recent era regardless of the occupancy of the leadership post. Contest for occupied posts decreased from 22 percent in Period II to 10 percent in Period III, while those for vacant posts decreased from 47 percent to 37 percent. The decrease, however, has been confined to the leadership of the Democratic party. Contests for occupied Democratic posts have declined by 24 percentage points (from 29 to 5 percent) and contests for vacant ones have dropped by 23 points (from 58 to 35 percent). Republican leaders have not been as fortunate; the rate of contests for occupied Republican posts has declined slightly (from 17 to 15 percent), but the number of contests for vacant ones has *increased* sharply (from 29 to 42 percent) in the post-1911 era.

Two party-minimizing explanations account for the general decline in contests. The first would be the institutionalization of the House leadership role. Greater acceptance of the authority of the leaders would presumably explain an increased reluctance of members to challenge either the sitting leadership or its anointed successors. The other explanation would stress the shift in power from the floor leaders to the committee chairmen in the years following the revolt against Speaker Cannon. The post-1911 diffusion of power has lowered the stakes involved in floor leadership contests and has thus led to a minimization of conflict. As plausible as each of these explanations may be, the fact that the decline in contests has been limited to Democratic caucuses limits their utility.

TYPES OF MAJORITIES AND MINORITIES

One very important interperiod difference emerges from the data in both tables. The Democrats had a higher proportion of contests in Period II regardless of their party status or office occupancy. In the subsequent period, the Republicans had a greater frequency of contests in these categories. One factor which characterizes both the Period II Democrats and the Period III Republicans is that both had difficulty holding control of the House. The Period II Democrats held the House for three spans totaling 16 years (an average of 5.3 years per span). The Period II Republicans were more successful. They held control of the House during four spans totaling 32 years (an average of 8.0 years). In Period III, the Republicans averaged 5.3 years per span (16/3), while the Democrats averaged 13.0 years (52/4). Thus, it is possible that the certainty (or lack of it) of gaining and keeping control of the House may have an impact upon the frequency of leadership contests.

Some support for this proposition appears when the Democratic party leaders are analyzed. From 1863 through 1899, the Democrats had 11 contests for the leadership. During this time, they emerged from near-extinction as a party to become a very competitive force in the House. Despite their frequent majorities in the House, however, only once did they control the Senate and the presidency at the same time.

Certainly, this was a continual reminder of their tentative status even when they held the House. They were an uncertain minority at this time, and leadership contests were one way of gaining access to the perquisites of power. Following their sizeable defeats in the congressional elections of the late 1890s they became a secure minority. Even their consecutive victories in the House elections of 1910–1916 were marred by the fact that their presidential standard-bearer had gained the White House twice with less than half of the votes. Their majority was insecure. In keeping with the expectation that contests will be infrequent for such insecure majorities, as for secure minorities, there were no contests for the 22 elected Democratic leaders from 1901 through 1931.

Following Roosevelt's landslide victory in 1932 and the ever-mounting number of House Democrats in subsequent elections, contests for the leadership reappeared. Five of the eleven elected Democratic leaders were challenged in the caucus between 1933 and 1940. The next quarter century, 1942–1967, was free of contests, largely because of the Rayburn–McCormack power combine. The Democratic party's majority throughout segments of this period, however, was not as secure as it had been in the 1930s nor as it has been in the past decade. Five of the 10 leadership selections since 1969 have been contested and the caucus defeats for committee chairmanships[78] lend substance to the "secure majority" thesis as an explanation.

The Republican pattern is not as clear. Four of their contests occurred in one eight-year span between 1881 and 1889, during which they alternated with the Democrats in controlling the House. Whether or not they were an insecure minority at the time is difficult to determine. Their next spate of contests appeared in the 1919–1925 period when they contested six leadership elections as a majority. One can speculate that having two presidential landslides behind them, they had become a secure majority which could afford to allow intraparty contests. But the proposition fails when the 1863–1875 and the 1895–1911 spans of Republican control are examined. No contests occurred in the first period, and only one (a minor challenge in 1909) occurred in the second. Secure Republican majorities do not always unleash a multitude of leadership contenders.

In one further effort to test the impact of party status upon House leadership change, the "declining minority" hypothesis will be explored. This proposition, advanced by Peabody, holds that severe losses in congressional elections will enhance the likelihood of minority party challenges.[79] Peabody's initial assessment was based upon his analysis of Republican revolts in the 84th–89th Congresses (1955–1966). When pushed back in time this proposition has some validity for the Republican party. In addition to the Martin and Halleck overthrows, there is the replacement of ex-Majority Leader John Q. Tilson by Bertrand Snell in 1931 after the Republicans lost control of the House and the challenge to ex-Speaker J. Warren Keifer in 1883 after a similar loss. Keifer was the only Speaker to be challenged for renomination in the caucus following his party's defeat at the polls.[80]

Looking at the Democrats, one sees a different picture. There have been ten instances since 1863 when the Democrats have convened as a minority after having lost either 20-plus seats or 10 percent of their membership from the previous Congress.[81] No Democratic leader who remained in the House and stood for renomination following these defeats was either overthrown or challenged in the caucus. Electoral success may have an impact upon the amount of discomfort which Democratic leaders face but electoral defeat apparently has none.

From this interpretation of the data, it appears that party status—be it majority or minority, secure, insecure, or declining—does not consistently explain the frequencies of House leadership contests and changes. The failure of party status as an explanatory variable forces a return to the concept of party distinctiveness: Democrats select their leaders differently than Republicans do.

SUMMARY AND IMPLICATIONS

The most direct finding in this study is that the two parties differ significantly in their patterns of House leadership change. Consequently, theories of House development which minimize the party variable in quest of institutional norms and electoral status predictors may slow our understanding of the dynamics of leadership change.

It is important to note however that institutionalized norms have appeared. Over time the number of House organizational posts has steadily increased as the leadership has become more bureaucratized. The increased importance of minor elective posts in the Republican organization (e.g., the chairmanships of the Republican Conference and Policy Committee) and the emergence of new appointive posts in the Democratic party (e.g., the Deputy Whips) indicates that this trend will continue.

Other signs of institutionalization may be found in the increased selection frequencies for House leaders and the greater incidence of continuations either in specific posts or party ranks during this latest House era. These developments contribute to the greater professionalization of the House leadership career, as does the decline in the number of departures arising from the leaders' own extra-House ambitions and the vagaries of their constituents.

It is the interparty differences, however, which hold the most meaning, for these differences appear to be related to fundamental questions of each party's social composition and governing philosophy. In this analysis of leadership change over time, the following observations were made for the Democrats: They have a higher proportion of appointed leaders than Republicans; their leaders moved between posts within the party hierarchy in an ordered succession; their appointed leaders are often "removed from above" by their elected ones; and their elected leaders are subjected to infrequent and unsuccessful contests in their caucuses. Republicans, on the other hand, were found to rely more upon election to select their leaders; their rate of interpositional mobility among leaders is very low; their appointed leaders were never removed by the elected one; and while their leaders face contests at the same rate that the Democrats do, the incidence of successful challenges is much greater in their caucuses. Republican leaders, in short, are often "removed from below."

Regarding the impact of majority versus minority status upon leadership challenges, contests appeared to occur more frequently in the majority party than in the minority one. Since the stakes are higher and the rewards are greater in the majority, the high incidence of contests for posts which contain real power should not be surprising. The last three intraparty contests which toppled leaders occurred during minority situations, but all three involved Republicans. The Democratic leadership's general invulnerability to caucus challenges, regardless of party circumstances, reduces the power of this variable in explaining change.

These interparty differences reveal two distinct leadership succession systems. The Democratic House organization is hierarchically arranged in a tightly controlled system which is designed to minimize internal conflict. The end result is a leadership with wide ranging "inclusive" attitudes toward issues that face the House. In contrast, the House Republicans appear to be relatively egalitarian in their leadership succession system, with open competition and a dominant role for the membership. The Republican leaders who emerge from this system appear to have "exclusive" attitudes toward House issues.

At this point, a possible reason for the difference in the functioning of the two parties may lie in the difference in their composition: the House Democrats are a large and heterogeneous mix of contending social groups, regions, and ideologies, while the House Republicans are a smaller and more homogeneous band of predominantly conservative small-town and small-city white males. Conflict within a homogeneous setting will not result in one social or ideological group's triumphing over another. Only the names in the offices will change, and in such a context, change of style will be more common than change of substance.

When a party is divided as the Democrats are, leadership change can result in a complete reshuffling of power. Formerly excluded groups can gain access to key posts and deny others this privilege. The legislative agenda may undergo an enormous transformation following an upheaval in the leadership. Any observer of the last few Democratic nominating conventions can readily see the consequences of such leadership change upon the party's presidential wing. It certainly would appear as if the controlled succession system which the House Democrats have carefully constructed is designed to avoid a similar outbreak of internecine warfare in the House.

Projections are always tentative, but it seems as if the Republican leadership succession system will remain relatively open and competitive. The party has undergone no fundamental reorientation in recent years. Hence, it is likely that its operating procedures will remain intact. The Democratic succession system has entered a transitional period as younger and more assertive members have joined the party's congressional ranks. Congressman Jim Wright is the first newly elected Democratic floor leader in 36 years who did not previously hold the position of Whip. His election against a backdrop of deposed committee and subcommittee chairpersons indicates change for the floor leadership of the party. As the Democratic party becomes more philosophically united, and as the ancient regional conflicts recede, it is likely that the Democratic leadership will no longer need their controlled succession system and that the membership will no longer tolerate it.

CHAPTER

6 Structural Characteristics III: Legislative Procedures

The congressional decision process is labyrinthlike, involving multiple, successive decision stages and an abundance of decision points. For a bill to become a law, it must successfully circumnavigate numerous obstacles and hurdles. This affords opponents of legislation numerous opportunities for delay, deadlock, and defeat of a proposed bill. Once a proposed bill is introduced in both houses, it must be referred to committee, favorably reported by the relevant subcommittee and full committees in each house, scheduled on the floor, debated and voted on the floor, and, if necessary, sent to conference to iron out differences between the House and Senate before being forwarded for presidential approval. So complicated is the congressional process that Woodrow Wilson was moved to write, "Once begin the dance of legislation, and you must struggle through its mazes as best you can to the breathless end—if any there be."

Additionally, the legislative process is complicated by the requirement that Congress act twice if a government activity is to materialize: once in the form of an authorization, entitling the government to undertake certain actions; and second with an appropriation, allocating public money to fund such an action. Thus, this two-track requirement means that for almost every government purpose, Congress must complete two separate legislative processes in each house. Of course, all of this means that most legislation will be compromised and watered down as efforts are made by proponents to neutralize potential intensely opposed, strategically located opponents.

Selections in this chapter examine the functions and politics of rules and offer authoritative explications, with illustrations, of congressional procedures.

As one studies legislative procedures, it should be kept in mind that these rules are not neutral. Procedures significantly affect the group struggle by favoring one group rather than another, affecting who wins and thus affecting the distribution of policy benefits. Also, procedures frequently become the focus of the ploys and strategies of various interests as they aspire to increase their political advantage.

6.1 Functions of Rules and Procedures*

Walter J. Oleszek

The rules and procedures of Congress satisfy important institutional requirements. Oleszek lists these and discusses how they facilitate the business of Congress and are augmented by the norms or informal rules of Congress.

FUNCTIONS OF RULES AND PROCEDURES

Any decision-making body, Congress included, needs a set of rules, procedures, and conventions, formal and informal, in order to function. In the case of Congress, the Constitution authorizes the House and Senate to formulate their own rules of procedure. Thomas Jefferson, who, as Vice President, compiled the first parliamentary manual for the U.S. Senate, emphasized the importance of rules to any legislative body.

> It is much more material that there should be a rule to go by, than what the rule is; that there may be uniformity of proceeding in business not subject to the caprice of the Speaker or captiousness of the members. It is very material that order, decency, and regularity be preserved in a dignified public body.[1]

Rules and procedures in an organization serve many functions. Among them are to provide stability, legitimize decisions, divide responsibilities, reduce conflict, and distribute power. Each of these functions will be illustrated both by examples drawn from a college or university setting and by parallel functions in Congress.

Stability

Rules provide stability and predictability in personal and organizational affairs. Individuals and institutions can conduct their day-to-day business without having to debate procedure. Universities, for example, have specific requirements for bachelor's, master's, and doctorate degrees. Students know that if they are to progress from one degree to the next they must comply with rules and requirements. Daily or weekly changes in those requirements would cause chaos on any campus. Similarly, legislators need not decide each day who can speak on the floor, offer amendments, or close debate. Such matters are governed by regularized procedures that continue from one Congress to the next and afford similar rights and privileges to every member.

Legitimacy

Students typically receive final course grades that are based on their classroom performance, examinations, and term papers. They accept the professors' evaluations if they believe in their fairness and legitimacy. If professors suddenly decided to use students' political opinions as the basis for final grades, there would be a storm of protest against such arbitrary procedures. In a similar fashion, members of Congress and citizens accept legislative decisions when they believe the decisions were approved according to orderly and fair procedure.

---

* From Walter J. Oleszek, *Congressional Procedures and the Policy Process* (Washington, D.C.: Congessional Quarterly Press, 1978), pp. 5–12.

DIVISION OF LABOR

Any university requires a division of labor if it is to carry out its tasks effectively and responsibly, and rules establish the various jurisdictions. Hence there are history, chemistry, and art departments; admissions officers and bursars; and food service and physical plant managers, all with specialized assignments. For Congress, committees are the heart of its legislative process. They provide the division of labor and specialization that Congress needs in order to handle the more than 20,000 measures introduced biennially, and to review the administration of scores of federal programs. Like specialized bodies in many organizations, committees do not make final policy decisions but propose recommendations to their respective chambers.

CONFLICT RESOLUTION

Rules reduce conflicts among members and units of organizations by distinguishing appropriate actions and behavior from the inappropriate. For example, universities have procedures by which students may drop or add classes. There are discussions with faculty advisers, completion of appropriate paperwork, and the approval of a dean. Students who informally attempt to drop or add classes may encounter conflicts with their professors as well as sanctions from the dean's office. Most of the conflicts can be avoided by observance of established procedures. Similarly, congressional rules reduce conflict by, for example, establishing procedures to fill vacancies on committees when several members are competing for the same position.

DISTRIBUTION OF POWER

A major consequence of rules is that they generally distribute power in any organization. As a result, rules are often a source of conflict themselves. During the 1960s, for example, many campuses witnessed struggles among students, faculty, and administrators involving the curriculum. The charge of irrelevance in course work was a frequent criticism of many students. As a result, the "rules of the game" for curriculum development were changed on many campuses. Students, junior faculty, and even community groups became involved in reshaping the structure and content of the educational program.

Like universities, Congress distributes power according to its rules and customs. Informal party rules, for example, establish a hierarchy of leadership positions in both chambers. And House and Senate rules accord prerogatives to congressional committee chairmen that are unavailable to noncommittee leaders. Rules are, therefore, not neutral devices. They help to shore up the more powerful members as well as protect the rights of the minority. Thus, efforts to change the rules are almost invariably efforts to redistribute power.

RULES AND POLICYMAKING IN THE CONGRESSIONAL CONTEXT

Rules play similar, but not identical, roles in most complex organizations. Congress has its own characteristics that affect the functions of the rules. First, members of Congress owe their positions to the electorate, not to their congressional peers or to influential congressional leaders. No one in Congress has authority over the other members comparable to that of university presidents and tenured faculty over junior faculty or to that of a corporation president over lower level executives. Members cannot be fired except by their constituency. And each member has equal voting power in committees and on the floor of the House or Senate.

Congress' rules, unlike those of many organizations, are especially sensitive to the rights of *minorities,* including the minority party, ideological minorities, and individual members. Skillful use of the rules enables the minority to check majority action by delaying, defeating, or reshaping legislation. Intensity often counts as much as numbers—an apathetic majority may find it difficult to prevail over a well-organized minority. Except in the few instances when extraordinary majorities are needed, such as overriding presidential vetoes (two thirds), Senate ratification of treaties (two thirds), and the decision to stop extended debate in the Senate (three fifths), the rules of the House and Senate require a simple majority to decide public policies.

Congress is also different from other organizations in its degree of responsiveness to external groups and pressures. The legislative branch is not as self-contained an institution as a university or a corporation. Congress is involved with every significant national and international issue. Its agenda compels members to respond to changing constituent interests and needs. Congress is also subject to numerous other influences, such as the President, pressure groups, political parties, and state and local officials.

Finally, Congress is a collegial and not a hierarchical body. Power does not flow from the top down, as in a corporation, but in practically every direction. There is only minimal centralized authority at the top; congressional policies are not "announced" but are "made" by shifting coalitions that vary from issue to issue. Congress' deliberations are also more accessible and public than those of perhaps any other kind of organization. These are some of the characteristics that set Congress apart from other organizations; inevitably these differences affect the decision-making process.

Procedure and Policy

Legislative procedures and policymaking are inextricably linked in at least four ways. First, procedures affect policy outcomes. Congress processes legislation by complex rules and procedures that permeate the institution and touch every public policy. Some matters are only gently brushed by the rules, while others become locked in their grip. Major civil rights legislation, for example, failed for decades to pass Congress because southern Senators used their chamber's rules and procedures to kill or modify such measures.

A second point is that very often policy decisions are expressed as procedural moves. Representatives and Senators, on various occasions, prefer not to make clear-cut decisions on certain complex and far-reaching public issues. Should a major weapons system be continued or curtailed? Should the nation's energy production needs take precedence over environmental concerns? Should financial assistance for the elderly be reduced and priority be given to aiding disadvantaged children? On questions like these, members may be "cross-pressured." (The President might be exerting influence one way while constituent interests dictate the opposite.) Legislators may lack adequate information to make informed judgments. They may be reluctant to oppose powerful pressure groups. Or the issue, they believe, does not lend itself to a simple yes or no vote.

As a result, legislators employ various procedural devices to handle knotty problems. A matter may be postponed on the ground of insufficient committee hearings. Congress may direct an agency to prepare a detailed report before an issue is considered. Or a measure may be "tabled" by the House or Senate, a procedural vote that effectively defeats a proposal without rendering a judgment on its substance. When the 95th Congress convened, for example, the Senate debated a proposal that would put it on record against blanket amnesty for Vietnam draft evaders. The controversial measure was tabled on a 48-to-46 vote, leaving the whole matter to the President.

Third, the nature of the policy can determine the use of certain procedures. The House and Senate generally consider noncontroversial measures under expeditious procedures, whereas controversial proposals normally involve lengthy deliberation. Extraordinary circumstances might prompt Congress to invoke rarely used practices to enact legislation with dispatch. For example, because of the severe winter of 1977, President Carter urged Congress to approve quickly a law granting him authority to order transfers of natural gas to states hard hit by gas shortages. On January 26, 1977, the measure was introduced in the Senate. To speed the bill's passage, the Senate employed a rarely used procedure that brought the measure immediately to the floor for debate, bypassing the usual committee stage entirely.[2] Moreover, under pressure from its leadership, the Senate rejected all substantive amendments and passed the measure 91 to 2 after two days of debate. As national issues change, moreover, some procedures become nearly extinct, while others are used more and more frequently to meet new needs.

Finally, policy outcomes are more likely to be influenced by members with procedural expertise. Members who are skilled parliamentarians are better prepared to gain approval of their proposals than those who are only vaguely familiar with the rules. Just as carpenters and lawyers must learn their trade, members of Congress need to understand the rules if they expect to perform effectively. And congressional procedures are confusing to newcomers. "To table, to refer to committee, to amend—so many things come up," declared freshman Senator S. I. Hayakawa (R–Calif.), "you don't know whether you are coming or going."[3] Former Speaker of the House John McCormack once advised freshmen House members:

> Learn the rules and understand the precedents and procedures of the House. The Congressman who knows how the House operates will soon be recognized for his parliamentary skills—and his prestige will rise among his colleagues, no matter what his party.[4]

Members who know the rules well always have the potential to shape legislation to their ends. Those who do not reduce their proficiency and influence as legislators.

PRECEDENTS AND FOLKWAYS

Congress is regulated not only by formal rules, but by informal ones that influence legislative procedure and member behavior.[5] Two types of informal rules are precedents and "folkways." Precedents, the accumulated past decisions on matters of procedure, represent a blend of the formal and informal. They are the "common law" of Congress and govern many procedures not explicitly covered in the formal rules. For example, formal rules prescribe the order of business in the House and Senate, but precedents permit variations through the unanimous consent of the members. The rulings of the Speaker of the House and presiding officer of the Senate form a large body of precedents. They are given formal status by the parliamentarians in each chamber and distributed to Representatives and Senators.[6]

Folkways, on the other hand, are unwritten norms of behavior that members are expected to observe. "Without these folkways," concluded Donald Matthews, "the Senate could hardly operate with its present organization and rules."[7] Several of the more important are "legislative work" (members should concentrate on congressional duties and not be publicity seekers), "courtesy" (members should be solicitous toward their colleagues and avoid personal attacks on them), and "specialization" (members should master a few policy areas and not try to be a jack-of-all-trades). Those who abide by these and other norms are often rewarded with increased influence in the policy process, for example, by being appointed to prestigious committees. Conversely, legislators who persistently violate Congress' informal customs are apt to see legislation they support blocked in committee or on the floor. Congressional decision making, then, is shaped by each chamber's formal and informal structure of rules, precedents, and traditions.

6.2 Enactment of a Law (or How Our Laws Are Made)*

J.S. Kimmit and Murray Zweben; Edward F. Willett

Two most authoritative treatments of legislative procedure are Kimmit and Zweben's *Enactment of a Law* and Willett's *How Our Laws Are Made*. Both are publications of Congress written while the authors were congressional staff employees and they are usually available at the offices of your Senator or Representative. Kimmit and Zweben focus on the Senate; Willett stresses the House. Here we excerpt from both to give a total view of congressional procedures.

(The following is from Kimmitt and Zweben:)

FORMS AND DESIGNATION OF LEGISLATIVE BUSINESS

All proposed legislation, and nearly all formal actions by either of the two houses, take the form of a bill or resolution. When bills and resolutions are introduced or submitted, they take one of the following forms: In the Senate, they are designated with the prefix "S. ———" for Senate bills; "S.J. Res. ———" for Senate joint resolutions; "S. Con. Res. ———" for Senate concurrent resolutions; and "S. Res. ———" for Senate resolutions. In the House of Representatives, they have the following designations: "H.R. ———" for House bills; "H.J. Res. ———" for House joint resolutions; "H. Con. Res. ———" for House concurrent resolutions; and "H. Res. ———" for House resolutions. The bills and resolutions are numbered ad seriatim, in the chronological order in which they are introduced.

Senate and House bills and Senate and House joint resolutions, when passed by both houses in identical form and approved by the President, become public or private law. Public laws affect the nation as a whole; private laws benefit only an individual or a class thereof. The procedure on both is identical, with the exception of joint resolutions proposing amendments to the Constitution of the United States, which under the Constitution must be passed in each house by a two-thirds vote of the members present and voting, a quorum being present. They are not sent to the President for his approval but to the Administrator of the General Services Administration, who transmits them to the various states for ratification by at least three fourths thereof. When so ratified, such amendments are valid.

Concurrent resolutions by either house do not become law; they are not signed by the President, nor by the Speaker and the Vice President. They are attested by the Secretary of the Senate and Clerk of the House and transmitted after approval to the Administrator of the General Services Administration for publication in the Statutes at Large. Concurrent resolutions have the force of both houses and must be approved by them in identical form to be effective—they are used for joint housekeeping matters such as the creation of a joint committee or to express the sense of Congress.

A House or Senate resolution (H. Res.

---

* From J. S. Kimmit and Murray Zweben, *Enactment of a Law: Procedural Steps in the Legislative Process* (Washington, D.C.: U.S. Government Printing Office, 1979, Senate Document 96–98), pp. 2–8, 10–16; Edward F. Willett, *How Are Laws Made?* (Washington, D.C.: U.S. Government Printing Office, 1980, House Document No. 96–352), pp. 9–18, 20–34. Reprinted from the public domain.

——— and S. Res. ———) only has the force of that house passing it, and the action by the one house is all that is necessary. Such resolutions are used for the housekeeping matters of the house passing it, such as creating an ad hoc investigating committee. They are also used to express the sense of the body passing them.

ORIGIN OF LEGISLATION

Legislation originates in several ways. The Constitution provides that the President "shall from time to time give to the Congress information of the state of the Union, and recommend to their consideration such measures as he shall judge necessary and expedient."

The President fulfills this duty either by personally addressing a joint session of the two houses or by sending messages in writing to the Congress or to either body thereof, which are received and referred to the appropriate committees. The President usually presents or submits his annual message on the state of the Union shortly after the beginning of a session.

The right of petition is guaranteed the citizens of the United States by the Constitution, and many individual petitions and memorials from state legislatures are sent to Congress. They are laid before the two houses by their respective presiding officers or submitted by individual members of the House and Senate in their respective bodies, and are usually referred to the appropriate committees of the house in which they were submitted.

Bills to carry out the recommendations of the President are usually introduced by the chairmen of the various committees or subcommittees thereof which have jurisdiction of the subject matter. Sometimes the committees themselves may submit and report to the Senate "original bills" to carry out such recommendations.

The ideas for legislative proposals may come from an individual Representative or Senator, from any of the executive departments of the government, from private organized groups or associations, or from any individual citizen. However, they can be introduced in their respective houses only by Senators and Representatives. When introduced they are referred to the standing committees which have jurisdiction of the subject matter.

Members frequently introduce bills that are similar in purpose, in which case the committee considering them may take one of the bills, and add the best features of the others for reporting to the parent body, or draft an entirely new bill and report it (known as an original bill) in lieu of the others.

Under Article 1, Section 7 of the Constitution of the United States, all bills for raising revenue shall originate in the House of Representatives; but the Senate may propose or concur in amendments as on other bills.

(The following is from Willett:)

THE HOUSE

INTRODUCTION AND REFERENCE TO COMMITTEE

Any member, the resident commissioner, and the delegates in the House of Representatives may introduce a bill at any time while the House is actually sitting by simply placing it in the "hopper" provided for the purpose at the side of the Clerk's desk in the House chamber. He is not required to ask permission to introduce the measure or to make a statement at the time of introduction. Printed blank forms for use in typing the original bill are supplied through the stationery room. The name of the sponsor is endorsed on the bill. Under a change in the rules of the House effective in January 1979, sponsorship of a public bill is no longer limited to 25 members, but may be by an unlimited number of members. On his request, a member may be added as a sponsor no later than the day the bill is reported to the House. In addition, a member listed as a sponsor (other than the first sponsor) may have his name deleted as a sponsor no later than the day the bill is reported to the House. To forestall the possibility that a bill might be introduced in the House on behalf of a member without that member's prior approval, the sponsoring member's signature must appear on the bill before it is accepted for introduction. In the case where there are multiple sponsors of a bill, the signature must be that of the member first named thereon. In the Senate, unlimited multiple sponsorship of a bill also is permitted. Occasionally, a member may insert the words "by request" after his name to indicate that the introduction of the measure is in compliance with the suggestion of some other person.

In the Senate, a Senator usually introduces a bill or resolution by presenting it to the clerks at the presiding officer's desk, without commenting on it from the floor of the Senate. However, a Senator may use a more formal procedure by rising and introducing the bill or resolution from the floor. A Senator usually makes a statement about the measure when introducing it on the floor. Frequently, Senators obtain consent to have the bill or resolution printed in the body of the *Congressional Record,* following their formal statement.

If any Senator objects to the introduction of a bill or resolution, the introduction of the bill or resolution is postponed until the next day. If there is no objection, the bill is read by title and referred to the appropriate committee.

In the House of Representatives it is no longer the custom to read bills—even by title—at the time of introduction. The title is entered in the Journal and printed in the *Congressional Record,* thus preserving the purpose of the old rule. The bill is assigned its legislative number by the Clerk and referred to the appropriate committees by the Speaker (the member elected to be the presiding officer of the House) with the assistance of the parliamentarian. These details appear in the daily issue of the *Congressional Record.* It is then sent to the Government Printing Office, where it is printed in its introduced form, and printed copies are available shortly thereafter in the document rooms of both houses.

One copy is sent to the office of the chairman of the committee to which it has been referred, for action by that committee. The clerk of the committee enters it on the committee's Legislative Calendar.

Perhaps the most important phase of the congressional process is the action by committees. That is where the most intensive consideration is given to the proposed measures and where the people are given their opportunity to be heard. Nevertheless, this phase where such a tremendous volume of hard work is done by the members is sometimes overlooked by the public, particularly when complaining about delays in enacting laws.

The Legislative Reorganization Acts of 1946 and 1970, the result of widespread proposals for "streamlining" Congress, establish the existing committee structure of the House and the Senate. Prior to the Reorganization Act of 1946, the House had 48 standing (permanent) committees and there were 33 in the Senate. In addition there were a number of select or special committees, usually of an investigative character, that normally did not consider pending legislation. There are, at present, 22 standing committees in the House and 15 in the Senate, as well as several select committees. In the House there are two permanent select committees, the newer being the Permanent Select Committee on Intelligence established in 1977 with legislative jurisdiction. In addition, there are several standing joint committees of the two houses, two of which are the Joint Committee on Taxation and the Joint Economic Committee.

Each committee has jurisdiction over certain subject matters of legislation and all measures affecting a particular area of the law are referred to that committee that has jurisdiction over it. For example, the Committee on the Judiciary has jurisdiction over measures relating to judicial proceedings, civil and criminal, generally, and 18 other categories, of which constitutional amendments, revision and codification of statutes, civil liberties, antitrust, patents, copyrights and trademarks, are but a few. In all, the rules provide for approximately 220 different classifications of measures that are to be referred to the respective committees in the House and nearly 200 in the Senate. Membership on the various committees is divided between the two major political parties in proportion to their total membership in the House, except that one half of the members on the Committee on Standards of Official Conduct are from the majority party and one half from the minority party. Until 1953, with certain exceptions, a member could not serve on more than one standing committee of the House. This limitation was removed in January 1953, and now all members may serve on more than one committee. In January 1971, the majority party of the House determined in caucus that (1) the chairman of a full committee may not be the chairman of more than one subcommittee of that committee, (2) a member may not be chairman of more than one legislative subcommittee, and (3) a member may not serve on more than two committees having legislative jurisdiction. These limitations do not apply to certain committees performing housekeeping functions and joint committees.

A member usually seeks election to the committee that has jurisdiction over a field in which he is most qualified and interested. For example, the Committee on the Judiciary is composed entirely of lawyers. Many members are nationally recognized experts in the specialty of their particular committee or subcommittee.

Members rank in seniority in accordance with the order of their appointment to the committee, and until recently the ranking majority member was elected chairman. The rules of the House require that committee chairmen be elected from nominations submitted by the majority party caucus at the commencement of each Congress.

Most of the committees have two or more subcommittees that, in addition to having general jurisdiction, specialize in the consideration of particular classifications of bills. Each standing committee of the House, except the Committee on the Budget, that has more than 20 members must establish at least four subcommittees.

Each committee is provided with a professional and clerical staff to assist it in the innumerable administrative details and other problems involved in the consideration of bills. For the standing committees, the professional staff (consisting of not more than 18, six of whom may be selected by minority) is appointed on a permanent basis solely on the basis of fitness to perform the duties of their respective positions. The clerical staff (consisting of not more than 12, four of whom may be selected by the minority) is appointed to handle correspondence and stenographic work for the committee staff and the chairman and ranking minority member on matters related to committee work. All staff appointments are made by a majority vote of the committee without regard to race, creed, sex or age. The minority staff provisions do not apply to the Committee on Standards of Official Conduct because of its bipartisan nature. The Committee on Appropriations and the Committee on the Budget have special authority under the House rules for appointment of staff and assistants for the minority.

Under certain conditions a standing committee may appoint consultants on a temporary or intermittent basis and may also provide financial assistance to members of its professional staff for the purpose of acquiring specialized training, whenever the committee determines that such training will aid the committee in the discharge of its responsiblities.

CONSIDERATION BY COMMITTEE

The rules adopted by the majority party caucus provide that the chairman of the committee to which a bill has been referred must refer the bill to the appropriate subcommittee within two weeks, unless a majority of the members of the majority party on the committee vote to have the bill considered by the full committee. One of the first actions taken is the transmittal of copies of the bill to the departments and agencies concerned with the subject matter and frequently to the General Accounting Office with a request for an official report of views on the necessity or desirability of enacting the bill into law. Ample time is given for the submission of the reports and when received they are accorded serious consideration but are not binding on the committee in determining whether or not to act favorably on the bill. The reports of the executive departments and agencies are submitted first to the Office of Management and Budget to determine whether the bill is consistent with the program of the President.

COMMITTEE MEETINGS

Standing committees are required to have regular meeting days no less frequently than once a month, but the chairman may call and convene additional meetings. Three or more members of a standing committee may file with the committee a written request that the chairman call a special meeting. The request must specify the measure or matter to be considered. If the chairman fails, within three calendar days after the filing of the request, to call the requested special meeting, to be held within seven calendar days after the filing of the request, a majority of the members of the committee may call the special meeting by filing with the committee written notice specifying the time and date of the meeting and the measure or matter to be considered.

With the exception of the Committees on Appropriations, on the Budget, on Rules, and on Standards of Official Conduct, committees may not, without special permission, meet while the House is reading a measure for amendment under the "five-minute rule." Special permission to meet will be given unless ten or more members object. Committees may meet during a recess up to the expiration of the constitutional term.

PUBLIC HEARINGS

If the bill is of sufficient importance, and particularly if it is controversial, the committee will usually set a date for public hearings. Each committee (except the Committee on Rules) is required to make public announcement of the date, place, and subject matter of any hearing to be conducted by the committee on any measure or matter at least one week before the commencement of that hearing, unless the committee determines that there is good cause to begin the hearing at an earlier date. If the committee makes that determination, it must make a public announcement to that effect at the earliest possible date. Public announcements are published in the Daily Digest portion of the *Congressional Record* as soon as possible after the announcement is made by the committee, and are often noted in newspapers and periodicals. Personal notice, usually in the form of a letter, but possibly in the form of a subpoena, is sent frequently to individuals, organizations, and government departments and agencies that are known to be interested.

Committee and subcommittee hearings are required to be public except when the committee or subcommittee, in open session and with a majority present, determines by roll call vote that all or part of the remainder of that hearing on that day shall be closed to the public because disclosure of testimony, evidence, or other matters to be considered would endanger the national security or would violate a law or Rule of the House of Representatives. The committee or subcommittee may by the same procedure vote to close one subsequent day of hearing. In 1979, the House amended its rules to provide that when a quorum for taking testimony is present a majority of the members present may close a hearing to discuss whether the evidence or testimony to be received would endanger national security.

Hearings on the budget are required to be held by the Committee on Appropriations in open session within 30 days after its transmittal to Congress, except when the committee, in open session and with a quorum present, determines by roll call vote that the testimony to be taken at that hearing on that day may be related to a matter of national security. The committee may by the same procedure close one subsequent day of hearing.

On the day set for the public hearing an official reporter is present to record the testimony in favor of and against the bill. Suitable accommodations are provided for the public and witnesses.

The bill may be read in full at the opening of the hearings and a copy is inserted in the record. After a brief introductory statement by the chairman and often by the ranking minority member or other committee member, the first witness is called. Members or Senators who wish to be heard are given preference out of courtesy and because of the limitations on their time. Cabinet officers and high-ranking civil and military officials of the government, as well as any private individual who is interested, may appear and testify either voluntarily or at the request or summons of the committee.

Committees require, so far as practicable, that witnesses who appear before it file with the committee, in advance of their appearance, a written statement of their proposed testimony and limit their oral presentations to a brief summary of their arguments.

Minority party members of the committee are entitled to call witnesses of their own to testify on a measure during at least one day of the hearing.

All committee rules in the House must provide that each member shall have only five minutes in the interrogation of witnesses until each member of the committee who desires to question a witness has had an opportunity to do so.

A typewritten transcript of the testimony taken at a public hearing is made available for inspection in the office of the clerk of the committee and frequently the complete transcript is printed and distributed widely by the committee.

BUSINESS MEETINGS

After hearings are completed the subcommittee usually will consider the bill in a session that is popularly known as the "markup" session. The views of both sides are studied in detail and at the conclusion of deliberation a vote is taken to determine the action of the subcommittee. It may decide to report the bill favorably to the full committee, with or without amendment, or unfavorably, or suggest that the committee "table" it, that is, postpone action indefinitely. Each member of the subcommittee, regardless of party affiliation, has one vote.

All meetings for the transaction of business, including the markup of legislation, of standing committees or subcommittees must be open to the public except when the committee or subcommittee, in open session with a majority present, determines by roll-call vote that all or part of the remainder of the meeting on that day shall be closed to the public. However, the members of the committee may authorize congressional staff and departmental representatives to be present at any business or markup session that has been closed to the public. These provisions do not apply to open committee hearings, hearings on the budget, or to any meeting that relates solely to internal budget or personnel matters.

COMMITTEE ACTION

At committee meetings reports on bills may be made by subcommittees. Reports are fully discussed and amendments may be offered. Committee amendments are only proposals to change the bill as introduced and are subject to acceptance or rejection by the House itself. A vote of committee members is taken to determine the action of the full committee on the bill, that is usually either to report the bill favorably to the House, with or without amendments, or to table it. Because tabling a bill is normally effective in preventing action on it, adverse reports to the House by the full committee are not ordinarily made. On rare occasions, a committee may report a bill without recommendation or unfavorably.

Generally, a majority of the committee constitutes a quorum, the number of members who must be present in order for the committee to act. This ensures adequate participation by both sides in the action taken. However, the rules allow committees to vary the number of members necessary for a quorum for certain actions.

For example, each committee may fix the number of its members, but not less than two, necessary for a quorum for taking testimony and receiving evidence. The rules allow committees (except the Committees on Appropriations, on the Budget, and on Ways and Means) to fix the number of its members, but not less than one third, necessary for a quorum for taking certain other actions. The absence of a quorum is the subject of a point of order—that is, an objection that the proceedings are out of order—i.e., that the required number of members is not present.

PUBLIC INSPECTION OF RESULTS OF ROLL-CALL VOTE IN COMMITTEE

The result of each roll-call vote in any meeting of a committee must be made available by that committee for inspection by the public at reasonable times in the offices of that committee. Information available for public inspection includes a description of each amendment, motion, order, or other proposition; the name of each member voting for and each member voting against the amendment, motion, order, or proposition, and whether by proxy or in person; and the names of those members present but not voting.

With respect to each roll-call vote by a committee on a motion to report a bill or resolution of a public character, the total number of votes cast for, and the total number of votes cast against, the reporting of the bill or resolution must be included in the committee report.

PROXY VOTING

A vote by a member of a committee with respect to a measure or other matter may not be cast by proxy unless that committee adopts a written rule that permits voting by proxy and requires that the proxy authorization (1) be in writing, (2) assert that the member is absent on official business or is otherwise unable to be present at the meeting of the committee, (3) designate the person who is to execute the proxy authorization, and (4) be limited to a specific measure or matter and any amendments or motions pertaining to the measure or matter. A member may authorize a general proxy only for motions to recess, adjourn or other procedural matters. A proxy must be signed by the member and must contain the date and time of day that it is signed. A proxy may not be counted for a quorum.

POINTS OF ORDER WITH RESPECT TO COMMITTEE PROCEDURE

A point of order does not lie with respect to a measure reported by a committee on the ground that hearings on the measure were not conducted in accordance with required committee procedure. However, certain points of order may be made by a member of the committee which reported the measure if, in the committee, that point of order was (*a*) timely made and (*b*) improperly overruled or not properly considered.

BROADCASTING COMMITTEE HEARINGS AND MEETINGS

It is permissible to cover open committee hearings in the House by television, radio, and still photography. This permission is granted under well defined conditions outlined in clause 3(*d*) of Rule XI of the Rules of the House of Representatives. As stated in the rule:

> The coverage of committee hearings and meetings by television broadcast, radio broadcast, or still photography is a privilege made available by the House and shall be permitted and conducted only in strict conformity with the purposes, provisions, and requirements of this clause.

REPORTED BILLS

If the committee votes to report the bill favorably to the House, one of the members is designated to write the committee report. The report describes the purpose and scope of the bill and the reasons for its recommended approval. Generally, a section-by-section analysis is set forth in detail explaining precisely what each section is intended to accomplish. Under the rules of the House all changes in existing law must be indicated and the text of laws being repealed must be set out. This is known as the Ramseyer Rule; a similar rule in the Senate is known as the Cordon Rule. Committee amendments must also be set out at the beginning of the report and explanations of them are included. Executive communications requesting the introduction and consideration of the bill are usually quoted in full.

If at the time of approval of a bill by a committee (except the Committee on Rules) a member of the committee gives notice of his intention to file supplemental, minority, or additional views, that member is entitled to not less than three calendar days (Saturdays, Sundays, and legal holidays excluded) in which to file those views with the clerk of the committee and they must be included in the report on the bill. Committee reports, with certain exceptions, must be filed while the House is actually sitting unless unanimous consent is obtained from the House to file at a later time.

The report is assigned a report number when it is filed, and it is delivered to the Government Printing Office for printing during that night. Beginning with the 91st Congress, in 1969, the report number contains a prefix-designator, which indicates the number of the Congress. For example, the first House report in 1969 was numbered 91–1.

The bill also is printed when reported and committee amendments are indicated by showing new matter in italics and deleted matter in stricken-through type. The report number if also printed on the bill and the calendar number is shown on both the first and back pages of the bill. However, in the case of a bill that was referred to two or more committees for consideration in sequence, the calendar number is printed only on the bill as reported by the last committee to consider it.

Committee reports are perhaps the most valuable single element of the legislative history of a law. They are used by the courts, executive branch departments and agencies, and public generally, as a source of information regarding the purpose and meaning of the law.

CONTENTS OF REPORTS

The report of a committee on a measure that has been approved by the committee must include (*a*) the committee's oversight findings and recommendations; (*b*) the statement required by the Congressional Budget Act of 1974, if the measure provides new budget authority or new or increased expenditures; (*c*) the estimate and comparison prepared by the Director of the Congressional Budget Office whenever the Director has submitted that estimate and comparison to the committee prior to the filing of the report; and (*d*) a summary of the oversight findings and recommendations made by the Committee on Government Operations whenever they have been submitted to the legislative committee in a timely fashion to allow an opportunity to consider the findings and recommendations during the committee's deliberations on the measure. Each of these items are separately set out and clearly identified in the report.

INFLATIONARY IMPACT AND COST ESTIMATES IN REPORTS

Each report of a committee on a bill or joint resolution of a public character reported by the committee must contain a detailed analytical statement as to whether the enactment of the bill or joint resolution into law may have an inflationary impact on prices and costs in the operation of the national economy.

Each report also must contain an estimate, made by the committee, of the costs which would be incurred in carrying out that bill or joint resolution in the fiscal year reported and in each of the five fiscal years thereafter or for the duration of the program authorized if less than five years. In the case of a measure involving revenues, the report need contain only an estimate of the gain or loss in revenues for a one-year period. The report must also include a comparison of the estimates of those costs with the estimate made by any government agency and submitted to that committee. The Committees on Appropriations, on House Administration, on Rules, and on Standards of Official Conduct are not required to include cost estimates in their reports.

FILING OF REPORTS

Measures approved by a committee must be reported promptly after approval. A majority of the members of the committee may file a written request with the clerk of the committee for the reporting of the measure. When the request is filed, the clerk immediately must notify the chairman of the committee of the filing of the request, and the report on the measure must be filed within seven days (exclusive of days on which the House is not in session) after the day on which the request is filed. This does not apply to the reporting of a regular appropriation bill by the Committee on Appropriations prior to compliance with requirements set out in the next paragraph, nor does it apply to a report of the Committee on Rules with respect to the rules, joint rules, or order of business of the House or to the reporting of a resolution of inquiry addressed to the head of an executive department.

Before reporting the first regular appropriation bill for each fiscal year, the Committee on Appropriations must, to the extent practicable and in accordance with the Congressional Budget Act of 1974, complete subcommittee markup and full committee action on all regular appropriation bills for that year and submit to the House a summary report comparing the Committee's recommendations with the appropriate levels of budget outlays and new budget authority as set forth in the most recently agreed to concurrent resolution on the budget for that year.

Generally, bills or resolutions that directly or indirectly authorize the enactment of new budget authority for a fiscal year must be reported to the House on or before May 15 preceding the beginning of that fiscal year. This deadline may be waived in emergency situations.

AVAILABILITY OF REPORTS AND HEARINGS

With certain exceptions (relating to emergency situations, such as a measure declaring war or other national emergency), a measure or matter reported by a committee (except the Committee on Rules in the case of a resolution making in order the consideration of a bill, resolution, or other order of business) may not be considered in the House until the third calendar day (excluding Saturdays, Sundays, and legal holidays) on which the report of that committee on that measure has been available to the members of the House. In addition, the measure or matter may not be considered unless copies of the report and the reported measure or matter have been available to the members for at least three calendar days (excluding Saturdays, Sundays, and legal holidays during which the House is not is session) before the beginning of consideration; however, it is always in order to consider a report from the Committtee on Rules specifically providing for the consideration of a reported measure or matter notwithstanding this restriction. If hearings were held on a measure or matter so reported, the committee is required to make every reasonable effort to have those hearings printed and available for distribution to the members of the House prior to the consideration of the measure in the House. General appropriation bills may not be considered until printed committee hearings and a committee report thereon have been available to the members of the House for at least three calendar days (excluding Saturdays, Sundays, and legal holidays).

CALENDARS

A calendar of the House of Representatives, together with a history of all measures reported by a standing committee of either house, is printed each day the House is sitting for the information of those interested.

As soon as a bill is favorably reported, it is assigned a calendar number on either the Union Calendar or the House Calendar, the two principal calendars of business. The calendar number is printed on both the first and the back pages of the bill. In the case of a bill that was referred to two or more committees for consideration in sequence, the calendar number is printed only on the bill as reported by the last committee to consider it.

UNION CALENDAR

The rules of the House provide that there shall be:

> First: A Calendar of the Committee of the Whole House on the state of the Union, to which shall be referred bills raising revenue, general appropriation bills, and bills of a public character directly or indirectly appropriating money or property.

This is commonly known as the Union Calendar and the large majority of public bills and resolutions are placed on it on being reported to the House.

HOUSE CALENDAR

The rules further provide that there shall be:

> Second: A House Calendar, to which shall be referred all bills of a public character not raising revenue nor directly or indirectly appropriating money or property.

The public bills and resolutions that are not placed on the Union Calendar are referred to the House Calendar.

CONSENT CALENDAR

If a measure pending on either of these calendars is of a noncontroversial nature it may be placed on the Consent Calendar. The House rules provide that after a bill has been favorably reported and is on either the House or Union Calendar any member may file with the Clerk a notice that he desires the bill placed upon the Consent Calendar. On the first and third Mondays of each month immediately after the reading of the Journal, the Speaker directs the Clerk to call the bills in numerical order (that is, in the order of their appearance on that calendar) that have been on the Consent Calendar for three legislative days. If objection is made to the consideration of any bill so called it is carried over on the calendar without prejudice to the next day when the Consent Calendar is again called, and if then objected to by three or more members it is immediately stricken from the calendar and may not be placed on the Consent Calendar again during that Session of Congress. If objection is not made and if the bill is not "passed over" by request, it is passed by unanimous consent without debate. Ordinarily the only amendments considered are those sponsored by the committee that reported the bill.

To avoid the passage without debate of measures that may be controversial or are sufficiently important or complex to require full discussion there are six official objectors—three on the majority side and three on the minority side—who make a careful study of bills on the Consent Calendar. If a bill involves the expenditure of more than a fixed maximum amount of money or if it changes national policy or has other aspects that any of the objectors believes demand explanation and extended debate, it will be objected to and will not be passed by consent. That action does not necessarily mean the final defeat of the bill since it may then be brought up for consideration in the same way as any other bill on the House or Union Calendars.

PRIVATE CALENDAR

All bills of a private character—that is, bills that affect an individual rather than the population at large—are called private bills. A private bill is used for relief in matters such as immigration and naturalization and claims by or against the United States. A private bill is referred to the Private Calendar. That calendar is called on the first and third Tuesdays of each month. If objection is made by two or more members of the consideration of any measure called, it is recommitted to the committee that reported it. As in the case of the Consent Calendar there are six official objectors, three on the majority side and three on the minority side, who make a careful study of each bill or resolution on the Private Calendar and who will object to a measure that does not conform to the requirements for that calendar, thereby preventing the passage without debate of nonmeritorious bills and resolutions.

DISTRICT OF COLUMBIA BUSINESS

The second and fourth Mondays in each month, after the disposition of motions to discharge committees and after the disposal of business on the Speaker's table requiring only referral to committee, are set aside, when claimed by the Committee on the District of Columbia, for the consideration of any business that is presented by that committee.

Obtaining Consideration of Measures

Obviously certain measures pending on the House and Union Calendars are more important and urgent than others and it is necessary to have a system permitting their consideration ahead of those that do not require immediate action. Because all measures are placed on those calendars in the order in which they are reported to the House, the latest bill reported would be the last to be taken up if the calendar number alone were the determining factor.

SPECIAL RESOLUTIONS

To avoid delays and to provide some degree of selectivity in the consideration of measures, it is possible to have them taken up out of order by procuring from the Committee on Rules a special resolution or "rule" for their consideration. That committee, which is composed of majority and minority members but with a larger proportion of majority members than other committees, is specifically granted jurisdiction over resolutions relating to the order of business of the House. Usually the chairman of the committee that has favorably reported the bill appears before the Committee on Rules accompanied by the sponsor of the measure and one or more members of his committee in support of his request for a resolution providing for its immediate consideration. If the Rules Committee is satisfied that the measure should be taken up it will report a resolution reading substantially as follows with respect to a bill on the Union Calendar:

> *Resolved,* That upon the adoption of this resolution it shall be in order to move that the House resolve itself into the Committee of the Whole House on the State of the Union for the consideration of the bill (H.R. ———) entitled, etc, and the first reading of the bill shall be dispensed with. After general debate, which shall be confined to the bill and shall continue not to exceed ——— hours, to be equally divided and controlled by the chairman and ranking minority member of the Committee on ———, the bill shall be read for amendment under the five-minute rule. At the conclusion of the consideration of the bill for amendment, the Committee shall rise and report the bill to the House with such amendments as may have been adopted, and the previous question shall be considered as ordered on the bill and amendments thereto to final passage without intervening motion except one motion to recommit.

If the measure is on the House Calendar the resolution reads substantially as follows:

> *Resolved,* That upon the adoption of this resolution it shall be in order to consider the bill (H.R. ———) entitled, etc., in the House.

The resolution may waive points of order against the bill. When it limits or prevents floor amendments, it is popularly known as a "closed rule."

CONSIDERATION OF MEASURES MADE IN ORDER BY PREVIOUS RESOLUTION

When a "rule" has been reported to the House, and is not considered immediately, it is referred to the calendar, and if not called up for consideration by the member of the Rules Committee who made the report, within seven legislative days thereafter any member of the Rules Committee may call it up as a question of privilege and the Speaker will recognize any member of that Committee who seeks recognition for that purpose.

If, within seven calendar days after a measure has, by resolution, been made in order for consideration by the House, a motion has not been offered for its consideration, the Speaker may, in his discretion, recognize a member of the committee that reported the measure to offer a motion that the House consider it, if the member has been duly authorized by that committee to offer the motion.

There are several other methods of obtaining consideration of bills that either have not been reported by a committee or, if reported, for which a special resolution or "rule" has not been obtained.

MOTION TO DISCHARGE COMMITTEE

A member may present to the Clerk a motion in writing to discharge a committee from the consideration of a public bill or resolution that has been referred to it 30 days prior thereto. A member may also file a motion to discharge the Committee on Rules from further consideration of a resolution providing either a special order of business, or a special rule for the consideration of a public bill or resolution favorably reported by a standing committee, or a special rule for the consideration of a public bill or resolution that has remained in a standing committee 30 days or more without action. This motion may be made only when the resolution, from which it is moved to discharge the Committee on Rules, has been referred to that committee at least seven days prior to the filing of the motion to discharge. The motion is placed in the custody of the Clerk, who arranges some convenient place for the signature of members. When a majority of the total membership of the House have signed the motion it is entered on the Journal, printed with the signatures thereto in the *Congressional Record,* and referred to the Calendar of Motions to Discharge Committees.

On the second and fourth Mondays of each month, except during the last six days of a session, a member who has signed a motion to discharge, that has been on the calendar at least seven days, may seek recognition and be recognized for the purpose of calling up the motion. The bill or resolution is then read by title only. After 20 minutes' debate, one half in favor of the proposition and one half in opposition, the House proceeds to vote on the motion to discharge.

If the motion to discharge the Committee on Rules from a resolution pending before the committee prevails, the House immediately votes on the adoption of that resolution.

If the motion to discharge one of the standing committees of the House from a public bill or resolution pending before the committee prevails, a member who signed the motion may move that the House proceed to the immediate consideration of the bill or resolution under the general rules of the House. If the House votes against the motion for immediate consideration, the bill or resolution is referred to its proper calendar with the same rights and privileges it would have had if reported favorably by the standing committee.

MOTION TO SUSPEND THE RULES

On Monday and Tuesday of each week and during the last six days of a session, the Speaker may entertain a motion to suspend the operation of the regular rules and pass a bill or resolution. Arrangement must be made in advance with the Speaker to recognize the member who wishes to offer the motion. Before being considered by the House, the motion must be seconded by a majority of the members present, by teller vote, if demanded. However, a second is not required on a motion to suspend the rules when printed copies of the proposed bill or resolution have been available for one legislative day before the motion is considered. The motion to suspend the rules and pass the bill is then debated for 40 minutes, one half by those in favor of the proposition and one half by those opposed. The motion may not be amended and if amendments to the bill are proposed they must be included in the motion when it is made. The rules may be suspended and the bill passed only by affirmative vote of two thirds of the members voting, a quorum being present.

The Speaker may postpone all recorded and yea–nay votes on motions to suspend the rules and pass bills and resolutions until the end of that legislative day or the next legislative day. At that time the House disposes of the deferred votes consecutively without further debate. By eliminating intermittent recorded votes on suspensions, this procedure reduces interruptions of committee meetings and also reduces the time members spend on suspension days going back and forth between the floor and their committee rooms or offices.

If the Speaker intends to defer recorded and yea–nay votes on motions to suspend the rules and pass bills and resolutions, he must announce his intention before he entertains the first motion to suspend on any suspension day. After the first deferred vote is taken, the Speaker may reduce to not less than five minutes the time period for subsequent deferred votes. If the House adjourns before completing action on one or more deferred votes, these must be the first order of business on the next suspension day. On Private Calendar days, however, that calendar will be disposed of before the deferred suspension votes.

CALENDAR WEDNESDAY

On Wednesday of each week, unless dispensed with by unanimous consent or by affirmative vote of two thirds of the members voting, a quorum being present, the standing committees are called in alphabetical order. A committee when named may call up for consideration any bill reported by it on a previous day and pending on either the House or Union Calendar. Not more than two hours of general debate is permitted on any measure called up on Calendar Wednesday and all debate must be confined to the subject matter of the measure, the time being equally divided between those for and those against it. The affirmative vote of a simple majority of the members present is sufficient to pass the measure.

PRIVILEGED MATTERS

Under the rules of the House certain matters are regarded as privileged matters and may interrupt the order of business, for example, reports from the Committee on Rules and reports from the Committee on Appropriations on the general appropriation bills.

At any time after the reading of the Journal, a member, by direction of the appropriate committee, may move that the House resolve itself into the Committee of the Whole House on the State of the Union for the purpose of considering bills raising revenues, or general appropriation bills. General appropriation bills may not be considered in the House until three calendar days (excluding Saturdays, Sundays, and legal holidays) after printed committee reports and hearings on them have been available to the members. The limit on general debate is generally fixed by unanimous consent.

Other examples of privileged matters are conference reports, certain amendments to measures by the Senate, veto messages from the President of the United States, and resolutions privileged pursuant to statute. The member in charge of such a matter may call it up at practically any time for immediate consideration. Usually, this is done after consultation with both the majority and minority floor leaders so that the members of both parties will have advance notice and will not be taken by surprise.

CONSIDERATION

Our democratic tradition demands that bills be given consideration by the entire membership with adequate opportunity for debate and the proposing of amendments.

COMMITTEE OF THE WHOLE HOUSE

In order to expedite the consideration of bills and resolutions, the House resorts to a parliamentary usage that enables it to act with a quorum of only 100 members instead of the normally requisite majority—that is, 218. This consists of resolving itself into the Committee of the Whole House on the state of the Union to consider a measure. All measures on the Union Calendar—involving a tax, making appropriations, or authorizing payments out of appropriations already made—must be first considered in the Committee of the Whole.

Members debate and vote on the motion that the House resolve itself into the Committee of the Whole. If the motion is adopted, the Speaker leaves his chair after appointing a chairman to preside.

The special resolution or "rule" reported by the Committee on Rules to allow for immediate consideration of the measure fixes the length of the debate in the Committee of the Whole. This may vary according to the importance and controversial nature of the measure. As provided in the resolution the control of the time is divided equally—usually between the chairman and the ranking minority member of the committee that reported the measure. Members seeking to speak for or against the measure usually arrange in advance with the member in control of the time on their respective side to be allowed a certain amount of time in the debate. Others may ask the member speaking at the time to yield to them for a question or a brief statement. Frequently permission is granted a member by unanimous consent to extend his remarks in the *Congressional Record* if sufficient time to make a lengthy oral statement is not available during actual debate.

The conduct of the debate is governed principally by the standing rules of the House that are adopted at the opening of each Congress. Another recognized authority is *Jefferson's Manual* that was prepared by Thomas Jefferson for his own guidance as President of the Senate from 1797 to 1801. The House, in 1837, adopted a rule that still stands, providing that the provisions of *Jefferson's Manual* should govern the House in all cases to which they are applicable and in which they are not inconsistent with the standing rules and orders of the House. In addition there is a most valuable compilation of precedents up to the year 1935 set out in *Hinds' Precedents* and *Cannon's Precedents of the House of Representatives,* consisting of 11 volumes, to guide the action of the House. A later compilation, *Deschler's Precedents of the House of Representatives,* covering years 1936 to 1974 is in preparation—of which volumes 1 to 3 are now published. Summaries of the House precedents prior to 1959 can be found in a single volume entitled *Cannon's Procedure in the House of Representatives*. A later volume, *Deschler's Procedure in the House of Representatives,* third edition, is a compilation of the parliamentary precedents of the House, in summary form, together with other useful related material, from 1959 to March 1978. Also, various rulings of the Speaker since 1931 are set out as notes to the current *House Manual*. Most parliamentary questions arising during the course of debate are susceptible of ruling backed up by a precedent of action in a similar situation. The Parliamentarian of the House is present in the House chamber in order to assist the chairman or the Speaker in making a correct ruling on parliamentary questions.

SECOND READING

During the general debate an accurate account is kept of the time used on both sides and when all the time allowed under the rule has been consumed the chairman terminates the debate. Then begins the "second reading of the bill," section by section, at which time amendments may be offered to a section when it is read. Under the House rules, a member is permitted five minutes to explain his proposed amendment, after which the member who is first recognized by the chair is allowed to speak for five minutes in opposition to it; there is no further debate on that amendment, thereby effectively preventing any attempt at filibuster tactics. This is known as the "five-minute rule." There is, however, a device whereby a member may offer a pro forma amendment—"to strike out the last word"—without intending any change in the language, and be allowed five minutes for debate, thus permitting a somewhat more comprehensive debate. Each amendment (except a pro forma amendment) is put to the Committee of the Whole for adoption.

At any time after a debate is begun under the five-minute rule, on proposed amendments to a section or paragraph of a bill, the committee may by majority vote of the members present, close debate on the section or paragraph. However, if debate is closed on a section or paragraph before there has been debate on any amendment that a member has caused to be printed in the *Congressional Record* after the reporting of the bill by the committee but at least one day prior to floor consideration of the amendment, the member who caused the amendment to be printed in the *Record* is given five minutes in which to explain the amendment, after which the first person to obtain the floor has five minutes to speak in opposition to it, and there is no further debate on that proposed amendment; but time for debate is not allowed when the offering of the amendment is dilatory. Material placed in the *Congressional Record* must indicate the full text of the proposed amendment, the name of the proponent member, the number of the bill to which it will be offered and the point in the bill or amendment thereto where the amendment is intended to be offered, and must appear in a portion of the *Record* designated for that purpose.

When an amendment is offered, while the House is meeting in the Committee of the Whole, the Clerk is required to transmit five copies of the amendment to the majority committee table, five copies to the minority committee table, at least one copy to the majority cloak room, and at least one copy to the minority cloak room.

THE COMMITTEE "RISES"

At the conclusion of the consideration of a bill for amendment, the Committee of the Whole "rises" and reports the bill to the House with the amendments that have been adopted. In rising the Committee of the Whole reverts back to the House and the chairman of the Committee is replaced in the chair by the Speaker of the House. The House then acts on the bill and any amendments adopted by the Committee of the Whole.

ACTION BY THE HOUSE

Under the rules of the House, debate is cut off by moving "the previous question." If this motion is carried by a majority of the members voting, a quorum being present, all debate is cut off on the bill on which the previous question has been ordered. The Speaker then puts the question: "Shall the bill be engrossed and read a third time?" If this question is decided in the affirmative, the bill is read a third time by title only and voted on for passage. In 1965, the House rules were amended to abolish the third reading of the bill in full on demand of a member—a practice that was sometimes used as a dilatory tactic.

If the previous question has been ordered by the terms of the special resolution or "rule" on a bill reported by the Committee of the Whole, the House immediately votes on whatever amendments have been reported by the Committee in the sequence in which they were reported. After completion of voting on the amendments, the House immediately votes on the passage of the bill with the amendments it has adopted.

In those cases where the previous question has not been ordered, the House may engage in debate lasting one hour, at the conclusion of which the previous question is ordered and the House votes on the passage of the bill. During the debate it is in order to offer amendments to the bill or to the Committee amendments.

In 1979, the House amended its rules to allow the Speaker to postpone a vote on final passage of a bill or resolution or agreement to a conference report. A vote may be postponed for up to two legislative days.

Measures that do not have to be considered in the Committee of the Whole are considered in the House in the first instance under the hour rule or in accordance with the terms of the special resolution limiting debate on the measure.

After passage of the bill by the House, a pro

forma motion to reconsider it is automatically made and laid on the table—i.e., action is postponed indefinitely—to forestall this motion at a later date, because the vote of the House on a proposition is not final and conclusive on the House until there has been an opportunity to reconsider it.

MOTIONS TO RECOMMIT

After the previous question has been ordered on the passage of a bill or joint resolution, it is in order to make one motion to recommit the bill or joint resolution to a committee and the Speaker is required to give preference in recognition for that purpose to a member who is opposed to the bill or joint resolution. This motion is normally not subject to debate. However, with respect to a motion to recommit with instructions after the previous question has been ordered, it is in order to debate the motion for ten minutes before the vote is taken, the time to be equally divided between the proponents and opponents of the motion.

QUORUM CALLS AND ROLL CALLS

In order to speed up and expedite quorum calls and roll calls, the rules of the House provide alternative methods for pursuing these procedures.

The rules provide that in the absence of a quorum, 15 members, including the Speaker, if there is one, are authorized to compel the attendance of absent members. A call of the House is then ordered, and the Speaker is required to have the call taken by electronic device, unless in his discretion he names one or more clerks "to tell" the members who are present. In that case the names of those present are recorded by the clerks, and entered in the Journal of the House and absent members have not less than 15 minutes from the ordering of the call of the House to have their presence recorded. If sufficient excuse is not offered for their absence, by order of a majority of those present, they may be sent for by officers appointed by the Sergeant-at-Arms for that purpose, and their attendance secured and retained. The House then determines the conditions on which they may be discharged. Members who voluntarily appear are, unless the House otherwise directs, immediately admitted to the Hall of the House and they must report their names to the Clerk to be entered on the Journal as present. However, the former practice of presenting members at the bar of the House during a call is now obsolete, and members now report to the Clerk and are recorded without being formally excused unless brought in under compulsion.

Whenever a quorum fails to vote on any question, and a quorum is not present and objection is made for that reason, unless the House adjourns, a call of the House is required to be taken by electronic device, unless the Speaker orders the call in the manner described above, and the Sergeant-at-Arms proceeds to bring in absent members. The yeas and nays on the pending question are at the same time considered as ordered and an automatic roll-call vote is taken. The Clerk calls the roll and each member who is present may vote on the pending question as he answers to his name. After the roll call is completed, each member, whose attendance was secured, is brought before the House by the Sergeant-at-Arms, where his presence is noted, he is given an opportunity to vote, and his vote is recorded. If those voting on the question and those who are present and decline to vote together make a majority of the House, the Speaker declares that a quorum is constituted, and the pending question is decided according to the will of the majority of those voting. Further proceedings under the call are considered as dispensed with. At any time after the roll call has been completed, the Speaker may entertain a motion to adjourn, if seconded by a majority of those present as ascertained by actual count by the Speaker; and if the House adjourns, all proceedings under this paragraph are vacated.

The rules prohibit points of no quorum (1) before or during the daily prayer, (2) during administration of the oath of office to the Speaker or any member, (3) during the reception of messages from the President or the Senate, (4) in connection with motions incidental to a call of the House, and (5) against a vote in which the Committee of the Whole agrees to rise. (But an appropriate point of no quorum would be permitted against a vote defeating a motion to rise.) If the presence of a quorum has been established at least once on any day, further points of no quorum are prohibited (1) during the reading of the Journal, (2) between the time a Committee of the Whole rises and its chairman reports, and (3) during the period on any legislative day when members are addressing the House under special orders. The language prohibiting quorum calls "during any period" when members are speaking under special orders includes the time between addresses delivered during this period as well as the addresses themselves. Furthermore, a quorum call is not in order when no business has intervened since the previous call. For the purposes of this provision, all the situations described above are not to be considered as "business."

The rules prohibit points of no quorum when a motion or proposition is pending in the House unless the Speaker has put the motion or proposition to a vote. However, the Speaker has the discretion to recognize a member of his choice to move a call of the House.

The first time the Committee of the Whole finds itself without a quorum during any day the chairman is required to order the roll to be called by electronic device, unless, in his discretion, he orders a call by naming clerks "to tell" the members, as described above. If on a call a quorum appears, the Committee continues its business. If a quorum does not appear, the Committee rises and the chairman reports the names of the absentees to the House. The House rules provide for the expeditious conduct of quorum calls in the Committee of the Whole. The chairman may suspend a quorum call once he or she determines that a bare or minimum quorum has been reached—that is, 100 or more members. Under such a short quorum call the Committee will not rise and therefore members' names will not be published. Once the presence of a quorum of the Committee of the Whole has been established for the day, quorum calls in the Committee are only in order when the Committee is operating under the five-minute rule and the chairman has put the pending motion or proposition to a vote.

VOTING

There are four methods of voting in the Committee of the Whole that are also employed, together with an additional method, in the House. These are the voice vote (viva voce), the division, the teller vote, the recorded vote, and the yea-and-nay vote that is used only in the House. If a member objects to the vote on the ground that a quorum is not present in the House, there may be an automatic roll-call vote.

To obtain a voice vote the chair states, "As many as are in favor (as the question may be) say 'aye'." "As many as are opposed, say 'no'." The chair determines the result on the basis of the volume of ayes and noes. This is the form in which the vote is ordinarily taken in the first instance.

If it is difficult to determine the result of a voice vote, a division may be demanded. The chair than states that a division has been demanded and says, "As many as are in favor will rise and stand until counted." After counting those in favor he calls on those opposed to stand and be counted, thereby determining the number in favor of and those opposed to the question.

If a demand for a teller vote is supported by one fifth of a quorum (20 in the Committee of the Whole, and 44 in the House), the chair appoints one or more tellers from each side and directs the members in favor of the proposition to pass between the tellers and be counted. After counting, a teller announces the number in the affirmative, and the chair then directs the members opposed to pass between the tellers and be counted. When the count is stated by a teller, the chair announces the result.

If any member requests a recorded vote and that request is supported by at least one fifth of a quorum of the House, or 25 members in the Committee of the Whole, the vote is taken by electronic device, unless the Speaker, in his discretion, orders clerks "to tell"—that is, record the names of those voting on each side of the question. After the recorded vote is concluded, the names of those voting together with those not voting are entered in the Journal. Members usually have 15 minutes to be counted from the time the recorded vote is ordered or the ordering of the clerks "to tell" the vote. However, the House rules allow the Speaker to reduce the period of voting to five minutes in certain situations.

In addition to the foregoing methods of voting, in the House, if the yeas and nays are demanded, the Speaker directs those in favor of taking the vote by that method to stand and be counted. The assent of one fifth of the members present (as distinguished from one fifth of a quorum in the case of a demand for tellers) is necessary for ordering the yeas and nays. When the yeas and nays are ordered (or a point of order is made that a quorum is not present) the Speaker directs that as many as are in favor of the proposition will, as their names are called, answer "aye"; as many as are opposed will answer "no." The Clerk calls the roll and reports the result to the Speaker who announces it to the House. The Speaker is not required to vote unless his vote would be decisive.

ELECTRONIC VOTING

Under modern practice that went into effect on January 23, 1973, recorded and roll-call votes are usually taken by electronic device, except when the Speaker, in his discretion, orders the vote to be recorded by other methods prescribed by the rules of the House, and in emergency situations, such as the failure of the electronic device to function. In addition, quorum calls are generally taken by electronic device. Essentially the system works as follows. A number of vote stations are attached to selected chairs in the Chamber. Each station is equipped with a vote card slot and four indicators, marked "yea," "nay," "present," and "open." The "open" indicator is used only when a vote period is in progress and the system is ready to accept votes. Each member is furnished with a personalized vote–ID card. A member casts his vote by inserting his card into any one of the vote stations and depressing the appropriate push botton indicator according to his choice. The machine records the votes and reports the result when the vote is completed. In the event the member finds himself without his vote–ID card, he may still cast his vote by paper ballot, that he hands to the tally clerk, who may then record the vote electronically according to the indicated preference of the member. The paper ballots are green for "yea," red for "nay," and amber for "present."

PAIRING OF MEMBERS

When a member anticipates that he will be unavoidably absent at the time a vote is to be taken he may arrange in advance to be recorded as being either in favor of, or opposed to, the question by being "paired" with a member who will also be absent and who holds contrary views on the question. A specific pair of this kind shows how he would have voted if he had been present. Occasionally a member who has arranged in advance to be paired, actually is present at the time of voting. He then votes as he would have voted if he had not been paired, and subsequently withdraws his vote and asks to be marked "present" to protect his colleague. This is known as a "live pair." If his absence is to continue for several days during which a number of different questions are to be voted upon he may arrange a "general pair." A general pair does not indicate how he would have voted on the question, but merely that he and the member paired with him would not have been on the same side of the question.

Pairs are not counted in determining the vote on the question, but, rather, provide an opportunity for absent members to express formally how they would have voted had they been present. Pairs are announced by the Clerk of the House and are listed in the *Congressional Record* immediately after the names of those members not voting on the question.

SYSTEM OF LIGHTS AND BELLS

Because of the large number and the diversity of daily tasks that they have to perform, it is not practicable for members to be present in the House (or Senate) chamber at every minute that the body is actually sitting. Furthermore, many of the routine matters do not require the personal attendance of all the members. In order to procure their presence when needed for a vote or to constitute a quorum, systems of electric lights and bells or buzzers are provided in various parts of the Capitol Building and of the House and Senate Office Buildings.

In the House the Speaker has ordered that the bells and lights comprising the system be utilized as follows:

One ring and one light on the left—Teller vote.

One long ring followed by a pause and then three rings and three lights on the left—Start or continuation of a notice or short quorum call in the Committee of the Whole that will be vacated if and when 100 members appear on the floor. Bells are repeated every five minutes unless the call is vacated or the call is converted into a regular quorum call.

One long ring and extinguishing of three lights on the left—Short or notice quorum call vacated.

Two rings and two lights on the left—Recorded vote, yea-and-nay vote, or automatic roll-call vote by electronic device or by tellers with ballot cards. The bells are repeated five minutes after the first ring.

Two rings and two lights on the left followed by a pause and then two more rings—Automatic roll-call vote or yea-and-nay vote taken by a call of the roll in the House. The bells are repeated when the clerk reaches the Rs in the first call of the roll.

Two rings followed by a pause and then five rings—First vote under Suspension of the Rules when the Speaker has announced his intention to defer recorded votes until the end of the suspension business. Two bells are repeated five minutes after the first ring. Five bells are rung at the beginning of each subsequent postponed vote, on which the Speaker has reduced the vote time to the five-minute minimum.

Three rings and three lights on the left—Regular quorum call in either the House or in the Committee of the Whole by electronic device or by clerks. The bells are repeated five minutes after the first ring.

Three rings followed by a pause and then three more rings—Regular quorum call by a call of the roll. The bells are repeated when the Clerk reaches the Rs in the first call of the roll.

Three rings followed by a pause and then five more rings—Quorum call in the Committee of the Whole that may be followed immediately by a five-minute recorded vote.

Four rings and four lights on the left—Adjournment of the House.

Five rings and five lights on the left—Any five-minute vote.

Six rings and six lights on the left—Recess of the House.

Twelve rings at two-second intervals with six lights on the left—Civil Defense Warning.

The red light indicates that the House is in session.

BROADCASTING LIVE COVERAGE OF FLOOR PROCEEDINGS

Recently, the House amended its rules to provide for unedited audio and visual broadcasting and recording of proceedings on the floor of the House. House rules prohibit the use of these broadcasts and recordings for any political purpose or in any commercial advertisement.

(The following is from Kimmit and Zweben:)

THE SENATE

Introduction and Reference of Proposed Legislation in Senate

During the morning hour of each legislative day, Rule VII of the Senate provides that, after the Journal is read and the presiding officer lays before the Senate messages, reports, and communications of various types, he shall call for, in the following order:

The presentation of petitions and memorials.

Reports of standing and select committees.

The introduction of bills and joint resolutions.

Concurrent and other resolutions.

Under recent practices, however, nearly all of the bills and resolutions are presented by a Senator to the clerks at the presiding officer's desk for processing throughout the day, and without any comments from the floor. A few of them are still introduced from the floor, and any Senator, when making such introductions, usually discusses his proposal when he presents it. Only one Senator may introduce a bill or resolution, but commonly he does it for himself and other Senators as cosponsors.

The rules require that every bill and joint resolution have three readings, each on a different legislative day, before passage—two of these to occur before reference to a committee. This is seldom done anymore, however, since all bills and resolutions are available in printed form. The reading requirement on different days is rarely invoked, usually only when there are procedural conflicts, but it can be forced on the Senate by a single Senator.

A legislative day is the period between the meeting of the Senate following an adjournment and its next adjournment, which period, by recessing (as opposed to adjourning) from day to day, may include several calendar days.

After the second reading of a bill, it is referred by the presiding officer to the standing committee of the Senate which, in his judgment, has jurisdiction of the subject matter, or a preponderance thereof. The reference by the presiding officer is subject to an appeal to the Senate, which, by a majority vote, has power to overrule his decision and bring about a reference to a different committee. In the Senate unanimous consent is required to refer a bill jointly and/or sequentially to two or more committees having jurisdiction over the subject matter.

Endorsements showing the author and reference are made at the presiding officer's desk on each bill. These various proceedings are shown in the *Congressional Record* of that day and are noted in the Minute Book kept by the journal clerk. After being referred, the bill is sent by a page to the Office of the Secretary of the Senate and numbered by the *Congressional Record* clerk. He delivers it to the bill clerk, who makes entries in the Bill Book and the computer-controlled data storage and retrieval system, showing the number, author, title, date, and reference. It is then turned over to the assistant journal clerk for proper notation in the Senate Journal of the proceedings of that day, and is subsequently sent to the Government Printing Office to be printed. Printed copies of the bill are delivered (usually the next morning) to the Secretary's office, and to the Senate and House document rooms, and are thus made available to the public. The original bill is then returned by the Printing Office to the Secretary of the Senate, who retains it in his files.

Senate Committee Consideration

A clerk in the Secretary's office delivers a printed copy of each bill to the committee to which it was referred, taking a receipt therefor. The clerk of the committee enters it upon the committee's Calendar of Business.

Committees as a rule have regular meeting days, but they may meet at the call of their chairman or upon the request of a majority at other times. At these meetings matters on the committee calendar are usually the order of business, but any matter within the committee's jurisdiction may be considered—for example, an investigation of an agency of the government over which it has jurisdiction, or to hear an official discuss policies and operations of his agency.

Any committee may refer its pending bills to its subcommittees for study and reports thereon. Most of the committees have standing subcommittees, and frequently ad hoc subcommittees are appointed to study and report on particular pieces of legislation or to make a study of a certain subject.

Committees or subcommittees generally hold hearings on all major or controversial legislation before drafting the proposal into a final form for reporting to the Senate. The length of hearings and the number of witnesses testifying vary, depending upon the time element, the number of witnesses wanting to be heard, the desires of the committee to hear witnesses, et cetera. Recommendations of the administration, in conjunction with the Office of Management and Budget, are sought by the committees on nearly all major legislation, but they are in no way obligated to accept such recommendations.

A subcommittee makes reports to its full committee, and the latter may adopt such reports without change, amend them in any way it desires, reject them, or adopt an entirely different report.

After consideration of any bill, the full committee may report it to the Senate favorably with or without amendments, submit an adverse report thereon, or vote not to report anything.

Committees need not act on all bills referred to them. Under the rules, a Senator may enter a motion to discharge a committee from the further consideration of any bill, but this is rarely done. By unanimous consent, some bills are discharged from one committee and sent to another. If a motion to discharge is agreed to, the bill is thereby taken out of the jurisdiction of that committee and placed on the Senate Calendar of Business. It may subsequently be referred to another committee.

Committee Reports

The chairman, or some other member of the committee designated for that purpose, reports bills to the Senate, and when reported they are placed on the Senate Calendar of Business, unless unanimous consent is given for immediate consideration.

The action taken by the committee appears on the copy of the bill reported, and a written report, which is numbered ad seriatim, nearly always accompanies the bill. The reports, like the bills, are printed by the Government Printing Office for distribution.

A reported bill passes through the same channels in the Secretary's office as an introduced bill, for notation of the proper entries on the records. It is reprinted, showing the calendar and report numbers, the name of the Senator reporting it, the date, and whether with or without amendment. Matters proposed to be stricken out of a bill by the committee are shown in line type, while matters proposed to be inserted are shown in italic. The committee report may include minority, individual, supplemental, and/or additional views, and these are printed as a part of the committee report on the measure.

Senate Consideration

The Majority and Minority Leaders, as the spokesmen for their parties, and in consultation with their respective policy committees, implement and direct the legislative schedule and program.

Most measures are passed either on the call of the Calendar or by unanimous consent procedure. The more significant and controversial matters are considered under a unanimous consent agreement limiting debate and controlling time on the measure, amendments thereto, and debatable motions relating to it, when possible. This is done because otherwise debate is unlimited. Measures may be brought up on motion by a simple majority vote if they have been on the Calendar one legislative day. Such a motion is usually made by the Majority Leader or his designee and is usually debatable. The motion to proceed to the consideration of a measure on the Calendar is usually only made if unanimous consent to proceed to its consideration is objected to.

On highly controversial matters, the Senate

frequently has to resort to "cloture" to work its will on the bill. Under Rule XXII, if three fifths of the Senators duly chosen and sworn (60 if the Senate is at full membership of 100) vote in the affirmative, further debate on the question shall be limited to no more than one hour for each Senator, and the time for consideration of the matter shall be limited to 100 hours unless increased by the same three-fifths vote indicated above. On a measure or motion to amend the Senate Rules, it takes two thirds of the Senators present and voting, a quorum being present, to invoke cloture.

Although under Rule VIII, which governs the consideration of bills on the call of the Senate Calendar, there is supposed to be a Calendar call each day at the end of the morning business, under current practice this very rarely occurs—the Calendar is usually called pursuant to a unanimous consent order. Rule VII makes a call of the Calendar mandatory on Monday if the Senate had adjourned after its prior sitting. This requirement may only be waived by unanimous consent, and it has become the practice of the leadership to almost invariably request that the requirement be waived.

Once a bill or resolution is before the Senate, it is subject to the amendatory process, both by the committee reporting it and by individual Senators offering amendments from the floor. A committee amendment reported as a total substitute (strikes all after the enacting clause and inserts new language for the entire bill) for the pending measure is always voted on last inasmuch as once a total substitute is agreed to, further amendments are precluded. With this exception, however, committee amendments take priority and are considered in order as they appear in the printed copy of the measure before the Senate. The only amendments from the floor in order during the consideration of these committee amendments are amendments offered to the committee amendments. Once the committee amendments have been disposed of, however, any Senator may propose amendments to any part of the bill not already amended, and while an amendment is pending, an amendment to the amendment is in order. By precedent, an amendment to an amendment to an amendment, being an amendment in the third degree, is not in order. However, the first amendment in the nature of a substitute for a bill, whether reported by a committee or offered by an individual Senator, does not kill a degree, being amendable in two more degrees.

There are certain special procedures in the Senate which limit the amendatory process. For example, during the consideration of general appropriation bills, amendments are subjected to the strictures of Rule XVI, under which amendments proposing new or general legislation, nongermane amendments, and amendments increasing the amount of an appropriation, which increase has not been previously authorized or estimated for in the President's budget, are not in order. Likewise, when operating under a general unanimous consent agreement in the usual form on a bill or resolution, amendments must be germane. Germaneness of amendments is also required once the Senate has invoked cloture, and in addition any amendments considered under cloture must have been submitted prior to the Senate's vote on cloture.

When all committee amendments and individual floor amendments offered by Senators have been disposed of, the bill is ordered engrossed and read a third time, which step ends the amendatory process.

The next step, after the amendment stage, is the engrossment and third reading of the bill. This reading is usually also by title only, but, upon demand, the engrossed bill must be read in full. The question is then put upon its passage, which is carried by a majority vote. If a bill has a preamble, sometimes referred to as "Whereases," it may be agreed to, amended, or striken out, after the bill has been passed. The title to a bill is also acted upon after its passage, and if amendments are made that necessitate a change in the title, the bill is accordingly amended. At any time before its passage, a bill may be laid on the table or postponed indefinitely, either of which motions has the effect of killing the bill; made a special order for a day certain, which requires a two-thirds vote; laid aside temporarily; recommitted to the committee which reported the bill; referred to a different committee; or displaced by taking up another bill by a majority vote.

Most bills are passed by a voice vote only, but where a doubt is raised in such a case, the presiding officer, or any Senator, before the result is announced, may request a division of the Senate to determine the question. Before the result of a voice or division vote has been announced, a roll-call vote may be had upon the demand of one fifth of the Senators present, but at least eleven—one fifth of the presumptive quorum of 51.

In the case of a yea-and-nay vote, any Senator who voted with the prevailing side or who did not vote may, on the same calendar day or on either of the next two days the Senate is acutally in session, make a motion to reconsider a question. On a voice vote or division vote, however, any Senator may make the motion. If made before other business intervenes, it may be proceeded with and is debatable. It may be laid on the table without prejudice to the main question and is a final disposition of the motion. A majority vote determines questions of reconsideration. If the motion is agreed to, another vote may be taken on the question reconsidered; if disagreed to, the first decision of the Senate is affirmed. The making of such a motion is privileged and may be made while another matter is pending before the Senate, in which case its consideration cannot be proceeded with except by unanimous consent or on motion. In such latter case the pending business would be displaced by agreeing to the motion.

Only one motion to reconsider the same question is in order. Such a motion, under Rule XXI, may be withdrawn by the mover by leave of the Senate, which may be granted by a majority vote, or by unanimous consent. A bill cannot be transmitted to the House of Representatives while a motion to reconsider remains unacted upon.

Engrossed Bills

The printed bill used at the desk by the Senate during its consideration as the official desk copy, showing the amendments adopted, if any, and endorsed as having passed, is sent to the Secretary's office and delivered to the bill clerk. Again, he makes the proper entries on his records and the data retrieval system. He then turns it over to the enrolling clerk who makes an appropriate entry on his records and sends it to the Government Printing Office to be printed on special white paper in the form in which it passed the Senate. This printed act is attested by the Secretary as having passed the Senate as of the proper date, and is termed the official engrossed bill.

After the passage of a bill by one body, it technically becomes an act (not yet effective as a law), but it nevertheless continues to be generally referred to as a bill.

Bills Sent to House

Engrossed bills are messaged to the House of Representatives by one of the clerks in the Secretary's office, who is announced by the Doorkeeper of the House.[1] Upon being recognized by the Speaker, the clerk announces that the Senate has passed a bill (giving its number and title) in which the concurrence of the House is requested.

Upon receipt of the message from the Senate, the Speaker refers the measure contained therein to appropriate committees. If, however, a substantially similar House bill has been favorably reported by a committee, the Senate bill, unless it creates a charge upon the Treasury, may not be referred but remains on the Speaker's table. It may subsequently be taken up or substituted for such House bill when consideration of the latter occurs.

Senate Action on House Amendments

Senate bills returned with House amendments are held at the desk and almost always subsequently laid before the Senate by the presiding officer upon request or motion of a Senator (usually the manager of the bill). The presiding officer may also do this upon his own initiative, but this is rarely done. After the House message has been laid down, the amendments may be considered individually or en bloc by unanimous consent. Any one of the following motions relating to the amendment or amendments may then be made, taking precedence in the order named: (1) a motion to refer the amendments to a standing committee of the Senate; (2) a motion to amend the amendments; (3) a motion to agree to the amendments; and (4) a motion to disagree to the amendments and ask a conference with the House. Usually number (4) includes authority for the presiding officer to appoint conferees on the part of the Senate, although the power to name conferees is in the Senate, not in the chair. The number of conferees named varies widely. The usual range is seven to eleven, but occasionally a larger number is appointed, especially in the case of general appropriation bills.

In the case of motion number (2), the amendments made by the Senate to the House amendments are transmitted to the House, with a request for its concurrence therein. If the House concurs or agrees in all the amendments (the words being used synonymously), the legislative steps in the passage of the bill are completed. The House, however, may amend the Senate amendments to the House amendments, this being the second, and therefore the last, degree in which amendments may be made. The House amendments to the Senate amendments are transmitted to the Senate, usually with a request for concurrence therein. As in the case of the original amendments, the Senate may agree to some, disagree to others, or ask for a conference with the House thereon. A conference may be requested at any stage of the consideration of these amendments in disagreement. If the Senate agrees to all of the House amendments to the Senate amendments, such action brings the two Houses into complete agreement, and likewise completes the legislative steps.

With respect to motion number (3), the concurrence of the Senate in the House amendments also completes the legislative steps.

With respect to motion number (1), the standing committee, after consideration, may recommend action indicated in motions (2), (3), or (4), and may make such motion accordingly.

BILLS ORIGINATING IN THE HOUSE

If a bill or resolution originates in the House, it follows the same steps as set forth above, except in reverse—i.e., a House committee considers it first, it is passed by the House, it is messaged to the Senate and referred to a Senate committee, the committee reports it to the Senate and it is then acted on by that body. If amended, it is returned to the House for concurrence in the Senate amendments.

CONFERENCES

When the Senate requests a conference or agrees to a request for a conference and names its conferees, it informs the House of its action by message. After the second house agrees to the conference, appoints conferees, and apprises the first house of its action by message, all the papers relating to the measure sent to conference (referred to as the "official papers") are transmitted to the conference. This includes the original engrossed bill, engrossed amendments, and the various messages of transmittal between the houses.

Since the conferees of each house vote as a unit, the House, like the Senate, may appoint as many conferees as it chooses to meet with the Senate conferees to reconcile the differences between the two houses—the sole purpose of a conference. Thus, having a larger number of conferees than the other house does not provide an advantage.

After deliberation the conferees may make one or more recommendations—for example, (1) that the House recede from all or certain of its amendments; (2) that the Senate recede from its disagreement to all or certain of the House amendments and agree to the same; or (3) that they report an inability to agree in all or in part. Usually, however, there is compromise.

Conferees dealing with an amendment or a series of amendments, as opposed to an amendment in the nature of a substitute, are more limited in their options than conferees dealing with a bill passed by the second house with an amendment in the nature of a substitute. They can only deal with the matters in disagreement. They cannot insert new matter or leave out matter agreed to by both houses, and if they exceed their authority, a point of order will lie against the conference report. Each house may instruct its conferees, but this is rarely done. Such instructions are not binding since conferences are presumed to be full and free—one house cannot restrict the other houses's conferees.

Where one house passes a bill of the other house with an amendment in the nature of a substitute and the measure then goes to conference, the conferees have wider latitude since the entire matter is in conference. They may report a third version on the same subject matter; all of its provisions, however, must be a germane modification of either the House or Senate version, or it will be subject to a point of order.

Conference Reports

The recommendations of the conferees are incorporated in a written report and a joint statement of managers, made in duplicate, both of which must be signed by a majority of the conferees of each house. If there are amendments upon which they were unable to agree, a statement to this effect is included in the report. These are referred to as amendments in disagreement. The conferees cannot report amendments in disagreement where the bill had gone to conference after one house had amended it with a complete substitute for the other house's bill.

One report, together with the papers if the House is to act first, is taken by the House conferees, or managers, as they are termed in that body, and subsequently presented by them to the House, with an accompaning explanatory statement as to its effect upon the matters involved. The report must lie over three days in the House for printing, except during the last six days of a session. The Senate conferees take the other copy which is presented for printing under the requirements of the Legislative Reorganization Act, as amended in 1970. To save time and expense, this requirement is frequently waived in the Senate by unanimous consent.

Normally, the House agreeing to a conference on a bill acts first on a conference report, but either house can act first if it has the official papers. Conference reports are privileged in both the Senate and the House. They cannot be amended, but must be voted upon as an entirety. If amendments in disagreement were reported by the conferees, they are acted on after the conference report is adopted. After adoption by the first house, the conference report is transmitted with the official papers to the other house with a message announcing its action.

Assuming action by the House first, the Senate conferees could then present their report and ask for its immediate consideration. It does not have to lie over three days in the Senate, as it does in the House, and the motion to proceed to its consideration is not debatable; thus the Senate may act immediately. A motion to recommit a conference report may not be made in the second house acting on the report since the conferees of the first house were discharged when their body agreed to the report.

If conferees reach a complete agreement on all of the House amendments to a Senate bill, and the House adopts that report, the adoption of the report by the Senate completes the legislative action on the bill. If, however, there were amendments upon which an agreement had not been reached by the conferees, the adoption of the report by both houses leaves the parliamentary status of these particular amendments in disagreement the same as if no conference had been held.

If the amendments on which an agreement could not be reached were House amendments, and the House acted on the report first, it could then recede from its amendments, eliminating the amendments in disagreement; and then, if the Senate adopts the report, the bill would have been cleared for the President's signature. If they were Senate amendments and the House acted first, the House could concur in the Senate amendments or concur in them with amendments. If the Senate amendments were concurred in by the House, that would clear the amendments in disagreement, and when the Senate agreed to the conference report, the bill would be cleared for the President's signature. If the House should concur in the Senate amendments reported in disagreement with amendments, after the Senate agreed to the report, it could concur in the House amendments to the Senate amendments which would clear the bill for the President's signature. If the amendments reported in disagreement are not so disposed of, a further conference on these amendments could be requested by one House and agreed to by the other. When this happens, the two houses usually appoint the same conferees. Until all the amendments in disagreement are reconciled by the two houses, the bill cannot become a law.

If a conference report is rejected by one of the houses, it so notifies the other body by message and usually requests another conference; however, it may merely notify the second body of its action without requesting a further conference, leaving further steps to be taken by the other house. Endorsements showing these various legislative steps and when taken are made on the engrossed bill.

When the two houses reach a complete agreement on all the amendments, the papers are delivered to the enrolling clerk of the house where the bill originated. He prepares a copy of the bill in the form as finally agreed upon by the two houses and sends it to the Government Printing Office for "enrollment," which means historically "written on parchment." The original papers on the bill are retained in the files of the originating house until the end of a Congress, when they are sent to the Archives.

SIGNATURES OF SPEAKER AND VICE PRESIDENT

Upon receipt of an enrolled bill from the Government Printing Office, either the Secretary of the Senate or the Clerk of the House endorses it, certifying where the bill originated. If, after examination by the enrolling clerk of that House, the bill is found to be in the form agreed upon by both houses, a slip is attached thereto stating that the bill, identified by number and title, has been examined and found truly enrolled. It is then presented to the Speaker of the House for his signature, which is announced in open session. As a matter of custom, all enrolled bills are signed first by the Speaker. The bill is then transmitted by messenger to the Senate, where it is signed by the Vice President.[2]

Under the rules of the House, the Committee on House Administration is charged, when an enrolled bill has been duly signed by the Speaker and the Vice President, to present the same, when the bill originates in the House, to the President of the United States for his signature "and report the fact and date of such presentation to the House." If it is a Senate bill, this responsibility of presenting the bill to the President falls on the Secretary of the Senate.

An error discovered in a bill after the legislative steps in its passage have been completed may be corrected by the authority of a concurrent resolution, provided it has not been approved by the President. If the bill has not been enrolled, the error may be corrected in the enrollment; if it has been enrolled and signed by the presiding officers of the two houses, or by the Speaker, such action may be rescinded by a concurrent resolution agreed to by the two houses, and the bill correctly reenrolled. If it has been presented to the President, but not acted upon by him, he may be requested by a concurrent resolution to return it to the Senate or the House for correction. If, however, the President has approved the bill, and it has thereby become a law, any amendment thereof can only be made by the passage of another bill, which must take the same course as the original.

PRESIDENTIAL ACTION—APPROVAL OR VETO

The President, under the Constitution, has 10 days[3](Sundays excepted)[4] after the bill has been presented to him in which to act upon it. If the subject matter of the bill is within the jurisdiction of a department of the government, or affects its interests in any way, he may, in the meantime, at his discretion, refer the bill to the head of such department for investigation and a report thereon. The report of such official may serve as an aid to the President in reaching a decision on the question of approval. If the President approves the bill, he signs it, giving the date, and transmits this information, by messenger, to the Senate or the House, as the case might be. In the case of revenue and tariff bills, the hour of approval is usually indicated. The enrolled bill is delivered to the Administrator of the General Services Administration, who designates it as a public or private law, depending upon its purpose, and gives it a number. Public and private laws are numbered separately and serially. An official copy is sent to the Government Printing Office, to be used in making the so-called slip law print. The enrolled bill itself is deposited in the files of the General Services Administration.

In the event the President does not desire to approve a bill, but is unwilling to veto it, he may, by not returning it within the 10 day period after it is presented to him, permit it to become a law without his approval. The Administrator of the General Services Administration makes an endorsement on the bill that, having been presented to the President of the United States for his approval and not having been returned to the House of Congress in which it originated within the time prescribed by the Constitution, it has become a law without his approval.

The Supreme Court of the United States, in the case of *Edwards* v. *U.S.* (286 U.S. 482), decided that, where the 10-day period extends beyond the date of the final adjournment of a session of the Congress, the President may, within such time, approve and sign the bill, which thereby becomes a law. If, however, in such a case, the President does not approve and sign the bill prior to the expiration of that period, it fails to become a law. This is what is known as a pocket veto. The U.S. Court of Appeals, in the case of *Kennedy* v. *Sampson,* 511 F.2d 430 (D.C. Cir., August 14, 1974), held that a Senate bill could not be pocket-vetoed by the President during an "intrasession" adjournment of Congress to a day certain for more than three days, where the Secretary of the Senate had been authorized to receive presidential messages during such adjournment.

If the President does not favor a bill and vetoes it, he returns it to the house of origin without his approval, together with his objections thereto (referred to as the "veto message"). It should be noted that after the final adjournment of the 94th Congress, first session, the President, although he could have exercised the pocket veto, chose to return two bills in this fashion, giving Congress the opportunity to reconsider and "override" the vetoes.

The constitutional provision for reconsideration by the Senate is met, under the precedents, by the reading of the veto message, spreading it on the Journal, and adopting a motion (1) to act on it immediately; (2) to refer it, with the accompanying papers, to a standing committee; (3) to order that it lie on the table to be subsequently considered; or (4) to order its consideration postponed to a definite day. The House procedure is much the same.

If, upon reconsideration by either house, the house of origin acting first, it does not receive a two-thirds vote, the President's veto is sustained and the bill fails to become a law.

If a bill which has been vetoed is passed upon reconsideration by the first house by the required two-thirds vote, an endorsement to this effect is made on the back of the bill, and it is then transmitted, together with the accompanying message, to the second house for its action thereon. If likewise reconsidered and passed by that body, a similar endorsement is made thereon. The bill, which has thereby been enacted into law, is not again presented to the President of the United States, but is delivered to the Administrator of the General Services Administration for deposit in the Archives, and is printed, together with the attestations of the Secretary of the Senate and the Clerk of the House of its passage over the President's veto.

ILLUSTRATION 6A HOW A BILL BECOMES A LAW

This figure shows the long, complex, arduous, and multistaged process by which a bill becomes a law.

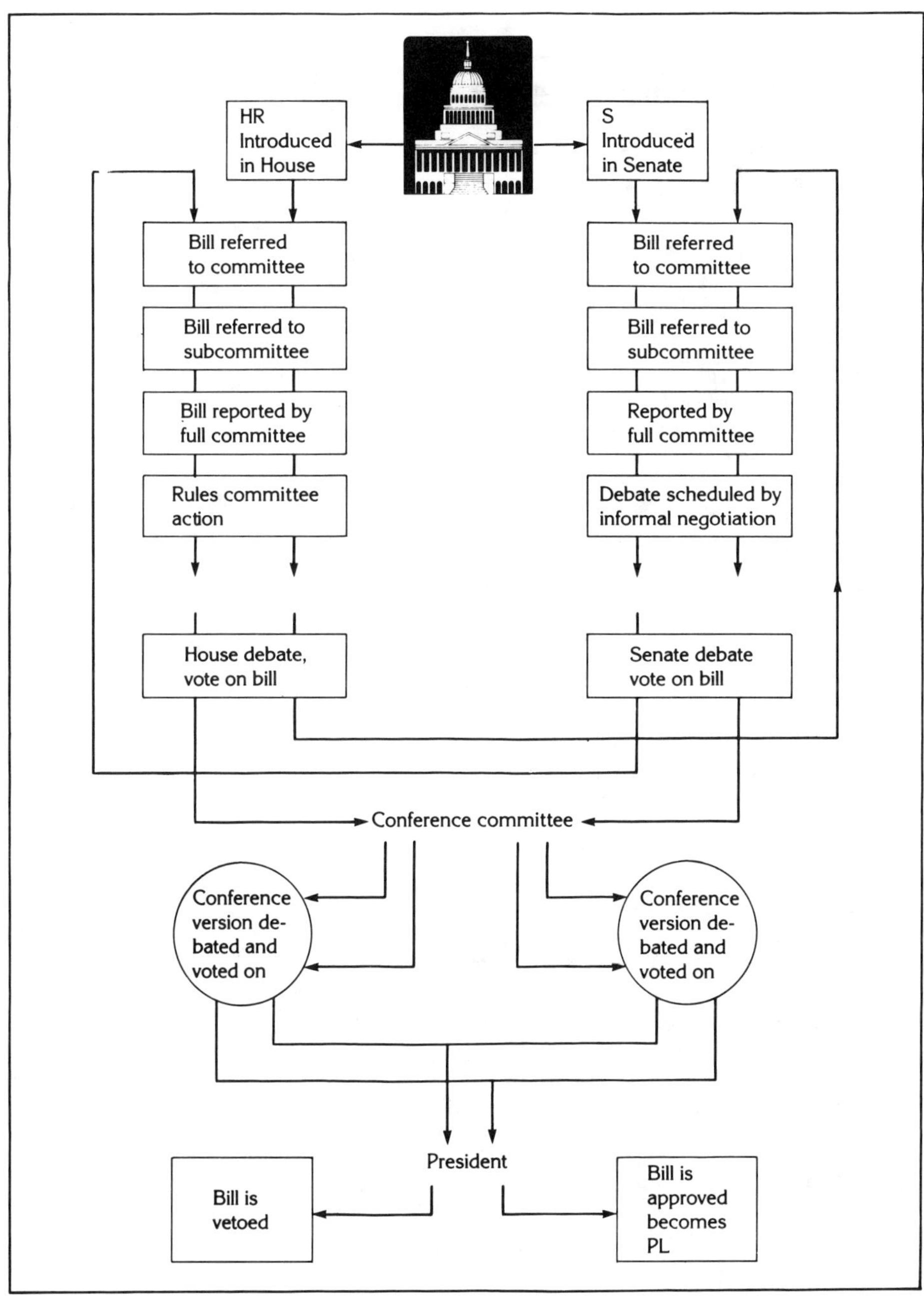

ILLUSTRATION 6B A HOUSE RULE

The House Rules Committee functions as a traffic cop, governing the routing of bills to the floor and the general flow of traffic. Notice how the rule stipulates the time and means of debate and the way amendments can be offered.

House Calendar No. 127

96TH CONGRESS
1ST SESSION

H. RES. 368

[Report No. 96–347]

Providing for the consideration of the bill (H.R. 4040) to authorize appropriations for fiscal year 1980 for procurement of aircraft, missiles, naval vessels, tracked combat vehicles, torpedoes, and other weapons, and for research, development, test, and evaluation for the Armed Forces, to prescribe the authorized personnel strength for each active duty component and the Selected Reserve of each Reserve component of the Armed Forces and for civilian personnel of the Department of Defense, to authorize the military training student loads, to authorize appropriations for fiscal year 1980 for civil defense, and for other purposes.

IN THE HOUSE OF REPRESENTATIVES

JULY 17, 1979

Mr. FROST, from the Committee on Rules, reported the following resolution; which was referred to the House Calendar and order to be printed

---

RESOLUTION

Providing for the consideration of the bill (H.R. 4040) to authorize appropriations for fiscal year 1980 for procurement of aircraft, missiles, naval vessels, tracked combat vehicles, torpedoes, and other weapons, and for research, development, test, and evaluation for the Armed Forces, to prescribe the authorized personnel strength for each active duty

Illustration 6B ***(continued)***

component and the Selected Reserve of each Reserve component of the Armed Forces and for civilian personnel of the Department of Defense, to authorize the military training student loads, to authorize appropriations for fiscal year 1980 for civil defense, and for other purposes.

Resolved, That upon the adoption of this resolution it shall be in order to move that the House resolve itself into the Committee of the Whole House on the State of the Union for the consideration of the bill (H.R. 4040) to authorize appropriations for fiscal year 1980 for procurement of aircraft, missiles, naval vessels, tracked combat vehicles, torpedoes, and other weapons, and for research, development, test, and evaluation for the Armed Forces, to prescribe the authorized personnel strength for each active duty component and the Selected Reserve of each Reserve Component of the Armed Forces and for civilian personnel of the Department of Defense, to authorize the military training student loads, to authorize appropriations for fiscal year 1980 for civil defense, and for other purposes, and the first reading of the bill shall be dispensed with. After general debate, which shall be confined to the bill and shall continue not to exceed four hours, three hours to be equally divided and controlled by the chairman and ranking minority member of the Committee on Armed Services, and one hour to be equally divided and controlled by a Member opposed to, and a Member in favor of, the provisions of section 812 of the bill, the bill shall be read

ILLUSTRATION 6B (*concluded*)

for amendment under the five-minute rule by titles instead of by sections. At the conclusion of the consideration of the bill for amendment, the Committee shall rise and report the bill to the House with such amendments as may have been adopted, and the previous question shall be considered as ordered on the bill and amendments thereto to final passage without intervening motion except one motion to recommit. After the passage of H.R. 4040, it shall be in order to move to take from the Speaker's table the bill S. 428 and it shall then be in order in the House to move to strike out all after the enacting clause of the said Senate bill and to insert in lieu thereof the provisions contained in H.R. 4040 as passed by the House.

ILLUSTRATION 6C A SENATE BILL

The following is an example of an actual Senate bill. The lines on p. 250 indicate a modification of the original bill.

Calendar No. 240

96TH CONGRESS
1ST SESSION

S. 109

[Report No. 96–226]

To require the reinstitution of procedures for the registration of certain persons under the Military Selective Service Act, and for other purposes.

IN THE SENATE OF THE UNITED STATES

JANUARY 23 (legislative day, JANUARY 15), 1979

Mr. HARRY F. BYRD, Jr. (for himself, Mr. NUNN, Mr. CHILES, and Mr. CANNON) introduced the following bill; which was read twice and referred to the Committee on Armed Services

JUNE 19 (legislative day, MAY 21), 1979

Reported by Mr. NUNN, with an amendment to the text of the bill and an amendment to the title

[Strike out all after the enacting clause and insert the part printed in italic]

A BILL

To require the reinstitution of procedures for the registration of certain persons under the Military Selective Service Act, and for other purposes.

Be it enacted by the Senate and House of Representatives of the United States of America in Congress assembled,

Illustration 6c (***continued***)

~~That section 3 of the Military Selective Service Act (50 App. U.S.C. 453) is amended by inserting "(a)" before "Except at the beginning of such section and by adding at the end of such section a new subsection as follows:~~

~~"(b) The President, within one hundred and twenty days after the date of enactment of this subsection, shall institute procedures for the registration of citizens and other persons in accordance with the provisions of this title. After registration procedures have been instituted under this subsection, the President may thereafter suspend the registration of persons under this title only for the purpose of revising existing registration procedures or instituting new registration procedures, but in no event may the President suspend or otherwise discontinue the registration of persons required to be registered under this title for a period of more than ninety consecutive days, and in no event may the President suspend or otherwise discontinue registration under this title more than once in any one-year period.".~~

That section 3 of the Military Selective Service Act (50 App. U.S.C. 453) is amended by inserting "(a)" before "Except" at the beginning of such section and by adding at the end of such section the following new subsection:

"(b) The President shall commence registration of citizens and other persons in accordance with the provisions of this title by January 2, 1980. The President may suspend

ILLUSTRATION 6C (*continued*)

the registration of persons under this title only for the purpose of revising existing registration procedures or instituting new registration procedures, but may not suspend or otherwise discontinue the registration of persons under this title for a period of more than ninety consecutive days. In no event may the President suspend or otherwise discontinue registration under this title more than once in any one-year period.".

SEC. 2. The President may not, after the date of enactment of this Act and before January 1, 1981, classify or examine any person registered under the provisions of the Military Selective Service Act (50 App. U.S.C. 451 et seq.) unless he determines that it is in the national interest to do so.

SEC. 3. The President shall submit a written report to the Congress not later than July 1, 1980, containing his recommendations (1) for revision of the categories and standards for deferment and exemption of persons under the Military Selective Service Act, (2) for the revision of the procedures to be followed for registration and classification under such Act, and (3) for other changes in such Act he determines necessary to improve the fairness and effectiveness of such Act. The President shall include in such report a certification to the effect that the Military Selective Service Act, including any changes recommended by him, is in his judgment, equi-

ILLUSTRATION 6C (*continued*)

table and will provide the means necessary to meet effectively the military manpower needs of the United States.

SEC. 4. (a) The first sentence of subsection (b) of section 135 of title 10, United States Code, is amended to read as follows: "The Under Secretary of Defense for Policy shall supervise manpower mobilization planning in the Department of Defense and shall perform such other duties and exercise such other powers as the Secretary of Defense may prescribe.".

(b) Paragraph (3) of section 138(c) of such title is amended—

(1) by inserting "(A)" after "(3)" at the beginning of such paragraph;

(2) by redesignating clauses (A), (B), and (C) of the second sentence of such paragraph as clauses (i), (ii), and (iii), respectively;

(3) by striking out "It shall include" at the beginning of the third sentence of such paragraph and inserting in lieu thereof the following:

"(B) The Secretary of Defense shall also include in the report required under subparagraph (A) of this paragraph"; and

(4) by adding at the end of such paragraph the following new subparagraph:

ILLUSTRATION 6C (*continued*)

"(C) The Secretary of Defense shall also include in the report required under subparagraph (A) of this paragraph an assessment of the Nation's capability of mobilizing the military manpower that may be needed to meet national security requirements during periods of national emergency. In making such assessment, the Secretary of Defense shall determine the Nation's capability of mobilizing the active military forces, selected reserve forces, other reserve force personnel, retired military personnel, and persons not members of the armed forces and shall include in such assessment a statement and explanation regarding the Nation's capabilities for mobilizing each of the personnel categories named.".

Amend the title so as to read: "A bill to require the reinstitution of registration of certain persons under the Military Selective Service Act, and for other purposes.".

ILLUSTRATION 6C (*concluded*)

Calendar No. 240

96TH CONGRESS
1ST SESSION

S. 109

[Report No. 96–226]

A BILL

To require the reinstitution of procedures for the registration of certain persons under the Military Selective Service Act, and for other purposes.

JANUARY 23 (legislative day, JANUARY 15), 1979

Read twice and referred to the Committee on Armed Services

JUNE 19 (legislative day, MAY 21), 1979

Reported with an amendment to the text of the bill and an amendment to the title

ILLUSTRATION 6D HOUSE CALENDAR

The calendars of the two houses are a major information source concerning the flow of legislation. The following is an excerpted House calendar, revealing the major sources contained within it.

NINETY-SEVENTH CONGRESS

FIRST SESSION { CONVENED JANUARY 5, 1981

CALENDARS
OF THE UNITED STATES HOUSE OF REPRESENTATIVES
AND
HISTORY OF LEGISLATION

LEGISLATIVE DAY 106 CALENDAR DAY 106

Tuesday, August 4, 1981

CONSENT CALENDAR—PRIVATE CALENDAR—SUSPENSIONS

HOUSE MEETS AT 12 NOON

SPECIAL ORDERS

ADJOURNMENT UNTIL TUESDAY, AUG. 4, 1981 — On motion of Mr. Murtha, by unanimous consent, *Ordered*, That when the House adjourns today (Friday, July 31, 1981), it adjourn to meet on Tuesday, Aug. 4, 1981. (*Agreed to July 31, 1981.*)

CONSENT CALENDAR — On motion of Mr. Murtha, by unanimous consent, *Ordered*, That notwithstanding clause 4, Rule XIII, it shall be in order to call the consent calendar on Tuesday, Aug. 4, 1981. (*Agreed to July 31, 1981.*)

(SPECIAL ORDERS CONTINUED ON P. 2)

PREPARED UNDER THE DIRECTION OF EDMUND L. HENSHAW, JR., CLERK OF THE HOUSE OF REPRESENTATIVES: JOHN P. JENKINS, Tally Clerk; MAXINE W. SNOWDEN, MARK D. O'SULLIVAN, THOMAS K. HANRAHAN, Assistant Tally Clerks

Calendars shall be printed daily—Rule XIII: clause 6 } *Index to the Calendars will be printed on Monday of each week the House is in session: otherwise first day of session thereafter*

U.S. GOVERNMENT PRINTING OFFICE : 1981 O—79-038

ILLUSTRATION 6D (*continued*)

(SPECIAL ORDERS CONTINUED FROM P. 1)

TAX INCENTIVE ACT, 1981	On motion of Mr. Rostenkowski, by unanimous consent, *Ordered,* That it may be in order on Tuesday, Aug. 4, 1981, or any day thereafter, to consider the conference report on H.R. 4242, Tax Incentive Act of 1981. (*Agreed to July 31, 1981.*)
CALENDAR WEDNESDAY BUSINESS	On motion of Mr. Murtha, by unanimous consent, *Ordered,* That business in order under the Calendar Wednesday rule be dispensed with on Wednesday, Aug. 5, 1981. (*Agreed to July 31, 1981.*)

UNFINISHED BUSINESS

1981	

SPECIAL LEGISLATIVE DAYS

Calendar Wednesday	Wednesday of each week, except during the last 2 weeks of a session (clause 7, rule XXIV).
Consent Calendar	First and third Mondays of each month (clause 4, rule XIII).
Discharge Calendar	Second and fourth Mondays of each month, except during the last 6 days of a session (clause 4, rule XXVII).
District of Columbia business	Second and fourth Mondays of each month (clause 8, rule XXIV).
Private Calendar	First and third Tuesdays of each month (clause 6, rule XXIV).
Suspension of rules	Mondays and Tuesdays and during the last 6 days of a session (clause 1, rule XXVII).

RESTRICTION OF POWER TO REPORT APPROPRIATIONS

Clause 5, rule XXI:

"5. No bill or joint resolution carrying appropriations shall be reported by any committee not having jurisdiction to report appropriations, nor shall an amendment proposing an appropriation be in order during the consideration of a bill or joint resolution reported by a committee not having that jurisdiction. A question of order on an appropriation in any such bill, joint resolution, or amendment thereto may be raised at any time."

ILLUSTRATION 6D (*continued*)

THE MORNING HOUR FOR THE CALL OF COMMITTEES

Clause 4, rule XXIV:

"4. After the unfinished business has been disposed of, the Speaker shall call each standing committee in regular order, and then select committees, and each committee when named may call up for consideration any bill reported by it on a previous day and on the House Calendar, and if the Speaker shall not complete the call of the committees before the House passes to other business, he shall resume the next call where he left off, giving preference to the last bill under consideration: *Provided,* That whenever any committee shall have occupied the morning hour on 2 days, it shall not be in order to call up any other bill until the other committees have been called in their turn."

NOTE.—See committee list below.

CALENDAR WEDNESDAY BUSINESS

Clause 7, rule XXIV:

"7. On Wednesday of each week no business shall be in order except as provided by paragraph 4 of this rule unless the House by a two-thirds vote on motion to dispense therewith shall otherwise determine. On such a motion there may be debate not to exceed 5 minutes for and against. On a call of committees under this rule bills may be called up from either the House or the Union Calendar, excepting bills which are privileged under the rules; but bills called up from the Union Calendar shall be considered in Committee of the Whole House on the State of the Union. This rule shall not apply during the last 2 weeks of the session. It shall not be in order for the Speaker to entertain a motion for a recess of any Wednesday except during the last 2 weeks of the session:

"*Provided,* That not more than 2 hours of general debate shall be permitted on any measure called up on Calendar Wednesday, and all debate must be confined to the subject matter of the bill, the time to be equally divided between those for and against the bill: *Provided further,* That whenever any committee shall have occupied one Wednesday it shall not be in order, unless the House by a two-thirds vote shall otherwise determine, to consider any unfinished business previously called up by such committee, unless the previous question had been ordered thereon, upon any succeeding Wednesday until the other committees have been called in their turn under this rule: *Provided,* That when, during any one session of Congress, all of the committees of the House are not called under the Calendar Wednesday rule, at the next session of Congress the call shall commence where it left off at the end of the preceding session."

NOTE.—See committee list below.

COMMITTEE LIST ACCORDING TO RULE X, WITH DATES OF THE CALLS OF COMMITTEE UNDER RULE XXIV

	Clause 4—Morning hours		Clause 7—Calendar Wednesday			
	1981	1981	1981	1981	1981	1981
1. Committee on Agriculture				(*)		
2. Committee on Appropriations						
3. Committee on Armed Services						
4. Committee on Banking, Finance and Urban Affairs						
5. Committee on the Budget						
6. Committee on the District of Columbia						
7. Committee on Education and Labor						
8. Committee on Energy and Commerce						
9. Committee on Government Operations						
10. Committee on House Administration						
11. Committee on Interior and Insular Affairs						
12. Committee on Foreign Affairs						
13. Committee on the Judiciary						
14. Committee on Merchant Marine and Fisheries						
15. Committee on Post Office and Civil Service						
16. Committee on Public Works and Transportation						
17. Committee on Rules						
18. Committee on Science and Technology						
19. Committee on Small Business						
20. Committee on Standards of Official Conduct						
21. Committee on Veterans' Affairs						
22. Committee on Ways and Means						

***Call rests with Committee on Agriculture.**

ILLUSTRATION 6D (*continued*)

BILLS IN CONFERENCE

Jefferson's Manual, sec. 555:
"And in all cases of conference asked after a vote of disagreement, etc., the conferees of the House asking it are to leave the papers with the conferees of the other * * *."
The House agreeing to the conference acts on the report before the House requesting a conference.

CONFEREES MAY NOT AGREE TO CERTAIN SENATE AMENDMENTS

Clause 2, rule XX:
"2. No amendment of the Senate to a general appropriation bill which would be in violation of the provisions of clause 2 of rule XXI, if said amendment had originated in the House, nor any amendment of the Senate providing for an appropriation upon any bill other than a general appropriation bill, shall be agreed to by the managers on the part of the House unless specific authority to agree to such amendment shall be first given by the House by a separate vote on every such amendment."

Bill No. Date Conference Asked / Agreed to	Brief of title	Conferees		Report filed in—		Report agreed to in—	
		House	Senate	House	Senate	House	Senate
1981 S. 694 June 23 July 9 (*Legislative day July 8*)	Defense, Department of, Supplemental Authorization Act, 1981.	Messrs. Price, Bennett, Stratton, White, Nichols, Brinkley, Mollohan, Daniel, Dan, Dickinson, Whitehurst, Spence, Beard, Mitchell of New York, and Mrs. Holt. (*House asks.*)	Messrs. Tower, Thurmond, Goldwater, Warner, Humphrey, Cohen, Jepsen, Quayle, Denton, Stennis, Jackson, Cannon, Byrd, Harry F. Jr., Nunn, Hart, Exon, and Levin. (*Senate acts first.*)	1981 July 27 97-204	1981 ---------	1981 ---------	1981 July 30 (*Legislative day July 8*)
H.R. 3982 July 14 (*Legislative day July 8*) July 15	Reconciliation Act of 1981, Omnibus.	Messrs. Jones of Oklahoma, Mineta, Solarz, Panetta, Gephardt, Aspin, Latta, Regula, Shuster, and Ms. Fiedler. (Budget Committee for considerations of the entire bill and Senate amendment.) AGRICULTURE, Solely for the consideration of—	Messrs. Domenici, Armstrong, Mrs. Kassebaum, Messrs. Boschwitz, Hollings, Chiles, and Biden. Title I (Agriculture, Nutrition and Forestry Committee): Messrs. Helms, Hayakawa, Lugar, Cochran, Huddleston, Leahy, and Zorinsky.	July 29 97-208	---------	July 31	

ILLUSTRATION 6D (*continued*)

1. UNION CALENDAR

Clause 1, rule XIII:
"First. A calendar of the Committee of the Whole House on the State of the Union, to which shall be referred bills raising revenue, general appropriations bills, and bills of a public character directly or indirectly appropriating money or property."

			No.
1981 Jan. 19	Referred to the Committee of the Whole House on the State of the Union.	Message of the President of the United States to the Congress on the State of the Union.	1
H. Rept. 97–3 Feb. 5	Mr. Rostenkowski Ways and Means. Rept. 97–3	Report pursuant to sec. 302(b) of the Congressional Budget Act of 1974.	3
Feb. 18	Referred to the Committee of the Whole House on the State of the Union.	Message of the President of the United States to the Congress on the subject of a Program for Economic Recovery.	4
H. Rept. 97–5 Mar. 2	Mr. Reuss Joint Economic Committee.	Report on the January 1981 Economic Report of the President.	5
H. Rept. 97–6 Mar. 3	Mr. Brooks Government Operations.	Report on Oversight Plans of the Committees of the U.S. House of Representatives.	6
H. Rept. 97–10 Mar. 19	**Mr. St Germain Banking, Finance and Urban Affairs.**	**Report on Monetary Policy for 1981**	**8**
Apr. 28	Referred to the Committee of the Whole House on the State of the Union.	Message of the President of the United States to the Congress on the Subject of the Economic Recovery program.	15
H.R. 3400 **May 4**	Mr. Whitten Appropriations. Rept. 97–29	**Making supplemental and further continuing appropriations for the fiscal year ending Sept. 30, 1981, rescinding certain budget authority, and for other purposes.**	**18**

Illustration 6d (*continued*)

2. HOUSE CALENDAR

Clause 1, rule XIII:
"Second. A House Calendar, to which shall be referred all bills of a public character not raising revenue not directly or indirectly appropriating money or property."

1981 H. Rept. 97–110 May 20	Mr. Stokes Standards of Official Conduct.	Report in the matter of Representative Raymond F. Lederer.	No. **15**
H. Res. 179 July 14	Mr. Beilenson Rules. Rept. 97–176	A resolution waiving certain points of order against H.R. 4120, a bill making appropriations for the legislative branch for the fiscal year ending Sept. 30, 1982, and for other purposes.	**30**
H. Res. 182 July 16	Mr. Hall of Ohio Rules. Rept. 97–182	A resolution providing for the consideration of H.R. 3518, a bill to authorize appropriations for fiscal years 1982 and 1983 for the Department of State, the International Communication Agency, and the Board for International Broadcasting, and for other purposes.	**31**
H. Res. 183 July 16	Mr. Bonior Rules. Rept. 97–183	A resolution providing for the consideration of H.R. 1520, a bill to authorize appropriations for the National Science Foundation for the fiscal year 1982.	**32**
H. Res. 184 July 16	Mr. Moakley Rules. Rept. 97–184	A resolution providing for the consideration of H.R. 2979, a bill to extend the authorizations of appropriations for the National Historical Publications and Records Commission for fiscal years 1982 and 1983.	**33**
H. Res. 189 July 21	Mr. Bonior Rules. Rept. 97–189	A resolution providing for the consideration of H.R. 3275, a bill to amend the Civil Rights Act of 1957 to authorize appropriations for the Civil Rights Commission.	**37**
H. Con. Res. 106 July 27	Mr. Gaydos House Administration. Rept. 97–203	To provide for the printing of the brochure entitled "How Our Laws Are Made".	**39**
H. J. Res. 207 July 29	Mr. Udall Interior and Insular Affairs. Rept. 97–206 (Placed on consent calendar 8.)	To require the Secretary of the Interior to place a plaque at the United States Marine Corps War Memorial honoring Joseph Rosenthal, photographer of the scene depicted by the memorial.	**41**
H.R. 772 July 29	Mr. Udall Interior and Insular Affairs. Rept. 97–207 (Placed on consent calendar 9.)	To provide for the retention of the name of Mount McKinley.	**42**

ILLUSTRATION 6D (*continued*)

3. PRIVATE CALENDAR

Clause 1, rule XIII:

"Third. A calendar of the Committee of the Whole House, to which shall be referred all bills of a private character."

Clause 6, rule XXIV:

"6. On the first Tuesday of each month after disposal of such business on the Speaker's table as requires reference only, the Speaker shall direct the Clerk to call the bills and resolutions on the Private Calendar. Should objection be made by two or more Members to the consideration of any bill or resolution so called, it shall be recommitted to the committee which reported the bill or resolution, and no reservation of objection shall be entertained by the Speaker. Such bills and resolutions, if considered, shall be considered in the House as in the Committee of the Whole. No other business shall be in order on this day unless the House, by two-thirds vote on motion to dispense therewith, shall otherwise determine. On such motion debate shall be limited to 5 minutes for and 5 minutes against said motion.

"On the third Tuesday of each month after the disposal of such business on the Speaker's table as requires reference only, the Speaker may direct the Clerk to call the bills and resolutions on the Private Calendar, preference to be given to omnibus bills containing bills or resolutions which have previously been objected to on a call of the Private Calendar. All bills and resolutions on the Private Calendar so called, if considered, shall be considered in the House as in the Committee of the Whole. Should objection be made by two or more Members to the consideration of any bill or resolution other than an omnibus bill, it shall be recommitted to the committee which reported the bill or resolution and no reservation of objection shall be entertained by the Speaker.

"Omnibus bills shall be read for amendment by paragraph, and no amendment shall be in order except to strike out or to reduce amounts of money stated or to provide limitations. Any item or matter stricken from an omnibus bill shall not thereafter during the same session of Congress be included in any omnibus bill.

"Upon passage of any such omnibus bill, said bill shall be resolved into the several bills and resolutions of which it is composed, and such original bills and resolutions, with any amendments adopted by the House, shall be engrossed, where necessary, and proceedings thereon had as if said bills and resolutions had been passed in the House severally.

"In the consideration of any omnibus bill the proceedings as set forth above shall have the same force and effect as if each Senate and House bill or resolution therein contained or referred to were considered by the House as a separate and distinct bill or resolution."

1981 H.R. 1547 May 20	Mr. Sam B. Hall of Texas____ Judiciary. Rept. 97-116	For the relief of Remedios R. Alcudia, Christopher, Ezra, Vermillion, and Peristello Alcudia. (By Mr. Dornan.)	No. 7
H.R. 1946 July 13	Mr. Udall__________________ Interior and Insular Affairs. Rept. 97-173	To reinstate and validate United States oil and gas leases numbered OCS-P-0218 and OCS-P-0226. (By Mr. Patterson.)	15

ILLUSTRATION 6D (*continued*)

CONSENT CALENDAR

Clause 4, rule XIII:
"**4.** After a bill has been favorably reported and shall be upon either the House or Union Calendar **any** Member may file with the Clerk a notice that he desires such bill placed upon a special calendar to be **known as** the 'Consent Calendar.' On the first and third Mondays of each month immediately after the **reading of** the Journal, the Speaker shall direct the Clerk to call the bills in numerical order which have **been for** three legislative days upon the 'Consent Calendar.' Should objection be made to the con**sideration** of any bill so called it shall be carried over on the calendar without prejudice to the next day **when the** 'Consent Calendar' is again called, and if objected to by three or more Members, it shall imme**diately** be stricken from the calendar, and shall not thereafter during the same session of that Congress **be placed** again thereon: *Provided,* That no bill shall be called twice on the same legislative day."

1981			No.
H.R. 2015 July 22	Mr. Udall Interior and Insular Affairs. Rept. 97–191 (Union Calendar 131.)	To enable the Secretary of the Interior to erect permanent improvements on land acquired for the Confederated Tribes of Siletz Indians of Oregon.	7
H. J. Res. 207 July 29	Mr. Udall Interior and Insular Affairs. Rept. 97–206 (House Calendar 41.)	To require the Secretary of the Interior to place a plaque at the United States Marine Corps War Memorial honoring Joseph Rosenthal, photographer of the scene dipicted by the memorial.	8
H.R. 772 July 29	Mr. Udall Interior and Insular Affairs. Rept. 97–207 (House Calendar 42.)	To provide for the retention of the name of Mount McKinley.	9
S. 875 July 30	Mr. Udall Interior and Insular Affairs. Rept. 97–209 (Union Calendar 142.)	To authorize the generation of electrical power at Palo Verde Irrigation District Diversion Dam, California.	10

ILLUSTRATION 6D (*continued*)

CALENDAR OF MOTIONS TO DISCHARGE COMMITTEES

Clause 4, rule XXVII:

"4. A Member may present to the Clerk a motion in writing to discharge a committee from the consideration of a public bill or resolution which has been referred to it 30 days prior thereto (but only one motion may be presented for each bill or resolution). Under this rule it shall also be in order for a Member to file a motion to discharge the Committee on Rules from further consideration of any resolution providing either a special order of business, or a special rule for the consideration of any public bill or resolution favorably reported by a standing committee, or a special rule for the consideration of a public bill or resolution which has remained in a standing committee 30 or more days without action: *Provided*, That said resolution from which it is moved to discharge the Committee on Rules has been referred to that committee at least 7 days prior to the filing of the motion to discharge. The motion shall be placed in the custody of the Clerk, who shall arrange some convenient place for the signature of Members. A signature may be withdrawn by a Member in writing at any time before the motion is entered on the Journal. When a majority of the total membership of the House shall have signed the motion, it shall be entered on the Journal, printed with the signatures thereto in the Congressional Record, and referred to the Calendar of Motions To Discharge Committees.

"On the second and fourth Mondays of each month, except during the last 6 days of any session of Congress, immediately after the approval of the Journal, any Member who has signed a motion to discharge which has been on the calendar at least 7 days prior thereto, and seeks recognition, shall be recognized for the purpose of calling up the motion, and the House shall proceed to its consideration in the manner herein provided without intervening motion except one motion to adjourn. Recognition for the motions shall be in the order in which they have been entered on the Journal.

"When any motion under this rule shall be called up, the bill or resolution shall be read by title only. After 20 minutes' debate, one-half in favor of the proposition and one-half in opposition thereto, the House shall proceed to vote on the motion to discharge. If the motion prevails to discharge the Committee on Rules from any resolution pending before the committee, the House shall immediately vote on the adoption of said resolution, the Speaker not entertaining any dilatory or other intervening motion except one motion to adjourn, and, if said resolution is adopted, then the House shall immediately proceed to its execution. If the motion prevails to discharge one of the standing committees of the House from any public bill or resolution pending before the committee, it shall then be in order for any Member who signed the motion to move that the House proceed to the immediate consideration of such bill or resolution (such motion not being debatable), and such motion is hereby made of high privilege; and if it shall be decided in the affirmative, the bill shall be immediately considered under the general rules of the House, and if unfinished before adjournment of the day on which it is called up, it shall remain the unfinished business until it is fully disposed of. Should the House by vote decide against the immediate consideration of such bill or resolution, it shall be referred to its proper calendar and be entitled to the same rights and privileges that it would have had, had the committee to which it was referred duly reported same to the House for its consideration: *Provided*, That when any perfected motion to discharge a committee from the consideration of any public bill or resolution has once been acted upon by the House it shall not be in order to entertain, during the same session of Congress, any other motion for the discharge from that committee of said measure, or from any other committee of any other bill or resolution substantially the same, relating in substance to or dealing with the same subject matter, or from the Committee on Rules of a resolution providing a special order of business for the consideration of any other such bill or resolution, in order that such action by the House on a motion to discharge shall be *res adjudicata* for the remainder of that session: *Provided further*, That if before any one motion to discharge a committee has been acted upon by the House there are on the Calendar of Motions To Discharge Committees other motions to discharge committees from the consideration of bills or resolutions substantially the same, relating in substance to or dealing with the same subject matter, after the House shall have acted on one motion to discharge, the remaining said motions shall be stricken from the Calendar of Motions To Discharge Committees and not acted on during the remainder of that session of Congress."

Motion No. and date entered	Title	Committee	Motion filed by—	Calendar No.
1981				

ILLUSTRATION 6D (*continued*)

NUMERICAL ORDER OF BILLS AND RESOLUTIONS WHICH HAVE PASSED EITHER OR BOTH HOUSES, AND BILLS NOW PENDING ON THE CALENDARS

Complete history of all actions on each bill follows the number in chronological order. For subject of bill see index, using index key following bill number in this section

NOTE. **Similar or identical bills, and bills having reference to each other, are indicated by number in parentheses**

No.	Index Key and History of Bill

HOUSE BILLS

H.R. 31 (H.R. 3132) (S. 414).—Cash Discount Act. Rules suspended. Passed House Feb. 24. 1981. Passed Senate amended Mar. 12 (*Legislative day of Feb. 16*), 1981. In House, referred Senate amendment to Energy and Commerce on Mar. 26, 1981. for a period ending Apr. 8, 1981. Committee discharged. House asked for a conference Apr. 8, 1981. Senate agreed to a conference Apr. 29 (*Legislative day of Apr. 27*), 1981. Conference report filed in the House June 23, 1981; Rept. 97–159. House agreed to conference report June 24, 1981. Senate agreed to conference report July 14 (*Legislative day of July 8*), 1981. Approved July 27, 1981. Public Law 97–25.

H.R. 85.—Oil Pollution Liability and Compensation Act, Comprehensive. (Referred jointly to Merchant Marine and Fisheries, Public Works and Transportation, and Ways and Means Jan. 5, 1981.) Reported from Merchant Marine and Fisheries May 21, 1981; Rept. 97–120, Pt. I.

H.R. 618.—California, city of Angels, title to certain lands to, convey. Reported from Interior and Insular Affairs Mar. 24, 1981; Rept. 97–13. Union Calendar. Passed House Apr. 6, 1981. In Senate, referred to Energy and Natural Resources Apr. 7 (*Legislative day of Feb. 16*), 1981.

H.R. 661.—Private relief, Frei, Blanca Rosa Luna de. Reported from the Judiciary May 20, 1981; Rept. 97–111. Private Calendar. Passed House June 2, 1981. In Senate, referred to the Judiciary June 3 (*Legislative day of June 1*), 1981.

H.R. 688.—Private relief, Moncrieffe, Junior Edmund. Reported from the Judiciary May 20, 1981; Rept. 97–112. Private Calendar. Passed House June 2. 1981. In Senate, referred to the Judiciary June 3 (*Legislative day of June 1*), 1981.

H.R. 772.—McKinley, Mount, retention of name of, provide. Reported from Interior and Insular Affairs July 29, 1981; Rept. 97–207. House Calendar--House 42

H.R. 779.—Benbrook Dam, Texas, municipal use of storage water in, provide. Reported from Public Works and Transportation May 19, 1981; Rept. 97–95; House Calendar. Passed House June 1, 1981. In Senate, referred to Environment and Public Works June 2 (*Legislative day of June 1*), 1981.

H.R. 783.—Private relief, Vogel, Roland Karl Heinz. Reported from the Judiciary May 20, 1981; Rept. 97–113. Private Calendar. Passed House June 2, 1981. In Senate, referred to the Judiciary June 3 (*Legislative day of June 1*), 1981.

No.	Index Key and History of Bill

HOUSE BILLS—Continued

H.R. 1100 (S. 468).—Former Prisoners of War Benefits Act of 1981. Reported from Veterans' Affairs May 4, 1981; Rept. 97–28. Union Calendar. Considered June 1, 1981. Rules suspended. Passed House June 2, 1981. In Senate, ordered placed on the calendar June 3 (*Legislative day of June 1*), 1981. Passed Senate amended June 4 (*Legislative day of June 1*), 1981. House agreed to Senate amendments with amendments July 30, 1981. Senate agreed to House amendments July 30 (*Legislative day of July 8*), 1981.

H.R. 1257 (H. Res. 161) (S. 1098).—National Aeronautics and Space Administration Authorization Act, 1982. Reported from Science and Technology May 8, 1981; Rept. 97–32. Union Calendar. Passed House June 23, 1981. Proceedings vacated. Laid on table June 23, 1981. S. 1098, as amended, passed in lieu June 23, 1981.

H.R. 1309.—Land grant colleges research facilities, 1890, upgrade. Reported from Agriculture June 16, 1981; Rept. 97–151. Union Calendar. Rules suspended. Passed House July 13, 1981. In Senate, referred to Agriculture, Nutrition, and Forestry July 15 (*Legislative day of July 8*), 1981.

H.R. 1311 (S. 304).—Tourism Policy Act, National. Reported from Energy and Commerce May 19, 1981; Rept. 97–107, Pt. I. Referred to Post Office and Civil Service May 19, 1981. Discharged from Post Office and Civil Service June 19, 1981. Union Calendar. Rules suspended. Passed House July 28, 1981. Proceedings vacated. Laid on table July 28, 1981. S. 304, as amended, passed in lieu July 28, 1981.

H.R. 1371.—Contract Disputes Act of 1978, section 12 of, amend. Reported from the Judiciary May 18, 1981; Rept. 97–47. Union Calendar. Passed House June 1, 1981. In Senate, referred to Governmental Affairs June 2 (*Legislative day of June 1*), 1981.

H.R. 1400.—Veterans' Educational Assistance Act of 1981. (Referred jointly to Veterans' Affairs and Armed Services Jan. 28, 1981.) Reported from Veterans' Affairs May 19, 1981; Rept. 97–80, Pt. I.

H.R. 1469.—Private relief, Mesnager, Madeleine. Reported from the Judiciary May 20, 1981; Rept. 97–114. Private Calendar. Passed House June 2, 1981. In Senate, referred to the Judiciary June 3 (*Legislative day of June 1*), 1981.

H.R. 1480.—Private relief, Marachi, Omar. Reported from the Judiciary May 20, 1981; Rept. 97–115. Private Calendar. Passed House June 2, 1981. In Senate, referred to the Judiciary June 3 (*Legislative day of June 1*), 1981.

H.R. 1520 (H. Res. 183) (S. 1194) (S. 1200).—Science Foundation Authorization Act for Fiscal Year 1982, National. Reported from Science and Technology May 13, 1981; Rept. 97–34. Union Calendar-----Union 22

ILLUSTRATION 6D (*continued*)

INDEX

Subject index of all legislation, House and Senate, which has been reported by the committees and acted upon by either or both of the Houses (except Senate resolutions not of interest to the House), and special House reports. Complete legislative history of each bill is carried under the number of the bill in the numerical section. In this section the subject, number, and name of the Member introducing bill is printed.

MAJOR SUBJECT HEADINGS

AGRICULTURE

APPROPRIATIONS (MAJOR)

ARMED FORCES

BUDGET, COMMITTEES

COMMISSIONS

DISCHARGE PETITIONS

DISTRICT OF COLUMBIA

ENERGY

HOUSE OF REPRESENTATIVES

INDIANS

HOUSE REPORTS

MEMORIAL DESIGNATIONS

PRESIDENTIAL MESSAGES
(WHOLE HOUSE ON THE STATE OF THE UNION)

PRIVATE RELIEF

PROCLAMATIONS

PUBLIC HEALTH SERVICE ACT

SENATE

VACANCIES

VETERANS

WILDERNESS

ILLUSTRATION 6D (*continued*)

SPECIAL LEGISLATIVE DAYS

AUGUST 1981

Monday, 3rd
Consent Calendar—Suspensions.
Tuesday, 4th
Private Calendar—Suspensions.
Wednesday, 5th
Calendar Wednesday.
Monday, 10th
District of Columbia—Discharge Calendar—Suspensions.
Tuesday, 11th
Suspensions.
Wednesday, 12th
Calendar Wednesday.
Monday, 17th
Consent Calendar—Suspensions.
Tuesday, 18th
Private Calendar—Suspensions.
Wednesday, 19th
Calendar Wednesday.
Monday, 24th
District of Columbia—Discharge Calendar—Suspensions.
Tuesday, 25th
Suspensions.
Wednesday, 26th
Calendar Wednesday.
Monday, 31st
Suspensions.

▽ ▽ ▽ **1981** ▽ ▽ ▽

JANUARY

Sun	M	Tu	W	Th	F	Sat
				1	2	3
4	~~5~~	~~6~~	7	8	~~9~~	10
11	12	~~13~~	14	15	~~16~~	17
18	~~19~~	~~20~~	21	~~22~~	~~23~~	24
25	26	~~27~~	~~28~~	~~29~~	~~30~~	31

FEBRUARY

Sun	M	Tu	W	Th	F	Sat
1	~~2~~	~~3~~	~~4~~	~~5~~	~~6~~	7
8	9	10	11	12	13	14
15	16	~~17~~	~~18~~	~~19~~	20	21
22	~~23~~	~~24~~	~~25~~	~~26~~	27	28

MARCH

Sun	M	Tu	W	Th	F	Sat
1	~~2~~	~~3~~	~~4~~	~~5~~	6	7
8	~~9~~	~~10~~	~~11~~	~~12~~	~~13~~	14
15	16	~~17~~	~~18~~	~~19~~	20	21
22	~~23~~	~~24~~	~~25~~	~~26~~	27	28
29	~~30~~	~~31~~				

APRIL

Sun	M	Tu	W	Th	F	Sat
			~~1~~	~~2~~	3	4
5	~~6~~	~~7~~	~~8~~	~~9~~	~~10~~	11
12	13	14	15	16	17	18
19	20	21	22	23	24	25
26	~~27~~	~~28~~	~~29~~	~~30~~		

MAY

Sun	M	Tu	W	Th	F	Sat
					~~1~~	2
3	~~4~~	~~5~~	~~6~~	~~7~~	~~8~~	9
10	11	~~12~~	~~13~~	~~14~~	15	16
17	~~18~~	~~19~~	~~20~~	~~21~~	22	23
24	25	26	~~27~~	~~28~~	29	30
31						

JUNE

Sun	M	Tu	W	Th	F	Sat
	~~1~~	~~2~~	~~3~~	~~4~~	5	6
7	~~8~~	~~9~~	~~10~~	~~11~~	~~12~~	13
14	~~15~~	~~16~~	~~17~~	~~18~~	19	20
21	~~22~~	~~23~~	~~24~~	~~25~~	~~26~~	27
28	29	30				

JULY

Sun	M	Tu	W	Th	F	Sat
			1	2	3	4
5	6	7	~~8~~	~~9~~	~~10~~	11
12	~~13~~	~~14~~	~~15~~	~~16~~	~~17~~	18
19	~~20~~	~~21~~	~~22~~	~~23~~	~~24~~	25
26	~~27~~	~~28~~	~~29~~	~~30~~	~~31~~	

AUGUST

Sun	M	Tu	W	Th	F	Sat
						1
2	3	~~4~~	5	6	7	8
9	10	11	12	13	14	15
16	17	18	19	20	21	22
23	24	25	26	27	28	29
30	31					

SEPTEMBER

Sun	M	Tu	W	Th	F	Sat
		1	2	3	4	5
6	7	8	9	10	11	12
13	14	15	16	17	18	19
20	21	22	23	24	25	26
27	28	29	30			

OCTOBER

Sun	M	Tu	W	Th	F	Sat
				1	2	3
4	5	6	7	8	9	10
11	12	13	14	15	16	17
18	19	20	21	22	23	24
25	26	27	28	29	30	31

NOVEMBER

Sun	M	Tu	W	Th	F	Sat
1	2	3	4	5	6	7
8	9	10	11	12	13	14
15	16	17	18	19	20	21
22	23	24	25	26	27	28
29	30					

DECEMBER

Sun	M	Tu	W	Th	F	Sat
		1	2	3	4	5
6	7	8	9	10	11	12
13	14	15	16	17	18	19
20	21	22	23	24	25	26
27	28	29	30	31		

*Marked dates indicate days House in session.
Total Legislative days 106.
Total Calendar days 106.

ILLUSTRATION 6D (*concluded*)

STATUS OF MAJOR BILLS—FIRST SESSION

Number of bill	Title	Reported	Passed House	Reported in Senate	Passed Senate	Sent to conference	Conference report agreed to in—		Date approved	Law No.
							House	Senate		
	LEGISLATIVE BILLS	1981	1981	1981	1981	1981	1981	1981	1981	
H. Con. Res. 115	Budget, First, 1982 (H. Rept. 97-23)	Apr. 16	May 7		May 12	May 13	May 20	May 21		
H.R. 3982	Reconciliation Act of 1981, Omnibus (H. Rept. 97-158)	June 19	June 26		July 13	July 15	July 31			
H.R. 4242	Tax Incentive Act, 1981 (H. Rept. 97-201)	July 24	July 29		July 31	July 31				
	APPROPRIATION BILLS									
H.R. 3512	Supplemental, 1981 (See H. Rept. 97-29)		May 13	May 14	May 21	May 28	June 4	June 4	June 5	97-12
H.R. 4034	HUD, 1982 (H. Rept. 97-162)	June 25	July 21	July 23	July 30	July 31				
H.R. 4035	Interior, 1982 (H. Rept. 97-163)	June 25	July 22	July 23						
H.R. 4120	Legislative, 1982 (H. Rept. 97-170)	July 9								
H.R. 4121	Treasury, 1982 (H. Rept. 97-171)	July 9	July 30							
H.R. 4119	Agriculture, 1982 (H. Rept. 97-172)	July 9	July 27							
H.R. 4144	Energy and Water, 1982 (H. Rept. 97-177)	July 14	July 24							
H.R. 4169	Commerce, Justice, State, Judiciary, 1982 (H. Rept. 97-180.)	July 16								
H.R. 4209	Transportation, 1982 (H. Rept. 97-186)	July 17								
H.R. 4241	Military Construction, 1982 (H. Rept. 97-193)	July 23								
H.J. Res. 308	Supplemental, urgent, 1981 (H. Rept. 97-192)	July 23	July 23		July 23					97-26

ILLUSTRATION 6E SENATE CALENDARS

The Senate has two calendars: General Business and Executive Business. The following are excerpts.

SENATE OF THE UNITED STATES

NINETY-SEVENTH CONGRESS

FIRST SESSION { CONVENED JANUARY 5, 1981 } DAYS IN SESSION 102
SECOND SESSION { }

CALENDAR OF BUSINESS

Wednesday, September 9, 1981

SENATE CONVENES AT 12:00 NOON

UNFINISHED BUSINESS

S. 951 (ORDER NO. 118)

A bill to authorize appropriations for the purpose of carrying out the activities of the Department of Justice for fiscal year 1982, and for other purposes. (*June 25, 1981.*)

PREPARED UNDER THE DIRECTION OF WILLIAM F. HILDENBRAND, SECRETARY OF THE SENATE

BY WILLIAM F. FARMER, JR., LEGISLATIVE CLERK

ILLUSTRATION 6E (*continued*)

GENERAL ORDERS

UNDER RULE VIII

ORDER No.	NUMBER AND AUTHOR OF BILL	TITLE	REPORTED BY
8	S. 9 Mr. Robert C. Byrd	A bill to amend the Federal Election Campaign Act of 1971 to provide reforms with respect to campaign contributions.	Feb. 16, 1981.—Read the second time and placed on the calendar.
61	S. 1078 Mr. Mathias	A bill to authorize appropriations for the Federal Election Commission for fiscal year 1982.	Apr. 30, 1981.—Mr. Mathias, Committee on Rules and Administration, without amendment. (Rept. 47.) (An original bill.) (See Order No. 88.)
63	S. Con. Res. 19 Mr. Domenici	Concurrent resolution setting forth the recommended congressional budget for the United States Government for the fiscal years 1982, 1983, and 1984, and revising the congressional budget for the United States Government for the fiscal year 1981.	May 1, 1981.—Mr. Domenici, Committee on the Budget, without amendment. (Rept. 49.) (An original concurrent resolution.) (Additional and minority views filed.)
78	H.R. 3132	An act to amend the Truth in Lending Act to encourage cash discounts, and for other purposes.	May 6, 1981.—Placed on the calendar.
85	S. 306 Mr. Hatfield and others	A bill to authorize the Secretary of the Interior to construct, operate, and maintain hydroelectric powerplants at various existing water projects, and for other purposes.	May 8, 1981.—Mr. Murkowski, Committee on Energy and Natural Resources, with amendments. (Rept. 61.)

ILLUSTRATION 6E (*continued*)

STATUS OF APPROPRIATION BILLS, FIRST SESSION, NINETY-SEVENTH CONGRESS

NUMBER OF BILL	SHORT TITLE	PASSED HOUSE	RECEIVED AND RE-FERRED IN SENATE	REPORTED IN SENATE	PASSED SENATE	SENT TO CONFER-ENCE	CONFERENCE REPORT AGREED TO IN—		DATE AP-PROVED	NUM-BER OF LAW
							SENATE	HOUSE	1981	
H.R. 3512	Supplemental, 1981	May 13	May 14	May 14	May 21	May 28	June 4	June 4	June 5	P.L. 97–12
H.R. 4034	HUD, 1982	July 21	July 22	July 23	July 30					
H.J. Res. 308	Urgent Supplemental, HHS, 1981	July 23	July 23	* * *	July 23	* * *	* * *	* * *	July 29	P.L. 97–26
H.R. 4035	Interior, 1982	July 22	July 23	July 23						
H.R. 4144	Energy and Water, 1982	July 24	July 27							
H.R. 4119	Agriculture, 1982	July 27	July 28							
H.R. 4121	Treasury, 1982	July 30	Aug. 4							

O

ILLUSTRATION 6E (*concluded*)

Senate of the United States

NINETY-SEVENTH CONGRESS

FIRST SESSION { Convened January 5, 1981

SECOND SESSION {

EXECUTIVE CALENDAR

Prepared under the direction of WILLIAM F. HILDENBRAND, Secretary of the Senate
By GERALD A. HACKETT, Executive Clerk

Wednesday, September 9, 1981

TREATIES

Date of report	Calendar No.	Treaty No.	Subject	Action of committee
1981 June 17	3	Treaty Doc. No. 97-3.	Consular Convention with the People's Republic of China.	Reported favorably, without reservation, by Mr. Percy, Committee on Foreign Relations, with a printed report (Ex. Rept. 97-14).

NOMINATIONS

Date of report	Calendar No.	Message No.	Name of nominee	Office and predecessor	Reported by
			DEPARTMENT OF ENERGY		
1981 July 21	* 344	356	James R. Richards, of Virginia.	Inspector General of the Department of Energy, vice John Kenneth Mansfield.	Mr. McClure, Committee on Energy and Natural Resources.
			FEDERAL TRADE COMMISSION		
July 31	* 437	505	James C. Miller III, of the District of Columbia.	A Federal Trade Commissioner for the term of 7 years, Sept. 26, 1981, vice Paul Rand Dixon, term expiring.	Mr. Packwood, Committee on Commerce, Science, and Transportation.

Illustration 6F The Congressional Record

An indispensable information source for the congressional researcher is the *Congressional Record*. It is a record of debate and floor action in both houses, as well as a calendar of events to come. The following excerpts show sections of the *Record*.

United States of America

Congressional Record

PROCEEDINGS AND DEBATES OF THE 97th CONGRESS, FIRST SESSION

Vol. 127 WASHINGTON, MONDAY, JULY 13, 1981 *No. 103*

Senate

(Legislative day of Wednesday, July 8, 1981)

The Senate met at 12 noon, on the expiration of the recess, and was called to order by the President pro tempore (Mr. THURMOND).

PRAYER

The Chaplain, the Reverend Richard C. Halverson, LL.D., D.D., offered the following prayer:

Let us pray.

Holy, holy, holy, Lord God Almighty, which was, and is, and is to come. Thou art worthy, O Lord, to receive glory and honor and power: For Thou hast created all things, and for Thy pleasure they were and are created.

We give thanks to Thee, O Lord God Almighty, for the weekend recess. We thank Thee for time with our families and friends. We thank Thee for rest and relaxation. We thank Thee for the opportunity to visit with some of the people, to hear their concerns, their cares, and their desires.

Now we thank Thee for the prospect of continuing the work to which we have been called as public servants. We thank Thee for those who labor with us in the Senate, in the cloakrooms, in our offices, and on the Hill. Help us never to take for granted their faithful service and to be responsive to their needs. Help us, dear God, to love and serve one another.

In the name of Him who was the servant of servants. Amen.

RECOGNITION OF THE ACTING MAJORITY LEADER

The PRESIDENT pro tempore. Under the previous order, the acting majority leader is recognized.

Mr. McCLURE. Mr. President, I yield 2 minutes to the Senator from Arizona (Mr. GOLDWATER).

The PRESIDING OFFICER. The Senator from Arizona.

SANDRA O'CONNOR—THE CONSERVATIVE

Mr. GOLDWATER. Mr. President, having now reviewed all published legal opinions and articles written by Sandra O'Connor during her service as an Arizona appeals judge, I am delighted to find four prominent conservative themes that stand out in her papers.

It is clear that Sandra O'Connor is and will be a strict constructionist; tough on criminals; a strong defender of private property rights; and respectful of State sovereignty.

Now, Mr. President, Judge O'Connor's attachment to these four major principles means far more to me than whatever position she may have taken on any single issue. Her consistently correct stand in these four broad areas of basic conservative philosophy mark her as exactly the type of Supreme Court Justice that Ronald Reagan and the millions of Americans who voted for him want on the Court.

STRICT CONSTRUCTIONIST

Mr. President, on at least nine occasions Judge O'Connor was required to make decisions turning on the interpretation of State statutes. Often she had to construe a law as a threshold issue before reaching the final holding of the case. Thus, she had ample opportunity, if she was so inclined, of expanding statutes or putting her own imprint on the law by applying it to situations never contemplated by the drafters.

In every case she deferred to the plain legislative intent. Never once can Sandra O'Connor be charged with rewriting a State law.

It is clear she is one Supreme Court Justice who will know the difference between the Court and the Congress. As a conservative, I have no fear that Sandra O'Connor will use the Court as a superlegislature.

TOUGH ON CRIMINALS

Mr. President, there are numerous instances when Judge O'Connor was assigned criminal cases as a trial judge. There are also seven opinions she wrote for the appeals court which involved review of criminal cases.

It is accurate to say that she was tough, but fair, in each of these cases. She is clearly concerned about protecting society from violent crimes.

In fact, on March 14, 1977, Judge O'Connor told the Republican Forum at Sun City, Ariz., that she was disturbed at the rising crime rate. She warned that the emphasis on civil liberties has made it difficult to convict people of crimes they "obviously" have committed. She called upon the legislature to enact uniform, certain penalties for repeat offenders and for more serious crimes.

Judge O'Connor's no-nonsense stand toward criminal offenders and her fairness both can be seen in the decision she wrote in State of Arizona against Blevins on January 2 of this year.

The case involved a defendant who was charged with hitting and running, leaving the scene after his vehicle had struck the operator of a motorcycle. Only circumstantial evidence was offered by the prosecution. Judge O'Connor held that this evidence alone was sufficient to sustain a conviction of manslaughter.

She wrote:

> The prosecution is no longer required, in a case based wholly upon circumstantial evidence, to negate every conceivable hypothesis of innocence.

Now, this succinct statement proves she is a conservative. She definitely will be a welcome addition to the High Court by all who are concerned that the rights of society are being trampled on by liberal activists who put narrow technical points ahead of the community's ability to protect itself.

Yet Judge O'Connor is not harsh. She is not blind to justice. In the case I just discussed she ruled that the trial judge had failed to instruct the jury properly on the issue of the defendant's actual knowledge that anyone had been injured. While the conviction for manslaughter was upheld, the conviction of leaving the scene of the crime was reversed.

Also, in the case of State against Miguel in May 1980, Judge O'Connor reversed the conviction of a defendant because he was not given the benefit of a full 12-member jury. Only an 8-member jury had been impaneled. So while she is strongly on the side of society against obviously guilty criminals, she insists that express constitutional guar-

● This "bullet" symbol identifies statements or insertions which are not spoken by the Member on the floor.

S 7515

ILLUSTRATION 6F (*continued*)

□ 1100

THE PEOPLE WHO LIVE IN RURAL AMERICA

(Mr. WATKINS asked and was given permission to address the House for 1 minute and to revise and extend his remarks.)

Mr. WATKINS. Mr. Speaker, I would like to change our debate just a little bit. I have just introduced a bill that I think all of us can unite and help a group of people that are the forgotten people, the one-third of the people of this country who live in rural America.

I must say, Mr. Speaker, the bill I just introduced allows the jurisdiction of the small cities and rural communities to remain under HUD, but it transfers the delivery system, the administration, of the small cities and rural communities activities to the Farmers Home Administration so we will have a delivery system of the programs. It is a fraud on the citizens of rural America to tell them these programs include them when in reality a delivery system does not even expect to get the program to them.

I would like to address this to both sides of the aisle because at this time over 50 percent of the programs under Farmers Home Administration have been wiped out by the administration. If we are concerned about the citizens who live in rural America, who live in small cities and rural communities, being able to even compete for the programs, then I ask Members from both sides of the aisle, from the urban as well as the rural areas, to join with me in coauthoring this piece of legislation.

THEY HAD TO MAKE A CHOICE

(Mr. MARKEY asked and was given permission to address the House for 1 minute and to revise and extend his remarks.)

Mr. MARKEY. Mr. Speaker, I think, when they chronicle the history of this Congress, the most significant event will be that the moderate and liberal Republicans, so-called, of the Northeast and Midwest had to make a choice. That choice was between their party and the people they represent.

I think it is becoming very clear, in their decision not just to gag us but also to bindfold us as we vote upon programs that are going to have a very significant impact upon their constituents across the Northeast and Midwest, that they will have lost the ability to really contend that they represent the interests of the people who live in those regions of our country.

ANNOUNCEMENT BY THE SPEAKER PRO TEMPORE

The SPEAKER pro tempore. The Chair will remind the Members that the Speaker indicated that at the hour of 11 o'clock there would be a termination of the 1-minute speeches.

PARLIAMENTARY INQUIRY

Mr. LEVITAS. Mr. Speaker, I have a parliamentary inquiry.

The SPEAKER pro tempore. The gentleman will state it.

Mr. LEVITAS. Mr. Speaker, if the House resolves itself into the Committee of the Whole House on the State of the Union, is it in order while the Committee is sitting for a recess to take place to give Members time to read the 500-page document we have just received?

The SPEAKER pro tempore. The Speaker would indicate that a motion for a recess is not in order.

Mr. LEVITAS. It is not in order once we go into the Committee?

The SPEAKER pro tempore. That is correct.

Mr. LEVITAS. I thank the Speaker.

OMNIBUS BUDGET RECONCILIATION ACT OF 1981

Mr. PANETTA. Mr. Speaker, I move that the House resolve itself into the Committee of the Whole House on the State of the Union for the consideration of the bill (H.R. 3982) to provide for reconciliation pursuant to section 301 of the first concurrent resolution on the budget for the fiscal year 1982.

The SPEAKER pro tempore. The question is on the motion offered by the gentleman from California (Mr. PANETTA).

The question was taken; and on a division (demanded by Mr. LEVITAS), there were—yeas 65, nays 35.

Mr. LEVITAS. Mr. Speaker, I object to the vote on the ground that a quorum is not present and make the point of order that a quorum is not present.

The SPEAKER pro tempore. Evidently a quorum is not present.

The Sergeant at Arms will notify absent Members.

The vote was taken by electronic device, and there were—yeas 316, nays 84, not voting 31, as follows:

[Roll No. 109]

YEAS—316

Addabbo
Akaka
Albosta
Alexander
Anderson
Andrews
Annunzio
Archer
Ashbrook
Aspin
Atkinson
Badham
Bafalis
Bailey (MO)
Barnard
Beard
Benedict
Benjamin
Bennett
Bereuter
Bethune
Bevill
Biaggi
Bliley
Boland
Boner
Bonior
Bonker
Bouquard
Bowen
Breaux
Brinkley
Brodhead
Brooks
Broomfield
Brown (CA)
Brown (CO)
Brown (OH)
Broyhill
Burgener
Burton, John
Butler
Byron
Campbell
Carman
Carney
Chappell
Cheney
Clausen
Clinger
Coats
Coleman
Collins (TX)
Conable
Conte
Corcoran
Coughlin
Courter
Coyne, James
Craig
Crane, Daniel
Crane, Philip
D'Amours
Daniel, Dan
Daniel, R. W.
Dannemeyer
Daub
Davis
de la Garza
Deckard
DeNardis
Derrick
Derwinski
Dickinson
Dornan
Dreier
Duncan
Dunn
Dyson
Edwards (AL)
Edwards (OK)
Emerson
Emery
English
Erdahl
Erlenborn
Evans (DE)
Evans (GA)
Evans (IA)
Evans (IN)
Fary
Fazio
Fenwick
Fiedler
Fields
Findley
Fish
Flippo
Foglietta
Foley
Ford (TN)
Forsythe
Frenzel
Fuqua
Gejdenson
Gibbons
Gilman
Gingrich
Ginn
Glickman
Goldwater
Gonzalez
Goodling
Gradison
Gramm
Green
Gregg
Grisham
Guarini
Gunderson
Hagedorn
Hall (OH)
Hall, Ralph
Hall, Sam
Hamilton
Hammerschmidt
Hansen (ID)
Hansen (UT)
Hartnett
Hatcher
Heckler
Hefner
Heftel
Hendon
Hertel
Hightower
Hiler
Holland
Hollenbeck
Holt
Hopkins
Horton
Howard
Hoyer
Hubbard
Huckaby
Hunter
Hutto
Hyde
Ireland
Jeffries
Jenkins
Johnston
Jones (TN)
Kazen
Kemp
Kildee
Kindness
Kramer
Lagomarsino
Lantos
Latta
Leach
Leath
LeBoutillier
Lee
Lent
Lewis
Livingston
Loeffler
Long (MD)
Lott
Lowery
Lujan
Luken
Lungren
Madigan
Marks
Marlenee
Marriott
Martin (NC)
Martin (NY)
Mattox
Mazzoli
McClory
McCloskey
McCollum
McCurdy
McDade
McDonald
McEwen
McGrath
McKinney
Mica
Michel
Mikulski
Miller (OH)
Mineta
Minish
Mitchell (NY)
Molinari
Mollohan
Montgomery
Moore
Moorhead
Morrison
Mottl
Murphy
Murtha
Myers
Napier
Natcher
Nelligan
Nelson
Nichols
O'Brien
Oakar
Ottinger
Panetta
Parris
Pashayan
Paul
Pease
Perkins
Petri
Peyser
Pickle
Porter
Price
Pritchard
Pursell
Quillen
Railsback
Rangel
Regula
Rhodes
Rinaldo
Ritter
Roberts (KS)
Roberts (SD)
Robinson
Rodino
Roe
Roemer
Rogers
Rosenthal
Roth
Roukema
Rousselot
Roybal
Rudd
Russo
Santini
Sawyer
Scheuer
Schneider
Schulze
Seiberling
Sensenbrenner
Shamansky
Sharp
Shelby
Shumway
Shuster
Siljander
Simon
Skeen
Smith (AL)
Smith (NE)
Smith (NJ)
Smith (OR)
Snowe
Snyder
Solomon
Spence
Stangeland
Stanton
Stark
Staton
Stenholm
Stump
Swift
Synar
Tauke
Tauzin
Taylor
Thomas
Traxler
Trible
Udall
Vander Jagt
Walgren
Walker
Wampler
Watkins
Weber (MN)
Weber (OH)
White
Whitehurst
Whitley
Whittaker
Whitten
Williams (OH)
Wilson
Winn
Wirth
Wolf
Wortley
Wright
Wyden
Wylie
Yates
Yatron
Young (MO)
Zablocki
Zeferetti

NAYS—84

Anthony
Bailey (PA)
Barnes
Bedell
Beilenson
Bingham
Blanchard
Bolling
Burton, Phillip
Chisholm
Collins (IL)
Coyne, William
Crockett
Daschle
Dellums
Dicks
Dingell
Donnelly
Dorgan
Downey
Dwyer
Early
Eckart
Edgar
Edwards (CA)
Ertel
Ferraro
Fithian
Ford (MI)
Fountain
Fowler
Frank
Frost
Garcia
Gaydos
Gephardt
Gore
Gray
Hawkins
Hughes
Jacobs
Jeffords
Jones (NC)
Jones (OK)
Kastenmeier
Kogovsek
LaFalce
Leland
Levitas
Lowry
Lundine
Markey
Matsui
Mavroules
McHugh
Miller (CA)
Mitchell (MD)
Moakley
Neal
Oberstar

ILLUSTRATION 6F (*continued*)

Monday, July 13, 1981

Daily Digest

Senate

Chamber Action

Routine Proceedings, pages S7515–S7553

Bills Introduced: Five bills and two resolutions were introduced, as follows: S. 1463–1467, S.J. Res. 97, and S. Con. Res. 24.
Pages S7535, S7538–S7539

Measure Passed:

Budget Reconciliation: Senate passed H.R. 3982, providing for reconciliation pursuant to section 301 of the first concurrent resolution on the budget for fiscal year 1982, after striking all after the enacting clause and inserting in lieu thereof the text of S. 1377, Senate companion measure. Senate insisted on its amendment, requested a conference with the House thereon, and the Chair was authorized to appoint conferees on the part of the Senate.
Pages S7517–S7518

Department of Justice Authorizations, 1982: Senate continued consideration of S. 951, authorizing funds for fiscal year 1982 for the Department of Justice, with committee amendments, and additional amendments proposed thereto, as follows:

(1) Helms Amendment No. 69, to the first committee amendment, forbidding the Department of Justice from bringing or maintaining any action to require, directly or indirectly, the mandatory busing of schoolchildren; and

(2) Helms modified Amendment No. 96 (to Amendment No. 69, in the nature of a substitute), prohibiting the Department of Justice from maintaining suits involving, directly or indirectly, the mandatory busing of schoolchildren and to establish reasonable limits on the power of courts to impose injunctive relief involving the transportation of students. **Page S7519**

By 54 yeas to 32 nays, two-thirds of those Senators duly chosen and sworn not having voted in the affirmative, Senate failed to agree to a motion to close further debate on modified Amendment No. 96.
Page S7523

A second motion was filed to bring to a close debate on modified Amendment No. 96, with a vote to occur thereon on Wednesday, July 15.
Page S7523
Pages S7519–S7530

Confirmations: Senate confirmed the following nominations:

William H. Draper III, of California, to be President of the Export-Import Bank.

Donna Pope, of Ohio, to be Director of the Mint.

Warren T. Lindquist, of New York, to be a member of the Board of Directors of the New Community Development Corporation.

Carol E. Dinkins, as Assistant Attorney General, William G. Lesher, an Assistant Secretary of Agriculture, Roger W. Mehle, Jr., an Assistant Secretary of the Treasury, Darrell M. Trent, Deputy Secretary of Transportation, Philip D. Winn, an Assistant Secretary of Housing and Urban Development, Joseph Wright, Jr., Deputy Secretary of Commerce, and Albert Angrisani, and Assistant Secretary of Labor, each to be a Member of the Board of Directors of the National Consumer Cooperative Bank.
Pages S7553–S7554

Nominations: Senate received the following nominations:

Abraham Katz, of Florida, to be the Representative to the Organization for Economic Cooperation and Development, with the rank of Ambassador.

A. Melvin McDonald, to be U.S. Attorney for the District of Arizona.

R. Lawrence Steele, Jr., to be U.S. Attorney for the Northern District of Indiana.

Thomas E. Dittmeier, to be U.S. Attorney for the Eastern District of Missouri.

Richard A. Stacy, to be U.S. Attorney for the District of Wyoming.

Nancy H. Steorts, of Maryland, to be a Member and Chairman of the Consumer Product Safety Commission.

Albert E. Eckes, Jr., of Virginia, and Eugene J. Frank, of Pennsylvania, each to be a Member of the U.S. International Trade Commission.

Three Army nominations in the rank of General.
Page S7553

Messages from the President: **Page S7533**

Communications: **Pages S7533–S7534**

Statements on Introduced Bills: **Pages S7535–S7538**

Amendments Submitted for Printing:
Pages S7539–S7540

D 842

ILLUSTRATION 6F (*continued*)

Notices of Hearings: Page S7540

Committee Authority To Meet: Page S7540

Additional Statements: Pages S7540–S7550

Nominations: Page S7553

Confirmations: Pages S7553–S7554

Record Vote: One record vote was taken today. (Total—185) Page S7523

Recess: Senate convened at 12 noon, and recessed at 4:54 p.m., until 11 a.m., on Tuesday, July 14, 1981. (For Senate's program see remarks of Senator Baker in today's Record, on page S7553.)

Committee Meetings

(Committees not listed did not meet)

U.S. TRADE POLICY

Committee on Finance: Subcommittee on International Trade concluded joint oversight hearings with the Banking, Housing and Urban Affairs Committee's Subcommittee on International Finance and Monetary Policy on U.S. trade policy, focusing on the progress the Administration has made in formulating its trade policy and to evaluate it against the standard set by Congress in existing legislation, after receiving testimony from Senators Mathias and Huddleston; Lane Kirkland, AFL–CIO, and Susan L. Snyder, Pathfinder Corporation for International Trade, both of Washington, D.C.; Edmund Pratt, Pfizer Chemical Company, and Harry L. Freeman, on behalf of the American Express Company, both of New York City; Richard Simmons, Allegheny Ludlum Steel Corporation, Pittsburgh, Pennsylvania; and James Geier, Cincinnati Milacrom, Inc., Cincinnati, Ohio.

URBAN ECONOMIC GROWTH

Committee on Finance: Subcommittee on Savings, Pensions, and Investment Policy began hearings on S. 1310, proposed Urban Jobs and Enterprise Zone Act, providing Federal tax reductions designed to increase new jobs and business investment in depressed urban areas, receiving testimony from Maudine Cooper, National Urban League, M. Carl Holman, The National Urban Coalition, Robert Zdenek, National Congress for Community Economic Development, Arnold Cantor and Stephen Koplan, both on behalf of the AFL-CIO, Paul Pryde, Janus Associates, and Mark Frazier, Sabre Foundation, all of Washington, D.C.; Nesby Moore, Union-Sarah Economic Development Corporation, St. Louis, Missouri; Mayor Donald Fraser, Minneapolis, Minnesota, representing the U.S. Conference of Mayors; Jacques Schlenger, Venable, Baetjer and Howard, Baltimore, Maryland; George W. Haigh, Toledo Planning Council, Toledo, Ohio; and Jim Roberts, Free Zone Authority Services, Alexandria, Virginia.

Hearings continue on Thursday, July 16.

NOMINATIONS

Committee on Foreign Relations: Committee concluded hearings on the nominations of William L. Swing, of North Carolina, to be Ambassador to the Republic of Liberia, Parker W. Borg, of the District of Columbia, to be Ambassador to the Republic of Mali, Julius W. Walker, Jr., of Texas, to be Ambassador to the Republic of Upper Volta, Vernon A. Walters, of Florida, to be Ambassador at Large, H. Monroe Browne, of California, to be Ambassador to New Zealand and to serve concurrently as Ambassador to Western Samoa, and Richard L. Walker, of South Carolina, to be Ambassador to the Republic of Korea, after the nominees testified and answered questions in their own behalf. Mr. Richard Walker was introduced by Senators Thurmond and Hollings.

Committee will consider these nominations and other agenda items on tomorrow.

NOMINATION

Committee on Rules and Administration: Committee concluded hearings on the nomination of Danford L. Sawyer, Jr., of Florida, to be Public Printer, after the nominee, who was introduced by Senators Chiles and Hawkins, testified and answered questions in his own behalf. Testimony was also received from Jacob E. Worner and Ben Cooper, both of Printing Industries of America, Robert Willard, Information Industry Association, Jerry Nash, Coalition of Minority Workers, Timothy Burr, National Association of Government Communicators, and William J. Boarman, Cornelius V. McIntyre, Frederick P. Allen, and George B. Driesen, all of the Joint Council of GPO Unions, all of Washington, D.C.

Committee will consider the nomination of Mr. Sawyer on Friday, July 17.

ILLUSTRATION 6F (*concluded*)

House of Representatives

Chamber Action

Bills Introduced: 6 public bills, H.R. 4125–4130; 2 private bills, H.R. 4131–4132; and 1 resolution, H. Res. 177 were introduced.

Pages H4267–H4268

Bills Reported: Reports were filed as follows:

H.R. 1946, to reinstate and validate United States oil and gas leases numbered OCS–P–0218 and OCS–P–0226 (H. Rept. 97–173); and

H.R. 3975, to facilitate and encourage the production of oil from tar sand and other hydrocarbon deposits (H. Rept. 97–174). **Page H4267**

Suspensions: House voted to suspend the rules and pass the following bills:

Intelligence authorization: H.R. 3454, to authorize appropriations for fiscal year 1982 for the intelligence-related activities of the United States Government, for the Intelligence Community Staff, and for the Central Intelligence Agency Retirement and Disability System, to authorize supplemental appropriations for fiscal year 1981 for the intelligence and intelligence-related activities of the United States Government;

Pages H4235–H4241

Marine protection authorization: H.R. 2449, amended, to amend title III of the Marine Protection, Research, and Sanctuaries Act of 1972, as amended, to authorize appropriations for such title for fiscal years 1982, 1983, and 1984. Agreed to amend the title. Subsequently, this passage was vacated and S. 1003, a similar Senate-passed bill, was passed in lieu after being amended to contain the language of the House bill as passed. Agreed to amend the title of the Senate bill;

Pages H4245–H4247

Land-grant colleges: H.R. 1309, amended, to provide grants to the 1890 land-grant colleges, including Tuskegee Institute, for the purpose of assisting these institutions in the purchase of equipment and land, and the planning, construction, alteration, or renovation of buildings to strengthen their capacity for research in the food and agricultural sciences; and

Pages H4247–H4249

Defense Production Act: H.R. 2903, to extend by one year the expiration date of the Defense Production Act of 1950.

Pages H4249–H4250

Insular Areas Authorization: House completed all debate on the motion to suspend the rules and pass H.R. 3659, amended, to authorize appropriations for certain insular areas of the United States, on which the vote was postponed until Tuesday, July 14.

Pages H4241–H4247

Interior Appropriations: House completed all general debate on H.R. 4035, making appropriations for the Department of the Interior and related agencies for the fiscal year ending September 30, 1982; but came to no resolution thereon. Proceedings under the 5-minute rule will be scheduled later this week.

Pending when the Committee rose was an amendment that seeks to reduce by $10,000 the funding for acquisition, construction, and maintenance for the Bureau of Land Management.

Agreed to a technical amendment.

Pages H4251–H4262

Late Reports: Committee on Interior and Insular Affairs received permission to have until 5 p.m. today to file reports on H.R. 3975, to facilitate and encourage the production of oil from tar sand and other hydrocarbon deposits, and H.R. 1946, to reinstate and validate United States oil and gas leases numbered OCS–P–0218 and OCS–0–0226.

Page H4265

Referrals: Two Senate-passed measures were referred to the appropriate House committees.

Page H4267

Amendments Ordered Printed: Amendments ordered printed pursuant to the rule appear on page H4268.

Quorum Calls—Votes. No quorum calls or votes developed during the proceedings of the House today.

Adjournment: Met at noon and adjourned at 2:35 p.m.

Committee Meetings

DEFENSE APPROPRIATIONS

Committee on Appropriations: Subcommittee on Defense held a hearing on Operation and Maintenance, Air Force. Testimony was heard from Gen. Richard Murray, former Director, Air Force Budget.

INTERNATIONAL COMMUNICATION REORGANIZATION ACT

Committee on Foreign Affairs: Subcommittee on International Operations and the Subcommittee on International Economic Policy and Trade adversely approved for full Committee action H.R. 1957, International Communication Reorganization Act of 1981.

6.3 The Legislative History*

Robert S. Lockwood and Carol M. Hillier

Tracing the legislative history of a bill is an important and relatively easy task. Lockwood and Hillier specify the major ways of doing this.

Before examining the means by which the origins of a bill may be traced and its history compiled, a brief recapitulation of the legislative process is in order.

The legislative history of a bill or resolution begins with its introduction in either house of Congress and its referral to a committee. The committee may hold hearings on the bill and make a report to the full House or Senate. At this point the bill is placed on the calendar, brought up for consideration and discussed on the floor, and passed or rejected by the membership. The process may be halted at any stage, and the bill dies. If passage is successfully completed, the bill is sent to the other House, where it follows the same steps. (Frequently, identical bills are introduced in both Houses at the same time and simultaneously follow this legislative route.) When the Senate and House produce different versions of the same bill, the legislation is sent to a conference committee consisting of members from each house for resolution of areas of disagreement and the production of a bill which is again voted on by both Houses. The bill becomes law when signed by the President. (If Congress is in session and the President does not sign a bill within 10 days, it becomes law without his signature.)

An inquiry into the history of a piece of legislation may begin at any point in the above procedure. One might have hearings on a specific subject and want to find out who originally introduced the bill and why. Or one may want the background of a public law tracing its full legislative history including sponsor, hearings held, committee reports submitted, debates on the floor of the House or Senate, dates of passage, and presidential action. Primary sources for this information are five in number: (1) the *Calendar of the U.S. House of Representatives and History of Legislation;* (2) the *Congressional Record;* (3) the *Journals* of the Senate and House; (4) committee hearings; and (5) the reports of Senate and House committees.

The *Calendar of the House of Representatives* (referred to hereafter as the *House Calendar*) is an excellent source for checking the status of current legislation, as well as being essential in the compilation of legislative histories. Issued daily, it provides a cumulative and constantly updated history of action taken on specific bills and resolutions. A handy reference is the "Status of Major Bills" chart which appears on the back cover. The final edition of the *House Calendar* issued at the end of each Congress is a summary of legislative accomplishments during the period and is a primary reference tool retained in many libraries. The bills are listed by number, with access through subject index (see Figure 6.3.1).

The *Congressional Record* contains the full text of House and Senate proceedings, and it is here that one finds the actual introduction of all bills and resolutions (including the introductory remarks of the sponsor), the dates of submission of committee reports, verbatim accounts of debates held on the floor, and the record of vote on any bill or resolution. The index lists legislation by bill number as well as by subject and also

* From Robert S. Lockwood and Carol M. Hillier, *Legislative Analysis: With Emphasis on National Security Affairs* (Washington, D.C.: National Defense University Research Directory 1980), pp. 238–52. Reprinted from the public domain.

FIGURE 6.3.1 THE "STATUS OF MAJOR BILLS," AS LISTED IN THE HOUSE CALENDAR (95TH CONGRESS, 2D SESSION)

STATUS OF MAJOR BILLS—SECOND SESSION

Number of bill	Title	Reported	Passed House	Reported in Senate	Passed Senate	Sent to conference	Conference report agreed to in—		Date approved	Law No
							House	Senate		
	LEGISLATIVE BILLS	1978	1978	1978	1978	1978	1978	1978	1978	
H.R. 50	Full Employment and Balanced Growth Act of 1978 (H. Rept. 95-895).	Feb. 22 Mar. 3	Mar. 16		Oct. 13					
S. Con. Res. 80	Budget, First Concurrent, 1979 (H. Rept. 95-1055; S. Rept. 95-793).	Apr. 14	May 10	Apr. 14	Apr. 26	May 11	(1)	May 15		
H.R. 39	Alaska National Interest Lands Conservation Act (H. Rept. 95-1045, Pts. I & II).	Apr. 7 May 4	May 19	Oct. 9						
H.R. 15	Educational Amendments of 1978 (H. Rept. 95-1137)	May 11	July 13		Aug. 24	Sept. 6	Oct. 15	Oct. 12		
H. Con. Res. 683	Budget, Second Concurrent, 1979 (H. Rept. 95-1456; S. Rept. 95-1124).	Aug. 8	Aug. 16		Sept. 6	Sept. 8	(2)	Sept. 23[3]		
H.R. 13511	Revenue Act of 1978 (H. Rept. 95-1445)	Aug. 4	Aug. 10	Oct. 1	Oct. 10	Oct. 12	Oct. 15	Oct. 15		
S. 2640	Civil Service Reform Act of 1978 (H. Rept. 95-1403; S. Rept. 95-969).	July 31	Sept. 13	July 10	Aug 24	Sept. 14	Oct. 6	Oct. 4	Oct. 13	95-454
H.J. Res. 554	District of Columbia, Representation in Congress, Constitutional Amendment (H. Rept. 95-886).	Feb. 16	Mar. 3		Aug. 18					
S. 555	Ethics in Government Act of 1977 (H. Rept. 95-800; S. Rept. 95-170; S. Rept. 95-273).	Nov. 11*	Sept. 27	May 16* June 15*	June 27*	Oct. 4	Oct. 12	Oct. 7		
	APPROPRIATION BILLS									
H.J. Res. 746	Supplemental, urgent power (H. Rept. 95-914)	Feb. 28	Mar. 7		Mar. 9				Mar. 15	95-246
H.J. Res. 796	Supplemental, disaster relief (H. Rept. 95-990)	Mar. 20	Mar. 23		Mar. 23				Apr. 4	95-255
H.J. Res. 859	Supplemental U.S.R.A. (H. Rept. 95-1083)	Apr. 25	Apr. 27	May 10	May 11				May 19	95-282
H.J. Res. 873	Supplemental, SBA disaster loans (H. Rept. 95-1105)	May 2	May 8	May 10	May 11				May 21	95-284
H.J. Res. 944	Supplemental, Grain Inspection Service (H. Rept. 95-1223).	May 31	June 16		June 19				June 26	95-301
H.J. Res. 945	Supplemental, Black Lung Program (H. Rept. 95-1236).	June 1	June 9	June 19	June 23				Aug. 2	95-332
H.R. 12927	Military Construction, 1979 (H. Rept. 95-1246)	June 1	June 16	July 19	Aug. 3	Aug. 9	Aug. 17	Aug. 21	Sept. 18	95-374
H.R. 12928	Public Works, 1979 (H. Rept. 95-1247)	June 1	June 16	Aug. 7	Aug. 10	Aug. 11	Sept. 14	Sept. 27	(4)	
H.R. 12929	Labor, HEW, 1979 (H. Rept. 95-1248)	June 1	June 13	Aug. 16	Sept. 27	Sept. 29	Oct. 12	Oct. 12(5)		
H.R. 12930	Treasury, Postal, 1979 (H. Rept. 95-1249)	June 1	June 7	June 19	June 27	Sept. 7	Oct. 4	Oct. 4	Oct. 10	95-429
H.R. 12931	Foreign Assistance, 1979 (H. Rept. 95-1250)	June 1	Aug. 14	Sept. 15	Sept. 22	Sept. 26	Oct. 12	Oct. 13		
H.R. 12932	Interior, 1979 (H. Rept. 95-1251)	June 1	June 21	Aug. 2	Aug. 9	Aug. 10	Oct. 5	Oct. 7	Oct. 17	95-465
H.R. 12933	Transportation, 1979 (H. Rept. 95-1252)	June 1	June 12	June 19	June 23	June 26	July 19	July 20	Aug. 4	95-335
H.R. 12934	State, Justice, 1979 (H. Rept. 95-1253)	June 1	June 14	July 28	Aug. 7	Sept. 8	Sept. 28	Sept. 30	Oct. 10	95-431
H.R. 12935	Legislative Branch, 1979 (H. Rept. 95-1254)	June 1	June 14	July 19	Aug. 7	Aug. 8	Aug. 17	Sept. 19	Sept. 30	95-391
H.R. 12936	HUD, 1979 (H. Rept. 95-1255)	June 1	June 19	Aug. 1	Aug. 7	Sept. 12	Sept. 19	Sept. 20	Sept. 30	95-392
H.R. 13125	Agriculture, 1979 (H. Rept. 95-1290)	June 13	June 22	Aug. 1	Aug. 10	Sept. 8	Sept. 26	Sept. 27	Oct. 11	95-448
H.J. Res. 1024	Supplemental, Agriculture (H. Rept. 95-1326)	June 28	July 11	July 19	July 24				July 31	95-330
H.R. 13467	Supplemental, second, 1978 (H. Rept. 95-1350)	July 13	July 20	Aug. 1	Aug. 7	Aug. 9	Aug. 17	Aug. 25	Sept. 8	95-355
H.R. 13468	District of Columbia, 1979 (H. Rept. 95-1351)	July 13	July 21	Aug. 9	Aug. 14	Aug. 14	Aug. 17	Aug. 17	Sept. 18	95-373
H.R. 13635	Defense, 1979 (H. Rept. 95-1398)	July 27	Aug. 9	Oct. 2	Oct. 5	Oct. 5	Oct. 12	Oct. 12	Oct. 13	95-457
H.J. Res. 1139	Continuing, 1979 (H. Rept. 95-1599)	Sept. 21	Sept. 26	Oct. 11	Oct. 15					

* 1977.

[1] House agreed to Senate amendment to House amendment May 17, 1978.

[2] House receded and concurred in Senate amendment with an amendment Sept. 21, 1978.

[3] Senate agreed to House amendment Sept. 23, 1978.

[4] Vetoed Oct. 5, 1978. House sustained Presidential veto Oct. 5, 1978.

[5] Senate agreed to the bill with a further amendment Oct. 12, 1978. House agreed to the Senate amendment Oct. 14, 1978.

includes lists of legislation submitted by specific members of Congress. Each index also contains a "History of Senate and House Bills and Resolutions," which refers the researcher to the different points in the *Record* where legislative action occurred.

The *Senate Journal* and *House Journal* are annual volumes which contain the daily proceedings, but not the debates, of each session of Congress. The journals are a very convenient source for locating information on legislative action since they are one-volume summaries of a year's proceedings without the excess verbiage. The "History of Bills and Resolutions" in the journals is arranged by bill number and provides information on introduction, addition of cosponsors, reports, consideration on the floor of Congress, amendment, and passage. Since they are not published until the close of a session, the *Record* must be used for research on recent actions.

For serious legislative analysis, the hearings on a particular bill or resolution are essential to obtain information on a proposed piece of legislation. Through their study one can identify the premises underlying a bill's introduction, groups supporting or opposing it, and reasons which led to its eventual passage or defeat. They help clarify the positions of key groups—i.e., interest groups, the Administration, or congressional factions—and may offer insight into the prevailing climate of public opinion on a subject, as well as explore policy alternatives. Hearings on specific bills may be identified through the *Monthly Catalog of United States Government Publications,* calendars of individual congressional committees, and private services, such as the Congressional Information Services.

Senate and House Reports contain the findings and recommendations of a committee following its consideration of a bill or resolution. The report explains committee actions to the full House and accompanies the bill to the floor where it is debated. There is no report on a piece of legislation which "dies" in committee—i.e., is not acted on or reported out. Reports on specific pieces of legislation may be identified by means of the *House Calendar,* the indexes to the *Congressional Record* and Journals of the House and Senate, the *Monthly Catalog,* the calendars of individual congressional committees, and the Congressional Information Service indexes and abstracts.

The five primary sources for legislative analysis are issued by the Congress; however, there are aids which simplify the researcher's task by providing easy access to essential information, such as dates of key actions which can be checked in the *Congressional Record,* and titles of hearings and reports to be consulted. Four of these aids will be considered here: the *Digest of Public General Bills and Resolutions, Congressional Information Service Index to Congressional Publications,* the *CCH Congressional Index,* and the *Monthly Catalog of United States Government Publications.*

The *Digest of Public General Bills and Resolutions,* prepared by the Congressional Research Service of the Library of Congress, contains factual descriptions of the subject matter of each public bill and resolution introduced in Congress, changes made during the legislative process, and dates of committee and floor actions taken. It is indexed by sponsor, identical bills, short title, and subject, as well as providing a numerical list by bill numbers. The *Digest* is a good starting point for legislative analysis since it provides many essential facts, including a cross-reference to identical bills (a plus when the researcher is faced with checking on five similar bills introduced and only one acted upon). The cumulative and final editions of the *Digest* contain a "Public Laws" section, which provides full legislative histories of each public law enacted during that session and a cross-index to originating legislation (see Figure 6.3.2).

The Congressional Information Service publishes a monthly *CIS Index to Congressional Publications,* which abstracts and indexes publications issued by Congress during the previous month. Needed information can be accessed by bill number, report or document number, subject of hearings or specific testimony, names and affiliations of witnesses, names of authors, names of subcommittees holding hearings, and official and popular names of bills and public laws. The precise indexing allows a number of research approaches and enables one to locate abstracts of publications related to specific topics, particular pieces of legislation, and testimony by individuals with ease—searches that would require interminable lengths of time without CIS. The *CIS Annual* cumulates the information for the year and also provides an abstract and legislative history for each public law enacted during the year covered by the annual. The legislative history includes references to all associated hearings and reports, as well as pertinent sections in the *Congressional Record* and *Weekly Compilation of Presidential Documents.*

The *Congressional Index,* published by the Commerce Clearing House, provides weekly reports on the status of legislation pending in Congress. Bills and resolutions are indexed by subject and sponsor, and information is given on companion and identical bills introduced, as well as laws enacted. A separate section deals with congressional action on nominations, treaties, and reorganization plans. In addition to providing the current status of legislation, the *Index* also lists the members of Congress with biographical data and committee assignments, committee hearings held, and recorded votes.

The *Monthly Catalog of Government Publications* is issued monthly by the Superintendent of Documents, U.S. Government Printing Office. All congressional documents can be accessed by author, title, subject, or series/report number, with full bibliographic information

FIGURE 6.3.2 A LEGISLATIVE HISTORY OF PL 95–610 FROM THE *DIGEST OF PUBLIC GENERAL BILLS AND RESOLUTIONS*

Public Law 95-610 Approved 11/8/78; S. 274.

Makes it unlawful for members of the armed forces, knowing of the activities or objectives of a particular military labor organization, to join or maintain membership in such organization, or attempt to enroll any other member of the armed forces in such organization.

Makes it unlawful for any person to: (1) enroll any member of the armed forces in a military labor organization, or to solicit or accept dues or fees for such an organization from any member of the armed forces; (2) to negotiate or bargain with any civilian officer or employee, on behalf of members of the armed forces, concerning the terms or conditions of service of such members; (3) participate in strikes or other concerted labor union activities which are intended to induce a member of the armed forces to (A) negotiate or bargain concerning the terms or conditions of military services, (B) recognize an organization as a representative of armed forces personnel with respect to complaints or grievances concerning terms or conditions of service, or (C) make any change in the terms or conditions of service of individual members of the armed services; or (4) use any military installation or facility for such prohibited activities.

Makes it unlawful for any military labor organization to represent or attempt to represent any member of the armed forces before any civilian officers or employee or member of the armed forces in connection with grievances or complaints arising out of terms or conditions of military service.

Prohibits members of the armed forces and civilian officers and employees from: (1) negotiating or bargaining on behalf of the United States with any person who represents or purports to represent members of the armed forces; or (2) allowing the use of any military installation, facility, reservation. vessel, or other property of the United States for any meeting, march, picketing, demonstration or other similar activity for the purpose of engaging in activities prohibited by this Act. Stipulates that nothing in this Act shall prevent commanders or supervisors from giving consideration to the views of members of the armed forces, either as individuals or through advisory councils, committees, or organizations.

Defines "member of the armed forces" as one who is serving on active duty, or is a member of a Reserve component while performing inactive duty training.

Sets forth penalties for the violation of the provisions of this Act.

States that nothing in this Act shall limit the rights of members of the armed forces to: (1) join or maintain membership in any organization which does not meet the definition of a "military labor organization"; (2) present complaints or grievances in accordance with established military procedures; (3) seek or receive information, or counseling from any source; (4) be represented by counsel in legal or quasi-legal proceedings in accordance with applicable laws and regulations; (5) petition the Congress for redress of grievances; or (6) take administrative action to obtain administrative or judicial relief as authorized by applicable laws or regulations.

8-18-77	Reported to Senate from the Committee on Armed Services with amendment, S. Rept. 95-411
9-16-77	Measure called up by unanimous consent in Senate
9-16-77	Measure considered in Senate
9-16-77	Measure passed Senate, amended, roll call #388 (72-3)
9-19-77	Referred jointly to House Committees on Armed Services; and Post Office and Civil Service
2-22-78	Reported to House from the Committee on Armed Services with amendment, H. Rept. 95-894 (Pt.I)
8-04-78	Reported to House from the Committee on Post Office and Civil Service with amendment, H. Rept. 95-894 (Part II)
9-26-78	Measure called up under motion to suspend rules and pass in House
9-26-78	Measure considered in House
9-26-78	Measure passed House, amended, roll call #832 (395-12)
10-14-78	Senate agreed to House amendments
11-08-78	Public Law

SOURCE: *Digest of Public General Bills and Resolutions*, 95th Congress, 2d Session, 1978, Final Issue, Part 1, pp. 231–2.

provided under the listing by Superintendent of Documents classification number. The *Monthly Catalog* and the *Congressional Information Service Index* are the best tools to use when one has only subject information and wishes to locate the full titles and publication information on hearings and reports.

Outlined above are some of the basic tools essential for locating information on legislation, both primary sources and those which provide shortcuts in locating the needed information. There is no specific guideline on how to trace the legislation on a given subject, since the path of the search would depend on the information originally available as well as the type of results desired.

As noted above, if the number of a bill or resolution is known, research can begin by consulting the index to the *Congressional Record* (under "History of Bills and Resolutions"), a similar section in the *House Journal* and *Senate Journal*, the *Digest of Public General Bills and Resolutions*, or the *House Calendar*. If the number is unknown, the search must begin under subject, author, or title indexes in these publications or by using a service such as the *Congressional Index*. When locating the hearings and reports on a bill, the search would extend to the *Congressional Information Service Index* or the *Monthly Catalog*. Debates and passage of a bill would be recorded in the *Congressional Record* along with the recorded vote, and would be referred to in the *House Calendar, Congressional Index,* and *Digest of Public General Bills and Resolutions*. Presidential action on a measure is recorded in the *Weekly Compilation of Presidential Documents*—including statements made in support of a bill, remarks offered at the signing of a piece of legislation, or veto messages. References may be obtained from the *Digest of Public General Bills, CIS Index, Congressional Index,* or *Congressional Record.*

In tracing a legislative history, the researcher should be aware that the entry for a bill enacted into law may not reflect its entire legislative consideration. A committee may hold hearings on one bill and report out another with a new bill number, or bills may be substituted for others previously introduced. It may be necessary to consult the debates, reports, and hearing on several bills in order to fully analyze one piece of legislation (see Figure 6.3.3).

The discussion thus far has focused on the sources to be consulted when searching for a specific congressional document or in tracing the history of a piece of legislation. There are two publications—privately published by Congressional Quarterly, Inc.—that are indispensable aids in legislative analysis: the *Congressional Quarterly Weekly Report* and the annual *Congressional Quarterly Almanac*. The former reports on major current legislation, including Administration stands, committee hearings, lobbying efforts, and legislative actions taken, as well as recording votes of members on specific bills. The information is consolidated and categorized by subject for convenient research.

Each *Almanac* analyzes the major legislation of the past session of Congress—as divided into broad subject categories. Under "National Security," for example, all major defense related legislation is considered, with detailed legislative histories, pertinent committee and floor action, important behind-the-scenes arrangements

FIGURE 6.3.3 ANOTHER SOURCE FOR THE HISTORY OF A PARTICULAR PIECE OF LEGISLATION IS FOUND ON THE PUBLIC LAW ITSELF—EITHER IN THE "SLIP LAW" VERSION OR IN THE *STATUTES AT LARGE*.

PUBLIC LAW 95–610—NOV. 8, 1978 92 STAT. 3085

Public Law 95–610
95th Congress

An Act

To amend title 10, United States Code, to prohibit union organization of the armed forces, membership in military labor organizations by members of the armed forces, and recognition of military labor organizations by the Government, and for other purposes.

Nov. 8, 1978
[S. 274]

Be it enacted by the Senate and House of Representatives of the United States of America in Congress assembled,

Armed Forces, union organizations, prohibition. 10 USC 975 note.

SECTION 1. (a) The Congress makes the following findings:

(1) Members of the armed forces of the United States must be prepared to fight and, if necessary, to die to protect the welfare, security, and liberty of the United States and of their fellow citizens.

(2) Discipline and prompt obedience to lawful orders of superior officers are essential and time-honored elements of the American military tradition and have been reinforced from the earliest articles of war by laws and regulations prohibiting conduct detrimental to the military chain of command and lawful military authority.

(3) The processes of conventional collective bargaining and labor-management negotiation cannot and should not be applied to the relationships between members of the armed forces and their military and civilian superiors.

(4) Strikes, slowdowns, picketing, and other traditional forms of job action have no place in the armed forces.

(5) Unionization of the armed forces would be incompatible with the military chain of command, would undermine the role, authority, and position of the commander, and would impair the morale and readiness of the armed forces.

(6) The circumstances which could constitute a threat to the ability of the armed forces to perform their mission are not comparable to the circumstances which could constitute a threat to the ability of Federal civilian agencies to perform their functions and should be viewed in light of the need for effective performance of duty by each member of the armed forces.

(b) The purpose of this Act is to promote the readiness of the armed forces to defend the United States.

SEC. 2. (a) Chapter 49 of title 10, United States Code, is amended by adding at the end thereof the following new section:

"§ 975. Membership in military unions, organizing of military unions, and recognition of military unions prohibited

10 USC 975.

"(a) In this section:

Definitions.

"(1) 'Member of the armed forces' means (A) a member of the armed forces who is serving on active duty, or (B) a member of a Reserve component while performing inactive-duty training.

"(2) 'Military labor organization' means any organization that engages in or attempts to engage in—

"(A) negotiating or bargaining with any civilian officer or employee, or with any member of the armed forces, on behalf of members of the armed forces, concerning the terms or conditions of military service of such members in the armed forces;

92 STAT. 3088 PUBLIC LAW 95–610—NOV. 8, 1978

(b) The table of sections at the beginning of chapter 49 of title 10, United States Code, is amended by adding at the end thereof the following new item:

"975. Membership in military unions, organizing of military unions, and recognition of military unions prohibited."

Approved November 8, 1978.

LEGISLATIVE HISTORY:

HOUSE REPORT No. 95–894, Pt. I (Comm. on Armed Services) and Pt. II (Comm. on Post Office and Civil Service).
SENATE REPORT No. 95–411 (Comm. on Armed Services).
CONGRESSIONAL RECORD:
Vol. 123 (1977): Sept. 16, considered and passed Senate.
Vol. 124 (1978): Sept. 26, considered and passed House, amended.
Oct. 15, Senate concurred in House amendment.

and pressures, and final results for each bill or resolution. The appendices offer "Special Reports," "Voting Studies," "Lobby Registrations," "Presidential Messages," "Public Laws," and "Roll-Call Charts."[1]

In pursuing research of retrospective legislation, it may be necessary to consult the predecessor volumes to many of the bibliographic tools explored above—i.e., the *Annals of Congress, Register of Debates,* and *Congressional Globe* would be referred to for the periods 1789–1824, 1824–1837, 1833–1873, respectively, since the *Congressional Record* began publication in 1873.

This paper has highlighted five primary sources and four aids useful for legislative research and analysis. Further access to legislative materials can be obtained from additional documents, which are too numerous to be discussed here.[2]

Technological developments in modern telecommunications and information networks can also assist the researcher and analyst. On-line retrieval systems such as Lockheed "Dialog" and System Development Corporation "Orbit" have greatly expanded accessibility to bibliographic information and greatly eased its retrieval. The *Congressional Record, Federal Register,* and *CIS Index* are all available as on-line data bases on one or more commercially available information systems. The Library of Congress Information System (LOCIS), available to the public in the Library of Congress Reading Rooms, contains legislative information files for the 94th and succeeding Congresses, which monitor a bill's passage through Congress. Automated searching can reduce research done manually in a matter of hours to a matter of minutes—giving the analyst more time to ponder the facts before him.

It is hoped that the information provided here will provide the researcher with some guidelines by which he can begin and carry out an inquiry into the great array of legislative information available—information from which facts must be gleaned, sorted out, analyzed, and put into proper perspective.

6.4 The Politics of House–Senate Conferences*

Gerald S. Strom and Barry S. Rundquist

The constitutional requirement that a law must be enacted in identical languages by both houses has led to conference committees for ironing out House–Senate differences. These "third houses," although not used on all bills, usually are employed for the most controversial legislation of a session. Strom and Rundquist study the politics and procedures of House–Senate conferences.

ABSTRACT

The question, "Who wins in House–Senate conferences?" has largely been answered for recent Congresses. But the question, "Why does the Senate win?" has not been adequately answered. The research reported here presents and tests some necessary conditions of a theory that provides an answer to this question. The Senate wins because it is most frequently the second acting chamber and, because it has constitutionally derived power over House decisions, giving it the capacity to get the adjustments it makes in House bills accepted in conference. In the minority of cases in which the Senate acts first, the House "wins" in conference. Unlike earlier attempts to explain conference outcomes, the theory proposed here is consistent with the overall pattern of House dominance in the legislative process.

INTRODUCTION

The question "Who wins in House-Senate conferences?" has been answered, at least for recent Congresses.[1] Almost all evidence shows that the Senate wins more often than does the House.[2] Why the Senate wins, however, has not been adequately answered. Speculation and hypotheses abound, especially since much of what we know about Congress leads to the conclusion that the House rather than the Senate should win.

In this paper we examine the available explanations of why the Senate conferees tend to win and suggest that an alternative explanation is not only supported empirically but is more consistent with the prevailing understanding of the roles of the House and Senate in congressional policymaking.

CONFERENCE OUTCOMES

Senate dominance of conference decision making has been demonstrated repeatedly. Fenno, in his study of 331 appropriations conference decisions, found that the Senate won 56.6 percent of all outcomes and 65 percent of the outcomes other than those where the House and Senate split the differences; the House won 30.5 percent and 35 percent respectively.[3] Similarly, Manley found that the Senate won 56 percent of all tax legislation outcomes and 70 percent of the outcomes in which there was a

---

* From Gerald S. Strom and Barry S. Rundquist, "A Revised Theory of Winning in House–Senate Conferences," *American Political Science Review* 71 (1977): 448–53.

The authors wish to thank John Ferejohn, Susan Hansen, Lester Seligman, William Wilschke, and two anonymous referees for their comments on earlier drafts of this paper, as well as Cheryl Frank, James Gerl, and Beatrice Villar for their assistance.

winner; the House won 25 percent and 30 percent respectively.[4] In a study of conference outcomes during five Congresses, Vogler found that the Senate won an average of 65 percent of the time, while the House won 35 percent.[5] Kanter found that the House accepted the Senate's recommendations of defense appropriations bills 57 percent of the time.[6] Finally, in examining the 136 identifiable conference outcomes during the 92nd Congress, we found that the House won 30 percent of the time while the Senate won 46 percent, and, when only decisions which resulted in a victory for one side are considered, the Senate won 60 percent to 40 percent for the House ($N = 103$).[7] Thus, where there is a winner, the Senate generally wins between 60 and 70 percent of conference outcomes, while the House wins 30 to 40 percent.

EXPLAINING CONFERENCE OUTCOMES

The scholars cited above offer several different explanations for their findings. For appropriations conferences, Fenno suggests that the greater support provided Senate conferees by the Senate itself allows them to win:

> The Senate is stronger in conference because the Senate [Appropriations] Committee and its conferees draw more directly and more completely upon the support of their parent chamber than do the House [Appropriations] Committee and its conferees. . . . The position they defend will have been worked out with a maximum of participation by Senate members and will enjoy a maximum of support in that body.[8]

This explanation takes account of a custom, dating to the 1840s, for conferees to be drawn from the standing committees in each chamber to which the bill was originally referred.[9] Fenno also examines and rejects the alternative explanation that the Senate wins because it supports the higher budget estimate.[10]

Manley explains Senate victories in the tax social security tariff areas with another version of the outside support explanation:

> The reason the Senate does better in cases of conflict with the Ways and Means Committee is because politically Senate decisions are more in line with the demands of interest groups, lobbyists, and constituents than House decisions. Ways and Means decisions, made under the closed rule, tend to be less popular with relevant publics than Senate decisions.[11]

Finally, Vogler seems to suggest that the chamber represented by the most prestigious committee in conference will win. His analysis shows, however, that the opposite is true: "House conferees drawn from committees with lower prestige than that of the Senate committees involved in conference were generally more successful than were House conferees from committees with prestige rankings above those of their Senate counterparts."[12] Vogler offers no explanation of this finding, but Ferejohn shows that it is a special case of Fenno's chamber support explanation: "The less prestigious House committees may be more permeable to influence from the House as a whole than the prestige committees, which are expected to control some natural excesses of the House. Thus conferees from low-prestige House committees enjoy more floor support than do conferees of the prestige committees."[13]

That the emphasis of these explanations falls on the greater outside political support given Senate conferees as opposed to House conferees is not surprising. This is one of the few variables related to success in conference decision making that apparently favors the Senate. Most other sources of House–Senate differences lead one to expect that the House will win in conference. For example, the greater specialization of Representatives in their committee work makes them better prepared for conferences. Similarly, the tighter organization of House committees is reflected in preconference strategy sessions, smaller and more hierarchically structured bands of conferees, better conference attendance records, and "tougher" bargaining stances by the House conferees.[14]

We are troubled, however, by two related aspects of this explanation of Senate victories. First, how exactly does Senators' greater outside political support help them to win in conference? Both unit voting and the tendency for the House conferees to be major proponents of the House committee's bill appear to limit the utility of outside political support as a bargaining resource. Unit voting means that senators have to change the position of a majority or more of the House conference delegation, not just that of enough to form a majority with the Senate conferees. Moreover, it is unclear why any House conferee would be willing to defer to the outside support of the Senate conferees rather than hold out for the bill his committee shaped and obtained House support for.

Second, even assuming that in some way greater outside political support is an important conference resource, its mobilization and use by Senate conferees seems to imply that there are important victories to be won in conference. But most observers seem agreed that conferences are not as important as other stages of the legislative process. As Fenno states, "conferees make the least consequential decisions of all."[15] If there is so little to be won, why would outside support be mustered to win it? The outside political support explanations seem to require the assumption that conferences are worth winning.

Our alternative explanation assumes that conference committees are less like wars or battles to be won and more like the peace talks that occur after major battles have been fought. It predicts that the chamber that will lose in conference is the chamber that has won the most prior to the conference. We would expect that conferees from this chamber would have the most incentive to induce the other confereees to leave their prior gains intact by conceding to their conference requests. Thus for the victor, conferences are a means toward ensuring what has been won elsewhere, not an arena for new victories. Therefore, strategic considerations, not the things that lead to winning battles (e.g., outside support), should affect winning in conference.

Which chamber is likely to have gained the most prior to conference? We will argue that the chamber that acts first on a bill tends to have the greatest impact on the content of a bill prior to the conference. This argument, a version of which has been advanced by Froman to explain why chamber disagreements are not taken to conference (i.e., the first acting chamber accepts the second acting chamber's revisions), and by Ferejohn to explain the results of appropriations conferences on Corps of Engineers civil works bills, is based upon the conception of the legislative process which follows:[16]

1. Action on legislation usually begins in one chamber because two separate *de novo* considerations of the bill would be costly in time and resources and would make resolution of differences between the House and Senate versions more difficult. As a senior member of the House Public Works Committee told us: "Well, we have to delay awhile right now. The Senate has been ahead of us in working up a bill so we will wait until they have a basic version. Then we will work from that. [Is this because it will be easier to reach an agreement of conference?] Of course. You can't take two totally different bills to conference and hope to reach agreement."

2. The first acting chamber negotiates a compromise on the bill. The compromise reflects the preferences of various chamber actors (e.g., chairmen, subcommittee chairmen, other legislators interested in the bill for whatever reasons) and those of the Executive Branch agency most involved. If the bill did not originate with the agency, the appropriate committee requests the agency's position on the bill.

3. When the second acting chamber considers the bill, a preliminary compromise has been struck between the originating chamber and the agency, and the second acting chamber may be thought of as the minority member of a three-actor game. In this situation, members of the second acting chamber have two alternatives: they can either put together an entirely new bill, in effect forming a new majority coalition with the agency (or for that matter with the other chamber); or they can make marginal adjustments, and therefore the second acting chamber would prefer to make marginal adjustments.

4. Actors in both the first acting chamber and the agency have an incentive to grant the second acting chamber's marginal adjustments in order to pass as much of its original com-

promise as possible. Of course, both actors as well as outsiders would also have an incentive to have the second acting chamber insert preferences they had sacrificed in the initial compromise as marginal adjustments.

5. In conference committees the preferences inserted by the second acting chamber will be accepted by the first acting chamber.

6. To the extent that marginal adjustments added by the second acting chamber deviate from the first acting chamber's original position, legislators from the first acting chamber have a short-run incentive to resist the adjustments. Moreover, if the first acting chamber consistently agreed to the marginal adjustments of the second acting chamber, in the future it might add more and more adjustments. Hence the first acting chamber has both a short-run and long-run incentive to oppose some of the second chamber's proposals. The conferees from the first acting chamber therefore have an incentive to grant some marginal adjustments so as to pass the legislation, but it is clearly in their interests as well to resist granting all the requests of the second acting chamber.

This view, which is consistent with the evidence that the Senate usually wins in conference, does not mean that the Senate's version of a bill usually predominates. Just the opposite is true: the House has more influence on the content of the bill because it acts first.

EVIDENCE

If this explanation of conference outcomes is correct, it must follow either that the Senate is always the second acting chamber, or that the House also tends to win in conference when it acts second. Table 6.4.1 shows that the Senate is *not* always the second acting chamber, and that, when the Senate does act first, the House wins in conference. In the 92d Congress, when the House acted first, the Senate won 72 percent of the conference outcomes; when the Senate acted first, the House won 71 percent of the conference outcomes.[17]

Of course one reason the House acts first so often is that it is constitutionally required to initiate action on revenue bills and by custom initiates action on appropriations bills. When money bills are separated out, the House is still found to act first on 60 percent of the bills that went to conference (see Table 6.4.2). More important, however, little difference exists in the proportion of conferences won by the Senate and the proportion of conferences on nonmoney bills won by the second acting chamber (see Table 6.4.3).

This strongly supports the inference that acting second is the general explanation of Senate predominance on both money and nonmoney bills.

These results may, however, be artifacts of the peculiarities of the 92d Congress. To determine whether these findings could be generalized beyond the 92d Congress, we hypothesized that the percentage of Senate victories in the five Congresses studied by Vogler[18] could be "predicted" by the following regression equation, derived from Table 6.4.1:

> Number of Senate conference victories during a Congress = 0.72 (No. of House first bills) + 0.29 (No. of Senate first bills).

And where, using Table 6.4.2:

> No. of House first bills = 0.72 (Total of bills resulting in conference).
>
> No. of Senate first bills = 0.28 (Total of bills resulting in conference).

Applying these equations to the numbers presented by Vogler, one can generate a set of predictions which can then be compared to Vogler's actual results. The more accurate the predictions, the more confidence we have that the assumptions and conclusions of the theory presented above are general.

Table 6.4.4 indicates the results of the application of these equations to Vogler's data.[19] The equations predict well, even with the strong assumptions that the percentages of bills passed first by the House and the percentage of Senate victories are constant. In fact, the results give strong support to both the theory and the corollary assumptions.

TABLE 6.4.1 CONFERENCE OUTCOMES IN THE 92D CONGRESS IN RELATION TO WHICH CHAMBER ACTED FIRST

	HOUSE WINS	SENATE WINS	
House passes bill first	28%	72%	100% (N=75)
Senate passes bill first	71%	29%	100% (N=28)

TABLE 6.4.2 CONFERENCE OUTCOMES ON MONEY AND NONMONEY BILLS IN RELATION TO WHICH CHAMBER ACTED FIRST

	MONEY BILLS	NONMONEY BILLS	TOTAL BILLS
House passes bill first	41	57 (60%)	98 (72%)
Senate passes bill first	0	38 (40%)	38 (28%)
	41	95 (100%)	136 (100%)

TABLE 6.4.3 CONFERENCE OUTCOMES FOR MONEY AND NONMONEY BILLS PASSED FIRST BY THE HOUSE

	HOUSE WINS	SENATE WINS	
Tax and appropriations bills	27%	73%	100% (N=37)
Other House first bills	32%	68%	100% (N=38)

TABLE 6.4.4 COMPARISON OF ACTUAL AND PREDICTED CONFERENCE OUTCOMES

CONGRESS	PREDICTED SENATE VICTORIES	ACTUAL SENATE VICTORIES (FROM VOGLER)
79	25	23
80	28	33
83	35	42
88	29	34
89	43	42

IMPLICATIONS

One implication of these results is that there is nothing about the Senate *per se,* other than its tendency to act second on legislation, that explains its tendency to win more often in conference than the House does.[20] The almost perfect symmetry of our basic findings indicates that neither the greater openness of Senate as opposed to House decision making, nor indeed any other characteristic that differentiates the House and Senate, exerts an independent influence on winning in conference. When the House goes second, it wins 71 percent of the time. If outside political support or greater openness to this support affects conference outcomes, this symmetry would suggest that it does so equally for both chambers.

A second implication of our conception of the legislative process is that, in order to influence the *major* aspects of a bill, outsiders would concentrate on policymaking in the first acting chamber and/or the relevant agency. This implication is further supported by Ferejohn's study of new starts added to the Army Corps of Engineers appropriations bills (where the House always acts first). Ferejohn concludes that "conference outcomes generally follow the pattern of House dominance," adding, "if the House adds a new start to the Corps' budget it almost always is funded in the final budget. A Senate-initiated new start usually has a much smaller chance of being in the conference budget. . . . House approval generally implies Senate approval, but the converse is not true."[21] Thus, although the Senate conferers prevailed in 65 percent of the new starts over which the conferees disagreed, more House-initiated than Senate-initiated new starts were included in the ultimate statute.[22]

CONCLUSIONS

We have suggested that the reason Senate conferees win more often in conference is that the Senate more often acts second to the House on legislation. We contend that the conferees from the first acting chamber have an incentive to exchange marginal amendments in the bill with conferees from the second acting chamber to obtain the latters' support for the major aspects of the bill their chamber has passed. Thus conferences are best understood as the contexts in which conferees from the first acting chamber bargain for the support of the conferees from the second acting chamber, rather than as "the third house" in which the forces that lead to legislative victories are similar to those that lead to legislative victories at earlier stages of the legislative process.

In support of this explanation we demonstrated that the House wins about as many conferences when the Senate initiates legislative action as the Senate wins when the House initiates legislative action. This finding rather clearly indicates that the greater openness of Senate proceedings and the greater outside support for Senate bills does not cause the Senate victories. The Senate wins because it acts second and for the reasons we have suggested.

This is not to say that outside groups, bureaucrats, or Congressmen do not wish to have their preferences prevail in conference. They clearly do. For example, agencies submit a reclama to the second acting chamber in hopes that the second acting chamber will pass a bill that includes their preferences and that will be upheld in conference. We suggest, however, that second chamber's conferees win not because they have more outside support, but because they have a strategic advantage in conference—namely, the ability to veto the compromise arranged by the first chamber.

Our theory also subsumes Froman's argument that the first acting chamber often accepts the second acting chamber's amendments without going to conference. The first acting chamber accepts the second acting chamber's amendments to protect its own version of the bill. The sending of bills to conference in the first place can be understood as an effort on the part of the first acting chamber to limit the number and extent of adjustments made by the second acting chamber. In this sense, conferences are a check on the logrolling between chambers that often characterizes House–Senate interaction.

Finally, this paper emphasizes the importance of the House in congressional policymaking. We have shown that 72 percent of the bills that went to conference in the 92d Congress originated in the House. Moreover, of the 607 bills that became public laws during the 92d Congress, 61 percent (or 327) originated in the House, while only 39 percent (or 237) originated in the Senate. If we are correct that acting first allows a chamber to have greater impact on the content of legislation, then clearly the House has more legislative impact than the Senate.

CHAPTER 7

Congressional Decision Making: The Micro Focus

In addition to studying congressional policymaking from the macro perspective of following how bills become law, congressional scholars also have employed a micro focus, studying how individual Congressmen reach decisions.

Micro studies vary in terms of what they study and how they gather data. Four separate components of the member cognitive map—force field (communications), information sources, decision shortcuts and determinants, and role orientations—have been the object of study. Table 7.1 displays these different components and the facet of decision making on which they focus. Sources for micro studies have been content analysis, direct interviewing, and analyses of roll-call data. The selections that follow address these various components and give examples of studies based on these different sources.

TABLE 7.1 FOUR COMPONENTS OF THE MEMBER'S COGNITIVE MAP

COMPONENT	DECISION-MAKING ASPECT
Force field/policy arena	Communications input—attempts to influence to which member pays attention in making a decision.
Information sources	Actors/sources from which member learns about the factual aspect of a bill.
Determinants	Actors/decision rules on which members rely when making a decision.
Role orientations	Broad philosophical perspective with which members observe the representational aspects of a bill.

7.1 An Overview of Information Sources for Congressional Decision Making*

David C. Kozak

This article lists the major sources of information available to House members when they make decisions concerning floor votes. It concludes with an attempt to classify these various sources of information.

This article reports the results of a study of congressional information sources based on 361 interviews with members of the U.S. House in 1977. (An elaboration of the procedures and instrument employed in the study are detailed in article 7.3 of this collection.)

Table 7.1.1 presents a frequency distribution of sources mentioned by the members in response to the question, "Where did you get your information—i.e., where did you turn to find out about the facts of the bill."

These major congressional information sources can be grouped as follows: personal contacts with other members, impersonal contact with other members, in-house publications, personal staff, outside sources, and members' experience and reading. During the course of the interviews, members provided a number of insights concerning the utility and contributions of these major sources.

TABLE 7.1.1 AGGREGATE FREQUENCY DISTRIBUTION OF INFORMATION SOURCES: THE PERCENTAGE OF INTERVIEWS IN WHICH MEMBERS MENTIONED VARIOUS INFORMATION SOURCES

Source	%
Committee chairman	5%
Committee members	13
State delegation	4
Party leader	4
Party Whip Notice	22
Floor debate	18
Committee report	14
Other members	9
Committee staff	3
Personal staff	33
Constituents	5
Interest groups	5
White House	3
Media/reading	18
Democratic Study Group (DSG)	30
Republican ad hoc group	1
Steering/Policy Committee membership	1
Personal experience/learning	5
Membership on other committee	2
Committee membership	6
Dear Colleague letter	5
Environmental study group (ESG)	2
Last time through	8

361 interviews were conducted.

MEMBERS AS INFORMATION SOURCES

Information concerning a floor vote comes from committee chairmen, committee members, other members, party leaders, and state delegation members.

Committee chairmen, cited 5 percent of the time, were mentioned as an information source in instances where the chairman was an obvious, dynamic actor, such as Morris Udall on strip mining, Robert Giaimo on the budget, and Louis Stokes on the Assassinations Committee.

* From David C. Kozak, *Contexts of Congressional Decision Making*. Forthcoming, University of Tennessee Press.

Committee members were mentioned 13 percent of the time. Other members note the information utility of committee members in two ways. First, those on committee are often turned to for clarification of bills that originate from their committee. As one member described: "I'll seek committee people out if I don't understand. If I have no trouble, no questions—there's no need to visit with them." Another noted, "I usually talk to committee proponents to get a clearer view." Second, committee members "at the door" often provide information. The function of committee members positioned as such is ". . . to discuss. They do not tell you how to vote." One freshman Republican illustrated the use of committee members at the House door with his reconstruction of his decision with regard to the FAA authorization. "I walked on the floor cold on that one. I got all of my information by asking a committee member at the door." Many members emphasized the selective use of committee members. Again and again members noted how they turn to committee members in whom they have confidence. In the words of one member, "I usually talk to friends on the committee to find out about the bill."

Other members not on the committee were mentioned in 9 percent of the decision cases. Other members mentioned as an information source are (1) class members, (2) those who closely monitor floor debate on behalf of the Republicans, (3) those who offer amendments ("I talked to Baucus to find out how his amendment would affect the strip mining bill"), (4) those who have pork-barrel projects at stake in any given vote (especially on snow removal and the water projects), and (5) those with recognized expertise on an issue (e.g., the Michigan delegation on clean air, doctors on saccharin). Many members pointed out that their fellow members are a natural source of information. As one noted, "You always survey the guys to find out about things that seem to be ambiguous."

Party leaders were mentioned in only 4 percent of the cases. Three forms of contact were mentioned. One is through official leadership positions issued on major issues. Democrats disseminate leadership positions in the form of published endorsements of the House Democratic Steering and Policy Committee. Republican leaders have two forums: publications of the House Republican Policy Committee and publication of the Republican Research Committee. These endorsements and stands primarily provide ". . . general information. They do not advise." As one Republican described Republican party pronouncements, "They are factual materials that help a guy make up his mind. Usually you'll go with them unless there is an overriding philosophical or local interest."

A second way party leaders provide information is meetings with party Whips. As a Democratic Zone Whip noted, "These meetings are used primarily to get information out through the Whip network."

A third type of party leader information input is through doormen and cloakroom recordings. The leadership of both House parties station partisan members of the doorkeeper's staff at all entrances to the House floor. These doorkeeps closely follow parliamentary developments and are prepared to give both a synopsis of the facts of a bill under consideration and the party's stand on it. Also, both leaderships provide telephone-accessed information lines in their cloakrooms so members away from the floor at the time of a vote can call to find out "what is up."

State delegations also were reported in fewer than 5 percent of the interviews, despite the fact that several studies have emphasized the "information sharing" utility of state delegations.[1] Members mentioned several occasions in which delegations provided information: reliance by delegation members on a member of the delegation ("On those kinds of things we all turn to—"); delegation meetings where each member briefs the delegation on developments in his committee ("These rundowns by committee are really helpful"); and, finally, consultation by delegation members with U.S. Senators from the same state.

IMPERSONAL CONTACT WITH OTHER MEMBERS

Impersonal contact that members have with other members also provides information for floor voting. Two very noteworthy impersonal contacts are "Dear Colleague" letters and debate.

Dear Colleague letters were mentioned overall in approximately 5 percent of the decision cases. These communications are sent to all colleagues by a member—on or off the parent committee—concerned with a particular bill. The letters give a concise, but biased, statement of the issue and the member's position on it. (See Illustration 7a, p. 298.) Although some members said that these kinds of communications are "simply too much to read, I don't have the time," many members mentioned their utility for "getting the pros and cons." One member stated that "due to their information value and the political situation around here, I always read them to see who is doing what."

General floor debate on a bill was mentioned in 18 percent of the interviews as an information source. Academic literature tends to downplay the importance of debate. Clapp notes that "legislators commonly believe that debate is more important in terms of public education than for member education."[2] Matthews argues that debate "lacks drama and excitement. . . . Most members have already made up their minds."[3] Nevertheless, many members interviewed in this study stressed the informativeness of debate. A freshman Democrat stated that "listening to debate affords a way to hear the arguments." A senior southern Democratic mentioned the information value of debate as follows: "From debate I learn what a bill and its amendments do. Nine times out of 10, if you have a question on a bill, someone will answer it during debate." The information value of debate is also emphasized by widespread support by members for closed circuit telecasting of debate into House offices. As one member noted, "The TV allows me to conduct business in my office without missing the value of debate." Finally, it should be noted that committee members indirectly provide information through debate, since they usually serve as floor managers for a bill and thus dominate debate.

IN-HOUSE CONGRESSIONAL PUBLICATIONS

Members identified three in-house congressional publications that have an information value: committee reports, party Whip Notices, and DSG materials.

The report a committee issues on a bill was mentioned as a source in 14 percent of the decisions. As Zinn notes,

> The report describes the purpose and scope of the bill and the reasons for its recommended approval. Generally, a section-by-section analysis is set forth in detail, explaining precisely what each section is intended to accomplish."[4]

Also, the report lists all changes the proposed bill will make in existing law, cost estimate, and new budget authority.[5] Finally, the report records the views of the committee majority together with any concurring, dissenting, or minority views. (See Illustration 4e.)

Many members noted that the report is invaluable as an information source. "It is just a good background summary of the bill," one member stated. Several members mentioned that members can determine their need for further study by examining the report. In one member's words, "If there are minority or dissenting views, that indicates to me that there was trouble in committee and there is likely to be a floor fight. For that reason I conscientiously read them." This member also noted that members probably don't have to read the report to get the information from committee. "You'll get the points of view of the committee from committee members on the floor."

Party information packets distributed through Whip networks were mentioned in 22 percent of the interviews, the third most frequently mentioned information source. Both parties distributed packages of information to their members. The Democrats title their packet *Whip Advisory*. It is prepared a week in advance, and members receive it usually the Friday before each new legislative week. It consists of a schedule of all bills to be called up to the floor for the following week, together with a synopsis of each bill. The synopsis lists the floor manager of the bill, gives a title-by-title summary of the bill, a background of the bill, dissenting views, and estimated cost. (See Illustration 5b.) Republicans call their notice *Legislative Digest*. It is published under the auspices of the House Republican Conference. (See Illustration 5c.) Like the Democratic *Whip Advisory,* it provides a schedule and summary of bills. The Republicans supplement the *Legislative Digest* with publications from the Minority Leader's office entitled *Legislative Alert*. These are in-depth studies of major bills prepared by minority counsels to the parent committee. It should also be noted that the Democratic and Republican packages are made available on the floor as well as through the mail. Many members—especially those who seem to be on the fringes of their parties—acknowledged that they try to read information packages from both parties.

Publications of the Democratic Study Group (DSG) rank as the second most frequently cited information sources, having been mentioned by 30 percent of the interviewees.

As both Stevens, et al.[6] and Ferber[7] have written, the DSG was originally intended as a counterbalance to the conservative coalition. The DSG constituted an attempt—and there is some evidence available to conclude that it has been a moderately successful one[8]—to develop higher voting cohesion among liberal Democrats. The contemporary DSG, although continuing these efforts, has also secured a reputation on both sides of the aisle and among those of all persuasions as the congressional information source par excellence. In the first session of the 95th Congress, it had approximately 230 members.

The DSG distributes four different publications: *Legislative Report, Daily Report, Special Reports,* and *Fact Sheets*. *Legislative Report* is issued weekly. (See Illustration 7b, p. 299.) It gives a complete schedule of the upcoming week's activities together with a summary of all bills. The particular utility of the *Legislative Report* in comparison to party publications is that it anticipates the amendments that are expected to be offered. It also lists the arguments pro and con for each amendment. In a commentary section, the *Legislative Report* lists the support and opposition of the Administration and major interest groups. The *Daily Report* is issued each day and provides a detailed, updated schedule for the particular day plus a last minute listing of possible amendments. The *Special Reports* (see Illustration 7c, p. 301) are in-depth discussions of issues that, although not presently up, are imminent. They are compiled by the legislative staff of the DSG and are intended to provide background information on the major bills of the session. The *Fact Sheets* (see Illustration 7d, p. 302) are detailed studies of major, controversial pieces of information that are coming up.

Members were effusive in their praise of the information value of the DSG. Several Republicans confided that they belonged to the DSG solely to receive the information packets. As one Republican noted, "It's the best information source up here." A Democrat pointed out that "it is a quick summary of issues that is put forth without pressure." Another Democrat said that "it is useful in telling us what is coming up, that it's coming up, and what consent and suspension stuff and amendments entail." Of a different order one member observed, "When the membership of a committee splits, the DSG is good for an objective statement of pros and cons." Members frequently mentioned the information value of the special reports on the strip mining and clean air bills. These special reports seem obligatory reading for members. "If it's something I feel the DSG will cover and review, I go to it," one member stated.

PERSONAL STAFF

The personal staff of a member was the most frequently cited source, mentioned in 33 percent of the decision cases.

The interviews revealed three uses of personal staff in information gathering: filtering and preparing, researching, and following debate.

The usual information input of staff is through the preparation of information packages and briefing papers. (See Illustration 7e, p. 303.) In this way, staff filters and distills information received from the DSG, committee, other members, interest groups, party organizations, the Administration, and constituents. The following comment from a member serves to illustrate this staff function: ''The staff breaks down a bill for me. They digest the information forwarded from the DSG, sponsors, and constituency mail and then synthesize it.''

Other members pointed to a research contribution. One member noted, ''I don't get briefed by staff. I pick up basic information on the floor, especially in conversations with other members and the party stuff they have on the floor. For me, staff contributes by looking into questions.'' Another member, a Republican, stated that his staff ''goes on the assumption that I've read *Legislative Alert*. Their job is to get into it. If there is controversy in the report, that serves as a red flag to get to work on it.'' Another mentioned that he used staff to research things in which he gets interested and involved. ''On those kinds of things where I see a problem, I put them to work. On the pay raise deal I had them do research on salary systems.'' Several members noted that staff research usually involves consultation with committee people and committee staffs and the staffs of other members, especially those in the state delegation and those with whom the member has ideological compatibility.

A final information contribution of staff stems from positioning staff in the House gallery to follow debate on hotly contested issues when the member cannot be present. Several members noted the utility of doing this when they are in committee and unable to be on the floor. In one member's words, ''This way I can keep abreast of developments in the committee of the whole and the business of amendments.''

OUTSIDE SOURCES

Constituents and interest groups constituted the only real outside actors contributing information, and this contribution must be regarded as minimal since both were mentioned equally—only 5 percent of the time. The White House, a potential outside source, was mentioned only 3 percent of the time.

Members noted that information from the constituency is only rarely forwarded by average citizens. In fact, the only information input from individual constituents seems to come through members' district opinion polls. These tell the member what constituents know and think about bills. Information from constituents usually comes from groups in the district that are somehow affected by the bill in consideration—e.g., local public officials on grant programs, district industrial plants and auto dealers on clean air, and postal workers on Hatch Act revisions.

Although Clapp,[9] Jewell and Patterson,[10] Milbrath,[11] and Tacheron and Udall[12] have written of the information value of interest groups and lobbyists, it is surprising to discover that groups and their lobbyists were mentioned for only 5 percent of the decisions.

The few who did mention interest groups viewed them as providing information in one of two ways. First, as a senior Republican noted, ''Pressure groups help by providing background materials.'' Such background information on bills is often routinely forwarded to members through the mail. Second, hearing from competing interest groups on a policy question provides the pros and cons of an issue. Those situations where groups were mentioned as information sources mainly involved narrow groups on specific issues such as tuna fishermen, grocers, and the Heinz Corporation on marine mammals; ''right to work'' committees and labor on common situs; coal companies on strip mining; government labor unions on the Energy Department; United Auto Workers on clean air; National Organization of Women (NOW) on the Hyde Amendment; postal workers on the Hatch Act; and pharmaceutical concerns and the American Diabetic Association on saccharin. In commenting on interest groups and legislation, many members corroborated the notion of Bauer et al. that interest groups deal only with legislators who are already sympathetic with the group's objectives.[13]

MEMBERS' EXPERIENCE AND READING

Members noted that information is often provided by their general learning and experience, their experience with a similar bill in a previous session of Congress, and their general reading.

Five percent listed personal experience. Personal experience was felt to be helpful in the following ways. First, expertise accumulated before one comes to Congress can be relied on. Second, experience that results from a member's following of a policy issue for several years can be a source of information. In this way, one member felt sufficiently informed on the FAA vote since he had "followed FAA matters for years." Another felt that his interest in foreign policy provided sufficient background on the Miller Amendment. Finally, a member's involvement with a bill provides him with information. Several members not on the parent committee of a bill emphasized that, due to constituency or personal interest, they had become active at the committee stage of a bill, giving testimony, debating, following the hearings, etc. This kind of involvement was felt to provide "all the guidance one needs."

The experience one has with a policy issue "the last time it was through" was cited in 8 percent of the interviews. For experienced members, routine authorizations and appropriations and bills, such as strip mining, countercyclical aid, common situs, and the Hyde Amendment, that "have been around for a while" pose no information problems. As one member noted, "These things tend to be the same as before. I don't have to look into them again." Another emphasized, "When they have been around for a few years, I have low information needs. I know what the bill is." Even in the case of amendments, prior experience is helpful. "If you've experienced it once before, you know what the major issues are and you can let your personal experience guide you—even on the amendments."

Media and general reading were mentioned in 18 percent of the interviews. Those who mentioned the media felt that the media provided them with background information on the ethics bill and on the saccharin debate. The media most frequently mentioned were the *Washington Post, The Wall Street Journal,* and *Congressional Quarterly.*

MISCELLANEOUS

In addition to the above-noted sources, a number of miscellaneous information sources were identified, although not by any great numbers of members. These miscellaneous sources of information are: committee staff ("Especially the staffers on subcommittee who wrote the bill—more than anyone they can help members understand what the bill does"); membership on another committee (Ways and Means and Budget Committee members mentioned they received information on major bills by virtue of their membership on those committees); copies of the actual bill and amendments, class organizations, Republican ad hoc groups (such as the Society of Statesmen and the Republican Study Committee); study organizations, such as the Democratic Research Organization that services southern Democrats, the bicameral, bipartisan Environmental Study Group, and the liberal Members of Congress for Peace Through Law. Republicans noted that their party's practice of scheduling and stationing younger members on the floor as monitors was an additional source of information for the monitor and others who could turn to him.

Also mentioned were the White House and federal bureaucrats. The White House was seen as a source of information on the Energy Department vote and on the HUD vote, where the

Carter Administration provided the breakdown of aid by states and congressional districts for alternative allocation formulas. Bureaucrats were viewed as helpful on the school lunch vote (HEW), saccharin vote (HEW, FDA), and water projects vote (Army Corps of Engineers).

Finally, sponsorship of a bill and, more important, membership on the parent committee are seen as sources of information. Holbert Carroll has argued that less than a majority of the membership of a committee's membership are "efficient" in terms of the committee's business.[14] For those who are, however, hearings and the testimony of witnesses is a valuable information resource. In the words of one member, "If I pay attention on committee, I have no reason to read party, committee, or group synopses."

CONCLUSIONS

Four major conclusions can be drawn from the above general descriptions. First, congressional information stems from what John Saloma refers to as a system of "multiple information channels."[15] As displayed in Table 7.1.1, 14 different sources were mentioned at least 5 percent of the time. Seven were mentioned in more than 10 percent of the interviews. The findings in Table 7.1.1 corroborate Clapp's finding that

> legislators use many sources in the course of their deliberations . . . such as . . . individual colleagues, informal organizations of Congressmen to which a legislator belongs, committee and personal staffs, the hearings and reports of committees, pressure groups, executive departments, the mail, and floor debate.[16]

Second, in John Kingdon's words, "Certain actors in the legislative system are more prominent in the decision-making of Congressmen than others."[17] The most frequently mentioned information source is personal staff, followed by publications of the DSG, party Whip Notices, floor debate, media and general reading, committee reports, and committee members. These findings provide several surprises. Contrary to both Kingdon[18] and Matthews and Stimson,[19] other members (including both members on the relevant committee and those not on it) are not the most frequently mentioned source of information. Also, despite the emphasis in recent publications on the information value of "books and scholarly studies,"[20] congressional research and investigatory agencies[21] (such as the General Accounting Office, Congressional Budget Office, and Office of Technological Assessment), and information technologies[22] (such as the Legislative Reference Service of the Library of Congress), few members mentioned them as a significant source of information.

Third, some sources of information, such as personal staff, DSG publications, Whip Notices, and the committee report, perform what both Kingdon[23] and Schneier[24] refer to as a filtering or "gatekeeper" function. These sources act to synthesize and forward information from a number of diverse sources and act as carriers. For example, both the DSG and Whip Notices give the committee position. The DSG provides positions taken by interest groups and by the Administration. The committee report contains the positions of key Congressmen and interest groups. Staff input often involves con-

TABLE 7.1.2 CLASSIFICATION OF MAJOR CONGRESSIONAL INFORMATION SOURCES BY PROXIMATENESS AND DIRECTNESS

	DIRECTNESS	
PROXIMITY	PERSONAL	IMPERSONAL
Proximate	Committee chairman Committee members Other members Party leaders State delegation Personal staff	Doormen Caucus recording Debate
Antecedent	Committee members Other members State delegation Personal staff Dear Colleague Interest groups Constituents	DSG publications Whip Notice Media/reading Committee report Policy committees

sultation with the committee and the staffs of other members, constituents, and bureaucrats. As such, these sources constitute collective channels of information.

Finally, congressional information sources can be differentiated on two bases: directness and proximity. With regard to directness, there are (1) direct contacts that involve a personal, face-to-face relationship between the member and the source, and (2) indirect sources that involve impersonal relationships. With regard to proximity, some sources provide information to the member at a point most proximate to the point of the decision while others are antecedent. Table 7.1.2 shows the classification of major sources according to these two variables.

ILLUSTRATION 7A DEAR COLLEAGUE LETTER

COMMITTEES:
ARMED SERVICES
MERCHANT MARINE AND
FISHERIES

Congress of the United States
House of Representatives
Washington, D.C. 20515

DENNIS M. HERTEL
14TH DISTRICT, MICHIGAN

DISTRICT OFFICE:
20491 VAN DYKE
DETROIT, MICHIGAN 48234
(313) 892-4010

1017 LONGWORTH OFFICE BUILDING
WASHINGTON, D.C. 20515
(202) 225-6276

October 2, 1981

Dear Colleague:

What has happened to international human rights?

The Congress has maintained a steadfast interest in this important area. Approximately 20 pieces of legislation have been introduced on the topic of international civil liberties. The latest example was the passage by the Senate of human rights requirements with respect to aid to El Salvador.

The Administration appears to be totally abandoning the quest for human liberties. Since the withdrawal of the President's nominee for the post of Assistant Secretary of State for Human Rights, no effort has been made to fill the position. The Assistant Secretary of State for Human Rights was established in response to a continuing concern of the Congress for the fundamental rights which are entitled to all individuals.

The cause of worldwide human rights is much too important for our Nation to lack a spokesman. I am asking you to join me and more than 30 of our colleagues in sponsoring House Resolution 164 urging a swift appointment of a qualified and dedicated individual for the post of Assistant Secretary of State for Human Rights.

Should you wish to join me in cosponsoring this resolution, please contact Salome Williams in my office at 56276.

Sincerely,

Dennis M. Hertel
Member of Congress

THIS STATIONERY PRINTED ON PAPER MADE WITH RECYCLED FIBERS

ILLUSTRATION 7B DSG LEGISLATIVE REPORT

DEMOCRATIC STUDY GROUP — U.S. HOUSE OF REPRESENTATIVES — WASHINGTON, D.C. Tel.: 225-5858
HON. WILLIAM M. BRODHEAD (Michigan)—Chairman RICHARD P. CONLON—Staff Director

SCHEDULE FOR THE WEEK OF JULY 27, 1981

MONDAY, JULY 27
(House meets at noon)

* Suspensions -- Ten bills are scheduled for consideration under suspension of the rules (pages 1-11).

* District Bills -- Two bills dealing with the District of Columbia are also scheduled for House consideration (page 11).

* Agriculture Appropriations -- H.R. 4119, FY 1982 Agriculture Appropriations, is scheduled for Floor action (page 13).

TUESDAY, JULY 28
(House meets at noon)

* Record Votes -- Record votes on suspensions postponed from Monday will be taken.

* Treasury-Postal Service Funds -- H.R. 4121, Treasury-Postal Service-General Government Appropriations for FY 1982, will be considered (page 19).

* Legislative Appropriations -- H.R. 4120, FY 1982 Legislative Branch Appropriations, will be acted on (page 26).

WEDNESDAY THROUGH FRIDAY, JULY 29 - 31
(House meets at 9 a.m. Wednesday and at 10 a.m. Thursday and Friday)

* Tax Incentives -- H.R. 4242, Tax Incentive Act, is scheduled for Floor consideration. A DSG Fact Sheet will be available prior to Floor consideration.

* Commerce-State-Justice Funds -- H.R. 4169, Commerce-State-Justice and Related Agencies Appropriations for FY 1982, will be brought up (page 31).

* Transportation Funds -- H.R. 4209, Transportation Appropriations for FY 1982, may be considered. A DSG Supplement will be available prior to Floor consideration.

(Continued on p. 300)

ILLUSTRATION 7B (*concluded*)

DSG LEGISLATIVE REPORT

MONDAY, JULY 27, 1981

SUSPENSIONS (10 Bills)

1 NOAA ATMOSPHERIC, CLIMATIC, AND OCEAN POLLUTION AUTHORIZATION (H.R. 2803)

FLOOR SITUATION: The bill will be considered under suspension of the rules; 40 minutes of debate; not subject to amendment; two-thirds majority vote required for passage. The measure will be managed by Chairman Fuqua.

BACKGROUND: The Science and Technology Committee reported the bill with additional and dissenting views by voice vote (H.Rept. 97-61).

The National Oceanic and Atmospheric Administration (NOAA) was established in 1970. It is responsible for a wide range of oceanic and atmospheric research and resource management, as well as for providing a variety of weather services. Until this year, NOAA was funded primarily through direct appropriations, except for authorizations in a few specific areas. This year, in order to develop a more comprehensive overview of NOAA programs, the committee decided to authorize more than half of all NOAA programs. It is the committee's intent to work toward authorization of all NOAA programs.

SUMMARY: This bill authorizes $498.5 million in FY 1982 for atmospheric, climatic, and ocean pollution activities of the National Oceanic and Atmospheric Administration (NOAA). This figure is virtually identical to the Administration's request and approximately $65 million above the FY 1981 funding level.

The measure authorizes $159.8 million for basic environmental services which provide satellite and radar support for weather observation and communication, and $98.9 million for public weather forecast and warning services. Environmental satellite services would receive $127.3 million, including $5.1 million specifically earmarked for the development of a civilian land observing system in conjunction with the LANDSAT program.

The bill also provides $44.5 million for specialized services that supply environmental information to the agricultural, aviation, and communication industries. This includes $1.9 million to develop a comprehensive research program on acid rain. The authorization for marine ecosystems analysis and ocean dumping research is $18.3 million, and funds for related programs total $24.6 million. Finally, the measure targets $2.2 million for the National Climate Program Office.

ILLUSTRATION 7C DSG SPECIAL REPORT

DEMOCRATIC STUDY GROUP • U.S. HOUSE OF REPRESENTATIVES
225-5858 • 1422 HOUSE OFFICE BUILDING • WASHINGTON, D.C. 20515

HON. WILLIAM M. BRODHEAD (Michigan) – Chairman   RICHARD P. CONLON – Staff Director

SPECIAL REPORT

No. 97-23   June 17, 1981

THE CASE AGAINST BLOCK GRANTS

The Republican substitute to the reconciliation bill that may be offered on the House Floor next week is expected to contain President Reagan's block grant proposals.

The Administration's block grant proposals would consolidate nearly 100 categorical programs, slash funding levels, and repeal the authorizations for dozens of programs.

The Administration contends that its program would result in greater efficiency, responsiveness, and innovation. Critics contend that the net result would be the elimination of numerous federal health, education, social services, and community development programs, and the serious underfunding of many others.

This DSG Special Report contains the following sections:

Note: *See DSG evaluation form at end of report.*

Illustration 7D DSG Fact Sheet

DEMOCRATIC STUDY GROUP • U.S. HOUSE OF REPRESENTATIVES
225-5858 • 1422 HOUSE OFFICE BUILDING • WASHINGTON, D.C. 20515

HON. WILLIAM M. BRODHEAD (Michigan) – Chairman RICHARD P. CONLON – Staff Director

FACT SHEET

No. 97-7 July 26, 1981

THE TAX BILL -- PART I

This DSG Fact Sheet deals with H.R. 4242, Tax Incentive Act of 1981, which is scheduled for Floor consideration on Wednesday, July 29.

This report is being divided into three parts because neither the committee report nor other information on the cost of the committee bill, the Republican substitute,or the Udall-Obey-Reuss balanced budget alternative, are available, and because it is unclear what amendments will be made in order (see Parliamentary Situation on page 4).

Part I deals with the basic provisions and arguments for and against the Ways and Means Committee bill, the Republican substitute, and the balanced-budget alternative. Part II, which will be available on Tuesday, will compare tax cut and revenue loss impacts, and major differences between the three measures. Part III, which will be available on Wednesday, will summarize the Rules Committee's action with respect to other amendments.

This Fact Sheet contains the following sections:

Note: *See evaluation form at end of Fact Sheet.*

ILLUSTRATION 7E STAFF-PREPARED LEGISLATIVE SUMMARY FOR REPRESENTATIVE JIM SANTINI (D–NEV.)

COMPLETE LEGISLATIVE SUMMARY

Number: H.R. 3965

Cost: $85 M in authorization for FY 78

Plus pay raise & benefits costs for FY 78

Title: Federal Aviation Administration Authorization Act: FY 78

Floor situation: Open rule: 1-hour debate

Date: March 24, 1977

Summary: Authorizes $85 M in FY 78 appropriations from Airport & Airway Trust Fund for research, development, & demonstration projects. Restricts funding for Aerosat program to $1.5M for feasibility study, although FAA requested $14.7M in its FY 78 budget. Terminates $50M annual FAA R&D authorization for RY 78-80 by amending Airport & Airway Development Act and initiates a requirement for annual authorization for FAA R&D commencing with this bill for FY 78. Reduce FY 76 authorization by $0.4M & FY 77 by $0.4M.

Amendments: 1. to raise funding level for Aerosat to FAA's original request of $14.7M (Rationale for program was based on increases in trans-Atlantic air routes & limitations of existing communications systems, but now travel levels have been reduced. Committee has reservations about high cost of total program & its effect on other expenditures)

Support Opposition: FAA supports the bill. State Department supports continuation of Aerosat program. Air Transport Association & International Air Transport Association oppose continuation of Aerosat.

Prior votes:

Nevada concern: None noted

Recommendation comment:

ILLUSTRATION 7F TODAY IN CONGRESS

A valuable information source for both insiders and citizens in the schedule of the day's events in Congress found daily in the *Washington Post*.

A4 *Tuesday, October 20, 1981* THE WASHINGTON POST

TODAY IN CONGRESS

Senate

Meets at 10:30 a.m.

Committees:

Agriculture, nutrition, and forestry agric. credit and rural electrification subc.—9:30 a.m. Open. Oversight hrng. on the bidding, purchasing, and elections processes of the Rural Electrification Administration. 322 Russell Office Building.

Banking, Housing, and Urban Affairs—9:30 a.m. Open. Bills promoting competition among certain financial institutions, expanding their range of services, and protecting the depositors and creditors of such institutions. 5302 Dirksen Office Building.

Budget—10 a.m. Open. Second budget resolution for FY82. 6202 DOB.

Commerce, science, and transportation surface transportation subc.—9:30 a.m. Open. Oversight hrngs. on the implementation of the Household Goods Transportation Act. 1318 DOB.

Commerce, science, and transportation business, trade, and tourism subc.—10 a.m. Open. Legislation on establishment of a service industries development program in the Commerce Dept. 235 ROB.

Energy and Natural Resources—10 a.m. Open. Hrngs. with the comte. on environment and public works subc. on nuclear regulation on legislation to provide for a nuclear property damage insurance fund, and to provide additional funds for the clean-up of the contaminated nuclear facility at TMI. DOE Sec. James Edwards. 3110 DOB.

Environment and Public Works—10 a.m. Open. Business meeting, to mark-up legislation providing for the completion of Union Station-Natl Vistors Ctr., and legislation on water projects deauthorization, other pending calendar business. 4200 DOB.

Foreign Relations—10 a.m. Open. Treaty protocol concerning the importation of education, scientific, and cultural materials to the U.S. 4221 DOB.

Governmental affairs civil service, post office, and genl services subc.—9:30 a.m. Open. Legislation to establish the Natl Archives and Records Admin. as an independent executive agency. 3302 DOB.

Judiciary—10 a.m. Open. Pending calendar business. 2228 DOB.

Labor and Human Resources—9 a.m. Open. Oversight hrng. on the activities of the Comprehensive Employment and Training Administration. 4232 DOB.

Republican Policy—12:30 p.m. Closed. Regular luncheon meeting. S-207 Cap.

Republican Conference—(immediately after policy luncheon) Closed. Business meeting of Republican senators. S-207 Cap.

Democratic Policy—2 p.m. Closed. Regular luncheon meeting. S-211 Cap.

House

Meets at noon.

Committees:

Armed Services—9:15 a.m. Open (may close). Jnt. hrng.: investigations, & readiness subcs. On U.S. participation in intl. military evaluations. 2118 Rayburn House office Building.

Banking, Finance & Urban Affairs—9:30 a.m. Open. Consumer aff. & coinage subc. Hrng. on federal preemption of state interest ceilings. 2128 RHOB.

Education & Labor—9:30 a.m. Open. Foreign Language Improvem. Act; Carl Albert Congressional Res. & Studies Center. 2175 RHOB.

Education & Labor—9:30 a.m. Open. Elem., secondary & voc. edu. subc. Alien Education Impact Aid Act. 2175 RHOB.

Energy & Commerce—10 a.m. Open. Fossil & synthetic fuels subc. Mark-up Standby Petroleum Emergency Auth. Act; hrng. on Alaska Natural Gas Transportation Act waivers. Energy Sec. Edwards. 2123 RHOB.

Energy & Commerce—9:45 a.m. Open. Health & environ. subc. Cont. hrngs. on acid rain. 2322 RHOB.

Government Operations—9:30 a.m. Open. Intergovl. rel. & human res. subc. Cont. hrngs. on payments in lieu of taxes legis. 2247 RHOB.

Government Operations—10 a.m. Open. Comm., consumer & monetary aff. subc. Cont. hrngs. on OPEC investment in U.S. energy companies. 2154 RHOB.

Interior & Insular Affairs—9:45 a.m. Open. On misc. Indian legis. 1324 Longworth House Office.

Interior & Insular Affairs—9:45 a.m. Open. Public lands & natl. parks subc. Oversight hrngs. on public lands policies: budget reductions. 2218 RHOB.

Interior & Insular Affairs—9:45 a.m. Open. Mines & mining subc. Natl. Minerals Security Act. 1302 LHOB.

Judiciary—9:30 a.m. Open. Mark-up misc. charter legis.; & Regulatory Procedure Act. 2141 RHOB.

Merchant Marine & Fisheries—10 a.m. Open. Mark-up Deep-water ports policy. 1334 LHOB.

Post Office & Civil Service—10 a.m. Open. Cont. hrngs. on air traffic control system. (2:30 p.m.) Hrng. with PATCO Pres. Poli. 311 Cannon House Office Building.

Public Works & Transportation—10 a.m. Open. Invest. & oversight subc. Review of intl aviation matters. 2167 RHOB.

Rules—10:30 a.m. Open. Federal Water Pollution Control Act Amends. H-313 Capitol.

Science & Technology—10 a.m. Open. Sci., res. & tech. subc. Mark-up pending legis. 2318 RHOB.

Small Business—9:30 a.m. Open. Export opportunities subc. Cont. on Regulatory Flexibility Act. 2359-A RHOB.

Veterans Affairs—9:30 a.m. Open. On OMB circular relating to private sector contracting for VA services. 334 CHOB.

Joint Economic—10 a.m. Open. Hrng. on incomes policy: The Case of Scandinavia. 2237 RHOB.

7.2 Resource Usage, Information, and Policymaking in the Senate*

Norman J. Ornstein and David Rohde

These two authors identify the major forces governing the information searches of U.S. Senators. They close by discussing the different types of staff networks utilized for providing information.

The purpose of this paper is to examine the policymaking process in the U.S. Senate from the perspectives of the legislative staffs of Senators and of Senators themselves. To evaluate various possible changes in the process by which the Senate makes policy, it is important to have a clearer picture of the ways in which Senators organize and carry out their legislative efforts. Despite growing interest in the congressional policy process in general,[1] or in various aspects of it,[2] research on congressional legislative staff, and particularly on personal staff, has been relatively limited.[3] Yet, the role which Senate professional staff play in legislative decision making is a crucial one. Every Senator has a legislative staff, although size and organization vary, and Senators depend heavily on these support personnel. For example, in more than 50 interviews with Senators for another research project, all but two of the Senators indicated that staff members were their primary source of information for legislative decisions.[4] In addition, staff personnel perform many other tasks, often acting as surrogates for their employers.

Thus Senators' legislative staffs are both ubiquitous and important in the policy process.

METHOD

Five Democratic and four Republican Senators were chosen with the attempt made to interview all members of each Senator's legislative staff, including those professional staff members, regardless of payroll source, who are directly involved in advising a Senator on legislative matters. This included some committee staff members and, for some offices, administrative assistants.

In selecting the Senators whose staffs would be studied, no attempt was made to draw a random sample of the Senate. In fact, the selection was deliberately biased by selecting Senators who were qualitatively judged to be among the more active participants in policymaking. It was decided that weaknesses or problems in the process would be more likely to be visible by examining this group. In all other ways, however, the group selected was broadly representative of the Senate according to various criteria: party, state size, ideology, committees served on, regional origin, and seniority. The interviews were semistructured in form and were taped; anonymity was promised to all interviewed. More than 40 interviews with staff were conducted. In addition, two roundtable discussions were held with the Senators in the sample. The interviews and the roundtables form the basic data for the following descriptions and analyses.

This paper examines the variety of structural and behavioral patterns exhibited within Senate staffs to meet the legislative goals established by members. Subsequent discussion analyzes

* From Norman J. Ornstein and David Rohde, "Resource Usage, Information, and Policymaking in the Senate," in *Senators: Offices, Ethics, and Pressures, A Compilation of Papers Prepared for the Commission on the Operation of the Senate,* 1977, pp. 37–46. Reprinted from the public domain.

possible changes to improve the ability of Senators to deal with policy questions within the constraints established by the level of their involvement.

SENATORS AND THE POLICY ENVIRONMENT

Types of Senators: Legislative Involvement

When discussing legislators and legislative activity, the mistake is often made of treating all individuals as equals. If one is merely concentrating on the product of legislative activity—roll call votes—no differentiation may be necessary. But, if one wishes to examine legislative activity in the broader context of the policy process, a basic important feature of the legislative process in the Senate can be captured by drawing a distinction between Senators as decision makers and Senators as activists or initiators.[5]

On every issue that comes to the Senate floor, the "decision makers" include all Senators who are present and voting. Each Senator is empowered to vote "yea" or "nay" on every legislative question put to the Senate. Thus, all Senators must acquire some information on each of the myriad issues that they are forced by circumstance to consider. The role of "decision maker" is essentially a passive one: Issues are brought before Senators and they must decide.

There is, however, much more to the legislative process in the Senate than the set of final floor decisions. In these other aspects of the policy process, the participation of Senators varies widely in any given issue area. Some Senators are not involved at all. Others are "activists": They initiate bills, organize support for proposals, offer amendments, speak publicly on positions, etc. The "activists" bear the main burden of policymaking in a given issue area.

Continuum of Involvement

Of course, the variety of levels of involvement with issues in the Senate cannot be adequately captured by a simple dichotomy; it is offered only for purposes of contrast. Actually, the situation is better represented by an imaginary continuum anchored at one end by those members whose involvement with a given issue is limited to the relatively passive act of making floor judgments (the "decision makers") with the remainder of the Senators ranked according to their degree of actitivism in that area.

The point of this fairly commonplace distinction is that this variation in activity among members has important implications as to how the policy process works in the Senate. Why this variation occurs and whether or how it can be changed (e.g., is it possible to increase the degree of involvement of "decision makers"?) are focal points of this paper.

The Determinants of Involvement

The main elements which determine whether a Senator becomes active in a policy area are three: possession of committee jurisdiction over the matter, a link between the policy and the Senator's constituency, or a personal interest on the part of the Senator.[6] Any one of these elements may be sufficient to cause active involvement by a Senator with an issue, although such involvement is not automatic.

A Senator may become actively involved with an issue because he has been assigned to a committee or subcommittee with jurisdiction over the matter, although neither of the other elements is present. This may be a short-term, pro forma involvement, with the Senator leaving the committee and policy area as soon as he can. This was the case of one Senator who became involved with the Public Works Committee, Buildings and Grounds Subcommittee because he was assigned to the Committee without requesting it, and was named chairman of the Subcommittee. He left the Committee after two years. It may also be a long-term, deeper involvement which begins with an undesired committee assignment, but which endures as the Senator gains seniority and develops interest in the policy area. This was the case with another Senator in our sample in the area of the Banking, Housing, and Urban Affairs

Committee, where he chairs a subcommittee.

It is not true, however, that a Senator will automatically be active on an issue simply because of a committee assignment. Many Senators simply ignore some areas within their committees, preferring to concentrate on others. A committee assignment, a vital state-related concern or a personal interest each make senatorial activity more likely, while the absence of all three almost certainly means that the only involvement a Senator will have on an issue will be as a passive "decision maker."

These three elements are not mutually exclusive. Indeed, in many cases they are closely linked. One obvious example is that members often seek assignment to a committee because it has jurisdiction over matters of concern to their constituencies or of personal interest. Such mutual reinforcement often leads to a higher level of activity on an issue. While the element of personal interest is idiosyncratic, the other two elements are not, rendering the likelihood of involvement with a particular issue predictable to some degree.

Since Senators cannot be forced to become personally interested in an issue, and since the nature of their constituencies cannot be altered at will, the only elements of involvement subject to control and manipulation are committee assignments and jurisdictions. At the moment, jurisdictions are stable and assignments are generally voluntary. Therefore, the likelihood of a Senator's involvement with an issue is the consequence of a set of determined elements, and not subject to systematic control or alteration. It is thus necessary to consider modifications in the policy process with the pattern of activity and interest that presently exists.

STAFF AND THE POLICY ENVIRONMENT

Senators and Staff: Patterns of Involvement

Among the Senators studied, there was substantial variation in the breadth and intensity of issue involvement. Senator A demonstrates a fairly conventional pattern. He serves on three committees. One related to his constituency's most important economic interest, and the other two involving personal interests. Of his six legislative assistants, one is assigned solely to the first committee, while one each is assigned to the other two committees as well as handling some limited additional areas. A fourth is assigned to matters of a subcommittee that the Senator chairs on one of the two "personal interest" committees, and the fifth and sixth divide all other legislative matters between them.

This Senator has secured committee assignments which serve personal or constituency interests, and he limits his legislative activity mainly to matters within his committee jurisdictions. His most intensive use of staff is where he has the most direct legislative responsibility (the subcommittee he chairs), and his initiatives outside his committees are few. Considering the other eight offices analyzed and some familiarity with many others, this appears to be a typical pattern of legislative involvement.

Senator B's legislative activities differ from those of Senator A in a number of ways. First, he is more senior than Senator A by about 10 years. One consequence is that he is the ranking Republican on a major committee, which gives him a number of staff members on that committee. He has chosen to concentrate most of his activity there. He has two other legislative assistants: one recently acquired under Senate Resolution 60 with responsibility for his other committee, and one who handles all other matters. This allocation is a deliberate choice; the Senator has sufficient staff funds to afford additional assistants. He chooses to specialize intensively in the area where he has the most "leverage."

Senator C exhibits a third pattern, one that is partly a consequence of the nature of the state he serves, which is one of the more populous in the Union. The size of the state means that almost all legislative matters are linked to constituency interests. The Senator serves on four committees on which he has a total of six assistants. In addition, he has four assistants on his personal staff. And, his assistants in effect have their own staff. Most have at least three persons under them: a legislative correspondent to answer mail, a secretary, and a researcher. Senator C is active in many areas outside the jurisdiction of his committees, largely because of the breadth of constituency interests, but also partly because of personal inclination. Because of a life-long interest in foreign affairs, Senator C spends a great deal of his time on foreign policy questions. He is not a member of a Foreign Relations Committee, and indeed, deliberately avoided assignment to the Committee to maintain freedom in his activity in the area.

These three Senators demonstrate patterns of legislative involvement which are, with certain variations, representative of the Senate—Senator B narrowly specializes, Senator C is active across most of the policy spectrum, and Senator A represents the modal intermediate pattern.

Types of Staff: Legislative Involvement

Just as there is considerable variation among Senators in their styles and ranges of legislative activity, there is a similar variation among staff members in terms of their responsibilities and roles. Among legislative staff members, the primary contrasting roles may be termed specialists and generalists. The "specialist" concentrates exclusively on a narrow range of legislative activity (e.g., matters within the jurisdiction of a single subcommittee), while the responsibilities of "generalists" range far and wide (as in the case of one staff member whose responsibilities covered the jurisdictions of 15 Senate committees).

Senators invariably acquire staff "specialists" in those areas where they are "activists" or "initiators." These staff are used to support the Senators' initiatives in those areas chosen for concentration.

However, some Senators also acquire "specialists" in those areas in which they would be expected to be personally active according to the three determinants discussed above, but are not. For example, Senator D comes from New England and recognizes that energy matters are politically important in his state. He does not, however, serve on any committee which deals with energy, nor does he have any personal interest in the subject. Because of the crucial constituency importance, he has chosen to allocate one staff member solely to energy matters. The staff member is one of four who handle matters outside of the Senator's committees. The Senator does not give much personal attention to energy policy, but when energy questions come up on the floor, he has access to good, detailed information on which to base his decisions. In this politically sensitive area he has chosen to use a staff specialist as a surrogate, reserving his personal attention for other matters.

Staff "generalists" handle a variety of areas, usually those in which the Senator himself does not specialize. They vary considerably in their level and scope of activity. Some—often those employed by Senators from the less populous states—merely monitor the legislation in their areas as it approaches and reaches the Senate floor. Others—more often those employed by Senators from the populous, industrial states—may be quite active with some degree of independence to make initiatives. Since these states are socially and economically heterogeneous, and the Senators often have public visibility, staff involvement alone can produce an impact, with little activity by the Senator. Moreover, a large share of the floor amendments offered by noncommittee members undoubtedly come from the "generalist" staff of interested Senators.

Other legislative decisions, such as cosponsorship of bills, are also handled, often with great independence, by staff. One legislative aide to a "large state" Senator, after emphasizing the strong committee-centered focus of the Senator's activity, commented on his own behavior in more peripheral legislative areas: "He is willing to delegate to me almost complete responsibility for everything. I sometimes think that if I could go over and vote for him on these matters, he'd defer that to me; it is literally to that degree."

There is little, if any, hyperbole here; the Senators themselves corroborate staff assertions like this one. Clearly, any initiatives which this particular Senator makes in the areas covered by this staff member—agriculture, environment transportation, etc.—come from the staff man. Just as clearly, these initiatives are few, since the Senator has only a limited amount of time, attention and desire to spend on areas he deems secondary.

Senators' Use of Staff

In the case of both "specialist" and "generalist" staff, the interviews and the roundtables suggested that they are important information conduits for Senators, both within and outside their Senators' areas of specialization. The punishing and frenetic schedule of the Senate leaves little time for Senators to read or reflect upon broad issues. In areas outside their principal interests, Senators rely on staff to follow legislation, to determine if it has a state-related interest, to provide information as the bills and amendments come to the Senate floor, and perhaps, to draft answers to letters inquiring about their position on a bill. In their areas of concentration, Senators rely on staff to keep up with trends in the field, and to refer to or summarize important or interesting articles or books. Even Senators who enjoy reading have little time for books or lengthy articles; their reading, beyond government documents, is usually limited to the major newspapers such as *The New York Times* and *The Washington Post*.

The previous assertion is overstated, of course. Senators have sources of information other than their personal and committee staffs. One Senator emphasized the importance of hearings:

> Hearings—you have to pay attention. You're running the show. I find that after hearings for two hours I feel drained. Particularly if it's my own subcommittee and I'm the only one there. There may be four or five guys who filter in or out, but I'm running it. I'm asking the questions. And I want to make sure I have got a record.

Senators call upon experts like Walter Heller, Paul McCracken, John K. Fairbank, Paul Warnke, etc., for advice or information on public policy issues. Several Senators in the roundtables commented on the invaluable information role of lobbyists.

It is clear that, while Senators absorb a good deal through the legislative process about their major areas over a period of time, the vast bulk of the information they receive comes from or through their staffs. They simply do not have the time to do much independent information gathering. This is, of course, especially true in areas in which the Senator is a "decision maker" rather than an "activist." Occasionally a Senator will do more. One Democratic Senator arranged a grueling series of expert briefings which ran three hours a night, five nights a week, for several weeks. To do this while the Senate is in session requires a superhuman endurance and dedication, and such efforts are rare.

Information and Knowledge

What does this imply about Senators' information needs on policy topics? Overall, Senators perceive no special needs or gaps in the policy information available to them. As one Republican Senator commented:

> I have no problems with it (information). I have too much information. There is no scarcity of any information that I've found on any of my committees. I can't keep up with all of the material that is already available.

Senators are able to get by quite nicely, in their own view, with the current situation of information flow and availability. They are rarely at a loss for questions to ask at a committee or subcommittee hearing, for comments to make on the floor or in speeches in their states or elsewhere, and they normally are able to cast floor votes which are consistent with their overall views, and which don't return to haunt them.

When Senators express dissatisfaction with their current policymaking system, it is generally in terms of time or management:

> The only precious commodity up here is time. You make an inquiry to the Library of Congress.

> You get back a stack of volumes that high—that's utterly useless.
>
> We launch ourselves with no administrative philosophy, or we have no systems, or we have few tools. To me, the greatest frustration of being a Senator is not having the tools of administration.

Why the emphasis on time? Basically, Senators see the decision-making process in terms of the frenetic pace of the Senate, and the haphazard, overcommitted scheduling of their daily activities. Whenever Senators need or want specific information or data, they can get it—from staff, lobbyists, the Library of Congress, etc. When they think of information, they think of reports of several hundred pages which they have no time to read—of too much information, in other words. They rarely think of unfulfilled needs.

Senators do not feel a lack of information. What they are missing, however, is the ability to place the information they have in broader contexts, and the time to think about the broader questions. Therefore, in analyzing the ability of Senators and the Senate to do in-depth, long range, crosscutting examination of policy alternatives, the distinction must be made between information or data, and knowledge.

The opportunity to study a policy area in an in-depth way, to take a concentrated period to reflect on a problem, is almost unavailable to contemporary Senators. They have a surplus of information from multiple sources, but no mechanism for assimilating broad knowledge due to a fragmented committee system, ineffective floor debates, and schedules which keep them constantly on the run. Senators devote all their attention and energy to getting through each legislative day. They have lost the opportunity to place policy considerations in broader contexts. Their concerns are more shortsighted. As one Republican Senator commented: "I'm trying to figure out what my schedule is at 4. That's my problem."

The knowledge gathering that Senators do comes, by osmosis, through years of legislative work or through individualized extra efforts.

This is the reality, with few expected dramatic changes. Even with a major restructuring of the Senate's schedule and its committee system, there is still a certain amount of work which 100 Senators must do in a session of Congress, and the workload is not going to decrease. Rather, with ideas like "sunset" legislation and "zero-based" budgeting, the workload of the Senate will continue to escalate.

RECOMMENDATIONS

The analytical scheme has highlighted the fact that there are significant differences among Senators and staff in the ways they approach their jobs in various policy areas. Proposals for changes in the way the Senate approaches investigation and legislation in crosscutting policy areas will be most successful if these differences are taken into account.

Senators: Opportunities for Briefings

It is important to reiterate one point made earlier: Since it is impossible or infeasible to manipulate the elements which determine whether or not a Senator will become involved in a policy area, the present patterns of activity and interest must be taken as given. Therefore, recommendations relating directly to members will be few. It is also essential to note that proposals which may assist one type of member will not be of use to another.

As noted earlier, it is not a lack of information but a lack of assimilated knowledge about issues which Senators feel. However, it is only in those issue areas in which a Senator is an "activist" that he has incentive to make the investment that the acquisition of such knowledge requires. One way to do this would be for the Senate, perhaps through the Library of Congress, to maintain lists of experts in various policy areas who could be tapped by individual Senators who desired briefings in their fields. A better, although more expensive, way would be for the Senate to keep a range of policy experts on retainer, to be available for individual Senators to obtain their views on upcoming legislation or for longer briefing sessions. Whatever means are chosen, Senators feel that these experts must be made available to members on an individual basis; Senators do not seem to regard group efforts as feasible or desirable.

With respect to Senators who have limited their role in a given area to that of "decision makers," little can be done directly. More assistance for those members can be given through their staffs, and these recommendations follow.

One possibility, however, would be to take better advantage of Senators' other major source of decision information: fellow members. A number of Senators have indicated that the few well-structured, well-attended debates (e.g., on weapons procurement) that have taken place in the Senate in recent years were valuable in reaching their decisions. If more of these debates could be held—particularly if they were scheduled in the middle of the week with other activities (such as committee meetings) prohibited at the same time to minimize distractions—they could be invaluable to decisionmaking.

The remainder of our recommendations relate directly to Senators' most important information source: staff.

Staff: Physical Conditions and Management of Space

Working conditions on Capitol Hill are the least conducive imaginable for considering broad policy questions. Staff people are packed like sardines in a noisy and hectic office environment with little privacy. It may be that the hectic character of work is natural to a legislative body, but some improvement in the physical environment of Senate offices can be achieved, and is essential. The office arrangements, with 8 to 10 people in an open room, phones continually ringing, and people wandering in and out, create an atmosphere where the only decisions that take place are short term and immediate. Additional office space and a limitation of two or three professionals per room are essential: office and room partitions might be utilized more effectively as well. In addition, rooms where staff could go for writing, thinking or research purposes, as part of each Senator's office allotment or as common areas within each office building, would be useful. The Library of Congress is simply too inconvenient for most staff.

Access to Operational Information

There are two basic areas which affect the Senate's capacity for crosscutting policy deliberations where staff information and resources could be improved. The first is in the area of the available information for floor votes on bills and amendments. Professional staff in the Senate spend an inordinate amount of time covering upcoming votes and monitoring floor debate. Much of this time is duplicative and largely wasted. Any time that could be saved from these duties would be available for other things; long-range and broader thinking would be one area that might benefit.

MEMOS

Regular memos, similar to the House Democratic Study Group Supplements to the Whip Notices, which describe bills and likely amendments as they are due for floor action and which list the pros and cons, would be a major improvement. These memos could be done weekly or twice a week by the party policy committees, or by a small staff out of the Office of the Secretary of the Senate.

There are a number of additional ways in which information about bills going to the floor could be transmitted to staff or to Senators.

STAFF BRIEFINGS

Committees could hold briefings on important bills which will be on the floor for a substantial period of time, or on which there will be a number of amendments. Another improvement would be to require committees to distribute information sheets on bills and prospective amendments. A more grandiose alternative would be to have staff or Senators videotape debates on controversial legislation, with tape copies going to Senators or staff who wished to consider a forthcoming bill. Each office could easily be equipped with a videocassette recorder.

MONITORING FLOOR DEBATE

In addition, a much better system should be devised to enable staff to keep abreast of floor activity at any given time. Much staff time and resources are wasted by having people monitoring floor action. Closed-circuit television of Senate floor debate, beamed to each Senate office, would be the best solution. Televising floor debate to the Senate offices would result in a great savings of staff and senatorial time and effort. Next best would be an audio hookup, or a teletype arrangement.

Finally, there are reforms to improve directly the staff capacity to engage in crosscutting policy analysis. To do this, ways must be devised in which Senate staff can assimilate new information, or put their knowledge into broader or different frameworks or time perspectives. This is not an easy task; even if the resources are readily available, the motivations of staff people cannot be easily changed. Many Senate staff will have little interest in developing their capacities to analyze crosscutting problems. They will be content to perform their jobs as now defined. Thus, opportunities can be provided only for those staff who wish to utilize them. This will probably mean that such devices as retreats, briefings, and videotaped debates will be used largely by staff of activist Senators.

STAFF RETREATS

One interesting possibility are retreats for Senate professional staff, away from Washington, during recesses, lasting two or three days. Perhaps Airlie House, or its equivalent, would be a good location. Retreats would focus on a broad policy area, such as energy or solar energy policy, defense strategy, transportation policy, health policy, etc. They would be run by a small group of experts who would try to "stretch" the minds of the staff people, and to alert them to possible future trends in the issue areas. The retreats would be small (perhaps six to eight staff at each one) and frequently run. They would be paid for by the Secretary of the Senate.

In addition, the Senate might try organized, publicized one-day briefings in Washington on selected topics (the Library of Congress has done some of this); or a series of videotaped discussions or debates on broad policy topics or on major bills which could be replayed at the convenience of the staff on a videocassette tape player in the Senate.

ADEQUACY OF STAFF

In closing, note should be taken of one recommendation *not* being made: increased Senate personal office staff. There was surprisingly overwhelming agreement among both Senators and staff that the present staff levels are sufficient for members' needs. The only disagreement was among staff "generalists" who wished they were "specialists"; they wanted more staff who would take their unwanted areas off their hands and permit them to concentrate on their particular areas of expertise. Otherwise the feeling is virtually unanimous that the human resources in the Senate are basically sufficient for the body to accomplish its tasks.

It is not that number of staff must be increased, but that the means of employing them and the support services available to them—as discussed above—must be improved.

7.3 Decision Settings in Congress*

David C. Kozak

This piece emphasizes variations in congressional decision making at the micro level. It contends that there are different patterns of congressional decision making corresponding to different kinds of issues.

ABSTRACT

This paper attempts to document contextual decision behavior in House floor voting and to foster an approach to congressional decision making that emphasizes decision settings. After presenting a synopsis of recent interview research among House members that reveals variable decision behavior, this paper argues that Congressmen encounter at least five different decision settings during the act of floor voting: hot votes, nonvisible votes, complicated bills, grant aid votes, and routine votes. Each setting is associated with distinctive decision behavior and decision rules. Therefore, universal or general models of legislative behavior that attempt to describe typical, normal, or modal behavior, although, providing a significant glimpse of legislative life, necessarily oversimplify what is a highly complex and contextual proces. A sophisticated approach to congressional decision making requires a multiple model approach and an appreciation for the decision setting within which each model is likely to apply. The paper concludes with an optimistic assessment of the potential for constituency–Representative linkages in House voting.

INTRODUCTION

Congressmen make up their minds in different ways on different kinds of issues. Although this is a rather obvious conclusion, it has not been emphasized nor researched in the scholarly literature of congressional voting behavior.

Previously, various authors have focused on what they conclude is the dominant behavioral pattern or decision determinant affecting congressional decision making. For example, Julius Turner, in his roll-call study, *Party and Constituency: Pressures on Congress,* argues that "party continues to be more closely associated with congressional voting behavior than any other discernible factor."[1] For Donald Matthews and James A. Stimson in *Yeas and Nays,* as the subtitle of their work states, cue-taking (i.e., following the position of another actor presumed to be an expert) is the "normal" decision-making procedure in the House.[2] For Aage Clausen in *How Congressmen Decide,* most decisions are made on the basis of policy dimensions. In his words,

> Legislators reduce the time and energy requirements of policy decision making by (1) . . . sorting specific policy proposals into a limited number of general policy content categories and by (2) establishing a policy position for each general category of policy content, one that can be used to make decisions on each of the specific proposals assigned to that category.[3]

John Kingdon, in *Congressmen's Voting Decisions,* develops a consensus model of decision making. To him,

---

* Published here for the first time, this paper is an edited and revised version of one prepared for delivery at the 1980 annual meeting of the Legislative Studies Group, held in conjunction with the 1980 annual meeting of the American Political Science Association, Washington, D.C., August 28–31, 1980.

> Congressmen begin their consideration of a given bill or amendment with one overriding question: Is it controversial? . . . When there is no controversy in the Congressman's environment at all, his decision rule is simple: vote with the herd. . . . If the Congressman does see some conflict in total environment . . . he proceeds . . . to the next step in the decisional flow chart.[4]

Usually, findings have been presented in terms of general propositions that attempt to describe typical or normal behavior, such as:

A congressman hears from few actors when making a decision, "most often from those who agree with him."[5]

"Fellow Congressmen appear to be the most important influence on voting decisions, followed by constituency."[6]

"Other members are the major source of a Congressman's information."[7]

"Congressmen confine their searches for information only to the most routine and easily available sources."[8]

Congressmen generally are not well informed when making a decision.[9]

Party affiliation is the factor most strongly related to congressional voting.[10]

Members base most votes on ideology.[11]

Most members have a "politico" style of representation and a district focus.[12]

The result of these research efforts has been both informative and frustrating—informative because each author gives us a glimpse of the forces and decisions rules that affect congressional voting, but frustrating because we are presented with a series of conflicting, single-factor theories and single-eye interpretations with little attempt to integrate them. For example, four different single-eye interpretations have evolved as alternative explanations for congressional decision making. They are the organizational explanation (cue-taking), the representational (instructed delegate) explanation, the trustee (public-interest statesman) model, and the ideologist model. With few exceptions, there have been no concentrated efforts to reconcile these disparate perspectives. This lack of integration frequently has been lamented by those who have made epistemological inventories of the legislative process field.[13] For example, Robert Peabody has emphasized that "the critical need is for theory at several levels for, quite clearly, in congressional research the generation of data has proceeded much more rapidly than the accumulation of theory.[14] Norman Meller has written that:

> Like raindrops on a dirty windowpane, legislative-behavior studies afford brief glimpses at a broader vision of the legislative process, but have failed to furnish a framework enabling its full comprehension. Studies are yet too disperse and lack replication; conflicting findings have not always served as stimuli for subsequent clarificatory research. Also, there has been too ready a subsuming of the basic unity of the legislative process and too little attention given to the generation of an inclusive theory.[15]

Recently, students of the policy process have taken to formulating a contextual approach to congressional decision making that offers the opportunity for overcoming the static quality of previous research. Examples are works by Theodore Lowi,[16] Randall Ripley and Grace Franklin,[17] John Bacheller,[18] Michael Hayes,[19] Charles O. Jones,[20] David Price,[21] and James Q. Wilson.[22] These works emphasize that there are different decision tracks or arenas in Congress, each associated with distinctive decision behavior. Through the construction of typologies—such as Lowi, and Ripley and Franklin's distinction between distributive, regulatory, and redistributive policy processes—they implicitly argue that no one model of legislative behavior is best. To them, congressional scholars are best served by multiple models and iterpretations, each of which best explains congressional decision making in a specific issue context.

Although the contextual approach has the potential for synthesizing divergent perspectives on decision making, it has neither been adequately conceptualized nor thoroughly researched. The most detracting limitation has been the failure to translate the typologies to the micro level of member decision making. For example, what is different about the decision environment of (again, to use Lowi's typology) distributive, regulatory, and redistributive issues that leads legislators to behave differently? What are the differences in the cognitive map of members when they decide on different kinds of issues? These concerns simply are not addressed in the aforementioned works that employ a contextual approach.

This paper will report some major findings of a research project that attempted to both explicate and test, at the micro level, propositions inherent in the contextual approach. It will be divided into two parts. The first part will give an overview of the project and its findings.[23] The second part will present some suppositions, drawn from the research, concerning decision settings in Congress.

RESEARCH SYNOPSIS

The micro-level theory deduced from work utilizing a contextual approach is that Congressmen utilize different decision rules, depending on the incentives for involvement present in different decision settings. On low-grade issues where few actors are involved or heard from, the member will make a decision by deferring to someone he perceives to be an expert in the field. Thus, the decision will reflect a narrow "subgovernment" phenomenon. Conversely, on hot, emotional, visible, controversial votes, where many are involved, members will feel sufficiently motivated to develop issue positions with which to cast, explain, and justify the vote. In David Price's words:

> The degree of conflict an issue is thought to entail and its perceived salience to the electorate . . . influence both the distribution of legislators' policy-making "investments" and the extent to which they take their bearings from broader interests.[24]

To test the theory, John Kingdon's method of direct interviewing of members was employed with three modifications. First, Kingdon asked questions about communications and then drew conclusions about decision determinants. In contrast, this research design asked questions about four separate components of the cognitive map: communications, information, decision rules, and role orientations. Second, this research design asked questions about issue characteristics (i.e., how the member perceived and defined the vote at hand). Third, Kingdon studied only, in his words, "big votes"[25]—those that were politically interesting and important. This research attempts to select a mixture of votes. Noncontroversial and routine votes, as well as high-profile votes, were studied. Table 7.3.1 displays the questionnaire used in this study.

Interviewing was undertaken in the first session of the 95th Congress (March–July 1977) under the sponsorship of Rep. Jim Lloyd (D—Calif.). Research efforts yielded 361 interview protocols from 80 sampled members concerning 31 separate House votes. Tables 7.3.2a and 7.3.2b display both the stratification of U.S. House at the time of interviewing and the distribution of interviewees per the different strata. As can be seen, there was considerable overrepresentation of northern Democrats with short service and underrepresentation of northern Democrats with long tenure. Other strata were fairly representative.

The results document contextual decision behavior in Congress, but in ways *more complicated* than the hot/low-profile distinction implied by contemporary contextual approaches.

With regard to communications, members heard from an average of three sources per vote. The actors most frequently mentioned as making input to congressional decision making were personal staff, constituency, committee members, and other members not on the committee. Table 7.3.3 displays the frequency with which various actors were mentioned. Interviews revealed that there were different kinds of communications to members. First, a distinction can be made on the basis of when the input was received. There are inputs proximate to the time of the vote, such as the partisan members who man the doorways, and inputs more antecedent

TABLE 7.3.1 QUESTIONNAIRE

1. Re the ________________ vote, who did you hear from or talk to concerning how to vote?
2. Was there anyone else to whom you paid attention?
3. I imagine that these kinds of communications and information sources are helpful to you in different ways.
   a. Who was helpful in informing you about the facts of the bill?
   b. In your estimation, who/what was most decisive in helping you make up your mind?
4. What kind of issue do you feel this is?
   a. Do you feel it is complex? yes no
   b. Do you feel it is technical? yes no
   c. Is there a lot of conflict and disagreement on this bill? yes no
   d. Is it major legislation? yes no
   e. (1) Is this legislation important to the people of your district? yes no
   (2) Are they aware of it? yes no
   f. Did you receive a lot of mail on it? yes no
   g. Do you feel that your vote on this could affect:
   (1) Your renomination? yes no
   (2) Your reelection? yes no
   h. Do you feel that this is a routine matter? yes no
   i. How strongly do you personally feel on this issue? 1 2 3
   j. When did you make up your mind on this issue?
   k. Is it a tough decision? yes no
5. When making up your mind on this piece of legislation on what did you rely?
   a. Constituency wishes.
   b. Your own opinion.
   c. Something else.
6. Was your focus the national interest, local interest, or both?
7. How informed do you feel about the issues raised in this legislation?
   a. Not at all.
   b. Somewhat.
   c. Very well.
8. Did you put much thought into it? yes no

TABLE 7.3.2a STRATIFICATION OF U.S. HOUSE OF REPRESENTATIVES, 95TH CONGRESS, PER TWO VARIABLES

LENGTH OF SERVICE	NORTHERN DEMOCRAT	SOUTHERN DEMOCRAT	REPUBLICAN	TOTAL
Short (0–5 years)	111 (27%)	38 (9%)	71 (17%)	220 (53%)
Medium (6–11 years)	30 (7%)	17 (9%)	38 (9%)	88 (21%)
Long (12+ years)	57 (14%)	22 (5%)	26 (6%)	105 (25%)
	198 (48%)	77 (19%)	135 (33%)	410 (100%)

TABLE 7.3.2b STRATIFIED DISTRIBUTION OF INTERVIEWS

LENGTH OF SERVICE	NORTHERN DEMOCRAT	SOUTHERN DEMOCRAT	REPUBLICAN
Short (0–5 years)	135 (38%)	22 (6%)	63 (18%)
Medium (6–11 years)	23 (6%)	31 (9%)	35 (10%)
Long (12*a* years)	23 (6%)	16 (4%)	11 (3%)

NOTE: Both tables based on 359 questionnaries. Due to an oversight, two questionnaires were not collated with the number with whom the interview was obtained.

TABLE 7.3.3 PERCENTAGE OF THE INTERVIEWS IN WHICH EACH ACTOR WAS MENTIONED BY MEMBERS IN RESPONSE TO THE QUESTION "WHO DID YOU HEAR FROM, PAY ATTENTION TO, CONSIDER CONCERNING THIS DECISION?

ACTOR	RESPONSES (PERCENT)
Committee chairman	20%
Ranking minority	3
Committee members	36
State delegation	31
Party leader	13
Other Congressmen	36
Committee staff	5
Personal staff	42
Individual constituents	37
Inspired mail	8
Group constituents	26
Private groups	22
Public-interest groups	5
Public groups	3
Bureaucrats	3
White House	14
Media	14

NOTE: Based on 361 interviews. Multiple responses permitted.

to the decision, such as constituency mail, staff briefing, and correspondence from interest groups. Second, communications vary according to whether or not there is an attempt to exert pressure. Some inputs involve active attempts to sway and influence. Examples are lobbying activities by those competing for a member's attention, such as other members, the President, constituents, and interest groups. Other inputs do not involve intense pressure. Rather, they are best thought of as latent factors and a member's self-referents for decision making. Examples are perceptions of constituency interests, opinions obtained through member-sponsored polls, inquiries a member makes to a trusted colleague, staff work on an issue, and communications received from congressional agencies such as the Library of Congress, Congressional Budget Office, and General Accounting Office.

The volume of communications a member receives and the sources he hears from vary by the kind of vote at hand. On hot votes, members received input from many sources; on low-grade issues, members heard from only a few sources. Variations in the mention of various sources are captured by the distinction between routine, grants to localities, hot, and specialized hot votes. On routine votes, members hear from staff and committee sources. On grant votes, members pay attention to staff, state delegation members, and the affected clientele in the district. On hot votes, members hear from major political actors: interest groups, congressional leaders, constituents, and the White House. Specialized hot issues involve input from segmental constituencies.

Three aspects of the congressional information process were studied: volume, sources, and level. With regard to volume, members acknowledged the use of an average of two sources for each vote. With regard to sources, information was received from direct contact with members, impersonal contact with members, in-house publications, staff, outside sources, and the general experience and reading of members. As noted in selection 1 of this chapter, information sources can be classified as being personal or impersonal and proximate to or distant from the vote. The most frequently utilized references were personal staff, Democratic Study Group (DSG) publications, party Whip Notices, and floor debate. Table 7.1.1 (p. 290) exhibits the frequency with which various information sources were mentioned. Concerning level or adequacy of information, on most votes members feel generally well-informed.

Variations in volume occur according to complexity, technicality, and parliamentary scheduling, as well as the low-profile/hot distinction. Members searched for more information when the vote was low-grade but hard to understand, hot, or did not come up at the last minute. Variations in the use of sources occurred according to a member's knowledge and need. If a member was unfamiliar with an issue but it was politically important to him, he would consult normal sources (i.e., staff and in-house publications). If a member was unfamiliar with a bill and it was not important to him, he would consult no source, save for members on the floor. Finally, if a member was unfamiliar with a bill but he perceived his vote to be very important, he would consult special, supplemental sources (i.e., members on the committee). Variations in the level of information occur according to the hot/low-profile distinction. On hot issues members feel better informed. On low-profile votes they feel less informed.

The decision rule (or decision ''determinant'' or ''referrent,'' as it is sometimes called) most frequently cited was, confirming Aage Clausen, ideology, or what might be called policy predisposition (i.e., standing commitments to support or oppose certain programs, policies, or agencies). In 65 percent of the decisions studied, members mentioned ideology as a decision referrent. The next most frequently mentioned referrents were constituency (13 percent), philosophy—support or opposition on moral grounds—(11 percent), and committee members (10 percent). The frequency with which various determinants were mentioned is displayed in Table 7.3.4. Determinants cited can be classified as proximate to or distant from the vote and internal or external to the legislator and legislature. Actors internal to or within the legislature and proximate to the vote that were identified as influential in congressional voting were the committee system, fellow members, party leaders, and a member's personal staff. Internal forces somewhat remote from the vote were party, ideology, legislator's demography, legislative procedures, and norms/folkways. External actors proximate to the vote were constituents, the President, bureaucrats, and lobbyists. Factors external to the legislature and antecedent to the vote were constituency characteristics, media, electoral outcomes, and public opinion. Table 7.3.5 classifies the major, identified causes according to the four possible categories.

Some variation in the mention of decision rules does occur according to a hot/low-profile distinction, although ideology is used as a decision rule in both issue contexts. For hot votes, decisions were likely to be based on ideology, philosophy, constituency interests, or constituent demands, and the member's assessment of the adequacy of the compromise. Low-profile issues were based on cue-taking and perception of consensus, as well as ideology.

TABLE 7.3.4 FREQUENCY DISTRIBUTION OF DETERMINANTS: THE PERCENTAGE OF INTERVIEWS IN WHICH VARIOUS DECISION DETERMINANTS WERE MENTIONED

ACTOR	RESPONSES (PERCENT)
Committee chairman	6%
Committee members	10
State delegation	3
Party leader	2
Other Congressmen	4
Personal staff	4
White House	6
Constituency	13
Compromise	7
Consistency	7
Consensus	7
Philosophical convictions	11
Policy assessments (ideology)	65
Campaign promises	3
Miscellaneous:	
Testimony before committee	1
Bureaucrats	2
Media/reading	1
Rule	1
No choice	2
Family/friends	1
Personal experience	2
On committee	7
Other items	1
Protect the process	2
Prioritization	2

NOTE: Based on 361 interviews. Multiple responses permitted.

Although ideology was overwhelmingly the most cited determinant, it was most frequently used in conjunction with other determinants. Thus, it seems that there are perhaps eight different, identifiable ways or modes of congressional decision making: philosophy, ideology, consensus, campaign promise, assessment of compromise, constituency representation, cue-taking from personal staff, and cue-taking from members. Each tended to be more frequently mentioned on certain kinds of issues.

With regard to role orientations, members mentioned a trustee (self-referrent) style much more frequently than a delegate (constituency

Table 7.3.5 Forces, Factors, and Actors Identified as Determinants of Legislative Voting

	External to the legislature or legislator	Internal to the legislature or legislator	
Proximate to the vote	Constituents	Committee system	
	President	Fellow members	Election classes Friends Ideological groups State delegations
	Bureaucrats	Party leaders	
	Lobbyists	Personal Staff	
Distant from the vote	Constituency characteristics	Party	
	Media	Ideology	
	Electoral outcomes	Legislator's demography	
	Public opinion	Legislative procedures	
		Norms/folkways	

referrent) or broker (combination of self and constituency) style. Table 7.3.6 displays the frequency of role orientation responses. Variations in role orientations occur according to hot votes with and without constituency relevance, grants to localities, and low-profile votes. On hot votes that are perceived by the member to be important to his constituency, a broker role is more prevalent. On hot votes without constituency relevance, members utilize a trustee role. On grant votes, members employ a broker role, while on low-profile votes a trustee style prevails.

An additional aspect of congressional decision making—time of decision—was researched starting midway through the study at the urging of several members. The most frequently cited times of decision were "on the floor" and "the last time the bill was up." Table 7.3.7 exhibits the frequency distribution of various temporal responses. Variations in time of decision occur according to the hot/low-profile distinction, members' information, parliamentary scheduling, and floor maneuvering. Early decisions are made when the vote is hot, has been scheduled well in advance, has been seen before, and does not involve last-minute floor wrangling. Late decisions are made on low-profile votes, new issues, votes that are brought up quickly, and votes on which there is some doubt concerning the final outcome due to the amendment process. It should

Table 7.3.6 Frequency Distribution of Role Conceptions in Response to the Question, "On What Did You Base Your Decision: Constituency, Self, A Combination of Both?"

Actor	Responses (percent)
Constituency (delegate)	2%
Self (trustee)	74
Both self and constituents (politico)	19
President	2
Staff	1

Note: Based on 352 interviews.

Table 7.3.7 Frequency Distribution of Responses to the Question: "When Did You Reach a Decision on This Vote?"

When decided	Percent
When member first entered politics	7%
Last time vote was up	18
During campaign	9
Automatic (when heard it was up)	6
On Committee	5
Week before	3
Day before	3
When read about it	6
When heard from constituents	4
On the floor	25
When change was made	5
Late	9

Note: Based on 141 interviews.

be emphasized that the precise time at which a member makes up his mind is also a function of his own idiosyncratic information process. If a member is briefed early in the week on that week's legislative activity, he will make up his mind early. If he is briefed day to day, he will make up his mind late.

Four major conclusions are supported by the research. First, there is contextual decision making in Congress. Neither the mode nor the mean yields a sophisticated view of congressional voting. The voting behavior of Congressmen is best understood in terms of decision contexts. Second, many of our major generalizations concerning congressional decision behavior—such as cue-taking is the normal mode of congressional decision making, Congressmen hear from only a few when making a decision, Congressmen engage in only a perfunctory search when making a decision, Congressmen do not feel informed when making a decision, members base voting on ideology, members have a broker role orientation, and other members are a major source of information—are highly contextual. There propositions are valid under certain conditions but invalid under others. Third, the hot/low-profile distinction implied by Lowi and by Ripley and Franklin is not the only difference that drives variations in legislative behavior. Variations occur according to a variety of factors, depending on the component of the cognitive map in question. Fourth, the involvement, contribution, and influence of various actors in congressional decision making varies by issue contexts and components of the cognitive map. For example, personal staff, which is mentioned in 33 percent of the decisions as an information source, is mentioned in only 4 percent of the decisions as a decision determinant. An emphasis on general patterns of influence fails to pick up these nuances.

SUPPOSITIONS CONCERNING ISSUE SETTINGS

There are two major limitations to the research design and the way data were analyzed. One is that there was no opportunity to interrelate the different components of cognitive map. Another is that, in analyzing the results, the Congressman is portrayed as a passive actor when an emphasis on the Congressman as an "active" contextual decision maker is perhaps more illuminating.

Moving away from the data arrays, it seems that—on the basis of this author's extensive interviewing among members concerning congressional decision making—there are at least five different decision settings that members encounter when voting on the floor. They are hot votes, nonvisible votes, complicated bills, votes on grant aids to localities, and routine votes. Although these settings may not be completely mutually exclusive (for example, a grant vote may also be routine or complicated), they seem to capture the major variations in decision making relayed by members during the interview sessions. For each setting there is a unique demand pattern that leads members to devise distinctive behavioral routines and shortcuts. Therefore, each decision setting is associated with a different combination of demand patterns, information search, level of information, decision rule, time of decision, and role orientation. Moreover, interview sessions indicate that members perceive and define the various settings with a degree of unanimity. For example, most will agree that a certain vote is hot and another is nonvisible.

HOT VOTES

A hot, or high-profile, vote is one that members feel is "controversial," "emotional," "salient," "major," and "visible." This kind of vote involves a lot of mail from the district, general constituency awareness, and a close, hard-fought battle based on strongly held positions. Examples of "hot" legislation in this study were votes on ethics, tax reform, the Hatch Act revisions, clean air (Dingell Amendment), abortion (Hyde Amendment), congressional pay raise, the saccharin ban, Rhodesian chrome, and common situs picketing. Several members also emphasized that other frequently seen hot votes involve minority and women's rights, military conscription, and gun control. Several members and staffers indicated that there are usually 10 or so extremely hot issues each session of Congress.

The input to members on hot legislation is extremely broad and voluminous, for it is these kinds of issues that attract heavy mail, press coverage, and party and presidential involvement. Most members recalled receiving a broad spectrum of input from a wide variety of interests. As one member stated:

> If there is an existence of contrary approaches on a bill, you do talk to a lot of people on it. When a lot of people are interested, when the range of opinion is wide, many attempt to talk to you and you have no alternative but to talk to them. On big, important bills, you will always hear from people.

For most members, the information search on hot issues is lower than normal, because most members are very familiar with the issues due to experience with the bill either in previous sessions of Congress or on the campaign trail. As one member stated, "On this kind of thing you don't need an extensive search for information. We know it already. Usually you've seen all the big ones before." If members utilize any information source on these votes it is usually a scan of normal materials (briefing by personal staff, DSG publications, Whip Notices, or committee reports) to learn the facts of a specific bill and possible amendments.

The level of a member's information on a hot vote is quite high. Several members addressed the reasons for this. One member noted,

> We are usually prepared on major bills and significant amendments to them. Divisions in committee which occur on important votes provide safeguards by communicating to the member that there will be a fight, and he better inform himself.

Another argued,

> The more controversy, the more you'll know about it. If you are to be respected by your colleagues, you should be able to talk the pros and cons on an issue.

Another noted,

> On major bills you get stuff from the Library of Congress, Congressional Research Organization, and party and factional groups. There is usually an abundance of information that allows you to get familiar with basic issues.

On hot votes, members will cast a vote on the basis of one of five decision rules: personal philosophy, ideology, campaign promise, constituency representation, or assessment of the adequacy of compromise. Many members state that on hot votes they rely on their own personal values or philosophy (e.g., "I believe it is morally wrong to have the government finance abortion"). If the member's personal values are not relevant, then he will cast the vote on the basis of ideology/policy predisposition (support for or opposition to certain programs and policies), a campaign pledge or commitment, and/or constituency representation (responding to citizen mail or voting what one perceives to be the interests or preferences of constituents). On a few hot issues, some members will employ the decision rule of voting their assessment of the adequacy of compromise. The statement, "I think it is a good compromise—all parties were able to deal" is given as the determinant of the vote. It should be emphasized that on hot votes members make no mention of cue-taking or following a consensus.

The time of decision on hot votes is usually very early, often stemming back to when one first got involved in politics. As one member elucidated,

> On these kinds of decisions you constantly are pressed for your opinion during primary and election campaigns and speaking engagements. Hell, I've been asked my opinion on ERA as much as I've been asked my name. By the time it comes up, I don't have to agonize. I know my position.

Several members emphasized that on hot votes they would reserve judgment only if major changes in the basic bill seemed a possibility.

Most members contend that on hot votes they employ a broker role that incorporates their own and their constituents' preferences. As a member stated, ''On hot issues, you better be in accord with your constituents or you may find yourself in trouble. But, you usually get to Congress because you are in agreement already.''

Nonvisible Votes

Most of the votes Congressmen face are not hot issues. They are not publicized and there is not much interest in them. Those kinds of votes are frequently referred to by members as ''low-grade,'' ''inside,'' or ''nonvisible'' votes.

Examples of nonvisible votes covered by this study were House Assassination Committee extension, regulation of the Arab boycott, the Debt Collection Practices Act, the Goldwater Amendment to a housing bill, and Rumanian earthquake relief.

On nonvisible bills, the input to members is low—almost nonexistent—and narrow, usually from only those interested or affected.

The search for information is confined primarily to normal, in-house sources or the usual pattern. The level of information is atypically low. Given the low political stakes involved, the floor voting member rarely will engage in an extensive search on this type of legislation.

The distinctive decision rule frequently employed in this setting, especially when the vote lacks controversy, is consensus—''following the herd,'' ''moving with your crowd,'' or ''flowing with the trend.'' For many members, this means watching the House voting board and paying attention to who is for or against and moving with the group with whom one identifies. Several members emphasized that consensus voting is an outshoot of the way Private, Consent, and Suspension Calendar items are handled. As one member stated, ''On those, I just float with the tide, figuring that if there are problems they would have come out in the committee report.'' Since many nonvisible votes pass by wide margins, many members acknowledge that consensus voting often involves ''voting yes unless you have a reason to vote no'' and ''staying out of a minority of 30 to avoid being targeted by the benefiting group.'' Members also stress that given their heavy load with committee work and case work, consensus voting is both an expeditious and rational way to decide.

The time at which members make up their minds on nonvisible votes depends on when they first learn or read about it. This, in turn, depends on the member's idiosyncratic staff system. However, many report on-the-floor decisions.

On nonvisible votes, members most frequently cite a trustee role orientation, arguing that they rarely get input from constituents. A few, with a basic delegate orientation, argue that they cast the vote on the basis of their perception of constituents' preferences. This, however, seems to be a rare practice in floor voting on these kinds of issues.

Complicated Votes

Frequently, members must vote on bills that are ''difficult,'' ''confusing,'' ''complex,'' ''hard to handle,'' and ''hard to zero in on.'' These usually are multifaceted votes that ''require a lot of thought'' on the member's part. Examples of complicated votes uncovered in this study were both the FAA and EPA reauthorization, strip mining regulations, the creation of the new Energy Department, and votes on budget targets. Either a hot or low-profile vote can be complicated.

The input pattern is moderate to high. Usually only those immediately affected communicate with floor voting members.

Because this type of vote is ''hard to understand,'' members engage in an extended search. They turn not only to normal sources of information, but frequently approach committee sources, either going directly to members or committee staff or relying on personal staff to check for detail and clarification. The level of information is best characterized as ''medium.'' After the extended search, members feel fairly comfortable with the vote.

The decision rule most utilized is cue-taking from members on the committee, who are also frequently in the cue-taker's state delegation and/or election class and have a similar ideological bent and a like constituency. "I voted that way because Congressman X on the committee assured me the bill was OK and recommended that I vote for it" is a frequently heard justification of the vote on complicated bills.

The time of decision for complicated votes occurs "late," after the extended search. The role orientation is almost always a trustee one. Given the technical nature of many complicated votes, members usually base the decision on their interpretation of the issue simply because constituency input is lacking.

Routine Votes

Many of the bills that members vote on can be classified as routine. They are less controversial but more salient than nonvisible votes. Routine votes are ones that "have been seen before" and therefore might be considered "normal" or "the usual." Examples from this study were votes on school lunch, a nuclear navy, snow removal, marine mammals, and the Miller Amendment of foreign aid reductions. The numerous uncontroversial, recurring authorization and appropriation measures that members see each year also serve as examples of routine votes.

The input pattern is low and narrow on routine votes. Only those affected are heard from. However, the lobbying activites of affected publics are usually very selective, zeroing in on those members who are bloc leaders, uncommitted, or wavering. Therefore, the force fields of average floor voting members are empty.

The information search process is a very normal one. Only normal sources are referenced. The level of information is very low due to a general lack of concern, interest, and relevance.

The decision is almost always based on ideology—standing policy positions to vote for or against certain programs. As one member noted,

> On recurring matters you simplify by attempting to achieve a consistent record pro or con certain programs. This allows you to develop little categories with which to classify and then act on relatively minor legislation that a member not on the committee can't affect anyway.

The time of decision on routine votes is either the time of the staff briefing that alerts members to a vote coming up or, for more experienced members, the last time the issue was before the Congress.

Like the nonvisible setting, the role orientation used on routine votes is a function of a member's basic orientation. Most use a trustee orientation, given the lack of communications from constituents, but a small minority of members attempt to represent their perceptions of constituency sentiment.

Grant Votes

Votes most relevant to members are those pertaining to federal grants to localities. These are high in political salience for the member and involve constituency awareness of the member's activities. The community development bloc grants, countercyclical aid, and public works are examples of grant votes studied during this research. Although grant votes may be routine, hot, complicated, or nonvisible, it is felt that members' behavior is so distinctive as to warrant classifying grants as a separate setting.

The communications members receive on grant votes come primarily from segmental constituencies—i.e., organized beneficiaries, including local public officials, in the district.

Members engage in an extended and intense information search on grant votes. Normal sources of information are supplemented by an exchange of information within the state delegation that involves interaction, both direct and through staff, with committee and agency sources.

On grant votes, members have a medium level of information. They do not know all facets, but the extended search yields more than average information—especially in terms of how the bill will affect the district.

Members follow two decision rules when making a decision on grant votes: cue-taking from staff and/or constituency representation. Usually members will assign personal staff to work on proposed grant formulas to ascertain how it affects their district. The vote is then made with deferrence to staff recommendations and with an effort to further constituency interests.

The time of decision for grant votes is typically the day before, once the mist has cleared on the likely impact of alternative schemes. Sometimes members suspend judgment, waiting to see the outcome of last-minute maneuvering and compromising on the allocation sections of a bill.

For almost all members, the role orientation used on grant votes is the delegate style. Members attempt to serve and further their perception of constituency interest.

SUMMARY, CONCLUSIONS, AND INTERPRETATIONS

The major conclusion to be drawn from this research is that congressional decision behavior varies according to different decision contexts. No single force drives decision making. No single model has a monopoly on truth. Congressmen do not all make up their minds in the same way or in a set fashion on each and every vote. This research provides the first empirical verification (based on systematic interviewing) for the proposition that different decision settings are associated with different behavior patterns and decision rules.

Members cast more than 1,500 votes on a wide variety of topics in the span of a single Congress. This research has detected five different decision settings that members confront when making these votes. It is felt that each is associated with rather distinguishable forms and styles of decision behavior. To cope with the high volume of decisions they are asked to make, members develop different programmed courses of behavior for each of the settings. On hot votes, members usually base the decision on their own personal values. If the member does not have strong feelings on a bill or if the bill is one of the vast majority that is not major, the vote will be cast on the basis of one of several decision shortcuts (constituency representation, cue-taking, consensus, or ideology) depending on (*a*) the member's familiarity with a bill, and (*b*) the bill's complexity, controversiality, and relevance to constuency.

Table 7.3.8 summarizes the suppositions concerning variations in members' cognitive maps associated with the five different decision settings. It should be emphasized that both the complicated and nonvisible settings approximate the subgovernment model (ratification of committee decisions), but the others do not. Only one setting (complicated) conforms to classic notions of cue-taking. Only two (hot and routine) approximate the model of ideological voting. All of this is to argue that a multiple model approach must be utilized if students of the legislative process are to have a complete understanding of congressional decision making, for each setting constitutes a very different kind of congressional decision-making process.

This documentation of contextual decision making in Congress confirms the speculation of several organization theorists that decision makers in large, complex organizations employ variable decision rules. For example, James D. Thompson emphasizes that there are different "types of decision issues" and "it seems clear that each type of decision issue calls for a different strategy."[26] Fredrick Cleaveland speculated in 1969 about "issue contexts" in Congress. For him, "issue contexts" are

> . . . the way members of Congress perceive a policy proposal that comes before them, how they consciously or unconsciously classify it for study, and what group of policies they believe it related to.[27]

To Cleaveland, "Such issue contexts strongly influence legislative outcomes because their structure helps determine the approach for analysis . . . as well as the advice and expertise that enjoys privileged access."[28] Surprisingly, until now there has not been much research on variable decision making in Congress.

The implications of a major finding presented here—that most floor decisions are

TABLE 7.3.8 VARIATIONS IN THE CONFIGURATION OF LEGISLATORS' COGNITIVE MAP ASSOCIATED WITH DIFFERENT DECISION SETTINGS

DECISION SETTING	INPUT PATTERN	INFORMATION SEARCH	LEVEL OF INFORMATION	DECISION RULE	ROLE ORIENTATION	TIME OF DECISION
Nonvisible	None	Atypically low due to lack of concern	Low	Consensus	Trustee or delegate (depending on basic inclination)	Floor
Complicated	Moderate to high	Extended	Medium	Cue-taking: members	Trustee	Late
Grant Aid	Low	Extended	Medium	Cue-taking: staff or constituency representation	Delegate	Day before
Routine	Low	Normal	Low	Ideology	Trustee (depending on basic inclination)	When briefed/ last time up
Hot	High	Atypically low due to familiarity	High	Assessment of compromise, campaign promise, philosophy, ideology, and/or constituency representation	Broker	Early (except when crucial amendments are pending)/ last time up

NOTE: This table summarizes suppositions, based on the research, concerning how each decision setting is associated with a distinctive input pattern, time of decision, information search procedure, level of information, decision rule, and role orientation.

based on ideology or extensions of it, such as cue-taking[29]—necessarily lead to a rather optimistic assessment of the potential for democratic linkage between representative and represented. A member's ideology, or policy predispositions as referred to here, better than any other factor predicts (*a*) the voting behavior of a member and (*b*) the sources of input and information on which he will rely. Although there are numerous ways representatives can evade public accountability, the opportunity for mass control of congressional elites is afforded by the ability of the masses to choose among competing policy approaches as presented in the debate of campaign issues, published voting records, and the ideological differences between political parties.

Finally, the five decision settings identified here may not be the only ones with which members must come to grips. Subsequent research may uncover additional settings—especially in the realm of foreign or defense policies, areas not covered by this study—or patterns of variation more refined than those offered here. One can only hope that others will contribute to a more sophisticated study of congressional behavior by attempting to identify decision contexts. As Roland Young sagaciously wrote more than than two decades ago:

> Legislative theories do not develop by themselves, as if wishing would make them so. . . . Unfortunately for those who want a general or easy answer, the dynamics of the legislative process do not relinquish their secrets readily.[30]

APPENDIX: SYNOPSIS OF SAMPLED VOTES

1. H Res 287. House Ethics Code (14 interviews). Adoption of the resolution to require comprehensive financial disclosure by House members, ban private office accounts, increase office allowance, ban gifts from lobbyists, limit outside earned income and impose other financial restrictions on members. Accepted, 402–22. March 2, 1977.
2. HR 3839. Second Budget Rescission, fiscal 1977 (10 interviews). Chappell (D–Fla.) amendment to the committee amendment to restore $81.6 million in the previously appropriated long-lead-time funds for a Nimitz-class nuclear aircraft carrier. Rejected, 161–252. March 3, 1977.
3. HR 3477. Stimulus Tax Cuts (10 interviews). Passage of the bill to provide for a refund of 1976 individual income taxes and other payments, to reduce individual and business income taxes, to increase the individual standard deduction, and to simplify tax preparation. Passed, 282–137. March 8, 1977.
4. HR 3843. Supplemental Housing Authorization (10 interviews). Goldwater Amendment to delete Title II of the bill establishing a National Commission on Neighborhoods. Adopted, 243–166. March 10, 1977.
5. HR 1746. Rhodesian Chrome Imports (11 interviews). Passage of the bill to halt the importation of Rhodesian chrome in order to bring the United States into compliance with U.N. economic sanctions imposed on Rhodesia in 1966 (repeals Byrd Amendment). Adopted, 250–146. March 14, 1977.
6. HR 4088. NASA Authorization (10 interviews). Passage of the bill to authorize $4.05 billion for NASA for fiscal 1978. Accepted, 338–44. March 17, 1977.
7. HR 4250. Common-Site Picketing (11 interviews). Passage of the bill to permit a labor union with a grievance with one contractor to picket all contractors on the same construction site and to establish a construction industry collective bargaining committee. Rejected, 205–217. March 23, 1977.
8. HR 3965. FAA Authorization (10 interviews). Passage of the bill to authorize $85 million for research and development programs for fiscal 1978. Accepted, 402–6. March 24, 1977.
9. HR 5045. Executive Branch Reorganiza-

tion Authority (13 interviews). Passage of the bill to extend for three years presidential authority, which expired in 1973, to transmit to Congress plans for reorganization of agencies in the Executive Branch. Accepted, 395–22. March 29, 1977.

10. H Res 433. House Assassination Committee (13 interviews). Adoption of the resolution to continue the Select Committee on Assassinations. Adopted, 230–181. March 30, 1977.
11. HR 5294. Consumer Credit Protection (11 interviews). Passage of the bill to prohibit debt collection agencies from engaging in certain practices alleged to be unfair to consumers. Passed, 199–198. April 4, 1977.
12. HR 5717. Rumanian Earthquake Relief (9 interviews). Motion to suspend the rules and pass the bill to authorize $120 million for the relief and rehabilitation of refugees and other victims of the March 4, 1977, earthquake in Rumania. Passed, 322–90. April 18, 1977.
13. HR 5101. Environmental Protection Agency Research and Development (6 interviews). Passage of the bill to authorize $313 million for fiscal 1978 research and development activities of the EPA and to promote coordination of environmental research and development. Accepted, 358–31. April 19, 1977.
14. HR 5840. Export Administration Act (10 interviews). Passage of the bill to revise U.S. export controls on sensitive materials and to prohibit U.S. firms from complying with certain aspects of the Arab boycott against Israel. Passed, 364–43. April 20, 1977.
15. HR 4877. First Regular Supplemental Appropriation, fiscal 1977 (11 interviews). Brademas (D–Ind.) motion that the House recede and concur with a Senate amendment to provide an additional $20 million to reimburse state and local governments for the costs of snow removal incurred during the 1976–77 winter emergency. Defeated, 124–279. April 21, 1977.
16. H Con Res 195. Fiscal 1978 Budget Targets (12 interviews). Passage of the resolution, as amended, providing for fiscal 1978 budget targets of revenues of $398.1 billion, budget authority of $505.7 billion, outlays of $466.7 billion and a deficit of $68.6 billion. Rejected, 84–320. April 27, 1977.
17. HR 2. Strip Mining Regulation (13 interviews). Passage of the bill to regulate surface coal mining operators and to acquire and reclaim abandoned mines. Passed, 241–64. April 29, 1977.
18. HR 11. Public Works Jobs Programs (9 interviews). Adoption of the conference report for the bill to authorize an additional $4 billion for the emergency public works employment program as requested in President Carter's economic stimulus package. Accepted, 335–77. May 3, 1977.
19. H Con Res 214. Fiscal 1978 Budget Targets (7 interviews). Adoption of the budget resolution setting fiscal 1978 targets of revenues of $398.1 billion, budget authority of $502.3 billion, outlays of $464.5 billion, a deficit of $66.4 billion, and binding limits for fiscal 1977. Adopted, 213–179. May 5, 1977.
20. HR 6655. Housing and Community Development Programs (12 interviews). Passage of the bill to authorize $12.45 billion for the Community Development Block Grant Program for fiscal 1978–80 and to authorize more than $2 billion for federally assisted, public and rural housing and to continue FHA mortgage and flood insurance programs. Passed, 369–20. May 11, 177.
21. HR 6810. Countercyclical Assistance Authorization (13 interviews). Passage of the bill to extend for an additional year, through fiscal 1978, a program of countercyclical grants to help state and local governments avoid cutbacks in employment and public services and to authorize

a maximum of $2.25 billion for the five quarters, beginning July 1, 1977. Passed, 243–94. May 13, 1977.

22. HR 1139. Child Nutrition Programs (9 interviews). Passage of the bill to extend through fiscal 1979 the summer food program and to make other changes in the school lunch and child nutrition programs. Passed, 393–19. May 18, 1977.
23. HR 6161. Clean Air Act Amendments (15 interviews). Dingell (D–Mich.) substitute for Title II to delay and relax automobile emissions standards, to reduce the warranties for emissions control devices, and to make other changes in existing law regarding mobile sources of air pollution. Adopted, 255–139. May 26, 1977.
24. HR 6970. Tuna-Dolphin Protection (12 interviews). Passage of the bill to limit the total number of dolphins that could be accidentally taken during the 1977 commercial tuna fishing operations, to authorize significant further reductions after 1977, to establish a 100 percent federal observer program on tuna boats, and to establish certain incentives and penalities to encourage conservation of dolphins. Adopted, 334–20. June 1, 1977.
25. HR 6804. Federal Energy Department (16 interviews). Passage of the bill creating a Cabinet-level Department of Energy by combining all powers currently held by the FPC, FEA, ERDA, and various other energy authorities and programs currently scattered throughout the federal bureaucracy. Passed, 310–20. June 3, 1977.
26. HR 10. Hatch Act Amendments (12 interviews). Passage of the bill to revise the Hatch Act to allow federal civilian and postal employees to participate in political activities and to protect such employees from improper solicitations. Approved, 244–164. June 7, 1977.
27. HR 7553. Public Works—ERDA Appropriations, Fiscal 1978 (16 interviews). Conte (R–Mass.)–Derrick (D–S.C.) Amendment to delete funding for 16 water projects and reduce funding for one more project, but to retain the total appropriations amount in the bill. Rejected, 194–218. June 14, 1977.
28. HR 7555. Labor–HEW Appropriation, fiscal 1978 (14 interviews). Hyde (R–Ill.) Amendment to prohibit the use of federal funds to finance or encourage abortions. Adopted, 201–155. June 17, 1977.
29. HR 7558. Agriculture Appropriations, fiscal 1978 (12 interviews). Voice vote to delay for one year the HEW-proposed saccharin ban. June 21, 1977.
30. HR 7797. Foreign Aid Appropriations, fiscal 1978 (11 interviews). Miller (R–Ohio) Amendment to cut 5 percent from the $7,046,454,000 recommended by the Appropriations Committee for foreign aid programs. Adopted, 214–168. June 23, 1977.
31. HR 7932. Legislative Branch Appropriations, fiscal 1978 (198 interviews) Grassley (R–Iowa) Amendment to prohibit use of funds appropriated in the bill for the 29 percent pay increase for high-level federal officials that took effect March 1, 1977. Rejected, 181–241. June 29, 1977.

7.4 | Analyzing Votes in Congress*

Jerrold Schneider

An enormous amount of scholarly effort has been expended studying recorded congressional roll-call votes. A dozen or so major studies have called attention to the correlation of party and constituency variables with congressional voting. In this essay, specifically written for this volume, Schneider identifies the three major approaches to analyzing votes in Congress. This piece is most useful in illustrating how each of these types of analyses are and can be done.

Votes in Congress are used as part of the basis for drawing a host of judgments about what Congress has done, and why, and what it might do under present or changed circumstances. Such votes are used to judge how a President and a Congress affect one another, and how Congress affects or is moved by other power centers, forces in the social structure, and voters. Roll-call votes are scrutinized to discover what policies might emerge or remain buried in the near or far future. Looked at across time, roll calls can reveal a great deal about change or the absence of it in the political system. If, as many have said, Congress is the nerve-end of the polity, roll-call votes in Congress are often the most definite indication of political trends.

Roll-call voting data constitute one of the more important kinds of archival sources for systematic inquiry in political science. One reason is that these data are easily and cheaply available.[1] More significantly, these votes involve many and perhaps most of the major political issues and, to a lesser extent, positions on these issues, of a given time. But careful attention should always be paid to issues and viewpoints *not* represented in Congress or at the roll-call voting stage of the legislative process. What issues and positions may be absent from the roll-call records may be discovered by examining the wider range of views found in congressional committee hearings, policy journals, and other political literature across the spectrum from left to right.

The unique advantage of roll-call votes lies with their *comparability:* (*a*) comparability of all legislators within the same chamber (House or Senate) with all other legislators on the same votes; (*b*) comparability of all issues with all other issues voted on by the same legislators; and (*c*) comparability of both legislators and issues across different time periods. When one considers the two alternative means of achieving such comparability, content analysis and systematic interviewing, one realizes why roll-call data are unique. Systematic interviews cannot assume more than a half-hour interview per Congressman under most circumstances, and one cannot cover very much ground in that amount of time. Content analyses are constrained by the fact that most Congressmen and Senators have said very little on most issues, at least on the record or in any recorded place; thus content analyses could seldom be used to compare statements on very many issues of a very wide range of members.

Roll-call votes are especially important for examining the roles played by parties, coalitions, blocs, and groups, and for discovering how the balance of power among them determines legislative outcomes. Roll calls also can be used to compare the differences in support and opposition among different issues, which

* Written specifically for this volume.

can illuminate differences in the politics of those issues. (For example, do Presidents of both parties have a freer hand in foreign policy than in domestic policy?) Finally, in a host of studies patterns of roll-call voting are correlated with variables drawn from outside Congress to determine what is affecting outcomes.

There are three main approaches to analysing votes in Congress. All three have their virtues and liabilities, and each is more suitable to some analytic situations than to others.

THE FIRST APPROACH—THE USE OF KEY VOTES

One of the most useful and frequently utilized approaches to employing congressional roll-call votes is the key vote approach. While some analysts have occasion to construct their own key vote index for a particular purpose, many more utilize the key vote indexes put out by lobby groups. These lobby groups rate each Congressman or Senator on a selected group of key votes important to that lobby, and the selection of which votes to use can be assumed to reflect the special competence of close observers who choose only the most indicative roll calls. Key vote indexes include those put forward by broad-gauged ideological groups, such as the liberal Americans for Democratic Action (ADA), the AFL–CIO Committee on Political Education (COPE), the U.S. Chamber of Commerce (CCUS), and the conservative Americans for Constitutional Action (ACA). ACA and ADA ratings are near mirror images of one another; invariably, if a member has a high rating on one of these two, he or she will have a proportionately low rating on the other.[2] ADA ratings are the most frequently used by academic analysts, probably because of the great importance of ideology in Congress, the weakness of party cohesion at least among the Democrats, and becasue ADA key votes bear an especially clear relationship to the principal dimensions of political conflict—foreign policy, economic policy, race, and civil liberties–democracy issues.

There are, in addition, many rating groups with narrower concerns. These include such groups as the right-wing American Security Council, whose National Security Index reflects support or opposition to major defense expenditures and programs, the pro consumer Consumers' Federation of America, the National Farmers Union, which represents small farmers, and Environmental Action, which publishes each year a "dirty dozen" list of the members with the worst environmental records. There are many more lobby groups publishing such ratings. They all want to put the voting records of members in the spotlight in order to increase their accountibility to voters and other more organized supporters of the lobby group's position. Care must be exercised, however, not to overinterpret the ratings. A member's voting record on a few, highly visible votes may be a poor indicator of legislative and political capabilities; a rating may reveal little or nothing of a legislator's leadership capability, particularly abilities relating to policy innovation, issue dramatization, the mobilization of support, negotiation of compromises, and advancement of the capacity of party or of the Congress as an institution, to name but some of the roles of a Congressman or Senator. It has even been true that members have had, from one point of view or another, an excellent voting record while turning out to be notoriously corrupt.

Analyses aimed at understanding congressional behavior as a whole have frequently made use of lobby ratings. An excellent recent example is a study that raised the question of the ideological differences between the Democrats and the Republicans in both the Senate and the House between 1965 and 1978. While some observers have claimed that there is little significant difference between the parties, this study, using ADA ratings, purports to demonstrate that nationally and regionally, excepting the 13 states of the South, there is a systematic ideological gulf of "dramatic" proportions separating the parties in both chambers. While the Democrats are a slightly left of center party, the Republicans are homogeneously clustered on the far right wing, with a half dozen Republican exceptions in the Senate and a very few exceptions in the House.[3]

In addition to the problem of the differences between visible and less visible votes, key votes also have the problem that many minor votes, which separately are of no great importance, cumulatively may add up to be quite significant. This is especially true in fiscal policy, though the new congressional budget process and the new era of near ubiquitous fiscal conservativism prompted by the onset of double-digit inflation make it much more likely that these so-called minor or "distributive" bills will come under much greater scrutiny for their larger cumulative effects.

Three other key vote indexes—all produced by the *Congressional Quarterly Weekly Report* (CQ)—are often used. They are (1) the Conservative coalition support and opposition ratings, (2) the party unity support and opposition scores, and (3) the ratings of presidential support. The Conservative coalition is considered by CQ to be operative in a vote when a majority of voting Republicans and a majority of southern Democrats oppose the stand taken by a majority of Northern Democrats. In the 1970s only 20 or 30 percent of all recorded votes manifested this coalition pattern, which seems low when viewed from the vantage point of studies that employ substantive definitions of "conservative" and "liberal." Use of ADA and ACA ratings to demarcate ideological coalitions with key votes seems preferable, as they at least give us some broad substantive basis for anchoring the meaning of these ideological categories.[4]

On firmer ground are CQ's party unity and presidential support scores. Party unity votes are those recorded votes in the Senate and House on which a majority of voting Democrats oppose a majority of voting Republicans. Between 1976 and 1979 the percentage of all recorded votes that were party unity votes varied in both chambers between about 35 percent and nearly 50 percent. A member's party unity score is simply the percentage of party unity votes on which a member votes with the majority of his or her party.[5] Presidential support and opposition scores involve the much more complex prior determinations by CQ on a vote-by-vote basis of what a President personally, as opposed to other Administration officials, does and does not want, and computing a member's support and opposition scores accordingly. These votes are sometimes used as a very rough basis for comparing differences in congressional support for different Presidents in various parts of their terms of office.[6]

A SECOND APPROACH—FORMAL ANALYSIS

A prominent mode of analysis among political scientists is formal analysis; the essence of this as defined here is to ignore information extrinsic to the body of roll-call votes to be analysed, treating roll calls as "hard data" to be considered *in vacuo,* while searching for patterns among the votes. Often patterns among roll calls so derived are subsequently examined in relation to other non-roll-call variables. Formal analysis relies solely on statistical analysis, usually dimensional analysis or cluster analysis more broadly. Since the range and character of these treatments are too complex to be summarized in this space, the reader is referred to the standard work on the subject.[7]

A major goal of formal analysis is objectivity of the research product. Even research motivated by partisan concerns, insofar as it attempts to discover the true character of reality, is concerned with objectivity. Objectivity merely means that a study is replicable; i.e., the findings of the study can be reproduced by other researchers operating under roughly the same conditions and using the same or equally defensible methods. But objectivity is different from validity. A study may be wholly objective and at the same time wholly wrong, if, for example, it ignores important aspects of a problem. Formal analyses of roll calls, by ignoring circumstances under which a roll-call vote takes place—i.e., by ignoring any information that might lead to different interpretations of what the vote accomplished or was meant to accomplish—may be wholly objective and quite wrong. In an important paper on this subject, a leading expert on congressional voting, who is accomplished in formal analyses, argues that dimensional studies are mistaken in suspending judgment regarding the substantive properties of roll-call data. He states:

> Whether the research is conducted by an initial choice of a single objective procedure of dimensional analysis or by trying different procedures, I am concerned mainly with the temptation to accept mindless dictates of the objective technique. This sometimes takes the form of an unwillingness to be subjectively selective regarding the data to be entered into an analytic operation, such as factor analysis, and at other times appears in the strenuous and tortured effort to find meaning in the results that are generated; indeed the latter effort may be required as compensation for the prior lack of selectivity.[8]

We shall have occasion below to make a great deal out of the general need for such prior selectivity. The same writer, in arguing for methods based on prior sorting into content categories, attributes a number of other major problems to formal analysis, including measurement error effects and inadequacies of mere demonstrations of scalar-consistent voting alignments, among others. He further adds: "The changing context of a longitudinal study tends to destroy one's confidence in the immutability of data patterns described at a single point in time with the use of objective methods."[9]

That roll calls are not "hard data" like births and deaths, but for most analytical purposes are only indicators of properties that we try to measure indirectly by reference to roll-calls, is explained in the section that follows.

This is *not* to say that a formal analysis *won't* arrive at a true representation of, for example, the coalition structure of voting in the Senate. Indeed, one such formal analysis[10] has recently reproduced the finding of a unidimensional ideological (left-right) structure that had been the result of the kind of "situational" analysis described in the next section. Rather, the point is twofold: (*a*) formal analysis is *unlikely* to be valid; and more important, (*b*) if it is valid, we would be so much less sure that it was valid, because so many of the relevant properties of votes were ignored, that we would be as likely as not to wonder if the results were mere artifacts of the methods.

A THIRD APPROACH— "SITUATIONAL" ANALYSIS

This approach, which has several variants,[11] combines the advantages of the formal approach—statistical subtlety and sensitivity along with replicability—with techniques that can also treat roll-call votes in a way that takes account of factors operative in the situation of each vote, while making clarity and theoretical meaningfulness of the results of analysis more probable than formal analyses would.

The major premise of a situational approach is that roll-call votes ought not to be analysed in a vacuum, separated from contextually based considerations, *because these votes are often false, misleading, or opaque as indicators of the operative intent* of a given legislator, group of legislators, or their cue-setters in casting a particular vote. Votes, in this view, must be looked at within the context of floor debates, committee hearings and reports, news stories, and, what is rarely done but is imperative, in the context of policy analyses and overviews such as the Brookings Institution's annual review of the issues and options of budget policy.[12]

Let us be very clear why and how roll-call votes are often false, misleading, or opaque as indicators of voting intent. One kind of vote that is misleading is what is usually called an "ends-against-the-middle" vote—a vote in which parts of ordinarily cohesive groups that are opposed to each other vote together for opposite reasons against the other parts, who vote together for a compromise. An instance of such a vote occurred when some conservatives and some liberals voted together against the Nixon Administration's welfare reform legislation, the former because it gave too much to welfare recipients and the latter because it gave too little.

Clearly, to treat a significant number of such votes as if everyone voting against the bill did so from similar motives would distort analysis. The error would be apparent if the floor debate was also scrutinized.

A second kind of error that stems from taking votes at face value can be called an error of "spurious comparability." Someone investigating the bases of support over time for a particular policy—e.g., foreign aid—might be tempted to assume that a vote on a foreign aid bill in 1949 involved the same policy content and reasons behind yeas and nays as a vote on a foreign aid bill in 1981, since they are both votes on "foreign aid." But such an assumption perhaps ought not to be made, given how much the goals of aid along with the list of recipient countries and multilateral institutions have changed between 1949 and 1981. If one wanted to establish, rather than baldly assume, the comparability of those two foreign aid votes, the reasons of supporters and opponents at the two times should be compared from floor debates and committee testimony.

A third major problem of roll calls taken at face value is that differences exist among them with respect to their *reversibility*—that is, to the extent to which a vote can be undone by another vote or by action or inaction in other parts of the legislative and administrative processes, and is cast with such anticipations. Some votes *are* truly decisive decisions in being strictly determinative of a policy or outcome that cannot be undone. The vote on the Clark Amendment barring U.S. intervention in Angola in December 1975 is a good example. The vote did indeed determine an outcome that, given the beliefs and dispositions of the Ford Administration and Secretary of State Kissinger, would have been quite different had either the Clark Amendment failed to pass or if there had been no vote either way. But many votes are *not* decisive and are meant to be undone. The former Republican Senator from Vermont, George Aiken, discussing his "sins" on the occasion of his retirement, noted:

> During the 34 years of my tenure as a United States Senator, I have committed many sins. I have voted for measures which I felt were wrong, comforting myself with the excuse that the House of Representatives, the conference committee, or, if necessary, the chief occupant of the White House would make the proper corrections.
>
> At other times, I have voted for measures with which I did not agree for the purpose of preventing the approval of other measures which I felt would be worse.[13]

No one would call his behavior at all unusual.

A fourth reason votes often are not what they appear to be can only be apparent by watching a vote take place. From the gallery one can regularly observe a clerk of the Senate calling out, after a preliminary vote tally, "Does any Senator wish to change his vote?" The *Congressional Record* prints no account of this or related events: not the initial vote and tally, not the vote changes, not that some Senators hold back until it is known whether their vote is needed, and not that some Senators change their vote to satisfy some attentive public after the test of strength has been made. There are similar problems associated with votes in the House.

Fifth, a wide variety of tactics may obscure the real character of a vote on an amendment or bill. Tactics include: tacking on riders or unrelated amendments (often to appropriations bills) to defeat otherwise passable legislation; proposing an amendment that destroys a carefully contrived but fragile compromise package; voting for a bill on final passage in order to appear favorable to the legislation to constituents after having voted to "gut" the bill with weakening amendments.[14] These are only a few of such tactics.

Sixth, taking bills at face value may be not merely inappropriate but impossible, because many bills voted on in Congress are such that their real content is *opaque*. The manifest bill content is opaque as to what the bill is intended to do and what the bill's different effects, directly and indirectly, in the short and long terms, would be on different groups. It is a complex task to determine the distribution of benefits and costs that would result from the passage of a piece of legislation. Much of what goes on in the legislative process hinges on that fact. The struggle to understand such effects, and to enable others within and outside Congress to be alerted to the distributional effects of a piece of legislation, or to obscure such understanding or prevent its dissemination, is a large part of the political process generally and the legislative process regularly.

Ideology is particularly important in determining roll-call voting[15] and yet is *particularly opaque*. Ideology usually involves claims of some against others, and the justification of those claims, that manifest the classic theme of deprivation versus privilege, refracted through theories of the economy, of international relations, and of democracy. For example, ideology in the realm of the economy draws on theories and policies related to economic growth of various kinds, capital supply and allocation, investment behavior, savings behavior, consumption behavior, labor market behavior (notably "implicit contracts"), theories of the causes, costs, and remedies of inflation, and the social stratification of various kinds of well-being and deprivation, all enmeshed in an international economic setting. Vast and complex as these matters are even to economists outside their fields of specialization, much of what Congress votes on involves these matters. No wonder, if such matters are the stuff of ideology, that ideology has been particularly opaque to political scientists. *But Congressmen,* acting on the cues of other key Congressmen, staff, experts, and interest-group leaders, respond to such opaque considerations even when they don't understand them!

Last, the body of roll-call votes itself can be misleading, particularly regarding the relations of majority and minority coalitions, if one fails to grasp that the universe of all roll-call votes is a *truncated agenda* of issues and positions. Since the committee stage reveals far more about minority issues and positions than appears at the stage of floor voting, one appropriate research strategy is to formulate hypotheses from the much more revealing committee stage, and then test those hypotheses with roll-call data.

To summarize the argument so far, if the comparability features of roll-call votes are to be taken advantage of, the misinterpretation of roll calls must be avoided. Heinz Eulau has written:

> There has always been trouble with studies of legislative behavior that rely solely on roll calls. . . . More statistical and methodological sophistication will not change the inherent weakness of the roll call as an indicator of either a legislator's "position" (vis-à-vis other legislators or on issues) or others' "influence" on his position. Simply too much happens in the legislative game before the yeas and nays are counted.[16]

SITUATIONAL ANALYSIS—METHODOLOGICAL ASPECTS

The core of a situational analysis is a three- or four-part method. Part I is the coding of each individual roll call within a chosen time period into categories derived from theoretical or situational considerations. Part II is the statistical analysis of patterns among roll-call votes in the derived categories. Part III is the tabular presentation of each roll-call assignment (by CQ number) under each category (and presentation of the item direction assignment of each roll call, where a situational assignment method is used) to facilitate precise replications and challenges by other researchers. Part IV, *if* called for by a particular research purpose, aims to examine the statistical relationship between (*a*) the patterns of roll-call voting derived in parts I and II, and (*b*) other variables extrinsic to congressional votes. Part IV will not be discussed below.

Part I: Coding Individual Roll Calls

Three kinds of coding are involved: excluding votes, coding votes into content categories, and item direction assignment. Let us take each in turn.

EXCLUDED VOTES

It has become traditional to adopt the rule of excluding votes in which 10 percent or less of the membership of the chamber, or 10 percent of those voting, vote in opposition. Omitting roll calls with such extreme splits is desirable because they are relatively weak tests of dimensionality; not to exclude such votes might have the effect of invalidly obscuring dimensionality that actually exists in the universe of other roll-call votes. It has been suggested that, for some analytic purposes, it might be appropriate to use a 15 to 20 percent cut-off point.[17] However, if one makes assumptions, implicit in the concern over public financing of congressional campaigns, about the unrepresentativeness of the electoral process, then to exclude votes with as much as 20 percent in opposition might be to ignore a segment of opinion in Congress that represented a much larger segment of public opinion. This might be especially true for the Senate of the 97th Congress. The customary 10 percent criterion seems, therefore, appropriate.

The following additional categories of roll-call votes that one might also exclude are especially appropriate to the study of coalition behavior, but should be considered tentatively vis-à-vis a broader list of analytic goals:

1. Votes to recess or adjourn. Such votes seldom have any policy content or relationship, rather reflecting the needs of overburdened legislators and a crowded legislative schedule.

2. Where partisanship is not a relevant variable in a given study, votes should be excluded on the partisan organization of the House and Senate at the beginning of the first session of each Congress.

3. Votes on unusually particularistic minor bills involving no funding or tiny amounts of money. These votes often occur in the House under suspension of the rules (requiring a two-thirds vote for passage) and would not be described as interest group votes exemplary of any wider pattern of voting. Examples include increases in pensions for widows of Supreme Court Justices, authorization of a monument to Mary McCleod Bethune, designation of a day to commemorate the 1915 massacre of Armenians by Turks, and amendments concerning the American Revolution Bicentennial. These votes are always very nearly unanimous votes by the 10 percent criterion.

These three categories of exclusion involve virtually no problem of coding reliability. Moreover, they involve a very small proportion of the total roll-call vote universe. The following categories of excluded votes involve a much more substantial question of intercoder reliability or replicability. Ways to meet this reliability problem are discussed below.

4. Votes in which a substantial issue of House or Senate prerogatives, norms or rules, or House versus Senate prerogatives or congressional versus presidential or executive branch prerogatives were explicitly raised in floor debate in such a way as to evidence both a substantial concern and clear independence from either policy or ideological considerations.

5. Following CQ's practice,[18] votes on final passage of appropriation and supplemental appropriations bills. Often these votes are on appropriations for several Departments, such as Commerce, Justice, and State, in a single vote. Members are uncomfortable voting against a broad category of legislation—e.g., defense appropriations as a whole—despite having voted for all manner of amendments that would have substantially altered the bill as it finally passed. Opposition at the point of final passage is not only useless; it also is uninterpretable and hence sends a signal to no one. For the same reasons, all votes on final passage could justifiably be excluded, as could most votes to adopt conference committee reports.[19] When these votes are not actually unanimous, they probably would be so counted if the unaminous vote exclusion criterion were 15 or 20 percent instead of 10 percent.

6. "Ends-against-the middle" votes, as described earlier, are the votes most important to exclude in *all* research contexts. They often involve the most recurrent political dilemma: whether to compromise or hold out for something more. It is never easy to decide whether a bill's good outweighs the harm. The propriety of excluding such votes derives from the fact that, as described above, such votes involve

groups voting together to defeat a compromise for contradictory reasons.

Some studies also exclude votes with high absenteeism, and this option should be carefully considered for earlier Congresses at least. Missing data procedures have been used in some circumstances to exclude the votes of legislators with high absenteeism.[20] Because of the recorded teller vote reform instituted in the House at the beginning of the 92d Congress, the problem of missing data in the House all but vanishes from that time for most analytic purposes, and simply ignoring missing votes is the most parsimonious approach. In the Senate, if one avoids rare years such as 1976, when so many Democratic Senators sought their party's presidential nomination, there is no serious problem of high absenteeism of any significant number of Senators on recorded votes. For pre-teller reform House votes—that is, pre-1972 Congresses—the invalidity of the votes as indicators of basic relationships is probably great enough that the researcher should only use carefully selected key votes.

Perhaps the wisest procedure, one allowing the greatest insights, is to statistically analyze one's results both with and without excluding all or some of the above kinds of excluded votes, thus allowing those who differ with the appropriateness of some or all of these exclusions to draw their own conclusions about the results. Moreover, if, as described below, the excluded votes are listed in an appendix by category of exclusion, other researchers can pinpoint disagreements with an analysis, allowing for closer comparisons among different studies.

It is sometimes thought that the formalist analyses described above exclude no roll-call votes and therefore are more "objective" than procedures that exclude votes on individual bases as just described. That is in fact often not the case. Votes are excluded but by a different and equally dubious method. One criticism of an influential study makes the point:

> Clausen first classifies roll calls into issue domains on the basis of their substantive content. He then applies a type of cluster analysis to the roll calls within each issue domain. Clausen uses the most comprehensive dimension to represent each domain in later analysis. The strict clustering criteria used insure that the roll calls constituting this primary dimension are homogenous, *but, at the same time limit it to the comprehensiveness of the primary dimension. Thus, on the average, 35 percent of the roll calls in the economic and welfare domains are not included in the primary dimensions. . . . A procedure which stays closer to the data than the sophisticated clustering and scaling techniques do is needed.* The smoothing of the data which these techniques accomplish is likely to smooth out just what one is looking for. (italics added.)[21]

This criticism can be extended to other studies.

CODING VOTES INTO CONTENT CATEGORIES

There is not space here to describe the theoretical bases for deriving content categories, as this will vary considerably from one study to another. But the importance and sometimes the difficulty of this part of an analysis is greater then any other part. In understanding congressional voting, Congress generally, and most political inquiry, the most successful theories—those that have accounted for the most variation in the most important behavior—have come from those observers with the deepest substantive knowledge of the interaction of politics, policy (especially economic policy and foreign policy), political subcultures of elites and mass publics, and institutions.

One major argument for the scientific status of content coding is that such coding of roll calls as indicators of dimensions (represented by coding categories) constitutes *a hypothesis* regarding the relationship between the indicator and the dimension it purports to indicate.[22] The confirmation of each hypothesis is obtained, in part, by results of analysis yielding high degrees of dimensionality or high correlation coefficients. Thus Duncan MacRae has stated:

> The use of *a priori* indices must therefore be considered as corresponding to the hypothesis

> stage of research; but the hypothesis that the index or category measures something must be tested. Again, methods such as scale analysis and cluster analysis provide a possibility for this test. They are not the only test since the verification of substantive hypotheses also supports by implication the measures of the variable used.[23]

In the same vein, Leslie Kish has stated:

> There are extraneous variables which are *controlled*. The control may be exercised in either or both the selection and the estimation procedures.[24]

High coefficients, when obtained, do not stand alone as confirming an hypothesis. Confirmation also involves simultaneous disconfirmation of competing hypotheses, substantive cogency of the theory from which the hypothesis is derived, cogency in terms of contextual factors, verisimilitude to the process modeled, and appropriateness of statistics and modes of measurement used. Above all, such hypotheses are further confirmed by replication. Thus we see how content coding is scientifically supported.

ITEM DIRECTION ASSIGNMENT

There are two methods of item direction assignments that one might choose. The best technique would be to use both and compare the results, but there is no such effort extant, probably because both alone are very time-consuming. Item direction assignment in either case is logically prior to interindividual analysis—i.e., to the analysis of patterns of relationship among groups of legislators.

The first method would utilize a correlational mode capable of distinguishing sign patterns to determine which of two polar values should be assigned to each roll call.[25]

The second method is a situational analysis of each vote. The discussion here is limited to the case of item direction coding according to a ''liberal equals yea'' or ''liberal equals nay'' coding of each roll call. Based on close observation of Congress and of particular Congressmen and Senators, a list is constructed of very liberal (progressive), moderately liberal, moderately conservative, and very conservative members, with particular emphasis on those who are most likely to be cue-setters. ADA and ACA ratings can be used for this purpose. Then CQ's presentation of how each member voted on each roll call is scrutinized by looking at these groups to see if they were cohesive on that vote. A quick way to scan for cohesion is to look at CQ's summary tally of northern Democrats, southern Democrats, and Republicans for splits among these normally cohesive groups. Where there are odd combinations, one follows a certain progression or ''paper trail'' to understand what happened on that vote—i.e., the basis of the voting alignment that took place. First, one reads CQ's story or stories as referenced by them, if any. If that fails, one reads the floor debate at the time of the vote. If that is insufficient, one reads the relevant committee hearings. If still confused, one reads expert analyses by policy analysts who have given testimony to the relevant congressional committees and other policy analysts in the field, striving always to encompass all views from left to right. Only a very small number of votes will require searching back as far as hearings and beyond. Macroeconomic policy and foreign policy votes require the greatest background.

This procedure is carried on simultaneously for all three parts of the coding of individual roll-call votes—excluding votes, coding votes into content categories, and item direction assignment.

PART II: STATISTICAL ANALYSIS OF ROLL-CALL PATTERNS—COHESION

While any number of research questions generate their own peculiar needs for statistical analysis, two particular foci have been central to the analysis of Congress and of legislatures generally. These two foci are the measurement of party cohesion and the measurement of bloc or factional cohesion, with special emphasis on ideological factions.

The centrality of the concern with cohesion flows from the nature of politics. Issues divide opposing sides. Concern with issues leads one to wonder over the character and strength of opposing forces, including their durability across time and across different issues. Some issues may divide forces that are cohesive on other issues. Some coalitions may come together only over a narrow band of issues and/or for a short time, while other coalitions' durability may be the most central characteristic of a whole political system in a particular period. Thus, the question of cohesion of wider or narrower groups of legislators over wider or narrow groups of issues over time is a fundamental concern. Parties are merely formalized coalitions that are weak or strong in part because of, or as reflected in, their degree of cohesion.

The essence of the most sensitive group of methods for the statistical analysis of cohesion is ''pairwise'' comparison of the votes or index scores of Senators, Congressmen, or, because the House has 435 members and a matrix of that size can't be managed by existing computer technology, a sample of Congressmen. A pairwise comparison constructs a matrix of all ''agreement'' scores, variously represented statistically, among all possible pairs of legislators or roll calls. Blocs or factions can be defined as subsets of legislators occupying the same parts of the space between maximum and minimum agreement scores. Typically, a nonparametric, ordinal-level statistic is judged most valid in representing the degree of agreement between two legislators. Then, one or another form of dimensional or cluster analysis is applied to the matrix of scores to derive a general characterization of the degree of cohesion within different blocs or factions. Alternately, matrices of relations between pairs of roll calls can reveal issue dimensions by cluster or dimensional analysis of the array of all possible pairs of all roll calls. However, the two types of matrices, those of legislator agreement scores and those of roll calls, often correspond closely, as do the indexes that summarize them.[26]

Part III: Facilitating Replication by Tabular Presentations of Coding Decisions

Many of the above coding decisions might be considered ''subjective''—i.e., not replicable—but for what we now introduce. There are three groups of coding decisions whose reliability or replicability is questionable in a situational analysis—excluding votes, coding votes into content categories, and item direction assignment by the situational technique. This problem is avoided by arraying for each vote the exclusion or content category to which it was assigned, and the assigned item direction, in an appendix, using CQ vote numbers. If space permits, the reason for the assignment can be given in a sentence, with citation of the place in the documentary record where the evidence for the coding decision was found. *Then,* scholars wishing to challenge the findings of an analysis can specify and test in a pinpointed way whether and how they disagree.[27]

CHAPTER

8 Policy Relationships in Congress: Constituents, Interest Groups, Executive

Policy making in Congress does not occur in a vacuum. Congress is the focus of lobbying efforts by individual constituents, organized interests, Executive Branch personnel, and the President. Thus, to understand the congressional policy process, one must have an appreciation for the policy relationships that exist between Congress and other actors and institutions seeking to influence congressional outcomes. Articles offered in this chapter examine policy relationships with constituents, groups, and the President.

A major point to be emphasized in studying policy relationships in that the activity, involvement, and influence of different actors is highly variable, depending on situational factors. Groups are most apt to be influential on highly particularized and nonvisible legislation. The President is likely to influence legislative affairs when his popularity is high, he has strong support in Congress, and a featured plank in his program is at stake. Congressional party leaders usually are most successful on procedural and low-profile votes not involving ideological, state or constituency concerns.

Another point is that Executive Branch lobbying is not monolithic. Not all Executive Branch lobbyists are pursuing the Administration's package. Frequently, agencies pursue their own narrow self-interests in the congressional process, even if at odds with or out of step with the President's program.

8.1 Why Do Americans Love Their Congressmen So Much More Than Their Congress?*

Glenn R. Parker and Roger H. Davidson

The topic of interaction between members of Congress and their constituents in their constituencies has been much neglected. A book by Richard Fenno—*Home Place: Congressmen in Their Constituencies*—is the first to really examine the "home-style" behavior of Congressmen. An important concept of member-constituency relationships examined by Fenno is that "We love our Congressmen but hate the Congress." Parker and Davidson examine this proposition and its implications.

ABSTRACT

This paper provides some evidence for answering the puzzle posed by Richard Fenno (1975, p. 286):† "We love our Congressmen so much more than our Congress." The data come from two national public opinion surveys dealing with attitudes and perceptions of Congress, conducted in 1968 and 1977. They show that Congress is judged, increasingly in unfavorable terms, on the basis of its performance on domestic policy, legislative–executive relations, and the style and pace of the legislative process. Congressmen, on the other hand, are judged—usually favorably—primarily on the basis of their service to constituents and their personal characteristics.

INTRODUCTION

The past decade has witnessed the spread of public cynicism concerning established political institutions. The available evidence suggests that alienation from the polity is a fairly widespread phenomenon, penetrating all countries, and bringing to the surface fundamental questions about the legitimacy of political institutions and authorities.

A recurring theme in critiques of the American political system is the citizen's dismay at the inability of government to perform, an impediment that Seymour Lipset (1963, pp. 64–70) singles out as detrimental to political stability. Felix Frankfurter (1930, p. 3) characterized distrust of Depression-era government as an indication that people felt that government was unable to satisfy the needs of a modern society. In a later and presumably more benign era, Morris Rosenberg (1951, p. 14) contended that politics meant "very little to people because it literally does little for them," and that governmental action was considered by many as "irrelevant to their lives" (1954, p. 364). Such a posture toward government probably affects the public's image of political officials. In fact, William C. Mitchell (1959, p. 693) has suggested that such officials are not viewed as performing vital services because political functions themselves are not considered as providing a societal contribution.

---

* From Glenn R. Parker and Roger H. Davidson, "Why Do Americans Love Their Congressman So Much More than Their Congress?" *Legislative Studies Quarterly* 4, no. 1 (February 1979): 53–61.

†Reference list in Endnotes.

Public assessments of governmental performance can be described in terms of three components: confidence, impact, and evaluation. *Confidence* reflects the degree to which individuals have faith in the actions of their officials and/or institutions. The extent to which governmental activity is perceived as affecting an individual's life is a measure of the *impact* of governmental performance. *Evaluations* are explicit judgments of the value the individual assigns to that impact. In this research note we focus on the last-mentioned component—the content of public evaluations of one political institution, the U.S. Congress.

Citizens' evaluations are certainly important in and of themselves. But in reporting these assessments, we too often overlook the bases of their judgments—that is, the criteria individuals use in forming their evaluations. Thus, the objective of this analysis is to describe the standards used in appraising Congress and its membership and to examine response categories in an effort to gauge the likelihood that certain standards generate favorable evaluations.

The findings are based on opinion surveys administered to national population samples (Harris, 1968; U.S. House of Representatives, 1977). Of particular interest are the responses elicited from two open-ended survey items concerning evaluations of Congress and the respondent's representative. In both surveys, individuals were first asked how they would evaluate the performance of Congress—excellent, pretty good, only fair, or poor. Respondents were then queried about the criteria upon which they based their evaluation. Later in the interview sessions, the same questioning was used to ascertain respondent's judgment of their representative's performance in the U.S. House of Representatives. The multiple-response nature of the open-ended questionnaire items allowed individuals the opportunity to provide as many different criteria as they desired. The responses to the above items were then coded and categorized on the basis of the criteria volunteered and, if discernible, the favorable or unfavorable nature of the responses.[1]

ANALYSIS

Domestic policy is the most frequently mentioned criteria for evaluating Congress (Table 8.1.1). Although the centrality of domestic policy appears to have declined somewhat since late 1968, it still is the most frequenlty cited basis for evaluating Congress. The valence associated with domestic policy has also changed in the last several years. While in 1968 domestic policy seemed to divide the electorate equally into those satisfied and dissatisfied with congressional actions, such policy actions had a distinctly negative effect in 1977: 93 percent of those citing domestic policy as a basis for their evaluations of Congress were negative in their assessments of congressional performance.

In late 1968, the Vietnam War's salience took its toll on the popularity of Congress. Of those who cited foreign policy as a basis for evaluation, nearly two thirds had negative evaluations. Several years later, in the absence of major American involvement in a foreign war, few people mentioned foreign policy considerations in evaluating Congress. As the Vietnam War and other foreign ventures began to fade from media attention and public consciousness, domestic policy conflicts gained greater saliency with the public. The ideological and partisan differences between those controlling the White House and Congress served to exacerbate the natural conflicts that the "sharing of power" produces. The resulting policy statements generated negative evaluations of congressional performances. In 1977, three of every four mentions of legislative–executive relations as a basis for evaluating Congress were negative.

Another frequently mentioned basis for assessing Congress is the style and pace of the legislative process. In fact, there appears to be an increase in the saliency of the congressional environment as a basis for congressional evaluations. In 1977, one of every three responses made reference to the congressional environment, and these references were distinctly negative. It seems clear that the congressional environment, like legislative–executive rela-

TABLE 8.1.1 BASES OF EVALUATIONS OF CONGRESS (IN PERCENTAGES)

	1968*			1977†		
BASES OF EVALUATION	PERCENT OF ALL RESPONSES (N=1370)	FAVORABLE	UNFAVORABLE	PERCENT OF ALL RESPONSES (N=1813)	FAVORABLE	UNFAVORABLE
Policy	51.8%			30.8%		
Domestic	46.3	54	46	30.1	7	93
Foreign-defense	5.5	35	65	0.7	100	—
Legislative-executive relations	6.5			19.6		
Presidential support	3.1	72	28	—	—	—
Presidential opposition	3.4	56	44	19.6	25	75
Congressional environment	16.0			37.1		
Congressional style and pace	10.2	38	62	23.1	30	70
Congressional ethics	2.4	—	100	4.9	—	100
Congressional self-seeking	3.4	—	100	9.1	—	100
Group treatment	4.2	66	34	1.4	50	50
Other	6.4	27	73	8.4	33	67
Repeat of closed-ended question	12.0					
Don't know/not ascertained	3.0			2.8		
Total	99.9			100.1		

* *Question:* "How would you rate the job Congress did this past year in 1968—excellent, pretty good, only fair, or poor? Why do you feel this way? Any other reasons?"

† *Question:* Overall, how would you rate the job Congress as a whole—that is, the House of Representatives—has done during the past two or three years—would you say Congress has done an excellent job, a pretty good job, only a fair job, or a poor job? Why do you feel this way? Any other reasons?"

tions, tends to foster negative evaluations of Congress.

In light of the saliency of the various criteria, it is not too surprising that evaluations of Congress are often negative. The range and volume of policies and problems for which Congress is held accountable—by the media and the public—create numerous opportunities for dissatisfaction with congressional performance. The cumbersome legislative process, which often gives the appearance of delay and inaction, may be a necessary evil for the constitutional system, but it is not an attribute that appeals to the public. Further, both domestic policy and the legislative environment are frequently mentioned as bases for evaluating Congress. In short, the most salient concerns of the public appear to be those that frequently generate negative impressions of congressional performance.

The criteria for evaluating Congress and those applied in evaluating individual Representatives show few parallels. Evaluations of Representatives tend to be based upon constituency service provided the district and the personal attributes of incumbents (Table 8.1.2). In addition, these criteria tend to place incumbent House members in a favorable light; most of what people hear (or retain) about incumbents is favorable. In fact, the reputation of House members was the most frequently mentioned criterion for evaluating the performance of incumbents. More than 70 percent of the responses refer to some aspect of the incumbents' constituency service or personal attributes.

Policy actions, in contrast, are infrequently cited as criteria for evaluating the Representative. This may be a blessing to House members, inasmuch as references to public policy tend to be negative in content. The infrequent use of policy criteria and the emphasis on personal characteristics and district service promote positive evaluations of the incumbent. Rarely are the latter elements viewed in a negative light. In sum, evaluation of Congress and of individual members are apt to differ in valence because of the disparate criteria that are applied to each. Congress is held resposible for policy and for management of the legislative environment, while individual Representatives are evaluated in terms of their personal characteristics or constituency service.

CONCLUSIONS

Clearly, quite disparate criteria are used in evaluating Congress and individual Representatives. Furthermore, one's evaluative criteria influence the nature of one's appraisal; *certain criteria are associated with positive evaluations, while other criteria are identified with negative appraisals*. That is, the features of congressional activity that attract the concern and attention of individuals affect how congressional performance is evaluated. It also seems clear that evaluations of Representatives rest more on service to the district than on policy concerns; moreover, such service generally is perceived in a favorable light by constituents. It is no wonder, then, that members of Congress pay so much attention to constituency service—it generates a positive image. Congress, on the other hand, is assessed more in terms of its policy actions, which tend to produce mixed (or negative) evaluations of the institution.

These findings cast new light on a paradox posed by Richard F. Fenno, Jr.: How can we account for the contrast in the popularity of Congress on the one hand, and individual Representatives on the other? "If our Congressmen are so good," he asks (1975, p. 278), "how can our Congress be so bad? If it is the individuals that make up the institution, why should there be such a disparity in our judgments?"

One possible explanation for this disparity is that people simply apply divergent standards of judgment to Congress as an institution and to individual legislators. Fenno speculates (1975, pp. 278–80) that individual legislators are judged on the basis of personal style and policy views. Stylistically, we expect our legislators to display a solicitous attitude toward constituents—to appear frequently in the district, to maintain contact through the media, and to work on local projects and individual cases. As

TABLE 8.1.2 BASES OF EVALUATIONS OF MEMBERS OF CONGRESS (IN PERCENTAGES)

	1968*			1977†		
BASES OF EVALUATION	PERCENT OF ALL RESPONSES (N=1,258)	FAVORABLE	UNFAVORABLE	PERCENT OF ALL RESPONSES (N=1,232)	FAVORABLE	UNFAVORABLE
Policy	11.2%			3.0%		
Vague-reference	7.9	69	31	1.5	—	100
Specific reference	3.3	46	54	1.5	—	100
Constituency service	49.8			37.7		
District service	28.1	74	26	13.3	100	—
Constituent assistance	2.1	100	—	12.6	100	—
District conditions	2.7	91	9	3.7	100	—
Informs constituents	16.9	18	82	8.1	82	18
Personal attributes	26.9			35.6		
Personal characteristics	16.5	84	16	6.7	100	—
Reputation	9.4	95	5	28.9	67	33
Personal acquaintance	1.0	—	—	—	—	—
Group treatment	6.4	58	42	3.7	100	—
Other	0.3	50	50	10.4	57	43
Repeat of closed-ended question	2.7					
Don't know/not ascertained	2.7			9.7		
Total	100.0			100.1		

* *Question:* "How would you rate the service your Representative gives in looking after this district in Washington—excellent, pretty good, only fair, or poor? Why do you feel this way? Any other reasons?"

† *Question:* "Overall, how would you rate the job the Congressman who has been representing this area during the past two or three years has done—would you say your Congressman has done an excellent job, a pretty good job, a fair job, or a poor job? Why do you feel this way? Any other reasons?"

for policy views, we ask merely that our legislators not stray too far from the norm as expressed by a majority of constituents.

Our data support Fenno's speculations, and they further indicate how much precedence stylistic considerations take over policy concerns. No more than 15 percent of our respondents, by the most generous reckoning, cited policies in explaining how they rated their Representative. Unless they were specific, these policy references tended to tilt in the incumbents' favor. Fortunately for incumbents, few voters voice specific policy concerns—indeed, few voice policy concerns of any kind—in evaluating members' performance.

For Congress as an institution, in contrast, citizens enunciate the task of resolving national problems. This is a far more hazardous assignment than citizens set for individual Representatives. Many problems are virtually insoluble on a national scale; even if they were solved, would we be able to ascertain that fact? As we have seen, in assessing Congress, respondents mention policy factors more frequently than any other considerations. In the late 1960s, domestic policy concerns tended to produce favorable assessments, while foreign policy concerns yielded critical assessments by almost a two-to-one margin. A decade later, the valences were reversed. Legislative–executive relations also produce mixed reviews: Some people expect Congress to fall into line behind the President; others want it to resist White House initiatives and act as a watchdog. Finally, what citizens read and hear of Capitol Hill style carries an overwhelmingly negative message. Scandal and venality are highly visible features of legislative institutions; expertise and courage are less well publicized.

The present data, in short, give eloquent testimony to the reasons why we "love our Congressmen so much" yet denigrate the institution of Congress. Individual legislators are evaluated in terms of personal style and district service—attributes upon which few voters are able to make comparisons with other legislators. But Congress-as-institution is evaluated largely on the basis of policies—which tend to be intractable and divisive.

In view of the divergence we have found in the public's premises in assessing Congressmen and Congress, incumbents are entirely rational in emphasizing constituency service and equipping themselves with the necessary staff and perquisites to do the job. Members of the U.S. House have historically had a firm grassroots base, cultivated by constituency service as well as by localist legislative roles. There is nothing novel about this; indeed, the House was designed to operate in this fashion (*Wesberry* v. *Sanders,* 1964). Yet, students of Congress agree that recently legislative roles have shifted perceptibly in the direction of constituency service. As Fiorina (1977, p. 61) puts it, "Congressmen are going home more, pressing the flesh, getting around. They are building a personal base of support, one dependent on personal contacts and favors."

The present emphasis upon constituency errand-running, which appears to date from the mid-1960s, contrasts with at least some of the dominant House norms of the previous generation or two.

If the push toward errand-running is conceded, there remains a critical issue of cause and effect. Put bluntly, the question is: In erecting the machinery for constituency communication and service, did legislators mainly contrive to ensure their own reelection, or did they simply respond to what they assumed the public demanded?

Perhaps this question will never be answered with certainty. At the very least, we need to review carefully the sequence of events that produced the present congressional establishment, with special attention to the decade of the 1960s. Survey data should be reanalyzed to determine legislators' and citizens' states of mind during this period of time, even though such data are bound to yield a fragmentary and inconclusive picture.

The present findings nonetheless leave little room for doubt concerning the public's expectations for legislators' performance. The data indicate that, whereas citizens' expectations for Congress are vague and anchored to generalized policy and stylistic concerns, their expectations for their own Representatives are unmistakable. Legislators are judged very largely on the way they serve their districts and communicate with them. Successful performance of this aspect of the Representative's job typically pays off handsomely, as indicated by incumbents' high rates of reelection. Yet such judgments on the part of voters imply sanctions as well; legislators who lose touch or who seem preoccupied with national issues may be disciplined by declining support or even defeat. A few "lessons" of this type will suffice to persuade other legislators, who after all are politicians, to shift their job priorities.

Is it possible then that public expectation, rather than legislative connivance, is the cause of the bureaucratic establishment that supports constituency-oriented policymaking? If so, we may wish to modify the currently popular notion (Fiorina, 1977, p. 3) that Congressmen are to blame for this state of affairs. The public may well be the key to the Washington establishment. If the public did not create this establishment, they have inspired and sustained it, and are apt to continue to do.

8.2 Lobbyists and the Legislative Process*

John M. Bachellor

Lobbyists illustrate the good and the bad in the legislature. The good is that they provide a major source of communications and input to Representatives from the represented. The bad is that they frequently convey highly distorted and particularistic demands. This piece looks at the differential impact of lobbying activities. It spells out those conditions under which interest groups are likely to sway public policy.

ABSTRACT

In this study of lobbyists' techniques and perceptions of the legislative process, the impact of several aspects of the legislative environment is examined, including group competition and the use of issues by candidates in presidential campaigns. Data from a sample of lobbyists indicates that nonconflictual issues are treated differently by lobbyists and the Congress from issues involving group conflict. Similarly, issues used in presidential campaigns are treated differently from those developed outside them. Finally, group size is shown to be a further

* From John M. Bachellor, "Lobbyists and the Legislative Process: The Impact of Environmental Constraints," *American Political Science Review* 71 (1977): 252–63.

The author is indebted to Thomas Patterson and Robert deVoursney for their criticisms of the author's doctoral dissertation, from which this article has been adapted. The author is also indebted to Eugene Lewis, David Rosenbloom, Robert Kweit, and Jeffery Ross, and two anonymous editorial readers for their criticisms and advice. Financial support was provided by the Syracuse University Department of Political Science and the Huber Foundation through Kirkland College. Computing was done using the facilities of Hamilton and Kirkland Colleges and Cornell University.

influence on lobbyists' techniques in dealing with Congress.

INTRODUCTION

In the recent past we have seen a number of disparate studies describing the legislative process. The studies differ in the relative significance attached to committee and floor activity in Congress. Berman, for example, devotes considerable attention in his study of the 1960 Civil Rights Act to action and maneuvering on the floor.[1] Floor action in this case was a crucial aspect of the process and a serious potential obstacle to enactment. Since the time of Wilson, however, the congressional process has been described as being dominated by committees.[2] Leroy Rieselbach, for example, argues that "the central fact is, of course, that the autonomous committees make the major choices and that these are merely ratified at a later point in the proceedings by the entire chamber."[3]

Clearly, neither picture comprehensively portrays congressional action. Recent data from a study by Richard Fenno shows comparative committee success in getting favorable floor action. Fenno found that the Ways and Means Committee has managed to get more than 90 percent of its major legislation passed by the House, while Education and Labor has had a success rate of only about 60 percent in the recent past.[4] While both committees were more likely to be successful than not, one did considerably better than the other.

Studies of the relationships between interest groups and legislators differ about the nature of interaction between them. Milbrath argues, for example, that lobbyists generally use direct methods of contacting legislators (such as through personal presentation of viewpoints and research findings or through testimony at hearings). Yet he and others have also acknowledged that lobbyists at times use indirect approaches to Congressmen (i.e., through constituents).[5]

To explain the variations in patterns of interaction discussed above, a number of political scientists have provided theoretical overviews of legislative policymaking and the role of interest groups in it. Theodore Lowi, for example, argues that legislation can be classified according to its expected impact on society. The "arenas" he posits are said to show distinctive "political structure, political process, elites, and group relations."[6] Lowi argues that one may distinguish three kinds of policies. Those of narrow impact are made without respect to resources and are called *distributive* legislation. Policies of somewhat broader impact, involving choices about who will be deprived or indulged, are called *regulative*. Finally, those of still broader impact, affecting social classes or races, for example, are called *redistributive*. It is doubtful, however, whether Lowi's categories can be operationalized.

One difficulty comes in attempting to distinguish between arenas. Determining how broad an impact an issue has can be difficult. Some actors involved in policy making see the impact of issues differently than others. Take for example, the question of freight rate setting. Is the impact of that matter to be judged as involving competing claims of operators of different modes of transportation, or is it to be judged as primarily a controversy between users and transporters? If the issue involves users, which ones are most important? Differing perceptions of issues are inescapable. Bauer, Pool, and Dexter, for example, point out that some actors involved in the free trade controversy primarily perceived it in terms of the impact of low tariffs on workers in their particular constituencies, while others saw it in terms of its impact on the position of the United States in its trade relations with other nations.[7] If policymakers cannot agree on the impact of issues, it seems unlikely that a classification based on impact can be operationalized.

Although "impact" does not appear to be useful as an explanation of interactions among policy makers, it suggests a fruitful direction for further inquiry. Clearly, the environment of legislative decision making varies in different policy areas. Fenno, for example, argues in *Congressmen in Committees* that

> if one is searching for the antecedents [of the influence outsiders have on committee members] one finds that the subject of the policy and its associated characteristics must be given a central place. We have compared the relative prominence of four categories of interested outsiders. But we have found again and again that similarities and, more often, differences in their interest and prominence are related to the policy area itself.[8]

To understand why different kinds of legislation are treated differently, we should look at variations in political processes outside the legislature that affect the way demands are placed on legislative policymakers.

One way in which the environment of legislative policymaking varies is the process by which issues come to Congress for action. Some issues, for example, are used by presidential candidates in public speeches and statements in attempting to put together a winning coalition. If these are reported by the media, the public (or some part of it) is likely to become aware of the fact that an issue is being discussed among political decision makers. Whether these issues are raised originally by interest groups, by political candidates, by the media, or by other means is not relevant. What is important to the political decision maker is that they have been brought to the public by candidates through the media and that the public is presumably aware of and concerned about them. The salience of these issues to the reelection of candidates and to the political party in the legislature is likely to affect legislative behavior. Further, once elected, the victorious candidate develops a program for congressional action which he works to get passed on becoming head of the administration. Issues used by presidential candidates have an impact on the whole decision-making system. Issues used in individual congressional campaigns usually have little electoral impact on other members of Congress. Thus, issues raised by presidential candidates will be called "campaign issues."

Other issues are brought directly to legislators and bureaucrats without going through the electoral process. These issues are settled with little public participation. By far the greatest number of government decisions fall within this category. These issues are primarily raised and defined by interest groups and the Executive Branch. They will be called "group issues."

A second relevant characteristic of the environment that affects the way that demands are placed on legislative policymakers is the controversiality of the issues involved. Some issues, such as pork-barrel programs and veterans benefits, have traditionally involved no opposition from other groups in the legislative environment. These "noncontroversial" issues do not place decision makers in the position of choosing among the demands of different groups in society. Although candidates for the presidency may attempt to exploit noncontroversial issues in their attempts to win office, these issues are less likely to be the subject of media coverage than others because stories about agreement are not as dramatic or "newsworthy" as areas of conflict. Groups seeking government action on such issues are not likely to use the electoral process because it is slow, expensive, and not likely to be necessary for the enactment of programs that have no organized opposition. Therefore, noncontroversial issues are likely to be group-defined rather than campaign-defined.

Other issues force decision makers to choose between alternative group claims. In dealing with these "controversial" issues, some groups may seek to work through the electoral process in attempting to get them satisfactorily resolved. McConnell, however, points out that groups will ordinarily seek to avoid raising issues in the electoral process because of the time, expense and uncertainty involved in it. Financial and organizational costs are likely to be heavy and the outcomes of such involvements are likely to be reached slowly. Nevertheless, under some circumstances some groups are likely to find that a group-defined settlement is more costly than electoral participation.[9] Thus, controversial issues may be group- or campaign-defined.

Not all organizations are likely to find that they are equally able to raise campaign-defined issues. Thus, organizational resources are likely to affect decision makers' interactions. While such resources as money, status and skill are likely to affect the success of all groups seeking policy decisions from the government, group membership has a particular impact on the ability of groups to have issues raised in campaigns. Groups with large memberships can use them to generate an appearance of public concern about issues. Their size makes them important to candidates seeking political office. As a result, several mass membership groups have developed partisan ties. These groups have gained privileged access to party platforms in return for their support and activity in electoral campaigns. Labor unions and farm groups are good examples of groups that have taken this route.[10] We may expect to find, then, that mass membership groups will be involved most frequently in campaign-defined issues. They should also be likely to participate in group-defined situations, because of the advantages of avoiding campaigns. Nonmass groups should be likely to avoid campaign issues, only participating when they are forced to.[11] They would be even more likely to deal with issues on a group-defined basis.

Three variables in the decision-making environment have been identified: (1) the definition of issues (group- or campaign-defined), (2) the controversiality of issues, (3) membership resources. This paper deals with the impact of these variables on the perceptions of legislative interactions held by lobbyists. Hypotheses will be derived that deal with the focus of lobbying activity and the techniques used by lobbyists.

From the model posited above, we may draw the following hypotheses: (*a*) lobbyists dealing with group-defined, noncontroversial issues should deal with them mostly while those issues are in committee; (*b*) lobbyists dealing with campaign-defined controversial issues should be most oriented to floor activity; (*c*) those dealing with group-defined, controversial issues should fall between the other two groups of lobbyists in committee and floor orientation.

These hypotheses should be valid because the main problem facing groups interested in noncontroversial issues should be getting the committee to act. If a bill is reported out, they do not have the problem faced by groups dealing with controversial issues—that the legislation may reflect the objectives of other groups with opposing interests. Therefore, noncontroversial legislation should be reported by the committee in a form which reflects the preferences of interested groups. In contrast, controversial issues should involve more frequent appeals from committee decisions. Campaign-defined issues are most likely to be appealed to the floor. All members of Congress are likely to be aware of and concerned about them because of their electoral impact. In contrast, congressional norms such as specialization and deference to committee decisions are more likely to operate with group-defined issues because of the smaller significance of such issues to most members.

Second, because the focus of legislative interactions should vary with respect to the nature of the legislative environment, we may expect that techniques employed by lobbyists will also vary. Lobbyists dealing with controversies settled in committees are most likely to use techniques most appropriate in the committee setting, while those dealing with legislation which involves floor controversy are likely to use techniques suited to that situation. Consequently, we may hypothesize that lobbyists dealing with noncontroversial issues will rely most on techniques appropriate in committee, while those dealing with campaign-defined issues will rely most on techniques appropriate for floor action. We may expect to find that lobbyists who deal with group-defined controversies fall between the other lobbyists in the use of these techniques.

In addition, the congressional personnel contacted by lobbyists should vary depending upon the kind of conflict involved. Noncontroversial issues are so routine that we may expect that they will be dealt with primarily by committee staff, while lobbyists dealing with more controversial issues, particularly campaign-defined ones, should approach Congressmen themselves in order to make sure that their messages get through.

Finally, we may expect that the use of constituent contact will vary depending on group resources. Groups with large memberships are most likely to use techniques that rely on mass contacting of legislators in attempting to keep them aware of public concern about these issues. In contrast, lobbyists representing nonmass organizations are likely to rely more on individually influential members of the constituency in attempting to affect congressional decisions.

THE DATA BASE

To examine these questions, a sample of 118 lobbyists was questioned about their lobbying techniques and perceptions of the legislative process during the period from January through June 1971. Forty-seven were interviewed at random, and 71 responded to a mail questionnaire sent to the remainder. Thus, 72 percent of the population of 163 eligible for inclusion in the study responded.[12] Lobbyists reporting less than $1,000 per quarter in income from lobbying were excluded from the study to eliminate those who had little interaction with other policymakers. Those not reporting a Washington, D.C., address were excluded on the same grounds.[13] Appendix B shows the types of organizations represented by the lobbyists studied.

Lobbyists were asked, "What legislation have you, in representing your organization, been primarily interested in during the past year?" [14] From their responses, the lobbyists interests were classified as noncontroversial; group-defined, controversial; or campaign-defined, controversial.[15] Controversial and noncontroversial issues were differentiated by reference to the *Congressional Quarterly Almanac, 1970* to determine whether or not opposition to them was present. Reports of activity at congressional committee hearings on each piece of legislation were examined to discover whether opposing positions on legislative proposals were taken by those testifying before the committee. Campaign-defined issues were found by referring to the 1968 *New York Times Index* for speeches made by the presidential candidates during the general election campaign.[16] Primary activity was excluded from the study, as were platform promises. Statements made during the presidential primaries do not relate so much to conflict between the significant organizations within Congress and in its environment that organize legislative coalitions; the political parties and the Administration; as they do to conflict within them. Platform promises are not good indicators of issues where the scope of conflict is so substantial as to include the public because they contain many elements which merely represent promises to loyal constituents and are consequently not thoroughly discussed by the media. In addition, the content of platforms represents compromise among party factions, not the campaign agenda of the individuals who hope to become the next President.

Mass membership groups were differentiated from nonmass groups by classifying those organizations whose members were other organizations (such as trade associations or businesses) as nonmass organizations, while those whose members were individuals (such as trade unions, farmers, and veterans' groups) were classified as mass organizations. See Table 8.2.1 for the list of issues included in each category.

FINDINGS

THE FOCUS OF LEGISLATIVE ACTIVITY

The first hypotheses held that lobbyists dealing with campaign-defined controversies would be most floor oriented, while those dealing with noncontroversial issues would be most committee oriented. Three indicators were examined to test the hypotheses. First, the lobbyists were asked, "How much time do you spend on legislation at the committee stage as opposed to when it reaches the floor?" In addition, they were asked: "How often do you have contact with members or staff of the House Rules Committee?" and "Has the House Rules Committee blocked any legislation that you have been interested in?" The second two measures were included because contact with the

Table 8.2.1 Lobbyists' Issue Interests

NONCONTROVERSIAL ISSUES
Veterans' programs
Industry subsidies (merchant marine, airport)
Public works
Research funding (health)
GROUP-DEFINED CONTROVERSIAL ISSUES
Civil service pay and benefits
Postal pay and benefits
Transportation regulation (trucking taxation and regulation, railway safety, highway safety, waterways transport)
Foreign trade legislation
Bank and savings and loan regulations
Consumer legislation (truth in lending, insurance legislation, food inspection)
Business regulation (antitrust)
Securities industry regulation
Communications regulation (cable TV)
CAMPAIGN-DEFINED CONTROVERSIAL ISSUES
Welfare legislation (Welfare reform, manpower retraining, war on poverty, Medicaid)
Health legislation (Medicare, national health insurance)
Social Security legislation
Civil rights legislation
Education legislation
Farm legislation
Vietnam
Cities
Labor-management relations
Housing legislation
Taxation
Environmental legislation

Rules Committee follows committee action. Therefore, greater contact indicates a shift in orientation away from the substantive committee.[17] Evidence from the first measure, "How much time do you spend on legislation at the committee stage as opposed to when it reaches the floor?", supports the hypotheses (See Table 8.2.2). Lobbyists dealing with noncontroversial issues reported overwhelmingly that their activities are concentrated in committee. On the basis of evidence gathered in interviews it appears that lobbyists representing groups with these interests develop close ties with the committees that they work with. Once the committees have acted, their recommendations are usually accepted with little conflict. This is unsurprising given the absence of outside groups acting in opposition to noncontroversial legislation.

Another reason the recommendations are accepted routinely is that the legislation usually has a rather narrow impact. Consequently, it is of little concern to policymakers who do not specialize in the particular area involved.

While committee relationships appear to be stable, one factor emphasized by these lobbyists as a key variable in leading to routine floor approval of bills is the attitude of the committee chairman about the legislation being considered. Since the committees act cohesively in dealing with these issues, their chairmen have a great deal of power in dealing with noncontroversial legislation. This can cause difficulties for outside groups at times:

> Over on the House side, Chairman ——— is a real strong chairman. He had some misunderstanding with the ——— agency a few years back when the Nixon Administration first came in on matters completely unrelated to our program. . . . [As a result,] Mr. ——— just didn't care a hoot about anything to do with the program. For that reason, and I think for that reason alone, we didn't get any action in the last Congress on bills that were important to us, even after they passed the Senate.

In most cases, lobbyists interested in noncontroversial legislation let the committee chairman guide the legislation through the subsequent procedures leading to passage. Thus, the job of lobbyists interested in this kind of legislation does not often involve contacting Congressmen in efforts to insure its passage once it reaches the floor. Passage is usually routine. One lobbyist pointed out that

> aside from [writing letters pointing out the value of the program], to come down to the popular notion of a lobbyist running around the Hill, buttonholding Congressmen saying, "I demand your vote," we've never had to do that.

Lobbyists dealing with group-defined controversial issues were more likely to report that they spend as much time dealing with legislation once it reaches the floor as they do when it is in committee. Nevertheless, although floor

TABLE 8.2.2 FOCUS OF LOBBYISTS' ACTIVITIES

	TYPE OF CONTROVERSY			
FOCUS OF ACTIVITY	NONCONTROVERSIAL	GROUP-DEFINED CONTROVERSIAL	CAMPAIGN-DEFINED CONTROVERSIAL	TOTAL
Almost entirely committee	17.6% (3)	18.8% (9)	7.7% (3)	14.4% (15)
Mostly committee	82.4% (14)	62.5% (30)	43.6% (17)	58.7% (61)
About equal or mostly floor	0% (0)	18.8% (9)	48.7% (19)	26.9% (28)
Total	16.3% (17)	46.2% (48)	37.5% (39)	100% (104)

$\chi^2 = 17.88$
D.f = 4
Sig. = 0.01

activity in this arena is significantly greater than in the case of noncontroversial legislation, most lobbyists' activities are concentrated in committee.

The committee writes the basic legislation which will be considered by the whole House or Senate. It chooses among a number of possible courses of action in dealing with each aspect of a piece of legislation. For this reason these lobbyists find the best committee to be the best place to work for legislation that conforms to their interests. The point was made by this lobbyist:

> We pretty much let legislation go once it gets out of committee, unless there is something in it that's particularly difficult. I'd say today that by the time a bill gets to the floor, the compromises and the amendments have been pretty well agreed upon. Once in a while when you get a real nationally controversial issue like the SST funding, then the floor vote is very important.

In itself, the fact that the committee performs the function of putting proposed legislation into the shape in which it will be considered on the floor would not explain why the actions of these lobbyists are so concentrated in committee. Other factors combine to make attempts to change legislation on the floor difficult and often futile for them. Lobbyists dealing with group-defined controversies perceive that other members of Congress usually defer to committee actions. One lobbyist pointed out that

> once a bill clears committee the battle is usually four fifths done, because they have a habit over there of backing up their committee actions in both houses. The main battle is to get proper appropriate legislation out of the committee. . . . Once that happens, you don't have any problem. Once in 10 times there'll be a floor fight. At that point you have to work with the entire Congress.

In addition, lobbyists note that working with the entire Congress can be difficult. The simple structural problem of the number of members who must be contacted on the floor can create serious difficulties for lobbyists who represent groups with limited resources.

Thus, most of these lobbyists deal primarily with congressional committees. The strategic position of committees and the deference which lobbyists perceive that members pay them, along with the difficulty of dealing with the large number of members who must be contacted to change legislation once it leaves committee, lead them to attempt to shape legislation before it reaches the floor, where possible.

Lobbyists dealing with campaign-defined controversies are considerably more floor oriented than those dealing with other kinds of legislation. Even though they are substantially more floor oriented than others, none reported that their activities are primarily concentrated on the floor, and a substantial number reported that their activities take place mostly at the committee stage. The committee, even here, is extremely important because of its role in shaping the content of legislative proposals. On the other hand, many of them reported that they spend as much time dealing with legislation once it reaches the floor as they do when it is in committee. One puts it this way:

> Obviously you spend as much time after you get out of committee. What good does it do you to concentrate on committees? No bill has ever passed in committee. You have to take it from committee to get it passed on the floor and through conference.

Clearly, these lobbyists face many of the same problems seen by those dealing with group-defined concerns. Yet at the same time, floor action is an important access point for them, unlike for other lobbyists:

> We concentrate in both areas, but I would think that in the committee stage the concentration is on dealing with the legislative concept when it is still jelling. The concentration when you get on the floor is with the reality of what the committee reported out. So that you really are dealing with two different concepts of concentration and development. Sometimes as far as success goes, there's greater success at the committee level. Other times it's at the floor stage.

In addition to the comparative measure of committee and floor activity, a second indicator of a shift in the focus of congressional decision making from the committee to the floor in campaign-defined controversies is greater contact with the Rules Committee on the part of lobbyists dealing with those issues. With this increase in contact, lobbyists dealing with campaign-defined issues should also report increased difficulties in getting legislation scheduled for floor action.

The data supported the hypothesis that argued that lobbyists dealing with campaign-defined controversies would report greater difficulties in getting legislation scheduled than those concerned with other issues (see Table 8.2.3). Lobbyists dealing with noncontroversial issues most often reported that they have no problems with the Rules Committee. Those dealing with group-defined issues reported difficulties somewhat more frequently while more than 70 percent of lobbyists dealing with campaign-defined issues encountered problems.

Lobbyists dealing with campaign-defined issues were likely to encounter problems for several reasons. One problem for them is that the Rules Committee works as an agent of the House leadership. A second problem was that at the time of this study, under Chairman Colmer the Rules Committee was an important access point to groups interested in preventing the enactment of legislation in the area of civil rights. One lobbyist pointed out that

> on some of the civil rights legislation it has been a problem. We lost several pieces last year at the

TABLE 8.2.3 LEGISLATION BLOCKED BY THE RULES COMMITTEE

	TYPE OF CONTROVERSY			
	NONCONTROVERSIAL	GROUP-DEFINED CONTROVERSIAL	CAMPAIGN-DEFINED CONTROVERSIAL	TOTAL
Yes	31.3%	45.7%	73.5%	53.1%
	(5)	(21)	(25)	(51)
No	68.8%	54.3%	26.5%	46.9%
	(11)	(25)	(9)	(45)
Total	16.7%	47.9%	35.4%	100%
	(16)	(46)	(34)	(96)

$\chi^2 = 9.79$
D.f = 2
Sig. = .01

> end, just because we couldn't get a discharge petition. I don't sense that other legislation had quite the difficulty. It's just that Colmer is the chairman and puts his stamp on it.

Other lobbyists stated that this problem is less severe than it was prior to the enlargement of the Committee.

Finally, these lobbyists noted that the Committee serves to protect members who feel that they cannot publicly oppose legislation themselves because of constituent pressure, but want to see it blocked anyway. It can protect the party leadership in the House in a similar fashion. As one lobbyist pointed out,

> The Rules Committee serves a lot more than its public image might lead one to expect. It serves the private interests and the private wishes of a good many members of Congress that aren't always exposed to the public for its immediate consideration. An individual may have terrific pressure from his constituency to get a piece of legislation out. The legislation may go through the committee and get to the Rules Committee but the member can call upon the Rules Committee chairman to in some manner delay or see that it doesn't come up or keep it from being scheduled. Personal commitments are made so that he will not be in any way criticized for holding this up. So these sort of things are not matters to which the public has an insight, but yet they are matters which affect legislation.

The hypothesis dealing with frequency of contact with the Committee was also supported by the data. Lobbyists dealing with noncontroversial issues were more than twice as likely to report that they had little or no contact with the Committee as were those dealing with campaign-defined controversies (Table 8.2.4). Nevertheless, evidence from the interviews indicated that lobbyists dealing with all kinds of issues were not likely to have much direct access to the Rules Committee because it operates primarily as an agent of the House leadership, and because the Committee has isolated its proceedings from outside influence.

> It has never been my experience that this organization or any other outside organization has been able to influence very directly the agenda of items which the Rules Committee will or will not take up. That has usually remained in the complete control of the Chairman of the Rules Committee and to a lesser extent of the membership of the Rules Committee. These are men chosen not only for their qualities of party loyalty, but also for their experience in how legislation should be handled. So they are not by any means a committee easily to be influenced in a casual manner from the outside.

Differences in Lobbyists' Techniques: Committee Specialization

The next hypothesis argued that the techniques employed by lobbyists would differ

Table 8.2.4 Lobbyists' Contact with the Rules Committee

	Type of Controversy			
Frequency of Contact	Noncontroversial	Group-Defined Controversial	Campaign-Defined Controversial	Total
Frequent	5.9% (1)	28.3% (13)	29.4% (10)	24.7% (24)
Occasional	29.4% (5)	21.7% (10)	44.1% (15)	30.9% (30)
Rare or Never	64.7% (11)	50.0% (23)	26.5% (9)	44.3% (43)
Total	17.5% (17)	47.4% (46)	35.1% (34)	100% (97)

$\chi^2 = 10.53$
D.f = 4
Sig. = 0.03

depending upon the nature of the controversy. I hypothesized that in dealing with noncontroversial issues, lobbyists would use techniques appropriate to influencing the committees. In handling campaign-defined matters, they should use techniques appropriate to influencing all of the Congress. In approaching group-defined controversies, lobbyists should be more likely than those dealing with nonconflictual issues to use techniques appropriate to influence all members of Congress, but less likely to do so than those involved in campaign-defined controversies.

Activities that lobbyists reported undertaking at the request of Congressmen were examined. Such activities as submitting statements to congressional committees and testifying before them were classified as "committee specialized." Contacting Congressmen or other interest groups to argue in support of a legislative position was classified as "nonspecialized."[18] While these techniques may be used in committee, they are not used exclusively there, as the others are.[19]

The data support this hypothesis. There were no significant differences between groups in the use of committee specialized techniques. Most groups reported both testifying and submitting statements to committees. In contrast, lobbyists dealing with campaign-defined controversies perform nonspecialized services more often than those dealing with noncontroversial issues and group-defined controversies (Table 8.2.5). Statements of lobbyists dealing with group-defined controversial issues showed that requests for support come most often when legislation is in committee. For example, one lobbyist pointed out,

> We will get one of their letters in. It will say, "We are interested in this bill. Is there any way you can support it?" They will ask us to testify or to write a letter to the chairman of the committee saying that the ——— supports this legislation introduced by so and so.

In responding to this question, lobbyists dealing with campaign-defined issues indicated that requests for support come at all points in the legislative process. For example, one lobbyists stated,

> If the request is in the initial stage, it's asking for our public endorsement. Later it may be with regard to helping to sell, and getting party sponsorship. Finally, we may be asked to provide help when it has reached the floor.

WHOM DO THE LOBBYISTS CONTACT?

It was hypothesized that lobbyists dealing with campaign-defined issues would be most likely to attempt to deal with Congressmen directly, while those dealing with noncontro-

TABLE 8.2.5 USE OF NONSPECIALIZED ACTIVITIES BY LOBBYISTS

NUMBER OF ACTIVITIES USED	TYPE OF CONTROVERSY: NONCONTROVERSIAL	GROUP-DEFINED CONTROVERSIAL	CAMPAIGN-DEFINED CONTROVERSIAL	TOTAL
None	0%	8.0%	4.3%	5.1%
	(0)	(2)	(1)	(3)
One	54.5%	32.0%	4.3%	25.4%
	(6)	(8)	(1)	(15)
Two	45.5%	60.0%	91.3%	69.5%
	(5)	(15)	(21)	(41)
Total	18.6%	42.4%	39.0%	100%
	(11)	(25)	(23)	(59)

$\chi^2 = 11.93$
D.f = 4
Sig. = .02

TABLE 8.2.6 CONGRESSIONAL DECISION MAKERS CONTACTED BY LOBBYISTS

	TYPE OF CONTROVERSY			
TARGET OF CONTACT	NONCONTROVERSIAL	GROUP-DEFINED CONTROVERSIAL	CAMPAIGN-DEFINED CONTROVERSIAL	TOTAL
Mostly members	5.9%	20.4%	21.1%	18.3%
	(1)	(10)	(8)	(19)
Members and staff equally	35.3%	38.8%	57.9%	45.2%
	(6)	(19)	(22)	(47)
Mostly staff	58.8%	40.8%	21.1%	36.5%
	(10)	(24)	(8)	(38)
Total	16.3%	47.1%	36.5%	100%
	(17)	(49)	(38)	(104)

$\chi^2 = 8.93$
D.f. = 4
Sig. = .06

versial issues would be most likely to deal with staff. The hypothesis was confirmed (see Table 8.2.6). The modal category for lobbyists dealing with noncontroversial interests was ''mostly staff'' while other lobbyists were more likely to reply ''about equal.'' Only about 20 percent of the lobbyists dealing with campaign-defined issues dealt mostly with staff members.

Getting a piece of noncontroversial legislation through Congress does not usually necessitate dealing with members.

> On something which has a narrow purview, like the bill to facilitate disposal of government-owned property, there are only a few members of either body who are interested in the legislation in the early stages and even after it goes through committee and onto the floor. It's rather routine if there is not opposition to it. You deal mainly with the staff on that sort of legislation.

Lobbyists with group-initiated interests reported that they dealt more with members of Congress and less with staff than did those representing interests with noncontroversial objectives. The greater controversiality of this legislation leads lobbyists to deal more with those having the ultimate decision-making powers than with those who deal with routine matters. One lobbyist made the point this way:

> I think probably on a time basis [we deal] more with the staff. But the times you are talking to a member, by then he has learned what you have given the staff. So on a time basis, you don't spend as much time with him, but you get as much done. For instance, he may have one or two questions that it has boiled to that maybe you can supply the information about. When you start out with the staff man, it may be 40 questions.

Lobbyists concerned with campaign-defined issues deal less with staff than do lobbyists in the other two areas. The greater contact that these lobbyists have with members occurs because of the greater controversiality and broader impact of campaign-defined issues. They involve larger segments of the public than do issues in other areas, and more conflict is associated with them. One lobbyist described the functions of staff and members in this way:

> We do talk to members of the staff a great deal to find out where things are in the process. They are not by and large partisan. So we look to them for information about what is going on. In terms of advocacy we approach the members directly or if we can't reach them that way we go through the personal staff.

GROUP SIZE, ISSUE AREA, AND CONTACTING TECHNIQUES

The differing resources available to mass and nonmass groups would lead one to expect that nonmass groups would avoid the use of presidential campaigns in seeking their political ob-

TABLE 8.2.7 ORGANIZATIONAL CHARACTERISTICS

NATURE OF CONTROVERSY	TYPE OF ORGANIZATION		
	NONMASS	MASS	TOTAL
Noncontroversial	15.0% (6)	18.2% (12)	17.0% (18)
Group-defined controversial	70.0% (28)	31.8% (21)	46.2% (49)
Campaign-defined controversial	15.0% (6)	50.0% (33)	36.8% (39)
Total	37.7% (40)	62.3% (66)	100% (106)

$\chi^2 = 16.29$
D.f. = 2
Sig. = .01

jectives, while mass groups should use them more frequently,[20] as Table 8.2.7 demonstrates. Only 15 percent of the lobbyists employed by nonmass groups reported being predominantly involved in campaign-defined controversies, while 50 percent of the mass-based groups were involved in such controversies.

Many observers of policymaking have emphasized the attention Congressmen pay to constituent contact which appears to be spontaneous. Lobbyists emphasize its use. Nevertheless, the differing problems faced by lobbyists with different resources leads to different uses of constituents. Lobbyists who represent mass organizations such as labor unions and veterans' groups can use the memberships of their organizations to write letters and send telegrams in an effort to make Congressmen feel that they are facing issues of concern to the constituency.

In contrast, while the nonmass organizations (primarily businesses and trade associations) do not have access to this resource, their ranks consist of prestigious members of the community, an economic elite which has the status and financial resources to get access to the Congressmen. In such groups we would expect a heavier reliance on the use of telephone calls from constituents to Congressmen and visits by constituents in the congressional office.

Tables 8.2.8 and 8.2.9 support the hypothesis.[21] Lobbyists representing mass organizations used personal and telephone contact less and letters and telegrams more than those representing nonmass organizations. Thus, the resources available to nonmass groups appear to lead them to become involved in group-defined controversies and to use office and telephone contact predominantly, while mass groups use their membership resources more often to influence the outcome of campaign-defined controversies.

TABLE 8.2.8 USE OF OFFICE AND TELEPHONE CONTACT BY LOBBYISTS

NUMBER OF DIFFERENT TYPES OF CONTACT EMPLOYED	TYPE OF ORGANIZATION		
	NONMASS	MASS	TOTAL
None	11.5% (3)	37.0% (17)	27.8% (20)
One	50.0% (13)	28.3% (13)	36.1% (26)
Two	38.5% (10)	34.8% (16)	36.1% (26)
Total	36.1% (26)	63.9% (46)	100% (72)

$\chi^2 = 6.09$
D.f. = 2
Sig. = .05

TABLE 8.2.9 USE OF LETTERS AND TELEGRAMS BY LOBBYISTS

NUMBER OF KINDS OF CONTACT EMPLOYED	TYPE OF ORGANIZATION		
	NONMASS	MASS	TOTAL
None	42.3% (11)	6.5% (3)	19.4% (14)
One	34.6% (9)	30.4% (14)	31.9% (23)
Two	23.1% (6)	63.0% (29)	48.6% (35)
Total	36.1% (26)	63.9% (46)	100% (72)

$\chi^2 = 16.49$
D.f. = 2
Sig. = .01

All kinds of lobbyists, however, emphasized the importance of using constituents to influence congressional decisions. For example, one reported:

> Most of our lobbying is done by letters, and through contacts with the Congress. Mostly through the committees. . . . It's by letters, by correspondence. We send back to our members and ask them to contact their Congressmen by letter or telegram because they're voting for them. If we walk in there from this office they ask where we are from and they aren't too interested, but if they are people from the lower echelon who call up, then it means something.

This is not the only reason lobbyists use constituent contact, however. Constituent contact is used by some organizations to give the membership a sense of participation.

> We do it for dual purposes. One is that we feel that keeping the constituent in touch with his member of Congress is an effective way of registering opinion. Second, we like to help keep in touch with the issue at hand so that he doesn't lose out and wonder at what point he missed the boat. With Congress being made up the way it is it gives a member of ——— or the membership of any organization a sense of real pride in helping out maybe some other section of the country or some other individual he has no real contact with.

CONCLUSIONS

In the research presented above, I have shown some ways that the legislative environment affects the behavior of lobbyists and their perceptions of the legislative process. Group characteristics and group relationships around specific issues affect legislative interactions. Legislative policymakers do not behave uniformly, regardless of issue.

Specifically, it was demonstrated that the legislative activity of lobbyists is most committee oriented in dealing with noncontroversial issues, while it is most floor oriented in dealing with campaign-defined, controversial issues. Lobbyists' techniques reflect this difference in focus of activity. Nonspecialized techniques are used least by lobbyists dealing with noncontroversial issues and most by those dealing with campaign-defined controversies. Constituent contact techniques were shown to be related to group resources. Mass groups were found to rely more on letter and telegram campaigns, while nonmass groups rely on telephone and direct contact by a few influential constituents.

Although this study was limited to an examination of the impact of environmental characteristics on legislator–lobbyist interactions, a number of other observed discrepancies in the behavior of legislative policymakers would appear to be related to environmental characteristics. Committee integration, for example, has been shown in a number of studies to vary markedly. It seems likely that integration is at least in part a response to the ways that demands are placed on congressional decision makers.[22] Similarly, findings showing differing degrees of constituency influence in different subject areas are probably affected by the same variables.[23] We may also expect to find that interactions between policymakers in the Congress and those in the executive branch vary for the same reasons.

The findings of this study point up the significance of the presidential campaign in the legislative process. Interest groups dealing with campaign-defined conflicts no longer may monopolize the issues presented to decision makers. The techniques employed by them demonstrate the perceived necessity of engaging a large constituency in favor of their positions. At the point when conflict leaves the group-committee-bureaucracy setting, one may no longer argue that the condition of subsystem semi-autonomy is present. Clearly, some degree of accountability to the larger constituency enters the policy process at this point.

Equally significant, however, is the fact that relatively few of the issues studied here were campaign defined Only about 35 percent of the lobbyists in this study dealt with issues that fell in this category. While one could not argue that this sample is a representative cross-section of all the issues dealt with by Congress, it is clear that one condition for interest-group effectiveness—maintenance of conflict within a small subset of decision makers—is more often present than not. In noncampaign defined issues, the focus on committee activity reported by lobbyists can be seen as an indicator of the significance of committee subsystems in the decision-making process. Thus, the recruitment of committee decision makers and the decision-making process in committees should be important topics of study for those who wish to understand policy outcomes.

APPENDIX A—QUESTIONS USED IN THE STUDY

1. How much time do you spend on legislation at the committee stage as opposed to when it reaches the floor? (check one)
   __ Almost entirely in committee
   __Mostly in committee
   __About equal
   __Mostly on floor
   __Almost entirely on floor.
2. How often do you have contact with members or staff of the House Rules Committee? (circle one)
   Frequently Occasionally Rarely Never
3. Has the House Rules Committee blocked any legislation that you have been interested in? (circle one) *Yes No*
4. How often do members of Congress request your support on legislation that they have introduced? (circle one) *Frequently Occasionally Rarely Never*
5. If you have been requested to provide support for legislation, please indicate which of the activities you have or have not pursued? (Circle *Y* (Yes) or *N* (No) in answering)
   Y N Testifying before committee
   Y N Filing statement with committee
   Y N Contacting members of congress
   Y N Contacting other interest groups
   Y N Informing your members of your support
   Y N Other (specify) ____________
6. Many lobbyists feel that getting constituents to contact their Congressmen is essential to a successful legislative program. Which of the following do you encourage most? (circle *Y* (Yes) or *N* (No) in answering)
   Y N Letters
   Y N Personal contact in D.C.
   Y N Personal contact in home district
   Y N Do not encourage constituent contact
   Y N Telephone calls
   Y N Telegrams
   Y N Other (specify) ____________

APPENDIX B—ORGANIZATIONAL AFFILIATIONS OF RESPONDENTS

	NUMBER	PERCENT
Labor unions (government employees)	11	10.5%
Labor unions (other)	25	23.8
Trade associations	37	35.2
Ideological organizations	5	4.8
Veterans organizations	7	6.7
Farmers organizations	10	9.5
Professional associations	8	7.6
Individual businesses	2	1.9
Total	105	100.0%

NOTE: Affiliations of 13 respondents were not ascertainable.

8.3 The Reassertion of Congressional Power: New Curbs on the President*

Harvey G. Zeidenstein

A major development of the 1970s—and a legacy of Vietnam and Watergate—was congressional assertion of power vis-à-vis the Presidency. This article chronicles these assertions and speculates about their future impacts.

The confrontations in the 1970s between the Nixon-Ford Administration and the Democratic-controlled Congress have left a legacy of restrictions on various kinds of presidential activities that are now operating on President Carter but which did not exist to limit "imperial" Presidents in the era from Franklin Roosevelt to Lyndon Johnson. These restrictions came as a reaction to what became recognized as a gradual erosion of congressional checks and balances against Presidents since the 1930s. They represented Congress' attempt to resurrect its disused legal powers to participate in policymaking—especially in the areas of declaration and termination of national emergencies, war-making, foreign policy, intelligence operations, budget policy, and impoundments of appropriated funds.

Our concern is with executive–congressional relations in legitimate and routine policy activities. Criminal or other impeachable offenses by Presidents are neither legitimate nor (we assume) routine. Consequently, restrictions unique to Watergate or to the attempted impeachment of former President Richard Nixon fall outside the scope of this study. Nonetheless, we are left with a lengthy catalog of restrictions on the President.

---

* From Harvey G. Zeidenstein, "The Reassertion of Congressional Power: New Curbs on the President," Reprinted with permission from the *Political Science Quarterly* 93 (1978): 393–409.

VARIETIES OF RESTRICTIONS ON PRESIDENTIAL ACTIONS

Through a variety of measures, Congress has increased its ability to restrict presidential actions and to hold the President and the Executive Branch more accountable to itself by allowing for formal congressional disapproval in some instances, requiring to be provided with critical information in others, and mandating that certain presidential initiatives cease automatically in other cases in the absence of congressional action to affirmatively approve those initiatives.

Termination or Continuation of Emergency Authority

In 1973 a Senate special committee found some 470 provisions of federal law that could be triggered during a "time of war" or a "national emergency" declared by Congress or the President.[1] Many were as innocuous as those providing for the presentation of soldiers' medals during conflict and assistance for current school expenditures in cases of certain disasters.[2] Other laws—such as those allowing the President to order private plants to manufacture necessary products "in time of war or when war is imminent," and to maintain lists of plants capable of war production—were potentially more sweeping in granting authority to the executive.[3]

Presidents have been far more willing to declare emergencies than to end them, so emergency periods, and the laws operative in them, typically have lasted many years beyond the end of the original emergency. This motivated passage of the National Emergencies Act in September 1976.[4] The act leaves most of the 470 wartime and emergency laws intact, but creates a system for declaring and terminating national emergencies.

Declaration is by the President. Of the three methods of termination, one (discussed later) is up to Congress and two leave the initiative to the President. As in the past, an emergency can be ended by presidential proclamation. A new wrinkle is that an emergency will terminate automatically in one year unless the President informs Congress within 90 days before the end of the year that the emergency is to continue.[5] As both methods are subject to presidential discretion, their purely legal restriction on his authority is minimal to nonexistent. But their effect may be important politically. A President who does not end an emergency, or who continues it, is subject to questions. Not the least of which is why an emergency still exists a year after his Administration presumably has been working on it.

Consultation with Congress before Military Operations

In November 1973 Congress overrode a Nixon veto and enacted the War Powers Resolution.[6] The resolution's avowed purpose is to "insure that the collective judgment of both the Congress and the President will apply" to sending American armed forces into hostilities or into situations where immediate involvement in hostilities is likely, and to the continued use of armed forces in hostilities or threatening situations.

Among other things, the resolution requires the President "in every possible instance" to "consult with Congress" before he introduces armed forces into hostilities or into situations leading to hostilities. He also must consult regularly with Congress until the forces have been withdrawn from combat or the threatening situation.[7]

The extent of consultation before the President commits forces to hostilities is open to varying interpretation. In reporting the War Powers Resolution, the House International Relations (then Foreign Affairs) Committee stated that it expected the President himself to seek congressional advice and opinion while his decision is still pending. The committee flatly rejected the notion that consultation occurs when a President informs Congress of decisions already made.[8]

But in the May 1975 rescue of the American merchant ship *Mayaguez,* what the administration called "consultation" was the White House informing about 20 congressional leaders after President Ford had ordered U.S. Navy jets and Marines to engage Cambodian forces. In the few hours between Ford's order and the first shots of combat, the leaders were able to submit their views to the President. But their opportunity to "advise" came after the military operations approved by the President had begun.[9]

Except for the grumblings of a few ultradoves, Congress winked at Ford's minimal consultation, largely because the rescue was considered a success. As the then Senate Majority Whip Robert Byrd told the President, he "might have been in a lot better position, had this operations not been successful," if he had actually sought advice from Congress.[10] But this observation would be nearly as trenchant had there been no legal requirement to consult, as President Truman learned when the Korean conflict went sour.

In a purely legal sense, then, the consultation provision adds no new curbs on the President's freedom to act. Even if he followed the intent of the law by seeking congressional advice before making up his mind, the President is not bound to accept it. On the other hand, future Presidents may follow Ford's precedent of defining after-the-fact briefings as consultation. The lesson of *Mayaguez* seems to be that in the future, as in the past, consultation—or lack of it—will be viewed in the context of existing political circumstances rather than according to a consistent legal definition. If the President embarks on a military venture opposed by Congress, or one that foments opposition because it fails, then lack of consultation will be a convenient legal springboard for criticism.

SENATE CONFIRMATION OF OMB HEADS

In 1970 President Nixon through a reorganization plan enlarged the old Bureau of the Budget into the more powerful Office of Management and Budget (OMB), which became a potent force for executing presidential policies. Among the more controversial policies was gutting domestic programs by impoundment—ordering the bureaucracy not to spend money appropriated by a liberal Democratic Congress.

Although the director and deputy director of OMB exerted far more authority than Cabinet officers, they were appointed by the President without the advice and consent of the Senate. This changed in March 1974, when President Nixon approved an amendment to the Budget and Accounting Act of 1921. The new measure exempted the incumbents, but required that future directors and deputy directors of OMB receive Senate confirmation.[11]

The Senate's role is probably a minor foray into the Executive's domain. Although confirmation hearings can be used to quiz prospective OMB heads on their views toward facets of fiscal policy, prospective appointees with enough political skill for the job probably will evade or finesse the more pointed questions. Also, traditionally, the Senate is strongly inclined to confirm whomever the President chooses for his Adminstration. Bert Lance is a case in point. In its eagerness to recommend Lance's confirmation, the Senate Governmental Affairs Committee was ignorant of or indifferent to his personal financial ethics.

For the near future, the Lance affair probably will make the President and the Senate more sensitive to personal ethics as grounds for withholding confirmation. For serious questions about the ethics of a potential presidential appointee would be of mutual concern to the President and the Senate. Both could be criticized in the media, as they were several months after Lance's confirmation. To avoid this, we expect the executive to rigorously screen an appointee's personal affairs before his name is submitted to the Senate. The Senate confirmation process will become a fail-safe device to backstop the executive's investigation. If this reading is correct, confirmation gives the Senate not a new check, but an added responsibility.

On the other hand, Congress may have gained an increased expectation that OMB directors will testify candidly before its committees. Many on Capitol Hill believe that Administration officials confirmed by the Senate are less protected by executive privilege than officials appointed exclusively by the President.

PRESIDENTIAL REPORTS TO CONGRESS

Three recent laws obligate the President to inform Congress about his current or anticipated activities with respect to executive agreements, national emergencies, and deploying U.S. armed forces abroad.

Stung by revelations that the Johnson and Nixon Administrations had made secret executive agreements with foreign governments, Congress, in 1972, reacted by requiring the Secretary of State to send it the text of any international agreement, other than a treaty, within 60 days after the agreement became effective. However, if the President judged that public disclosure would injure national security, the text would be submitted only to the Senate Foreign Relations Committee and the House International Relations Committee "under the appropriate injunction of secrecy to be removed only upon due notice from the President."[12] In effect, the President would inform Congress, or at his discretion only two of its committees, of faits accomplis. And short of a leak, they would be kept secret from the public as long as the President wished.

Still, Congress gained a significant inroad. It

can modify or hamstring executive agreements by refusing the funds to implement them. Even secret agreements known only to the two foreign policy committees are not immune. These committees could register strong displeasure, even threats, with the Administration. For example, without public disclosure of the secret details of an agreement, either committee could sponsor legislation which, in general language, nullifies its purpose. Such measures could be debated by Congress in secret sessions.

When the President declares a national emergency, the National Emergencies Act forbids him from exercising any statutory authority available during emergencies unless and until he informs Congress of the specific laws under which he proposes to act.[13] This alerts Congress to the President's probable future activities. To help Congress monitor the executive's ongoing activities during an emergency or declared war, all of the President's significant orders and all executive agency rules and regulations are to be filed, indexed, and promptly sent to Congress, by means to insure their confidentiality where appropriate. Finally, every six months during an emergency or declared war, and within three months after it has ended, the President must inform Congress of the total expenditures directly attributed to the emergency or war.[14]

When Congress has not declared war, the War Powers Resolution requires the President to inform Congress in writing within 48 hours after he has introduced U.S. armed forces into any of three situations: hostilities or circumstances where immediate involvement in hostilities is likely; the territory, air, or waters of a foreign nation while equipped for combat, except for such deployments which are nonhostile; or a substantial increase in the number of combat-equipped forces already stationed in a foreign country.[15]

The President's report must specify the reasons he introduced armed forces, the legal authority justifying their introduction, and the estimated scope and duration of the hostilities or involvement. The President must also give Congress any additional information it requests, and report every six months while American forces are involved in any of the three situations requiring his original report.[16]

The War Powers reports, as such, are not a severe encroachment on the President's authority. But the information given (or omitted) can be a basis for significantly influencing Congress' decision to support or throttle the President's military initiatives.

CIA REPORTS TO CONGRESSIONAL COMMITTEES

As a civilian agency, the CIA is outside the jurisdiction of the War Powers Resolution. Consequently, the resolution does not require the President to inform Congress of covert CIA operations, such as the secret war in Laos in the 1960s and a variety of other CIA military and political activities intended to establish or protect friendly regimes abroad.

This gap was plugged by other measures compelling CIA accountability to selected congressional committees. First came an amendment to the Foreign Assistance Act of 1961, sponsored by Senator Harold Hughes and Representative Leo Ryan, which took effect on December 30, 1974.[17] Except for gathering "necessary intelligence," the Hughes–Ryan Amendment prohibits the spending of money by or for the CIA for operations in foreign countries, "unless and until" the President finds each operation is important to national security, and the President reports, "in a timely fashion," a description and scope of each operation to the "appropriate committees" of Congress, including the Senate Foreign Relations Committee and the House International Relations Committee. Presidential approval and reports of covert operations are not required during military operations resulting from a declared war or from the President acting under the War Powers Resolution. The Hughes–Ryan Amendment does not require written reports.[18] Acting as the President's delegate, the director of the CIA gives oral briefings to "appropriate" committees.[19] There are currently eight of them: The Senate and House Armed Services Committees, the Senate Foreign Relations and the House International Relations Committees, the Senate and House Appropriations Subcommittees on Defense, and Senate and House Select Committees on Intelligence, which have oversight and legislative jurisdiction over the entire intelligence community. The Senate Select Intelligence Committee was created in May 1976, its House counterpart 14 months later. Both succeeded temporary committees in each house—one chaired by Sen. Frank Church, the other by Representative Otis Pike—which investigated the CIA in 1975 and disbanded in 1976.

A Hughes–Ryan report is not a prerequisite for a covert operation, so the committees may be briefed after the operation has begun.[20] However, as former CIA Director William Colby testified to the Senate Government Operations Committee early in 1976, on the day the CIA is informed that the President has signed a finding approving an operation, the CIA calls the committees' staffs to notify them that there is a finding to report at the committees' convenience. "We make a point of getting that notice out immediately."[21] Colby said he has reported as early as the next morning with some committees and some weeks later with others, depending on the committee.[22]

Because of the Hughes–Ryan Amendment no President or his apologists will be able to disclaim responsibility for any CIA operations in peacetime and as a result, the President is given stronger incentive to closely monitor the CIA and prevent it from undertaking operations without his authority (the so-called rogue elephant).

Although the Hughes–Ryan Amendment does not legally require reports until after covert operations have begun, the Senate has used the power of the purse to persuade the CIA and other intelligence agencies to give the Senate Select Committee on Intelligence advance notice of future covert activities also. The committee was established in May 1976 by Senate Resolution 400.[23] One section of the resolution expresses the "sense of the Senate" that Exectuive Branch agencies should keep the Select Committee informed of their intelligence activities, "including any significant anticipated activities," although prior notification is not a precondition to implementing the activity.[24]

No "sense of the Senate" resolution has legal force outside that chamber. But the Senate gave its Select Intelligence Committee exclusive jurisdiction over all authorization bills for the CIA, and shared jurisdiction with other committees over authorizations for the intelligence activities of other agencies in the intelligence community.[25] With its hand on the money authorizing spigot, it is not surprising that the committee has been fully briefed on covert operations prior to their implementation. The committee has even voted on every proposed covert operation.

In addition to its control over authorizations, the Select Intelligence Committee may make intelligence information available to any other committee or member of the Senate. With the approval of the full Senate, the committee may inform the public of information the President wants to keep classified.[26] These powers give the committee a strong bargaining position with the executive. After being briefed on a proposed covert operation, the committee reaction, if any, can include the following:

Comment to the Executive Branch.

Referral of information to other committees, if appropriate.

Public disclosure, if supported by a closed session vote of the Senate.

Funding restrictions.[27]

When the House created its own Select Intelligence Committee by passing House Resolution 658 in July 1977, it used language that was, in most parts, identical to that in Senate Resolution 400.[28] But in a notable departure from the Senate resolution, the House measure does not express the "sense of the House" that intelligence agencies should alert the House Intelligence Committee to anticipated activities. Without this mandate, it is too soon to tell whether the House Intelligence Committee will expect to receive prior notification of covert activities, although it is equal to its Senate counterpart in controlling authorizations, and equivalent to it is sharing classified information with other lawmakers and the public.

Mandate for Committee Disclosure of Classified Information

By providing a mechanism for public disclosure of classified information, the resolutions creating the Senate and House Select Intelligence Committees give these bodies a check against the President far stronger than what the other six committees have from the Hughes–Ryan Amendment alone.

Each Intelligence Committee may vote to disclose any information it receives from the Executive Branch. After informing the President of its decision, a committee can release the information in five days unless the President objects personally, in writing, states the reasons for his objection, and certifies that the threat to the national interest of disclosure outweighs any public interest in the information. If the committee still favors disclosure, it can vote to refer the matter to its parent body, the Senate or the House, as the case may be. Within four days of the referral, the parent body goes into closed session (required in the Senate, only if voted upon in the House). The Senate has a maximum of nine days to vote for one of three actions: to approve or disapprove disclosure of all or part of the information, or to refer all or any part of the information back to its Intelligence Committee, in which case the committee makes the final decision whether to go public.[29] The House procedure allows two hours of debate (rather than nine days), then requires a vote on whether to approve the recommendation for disclosure made by its Select Intelligence Committee. If the House votes against the recommendation, it is sent back to the Committee for further recommendation.[30] In both houses, the final vote is taken in open session without debate and without divulging the classified information at issue.[31]

The provision for public disclosure approved through these procedures is meant to inhibit the President from illegal or highly unpopular intelligence operations.

Centralizing or "Defragmenting" Committee Oversight

Friendly critics have argued that Congress's decentralized committee system leaves it impotent in any face-off with the executive, and incapable of adopting a coherent policy of its own. Fractionalized legislative and budgetary authority by numerous, sometimes competing, committees and subcommittees has led to desultory oversight of executive branch agencies, to some committees sitting on information that should be shared with their parent chambers, and to ineffective coordination by each house over the total legislative and fiscal output of its committees. In sum, Congress has been constipated by an inefficient decision-making structure and process. While this condition has often hurt the President by delaying his legislative agenda and hobbling executive programs, in other circumstances it has left him or executive branch agencies immune from congressional checks and balances.

OVERSIGHT OF INTELLIGENCE

As a case in point, both the executive and Congress were unhappy with what passed for oversight of intelligence and counterintelligence activities. After experience with the Hughes–Ryan Amendment, the executive implored the House of Representatives, in the words of Speaker Tip O'Neill, "to establish a process that could provide valid oversight of all intelligence activities . . . and at the same time reduce the possibilities of leaks that might occur from the Hill."[32] O'Neill was urging his colleagues to create the Permanent Select Committee on Intelligence 14 months after the Senate Select Intelligence Committee was established. The anticipated benefits to the House were expressed by Rep. Edward Boland (D–Mass.).

Noting that seven committees had some form of jurisdiction over various agencies in the intelligence community, Boland observed:

> All of them can secure access to the most vital secrets of our Nation, but none of them currently [July 1977] views the activities of the community as a composite.
>
> None of them, in practice, have developed a critical overview of the functioning and work-product of the entire community.
>
> [These committees] would . . . agree, I believe, that because of the lack of a strong, unified vehicle in this House—and previously in the other body—abuses occurred in the operations of some intelligence agencies, most notably the CIA.[33]

Traditionally, legislative jurisdiction over the FBI was held by the Senate and House Judiciary Committees. The Armed Services Subcommittees on Intelligence had comparable authority for the CIA and Defense Department intelligence agencies. Despite the contribution of the CIA in the formation and implementation of foreign policy, there was no role for the Senate Foreign Relations and the House International Relations Committees. Appropriations for intelligence activities were, and still are, processed by Appropriations subcommittees. But no total sum was available to Congress, for intelligence funding has been scattered throughout the budgets of several agencies.

This disjointed structure was rebuilt by establishing the Senate and House Select Intelligence Committees. Each combines unified oversight of all intelligence agencies with a mandate to share information with other committees and members of Congress. To insure liaison among other committees with jurisdiction in the field, the membership of both Intelligence Committees must include representatives from each of four committees in their respective houses: Appropriations, Armed Services, Judiciary, and Senate Foreign Relations or House International Relations.

To reduce the chance that the Intelligence Committees will fall into a protective relationship with the agencies they are supposed to monitor, no member may serve more than eight years on the Senate committee or six years on the House committee, and a third of the members of each committee is to be replaced every two years.

CONGRESSIONAL BUDGET POLICY

Nothing has the universal impact on all policy areas as the federal budget and the fiscal policy it represents: levels and incidence of taxation, spending, and debt. Yet until the mid-70s, Congressional budgetary decisions were clumsily arrived at and muddled in intent. Consider these historic problems:

Congress lacked sufficient information and expertise to effectively evaluate the President's annual budget. Most information and analytical skills rested principally in the President's Office of Management and Budget (OMB), and in the Executive Branch Departments which compiled the budget and were therefore able to defend it in Congress. Congress had no institutional staff agency comparable to the OMB.

Congress could not coordinate revenues and expenditures. One set of committees wrote the tax laws (Ways and Means in the House, Finance in the Senate), another set the spending bills (Appropriations Committees in each house). This decentralized jurisdiction, coupled with Congress' proclivity to spend money and reluctance to raise taxes, contributed, said the critics, to chronic budget deficits and inflation.

There was little or no coordination of expenditures. Each house's Appropriations Committee was (and is) fractured into some 13 specialized subcommittees, each autonomous in the amount of appropriations it recommended. Total spending was the sum of whatever their recommendations happend to be, as modified and adopted by Congress on a piecemeal basis during the legislative session. There was no disciplined look at total spending or its effect on inflation, budget deficits, the national debt, and federal borrowing to pay interest on the debt.

More important, perhaps, Congress had no mechanism for incorporating its own clear priorities for its spending, no coherent policy which dictated hard choices about where to spend a limited amount of money, because there was no predetermined limit. Since the President's budget reflected his priorities and hard choices, he was in a stronger position to argue with Congress when they disagreed, and to receive public support when he vetoed spending bills on the grounds of dampening inflation.

These chronic problems were addressed by the decision structure and process created by the Congressional Budget Act of 1974, which became fully effective in 1976.[34] Without getting into their fine points, the cardinal provisions of the Budget Act can be summarized as follows:

It establishes a new fiscal year beginning October 1. Since the President sends Congress his annual budget in mid or late January, this gives Congress more than eight months to work on it, instead of the less than six months available under the old fiscal year beginning July 1.

To match the technical knowledge and expertise of the President's OMB, the act creates the Congressional Budget Office (CBO), empowered to secure information from executive branch agencies. The act also establishes Budget Committees in each house of Congress, which, utilizing the staff studies of the CBO and staff studies of their own, recommend coordinated levels of revenues and expenditures and priorities for spending. In effect, these three new bodies were created to help Congress establish its own budget ceilings (targets) which, under the Budget Act, may not be exceeded.

The Budget Committees' recommendations are embodied in concurrent budget resolutions reported to their respective houses. A first resolution sets tentative or "target" ceilings for appropriations and actual expenditures (outlays) in each functional category, as well as ceilings for total appropriations and outlays, revenues, a budget surplus or deficit, and the national debt, and is due by April 15.

By May 15, standing committees must report new authorization bills, and Congress must adopt a first concurrent budget resolution. (As a concurrent resolution, it is not submitted to the President for approval or veto.) This resolution guides, but does not bind, subsequent congressional budgetary decisions. However, the CBO and the Budget Committees keep score on how close spending and revenue bills come to the first resolution's ceilings. And in the Senate, at least, Budget Committee Chairman Edmund Muskie is not above jawboning his colleagues into fiscal restraint.

By September 15 Congress must adopt a second, binding, concurrent budget resolution, which either affirms or revises the first resolution passed on May 15. If the money bills passed in the preceding four months do not conform to the ceilings in the second resolution, it can dictate changes in the amounts of appropriations, revenues, and the public debt. These changes are called reconciliations. Congress must then adopt a reconciliation measure to implement the second, binding, concurrent resolution and may not adjourn until this is done.

Despite some shakedown problems, the new budgetary process puts Congress on a level at least approaching the Presidency in making—and taking responsibility for—policy decisions on spending and revenue raising. To the Carter Administration, pledged to seek a balanced budget, the Budget Act can make Congress a competent ally. But should Congress break with the President, it would be a formidable adversary.

Stopping the President by Concurrent Resolution

Some of the laws defining the President's authority in selected policy areas have permitted Congress to remove his authority by adopting a concurrent resolution. Although they require a majority vote in each house, concurrent resolutions are not sent to the President, so they cannot be vetoed. Three recent laws provide for veto-proof concurrent resolutions.

The National Emergencies Act requires future national emergencies to end on the date specified in a presidential proclamation or in a concurrent resolution, whichever date comes first. No later than every six months after the emergency is declared, Congress must consider whether to end it by concurrent resolution. When the emergency ends, so do the President's special powers granted him by numerous statutes triggered by the emergency.[35]

The War Powers Resolution states that "at any time" U.S. armed forces are engaged in hostilies abroad without a declaration of war or specific statutory approval from Congress, such forces shall be removed by the President if Congress so directs by concurrent resolution.[36] Because of another provision of the War Powers Resolution discussed below, such a concurrent resolution would be practical only during the first 60 days of a conflict.

The National Emergencies Act and the War Powers Resolution contain similar rules for giving concurrent resolutions fast consideration in Congress. Unless waived by a majority vote in either house, these rules protect concurrent resolutions from committee pigeonholes in both houses and filibusters in the Senate.[37]

In 1974, Congress amended Section 36 of the Foreign Military Sales Act to require the President to give Congress advance notice of any offer to sell arms or services valued at $25 million or more. By the mid-1970s, the United States had become one of the leading exporters of armaments, but Congress had had little to say about what weapons were sold to which countries. Congress had 20 days to reject any offer to sell arms by concurrent resolution, unless the President stated that an emergency required the sale in the national security interests of the United States.[38] (The quick transfer of weapons to Israel during the 1973 Yom Kippur war is an example of the kind of emergency Congress had in mind.)

After some experience with this law, Congress determined that 20 days gave it insufficient time to investigate an arms sale, and that the $25 million floor allowed a series of smaller arms sales to escape its scrutiny.[39] So in 1976 Congress further amended Section 36 by giving itself up to 30 days to pass a concurrent resolution disapproving the sale of major defense equipment valued at $7 million or more, as well as any arms or services of $25 million or more.

In practice, at least some members of Congress have considerably more than 30 days to decide whether they want to support a concurrent resolution. First, by informal agreement with the executive branch the Senate Foreign Relations Committee and the House International Relations Committee receive "prenotification" of proposed sales 20 days in advance of formal notification to Congress. Formal notification initiates the 30-day disapproval period.

Second, members of Congress may be able to buy time by threatening to pass a resolution of disapproval before the end of 30 days. The President can prevent this by withdrawing formal notification before Congress kills the sale. The President may resubmit notification later, but that begins a new, full 30-day period. In the indefinite interim between withdrawal and resubmission of the proposed sale, Congress has ample time to influence the President and foreign governments to accept congressionally imposed compromises on foreign arms sales.

This has already occurred. In the 1975 sale of Hawk ground-to-air missiles to Jordan, and in the 1977 sale to Iran of Airborne Warning and Control System (AWACS) aircraft.[40] A third instance of compromise occurred in May

1978, when President Carter promised an additional 20 planes for Israel as part of his package sale of jet fighters to Saudi Arabia, Egypt, and Israel.

STOPPING PRESIDENTIAL ACTIONS BY SIMPLE RESOLUTION

A one house veto of a presidential recommendation by passage of a simple resolution is authorized in the Impoundment Control Act of 1974 (which appears as Title X of the Congressional Act of 1974).[41] In a special message to Congress, the President may propose that he defer spending specified amounts of money for certain purposes until a later time in the current fiscal year. (He may not propose deferrals beyond the end of the year.) But the funds must be available for expenditure if either house passes a resolution disapproving the proposed deferral. Both houses have procedures for discharging a resolution from a committee, for treating motions to consider a resolution as privileged, and for limiting debate before the final floor vote.[42]

STOPPING THE PRESIDENT AUTOMATICALLY BY INACTION

Sponsors of concurrent or simple resolutions cannot stop the President without convincing a majority of their colleagues to vote against him. Assembling a majority on any policy issue is hard enough; constructing one in opposition to the President's policy is even harder.

This problem is leapfrogged if Congress wants to stop the President from fighting an undeclared war or from permanently impounding appropriations. In both cases, the President must stop automatically by a specific deadline, unless majorities in both houses of Congress vote to approve his action. The problem of achieving a majority is faced by the President's supporters, not his opponents.

Recall that in the absence of a declaration of war, the War Powers Resolution directs the President to report to Congress within 48 hours after he introduces U.S. armed forces into hostilities or situations where hostilities are likely. The teeth of the resolution are in its provision that within 60 days after the report is due, the President shall terminate American involvement in hostilities or hostile situations, unless Congress has declared war or enacted a specifiic authorization for the fighting, has extended by law the 60-day deadline, or is physically unable to meet because of an armed attack against the United States.[43] Priority procedures provide that any measure supporting the President, that is, legislation authorizing the war or extending the deadline, shall be voted upon before the 60 days have elapsed. However, this is not guaranteed, for the procedures may be waived by majority vote in either house.[44]

The 60-day deadline could be extended up to 30 additional days if the President determines that "unavoidable military necessity" requires the extra time for the safe removal of U.S. forces. The President would have to certify this need to Congress in writing.[45] (As mentioned above, Congress could force the President to disengage from hostilities at any time by passing a concurrent resolution.)

A shorter deadline is written into the Impoundment Control Act. The President must propose permanent impoundments, called "recissions," to Congress. However, the appropriations proposed to be rescinded have to be available for expenditure unless, within 45 days of the President's request, Congress acts affirmatively and passes a rescission bill[46] approving the President's request. If passed, the recission measure would repeal or amend the amounts authorized in previous appropriations acts. Both houses have provisions for expediting floor action on recission bills.

ABOLISHING PREVIOUS PRESIDENTIAL AUTHORITY

The National Emergencies Act was signed into law on September 14, 1976. Two years from that date, all powers and authority held by the President and any other federal officer or employee as a result of past national emergencies will have terminated.[47] In effect, on September 14, 1978, the Act will have ended four emergencies: those declared by Presidents Roosevelt, in March 1933 to deal with the Depression, Truman, in December 1950 after the oubreak of the Korean War, and Nixon, in March 1970 in response to a postal strike, and in August 1971 to implement currency restrictions following an international monetary crisis.[48]

The two-year grace period was to give the executive time to seek enactment of new laws to continue programs operating under statutes triggered by past emergencies. Also, of the some 470 so-called ''emergency'' laws, eight grant the executive authority considered essential for normal government activities. These eight provisions are exempt from termination under the National Emergencies Act, although they were subject to congressional review and possible change within nine months after the act became law.[49] So, while the act strips the President of most past emergency authority, it leaves him with enough for normal operations and grants him time to try to gain more. And, of course, the President may declare new emergencies in the future.

PRESIDENT AND CONGRESS: THREE SCENARIOS FOR THE FUTURE

A combination of the Great Depression, World War II, the Cold War, and the early years of the Vietnam War left the Presidency with vastly expanded responsibilities and authority. Is the final legacy of Vietnam and of Presidents Johnson and Nixon to be a weakened Presidency? An ascendant Congress? More generally, in what way may the new restrictions shape the future relationship of Presidents and Congress?

While the definitive answer will be provided by future events, we can consider three scenarios, in order of their probability for the near future.

Scenario 1: A More Balanced Partnership

Assuming no major changes in the existing political environment, the next few years should see a more balanced partnership between President and Congress in the adoption of public policy. Congress will insure this by exerting many of the new restrictions as checks on the President. But while there will be some retrenchment of the President's influence, there will not be a period of congressional dominance reminiscent of the 19th century. The President has too many responsibilities, legal and political, for that. Rather, the President will continue to propose, but Congress will more often—and more effectively—dispose. This relationship should be institutional. That is, the growth in congressional checks will be mostly (but not completely) independent of changes in specific issues or in the partisan makeup of the White House and Capitol Hill. Several factors contribute to this conclusion.

The new restrictions make it easier for Congress to offset the President. Executive actions kept secret in the past now must be reported routinely, giving Congress substantive knowledge on which to act. Previously, Congress's ultimate weapon was the power of the purse—restricting the use of future appropriations or repealing past spending authority. Both techniques were subject to delay in the legislative process and a possible presidential veto. Now the President faces veto-proof simple and concurrent resolutions, protected against committee pigeonholes and filibusters, and automatic deadlines written into existing law.

Other things being equal, the more opportunities Congress has to impose restrictions, the more likely it will. Restrictions giving Congress the most opportunities are those permanently built into routine congressional activity. One example is the annual budgetary process, with its budget committees and timetable of deadlines for spending priorities and target ceilings. The routine workload of the Intelligence Committees includes drafing annual authorization bills and receiving annual, or more frequent, reports of executive branch intelligence activities. Finally, presidential impoundment requests, and their review by Congress, have become virtually routine.

In the aftermath of Vietnam and Watergate,

Congress appears to have developed a more confident self-image, a greater willingness to assert its institutional prerogatives. Consequently, Congress seems more inclined to oppose a President perceived as demeaning its dignity and downgrading its importance in the constitutional scheme of things.

With the possible exception of Lyndon Johnson, Presidents since Franklin Roosevelt have not had consistently strong political bases from which they could win a serious confrontation with a determined Congress. Republican Presidents Eisenhower and Nixon won huge popular pluralities in 1956 and 1972, respectively, but faced sizable Democratic majorities in Congress. Democratic Presidents—Truman in 1948, Kennedy in 1960, Carter in 1976—won very close elections and ran well behind their congressional party in popular votes. There is no evidence that this phenomenon—Presidents of both parties without coattails—will reverse itself in the immediate future.

SCENARIO 2: CONSTITUTIONAL CONFRONTATION

Given the necessary circumstances—President and Congress at loggerheads, with neither willing to back down or compromise—there could be a confrontation if the President challenges the constitutionality of some of the restrictions.

For example, a case can be made that Congress cannot stop the President with a veto-proof concurrent resolution. Article 1, Section 7 of the Constitution states that "every order, resolution, or vote" to which both houses must agree (with the exception of a resolution to adjourn) shall not take effect until after it has been signed by the President or passed over his veto," according to the rules and limitations prescribed in the case of a bill." Consequently, one can argue that any resolution ending an emergency or a war, or preventing a foreign arms sale, must be sent to the President for his approval or veto. The rebuttal is that veto-proof concurrent resolutions comply with the requirements of Article 1, Section 7, because they are authorized in statutes which have been signed by the President or passed over his veto. This constitutional argument has not been resolved by the Supreme Court.

A President might also refuse to continue reporting CIA activities, especially if they were compromised by leaks, by asserting executive primacy in the conduct of foreign policy and national security. Congress could retaliate by citing its legislative authority for oversight and investigation.

The Supreme Court would have to be willing to resolve such issues. If it were not, either the President would eviscerate any restrictions he chose to ignore, or Congress would enforce them by other means—not excluding impeachment.

SCENARIO 3: REASSERTION OF THE DOMINANT PRESIDENCY

Unlikely in the near term, but not in the more distant future, is the reassertion of presidential primacy on a footing equivalent to what it was from 1932 to 1972. The present restrictions (or most of them) might remain in the statutes, but they would be unused as politically unfeasible. The conditions for this scenario would include one or more of the following: the dimming of Vietnam and Watergate in Congress's institutional memory; a desire in Congress to escape the political heat that accompanies leadership in policymaking, with a consequent deferring to the President's initiatives; and some severe crisis or emergency (a prolonged energy crunch or world famine come to mind) comparable to the Depression or World War II, in which Congress and the public give the President virtual carte blanche.

CHAPTER

9

Congress and Public Policy: Contributions, Processes, and Impacts

Congress's contribution to public policy cannot be overemphasized. Almost all that the government does can be traced to some congressional action. Congress serves as policy incubator and initiator, formulator and legitimator. As a grand forum for debate and deliberation, Congress is the great coalition builder for the American polity.

The policy tools of Congress include much more than passing legislation. Among the extra legislative tools are oversight responsibilities, the ever-growing congressional veto, the power of the purse, advise-and-consent authority, and the "new" congressional budget process.

Selections in this chapter address these various formidable policy tools. Also examined are analytical perspectives on Congress's contributions to the broader political system and the total policy process.

The subject of congressional policymaking can be examined as both an independent and a dependent variable. As dependent variable, congressional policymaking can be viewed as the result of a combination of congressional organizational qualities and the reelection imperative. In other words, much of what Congress does in a policy sense can be explained by referencing the organization and underlying incentive system of Congress. As an independent variable, congressional policymaking can be studied with an eye toward detecting bias in policy outcomes, impacts, and consequences. From this vantage point, an effort is made to ascertain who wins and who loses from the configuration of power in Congress.

ILLUSTRATION 9A POWERS OF CONGRESS

POWERS OF CONGRESS

Article I, Section 8 of the Constitution defines the powers of Congress. Included are the powers to assess and collect taxes—called the chief power; to regulate commerce, both interestate and foreign; to coin money; to establish post offices and post roads; to establish courts inferior to the Supreme Court; to declare war; to raise and maintain an army and navy. Congress is further empowered "to provide for calling forth the Militia to execute the laws of the Union, suppress insurrections and repel invasions;" and "to make all laws which shall be necessary and proper for carrying into execution the foregoing powers, and all other powers vested by this Constitution in the government of the United States, or in any department or officer thereof."

AMENDMENTS TO THE CONSTITUTION

Another power vested in the Congress is the right to propose amendments to the Constitution, whenever two thirds of both houses shall deem it necessary. Should two thirds of the state legislatures demand changes in the Constitution, it is the duty of Congress to call a constitutional convention. Proposed amendments shall be valid as part of the Constitution when ratified by the legislatures or by conventions of three fourths of the states, as one or the other mode of ratification may be proposed by Congress.

SPECIAL POWERS OF THE SENATE

Under the Constitution, the Senate is granted certain powers not accorded to the House of Representatives. The Senate approves or disapproves certain presidential appointments by majority vote; and treaties must be concurred in by a two-thirds vote.

SPECIAL POWERS OF THE HOUSE OF REPRESENTATIVES

The House of Representatives is granted the power of originating all bills for the raising of revenue.

Both houses of Congress act in impeachment proceedings, which, according to the Constitution, may be instituted against the President, Vice President, and all civil officers of the United States. The House of Representatives has the sole power of impeachment, and the Senate has the sole power to try impeachments.

PROHIBITIONS UPON CONGRESS

Section 9 of Article I of the Constitution also imposes prohibitions upon Congress: "The privilege of the writ of habeas corpus shall not be suspended, unless when in cases of rebellion or invasion the public safety may require it." A bill of attainder or an ex post facto law cannot be passed. No export duty can be imposed. Ports of one state cannot be given preference over those of another state. "No money shall be drawn from the Treasury, but in consequence of appropriations made by law. . . ." No title of nobility may be granted.

SOURCE: From "Powers of Congress," *United States Government Manual,* 1980–81, pp. 40–41. Reprinted from the public domain.

9.1 Legislative Power*

Louis Fisher

This article discusses the full gamut of congressional power and the various modes through which it is exercised. Fisher focuses on the increasing importance of legislative vetoes.

The Constitution grants to Congress the basic responsibility and power over legislation, giving the President only a qualified veto and the right to make recommendations. Yet in the minds of many it is the President, particularly in the 20th century, who carries out the duties of "chief legislator." In part this reflects a real shift of power. In many ways, however, the notion of the President's influence in legislative affairs is an illusion nourished by academics, the news media, and Congress itself. This paper explores the principal issues that presently confront the Senate in its exercise of legislative power.

SPECIFICITY OF STATUTORY LANGUAGE

Not since 1935 has the Supreme Court struck down a delegation of power to the executive branch because legislative guidelines were inadequate. There were two such decisions in that year, both involving the National Industrial Recovery Act, which placed upon industrial and trade associations the responsibility for drawing up codes to minimize competition, raise prices, and restrict production. If the President regarded the codes as unacceptable he could prescribe codes and enforce them by law. The Court concluded that Congress had failed to provide adequate standards and guidelines for administrative action. In the *Schechter* case, Justice Cardozo exclaimed, "This is delegation running riot."[1]

What the Court found intolerable was not delegation per se but the lack of statutory guidelines. The Court has repeatedly recognized that the nature of government requires Congress to pass general legislation and leave to other branches the responsibility for "filling in the details."[2] While Congress cannot surrender the legislative power entrusted to it by the Constitution, neither is it possible for Congress to avoid delegating major powers and discretionary authority to the President. The tension between these two conflicting values was resolved by one author in the following syllogism: (1) Major premise: Legislative power cannot be constitutionally delegated by Congress; (2) Minor premise: It is essential that certain powers be delegated to administrative officers and regulatory commissions; (3) Conclusion: Therefore the powers thus delegated are not legislative powers.[3]

This kind of circular reasoning is evident in many Court decisions on delegation. The Court declares that it would be a breach of the Constitution for Congress to transfer its legislative power to the President, and yet in the very same decision the Justices will uphold the delegation in question.[4]

Why does the Court sanction such legislation? Often the statutory language is vague and ill-defined, such as general guidelines of "excessive profits," "reasonable rates," "unjust discrimination," and "in the public interest."

---

* From Louis Fisher, "The Senate's Legislative Power," in *Techniques and Procedures for Analysis and Evaluation: A Compilation of Papers Prepared for the Commission on the Operation of the Senate* (Washington, D.C.: U.S. Government Printing Office, 1977), pp. 3–13. Reprinted from the public domain.

Often the legislation is saved not because of specificity in the language but because Congress has supplied standards of due process to guide administrative officials. Such standards include the giving of notice and hearing by an agency prior to issuing a ruling or regulation. Also, findings of fact are supplied for the record and procedures exist for appeal. The Administrative Procedure Act of 1946 established various standards for agency rulemaking in order to guarantee fairness and equitable treatment. Through such standards Congress tries to eliminate or minimize the opportunity for executive caprice and arbitrariness.

Yet there is still a profound concern that Congress has handed over to executive branch officials too much of its legislative power. This is illustrated by the Economic Stabilization Act of 1970, which authorized the President to "issue such orders and regulations as he may deem appropriate to stabilize prices, rents, wages, and salaries at levels not less than those prevailing on May 25, 1970." Several parties took this statute to court to test its constitutionality. In one of the principal decisions, Circuit Judge Leventhal upheld the delegation by noting that some of the congressional guidelines had been included in the committee reports and legislative history: "Whether legislative purposes are to be obtained from committee reports, or are set forth in a separate section of the text of the law, is largely a matter of drafting style." It is more than that, however, for agencies are bound by law but not necessarily by nonstatutory controls (a point pursued in the next section). As for the 1970 act, it was subsequently amended to provide for more explicit standards and guidelines.[5]

In 1974 two members of the Supreme Court objected to excessive delegation of legislative power to the executive branch.[6] The issue was raised more prominently when President Ford imposed a fee on imported oil on January 23, 1975. The plan called for an initial fee of $1 a barrel, followed by increases to $2 on March 1 and to $3 on April 1. The Ford administration contended that there were three types of measures: taxes, tariffs, and fees. The first two had to be authorized by Congress while a fee on imported material "may be set for nonrevenue purposes and need not be legislated."[7]

As appeal was made to the courts to have the fee declared illegal. Congressman Robert Drinan, joining with other parties, argued that the imposition of "license fees" was a circumvention of the duty system established by the Constitution. U.S. District Court Judge John Pratt decided that the fee program was one of several actions covered by the Trade Expansion Act, which permitted the President "to adjust imports." In answer to those who regarded the section as an undue delegation of legislative authority, Judge Pratt remarked that the "nondelegation doctrine is almost a complete failure."[8]

Judge Pratt was reversed by the U.S. Court of Appeals for the District of Columbia. Circuit Judge Tamm, writing for a 2–1 majority, concluded that the Trade Expansion Act did not authorize the fees imposed by President Ford. A review of previous trade legislation convinced him that congressional delegations had been "narrow and explicit in order to effectuate well-defined goals." He also rejected the Administration's interpretation of a fee on imported materials. He cited a Tariff Commission report that called the license fee mechanism "substantially a duty system." Moreover, the fee imposed by President Ford would generate an estimated $4.8 billion a year, which was more than the total amount of revenue derived from customs in 1974.[9]

The fee-duty distinction was not addressed by the Supreme Court, in 1976, when it upheld the license fees. Justice Marshall, writing for a unanimous Court, stated that the fees were within the scope of the Trade Expansion Act. That the act itself delegated broadly—authorizing the President to "take such action, and for such time, as he deems necessary to adjust the imports of [the] article and its derivatives so that . . . imports [of the article] will not threaten to impair the national security"—did not disturb the Court. Justice Marshall was satisfied that the President's action was authorized by the language of the Trade Expansion

Act and its legislative history. He maintained that the legislative standards were clearly sufficient to meet any delegation doctrine attack.[10]

It is evident from these examples that the impulse for more explicit standards for administrative action must come from Congress itself, not the courts. But a number of practical hurdles discourage specificity.

REASONS FOR BROAD DELEGATION

Vague and general grants of legislative power have been criticized from various points of view. The are those who believe that political accountability depends on the establishment of clear guidelines for administrators.[11] A more contemporary concern is the stress on program evaluation. How can Congress, assisted by the General Accounting Office and other staff support, determine whether programs are being carried out effectively unless the original legislative goals are stated in clear terms?

Part of Congress' hesitancy in writing explicit statutory language reflects the dilemma of trying to legislate for future events. Courts for more than a century have recognized that it is essential to phrase statutes in general terms when events are future and impossible to be fully known. There are many subjects of government upon which wise and useful legislation must depend, which cannot be known to the lawmaking power, and must, therefore, be a subject of inquiry and determination outside of the halls of legislation.[12]

Toward the end of the 19th century and the first part of the 20th, administrative discretion was broadened because the conditions in the economy to be regulated were increasingly complex, interrelated, and in process of constant change.Courts repeatedly held that broadness and generality in statutes are unavoidable. Because of the unique circumstances existing in different regions and localities, Congress could only declare a general policy and leave to administrative officers the duty of applying the statute to particular cases.[13]

Kenneth Culp Davis, a prominent authority on administrative law, has identified a number of other reasons for broad delegation. Legislators and staff generally lack the expertise to draft specific language for highly specialized subjects. Even experts in the agencies and in the private sector find it difficult to suggest strict standards that will be practical and workable. These circumstances, faced by legislators and administrators alike, invite vague formulations of objectives. Furthermore, specificity of language may jeopardize the consensus needed to pass legislation and attract agency and interest group support. Under such conditions, Davis concludes, vague or meaningless standards may be preferable to precise and meaningful ones.[14]

This does not mean that administrators are free to work in an environment without guidelines. Instead of relying on more stringent legislative standards, Davis would rather have guides furnished by the administrators who have to implement the program. If Congress fails to provide adequate standards, agency officials have to use their rulemaking authority to establish criteria for further action. Congress may also control administrative action by changing authorization language or even by placing limitations in an appropriation act.[15] In the event that the President issues executive orders pursuant to delegated authority, and Congress wants to revoke the orders, such action is well within its power.[16] Congress may also include in a statute a requirement for review at stipulated periods, and may provide for a termination date for delegated authority (so-called sunset or self-destruct provisions).

NONSTATUTORY CONTROLS

Vagueness in legislation is often remedied, to some extent, by details that appear in the legislative history: committee reports, committee hearings, floor debates, correspondence from review committees, and other sources. This narrows considerably the range of agency discretion. For example, the Public Works Appropriations Act for fiscal 1976 contained a lump sum of $1.2 billion for construction by the Corps of Engineers. But the two houses of Congress had quite specific projects in mind in arriving at that sum. The projects are listed in the conference report, grouped together state-by-state so that each member knows the projects to be carried out.

Nonstatutory controls serve the purposes of both branches. Neither Congress nor the agencies are always certain of the specifics to be included in a statute. If judgments and predictions are wrong, the statute has to be rewritten. Putting the guidelines in nonstatutory sources introduces valuable flexibility to the legislative process. If adjustments are necessary after passage of the law, committee and agencies can depart from the nonstatutory scheme without having to write a new statute.

The nonstatutory system of legislative control is fragile; much depends on a "keep the faith" attitude among agency officials. They must want to maintain the integrity of their budget presentations and preserve a relationship of trust and confidence with congressional committees. If they ever violate that trust and abuse their discretionary power, they have to face the prospect of budget cutbacks, restrictive language in statutes, and line-item appropriations.

Part of this evolution can be illustrated by the history of reprogramming of funds by the Defense Department. Reprogramming consists of the shift of funds within an appropriation account (for example, aircraft procurement, Navy), in contrast to the shift of funds from one account to another (for example, from aircraft procurement, Navy to weapons procurement, Navy). The latter transactions are called transfers and require statutory authority. Reprogramming is basically a nonstatutory development; controls are exercised for the most part through committee reports, agency directives, and a complicated set of understandings between the two branches.

Several decades ago the technique of legislative control relied basically on review by two members from each of the Appropriations Committees: the chairman of the Defense Appropriations Subcommittee and the ranking minority member from that subcommittee. Gradually the subcommittee began to place restrictions in the committee report on the defense appropriations bill. Those restrictions, in turn, were incorporated in the Defense Department directives and instructions. Review extended to a greater number of committee members—from the chairman and ranking member to the full subcommittee, and sometimes to the full committee. The authorization committees (Armed Services) became involved. At times the committees would agree that the decision was so crucial that it should be made on the floor of Congress rather than worked out as an agency–subcommittee agreement.[17]

Although the procedure has worked well, occasionally there have been what Congress regards as bad-faith efforts to circumvent the understandings. Particularly serious to Congress was the practice of some defense agencies to request funds for a program, be turned down, and then reprogram other funds to that very program. This completely frustrated the congressional review and nullified legislative action. After warnings were issued by the committees having jurisdiction—both Appropriations and Armed Services—it was decided to place a restriction in statutory form. For a number of years now it has been the practice of Congress to insert this language in the Defense Appropriations Act: "No part of the funds in this act shall be available to prepare or present a request to the Committees on Appropriations for the reprogramming of funds, unless for higher priority items, based on unforeseen military requirements, than those for which originally appropriated and in no case where the item for which reprogramming is requested has been denied by the Congress."[18] The clause on "higher-priority items" is intended to discourage agencies from trying to use extra funds that become available on marginal and low-priority programs.

The tenuous nature of nonstatutory controls is evident from an incident in 1975. The conference report on the defense appropriations bill for fiscal 1975 had directed the Navy to produce, as its air combat fighter, a derivative of the plane selected by the Air Force.[19] Instead, the Navy picked an aircraft that was not a derivative. A contractor, who had bid on the expectation that the Navy would follow the understanding in the conference report, lodged a formal protest with the General Accounting Office to the effect that the action was null and void. Among the arguments presented by the contractor was the claim that directives placed in a conference report were binding on an agency.

The GAO disagreed. The Comptroller General ruled that such directives had legal force only when some ambiguity in the language of the public law required recourse to the legislative history; otherwise, agencies followed nonstatutory controls for practical, not for legal, reasons. Agencies may ignore nonstatutory controls, said the Comptroller General, but only "at the peril of strained relations with the Congress." To be legally binding the directive on the Navy aircraft had to appear in the public law.[20]

If there is litigation, the legislative history of a statute may be controlling. But Congress and the public cannot enter the courts to resolve every grievance. Generally the nonstatutory controls depend on good-faith efforts and a spirit of cooperation by agency officials.

Do agencies regard nonstatutory controls as less binding than in prior decades? If so, is that because of politicization at the top ranks of agencies and less influence by careerists? The experience during the Nixon years may be largely an aberration, yet similar breakdowns in executive–legislative understandings have marred the records of other recent Administrations. If some type of fundamental shift is underway, producing a heightened sense of agency independence and White House autonomy, Congress may have to depend more heavily on statutory provisions and sharper legislative guidelines.

LEGISLATIVE VETOES

Another technique used by Congress to retain control over delegated authority is to attach strings, or conditions, to a statute. One of the more controversial conditions is to subject presidential action to some type of legislative veto by both houses, by either house, or even by congressional committees.

An early use of this approach involved the delegation of reorganization authority to the President in 1938. President Roosevelt asked for authority to reorganize the executive branch, subject to disapproval by a joint resolution of Congress. The latter would have to be presented to the President for his signature. If a joint resolution were to be vetoed, legislators doubted that they could muster the necessary two-thirds majority in each house to override the President. In effect, they would have delegated an authority by majority vote but could not regain control without a two-thirds majority. Partly because of that misgiving, the proposed reorganization bill was not enacted in 1938.

The next year some members proposed that reorganization plans be subject to disapproval by a concurrent resolution, which requires passage by each house but is not presented to the President. This raised the question of whether a concurrent resolution would be "legislative in effect," for the Constitution provides that "every order, resolution, or vote to which the concurrence of the Senate and House of Representatives may be necessary (except on a question ofadjournment) shall be presented to the President. . . ." That language has not been strictly adhered to. For example, Congress adopted constitutional amendments by passing resolutions and referred them not to the President, but directly to the states for ratification. That procedure was upheld in *Hollingsworth* v. *Virginia* (1798).[21]

Also, Congress early developed the practice of passing simple resolutions (adopted by either house) and concurrent resolutions (by both houses) for internal, housekeeping matters. Since they were not regarded as "legislative in effect," there was no need to present them to the President. A Senate report in 1897 concluded that "legislative in effect" depended on the substance, not the mere form, of a resolution. If it contained matter that was "legislative in its character and effect, it must be presented to the President."[22]

Nevertheless, concurrent resolutions gradually became a vehicle to control executive actions. Congress relied on that procedure in 1906 to direct the Secretary of War to make investigations in river and harbor matters. A 1903 act provided that even simple resolutions were sufficient to direct the Secretary of Commerce to make investigations.[23]

It was against this background that Congress extended the use of concurrent resolutions to protect its legislative prerogatives. During the 1939 debate on the reorganization bill, Congressman Cox argued that the concurrent resolution feature was not legislative in effect. Instead, it was a condition attached to reorganization authority delegated to the President. If he disagreed with the condition he could exercise his veto power. Otherwise, the signing of the bill would indicate his willingness to abide by the condition. The House Select Committee on Government Organization defended the concurrent resolution procedure by pointing to a recent Supreme Court decision that upheld a delegation of authority to the Secreatry of Agriculture. That authority was contingent upon the votes of farmers during a referendum. To the committee it seemed absurd "to believe that the effectiveness of action legislative in character may be conditional upon a vote of farmers but may not be conditioned on a vote of the two legislative bodies of the Congress."[24]

As enacted in 1939, the Reorganization Act authorized the President to submit plans for executive reorganization. The plans would take effect after 60 days unless Congress, within that time, disapproved them by concurrent resolution. Extension of the authority in 1949 permitted disapproval by a single house. Presidents, whatever constitutional reservations they may have had over the legislative veto procedure, acquiesced in this type of conditional legislation. They realized that Congress would not delegate such authority without attaching strings to it.

That the legislative veto parts company with the procedures set forth by the Constitution is obvious. But so do many executive practices. Legislative recommendations by the Executive Branch do not always come to Congress for review and action; often they are accomplished unilaterally by executive order, proclamation, or agency rulemaking. In the words of Justice White, in a 1976 decision, legislative veto—even by a single house—"no more invades the President's powers than does a regulation not required to be laid before Congress."[25]

The legislative veto procedure is of special concern when used by Congress not for the purpose of retaining control over its own powers, which it may temporarily delegate, but to control actions and responsibilities that are executive in nature. In this type of situation Congress does not attach conditions to delegated authority; it attempts to control what the President claims belongs to him under the Constitution.

For example, suppose that the President enters into an armistice with a foreign country. Could Congress veto that action by passing a concurrent resolution, or simple resolution, as contemplated by pending legislation on executive agreements? Can Congress, under the War Powers Resolution, pass a concurrent resolution to order the President to withdraw troops when he determines that their presence is needed to protect American lives? While Congress is at liberty to pass such resolutions, the President may conclude that his obligations under the Constitution cannot be circumscribed by one-house or two-house vetoes. However obscure and ill-defined the realm of foreign affairs and national security, it is far different from reorganization authority, which is congressionally based and may be granted and withdrawn as Congress decides.

A different type of controversy is involved in the present effort of Congress to control administrative rulemaking. On September 21, 1976, the House of Representatives voted 265–135 in favor of H.R. 12048, which included a legislative veto over agency rules and regulations. The vote fell short of the two-thirds majority needed under suspension of the rules. Agency rulemaking cannot be categorized neatly as legislative or executive. It can be looked at as a fusion of both: legislative in the sense that agency regulations have the force of law, executive in the sense that agencies are carrying out the purposes enacted by Congress.[26]

The debate on the Administrative Rulemaking Reform Act of 1976 includes a variety of complex points made by proponents and opponents. Practical, as well as constitutional, issues are at stake.[27] For the purpose of this paper it is enough to discuss the potential impact of the legislation on delegated power. While the reform would permit Congress to review—and reject—regulations issued by agencies, it might also encourage Congress to legislate with even fewer guidelines. Advocates of vague delegations could always argue that Congress would be in a position to review regulations to make sure that they square with congressional intent. But if the statute is vague, and if the legislative history supplies inadequate or conflicting directives, it becomes impossible to know whether the agency is departing from the legislative purpose. Nor would courts, through their review of agency rules, be any better prepared to determine the appropriateness of a regulation.

A second question concerns the scope of the Administrative Rulemaking Reform Act. With few exceptions, all agency regulations would be subject to legislative review and legislative veto. Is agency abuse so widespread that all regulations should be scrutinized by Congress? Is there, in fact, abuse, or does the problem originate because of a lack of clear and understandable legislative standards? If the latter, Congress could devote more time and thought to clarifying statutory objectives instead of injecting itself so deeply in the administrative process. Congress could exercise its policymaking prerogative directly through legislation, as was the original intent of the Constitution, rather than placing upon agencies the responsibility for articulating national standards. Alternatively, Congress (as has been the practice), can apply the legislative veto more selectively to agencies that require special attention.

A third issue related to the purpose of the doctrine of separated powers. In part it was adopted by the framers to provide a system of checks and balances in the national government. But the creation of a separate executive was also meant to impart efficiency and accountability to administration. The actions of the Continental Congress, from 1774 to 1787, provided the framers with evidence of the limitations and frailties of a legislative body that had to both pass laws and administer them.[28]

Perhaps the goals of unity and responsibility in the executive branch are impossible to achieve in the 20th century, particularly with the growth of the federal government, the dozens of quasi-independent regulatory agencies, and the large number of off-budget agencies. No doubt the executive branch is splintered in ways never anticipated by the Founding Fathers. But before abandoning the scheme of separated powers, and the division of labor between Congress and the President, we ought to consider individual reform efforts in the broader context of fundamental principles. The demarcation between legislative and executive, though not precisely delineated in the Constitution, was done for a purpose and it has yet to be demonstrated that the purpose belongs to a day gone by.

LEGISLATIVE INITIATIVE

For a number of decades it has been the practice of scholars to characterize the President as "chief legislator." This image, which appears to satisfy some yearning for simplicity and idolatry, gives the executive branch undue credit. Every statute, Woodrow Wilson noted long ago, "may be said to have a long lineage of statutes behind it."[29] An executive branch agency, or the President, often puts into motion an idea already conceived and nurtured by legislators and private groups. Congressional staff assistants, who play a major role in initiating a bill, may prefer to conceal that fact out of deference to a member of Congress. Private organizations, responsible for drafting a bill and mobilizing support, may deliberately obscure their contribution in order to enhance prospects for passage.

After a presidential proposal reaches Congress, it is usually reworked considerably in committee and on the floor. Yet upon passage it may retain the designation "the President's bill." Even in cases where the President's proposal emerges unscathed from the legislative mill, that may demonstrate not his power to impose so much as his accurate assessment of what Congress and its members are willing to accept. Still, the President dominates the media, hands out the pens upon signing a bill, and manages to retain the largely fictitious title of chief legislator.

The responsibility for this misconception cannot be laid solely at the feet of academics and the media. Members of Congress often prefer to wait for an executive request for legislation rather than take the initiative. Even when they do initiate legislation, they submit to a lengthy review process by the Administration. A negative response by the Office of Management and Budget, stating that the proposal is "not in accord with the program of the President," is regarded as a near-fatal announcement. Only in a few cases, such as the War Powers Resolution and anti-impoundment legislation, will Congress persevere in the face of determined executive opposition.

And whereas Congress is expected to tolerate executive indifference or disdain regarding its proposals, there is strong pressure on Congress to act with alacrity on what the President wants. Failure to do so reinforces the image of Congress as a slothful and nay-saying institution, even when the executive proposal is lacking in merit or of low priority. Why is a legislative "no" resented by the public, and the media, while a presidential veto has the aura of a heroic act? Congress is consistently at a disadvantage when compared to the executive branch. If a member of Congress travels to a foreign country his activity is condemned as a "junket." A similar journey by an executive branch official is praised as a high mission of statecraft. If the President sends up a supplemental request for funds not contemplated in his budget, it appears to meet a new and pressing need. An effort by Congress to add to his budget, and reshape it along legislative priorities, is castigated as irresponsible and profligate.

This is not simply the fault of a biased or ill-informed press. Congress and the President behave differently when their institutions are under attack. It is characteristic of members of the executive branch to join ranks and present a solid front, defending the President's program and record. Frequent shifts of 180 degrees are made without apology or embarrassment. In contrast, members of Congress have a facility for demeaning their own institution. "I am frugal but Congress is spendthrift" is the message sent to constituents at home. In the words of Richard D. Fenno, Jr., "Members run for Congress by running against Congress."

The Senate could take steps to foster a more accurate image of Congress—to show the actual role of legislators in initiating policy, incubating ideas, and reshaping presidential proposals. Press announcements from Congress might be an effective means of claiming credit. This would require Congress to vest in some central agency—either for Congress as a whole or for each house—the authority and responsibility for preparing releases for the press.[30]

The difficulties in creating such a central office are not hard to imagine. The majority and minority parties will differ on the accomplishments of Congress. Individual Senators will prefer to handle their own media contacts without interference from a central office. Yet after a bill has emerged from conference, the very process that made accommodation possible between the House and the Senate, and between the majority and minority parties, should create a climate in which the legislative record can be set straight.

9.2 Legislative Oversight of Bureaucracy*

Morris S. Ogul

This article gives an overview of congressional oversight activities, drawing general conclusions about this important legislative function.

Legislative oversight of bureaucracy involves some of the most complex forms of behavior that the Congress undertakes. Not surprisingly then, legislative oversight is less understood than almost any other aspect of congressional behavior. Both Congressmen in interviews and scholars in their writings concede this lack of sustained insight. In this vortex of incomplete knowledge (recognizing that the best experts on congressional behavior are often Congressmen) an outsider may make a contribution by looking at familiar questions from a more detached viewpoint than that of the immersed participant.

What follows is based on perspectives derived from a variety of sources, from general reading and observation of the Congress and especially from intensive research in 1965 and in 1966 into the behavior of several committees and subcommittees. Then, and since, the writer has interviewed in depth some 40 House members, an equal number of staff persons, and more than a score of lobbyists and officials in the Executive Branch concerned with oversight.

Statements embodying general laws about oversight are scarce. It is possible, however, to provide some useful insights into the conduct of oversight. The materials that follow may qualify under this latter heading. Oversight is defined as the behavior of legislators, individually or collectively, formally or informally, which results in an impact on bureaucratic behavior in relation to the structure and process of policy implementation.

LEGAL EXPECTATIONS AND ACTUAL BEHAVIOR

There is a large gap between the oversight the law calls for and the oversight actually performed. The clearest single statement about the oversight that the law requires the Congress to perform comes from that often quoted and seldom heeded statement in the Legislative Reorganization Act of 1946 assigning each standing committee the responsibility to "exercise continuous watchfulness of the execution by the administrative agencies concerned of any laws, the subject matter of which is within the jurisdiction of such committee."

Members of the Congress agree that this provision provides a full and direct legal obligation to act. In addition, all those interviewed saw that obligation as an appropriate one for the Congress. In brief, there is consensus in the Congress that extensive and systematic oversight *ought* to be conducted.

One reason for the gap between expectations and behavior lies in the nature of the expectation. The plain but seldom acknowledged fact is that this task, at least as defined above, is simply impossible to perform. No amount of congressional dedication and energy, no conceivable increase in the size of committee staffs, and even no extraordinary boost in committee budgets will enable the Congress to carry out its oversight obligations in a comprehensive and systematic manner. The job is too large for any combination of members and staff to completely master. Congressmen who feel obligated to obey the letter of the law are doomed to feelings of inadequacy and frustration and are laid open

---

* From Morris S. Ogul, "Legislative Oversight of Bureaucracy," Working papers on House Committee Organization and Operation, Select Committee on Committees, 1973. Reprinted from the public domain.

to charges of neglect. Fortunately, at least for their own morale, the members of the Congress tend to focus on the immediate more than on the impossible.

The statements above are not intended to suggest that the Congress ignores the oversight function but rather that it performs it selectively. In fact, the Congress oversees formally and informally in many ways on a daily basis. The most visible and perhaps the most effective way is through the appropriations process; the most unnoticed is latently as it considers authorizations, performs casework, and goes about business not directly labeled as oversight.

The remaining part of the gap between expectations and behavior narrows as one considers why Congressmen act as they do. Two topics will be given central attention: the multiple priorities of the members of the Congress, and the impact of their policy preferences on their behavior. A discussion of these topics will reveal that there are sound reasons for this gap to exist and that most members do not really mind too much that the gap is as large as it is. Hence, their lack of willingness to do much about it.

MULTIPLE PRIORITIES

Although they seldom seem to articulate it, most members do seem to realize that the performance of oversight is best discussed not in the vacuum of legal expectations but in the more proximate context of multiple priorities and policy preferences. Each member is faced with a variety of obligations that are generally agreed to be legitimate, important, and demanding in time and energy. In principle, he should be working hard at all of them. In fact, since he does not weigh them equally, he is unlikely to give them equal attention.

When any action is perceived to contribute directly and substantially to political survival as well as to other legitimate functions, it is likely to move toward the top of any member's priority list. Extra incentives to oversee come from problems of direct concern to one's constituents or from issues that promise political visibility or organizational support. Conversely, problems not seen as closely related to political survival are more difficult to crowd onto the member's schedule. In the choice phrase of one member: "Our schedules are full, but flexible."

Not all congressional activity is linked directly to political survival. A Congressman seems to gain interest in pushing oversight efforts onto his active calendar under the following conditions: New executive requests are forthcoming calling for massive new expenditures or substantial new authorizations in controversial policy areas; a crisis has occurred that has not been met effectively by executive branch departments; the opposition political party is in control of the executive branch; he has not been treated well either in the realm of personal attention or in the servicing of his requests; he has modest confidence in the administrative capacity of Department or agency leaders. If key members have confidence in the way that executive branch department leaders are running their programs, pressure for oversight eases. Comparing the experience of two former heads of the now defunct Post Office Department is instructive. Because most members of the House Post Office and Civil Service Committee had great respect for Postmaster General Lawrence O'Brien, their willingness to give him wide latitude to run his department was immense. Because these same members lacked such confidence in John Gronouski, they probed somewhat more carefully into the affairs of the Post Office Department when he ran it. At issue was not comparative executive competence, but congressional perceptions about that competence.

In making his choices about what to do, each Congressman applies his own standards of relevance; all will be doing those things that they consider most important to them at that time. Problems seen as less pressing may be recognized but may remain untouched. In these calculations, oversight frequently falls into the semineglected category. Choice, not accident, governs this decision.

If one judges from the behavior of Congressmen rather than from their words alone, the conclusion seems clear that in oversight as in other congressional activities, selection and choice among worthy tasks is always necessary. Absolute mandates, even if accepted as desirable, will be obeyed only in relative terms. The price of effective action in one area may be the neglect of another.

Members of the Congress, like most other people, manage to compartmentalize their various beliefs and behaviors. Even in the face of continuing imperfect performance, Congressmen retain their belief in the desirability of doing a good job at oversight. Yet, concurrently, many members seem comfortable while not doing much to narrow the gap between expectations about oversight and the actual performance of it. One might reasonably conclude then that the main spurs to the conduct of oversight do not come from any abstract belief about its necessity or desirability, but from other sources.

Congressmen through their actions implicitly rank their priorities. A glance at the rules that many seem to use provides some help in trying to understand oversight.

All members have many tasks that they feel should be pursued. The finite limits set by time and energy require that some of these expectations will be met more fully than others. If there is widespread agreement about the contents of a list of high-priority tasks, there is less consensus on the relative ranking of them. Only a few things are known about why members choose to give primary attention to some activities and less to others. Even if we can presume that the omnipresent desire to survive politically serves as a major inspiration, still, member selection of other priorities remains a murky area of political analysis.

Because these factors change, the interests of each Congressman in oversight will wax and wane despite his continuing adherence to the notion that oversight is an important function for the Congress to be performing.

POLICY PREFERENCES

Examining the policy preferences of members of the Congress moves us toward a more adequate explanation of the gap between expectations and behavior. From interviews and observation, I conclude that Congressmen are seldom anxious to monitor those executive activities of which they approve. Oversight efforts to support administrative programs are the exception. A member essentially indifferent to a program is not likely to press for oversight efforts. One of the most important pressures to oversee flows from disagreements on policies, especially those that are of intense concern to the member. The words of members express the abstract desire to oversee; it is when that desire combines with policy disagreement that oversight is more likely to ensue.

A classic example is the experience of the House Judiciary Committee in 1965 and 1966 with civil rights issues relating to race relations. This committee was an able group vitally interested in civil rights policymaking and administration. Emanuel Celler ran the committee as a strong chairman. Superficially, the Committee was conducting almost no oversight activity on questions of civil rights. What was strange was that the civil rights concerns of the Committee were known to be strong and deep. Several not so obvious factors helped to explain the situation. First, the Committee chairman felt that he was having an impact on the activities of the Justice Department through informal consultation. Second, the chairman agreed in essence with what the Justice Department was doing and thus had no desire to interfere. Third, in the judgment of Chairman Celler, the net effect of any formal investigations would be harmful to the cause of civil rights since antirights forces might find the forum useful to articulate and publicize their views. In this case, the absence of formal oversight could be explained by a simple formula: When policy interests and the obligation to oversee clash, policy preferences will normally prevail as a guide to conduct.

The discussion thus far of member priorities, choices, and policy preferences concerns each member. The fact is that in oversight efforts, as in other activities, all Congressmen are not equal. So even an intense desire to oversee, clearly a rarity in the Congress, depends for its fruition on factors other than the individual member's wants. The ability to oversee depends on where one is situated in the legislative process. Individual members, on their own, conduct very little oversight. For reasons of authority, money, and staff, oversight efforts are centered in the standing committees and subcommittees. Where one is placed in the committee system becomes a vital element in translating desires into effective action. A brief look at committees and their oversight activity is thus warranted.

COMMITTEES AND OVERSIGHT

One key to understanding oversight can be discovered by examining those places in the Congress where the division of labor and specialization can most easily be found, the committees and subcommittees. Members individually rarely can expect to conduct much legislative oversight. A comment later in the paper will indicate how even individual members can partially overcome this limitation. The heart of legislative oversight lies in the committees and subcommittees. How and why these units function as they do will tell us a great deal about how legislative oversight is performed. How the committees function is related to their structures for decision making.

Perhaps the most effective means to enhance a committee's oversight performance is through the presence of an alert, shrewd, active chairman who wants to conduct oversight broad in scope and profound in depth. Most reforms pale in significance before this seemingly simple solution. No one, of course, really knows how to pretest prospective chairmen for these talents and interests. Nor is it clear that the members would want to pick their chairman on the basis of these criteria even if they could. The best practical bet seems to be to assume that a list of committee chairmen and subcommittee chairmen will include a few who are intensely interested in oversight and highly talented in pursuing it and a large number who are less keen and less talented.

Assuming some such mix of committee chairmen, is there any way to enhance the oversight efforts of those committees headed by chairmen whose appetites and talents for oversight are unimpressive? At least one suggestion merits discussion. The odds for active oversight are better, in the absence of an eager chairman, if there are some semi-autonomous subcommittees with established jurisdictions, budgets, and staffs. The objective is to create additional fields in which ambition may flower. Visibility and ambition are as effective stimulants for subcommittee chairmen as for any other members. An active subcommittee within a quiescent full committee is not an unknown phenomenon in the Congress.

Innovation always has its price. The flexibility of the full committee chairman, his personal power, and perhaps even committee efficiency could possibly suffer. Whether enhancing the prospects for oversight may be worth these costs has to be decided by the Congressmen themselves.

What promotes the personal power of the chairman is not necessarily good for committee oversight efforts. Fixed subcommittee jurisdictions may indeed remove some flexibility from the full committee chairman, but the price may be right: promoting the competence prerequisite to oversight activity. Numbered subcommittees without fixed jurisdictions may impede the development of expertise. Besides, from an oddsmaker's perspective, the presence of several subcommittee chairmen with defined jurisdictions, separate staffs, and separate budgets, increases the field from which an interest in oversight may emerge. This analysis does not ignore the problems that may arise in some decentralized communities, but merely adds another weight to the scales.

Committee leaders may not dominate all committee behavior, but they do control much of it. What they are willing to do is central. Of course, committee members may press committee leaders to act. One type of situation minimizes the likelihood of member pressure for leadership action: where the members of a committee are there involuntarily. Members view some committee assignments as highly desirable; other assignments are viewed as burdens to be endured. Members appointed to unsought committees frequently transfer to more satisfactory assignments as soon as they can muster sufficient seniority. Given the normal problems in allotting their time and energy, we can expect that few members who see their assignments as undesirable are likely to exert maximum effort on such committees. Some oversight behavior, or the lack of it, is explainable in part by the priority that members assign to their work on a particular committee. In low-status committees, those few members who choose to remain probably do so for reasons unrelated to any desire to actively pursue oversight.

SOME GRIST FOR CONTEMPLATION AND DISCUSSION

Four Myths About Oversight

Perhaps the first necessity in thinking more generally about oversight is to suggest that some widely held and deeply cherished ideas are myths. The first of these is that the Congress lacks sufficient authority to oversee properly. In fact, one can argue that the Congress has all of the authority that it needs to oversee much more extensively and effectively.

A second myth holds that the Congress lacks the budget to oversee effectively. With few exceptions, committees have the money that they need even if they wish to sharply augment their oversight efforts. One can uncover, of course, some relatively deprived committees or subcommittees, but these are the exceptions.

A third cherished belief states that the answer to how to improve oversight efforts is more staff. This answer might hold in a few cases, but not generally. Committee staff persons are hired to satisfy a variety of needs. If committee chairmen choose to take on staff exclusively for subject-matter competence, research skills, and investigative talents, they can quickly improve the prospects for oversight. But even then, staff behavior is largely a function of member preferences. A chairman passive about oversight is unlikely to have staff persons, however talented, who view oversight as a high priority. With a few conspicuous exceptions, staff behavior is more a function of member preferences than a determinant of them.

The Legislative Reorganization Act of 1970 spelled out some relationships between the Congress, its committees, and the GAO. The actual impact of the GAO on legislative oversight would be an intriguing study in itself. Such an analysis might well suggest useful paths in a rethinking of how the oversight function is performed.

Legal authority, staff, and money are all important prerequisites to congressional action, but none of these are grossly lacking now. Genuflections before the trilogy of authority, money, and staff do not reach the basic problems.

In my judgment, a fourth myth about oversight is that members of the Congress and their staffs lack the experience, training, intelligence, or creativity to conduct more and better oversight. To put it more bluntly, some critics charge that the members and their staff simply lack the competence, defined broadly in the terms just mentioned, to do the necessary work. One can unearth situations where members lack the competence needed for specific tasks, but one finds little evidence to support the proposition that these deficiencies are universal or, when found, that normally they are beyond remedy. As has been demonstrated in actual performance, useful oversight is practicable in the Congress. Deficiencies in competence in specific circumstances can frequently be remedied if the committees or subcommittees desire to do so.

It is true that even talented generalists (viz., the members of the Congress) can be intimidated by mountains of data, by exotic or technical vocabularies, or by arcane analyses. It is also true that some technical experts at times seem to relish prolix analyses presented in nearly incomprehensive language. The expert may indeed understand that obfuscation is his first line of defense. But legislators and their staffs are predestined neither to succumb nor to be deceived. Effective legislative oversight does not require that all members and all staff persons be competent in all aspects of public policy. If that were necessary the task indeed would be hopeless. The dual practices of division of labor and specialization provide the classical solution to this problem.

SOME SUMMARY PROPOSITIONS

1. Oversight is neither comprehensive nor systematic because that goal is beyond achievement.

2. Oversight is performed intermittently because the factors most relevant to stimulating it are not constantly present. Thus the quality and quantity of oversight varies between the two branches of the Congress, among the committees and subcommittees within each house, and in the same committees and subcommittees from session to session and from issue to issue.

3. It is not too difficult to produce a syndrome of factors which tend to maximize the possibilities for effective oversight. The elements might be: there is a legal basis for committee activity and there is an adequate budget for it; adequate staff resources, defined in terms of numbers, skills, and attitudes are present; the subject matter is not unusually complex or technical; the issue involved has high political visibility; the committee with relevant jurisdiction is decentralized in structure unless the chairman is a strong advocate of oversight in the given area; key committee members are unhappy with their treatment by executive branch personnel; key committee members lack confidence in top executive branch personnel; committee senior members harbor personal antipathy toward executive officials; the executive branch proposes vast changes in existing programs; committee control rests in the political party opposite to that of the President.

The ease of creating such a list obscures the more difficult problem of assigning weights to each element and to predicting the possible consequences of its presence or absence. Perhaps that is because the primary elements of explanation may well vary from case to case. There seems to be no single pattern which explains legislative oversight in all circumstances. There are only common factors which combine in different ways under specified sets of circumstances. Moreover, even casual inspection of congressional behavior suggests that all the conditions which are part of this syndrome are rarely present simultaneously.

4. Oversight is not a high priority much of the time for most members.

5. Congressional staff behavior is primarily determined by member priorities and policy preferences. The best way to alter staff behavior is to focus on its major determinant.

6. A sense of realism demands recognition of the fact that most members are relatively satisfied with the conduct of legislative oversight of the bureaucracy. They feel little stimulus to alter existing patterns.

SOME PROPOSALS PERHAPS WORTHY OF DISCUSSION

Casework and Oversight

For very fundamental reasons, most oversight activity will come from Congressmen acting not as individuals, but as members of committees and subcommittees. But Congressmen acting as individuals in their own offices can do something that most do not do now. Priorities are basic. Most members now view the mountains of casework processed in their offices simply as service for constituents. Members could instruct their caseworkers to be more alert to the patterns of problems revealed in cases so that this information could be passed on to the appropriate committees and subcommittees. Congressmen collect routinely a mother lode of information potentially useful for oversight. Members either have not understood the value of what they have or have not cared enough to order the modest effort that would make this information more useful.

Committee Structure and Oversight

Committees that are serious about improving their potential for oversight should carefully examine their subcommittee structure to see if more autonomy might be provided.

Recognition of the Full Dimensions of Oversight

Much oversight that now occurs in the Congress is not recognized. Because a session is called a legislative hearing, or because processing of constituent complaints is called casework does not mean that these activities are unrelated to oversight. Oversight should be viewed from a broader perspective than that of formal investigations.

Are Oversight Subcommittees Worthwhile?

Perhaps the most obvious step taken by a few standing committees to enhance their oversight efforts has been to create specific oversight subcommittees. To my knowledge, no one has systematically or intensively looked at whether having such subcommittees makes any appreciable difference in the conduct of oversight. Here is a structural solution which one could suspect has not had any great impact. But nobody knows for sure. The topic does deserve attention.

A FINAL NOTE

The standard answer to improving the conduct of the congressional oversight function usually seems to be: Elect smarter people to the Congress, make them work harder, and give them bigger staffs. After extensive observation of the Congress at work, it seems to me that most members have the talent necessary to perform their jobs well; many Congressmen probably cannot work much harder than they do now, although they can change what they do if they want to; few Congressmen argue that increasing staff size would have any significant impact on the conduct of oversight. Apparently, those members who publicly proclaim the general virtue of having more staff seemingly do not have the improvement of oversight specifically in mind.

Surely a more accurate answer than the standard one (although still not a fully satisfactory one) might be: If more and better oversight is to be achieved, members need to alter their priorities for allocation of their time and they need to insist on *better* staffs. In practice, how to achieve either of these objectives is far from obvious.

The idea that no problem, given human effort and enough money, is beyond solution stands at the center of the American ethos. As a goad to improve things, this view may have great utility; as an observation about reality, it may be sadly defective. If the goal is to increase the quantity of oversight and to improve its quality, one needs to look at underlying causes. From this perspective, structural changes in the Congress, by themselves, are unlikely to do the job. The basic limits to more adequate oversight seem to me to lie not in defective structures but peripherally in excessive expectations and centrally in an imperfect will to act. The latter comment necessarily implies neither a general criticism nor a weakness. Congressmen do what they do and slight what they slight for reasons that seem persuasive to them. In the words of an astute Senate staff member discussing staff behavior on oversight matters:

> Specialists in departmental interference must judge both the merits of the case and the costs in time, effort, and their own or the Congressman's "credit" with the agency, of attempting to achieve a given solution.

In other words, reality is complex. The bases for choice are many. Balancing reasonable requests for time and action is central. Most Congressmen feel that they can justify much of what they do in terms that their constituents would find quite acceptable. Most staff members feel that what they are doing is what their employers, the members of Congress, want them to do. Merely telling members or staff persons to do something else is just not much help. The incentives for conducting more intensive and extensive oversight are great in the abstract and yet are modest in most concrete situations. Any analysis of legislative oversight has to be grounded in these stern facts.

9.3 | Congressional Oversight*

Joel D. Aberbach

Here, Aberbach discusses recent trends in oversight and identifies the factors affecting both the incident and quality of oversight.

VARIETIES OF CONGRESSIONAL OVERSIGHT

Congress has shown increasing concern about oversight as the federal bureaucracy has expanded in size and program initiation has passed to the executive branch. In 1946, following the New Deal and World War II, a provision of the Legislative Reorganization Act prescribed "continuous watchfulness" over the actions of the executive branch agencies in carrying out the laws. In the 1970 amendments to the act, Congress required most committees to issue periodic reports on their oversight endeavors. This was an obvious attempt to spur them to action. Data gathered on congressional oversight in 1973 for the Bolling Committee staff and comments by Congressmen before the Committee indicated that this requirement had not produced the desired effect and the House amended its rules in an attempt to stimulate more activity and provide some coordination. There is sentiment in the Senate for similar action, as indicated by the *Interim Report of the Commission on the Operation of the Senate* (U.S. Congress, 1976) and by Senate support for "sunset" legislation in 1978.

When it comes to performance Bibby's (1968)* comment that oversight is "Congress' neglected function" is still the standard introductory observation in papers on the subject. The second definition of oversight found in *Webster's New Collegiate Dictionary* may be unintendedly appropriate: "an overlooking or something overlooked; (an) omission or error due to inadvertence." However, the first meaning, "watchful care or supervision" is surely what we have in mind when we speak about congressional oversight.

There is a debate within the scholarly literature about how to define oversight. Harris proposes a relatively narrow definition. For him, oversight "strictly speaking, refers to review after the fact. It includes inquires about policies that are or have been in effect, investigations of

---

* From Joel D. Aberbach, "The Development of Oversight in the United States Congress: Concepts and Analysis," in *Techniques and Procedures for Analysis and Evaluation: A Compilation of Papers Prepared for the Commission on the Operation of the Senate* (Washington, D.C.: U.S. Government Printing Office, 1977), pp. 53–69. Reprinted from the public domain. This piece subsequently has been published in *American Behavioral Scientist* 22 (May/June 1979): 493–516.

This is a revised version of papers originally prepared for the Commission on the Operation of the Senate and the 1977 annual meeting of the American Political Science Association. Generous support from the Institute of Public Policy Studies and the Rackham Faculty Development Fund at the University of Michigan and from the Brookings Institution allowed the author to recheck the original data analyzed in the Commission and Association papers. Most of the corrections from the rechecking process were entered on the data tape in time for inclusion in this paper. The paper, therefore, contains some modifications in the data reported in earlier papers, although none substantial enough to change any conclusions. Final data reflecting all corrections will be reported as part of the author's Brookings volume on oversight. The author wishes to express his thanks to the graduate students at Michigan who assisted so ably in the arduous task of coding, preparing, and analyzing the data used here, particularly Celinda Lake and Susan Van Alstyne, and to Cynthia Enquist, who did much of the checkcoding while a summer intern at Brookings. Thanks are also extended to Doug Neal of the Bureau of Social Science Research, who produced the graphic in Figure 9.3.1.

* Reference list in Endnotes.

past administrative actions, and the calling of executive officers to account for their financial transactions'' (Harris, 1964). Ogul takes a much broader approach and defines legislative oversight as ''behavior by legislators and their staffs, individually or collectively, which results in an impact, intended or not, on bureaucratic behavior'' (Ogul, 1976). The Ogul definition is useful in that it directs attention to the fact that oversight is a latent as well as a manifest function of Congress and that many of the things done by members and Senators contribute to oversight. It is so broad, however, that it is hard to exclude very many congressional activities from inclusion under the oversight rubric. I define oversight as congressional review of the actions of the federal departments, agencies, and commissions and of the programs and policies they administer. This includes review that takes place *during* program and policy implementation as well as afterwards, but excludes much of what Congress now does when it considers proposals for new programs or even for the expansion of current programs.

As noted above, it is often asserted that Congress neglects oversight. What does occur, with a few exceptions, is said to be neither continuing, comprehensive, nor systematic (Bibby, 1968). Agencies or programs are rarely overseen persistently, the focus of the oversight effort is often very narrow, and it is certainly the case that systematic oversight efforts (those involving a methodical approach governed by some rational principle which orders and gives unity to the elements of the effort) are just about impossible to uncover.

A basic assumption underlying much of the normative discussion in this chapter is that, simply stated, oversight of administration is desirable because it provides one mechanism by which those who administer the public policies which singly or cumulatively affect us in fundamental ways can be held accountable and their programs evaluated. I also assume that more oversight is usually better than less.[1] The idea behind this is quite simple: Even oversight performed sporadically, focused on fairly narrow subjects, and utilizing an unsystematic approach should at least hold down flagrant abuses of power by administrators, make them more responsive to the wishes of Congress, and provide Members and Senators with better knowledge and use in making judgments about the effectiveness of programs. Persistent oversight of programs or agencies is, I assume, more likely to yield these benefits than random reviews, but the benefits of regular efforts in an area may not be commensurate with the high costs in time and effort involved unless the quality of the oversight is improved.[2] And quality can only be significantly improved through efforts to evaluate programs in a comprehensive and systematic manner. Great difficulties are suggested by the latter point because our political system diffuses authority and promotes legislation which often enumerates unclear and even contradictory goals for programs.

The issue, then, is how to promote more and better oversight. Separating the elements of quantity and quality is, of course, a simplifying device. If one accepts it, a futher simplification will aid us in the analysis. This involves a division of the factors often thought to promote oversight into those whose effect is mainly to increase the quantity (incidence) of oversight and those which are very likely also to increase the quality of oversight. A further distinction, given our interest in change, will be drawn between those factors which are subject to planned manipulation (i.e., can be affected through policy changes) and those which are basically beyond our control.

Factors Mainly Promoting a Greater Incidence of Oversight

The literature is filled with propositions about factors which promote oversight.[3] A good number seem mainly to affect the quantity of oversight done. The following is a brief enumeration of some of these factors plus some commentary where appropriate.

1. SPLIT PARTISAN CONTROL OF THE PRESIDENCY AND CONGRESS

If different parties control the presidency and Congress, the majority in Congress has an incentive to harass and embarrass the executive for partisan gain. This is not a factor which is conducive to persistent oversight of a policy or agency and it is not something which we can control. However, there is one reform which has been suggested which would produce much the same stimulus to oversight and would always be as effective as split control; that is to give the minority party in Congress (if it does not also control the Presidency) control of the Government Operations Committees and of oversight subcommittees of the authorization committees.

2. CASEWORK PROBLEMS

If the bureaucracy is unresponsive to requests for assistance for the constituents of a strategically placed Senator or Representative (i.e., a committee or subcommittee chairman or ranking members, and the like), the oversight may be used as a means to set things aright. One would not expect this to happen very often or to require persistent oversight to correct the situation.

Casework problems are not something we can manipulate in the interest of increased oversight, but there might be a way to use casework information to stimulate oversight and perhaps improve its quality as well. Congress could establish a central office to collect and analyze information on casework requests and responses to them. A periodic report which highlighted recurrent problems might create pressure for (and information to be used in) a review of the agencies or programs involved.

3. ATTEMPTS TO SATISFY GROUP INTERESTS IMPORTANT TO THE SENATOR OR CONGRESSMAN

This is a broader category than two, but shares much in common with it. Most established interests are well represented in the bureaucracy; program administrators wish to provide them with services, and administrators are especially responsive to those groups of concern to important people in Congress. Every once in a while, however, vocal dissatisfied groups stimulate spurts of oversight as in the case of OSHA (Occupational Safety and Health Administration).

4. DESIRE TO PROTECT FAVORED AGENCIES

This factor is related to (3), only here the Senators and Congressmen are mobilized by bureaucrats as well as interest groups to protect a program which is threatened by the administration or which needs a boost for some other reasons. The purpose of the oversight effort is to show how marvelous or essential the program is and to demonstrate the depth of its support. Such efforts, I believe, are especially common when there is split partisan control of the Congress and the presidency, but probably occur at all times. "Sunset" laws of the type now under consideration in Congress would unintentionally stimulate this type of oversight on a regular schedule. While protective oversight is likely to be very superficial, every once in a while it will expose flaws in a program which even its most ardent supporter will want to see corrected.

EFFORTS TO PREEMPT OPPONENTS

Preemptive oversight is really a special case of protective oversight. As Scher says, some oversight (which he terms preventive) "results from an unenthusiastic determination that a limited examination of an agency by its friends may cost less than an uncontrolled one by its enemies" (Scher, 1963). Such oversight is likely to be superficial and brief, but the incentive to perform it is subject to some manipulation. A restructuring of committee jurisdictions which encouraged "unfriendly" committees to take a look at the program or agency in question would encourage this type of oversight. The new budget process may be a particularly important stimulus to preemptive oversight since authorization committees will want to present what looks like a strong case to the Budget Committees. I will return to this point later in describing factors leading to higher quality oversight (because should the budget process really work it is likely that superficial evaluations will be at a disadvantage in competition with more systematic efforts).

COMMITTEE STRUCTURE

We now turn to a factor which is very much subject to planned manipulation: committee structure. The more decentralized the committee, the greater the likelihood of oversight. As Ogul (1976) notes, "a decentralized committee—one in which power over money, staff, and program is largely in the hands of subcommittee chairmen and others—enhances the opportunity for oversight simply because decision-making is dispersed."

An additional factor which ought to lead to a greater incidence of oversight is the establishment of oversight subcommittees. Once established, many members of these subcommittees and their staffs should want to make something of their assignments and greater oversight activity is a likely result.

INCREASING STAFF RESOURCES

The latter point raises the general issue of staff resources. One would expect that increases in the number of staff members on committees and subcommittees and increases in staff assigned to individuals both in their offices and through their committee assignments would lead to more oversight activity. There would probably not be a one-to-one relationship between the number of staff and oversight, but one would expect some impact if only because of the greater number of people available to do things. However, when authority over staff is dispersed, increases in the number of staff are more likely to lead to increases in the level of oversight activity than to increases in systematic oversight. The problems of lack of coordination and lack of an orderly, methodical approach to oversight are, in fact, probably exacerbated by mere increases in the numbers of staff aides.

CORRUPTION, CRISIS, AND PUBLICITY

Evidence of corruption, the breakdown of a program, or the subversion of accepted governmental processes as revealed by Watergate make oversight attractive because the overseer is almost sure to make a favorable public impression. Most such oversight is not planned for in advance and is likely to be shortlived and somewhat superficial. But Watergate and the feeling that the Great Society programs of the 1960s were ineffective may well have had a profound impact on both the attentive public and the people in Congress themselves, alerting them to the need for "continuous watchfulness."

A related factor which may bring Congressmen who oversee the executive branch publicity previously unavailable is the rise of citizens' lobbies with wide memberships or favorable public recognition. These groups place oversight of target agencies and programs on their agendas and publicize congressional response. They also are sources of information previously unavailable. They seem to be a stimulus to more oversight, but whether they will sustain themselves through time or maintain a steady enough interest in an area to reward persistent congressional attention is not yet clear.

Factors Likely to Increase the Quality of Oversight

The analysis in the preceding section was inspired by recent academic work (especially Scher, 1963; Ogul, 1976) that approaches oversight from the perspective of the incentives of the Senators and Representatives. While more traditional scholars spend much time examining the techniques of oversight (hearings, investigations, and so on) and the resources available (staff, money, and so on), Scher and Ogul ask what net gains accrue to Senators and Representatives from performing oversight. Investigations, to take one example, can yield great publicity dividends if they expose corruption or harass unpopular agencies, but they may prove politically useless or even damaging if they turn up nothing newsworthy or threaten powerful interests. Persistent oversight of an agency or program is even more time-consuming than a one-shot investigation and the publicity rewards are likely to be much lower. In brief, when the disadvantages outweigh the advantages one assumes that Congressmen and Senators shy away from oversight, even though they may believe that it ought to be done.

When one looks at oversight in this way it is not surprising that performance has usually been spotty at best, with persistent oversight a rarity and really thorough systematic jobs almost nonexistent. However, over the last few years there have been changes in the environment which ought to make improvement in the quality of oversight more attractive to many in Congress. This certainly does not guarantee that such improvements will occur, but it does make it more than an academic exercise to discuss factors likely to increase the quality of oversight.

1. RELATIVE RESOURCE SCARCITY

Many of us are accustomed to thinking about an ever-growing economy with rapidly increasing resources available to government for the expansion of old programs and the establishment of new ones. This environment discourages the careful oversight of ongoing programs which usually have the support of entrenched constituencies. There is no pressing reason to worry much about efficiency or effectiveness in such an environment and, therefore, little oversight should be expected, let alone systematic oversight.

We are now in a period of relative resource scarcity. In addition to the strains brought on by the recent recession, many of the programs of the 1960s proved much more expensive than originally estimated. Together with the belief that many government programs are not working very well, these factors have created a growing interest in the attentive public in efforts to determine the effectiveness of programs and to weigh them against possible alternate uses of the resources they consume. There is a growing constituency which supports such efforts and public acclaim to be gained by backing them. In addition, if hard choices must be made, the political costs may be reduced by transferring responsibility for unpopular decisions—i.e., fixing the blame on the outcome of carefully conducted, technically respectable analyses. In short, relative resource scarcity has created a political climate which makes high-quality, systematic oversight more attractive than it was before.

2. INFLUX OF SKEPTICAL SENATORS AND REPRESENTATIVES

Contributing to this climate is the influx into Congress of Democrats described by Rep. Bob Carr as "skeptical of government intervention and solutions" (Singer, 1978). Their electoral success reinforces the belief that a skeptical view is popular with the public and may advance the notion that thorough, systematic oversight can yield some political payoff.

3. WIDESPREAD PROGRAM EVALUATION

In part as a consequence of the relative scarcity of resources described above, in part as a reflection of the spread of new analytic techniques, and in part as a function of new mandates given to the Executive Branch agencies, congressional support agencies, and congressional committees themselves, program evaluation is being done all over the government. It is not always well done and it is often self-serving, but it does put pressure on Congress to examine the findings and at least to consider the results.

A major problem is that low quality evaluations are encouraged by the types of programs Congress typically passes. In order to build a coalition large enough to pass a bill and in an effort to offend as few people as possible, Congress often establishes programs which lack clear, noncontradictory goals for the agencies to accomplish.

Schick (1976), however, notes that

> When Congress muddles through without a clear specification of purpose, the process of evaluation is not aborted. Rather, it must begin with executive implementation rather than with textbook clarity about objectives. Congress, in fact, has two legitimate tasks to get the Executive to produce relevant evaluations. First, Congress can write into law a mandate for the agency to evaluate its program; second, Congress can demand that the evaluative measures used by the agency reflect congressional interest and perspectives, not merely the orientation of the implementing agency. . . . What is required is the prescription in law of a process that agencies must adhere to in evaluating their activities, including milestones for the crucial events in the process, and a reporting schedule.

Schick's proposals are realistic and would improve the prospects for the intelligent utilization of program evaluations by Congress. They suggest a general point which is that congressional committees should work closely with any agency (for example, GAO) doing evaluations for them—or the products are unlikely to have much impact. The process Schick proposes will *not* eliminate all muddled program objectives and the problems they create (it does, after all, involve continuous bargaining between Congress and the agencies) and it will not result in high quality program evaluations as measured by a set of absolute professional standards, but it *will* increase the usefulness and impact of the evaluations done.

Effective congressional utilization of evaluation requires the active interest of Senators and Representatives, staff members who can skillfully direct the work of technical experts, and a congressional willingness to bite the bullet at times when evaluation results cause some political difficulties. No one can mandate such things, but changes in the political climate and in the composition of Congress give some encouragement that this might be possible.

It would be helpful, in this regard, to develop courses in evaluation for politically skilled but analytically untrained staff. This would help facilitate fruitful communication between Congress and evaluators from the congressional support agencies or the executive branch departments.

4. REFORMS IN THE BUDGET PROCESS

The most important *potential* stimulus to systematic oversight by the Congress is the new budget process established by the 1974 Budget Act. As Schick notes (1976):

> There is some possibility that the new congressional budget process might bolster the incentives for evaluation at [the authorization and appropriations] stages, if only because of the pressure to consider particular spending demands in the light of overall national priorities and other claims on the budget. Moreover, the new congressional process might contribute to a narrowing of the authorizations–appropriations gap, the proclivity to authorize one level of expenditure but to appropriate at a much lower level. More realistic authorizations might encourage committees to take more careful looks at the programs subject to their oversight.

A possible scenario is that some presentations to the Budget Committees by the authorization committees of their views and recommendations on matters to be covered in the budget resolutions (as required in Section 301(*c*) of the act) will be based on evaluations designed to make favored agencies and prorams look good. (''Preemptive oversight'' may also take hold here—a desire to evaluate programs before CBO or the Budget Committee staffs get to them.) With any luck, some authorization committees will seek to influence the Budget Committee by presenting more systematic evaluation than those of the competition in order to back up their claims to the available funds. The Budget Committees, if they reward such efforts, can thereby stimulate a continuing improvement in the quality of oversight.

5. ROTATION OF COMMITTEE MEMBERSHIPS

A final factor which might increase the quality of oversight would be the regular rotation of committee assignments. Such a procedure could have several benefits. First, it would loosen the ties which Senators and Representatives develop with the agencies whose programs their committees authorize or fund. This, in itself, would be a stimulus to more objective perspectives on programs and the agencies which administer them. Second, by moving from committee to committee, each individual might develop a better view of the overall situation. Third, because of the need to develop a quick comprehension of the agencies and programs involved, the Senators and Representatives might be more interested in seeing thorough studies of relevant policies, especially studies which compared benefits across programs or agencies.

The difficulties with this proposal are many, but two (leaving aside resistance to change) stand out. First, unless the staff attached to the committees had low turnover, committees would be even more reliant on the executive for information and expertise than they are now. Second, if the staffs remained in place, the perspectives of program clientele groups and the agencies might still dominate the process. Reserving some staff positions for people whose professional training is in policy analysis might help here.

AN ANALYSIS OF TRENDS IN CONGRESSIONAL COMMITTEE OVERSIGHT BEHAVIOR

As I indicated earlier, the notion that oversight is Congress' neglected function is widespread, shared alike by scholars and legislators. The survey of oversight activity by House Committees done by the Congressional Research Service for the Bolling Committee (1974), for example, showed that 11 percent of all hearing and meeting days in the first eight months of the 93d Congress (January 1 to September 5, 1973) were devoted to oversight.[4] The prevailing inference drawn from these data was the 11 percent was too low a number. Thus, the Committee's report expressed a firm belief that "the oversight responsibilities of the House Committees are important and too often shunted aside by the press of other business" and endorsed the view "that oversight of programs and agencies should be a principal function of the Congress." The significance of the 11 percent figure will be considered below in my examination of oversight activity over the last four Congresses.

This part of my article documents and provides some preliminary analysis of trends in congressional oversight behavior. The analysis is longitudinal, covering the 91st, 92d, 93d, and 94th Congresses, and comparative, contrasting the House and the Senate. The analysis has two major purposes:

1. To document the amount of oversight behavior in committee hearings and meetings for each of the last four Congresses.
2. To perform a preliminary analysis of the impact of some of the factors identified earlier as likely to promote a greater incidence of oversight.

The nature of the data I employ here requires me to place my major emphasis on the quantity of oversight, but I will also briefly consider the implications of the evidence for the quality of the oversight being done.

My data source is the Daily Digest which is appended to the *Congressional Record*. The Daily Digest lists and summarizes the meetings and hearings held by congressional committees. The time period coded for each Congress is January 1 to July 4 of the first year of each session—i.e., 1969, 1971, 1973, and 1975. The unit of analysis is a hearing and/or meeting series dealing with what I call a "matter," defined as a subject, theme, or topic. The coders were instructed to code as a unit a series of hearings and/or meetings on one subject, topic, or theme. The number of days of hearings and/or meetings per matter was also recorded so that the total amount of time spent on each matter can be recovered from the data where that is desirable.

All hearings or meetings listed in the Daily Digest were coded so that effort spent on oversight as measured from this source could be compared to activities devoted to other purposes such as authorizations, nominations, and so on. Oversight is defined here conceptually as congressional review of the actions of the Executive Branch and operationally as hearings or meetings held for any of the following purposes, either singly or in combination: (1) to review and/or control unacceptable forms of bureaucratic behavior; (2) to ensure that the bureaucracy implements the policy objectives of Congress; and (3) to determine the effectiveness of programs and policies. In addition committee hearings or meetings described in less precise terms than those above simply as efforts to review or oversee the activities of an agency were coded as oversight. The numbered elements of the operational definition were drawn from the CRS study for the Bolling Committee (U.S. Congress, 1974: 267). The difference between their study and mine is that I did not code as oversight hearings or meetings designed, in their words, "to analyze national (and international) problems requiring federal action" unless they were part of an effort to review government actions in the area.

Before proceeding, I should note some of the shortcomings of the data set. First of all, it understates the amount of committee activity to some extent because the descriptions in the Daily Digest are inserted by the committees themselves. If for any reason they fail to submit copy to the *Record,* there is no entry for any hearings or meetings they may have held. Second, the descriptions submitted are not always as clear as one might hope. We guarded against error by double-coding any questionable entries in the Digest. Third, the data are records of hearings and meetings, not other activities of the committees. They, therefore do not necessarily include such efforts as staff investigations and the like which can be important aspects of oversight, unless those efforts are reflected in hearings and meetings. Finally, oversight may occur as a by-product of hearings and meetings held by congressional committees for other purposes. Accordingly, the data analyzed in this article underestimate the amount of oversight because they consider only the primary purpose of each hearing or meeting as described in the Daily Digest.

Changes in Committee Oversight Activity

Most congressional committees are quite busy and the evidence indicates that the number of hearings and meetings held by them has increased significantly since 1969, the first year coded in our data set. Table 9.3.1 presents the number of hearings and/or meetings series coded in each of the four Congresses, the total number of days spent in hearings and meetings, and the mean days per series for all House and Senate committees except Appropriations, Rules, and Administration.[5] The committees dealing with rules and administation were excluded from the analysis because of their preoccupation with internal chamber business. The appropriations committees were excluded for reasons of comparability since the House Committee followed its unique tradition until the 93d Congress of reporting very few of its hearings or meetings for inclusion in the Daily Digest.

The total number of hearings and meetings series increased rapidly in both the House and the Senate in this period. The Senate workload shows some signs of leveling off in the 94th Congress (there was a dip in the total days column from the 93rd, perhaps indicating a rough saturation point in the area of 1,000 hearings or meetings in a six-month period for the Senate committees coded here. What is clear is that committees in both bodies meet even more often than they did just a few years ago and that more and more matters are taken up in each session.[6]

Table 9.3.2, which displays data on oversight hearings and meetings, shows a fairly con-

TABLE 9.3.1 FREQUENCY OF COMMITTEE OR SUBCOMMITTEE HEARINGS AND MEETINGS IN THE HOUSE AND SENATE, BY CONGRESS*

CONGRESS	TOTAL NUMBER OF SERIES†	TOTAL NUMBER DAYS‡	MEAN DAYS PER SERIES
House:			
91	340	1,087	3.20
92	398	1,184	2.97
93	467	1,448	3.10
94	593	1,641	2.77
Percent change from 91 to 94	+74.4	+51.0	−13.4
Senate:			
91	278	717	2.58
92	326	877	2.69
93	406	1,063	2.62
94	431	943	2.19
Percent change from 91 to 94	+55.0	+31.5	−15.1

NOTE: Entries are for the January 1 to July 4 period of the first year of each session of the 91st to 94th Congresses.

* Hearings and meetings held by the Appropriations, Rules, and Administration committees in each chamber have been excluded.

† A series is defined as a set of hearings and/or meetings on one subject, topic, or theme.

‡ The total number of days is derived by adding the number of days of hearings and/or meetings in each series.

TABLE 9.3.2 OVERSIGHT HEARINGS AND MEETINGS BY HOUSE AND SENATE COMMITTEES OR SUBCOMMITTEES, BY CONGRESS*

CONGRESS	NUMBER OF OVERSIGHT SERIES	OVERSIGHT SERIES AS PERCENTAGE OF TOTAL SERIES†	NUMBER OF DAYS OF OVERSIGHT HEARINGS AND MEETINGS	NUMBER OF DAYS OVER-SIGHT AS A PERCENT OF TOTAL NUMBER OF DAYS‡	MEAN DAYS OVERSIGHT	STANDARD DEVIATION DAYS OVERSIGHT
House:						
91	35	10.3	128	11.8	3.66	55.5
92	32	8.0	87	7.3	2.72	2.40
93	69	14.8	169	11.7	2.45	2.30
94	118	19.9	285	17.4	2.42	2.17
Senate:						
91	27	9.7	82	11.4	3.04	2.69
92	34	10.4	100	11.4	2.94	3.23
93	39	9.6	112	10.5	2.87	2.75
94	67	15.5	173	18.3	2.58	2.39

NOTE: Entries are for the January 1 to July 4 period of the first year of each session of the 91st to 94th Congresses.

* Hearings and meetings held by the Appropriations, Rules, and Administration Committees in each chamber have been excluded.

† See Table 9.3.1 for a count of the total number of series.

‡ See Table 9.3.1 for a count of the total number of days.

sistent pattern of increases both in the number of series and in the total days devoted to oversight. The one exception is found in the House where the number of oversight series decreased slightly from the 91st to the 92d Congress while the total number of oversight days dropped rather precipitously. This relatively steep drop in the number of days devoted to oversight is a function of a drop in the mean number of days spent on oversight per series. As the change from a standard deviation of 5.55 in the House in the 91st Congress to 2.40 indicates, there were fewer extreme cases in the 92d Congress. In fact, one oversight series of 33 days of hearings and meetings in the 91st Congress is the culprit. This was the largest series by far, the next longest oversight series recorded in the period covered by the data being 16 days long. At any rate, with the one exception described, oversight not only increased in absolute terms from Congress to Congress, but it held its own as a percentage of a rapidly increasing committee workload. It began to rise in the House in the 93d Congress as a percentage of total series of hearings and meetings and in the 94th Congress exploded into prominence in both chambers as a major percentage both of series and of hearings and meeting days.

How does one explain this change in congressional oversight behavior? Earlier, I outlined a group of factors which have been identified as promoting a greater incidence of oversight. Split partisan control of the Presidency and Congress has been a constant factor in the period covered by the analysis and unfortunately, therefore, its direct impact on oversight activity cannot be assessed using these data.[7] In addition, the data, because of limited information in the Daily Digest, are not appropriate to answer questions about the relationship between oversight activity and such factors as casework problems, attempts to satisfy group interests important to the Senator or Congressman, or the desire to protect favored agencies. Additional analytic work could be done in these areas by evaluating hearings transcripts and interviewing participants. However, the data collection problem will be a difficult one since the investigator would ideally like to know not only what motivated a given instance of oversight activity, but when similar conditions (casework problems and the like) existed and no oversight resulted.

Fortunately, there are some data presently available which can help to probe the relationships between the remainder of the factors identified earlier and oversight activity. Turning first to staff resources, it was hypothesized that oversight would increase as a function of the number of staff available to committees and subcommittees. Information collected by the Temporary Select Committee to Study the Senate Committee System on numbers of staff members available to House and Senate Committees is the basis of the rather remarkable plot found in Figure 9.3.1. The horizontal axis is the total number of permanent, inquiries and investigation staff available in 1969, 1971, 1973, and 1975 to all Senate committees as reported by the Temporary Select Committee (1976) and the vertical axis is the total number of days Senate committees spent on oversight in those years. The total number of days Senate committees spent on oversight during this period appears to bear an almost linear relationship to the total staff available.

Before declaring increases in staff the definitive factor promoting more oversight, a few cautions are in order. First of all, Figure 9.3.1 covers a very short time span and chance may be at work here. The data might not be quite so neat if a longer series could be examined.[8] Second, while complete data on staff growth for the House are not available, the data for 1969 and 1971 which are presented by the Temporary Select Committee present a problem. Staff in the House grew from 688 to 799 in this period, while a look at Table 9.3.2 will show that total days of oversight in the House fell during this same time span. Perhaps the relationship between staff and oversight only exists in the Senate, but one would want to see more data on both chambers before reaching that conclusion. Third, correlation does not indicate causation

FIGURE 9.3.1 STAFF SIZE VERSUS DAYS OF OVERSIGHT HEARINGS AND MEETINGS, SENATE

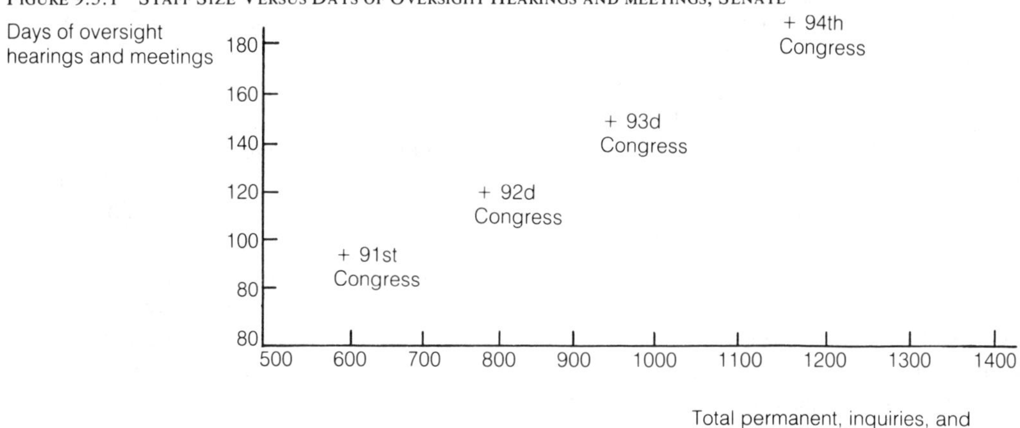

NOTE: Oversight entries are for the January 1 to July 4 period of the first year of each session of the 91st to 94th Congresses.

and in the case of these variables the direction of causality is not absolutely clear. More staff may be promoting oversight, but the reverse may also be true and the desire of Senators to oversee the bureaucracy may be leading them to hire more staff. If the latter is correct, when and if the desire abates, staff increases may well be associated with constant or even decreasing levels of oversight.[9] My own feeling on this point is that the system is a complex one in which additional people are slack resources some of whom find their way into oversight activity regardless of the priorities of their employers, but the key point for now is that one should be cautious in interpreting these data.

Next, let us examine the committee structure factor. This factor is an extremely important one for those interested in reform because, like the staff factor, it is very much subject to planned manipulation.

Two propositions were outlined earlier. The first is that the more decentralized the committee, the greater the likelihood of oversight. In order to make a satisfactory test of this proposition one would want to develop good measures of the dispersal of power over money, staff, and the agenda in each committee and then relate them to the level of oversight activity. Such measures are not currently available, but one crude indicator of decentralization—the number of subcommittees on the full committee[10]—does not show very promising results. The average correlation between the number of subcommittees and the amount of oversight conducted (the oversight indicator was coded here as a dummy variable—i.e., 1 = oversight and 0 = other) is .05 in the House and 0.1 in the Senate for the four Congresses in the data set. In addition, the correlations in the House for the 93d and 94th Congresses, those after the passage of the so-called Subcommittee Bill of Rights (Ornstein, 1975), were −.02 and .05, respectively.

The second proposition on committee structure outlined above, namely that the establishment of oversight committees or subcommittees is likely to lead to an increase in oversight activity, seems very promising. These units would have oversight as a major mandate and the assumption is that if they are active at all they will be more likely than other units to devote their efforts to overseeing the executive. Fortunately, it is fairly easy to identify existing oversight committees and subcommittees (which we will call oversight units) and to compare their behavior to that of nonoversight units.

In Table 9.3.3 the percentages of hearings and meetings series devoted to oversight are presented both for oversight units and for the remainder of the committees and subcommittees. The data are further divided by chamber and Congress. Oversight units are defined as the Government Operations Committees in both chambers and subcommittees of other committees which have such identifying labels as oversight and department operations in their titles.

A look at the table will show some very clear findings in the House. Oversight units do indeed devote more series of hearings and meetings to oversight than other committee units. The differences are quite pronounced. Indeed, the average correlation (r) between dummy variables for the oversight and committee units indicators is .28.[11]

Both oversight and nonoversight units have increased their oversight percentages since the 91st Congress. However, the House oversight units' share of the total oversight series—i.e., the percentage of the total oversight series in each Congress which they conducted—has dropped from 37.1 percent in the January 1 to July 4 period of 1969 (the 91st Congress) to 30.5 percent in the comparable period of 1975 (the 94th Congress).[12] This drop resulted from the fact that the percentages of series devoted to oversight rose more steeply for the nonoversight than for the oversight units. The difference in oversight percentage growth rates was enough to overcome the greater percentage increase in the number of series held by the oversight units.

In the end, then, one must conclude both that the oversight units on the House committees do spend a higher proportion of their time on oversight series than the nonoversight units *and* that the large increase in oversight found in the House cannot be accounted for simply by the increase in activities of the oversight units. What has happened is that most everyone is now getting into the act in a bigger way than before. Before discussing a factor which may have contributed to this substantial increase in oversight effort, let me say a few words about the data on oversight units in the Senate.

TABLE 9.3.3 PERCENTAGES OF HOUSE AND SENATE HEARINGS AND MEETINGS SERIES DEVOTED TO OVERSIGHT, BY COMMITTEE UNIT AND CONGRESS

CONGRESS	OVERSIGHT SERIES AS A PERCENTAGE OF TOTAL SERIES HELD BY OVERSIGHT UNITS*	OVERSIGHT SERIES AS A PERCENTAGE OF TOTAL SERIES HELD BY NON-OVERSIGHT UNITS
House:		
91	41.9 (31)†	7.1 (309)
92	28.2 (39)	5.8 (359)
93	41.7 (48)	11.7 (419)
94	52.2 (69)	15.6 (524)
Senate		
91	6.7 (15)	9.9 (263)
92	14.3 (14)	10.3 (312)
93	5.3 (19)	9.8 (387)
94	34.3 (35)	13.9 (396)

NOTE: Entries are for the January 1 to July 4 period of the first year of each session of the 91st to 94th Congresses.

* Oversight committee units are defined as the Government Operations Committees in both chambers and subcommittees of other committees which have such identifying labels as oversight and department operations in their titles. Hearings and meetings held by the Appropriations, Rules and Administration Committees in each chamber have been excluded.

† Numbers in parentheses are the bases upon which percentages are calculated.

The Senate data on the percentages of series devoted to oversight by oversight committee units resembles that found in the House (i.e., much higher percentages) only in the 94th Congress. One wonders why there are virtually no differences for any of the other Congresses. The main reason is that in the 91st, 92d, and 93d Congresses the Senate Government Operations Committee was the *only* oversight unit which held any hearings or meetings at all. (In fact, it was the only one in existence in the Senate.) This is important because the Government Operations Committee, unlike most of the oversight subcommittee units, has a firm legislative mandate and, therefore, is likely to be occupied with tasks other than oversight.[13] The committee, for instance, was very busy during much of the period before the 94th Congress shaping complex legislation such as the Budget and Impoundment Control Act. Only in the 94th Congress do oversight units from Senate committees other than Government Operations begin to appear in the data. I am reluctant, therefore, to reach any firm conclusions about the effectiveness or ineffectiveness of Senate oversight units in producing actual oversight activity. Before reaching such conclusions, I would wait until there are a few more oversight subcommittees on regular Senate authorization committees and then examine their behavior.

There is one final factor discussed above which is said to make oversight more attractive to legislators. The relationship between that factor, labeled "corruption, crisis and publicity," and increases in oversight is not the easiest to establish, but Watergate, which was a mixture of all three, seems to have had a clear impact. As Table 9.3.2 demonstrated, the absolute number of oversight series and days generally increased during the period of the 91st to 94th Congresses, but oversight really jumped into prominence as a major percentage of the daily activities of House and Senate committees in the post-Watergate (94th) Congress. While other factors are surely important, it is highly unlikely that the juxtaposition of the Watergate crisis and the literal explosion of oversight is mere coincidence.

CONCLUDING COMMENTS

The very rapid recent growth in oversight may well be a temporary phenomenon—a fad inspired by the political currents flowing from Watergate. There is certainly a faddish element to it at the moment and the level of oversight activity may well fade soon. However, there are reasons to think that a fairly solid foundation for substantial oversight activity does exist (although not necessarily at the very high levels found in the 94th Congress) and the data developed in this study indicate some factors which can be manipulated in an effort to maintain a high incidence of oversight activity by congressional committees.

The whole Nixon period brought into focus a growing imbalance of power between the executive and legislative branches. As the data show, congressional activity increased rather dramatically from the 91st to the 93d Congress. Yet during this time oversight held its own as a percentage of this growing activity, dipping only in the House in the 92d Congress and recovering quickly in the 93d Congress, a time when oversight reforms were an important item on the Bolling Committee agenda. Watergate may well have been the chief factor leading to the dramatic increase in oversight recorded in the 94th Congress, but there was already a substantial and growing base of oversight activity prior to that time. I suspect that the pre-Watergate increase in oversight activity derived from the suspicion of presidential power which developed in the Johnson Administration mainly as a result of the Vietnam war and a widespread disillusionment with many of the programs of the 1960s. Even during Nixon's first term Congress attempted to place limits on presidential war and spending powers and initiated serious debate on program priorities. Oversight tended to increase as a natural concomitant of these efforts (and related changes in congressional rules and resources), and as a response to a growing attentive public which showed an interest in congressional efforts to control the Executive Branch. My argument, in essence, is that Watergate stimulated oversight activity, but that it occurred in a context of related stimuli and reinforced them. If this is so, one would expect the observed increases in oversight activity to persist—although perhaps not at quite such high levels—even as memories of Watergate per se recede.

Turning now to factors which the data suggest might be manipulated to encourage oversight, two stand out: increased committee staffs and the establishment of more oversight units. On the first, some cautions against too simple an interpretation of the data are expressed in the article, but the evidence does at least suggest that increasing committee staff resources has an impact on oversight activity. As noted, the impact is probably less dramatic than a first glance at Figure 9.3.1 would lead one to think. However, even if one believes merely that some new staff people will haphazardly find their way into oversight, then further increases in staff will help maintain or even increase oversight activity. Staff earmarked for oversight duty are even more likely to have this effect, though one would realistically expect much slippage between the duties they are supposed to perform and their actual assignments.

The second factor, oversight units, potentially is important not because it is likely to increase oversight activity greatly, but because of its potential as a backstop. The data indicate that oversight units, particularly oversight subcommittees without major legislative authority, do spend a much higher proportion of their time in oversight activities than nonoversight units. They were by no means the major factor responsible for the increases in oversight activity reported in the data, but the empanelling of more oversight subcommittees should establish a base for a higher minimum level of oversight in the Congress.

In closing, let me say a few words about some priorities for future research. First, research of the type reported here will benefit from a longer time frame, particularly in terms of establishing a norm for oversight in the pre-Nixon years, testing the import of split partisan control, and gaining a better understanding of the relationship between committee staff size and oversight behavior. Second, oversight sometimes occurs in hearings and meetings held primarily for some other purpose such as authorizing or appropriating money for ongoing programs. A more comprehensive study design would take this fact into account through such means as content analysis of hearing and meeting transcripts and interviews with participants. It also would consider oversight which occurred outside of the formal hearing or meeting framework. Third, much more work needs to be done on the quality issue. Case studies of various types of oversight efforts probably would be the best way to begin to understand better the conditions leading to more comprehensive and systematic oversight. Finally, not enough is known about the impact of oversight activity on the actions of administrators. Just what effects does oversight really have? An assumption was made at the beginning of the study that more oversight, even if it is not comprehensive or systematic, is better than less because of its likely impact on administroatrs' behavior. This assumption, while plausible, is so central to making decisions about reforms aimed at increasing the quantity of oversight that we should find out all we possibly can about its validity.

9.4 Legislative Initiative*

John R. Johannes

A prevalent conventional wisdom in Washington is that "the President proposes and Congress disposes." Johannes argues that there are abundant examples of congressional initiation of policy. He highlights the factors associated with aggressive congressional policy initiation.

Recurring and fundamental questions about policymaking in the United States focus on Congress' ability to initiate legislation. Does Congress lead? How and when? Are conditions changing to enhance or inhibit congressional initiative?

LEGISLATIVE INITIATIVE: MIXED OPINIONS AND MISUNDERSTANDINGS

Nearly all commentators on the legislative process see the President's leadership as natural. But many have argued that he has become the dominant or even exclusive initiator of major legislation. House Republican Leader John Rhodes recently wrote, "Congress has served as little more than a glorified echo chamber for the Executive Branch of government—usually content to approve or disaprove [*sic*], rarely willing to initiate."[1] Former Senator Mike Monroney asked, "Is Congress still capable of initiating and enacting its own legislative program?"[2]

Journalist David Brinkley saw Congress moving toward a "state of honored irrelevance";[3] and Stewart Alsop insisted, "The only really important law originated, shaped, and passed by Congress since World War II is the Taft–Hartley Act . . . and there may never be another."[4] Political scientist James A. Robinson argued that "with rare exceptions, the President initiates, and Congress ratifies, delays, amends, or vetoes."[5] And an all too typical introductory textbook claimed that "it can rightly be said today that the President 'proposes' and the Congress 'disposes.' "[6]

Not everyone agrees. Rejoinders range from Rosenthal's statement that "When executive leadership is not forthcoming, the legislature can fill the vacuum"[7] to a Senator's remark that "These political scientists don't know a damn thing about Congress"[8] to Bertram Gross' "What rubbish!"[9] Most students of Congress concur in these responses, but until recently they offered little evidence or explanation.[10] Why the differences of opinion, the misperceptions, and the often wholesale acceptance of the presidential domination model?

One answer is that Congressmen and political scientists working in areas such as foreign policy peculiarly subject to presidential leadership have generalized too readily. Second, President Johnson's success with Congress in the mid-60s misled many observers. Third, most scholars have dismissed as outdated Chamberlain's study of legislative influence and initiative from 1880 to 1940. That study concluded "not that the President is less important than generally supposed but that Congress is more important."[11] Finally, counting initiatives

* From John R. Johannes, "The President Proposes and Congress Disposes—But Not Always: Legislative Initiation on Capitol Hill," *Review of Politics*, 1974, pp. 356–401.

to assign "credit" is practically impossible.[12] Definitions are in order before quantification, but few writers agree on specifics. Existing definitions do, however, point to two components of initiation. One is technical and substantive (policy ideas, information, analysis, draft bills); the other is political (publicizing and support-building). Both are commonly performed by subgovernments of congressional, executive, and interest-group personnel—making for what Stephen K. Bailey called an "almost unbelievably complex process."[13]

The best data to unravel this complexity have come from a proliferation of case studies in the late 1960s and early 1970s. The unmistakable thrust of the cases was that, although Congress expects executive recommendations, and although the President may indeed be termed *chief initiator* (especially if one uses a narrow defintion of initiation that cuts into the legislative process close to enactment), much of what had been considered presidentially inspired legislation had roots in and had been substantially modified by the Congress.[14] These studies, revealing congressional activism in virtually all policy areas, make it possible to describe Congress' role in, and the conditions that influence, policy initiation.

FORMS OF CONGRESSIONAL INITIATION

Congressional initiating activity forms a continuum, from cases of strong and direct initiation, in which elements of Congress perform nearly all the technical and political chores, to examples of very weak and indirect initiative, wherein Congress does little. The Taft–Hartley Act and the 1973 War Powers Act exemplify the former. The latter includes innumerable instances in which someone on the Hill had or was the first to articulate an idea subsequently claimed by the President.[15] Presidential "stealing" of congressional initiatives is common; and it often follows periods of policy gestation in Congress, where legislators frequently introduce bills and promote policies not in hopes of immediate success, but to prepare the way for future adoption or electoral gain.[16]

Congress can turn the tables on the executive, borrowing ideas, information, and bills from agencies or study commissions, and guiding them to enactment, sometimes against presidential wishes.[17] Congress has coaxed, embarrassed, and almost forced Presidents to propose legislation by threatening to take the lead if they did not. By enacting statutes requiring the executive to report to Congress on policy recommendations that arise from program evaluations and special studies, legislators theoretically can force the President to initiate. This tactic, however, seldom works.[18] Conversely, Presidents have tried to push the initiative onto Congress by inviting it to fill in details for vague administration proposals or by blatantly passing the whole buck to the lawmakers.[19]

FACTORS AFFECTING CONGRESSIONAL INITIATIVE

Four sets of conditions influence policy innovation by Congress: environmental, personal, institutional, and procedural. No condition is necessary or sufficient, but the likelihood and ease of congressional initiation increases in proportion to the presence of favorable factors. Naturally, exceptions to the following rules exist. And each should be read on an "other things being equal" (which they never are) basis.

Environmental Factors

POLICY GAPS

The presence or absence of actionable issues and problems is a key determinant of whether Congress initiates. Their availability is a function of at least: (1) past activity (are laws already on the books?); (2) complexity (the more technical and complicated the matter, the less likely Congress is to tackle it on its own); (3) executive action; and (4) outside pressures. The existence of what David Price calls "policy gaps'' marked congressional activity in the consumer, pollution, and election-financing fields, among others, in recent decades.

EXECUTIVE INVOLVEMENT

When the President is willing and able, initiation is his for the taking. Presidential willingness depends mainly on his ideology, priorities and preferences, and political standing on Capitol Hill. His ability to lead depends on the executive branch agencies. As a rule, congressional initiatives come when: (1) an issue is new and no agency is responsible for or interested in it; (2) interest groups find access to the executive difficult; and (3) the executive is divided on an issue, and no compromise between competing bureaucratic and/or White House interests can be achieved. Policy differences downtown often translate into covert support for congressional activists.[20]

NEED AND PRESSURE

Most successful initiatives are occasioned by manifest needs and pressures. Generally, pressures build gradually, leading to periods of intense lawmaking, and decline thereafter. Events contribute to the pressure, either triggering action or making it possible. Sputnik led to the 1957 Space Act; Vietnam paved the way for the 1966 Veterans Readjustment Act and the War Powers Act. Events need not be crises, although crises help—especially when Congress has been working on a problem before it became a crisis. Moreover, by adroit use of hearings, investigations, and public appearances, Congressmen can stimulate outside pressures to bolster *their* efforts at innovation.[21]

PARTISAN ALIGNMENTS

Their relative liberalism and control of Congress for 40 years have made Democrats the normal congressional initiators. Logic and examples from the 1950s suggest that their activism increases when a Republican is President. However, the case studies of congressional initiative during the Roosevelt, Kennedy, and Johnson years caution against conclusions that situations of split government are necessarily the most favorable to congressional initiation. It is likely that energetic Presidents find it uncomfortable to resist activism by their party cohorts and that they welcome additions to their programs, especially when the congressional initiatives are popular and inexpensive, as were consumer protection bills. Conversely, hesitant legislators may be encouraged by ambitious Presidents.

Party alignment affects how Presidents respond to congressional initiatives. If Eisenhower and Nixon are models, a President facing a hostile Congress will oppose, veto, or offer counterproposals; when one party controls both branches, Administration cooperation, endorsement of ''benevolent'' takeovers are forthcoming. Counterproposals and takeovers, of course, obscure Congress' role as initiator.

INTEREST GROUPS

Interest groups play a vital role in policy initiation. They supply ideas, bills, information (extremely valuable when issues are technical or complex and when Congress lacks resident expertise—especially when a well-informed executive stands in opposition), publicity, political muscle, strategy, and linkages between congressional activists and sympathetic executive officials.[22] The more skillful and committed are the relevant outsiders, the more frustrated they are by their inability to persuade the administration; and the more legitimate their requests, the greater the chance for successful congressional initiative. It would be erroneous to picture congressional initiatives as simple responses to outside demands, for interest-group activity frequently is stimulated by policy entrepreneurs in Congress.

PERSONAL FACTORS: WHO INITIATES?

SENATORS

Major policy initiatives seem to originate more often in the Senate than in the House.

Compared to the House, where committee work, specialization, and a nose-to-the-grindstone ethic make for expertise and influence, the Senate is more nationally oriented, more issue conscious, more tolerant and freewheeling, more publicity prone, probably more liberal, and more conducive to individualism.[23] Senators serve on more committees, and almost all majority-party Senators chair subcommittees, thus affording them more opportunities for action, but also spreading them thinner than their House colleagues.

IDEOLOGY AND ROLE ORIENTATION

Liberals and moderates (the former often proposing ideas and the latter modifying and supporting them) initiate more often than conservatives. Activists share the traits associated with the "inventor" and "tribune" purposive roles.[24] Representational style and focus are harder to pin down. Nation-oriented "trustees" are more prone to problem solving than district-oriented "delegates," but constituency-oriented legislators have successfully initiated legislation, particularly when salient local problems raise national issues and when Congressmen see a need to shore up their standing back home.

EXPERTISE

Anyone can offer suggestions or introduce bills, but successful initiatives, if not in their original sponsorship then certainly in their final form, are associated with legislators who are experts. This is less true for the Senate than for the House. Expertise normally derives from a committee or subcommittee chairmanship, but it also comes from one's experience, curiosity and hard work, personal staff help, and outside assistance. Substantive expertise without political acumen is usually insufficient, as it is when environmental constraints are severe. Price cites a Senate Finance Committee member's frustration: "I don't introduce bills in these areas. What kind of a bill could I introduce? You've got to let the executive take the lead."[25]

MOTIVATION

In addition to the obvious desire to solve problems, initiators have been moved by other reasons: improving relations with one's constituents, partisanship, carving out a policy niche for oneself, generating national publicity, and finding something to do with one's subcommittee. As Nadel discovered, good policymaking is often simply good politics.[26]

Several writers suggest that initiators tend to be low-seniority members from heterogeneous and competitive constituencies, but there is considerable evidence in opposition.[27] On the one hand, the precariousness of one's seat may incline him toward activism; on the other hand, members in the best positions to achieve success (chairmen and ranking committee members) enjoy those positions by virtue of seniority and electoral safety. In the House, seniority and formal position are more decisive than in the Senate.

INSTITUTIONAL AND STRUCTURAL FACTORS

COMMITTEE ASSIGNMENT

Committee assignments largely, but not totally, determine one's opportunities for initiation. This holds especially true for the House, where Congressmen receive only one major assignment, and where the norm of specialization is highly regarded.

COMMITTEE TYPE, JURISDICTION, AND ATMOSPHERE

Not all committees are equally innovative, nor is any one panel consistently active. Committees vary, and Fenno's classification of House committees into "corporate" and "permeable" types helps to distinguish them.[28] The former (Appropriations, Ways and Means, and Interior) are more self-sufficient, attract somewhat less activist legislators, are more oriented toward success on the floor, and thus are more cautious. The latter (Education and Labor, Banking and Currency) are more open to outsiders, and less concerned with prestige inside the House, attract activists, and are less inhibited in attacking—if not filling—policy gaps. Fenno argues that no Senate committee is of the corporate type, which may help explain the Senate's greater propensity for initiation.

Because of their jurisdictions, certain committees tend to be overshadowed by the executive or by their counterparts in the other chamber, thus placing restraints on their activism. At times, committees undertake initiatives partly to protect or expand their jurisdictions (several committees have been concerned with water pollution, for instance). At other times jurisdictional squabbles delay or kill initiatives.

The atmosphere in a committee does and doesn't provide incentives. Successful initiatives are more likely to emerge from relatively open, yet reasonably integrated, committees whose members are free and encouraged to pursue their policy interests and who share an activist outlook (Senate Commerce or Labor and Public Welfare Committees). Committees whose members are sharply split are less probable candidates for innovation—not because of a dearth of ideas but rather because the members may not be able to agree enough to report a bill and carry it on the floor.

COMMITTEE STRUCTURES

Centralized committees are less likely to initiate legislation; decentralized committees with relatively independent subcommittees—those with their own staffs, budgets, and missions—are more likely to. Subcommittees provide activist chairmen with staff assistance, a forum for publicity, and an arena for settling differences. However, autonomous subcommittees unrepresentative of their parent committees can go too far, causing the full committees (e.g., Senate Judiciary) to overrule the subcommittee (e.g., Antitrust and Monopoly) or to force a compromise.

CHAIRMEN

Most successful initiators are committee or subcommittee chairmen. Would-be innovators who do not chair subcommittees may provide ideas and some of the push behind them, but they lack the wherewithal to complete the job. Full committee chairmen, even on decentralized committees, are key to initiation. They, more than anyone else, create the committee's atmosphere. "Service" or "consensus" chairmen[29] who are open and fair, who allow committee members their head and assist them, promote policy innovation. Those who are conservative, who restrain members, and who keep a tight rein on staff discourage it.

Chairmen often supply what less senior members pursuing new policies lack: a sense of the possible, an ability to transform good ideas into viable bills, and a capacity for support-building. Usually, committee chairmen who claim certain issues for themselves preclude other committee members from activity in those areas.

COMMITTEE STAFFS

Absolutely crucial to congressional initiation are committee staffs. Though the 1946 Legislative Reorganization Act that made professional staffs available to committees intended those aides to be nonpolitical and nonpartisan, it appears that committees having such staffs are penalized in terms of initiative. Large, activist, and probably partisan entrepreneurial staffs promote policy innovation. Small, professional, and nonpartisan staffs do not.[30] Staff loyalty is important. When aides are closely attached to subcommittees, initiative is encouraged; when controlled by the full committee chairmen, their interests and aggressiveness dictate that committee's ability to lead. Congressmen lacking access to committee staff must look elsewhere for help—usually to their rather small, but growing and increasingly specialized, office staffs.[31]

Besides spotting problems and searching for solutions, staffs provide resident expertise and a research capability. Occasionally the research is of a primary investigatory nature; most often it is reworking, reanalyzing, and highlighting data acquired elsewhere. Furthermore, staffs provide linkages to interest groups and executive personnel.

POLITICAL PARTY

Although party leaders announce their programs almost every year, parties in Congress are rarely the sources of initiatives. Party policy committees seldom provide the kinds of research needed for initiation. Leaders themselves scarcely ever initiate. Their job is brokerage and mobilization for committee bills or for amendments. When initiatives come from majority party members, they come in scatter-gun fashion. The majority leadership during periods of divided government sometimes converts these proposals into party issues, but such laying-on-of-hands comes rather late in the game.

Minority members and leaders seeking to initiate face a dilemma, especially in the House where individualism is more difficult than in the Senate. Routinely, good minority proposals are preempted by the majority; bad ones cannot escape committees. The minority modifies and opposes; it does not initiate.[32]

PROCEDURE

TIME

Most congressional initiatives seem to take considerable time from idea to enactment. Part of this is a mirage caused by the open and visible nature of the congressional legislative process, compared to the closed "legislative" process within the executive branch in which the public sees only the final presidential recommendation. But part of the time problem stems from the very real congressional need for more time to accomplish the technical-substantive portion of policymaking, to publicize, and to gather support.

Congressional initiatives that have been enacted quickly share certain characteristics: (1) the issue is popular, often spectacular, and relatively uncomplicated; (2) similar legislation had been enacted or dealt with previously, and thus the proposal is ripe or at least familiar; (3) the initiative is partly intended to embarrass the President; (4) the committee involved has or has available substantial expertise; and (5) assistance is readily available from outsiders. Wage and price controls, the 1970–71 emergency public employment program, and the 1969 tax cut are examples.

Time affects individual initiators, for they must devote substantial effort to their pet projects. But time is a scarce commodity, so something must give—usually one's other duties.

POLICY MODIFICATION AND BARGAINING

The process of converting the conditions above into statutes requires adjustment at two levels. Within a committee or house of Congress, an individual's or subcommittee's proposal may have to be bargained down to size if it is to pass. Or, the committee chairman may exact a price for pushing a member's initiative through to enactment. Secondly, congressional initiatives often require help from an opposed or uninterested Administration. In either case, the price of assistance is paid in the coin of substantive concessions and credit for the new law.

CONCLUSION

Those who argue the "President proposes and Congress disposes" position are fond of quoting John Stuart Mill's remark that "a numerous assembly is as little fitted for the direct business of legislation as for that of administration."[32] But they overlook what follows: Laws "can never be well made but by a committee of a very few persons." Applied to Congress, Mill's words were never so true. Congress does initiate legislation, thanks mainly to its pluralistic and permeable committee and subcommittee structure and to its individual policy advocates, especially in the Senate. Granted, Congress does demand recommendations from the President (who remains chief initiator); but in their absence it can and does lead—not consistently, not programmatically, but as a reserve initiator employing several means to its end. More importantly, because it can initiate in any given case, Congress serves as a seedbed and greenhouse for long-range policy development. Congressmen, political scientists, and journalists would be wise to take note of and to make known these facts.

Congressional initiation implies that as an institution representing one of America's two majorities,[33] Congress is to a large degree organizationally and functionally autonomous.[34] Thus those who glory in a "constitutional balance" model of American political institutions can be satisfied; those who preach executive supremacy had better look again.[35]

Conditions affecting the legislature's ability to lead are changing, probably in a way to decentralize Congress and thus to enhance initiation. But Congress must be wary lest excessive decentralization and a pell-mell rush to initiate weaken its ability to do what it was designed for: coherently, cautiously, and accountably to reconcile in the name of all the people the needs, demands, and proposals put forth by the President or its own subcommittees in the name of some of the people.

9.5 The New Congressional Budget Process*

In response to Presidential impoundments (failure to spend authorized funds), piecemeal budgeting, and increasing "backdoor" spending, Congress in 1974 established a new budget process. The new congressional budget process has revolutionized the way in which Congress handles the federal budget. The following gives an overview of this process. As this collection of readings is being prepared, the new budget process was highlighted in the summer of 1981 as the Reagan Administration and its allies in Congress used it to significantly reduce the activities of the federal government.

The federal budget, like all public budgets, reflects what is proposed to be done for a specific period of time in the future, usually 12 months. It is a plan concerned with managing public funds, and it deals with how much government will spend and how those expenditures will be financed. When passed by Congress and signed by the President, the budget becomes law. The amount of funds specified in the legislation is then legally binding for all federal agencies for a given fiscal year. Agencies cannot spend more than is specified unless they are able to get supplemental or deficiency appropriations through the same legal channels as the original budget.

The budget, of course, is much more than a legally binding financial plan. Since funds are always limited, the act of budget making becomes a process of choosing among alternative expenditures, and the budget document itself becomes a description of national goals and priorities. The budget process, then, entails

* From *A Glossary of Terms Used for the Federal Budget Process,* 3d ed. U.S. General Accounting Office, 1981. Reprinted from the public domain.

political decisions (choices) as well as financial and economic analyses. In the United States that process is lengthy and complex. What our federal budget actually contains in any given fiscal year is the result of the interplay between the Executive Branch, and its many Departments and agencies, and Congress, with its system of committees and subcommittees.

Although the Constitution (Article I, Section 1) gives Congress the responsibility for budget decisions, by law the Executive Branch is charged with preparing and submitting the budget. Under the Budget and Accounting Act of 1921, every year the President transmits a proposed federal budget to Congress within 15 days after it convenes in the new calendar year. Until 1976, the President's annual budget message contained the proposed budget for the fiscal year that began July 1 and ended June 30. The Congressional Budget and Impoundment Control Act of 1974 (P.L. 93–344) changed those dates. The federal fiscal year now runs from October 1 through September 30. The act has not directly altered the executive budget process—agency officials continue to channel their budget requests through the Cabinet level, and in turn through the Office of Management and Budget, which reviews the requests in light of the President's proposed budget initiatives—but the act has strengthened the legislative side of budget making by introducing changes that have helped Congress form a clearer perspective of fiscal policy requirements.

Although federal budgeting is a continuous process, it can be understood and studied in terms of four phases: (1) executive preparation and submission, (2) congressional action or the congressional budget process, (3) implementation and control of the enacted budget, and (4) review and audit. Our discussion of these phases augments Figure 9.5.1, which describes and identifies the activities and actors in the federal budget process. Most of our discussion is devoted to phase 2 because, with the passage of the 1974 Budget Act, Congress acquired a new budget process. Rather than acting on the executive's budget proposals in a piecemeal fashion, as had been done in the past, Congress now has a system for looking at the budget as a unified proposal early in the budget cycle. The act has given both houses the opportunity to determine if the budget is consistent with national priorities.

PHASE 1: EXECUTIVE PREPARATION AND SUBMISSION

Preparing the President's budget starts many months before it is submitted to Congress in late January. Formulation begins at the agency level, where individual organizational units review current operations, program objectives, and future plans in relation to the upcoming budget. Throughtout this preparation period, there is a continuous exchange of information among the various federal agencies, OMB, and the President. Agency officials receive help in the form of revenue estimates and economic outlook projections from the Treasury Department, the Council of Economic Advisers, the Departments of Commerce and Labor, and OMB. The budget timetable in Table 9.5.1 highlights the key steps involved in preparing the President's budget and transmitting it to Congress. The months in parentheses indicate when agencies are expected to submit review materials to OMB.

PHASE 2: THE CONGRESSIONAL BUDGET PROCESS (AN ILLUSTRATIVE OVERVIEW)

The Budget of the United States Government, published each January, contains the President's proposals for the federal government's outlays and budget authority for the ensuing fiscal year. Congress can act as it wishes on these proposals. It can change funding levels, modify or eliminate programs, or add new ones not requested by the President, and it can act on legislation determining tax rates. The final outcome of Congress' actions is the expenditure (outlay) of federal funds. However, Congress does not act (vote) on outlays directly, but rather on requests for budget authority. Through

Figure 9.5.1 The Federal Budget-Making Process

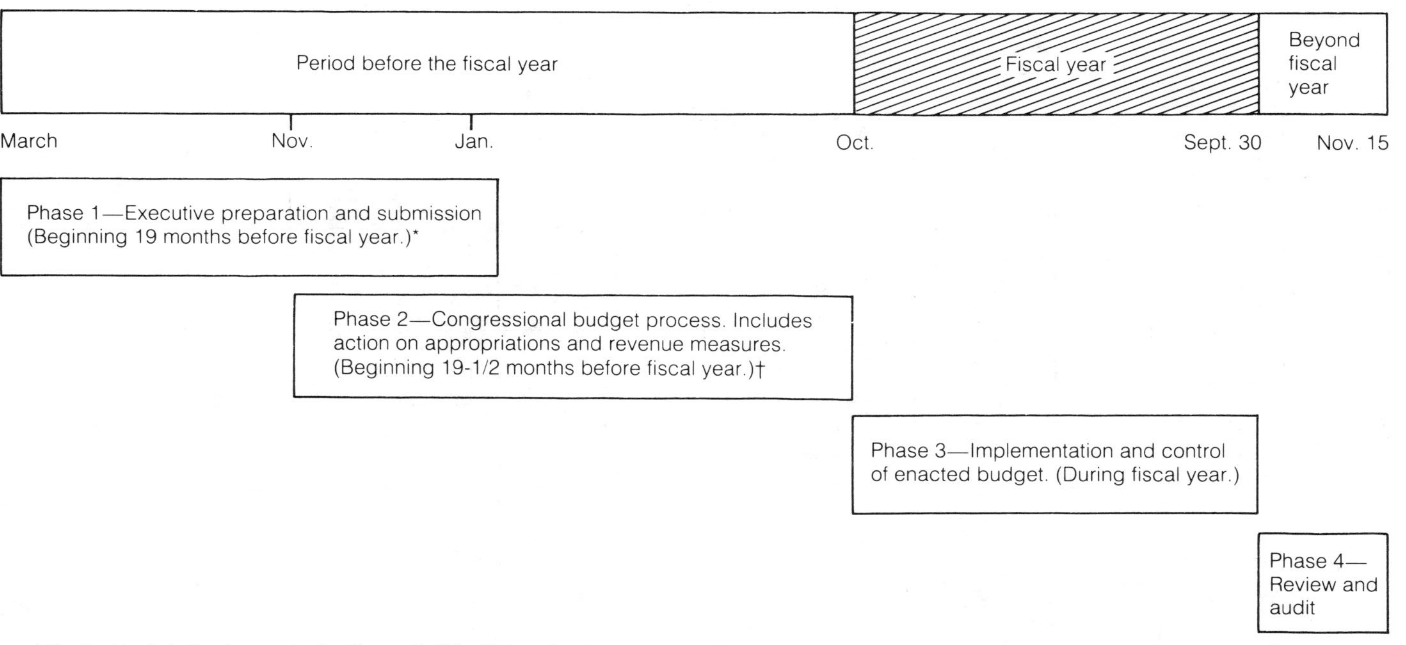

* The President's budget is transmitted to Congress within 15 days after Congress convenes.

† If appropriation action is not completed by September 30, Congress enacts temporary appropriation (i.e., continuing resolution).

FIGURE 9.5.1 (*continued*)

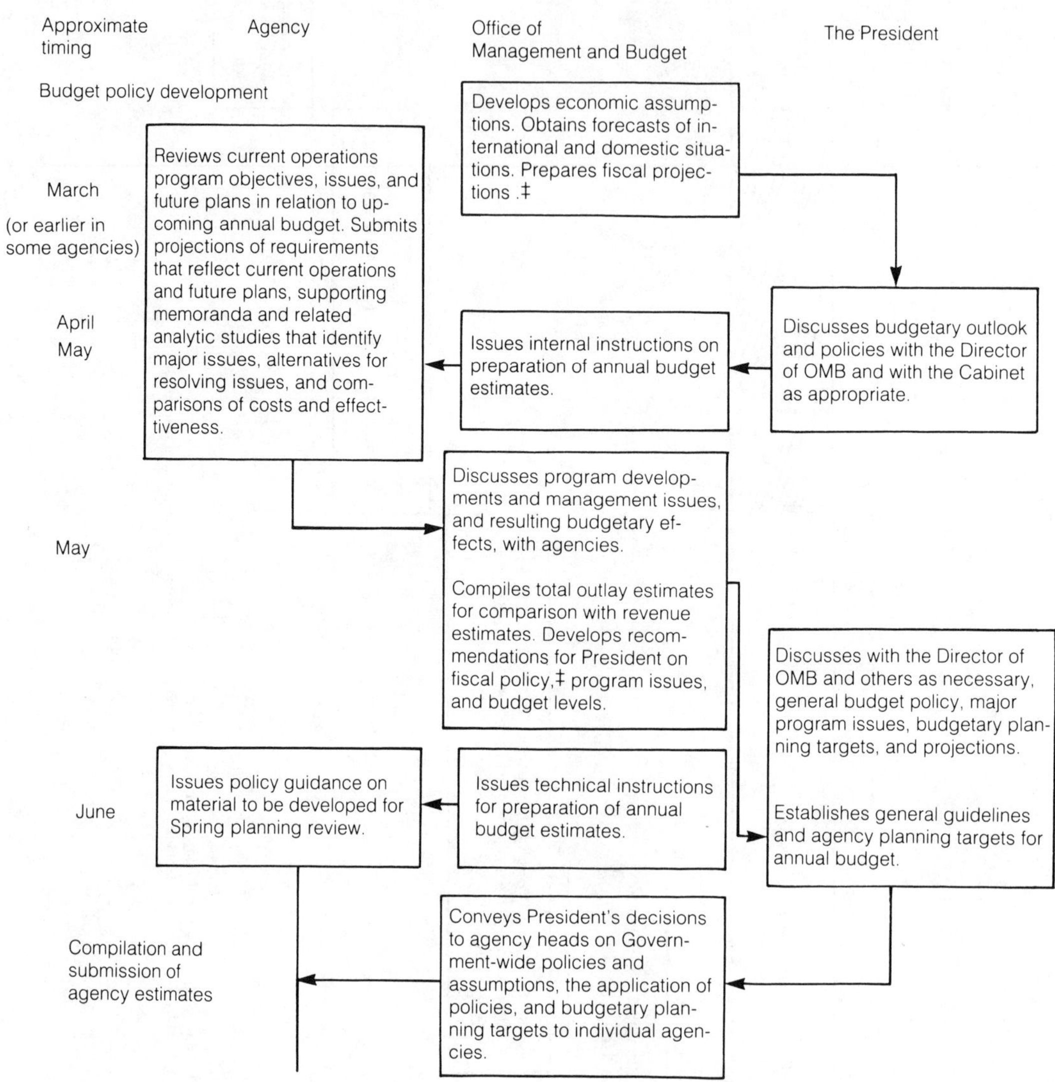

FIGURE 9.5.1 (*continued*)

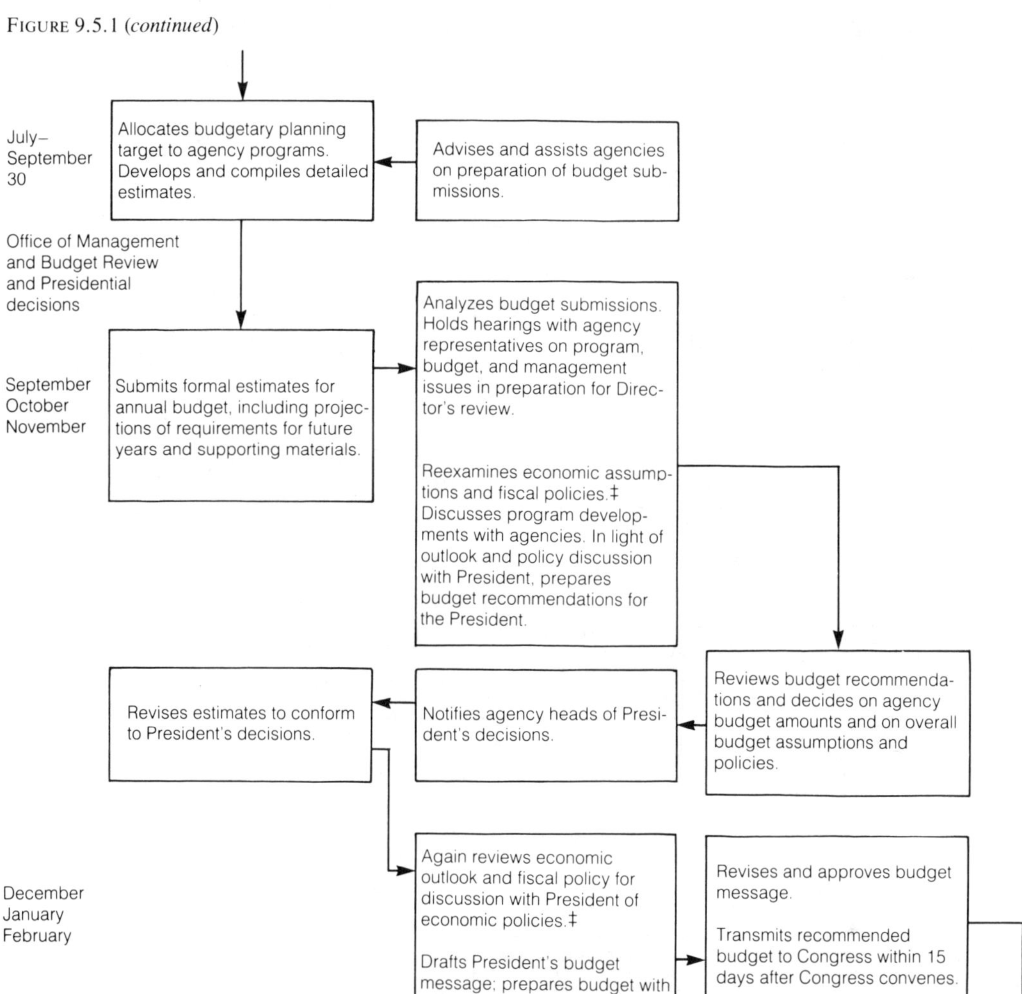

‡ In cooperation with the Treasury Department and Council of Economic Advisers.

FIGURE 9.5.1 (*continued*)

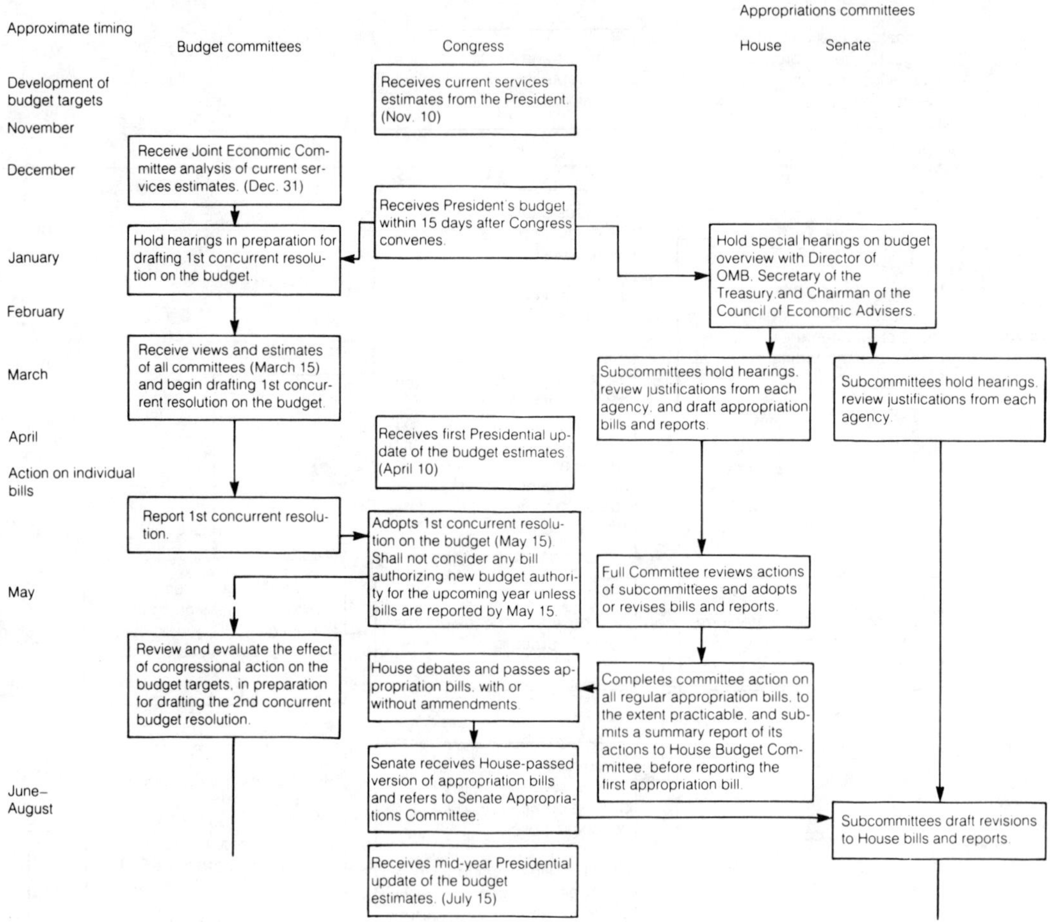

FIGURE 9.5.1 (*continued*)

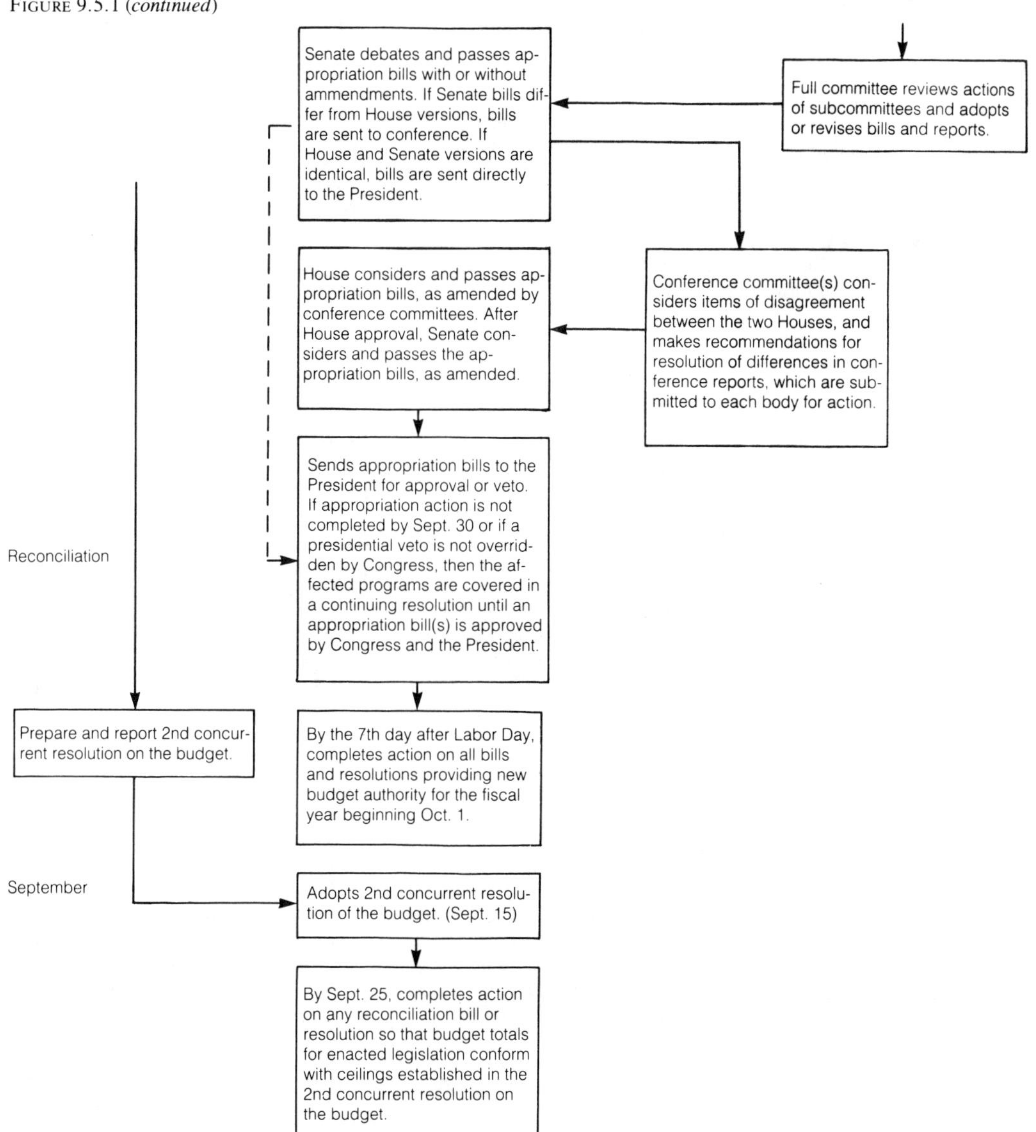

October New fiscal year begins October 1

FIGURE 9.5.1 (*continued*)

Phase 3—Implementation and control of enacted budget

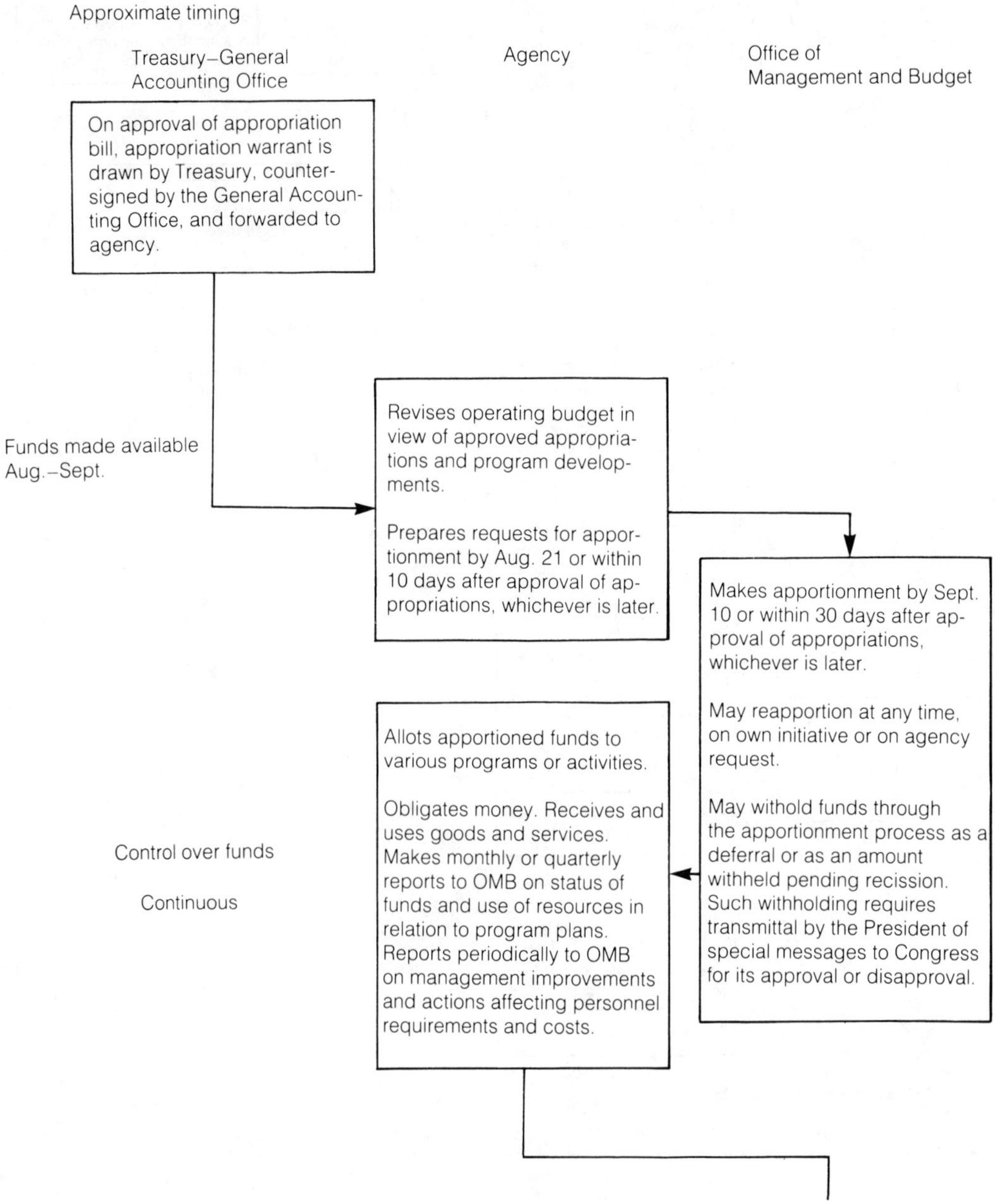

Approximate timing

Treasury–General Accounting Office

Agency

Office of Management and Budget

On approval of appropriation bill, appropriation warrant is drawn by Treasury, countersigned by the General Accounting Office, and forwarded to agency.

Funds made available Aug.–Sept.

Revises operating budget in view of approved appropriations and program developments.

Prepares requests for apportionment by Aug. 21 or within 10 days after approval of appropriations, whichever is later.

Makes apportionment by Sept. 10 or within 30 days after approval of appropriations, whichever is later.

May reapportion at any time, on own initiative or on agency request.

May withold funds through the apportionment process as a deferral or as an amount withheld pending recission. Such withholding requires transmittal by the President of special messages to Congress for its approval or disapproval.

Control over funds

Continuous

Allots apportioned funds to various programs or activities.

Obligates money. Receives and uses goods and services. Makes monthly or quarterly reports to OMB on status of funds and use of resources in relation to program plans. Reports periodically to OMB on management improvements and actions affecting personnel requirements and costs.

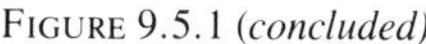
FIGURE 9.5.1 (*concluded*)

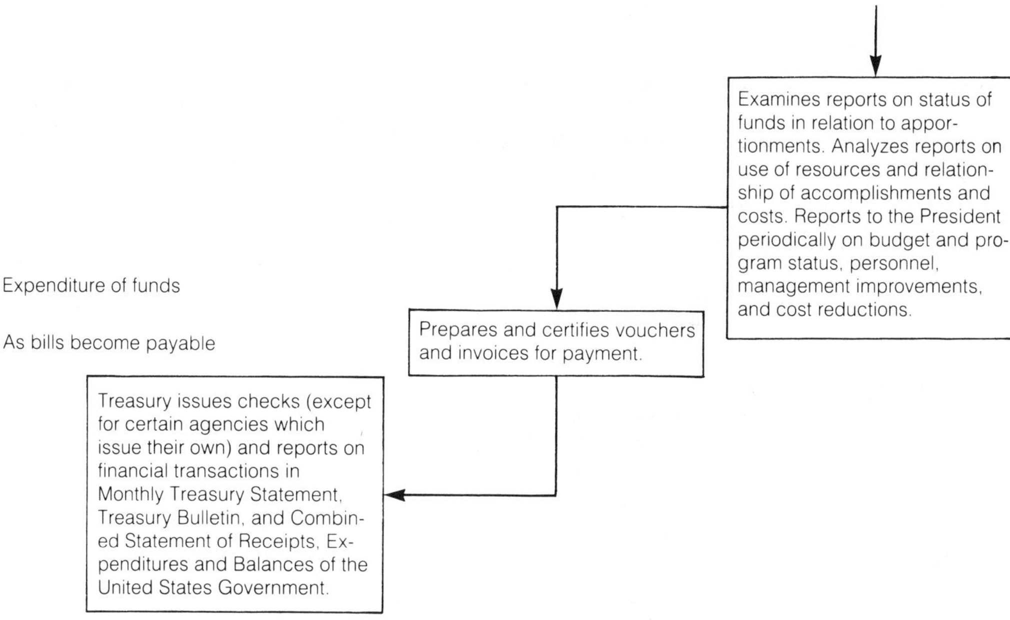

Phase 4—Review and audit

Approximate timing

Treasury–General Accounting Office	Agency	Office of Management and Budget
General Accounting Office performs independent audit of financial records, transactions, and financial management, generally. "Settles" accounts of certifying and disbursing officers. Makes reports to Congress including reports on special messages on deferrals and proposed recissions.	Reviews compliance with established policies, procedures, and requirements. Evaluates accomplishment of program plans and effectiveness of management and operations.	Reviews agency operations and evaluates programs and performance. Conducts or guides agencies in organization and management studies. Assists President in improving management and organization of the executive branch.

Program evaluation, management appraisal, and independent audit.

Periodic

SOURCE: Office of Management and Budget, January 1977.

TABLE 9.5.1 EXECUTIVE BRANCH BUDGET TIMETABLE

TIMING	ACTION TO BE COMPLETED
April–June (March)	Conduct spring planning review to establish presidential policy for the upcoming budget.
June	OMB sends policy letters to the agencies.
September 1	Smaller agencies submit initial budget request materials.
September 15	Cabinet departments and major agencies submit initial budget request materials.
October 15	Legislative Branch, judiciary, and certain agencies submit initial budget requests materials.
September–January (September)	OMB and the President review agency budget requests and prepare the budget documents.
January	The President transmits the budget during the first 15 days of each regular session of Congress.
January–February	OMB sends allowances letters to the agencies.
April 10 (February)	The President transmits an update of the budget estimates. (Note: Transmittal is often requested to be made earlier than the required date.)
July 15 (June)	The President transmits an update of the budget estimates. (Note: Transmittal is often requested to be made earlier than the required date.)

SOURCE: OMB Circular No. A–11, rev. (June 3, 1980).

the appropriations bills it passes, Congress grants budget authority to agencies, which permits them to incur obligations and hence to spend federal funds.

Before a request for budget authority can be considered, Congress must first enact legislation authorizing an agency to carry out a particular program, such as revenue sharing or food stamps. Authorizing legislation can set a limit on the funds for a given program or call for "such sums as may be necessary," but it cannot stipulate the dollar amount to be spent on the program. Some major programs, like space, defense procurement, and foreign affairs, are reauthorized by the standing legislative committee every year, while other programs are authorized for several years in advance.

How much money each department, agency, or program receives is determined by the House and Senate Appropriations Committees and their subcommittees, each of which has jurisdiction over specific numbers of federal agencies. Money bills (i.e., appropriations) may be for one year (the most common form), which allows an agency to spend only during one fiscal year, or they may be multiyear appropriations. The Constitution requires that all revenue (tax) bills originate in the House, and by custom the House also originates appropriations measures.[1]

Since appropriations are not usually considered until authorizing legislation is passed, in recent years many federal agencies have received their appropriations after the new fiscal year has begun. When an agency does not receive its appropriation before the old one lapses, it operates under a continuing resolution passed by Congress. A continuing resolution usually allows an agency to spend at the previous year's rate.

The 1974 Budget Act has introduced the following changes into the congressional budget process:

1. It requires Congress, before it enacts any appropriation bills, to adopt concurrent budget resolutions. The first resolution sets target totals for budget authority, outlays, receipts, and the public debt. These targets serve as a guide for Congress' subsequent considerations of appropriations and tax measures. The resolution also subdivides the targets into 17 functional spending categories, such as defense and health, which represent broad national priorities.

2. It established the House and Senate Budget Committees and has charged them with the responsibility of reporting the concurrent budget resolutions. The Committees also keep track of individual authorization, appropriations, and revenue decisions that Congress makes during the budget process.

3. By creating the Congressional Budget Office (the congressional counterpart to OMB) and granting it broad authority to obtain data from executive branch agencies, the act has provided Congress with a mechanism for obtaining impartial policy and cost analyses and five-year budget projections. CBO provides Congress with all available information related to the budget and conducts budget-related studies at Congress' request. It also monitors individual spending bills and issues periodic scorekeeping reports showing the status of congressional action on these bills.

4. It has provided Congress with a firm budget timetable that coordinates the authorization and appropriations cycles with the overall congressional budget as embodied in the concurrent budget resolutions.

5. It has changed the rules on presidential impoundment of funds by establishing a procedure for congressional involvement. The act requires that any money not spent must be reported to Congress in rescission or deferral messages. Impoundments take effect unless they are disapproved by both houses within 45 days of the President's notification. Deferrals (temporary withholding of funds from obligation) are effective until overturned by either house.

The congressional timetable laid down in Title III of the act is illustrated in Figure 9.5.1. Congress' activities with respect to the timetable are summarized below.

Congressional Budget Timetable

November 10

Congressional review of the budget begins when the President submits estimates of the current services budget, a five-year projection of federal spending based on current programs and existing funding levels, exclusive of any new programs. The Joint Economic Committee assesses these estimates, spelling out the economic assumptions (inflation, unemployment, rate of economic growth) that underlie them, and reports its evaluation to Congress by December 31. Congress uses the current services budget as a basis for examining the President's January budget submission.

January (15 days after Congress convenes)

Following the submission of the President's budget, the Senate and House Budget Committees begin hearings to examine the President's economic assumptions and spending priorities in preparation for drafting the first concurrent resolution on the budget.

March 15

Authorization and appropriations committees report to the Budget Committees their views and estimates of new budget authority to be enacted for the ensuing fiscal year. Some committees hold formal markup sessions to draft these views and estimates. The reports are used by the Budget Committees to gauge the total and functional spending estimates contained in the first concurrent budget resolution.

April 1

The Congressional Budget Office submits its report detailing alternative spending patterns and revenue levels associated with different budget options and their budgetary implications to the Budget Committees. The CBO report, which in theory is used in drafting the first budget resolution, presents Congress with spending scenarios above and below the President's.

APRIL 15

The Budget Committees of both houses report the first concurrent budget resolution to Congress. This initial resolution establishes targets for: (*a*) the appropriate level of total outlays (money to be spent in the ensuing fiscal year) and total new budget authority (money to be spent in the ensuing fiscal year and in future fiscal years) both in the aggregate and by functional category, (*b*) the appropriate budget surplus or deficit, (*c*) the recommended level of federal revenues, and (*d*) the appropriate level of public debt.

MAY 15

Budget Committees report legislation proposing new budget authority to the House and Senate. If a committee fails to meet this deadline, the legislation cannot be considered by the House or Senate unless a waiver is reported by the House Rules Committee or the Senate Budget Committee.

MAY 15

Congress completes action on the first budget resolution. Until the first budget resolution has been finalized, setting a "target" spending ceiling and revenue floor for the fiscal year, neither house can consider any spending or revenue measures that would take effect in that fiscal year.

SEPTEMBER (7TH DAY AFTER LABOR DAY)

Congress completes action on all regular authorization and appropriations measures. The only exception to this rule is consideration of bills that have been delayed because necessary authorizing legislation has not been enacted in time. When this happens, federal departments and agencies exist on "continuing resolutions"—the prior year's funding levels—until their regular appropriations are passed.

SEPTEMBER 15

There is no deadline for reporting the second budget resolution, but it normally occurs before the annual August recess (or immediately after), and it must be made final by September 15. In the first resolution, the total and functional spending levels are "targets," but in the second resolution they are "binding." This has the effect of "locking in" a congressional spending ceiling and revenue floor. Once the second budget resolution is in place, no legislation can be passed that would breach these limits, unless Congress places a subsequent budget resolution.

SEPTEMBER 25

Congress completes final actions on reconciliation for second budget resolution, which either affirms or revises the budget targets set in the first resolution. The House and Senate Budget Committees report any changes to the floor in the form of a reconciliation bill. Congress cannot adjourn for the year until the reconciliation legislation is passed.

OCTOBER 1

The fiscal bear begins.

PHASE 3: IMPLEMENTATION AND CONTROL OF THE ENACTED BUDGET

After the budget is approved by Congress, the President is responsible for executing it. Under law, most of the budget authority granted to the agencies of the executive branch is converted into outlays through an apportionment system regulated by the Office of Management and Budget. The Director of OMB apportions (distributes) budget authority to each agency by time periods (usually quarters) or by activities over the duration of the appropriation. This ensures both the economical and effective use of funds and obviates the need for agencies having to ask for supplemental authority. However, changes in law or economic conditions during the fiscal year may necessitate the enactment of additional budget authority. When this happens, supplemental requests are sent to Congress for its consideration. On the other hand, the Executive Branch, under the Antideficiency Act (31 U.S.C. 665), may establish reserves to fund contingencies or to effect savings made possible by more efficient operations or by changes in requirements.

Title X of the 1974 Budget Act permits the President to withhold appropriated funds for fiscal or other policy reasons, or because the President has determined that all or part of an appropriation is not needed to carry out a program. When these circumstances arise, the President sends a special message to Congress requesting that the budget authority be rescinded. If Congress does not pass a rescission bill within 45 days of continuous session, the budget authority is made available for obligation.

In order to defer—temporarily withhold—budget authority, the President must also send a special message to Congress indicating the reasons for the proposed delay in spending. Either house may, at any time, pass a resolution disapproving the President's request for deferral of budget authority, thus requiring that the funds be made available for obligation. When no congressional action is taken, deferrals may remain in effect until, but not beyond, the end of the fiscal year. If continued deferral is desired into the new fiscal year, the President must transmit a new special message to Congress.

PHASE 4: REVIEW AND AUDIT

Individual agencies are responsible—through their own review and control systems—for making sure that the obligations they incur and the resulting outlays adhere to the provisions in the authorizing and appropriations legislation, as well as to other laws and regulations governing the obligation and expenditure of funds. OMB exercises its review responsibility by appraising program and financial reports and by keeping abreast of agencies' efforts to attain program objectives.

In addition, the General Accounting Office, as an agency responsible to Congress, regularly audits, examines, and evaluates government programs. Its findings and recommendations for corrective action are made to Congress, to OMB, and to the agencies concerned. GAO also monitors the executive branch's reporting of messages on proposed rescissions and deferrals. It reports to Congress any differences it may have with the classifications (i.e., rescissions or deferrals) of the President's requests for withholding funds. Should the President fail to make budget authority available in accordance with the 1974 Budget Act, GAO may bring civil action to obtain compliance.

9.6 Policy Contributions of Congress*

Charles O. Jones

Utilizing a policy process framework, Jones identifies the major functional activities in which Congress is involved in the making of public policy.

CONGRESS AND PROGRAM DEVELOPMENT ACTIVITIES

We turn now to consider congressional involvement in program development activities—those associated with getting problems to government (perception, definition, aggregation, representation, and agenda setting) and with acting on them once there (formulation, legitimation, and appropriation)—see Table 9.6.1. Bear in mind that the focus in this section is on the *activities,* not on the *institution*. That is, we are not solely trying to explain how, for example, Congress establishes means for defining problems or setting an agenda, but rather how the actions of members and staff contribute to achieving these functions for a particular issue. It may well be, of course, that Congress will be the center of such activity for certain issues (see below), but we may not discover that fact unless attention is directed more broadly to the activity rather than to the institution.

Problem to Government

perception/definition of problem

Members of Congress are highly sensitive to public problems. The demands of the office itself insure that the successful Representative and Senator will organize his or her political life to search for and receive public problems (principally those in the state or district). Most notable in this regard is the campaign. For Representatives these events come so frequently that they are virtually in a perpetual search for district problems. The campaign experience is instructive but so are the frequent visits to the district, the mail, phone calls, and the work of the district office.

Much of this intelligence about state or district problems is gained by the members through an unsystematic but normally reliable process of personal absorption. Representatives in particular often know more about the geographical area that constitutes their district than anyone else. This knowledge is typically honed by the threat posed by a primary or general-election opponent. An exception to the more personally developed information is that gained by polls, a device increasingly used by members of both houses.

Members also can claim expertise in problem definition by virtue of their work in Washington. Personal staffs may be directed to study particular problems—often those affecting the state or district. And, of course, the committees and subcommittees are constantly engaged in problem identifying and defining activities in the hearings and staff reports. Similarly, the various congressional research agencies may also be requested to prepare analyses of the causes and effects of public problems.

These Washington-based definitional activities tend to be more systematic than those associated with the state- or district-based activities mentioned above, but less systematic than those

---

* From Charles O. Jones, *The United States Congress: People, Places, and Policy* (Homewood, Ill.: Dorsey Press, 1981), chapter 13, pp. 365–78.

TABLE 9.6.1 THE POLICY PROCESS

	PHASE	ACTIVITIES	INITIAL PRODUCT
Program development activities	Problem	Perception	Problem
		Definition	
	to	Aggregation/	
		Organization	Demand
	government	Representation	
		Agenda setting	Priorities
		Formulation	
		Research	
		Analysis	Proposal
		Selection	
	Action	Legitimation	
		Identification	
	in	of interests	
		Communication	Program
	government	Bargaining	
		Compromise	
		Appropriation	
		Formulation	Budget
		Legitimation	
Program execution activities	Government	Implementation	Structure
		Organization	Rules
	to	Interpretation	Service, payment,
	Program	Application	controls, etc.
	Program	Evaluation	Support, adjustment,
		Specification	Cancellation, etc
	to	Measurement	
		Analysis	
	government	Recommendation	
	Problem	Resolution	Relative solution,
	resolution or change	Termination	social change

SOURCE: Adapted from similar table in Jones (1981: 355).

of the bureaucracy. It is also the case that, whereas Representatives typically have an advantage over Senators in knowing their constituency, Senators have a staff advantage over Representatives that sometimes prepares them to comprehend better the relationships among various problems.

AGGREGATION AND REPRESENTATION

Senators and Representatives are likewise very active and experienced in facilitating the aggregation of those whom they perceive to be effected by a problem. This talent follows from their need for electoral support at home and their experience in enacting legislation in Washington. In some cases, members insist that those affected get together so as to present a stronger, more united front in Washington. And, conversely, they may discourage presentation of demands if groups are divided and in conflict. Again I must stress that we are merely noting how and why *members of Congress* get involved in other than the familiar policy approval activities. Policy actors from elsewhere in the government and from the private sphere are also involved in these early-stage activities of definition and aggregation.

It should also require no more than a brief mention that the members of Congress and their staffs are experts in representing. Just as they are well trained and organized to campaign and get reelected, so too are they well prepared to represent. In fact, the one activity follows from the other. This is not to say that they are always good at representing, or that others are not also involved in that activity, but only to stress that the members are predictably and legitimately active here.

AGENDA SETTING

Members of Congress, in particular the party and committee leaders, are often actively involved in the process of setting priorities among public problems to be treated. The leaders can provide important information about the mood and interests of the membership. They can supply predictions about how members will react to certain priorities. But not even party leaders are normally in a position to establish priorities on their own. As Richard E. Neustadt observes: "Congressmen need an agenda from outside, something with high status to respond to or react against. What provides it better than the program of the President?" (1960: 6–7).* The President and his aides often consult with members of Congress and their staff but priority setting has typically been an executive-centered activity.

What about those instances when the President is of a different party from that of the majority in Congress? As Neustadt mentions, the presidential program may also be something for Congress to react to. But what if the President doesn't want much of anything from Congress—or intends to let present programs expire, programs that a majority in Congress support? In such cases, members of Congress have been much more active in establishing priorities. For example, in his study of the Eisenhower Administration, James L. Sundquist concludes that congressional Democrats definitely established priorities to counter those of the Republican President, and in spite of a lack of cooperation by their own party leadership. Speaker Sam Rayburn and Senate Majority Leader Lyndon B. Johnson worked rather closely with the popular President.

> The [Democratic] activitists were constrained to proceed independently to organize their own bloc in each house of the Congress, rally support for specific measures inside and outside the legislature, and press for action on them. They could also work with the Democratic National Committee . . . and particularly with the Democratic Advisory Council established by [Paul] Butler late in 1956.
>
> The Senate activist bloc, the corresponding House bloc (organized as the Democratic Study Group), and the national committee and advisory council came to comprise a triangle of communication and mutual reinforcement that bypassed the party's leadership in Congress. By 1960 it had come close to isolating the leadership. (Sundquist, 1968: 395–396.)

The Nixon Administration also encouraged congressional Democrats to be more active in setting priorities. Ralph K. Huitt describes the situation as follows (in Mansfield, ed., 1975: 76).

> Nixon did not seem to want anything from Congress. To be sure, he initiated domestic programs and proclaimed priorities, but he seemed to lose interest in them quickly. In fact, Congress found itself upbraiding him for not really trying to get what he said he wanted, which many members wanted more than he did.

Nixon's style and lack of programmatic drive may have encouraged many congressional Democrats to establish their own priorities but they were not successful in creating a process for doing so. Weak party leadership and rather continuous reform were but two of many factors preventing the development of a coherent counterprogram.

In summary, neither house of Congress is well structured to set priorities. Bicameralism, the decentralized committee system, and a highly dependent party leadership are obstacles to this end. At the same time, members can provide information about what their con-

---

* Reference list in Endnotes.

stituents think is important. They can provide equally useful information on the many special interests likely to be touched by government programs. It is for these reasons, as well as the realization that Congress must approve government programs, that the members are drawn into agenda-setting activities.[2]

Action in Government

FORMULATION

As indicated in Table 9.6.1, program formulation may involve doing research on the various options for treating a problem, analyzing the advantages and disadvantages of these options (to include review of the effects from each), and eventual selection of one option or a combination of options. Members of Congress can bring a great deal of wisdom to these activities, again working in concert with others. Congressional hearings are often designed to explore policy options—typically including that of continuing an existing program. Committees and subcommittees are structured by membership and staff operations to provide political analysis of political options. Over time these units become impressive banks of information on the feasibility of proposals.

Political feasibility is a crucial consideration for program formulation. But Ralph K. Huitt questions whether it makes sense to speak of a total ''legislative system'' to include Congress, the interest groups, executive agencies, and the press, in making strategic choices on what is feasible (in Ranney, 1968: 272).

> It is more accurate, I think, to begin with the committees and speak of the *policy system,* which is focused about each pair of committees House and Senate that shares similar, if not identical jurisdiction.

Huitt observes that there are large national interest groups and high-level executive departments ''ranging across a broad sweep of the legislative spectrum.''

> More common than the giants by far are the groups with a single interest (albeit a broad one, like higher education), and the executive agency with one or a handful of bills, all of whose business is done with a single committee in each house. (in Ranney, 1968: 272.)

According to Huitt, ''this organization . . . around specialized concerns shapes the entire system that makes legislation'' (in Ranney, 1968: 274). For present purposes we can interpret these comments as reinforcing the view that it is the member's knowledge of specialized interests that contributes to program formulation—from the research into options to the selection of one proposal over another.

It should be pointed out that the participation of members of Congress in formulation activities is often highly subjective. The evidence they offer is biased in favor of the interests they represent. One is expected to have preferences on Capitol Hill. Selective presentation of data is a common and accpeted practice. Staff reports are typically prepared for some one or some group and for a clearly specified purpose. The objectivity or fairness is presumed to be a result over time of subjective arguments forcefully presented.

The reforms during the 1970s increased Congress' capacity to formulate programs independent of the executive. The creation of the Congressional Budget Office and the Office of Technology Assessment, the provision for a stronger research agency in the Library of Congress (the Congressional Research Service), and the large increases in personal and committee staffs contributed to greater research and analytical skills on Capitol Hill. Program formulation has been centered in Congress for certain issues in the past. We may expect it to occur there in the future, both as a consequence of inaction elsewhere and in response to, or as a counterforce to, proposals developed elsewhere. A further result of this increased analytical capacity may well be more active participation by members in executive-centered program formulation—partly due to demands by the members themselves, perhaps due as well to a recognition of their growing competence.

It is within this set of legitimation activities that legislators typically excel. Given the nature of our constitutional system, most national government programs must be traceable to majority support in Congress. Others besides legislators participate in building legislative majorities however, and there are all kinds of approval processes which take place outside Congress—in letting contracts, setting standards, issuing licenses, etc. (Jones and Matthes, 1982).

The activities associated with majority building in a legislature include the identification of the principal interests to be satisfied, communication among these interests, bargaining, and determination of a compromise. Virtually the entire legislative process as described in the previous chapters is designed to accomplish these goals—the organization and appointment of committees and subcommittees, assigning bills, the hearings and markup sessions, the scheduling of bills for floor debate, the amending process, and voting. The Congress is composed of two majority-building machines, which then must meld their products before legitimation is complete.

One must not be misled, of course, into believing that each proposal for government action on a public problem represents a significant challenge to the majority building talents of legislators. There are such cases, to be sure. It took several decades before majorities were fashioned for federal aid to education, medical care for the aged, federal civil and voting rights laws. If all legislative proposals were so conflictual, congressional turnover would no doubt be high—the result of fatigue. As it is, however, most proposals are to do a bit more of what is already being done, extend what is being done for some to others, or do something like that being in another area. As Huitt notes (in Ranney, 1968: 274):

> What is most feasible is what is purely incremental, or can be made to appear so. Paradoxically, it is politically attractive to tout a proposal as ''new'' so long as it is generally recognized that it is not new at all, but a variation on a familiar theme.

The advice contained in this wisdom is: Try to go where the majority already is. Even if you want to do something truly new, you are advised to begin with what is feasible. Huitt speaks of ''finding halfway houses . . . which supply at least part of what is needed under the guise of doing something else'' (in Ranney, 1968: 274). A classic case is the means by which we finally got a federal aid to education program. Having just enacted a popular ''War on Poverty'' program, the education aid proposal was based on the number of persons in a school district below the poverty line rather than the number of students, the economic base, the condition of the schools, etc.

R. Douglas Arnold notes a distinction between ''separate coalitions for each new expenditure program'' and ''a single umbrella coalition for a whole collection of diverse programs'' (1979: 210). In the first the necessary support is garnered by extending the program to each state and congressional district, regardless of need. The second ''umbrella'' type coalition relies on what Arnold calls ''multiple-program logrolls.'' The exchange of support between urban and rural Democrats for programs affecting each is an example of the umbrella coalition. Of course, building and maintaining such a group typically depends on strong party leadership and structure. As Arnold notes, however (1979: 212):

> The days of Lyndon Johnson and Sam Rayburn passed, and their successors, Mike Mansfield and Carl Albert, were much less inclined to function as coalition leaders. Yet party leaders are the only ones who *could* arrange and enforce the complex series of trades necessary to assemble an umbrella coalition for diverse programs.

We may also expect to find members of Congress getting involved in other legitimation processes. Certainly they will be attentive to federal contracts to be awarded in their states and districts. They may show up at public hearings for setting pollution standards or licensing a nuclear power plant (or be instrumental in organizing others to testify). And they may challenge the expertise of a government technician who has been given the authority to develop a procedure, build a dam, set a standard, design a weapon. The rationale for involvement by a member may again be constituency interest but it may also be the result of the member's understanding of the law which provides for the bureaucratic approval process.

APPROPRIATION

The budgetary process runs parallel to the substantive lawmaking process. Few laws can be enforced, few program goals can be realized without money. Until the passage of the Budget and Impoundment Control Act of 1974, the formulation of a budget was centered primarily in the executive. Though sensitive to the views of members, the Office of Management and Budget (and its predecessor, the Bureau of the Budget) had the responsibility of preparing the document for submission to Congress.

In essence, the 1974 act created a budgetary formulation process in Congress. Budget Committees were established in each house, a Congressional Budget Office with a professional staff was authorized, and a procedure was developed for setting money limits for the authorizing and appropriations committees. Congress now takes a comprehensive view of taxing and spending and seeks to control both. As Dennis S. Ippolito sees it, the new congressional participation in budget formulation offers several advantages (1978: 119):

> First, the new budget process provides Congress with the mechanism to act on fiscal policy and to challenge executive dominance in economic management. Second, Congress can use the budgetary process to make priority choices by considering spending decisions in relation to each other. The budget resolutions therefore also make it possible for Congress to specify how its priorities differ from those of the President. Third, Congress has developed budgetary staff and information resources that reduce considerably its reliance on the executive for budget data and analysis.

Approval of the taxing proposals is centered in the House Committee on Ways and Means and the Senate Committee on Finance. Authorization of expenditures must precede appropriations and this action is taken in the several authorizing committees. And appropriations are handled in the two Appropriations Committees. All of these actions are legitimation processes like those described above—i.e., actions requiring majority support in both houses. We needn't repeat the earlier discussion. But two points are worth mentioning.

First, approval of appropriations is a separate action from approval of a program. Therefore they may not come out the same. That is, the money appropriated for a program may be less (it can't be more) than the amount authorized. Thus different forces may be at work in the two legitimation processes.

Second, the new budget system has affected the approval processes for taxation, program authorization, and appropriation. When Congress approves budget resolutions, it is, in essence, establishing limits for the standing committees—limits which did not exist in the past. The potential for conflict is considerable (LeLoup, 1980; Schick, 1980). Thus, for example, in 1980 the House passed a budget resolution directing its committees to reduce spending by $6.4 billion. Appropriations Committee Chairman Jamie L. Whitten (D–Miss.) defied the resolution in regard to appropriations for Saturday mail delivery. Much to the chagrin of Budget Committee Chairman Robert N. Giaimo (D–Conn.), Speaker O'Neill appeared to support Chairman Whitten: "If the Budget Committee was to say to the Appropriations Committee, 'You can't do this,' they would be transgressing on the rights of the Appropriations Committee." Chairman Giaimo responded by charging that the Speaker was undermining the budget process. "It undermines what the leadership told us to do. The Budget Committee didn't dream this up by itself."[3]

To summarize, one may expect to find members of Congress and their staff actively involved in all functional activities associated with program development. They can justify involvement because of their knowledge and understanding of constituencies, and the many private and public interests affected by government programs, as well as expertise on the special topics of their committees and subcommittees, and, ultimately, their authority to approve laws. This general survey of activities suggests quite varied participation. We may expect:

1. Active participation by many members and staff in legitimation activities (including appropriations).
2. Variable participation by members and staff in problem definition, interest aggregation, program formulation, and formulation of the congressional budget.
3. Limited participation by members and staff in agenda setting.

Comparing Action on Specific Bills

The tremendous variation in legislator involvement in program development is illustrated by comparing what happens on specific bills at any one time or what happens over time in regard to a particular program. Consider a few of the many available studies of a bill becoming a law—campaign finance reform by Robert L. Peabody and colleagues (1972), the federal aid to education program by Eugene Eidenberg and Roy Morey (1969), civil rights legislation by Daniel M. Berman (1966), a national health service corps by Eric Redman (1973), and the classic study of the Employment Act of 1946 by Stephen K. Bailey (1950). Each of these studies provides quite different answers to the following questions.

1. Who participated in what program development activities?
2. Did this participation vary between the House and Senate? If so, how did it vary?
3. Which activities were centered in Congress? Which in the Executive Branch?
4. How and when did legislators and staff communicate with each other? With other participants?
5. How aware of program development were the less active legislators and staff?

These are but a few of the more obvious questions one might ask, with quite variable results.

David E. Price has conducted one of the few systematic analyses of legislators' participation in program development activities. Based on a study of 14 major bills, Price, like Huitt, first warns against generalizing about participation in policy activities, "particularly if the unit of analysis remains the entire executive or legislative establishment."

> Legislative initiatives are diverse and scattered phenomena, while various policymakers hardly find themselves possessed of equal incentives and resources, the system does display considerable "slack." Differences between individuals, committees, and agencies sometimes display fixed patterns attributable to "external" determinants. But the freedom of individuals and decision-making units to determine their own legislative roles is often considerable. (Price, 1972: 292.)

In what was a most useful exercise for our purposes, Price identified who was involved in six program development activities for fourteen bills. The activities closely parallel those relied on in Table 9.6.1.

Those listed in Table 9.6.1	Price's counterparts
Perception/definition	Information gathering
Aggregation/organization	Interest aggregation
Representation/agenda-setting	Instigation/publicizing
Formulation	Formulation
Legitimation	Mobilization Modification

Table 9.6.2 summarizes Price's observations about the relative involvement of executive, legislative, and interest-group participants—whether actors from these sources were primarily involved or whether they worked together with others, hence the several "mixed" categories. Several conclusions emerge from this table.

1. Information gathering tended to be centered more in the Executive Branch—six

Table 9.6.2 Variation in Participation in Program Development Activities (14 bills, 89th Congress)

Program Development Activity	Source of Participants (Number of Bills)						
	(A) Primarily Executive	(B) Primarily Legislative	(C) Primarily Interest Groups	Mixed			
				A,B	B,C	A,C	A,B,C
Information gathering* (perception/definition)	6†	—	1	4	1	2	—
Interest aggregation (aggregation/organization)	—	7	—	7	—	—	—
Instigation/publicizing (representation/agenda-setting)	1	2	—	3	2	5	1
Formulation (same)	2	3	—	2	—	—	7
Mobilization (legitimation)	—	2	—	8	1	—	3
Modification (legitimation)	—	13	—	1	—	—	—

* The labels in parenthesis represent the policy activities used here—see Table 9.6.1.

† Figure represents the number of bills on which participants drawn from the executive were primarily involved (N = 14).

Source: From David Price, *Who Makes the Laws?* (Cambridge, Mass.: Schenkman, 1972), Table 7, pp. 290–91.

bills where executive actors were primarily involved, six others where they worked with others (a, b and a, c).

2. Interest aggregation and modification tended to be centered more in the legislature—the latter heavily so.
3. Instigation/publicizing, formulation, and mobilization were characterized by considerable mixing of participants.
4. Legislators were primarily involved in more activities than either executive or interest-group actors—information gathering being the only activity in which they were not the principal actors for at least one bill.

The three groups of participants also varied in their involvement across policy activities for the different bills studied by Price. I assigned scores to each group depending on whether they were primarily involved in an activity (3 points), shared involvement with another group (1½ points each), or shared with the other two groups (1 point each). By this simple scoring system the following variations were identified:

1. Congressional dominance (members of Congress active in all activities, little sharing with others):
   Fair packaging
   Campaign finance
   Cold War GI benefits
2. Congressional sharing with interest groups (members of Congress active in most activities, some sharing with lobbyists):
   Traffic safety
3. Congressional sharing with executive (members of Congress active in most activities, some sharing with members of Executive Branch)
   Cigarette labeling
   Oceanography
   Poverty amendments
4. Executive sharing with Congress (members of Executive Branch active in most activities, some sharing with members of Congress):
   Foreign investors' tax

Medical complexes (heart disease, cancer, and stroke research)

5. Sharing among all groups (significant involvement of groups in several activities):
   Medicare
   Sugar Act amendments
   Unemployment insurance
   Elementary and secondary education
   Fair labor standards

James L. Sundquist also found important differences in policy responsibility and participation among several major bills during the Eisenhower, Kennedy, and Johnson Administrations. Though Sundquist's analysis of program development activities is less systematic than Price's, his rich descriptive material provides further support for the impressive variation in congressional policy participation (Sundquist, 1968: 390–91 and *passim*). Ripley and Franklin likewise identify variations among important bills—Executive Branch dominance, joint program development, congressional dominance, and stalemate—but as noted earlier they do not discriminate among the several program development activities (1980: 219).

The point to be emphasized from these variations is that they reinforce the utility of viewing Congress as a population variably drawn into the policy process as associated with different issues. It is clear that the members and their staffs participate broadly in policy activities and this participation varies greatly among various types of issues. Price contributes even more evidence to support this conclusion when he examines differences among congressional committees. As with individual members, he found that certain committees and subcommittees were active in different types of activities. He cautiously concluded that some committees specialize in "the formulation and publicizing of legislation," and other specialize in "the 'maturing' and compromising of proposals with an eye to eventual mobilization (Price, 1972: 311–312).

CONCLUSION

The Congress is the most critical government institution for maintaining a constitutional democracy. Its legitimacy as the lawmaker stems from the electoral connections with the people. This authority to pass on all government programs justifies congressional involvement in other program development activities (problem definition, aggregation, agenda-setting, formulation) and guarantees that those responsible for and benefitting from these programs (political executives and bureaucrats at all levels of government, as well as public and private interest groups) will often draw members and their staffs into fuller participation in the early stages of program development. For the student of legislatures the policy process perspective offers a different view of the role those institutions play in the political system. The formal structure and procedures of the lawmaking process are undeniably important for maintaining the legitimacy of government programs, thus justifying the scholar's attention. But focusing on issues, how they get to government and who acts on them there, provides quite a different window for studying legislative behavior. We have done no more in this chapter than provide clues as to where to look and what to look for. In summary, these clues are:

1. Look for congressional involvement (members and staff) in all activities logically associated with developing a government program.
2. Look for congressional participation in policy-associated networks (cozy little connections, cozy little triangles, sloppy large hexagons).
3. Above all, look for variation—in who participates in what, in how this participation changes over time, in how the participation differs between issues, bills, committees, the two chambers, the political parties.

9.7 Setting the Agenda in the United States Senate*

Jack L. Walker

Walker discusses agenda setting in the U.S. Senate by identifying different kinds of agenda items and how each is handled very differently. He concludes with proposals for improving the process.

INTRODUCTION

The past 15 years of American public life have been among the most turbulent in the nation's history. It has been a period marked by intense and bitter controversy, but also a time in which the Congress enacted some of the most far-reaching domestic social legislation in the country's history. The public sector has expanded steadily and the government has begun to intervene in many new areas of social and economic life. Besides the enactment of new programs, we have seen the beginning of serious public debate over many highly controversial issues—such as population control or national land use planning—long excluded from the legislative agenda of the Congress.

Many observers of the Congress have recognized the crucial importance of agenda setting. Bauer, Pool, and Dexter concluded that "the most important part of the legislative decision process was the decision about which decision to consider." The representative's major problem was "not how to vote, but what to do with his time, how to allocate his resources, and where to put his energy."[1]

Although the choice of issues for debate clearly has an important impact on the outcome of the legislative process, not much is known about how agenda items are chosen. A small number of thoughtful essays exist on the subject, but there have been few large-scale empirical studies.[2] Some of the work done on this subject has been insightful, but there remain many unanswered questions. Are most issues forced upon the legislature by forces beyond their control, or can representatives determine for themselves which questions to debate? Is agenda setting the sole province of the leadership, or can junior members make an impact on the process? What kinds of information are employed by those who set the agenda? Are agenda items chosen because of their relevance to certain social problems, their cost, their appeal to powerful constituents, their potential to bestow prestige or recogition on their sponsors, or some other criteria known only to Senate insiders?

---

* From Jack L. Walker, "Setting the Agenda in the United States Senate," in *Policymaking Role of Leadership in the Senate: A Compilation of Papers Prepared For the Commission on the Operation of the Senate* (Washington, D.C.: U.S. Government Printing Office, 1976), pp. 96–120. Reprinted from the public domain. A revised version of this paper appeared under the following title: "Setting the Agenda in the U.S. Senate: A Theory of Problem Selection," *British Journal of Political Science* 7, part 4 (October 1977): 423–45.

The author wishes to thank Louis Cornelius, Gregary Dow, Valerie Bunce Echols, Charles Honeyman, Richard Poole, and Judith Shribman, who collected data for this project; thanks to John Echols, who helped to construct measures and interpret findings; thanks to Douglas B. Neal, who managed the data set, drew the figures, and did essential bits of programming; and thanks to colleagues Joel Aberbach, George Downs, Edie Goldenberg, John Kingdon, Lawrence Mohr, Robert Putnam, Robert Rich, Everett Rogers, Kenneth Warner, and Sidney Winter, who attended the Institute of Public Policy Studies faculty seminar on policy formation.

A TYPOLOGY OF ITEMS ON THE SENATE'S AGENDA

The Senate's capacity to shape its own agenda definitely is increasing, but members still are able to exercise very little discretion over the scheduling of items for debate. Much of the business transacted by the Senate either is mandated by the Constitution or required for the daily maintenance of the vast federal establishment. Each year a budget must be created, innumerable amendments must be made to existing statutes, and presidential appointees must be confirmed or rejected. The daily schedules of individual Senators also are jammed with activities—subcommittee hearings, talks with constituents, lobbyists or reporters, roll calls on the Senate floor, consultations with staff members. These matters originate with other people and are virtually unavoidable.[3] Little time and energy remain for reflection or the promotion of bold new legislative departures.

With so many duties and responsibilities thrust upon them it is no surprise that most Senators spend little time promoting legislative change. There is more than enough to do without creating new problems. In Figure 9.7.1 the Senate's agenda is portrayed as a collection of items ranging from those with which the Senate is required to deal, toward another, smaller set of issues that Senators may take up at their own discretion.

The budgetary cycle produces a huge volume of periodically recurring agenda items that can be placed at the left-hand side of Figure 9.7.1. Action on appropriations, for example, is required each year along with decisions about a flood of requests from executive branch agencies and relevant interest groups for minor amendments or modifications of existing statutes. As the federal governments's responsibilities increase, the care and maintenance of the existing operations of the government take large amounts of time and attention.

Moving from left to right in Figure 9.7.1, one encounters portions of the agenda that the Senators are increasingly able to control. To begin with, there is a large class of items—labeled the sporadically recurring problems—that do not appear every year but, nevertheless, once they arise, are virtually forced upon the Senate's agenda. In these cases, major legislation already has been passed, agencies have been established, and grants have been made available or regulations have been drawn up. Those directly involved in these programs have organized themselves to shape and influence the government's activities in the area. Small political systems have been established, revolving around executive branch agencies, professional groups, suppliers, and clients, all of whom operate according to customary rules and understandings that have developed as the programs have evolved. The vocational educational field, labor relations, the merchant marine, highway construction, soil conservation, and hundreds of other specialized policy areas have become established as subgovernments whose immediate access to the Senate's agenda is assured.[4]

Once major disagreements arise within these systems as a result of social changes or shifts in political influence they exercise a compelling claim on the attention of key Senators who control the committees and subcommittees that oversee their activities. The Senate provides the natural forum in which disputes are settled and new legislative compromises created. The his-

FIGURE 9.7.1 A TYPOLOGY OF SENATE AGENDA ITEMS

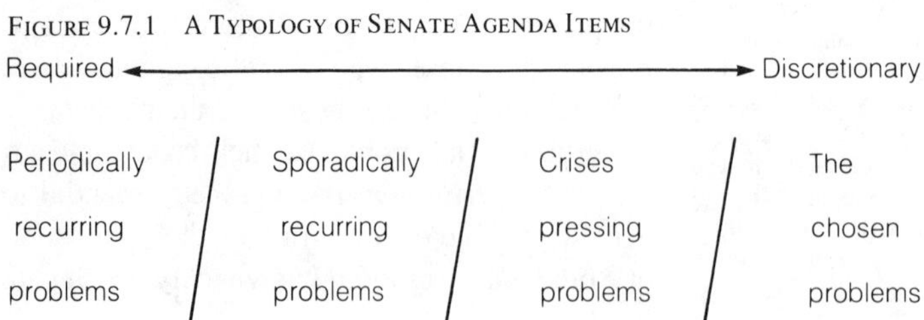

tory of any policy area usually can be traced through a series of legislative landmarks—from the Wagner Act to Taft–Hartley to Landrum–Griffin, for example—which represent points in the evolution of the area when fundamental changes in prevailing social or political balances have required major revisions of government policies. When dislocations arise in established program areas, the pressure to consider them is nearly irresistible. Since important Senators often play key roles in these active policy systems, they are able to place the concerns of these established areas at the top of the Senate's agenda.

Most of the Senate's agenda items appear each year at about the same time with great predictability. Yearly appropriations or the routine aspects of oversight sometimes create unforeseen difficulties, but knowledgeable observers of the legislative process can describe with fair accuracy exactly how much progress the Senate will have made on these problems a year in the future. The need for comprehensive revisions of welfare policies, federal aid to higher education, or industrial and labor relations also usually arise slowly over the course of several years. When the Senate finally begins serious debate over concrete proposals for change, there has been ample time to collect evidence and prepare for the discussion. Once again, knowledgeable observers would be aware of the emergence of such issues and could make good predictions about when they would appear on the Senate's agenda.

Not all issues, however, arise with such predictability. The violent civil disorders of the 1960s or the OPEC oil boycott blow up like summer thunderstorms and burst upon the country in magnified form via the mass media. A great national crisis suddenly is proclaimed by commentators and citizens alike, and Senators are expected to take immediate action to solve it. Pressing problems of this kind force their way immediately onto the Senate's agenda, whether or not feasible solutions are in sight. Action of some kind, even if it is merely symbolic, must be taken as quickly as possible. Problems of this type have arisen frequently in the past few decades, catching most Senators by surprise. They occur almost randomly and when they arise they displace all other agenda items that can be delayed or pushed aside.

In some years the Senate's agenda is jammed to overflowing by its extensive budgetary and housekeeping responsibilities, by fundamental revisions of established policies and by pressing problems arising from national crises. During such periods Senators are engaged mainly in reacting to the demands of outside political forces; they are able to exercise little choice in the establishment of the legislative agenda. In most years, however, several items appear on the Senate's agenda for debate that have been spawned and incubated principally within the Senate. These issues—the Senate's chosen problems—are the handiwork of the activist minority, the culmination of their promotional efforts. They are selected from the numerous possibilities offered up by the Senate's legislative activists who compete against each other and against all other forms of problems for this limited space on the agenda. Aspiring activists strive to guide their problems past the many obstacles in their path into the charmed circle of national concern, where there is room for only a few issues at a time. Once the problem begins to attract attention and is debated seriously by other Senators, it takes on a heightened significance in the mass media. Its activist sponsors, beyond the satisfaction of advancing the public interest as they see it, also receive important political rewards that come from greatly increased national exposure.

THREE FACTORS DETERMINING THE DISCRETIONARY AGENDA

How does an aspiring problem make its way into the charmed circle of serious national attention? Is the process of agenda setting in the Senate entirely fortuitous, each issue's emergence the result of some unique combination of events? Can any generalizations be made about the final process of issue selection? Caution certainly is in order when an explanation is offered of such a subtle process of persuasion and influence. But even in the face of extreme complexity, it is possible to offer a general explanation of the conditions that usually allow issues successfully to claim a place on the discretionary portion of the Senate's agenda.

The appeal of legislative proposals concerning issues that have not received serious attention in the recent past is determined mainly by three prominent features or conditions. First, an item's attractiveness increases if it has an impact on large numbers of people; Senators must believe that the proposed legislation will have broad political appeal.[5] Second, convincing evidence must exist that the proposed legislation is addressed to a serious and real problem. The more graphic and easily understood the evidence of trouble, the more creditable the sources of information upon which the case is based, the more appealing the aspiring agenda item becomes. Third, the case for inclusion on the agenda will be greatly strengthened if an easily understood solution exists for the problem being addressed. Again, the more comprehensible the solution and the more honorable or prestigious its origins, the more likely that an item will claim a place on the discretionary agenda. If proposed legislation has all three of these desirable characteristics, its chances of appearing on the Senate's agenda are greatly enhanced. These conditions are not sufficient in themselves to ensure success, but they certainly increase an issue's attractiveness and lower any barriers in its path.

When establishing the discretionary agenda, Senators create alliances that appear, disappear, and recombine as problems and solutions rise and fall in prominence. Often, solutions may become known before appropriate problems can be found to which they can be applied, or before a convincing case can be made for the seriousness of the problems they are meant to address. Activist Senators or special interest groups dedicated to the value of a given solution—such as income grants in lieu of services or administrative decentralization—frequently are out looking for social problems to which their nostrum can be applied. Or they are anxious to define problems in such a way that their pet solutions will be singularly applicable. There also are many problems—such as decay of central city housing—that can be documented easily, but they have attracted little serious debate for years because no politically or economically feasible solution seems to exist.

Careful observers of the Senate, studying its daily struggles and monitoring the informal conversations of its members, usually are able to make accurate forecasts of the attractiveness of any proposed legislation. Based on their intimate knowledge of the political affinities of the membership and the patterns of influence prevailing at the time, insiders can estimate whether a proposal (e.g., for the national chartering of corporations or the provision of subsidies to cities for the construction of mass transit lines) is likely to draw any interest or support. By offering a stream of new proposals, however, activist Senators constantly challenge the received wisdom concerning the political composition of the Senate, hoping that their initiative will lead to some unprecedented combination of support and a dramtic political breakthrough. At any time there are many possible combinations of votes that might be forged into a winning coalition if the right kind of issue can be found as a catalyst. The number of feasible possibilities for coalition building certainly is not infinite, but definitely exceeds those that actually have appeared. Activist Senators continually search for these potential new voting combinations and, in periods of intellectual and political ferment, often find them in policy areas never anticipated by Senate insiders.[6]

Once a breakthrough occurs in a policy area formerly ignored by the Senate, a surge of legislative activity often occurs, lasting over several years. Activist Senators are joined by lobbyists, ambitious agency chiefs, crusading journalists, and policy professionals of all kinds in a rush to exploit the newly discovered political pay dirt.

The sometimes frantic burst of activity that follows an initial political breakthrough may bring proposals on to the Senate's discretionary agenda that do not necessarily have broad appeal, where little evidence of a problem exists and where no feasible solutions are anywhere in sight. Legislation of this kind may not only be debated but often passes into law because the pressure on the Senate to act in such circumstances in nearly overwhelming. Once a topic such as pollution control or mass transit has achieved the status of a chosen problem and it becomes clear that the votes are there for passage of bills on the subject, powerful forces are unleashed that press for action. As the surge progresses, the relative importance of succeeding legislative proposals on the same topic tends to decline and the case for their passage becomes weaker. Although efforts are made to sustain the momentum created by initial legislative successes, the vein of interest and support is rapidly played out. Competition mounts for space on the discretionary agenda from other aspiring problems and the legislative surge comes to an end, leading eventually to new cycles of debate and legislation.

AUTO SAFETY LEGISLATION—1966: A CASE STUDY OF AGENDA SETTING

One of the best examples in recent years of agenda development that exhibits the characteristics described here began in 1962 with the election in Connecticut to the Senate of Abraham Ribicoff.[7] Coming to the Senate with experience as a state governor, House member, and former Secretary of HEW, Ribicoff adopted the promotional style of a legislative activist. His policy interests were broad and his assignment to the Government Operations Committee allowed him wide scope. Within two years he acquired a subcommittee chairmanship and almost immediately began an investigation of the federal government's efforts in the area of traffic safety—a subject to which he had devoted much time and attention while governor of Connecticut. In order to prepare for this investigation he hired as a consultant to his subcommittee a young attorney from Hartford, Ralph Nader, who had come to Washington to devote himself full-time to the cause of safety and consumer protection. In 1965 Nader published his book *Unsafe at Any Speed*[8] and the Ribicoff subcommittee's hearings were in full swing.

The time was certainly ripe for the promotion of traffic safety as an agenda item in the Senate. Reports issued annually by the National Safety Council, a highly respected private agency, clearly demonstrated that the country was experiencing an unprecedented increase in deaths on its highways. Traffic deaths per 100 million miles driven had declined almost every year since World War II, but beginning in 1960 the rate turned sharply upward and rose for four of the next five years—the longest and worst surge since yearly records had been kept. For those not moved by such abstractions as statistical rates there was clear evidence of a serious problem in the total number of deaths recorded. From 1946 to 1961 total yearly deaths, with a declining rate in ratio to an increasing number of cars, had remained within the 30,000 range—33,411 in 1946 to 38,091 in 1961—but with the increase in accidents the numbers climbed into the 40,000 range in 1962 and quickly moved to 53,041 in 1966. When the increase in the death rate hit its peak in 1966 it was still lower than it had been in the early 1950s, but the upward turn had attracted attention, and coupled with the rapid increase in the total number of deaths, it provided stark, unavoidable evidence that a major social problem existed. Since the issue involved almost every American family, the country's largest manufacturing industry, and some of its most powerful unions, it clearly had the potential for broad national appeal. Ribicoff, Nader, and Robert Kennedy, another subcommittee member who began to take an active interest in the problem, realized they were dealing with an issue that had great political potential.

As the Senators and their staff members began searching for solutions to the problem, they discovered that a rather elaborate policy community, including numerous voluntary and government agencies, already existed in the field of traffic safety.[9] They also found that this community was becoming increasingly divided over how to define the problem they faced. The majority of professionals in the field was committed to the established policies being pursued all over the country, which affected driver training courses in high schools, improved signs and lighting for highways, and mass media advertising campaigns promoting safe driving. All these programs aimed primarily at improving the performance of the driver.

A small group of traffic engineers, however, some of them in the Federal Highway Administration, backed by results from a mounting volume of empirical research, had begun to advocate reform of the automobile itself. Their studies showed that the impact on the accident rate of all policies meant to reform drivers was negligible. But they found that changes in the design of the auto or the addition of seat belts could significantly reduce the death rate by protecting the occupants of a car, once the accident took place. The political implications of these results also were clear—they pointed directly to the need for safety standards imposed by government on the manufacture of automobiles.

In Figure 9.7.2 both the yearly death rate from traffic accidents and the volume of literature on the subject of traffic safety are depicted for the years from 1952 to 1972.[10] The data in Figure 9.7.2 suggest that the technical literature on traffic safety was developing rapidly during this period, and that the surge of publication, measured by the number of articles on the subject appearing in technical journals each year, began in the mid-1950s, several years before the increase in death rate. This increased level of publication was primarily the result of an intellectual controversy and came in response to pioneering research results that challenged prevailing assumptions in the field. The experts, in other words, were engaged in debate over traffic safety several years before the public or political leaders became aroused about the problem. A challenging new approach to reducing the traffic death toll emerged from this debate—one that could be presented to laymen in a dramatic and persuasive way through stop-action photography and crash-sled demostrations.

The level of concern in the mass media over this issue is measured indirectly in Figure 9.7.2 by the number of column inches on traffic safety appearing each year in the *New York Times Index*. The amount of news generated on this topic declined fairly steadily from the mid-1960s until 1964 when it began to turn upward. There was a small increase in coverage during 1965—the year of the Ribicoff hearings—and then a massive upsurge in 1966, the peak year of traffic deaths and the year in which the highway safety act passed the Congress and was signed into law.

These data indicate that the *Times* was reacting to events in this case, not stimulating the controversy or providing leadership. The expert community had been engaged in debate for more than a decade prior to the emergence of traffic safety as an agenda item in the Senate, but the crucial ingredient of leadership needed to cause the political upheaval of 1966 was provided by an ambitious group of political entrepreneurs who were able to capture the attention of the Congress and the media. There were several unique characteristics of this issue that contributed greatly to their success—especially the spectacular technical shortcomings of the Chevrolet Corvair and the sinister but unsuccessful effort by General Motors to discredit Ralph Nader.[11] Still, the central elements of the agenda-building process were present. Once clear evidence from a respected source could be found that pointed unmistakably to the existence of a serious national problem, legislative activists had the political resources they needed to promote the solution being offered by the research community against the one favored by the automobile manufacturers.

By the time the traffic safety legislation reached the stage of serious formulation and debate in 1966 its original sponsors had been pushed aside by Senators better placed to create a winning coalition. Senators Ribicoff and Gaylord Nelson, both of whom had pressed for the legislation in the early stages, were displaced by Warren Magnuson, the powerful chairman of the Senate Commerce Committee. Under his leadership a legislative victory was achieved against the determined opposition of powerful industrial interests—a result that few

FIGURE 9.7.2 HIGHWAY SAFETY ACT—1966

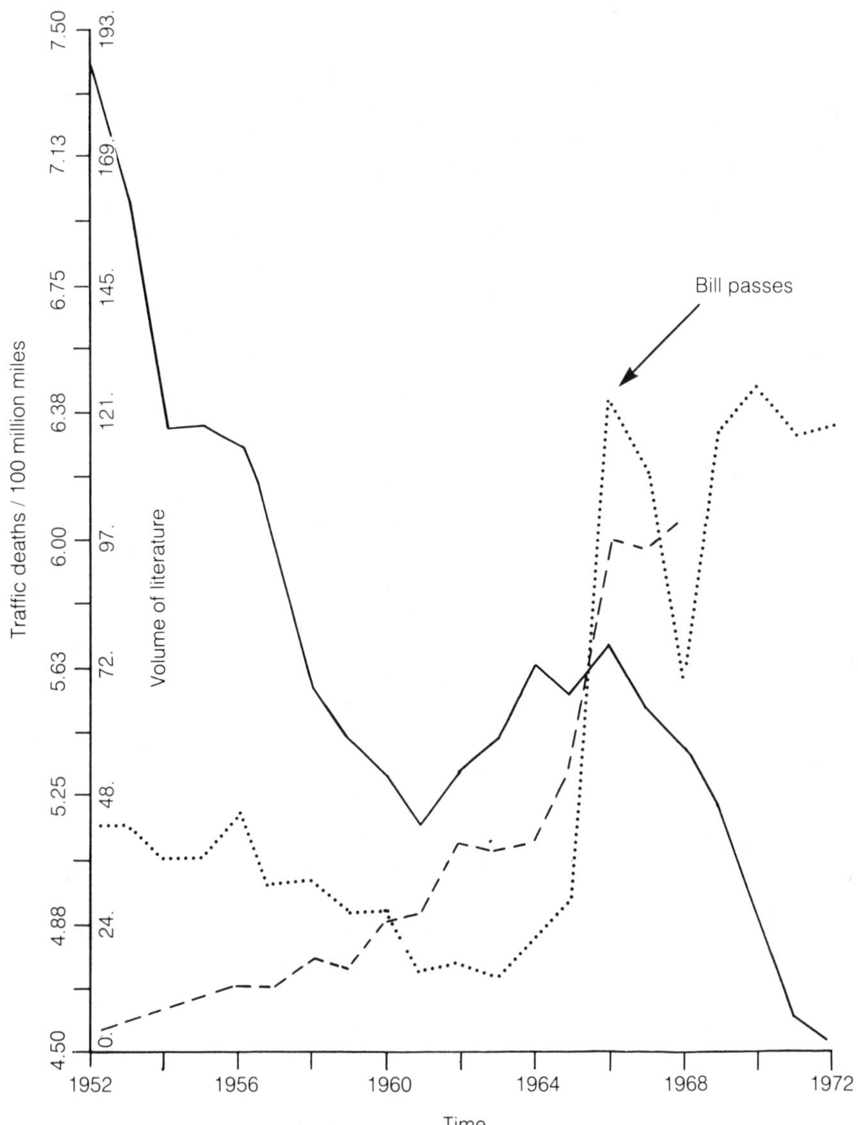

KEY: Solid line = Deaths per 100 million miles driven.
Dotted line = *N.Y. Times Index* column inches on traffic safety.
Dashed line = Technical traffic safety literature (x10).

Senate insiders would have predicted when debate began on the issue. As a result of the controversy, a majority coalition was discovered in the Senate for legislating an unprecedented expansion of the federal government's efforts to ensure the safety of its citizens. Both proponents and opponents of reform immediately were put on notice that new political opportunities existed in this policy area.

All the elements necessary for successful policy innovation were present in this case. An easily understood, widely respected social indicator pointed to the development of a serious national problem. Prevailing public policies were unable to handle it. A body of research with clear policy implication had emerged, providing justification for new legislation. Established agencies had either ignored or lost touch with the developing knowledge base in the field. They also had thrown their motives into question through illegitimate efforts to discredit their critics. And skillful political entrepreneurs were available who could tie all these elements together in a dramatic proposal for change.

THE SAFETY MOVEMENT IS BORN

The passage of traffic safety legislation in 1966 was a surprise to many and caused a pronounced shift of political ground throughout the national political system. The Senate's action not only secured the reputation of Ralph Nader as a national crusader for consumer protection and corporate responsibility. It also transmitted powerful cues concerning the nature of the legislative agenda to lobbyists, members of the President's staff, activist legislators, journalists, and agency chiefs all over the city of Washington. Traffic safety legislation became a benchmark—a widely acknowledged legislative triumph—which could be cited as an important precedent by advocates of other forms of safety legislation. In 1969 President Nixon introduced his proposal for an occupational safety bill by saying:

> Three years ago, following its study of traffic and highway safety, the Congress noted that modern technology had brought with it new driving hazards, and accordingly it enacted the National Traffic and Motor Vehicle Act and the Highway Safety Act. With the advent of a new workplace technology we must now give similar attention to workplace safety and health.[12]

In the same year, speaking before a meeting of the American Society of Safety Engineers, David A. Swankin, the Director of the Bureau of Labor Standards, explained:

> An aroused public conscience against needless highway accidents has had, I believe, a spin-off to work accidents, giving the whole safety movement a shot in the arm. . . . The whole area of safety is opened up.[13]

Beyond the halls of Congress, associations of professionals in the safety field—groups like the American Academy of Occupational Medicine, the American Association of Industrial Nurses, the American Public Health Association, the America College of Preventive Medicine, or the American Society of Safety Engineers—began active discussion of the new possibilities for greatly expanded government action in the field of safety and accident prevention.[14] Newspapers began to pay greater attention to any events having to do with aspects of individual or industrial safety. The *Congressional Quarterly,* the *Reader's Guide to Periodical Literature, Index Medicus* and the *Business Periodicals Index* created in 1967 or 1968 new categories labeled "Safety and Health," "Industrial Safety," or "Traffic Safety."

Lobbyists and activists in the consumer field in 1969, interviewed by Mark Nadel, said that their efforts were being devoted to safety and consumer protection at that particular time because it was a field where movement was taking place, one where large political payoffs were possible.[15] As George C. Guenther, another official of the Bureau of Labor Standards wrote in 1969: "It is said that each subject has its time. We sense a favorable and fair wind blowing for a new high level of safety and health in the American workplace."[16]

Within the Congress, activist Senators were moving quickly to capitalize on the rising interest in safety by proposing new legislation. Senator Magnuson's Commerce Committee staff organized itself as a small factory for producing legislative proposals on safety. The committee began an investigation of meat inspection in 1967—followed in 1968 by a study of poultry inspection and in 1971 by hearings on fish inspection—and also began preparing for hearings in 1968 on the safety of diet pills. Also in 1967, the committee cleared for passage the Toy Safety and Child Protection Act and a set of strengthening amendments to the Flammable Fabrics Standards Act—originally passed in 1953. A year later, in 1968, the Fire Research and Safety Act was passed, a program that led in 1974 to the passage of the Federal Fire Prevention and Control Act, a comprehensive reorganization and expansion of the federal government's efforts at fire prevention.

Sensing that legislative breakthroughs were possible in this area, President Johnson proposed in 1968 the creation of a National Commission on Product Safety, a study group whose mission was to collect evidence of problems in the area and propose solutions. Commissions of this kind provide the President with an investigatory tool that may produce important political gains but is unlikely to cause any serious losses. In the short run, knowledge of the extent of household accidents was almost nonexistent at the time. Estimates of the number of accidents caused yearly by faulty products varied by a factor of five. So there was a clear need at least for information on the extent of the product safety problem if any action was to be taken. Merely by proposing the commission, the President made an important symbolic gesture that lent visibility to the safety movement. And, since concrete proposals for change were several years away, no political enemies would be created immediately. The commission launched an ambitious program of fact-gathering and through its reports began to add to the national debate over safety. There was little knowledge of solutions for the problems being identified by the commission. Only a loosely organized network of professional associations were dedicated to working in the area. The Congress had evidence that a serious problem existed, however, and during this period that was all they needed. In 1972 the Consumer Product Safety Act was passed. This made the commission a permanent regulatory agency with the authority to continue its search for solutions to the problems it had uncovered and to begin setting standards for the production of thousands of items merchandized in all sectors of the American economy.

THE COAL MINE HEALTH AND SAFETY ACT: 1969

By 1968 it was clear that safety remained a chosen problem on the Senate's agenda, but the ultimate strength of the legislative surge that eventually would follow upon passage of the auto safety bill still was undetermined. A solid majority had appeared during 1967 for the enactment of several pieces of safety legislation. The Study Commission on Product Safety had been approved, but it still was possible that support would evaporate when additional pieces of legislation on the subject were proposed. In situations like this, legislative momentum often is sustained by a dramatic crisis that provides unchallengable proof of the need for action.

During the 1950s, for example, legislation intended to prepare the society against the threat of nuclear war—the Civil Defense Act, National Defense Interstate Highway Act—was slowly making its way through a cautious and skeptical Congress. This leisurely legislative surge was suddenly transformed into a frantic rush—the National Defense Education Act, creation of NASA—immediately after the launching of Sputnik in 1957.

Crises seldom can be manufactured, of course, but when they appear, it is up to political entrepreneurs to make use of them to get the legislation they want. Advocates of safety legislation tried throughout this period to capitalize on disastrous accidents that took many lives in order to build support for their cause. Large disasters take place often in all industrial societies but they seldom produce any legislative reaction. During the period from 1966 until 1972, however, when safety already had claimed a secure place on the Senate's discretionary agenda, any serious accident potentially was useful as a goad to action.

A midair collision of two aircraft over New Jersey in 1967 caused a flurry of debate over air safety during consideration of the Federal Aviation Agency's appropriations bill. The accident could not be capitalized upon, however, mainly because no concrete proposal had been developed for reform in this area. A year later, though, when 78 miners were killed in a coal mine in Farmington, West Virginia, legislative activists were fully prepared to move. Coal mine safety had been debated several times in the Congress during the past 30 years, and legislation setting some safety standards had been passed in 1952, once again in the wake of several disastrous accidents.[17] Technical literature on the subject was not plentiful, but a professional community did exist in this field, including experts with a continuing interest in mining safety. Medical researchers, in particular, had made significant progress during the early 1960s in discovering how to detect and treat pneumoconiosis or "black lung" disease. As a result, some had become crusaders for tougher legislation.[18] Safety equipment was available. Recognized mining procedures—some borrowed from standard practice in Japan, the Soviet Union, England, and Germany—were known that would increase the safety of the mines without steep declines in productivity.[19] Once again, it could be said that a solution existed that was in search of a problem.

The circumstances leading up to the debate and passage of the Coal Mine Health and Safety Act in 1969 are depicted in Figure 9.7.3.[20] The three variables recorded here are the same as those that appeared in Figure 9.7.2, but in this case they display slightly different patterns. Once again, as in the auto safety case, the problem of coal mine safety received little attention in the *New York Times* until it became the center of debate in the Congress. A small increase in coverage accompanied the Farmington mine disaster, but the newspaper seems to have been mainly reacting to Congressional initiatives rather than providing leadership for legislative activists. Technical literature in the area—recorded as the total number of papers and books published each year on the subject—was declining in the decade prior to passage of the bill. The sharp spurts of publication appearing from 1955 to 1957 and in 1972–74 are probably direct results of increases in government research funds, included in the new legislation passed in 1952 and 1969. They did not stem from within the professional community in response to research breakthroughs or intellectual controversy.

Legislative action in 1969 seems to have been the direct result of the abrupt increase in the death rate in 1968 caused mainly by the Farmington disaster. The 1952 legislation had established safety standards for coal mines, but limited its enforceability to mines with more than 15 employees. Since the investment necessary to meet the standards led to declines in worker productivity and increased costs, incentives were created to expand production in the industry's smaller mines, not covered by the safety legislation. Declines in the demand for coal throughout this period made these economic incentives even more powerful. Since the smaller mines, however, also were much more hazardous, the 1952 safety legislation ironically contributed to the steady increase in the death rate from 1955 into the early 1960s.[21] The impact of the 1969 safety legislation was delayed both by a dispute within the Nixon Administration on how the new standards were to be enforced and by another disaster in Hyden, Kentucky, that took 38 lives in December 1970.[22] Once its provisions began to be enforced, however, the death rate began to decline rapidly. Solutions were available to meet the problems of coal mining safety. What had been missing for decades was not the technology that would do the job but the right combination of political factors that would set the stage for action.

THE OCCUPATIONAL SAFETY AND HEALTH ACT: 1970

Passage of both the auto safety and coal mine safety bills within only three years was a political earthquake that provided enormous momentum for the safety movement. Legislative activists now had two powerful precedents that could be cited in support of safety legislation in many new areas. Bills covering all consumer products manufactured in the country, or all workplaces in all enterprises of any kind, would have been regarded as hopeless, visionary schemes in 1965. Only five years later they were at the top of the Senate's agenda and being given serious consideration. Once the opposition of the powerful automobile and coal mining industries had been pushed aside, it became difficult for Senators to resist appeals to complete the job by ensuring the safety of all the rest of the workers and products in the entire economy. These bills had broad potential appeal and, however uncertain the reports, there

FIGURE 9.7.3 COAL MINE HEALTH AND SAFETY ACT—1969

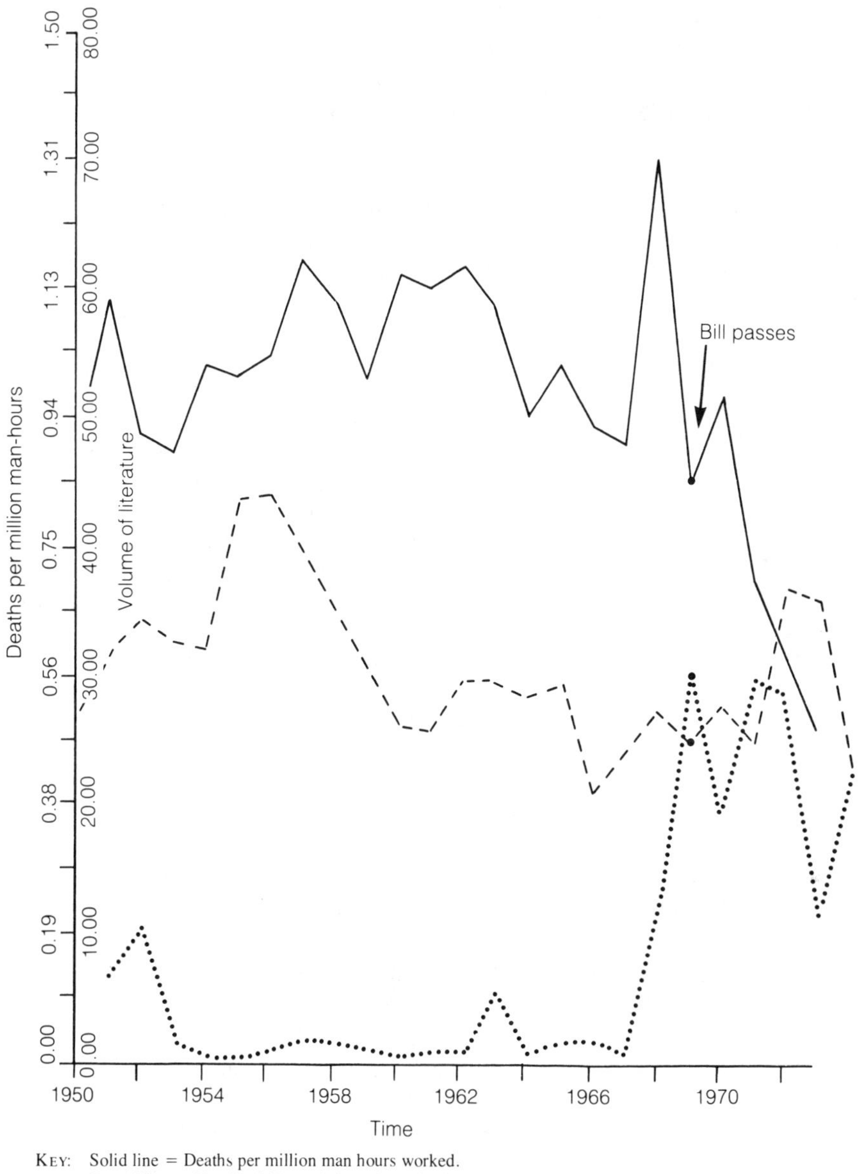

KEY: Solid line = Deaths per million man hours worked.
Dotted line = *New York Times Index* column inches on coal mine accidents and safety.
Dashed line = Coal mine health and safety technical literature (x5).

clearly were many serious accidents taking place that probably could be traced to shoddy products and dangerous working conditions. Even though there was little reliable knowledge of how to create safe products or workplaces, the argument was made that progress was possible only if agencies were created that could begin to perform the necessary research.

Occupational safety was a prime discretionary agenda item in the Senate in 1970 primarily because of the processes of political evolution set in motion by the passage of automobile safety legislation in 1966 and coal mine safety legislation in 1969. Support for this assertion is contained in Figure 9.7.4, where the conditions leading to the passage of the Occupational Safety and Health Act are depicted. This chart contrasts sharply with those that dealt with auto and coal mine safety. If analyzed alone, it would provide few clues as to why the Senate chose this policy area for consideration from among all those being offered up by legislative activists. The yearly death rate from job-related accidents recorded in this figure declines in all but two years of the period from 1950 to 1972. No distinctive upturn in the rate appears that might capture public attention as occurred in both the auto and coal mine safety cases. Advocates of occupational safety legislation argued that despite this decline in the death rate federal intervention was warranted to deal with new technical processes and industrial chemicals just coming into use. These were certain to be more hazardous than anything yet encountered. It seems unlikely that such hypothetical arguments would have been persuasive, had it not been for the momentum generated by the political struggles over safety legislation that had occurred during the preceding five years. The urge to create a comprehensive program—and to capitalize on the existence of an assured majority apparently ready to support further safety measures—led the Congress to disregard evidence that the prevailing safety policies of both government and industry had been steadily reducing the rate of deaths and injuries from job-related accidents for more than two decades.

There was no dramatic scientific breakthrough or sudden spurt of knowledge about occupational health and safety that would have stimulated the enactment of new legislation. This definitely was not a case where the solution appeared before the problem. Numerous professionals were already at work in the field with long-established interests in occupational diseases or job-related accidents. Most of them had close ties either to insurance companies or public health agencies. When representatives of professional societies in the field were called to testify during 1968 and 1969 Congressional hearings on the occupational safety legislation, many expressed great skepticism about the feasibility of the proposed new regulatory schemes. The executive director of the American Society of Safety Engineers, for example, argued against passage of any new mandatory regulations by pointing to the lack of effectiveness of similar programs in several of the larger industrial states:

> Since [these] states . . . have ongoing programs, substantial safety regulations, fairly adequate staffs, and consultation for employers, it is believed that these elements are not a great factor in changing injury frequency, since they show trends comparable with those of national data. . . . We conclude that injury data available does not indicate clearly a particular solution; rather, it does show a problem in reducing occupational injuries further. It is our judgment that more complete, reliable data is needed to determine the nature and scope of the problem as well as the relevancy of regulatory codes to specific types of accidents and injuries.[23]

The rapid upward surge in the volume of technical publications shown in Figure 9.7.4 begins in 1968—three years after the beginning of the Ribicoff hearings on auto safety—and turns abruptly downward a year after passage of the Occupational Safety and Health Act in 1970. Many of the papers published during this period were commissioned by agencies within the Department of Labor or HEW and must be regarded as part of the campaign mounted by advocates of new safety legislation. The renewed concern did lead to the founding of new centers of research in the area. This initial surge of publication appeared more because of the increased availability of federal research funds and the heightened interest shown by the Congress in industrial and occupational safety than because of any new scientific discovery or broad-based intellectual revolution in the field.

Newspaper coverage of the occupational safety issue, after being virtually nonexistent for a decade, rose slightly in 1968, but once again did not surge upward until the year in

FIGURE 9.7.4 OCCUPATIONAL HEALTH AND SAFETY ACT—1970

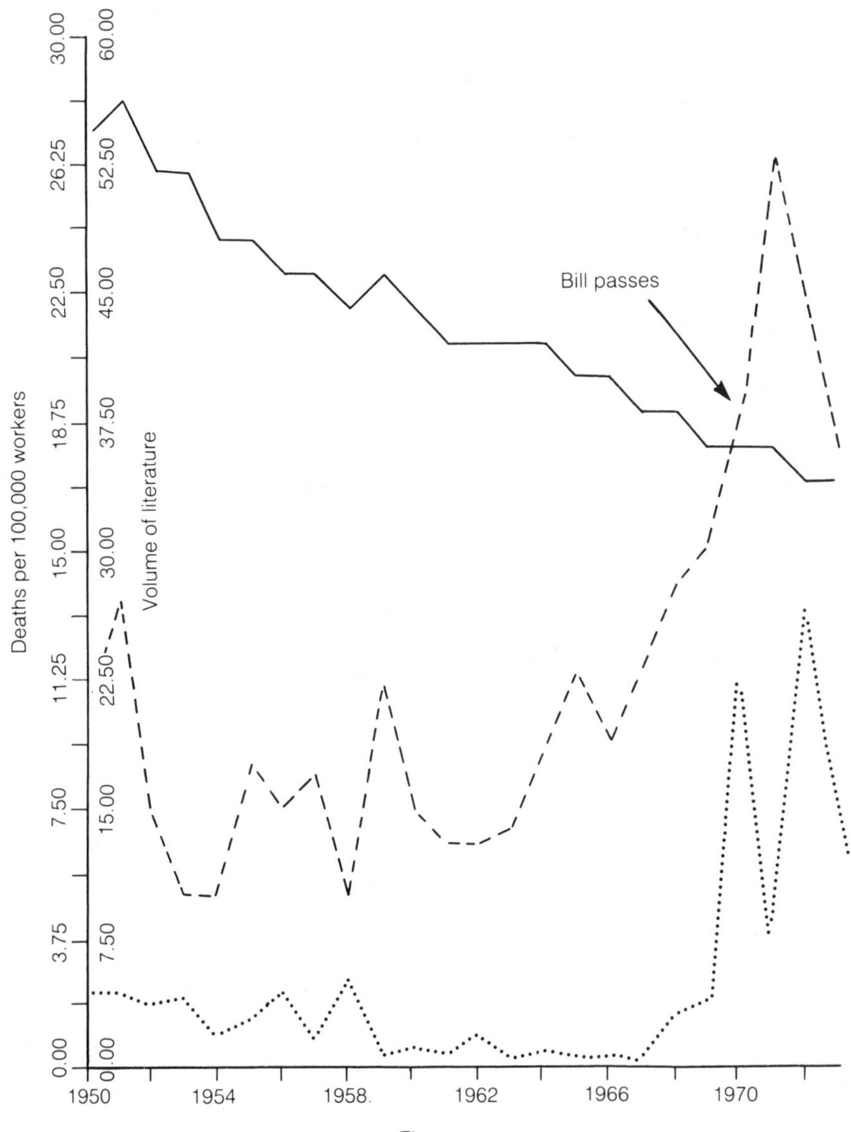

KEY: Solid line = Deaths per 100,000 workers.
Dotted line = *New York Times Index* column inches on occupational safety.
Dashed line = Technical literature on occupational health and safety.

which the subject became a major focus of debate in the Congress. The *New York Times* seems to have followed the lead of Congress as it cycled from one safety issue to another. In each case the newspaper began extensive coverage of an issue in the year it moved to the floor of the Congress and then maintained an interest in the issue for a few years afterward while the new legislation was being implemented and while the general topic of safety remained a chosen problem on the discretionary agenda of the Congress.

THE SURGE OF SAFETY LEGISLATION IS ENDED

By 1972 the surge of safety legislation was coming to an end. Once bills with such broad scope as the Consumer Product Safety Act and the Occupational Safety and Health Act had been passed, there were few matters of consequence left to consider. After the disastrous collapse of a coal slag dam in West Virginia in 1972, a bill was quickly passed entitled the Federal Safety of Dams Act. It granted new powers of inspection and regulation over the construction of dams to the Army Corps of Engineers, showing that the safety majority still existed and could be counted upon to act if given a plausible context.[24] The Senate's concern over safety had not completely evaporated by any means, but other issues arising from the gathering problems facing the nation's economy and the first rumblings of the Watergate affair were beginning to crowd onto the discretionary agenda, pushing safety into the background.

Moods shift rapidly in the Senate. No sooner had a new set of safety agencies with increased regulatory power been created than the economy began to slide into a serious double illness of recession and hyperinflation. Freshly written safety requirements and rules came under fire from those concerned over the increased costs caused by the expansion of federal regulatory powers. ''Deregulation'' became the slogan of these counterattacking forces. Worries over inflation and declining industrial productivity led to general criticisms of any federal regulation—whether it arose from efforts to ensure safety, prevent racial or sexual discrimination, or reduce pollution—that could be characterized as an obstacle to economic growth. The safety issue had appealed to liberals in 1968 and 1969 because reform in this area did not create hugh new financial burdens for the federal budget. However, these new regulations did impose costs on the companies and enterprises that were required to install new equipment or keep records and make reports about activities that never had been monitored before. The agencies receiving the most criticism were those enforcing the safety legislation that was passed toward the end of the legislative surge; the dimensions of the problems often were in dispute and feasibility solutions were not readily at hand.[25]

Even though safety began to give way in the Senate to a new set of ''hot'' issues—public service employment, national health insurance, and reorganization of the Congress itself, among others—safety issues could not be removed entirely from the agenda. The surge of legislative activity had left in its wake new regulatory agencies such as the Consumer Product Safety Commission and the Occupational Health and Safety Administration and had granted new powers and greater responsibilities to established ones such as the National Bureau of Standards and the Federal Highway Administration. This enlarged administrative complex—with all its newly acquired clients, political allies, interest groups, suppliers, consultants, professional societies, trade associations, and research centers—provided a new focus for public attention, the concrete embodiment of government concern for the safety of its citizens. Now that this machinery had been put into place, it required annual appropriations, approval of appointments to its top administrative positions, periodic investigations of its operations, and the settlement of disputes over the implementation of the new policies. Safety was not removed from the Senate's attention—its status simply had shifted from that of a chosen problem on the discretionary agenda to a sporadically recurring problem on the required agenda.

A SUMMARY OF THE ARGUMENT

There is no single, simple process governing the assembly of the Senate's legislative agenda. Many items appear as part of the annual budgetary cycle—a highly routinized process that follows a clear timetable and employs widely known operating procedures—while others are generated by visionaries and guided past innumerable obstacles by shrewd and energetic political entrepreneurs. Activist legislators, motivated by a desire to promote social change and anxious to gain reputations as reformers, constantly search for issues that might be transformed into new items on the Senate's discretionary agenda. These activists compete with each other as well as the opponents of their proposals, fashioning arguments and justifications for action that will catch the imagination of fellow Senators.

Issues aspiring to be included on the discretionary agenda are more likely to achieve success if they exhibit three prime characteristics: First, a proposal should affect large numbers of people and have the potential for broad political appeal. Second, there should be arresting proof of the existence of the problem—the more graphic and newsworthy the better. Third, an easily understood solution should be available that is both technically and politically feasible.

Aspiring agenda items that have all three of these characteristics, even if they break new policy ground, will, very likely, reach the stage of serious debate in the Senate.

If an issue of the discretionary agenda successfully passes into law—especially if it is in a policy area where little activity has taken place before—a strong impetus is created for further legislation in the same field. Activists inside and outside the Senate sense that legislative progress may be possible in areas that are logically related to the original breakthrough. Word that the policy area is beginning to open up passes quickly through innumerable professional and political contact networks. A surge of legislative activity is launched in which reformers urge that benefits conferred in the original breakthrough be extended to similar areas. Activity continues until the logical possibilities for extension of the reform are exhausted or until the justifications offered for new proposals become so weak and unappealing that more attractive proposals in other policy areas force their way onto the agenda and bring the legislative surge to an end.

A complicated set of political processes produces the Senate's agenda, but the results are not completely random and unpredictable. Even the discretionary agenda usually contains items that are logically compatible. Issues seem to group themselves into clusters that include complementary topics which provoke similar political alignments and impel government to perform similar functions. Proposals to toughen safety regulations, for example appeared during a period in which many other forms of consumer protection and pollution control legislation were being debated. They began to recede from the agenda when essentially competitive proposals to encourage economic growth or increase worker productivity came into prominence. As Crenson has argued in his book on the politics of air pollution in cities:

> By promoting one political agenda item, civic activists may succeed in driving other issues away. . . . A community that commits itself to the consideration of one local concern may, in effect, commit itself to a whole chain of rationally related issues and diminish its ability to consider rationally antagonistic issues.[26]

Those who manage to shape the legislative agenda, in other words, are able to magnify their influence many times over by determining the focus of attention and energy in the entire political system. By dictating the issues to come under debate, they indirectly determine the kind of political alliances likely to be formed, and prevent others from gaining a hearing for logically incompatible or competitive issues.[27]

AN EVALUATION OF THE PROCESS

This description of the agenda-setting process provides support for Polsby's assertion that the Senate has become one of the best places in the American "political system for the incubation of new policy and the building of national constituencies."[28] The clubby, slow-moving Senate of the 1940s and 1950s was dominated by southern conservatives engaged in a stubborn holding action against activist, liberal Presidents. The body is described with much clarity by Donald Matthews in his *U.S. Senators and Their World.*[29] The Senate has slowly but steadily been transformed in recent years into a prime launching pad for liberal initiatives and one of the most persistent forces for change in the American government system.

Because of the distinctly liberal bias in the highly decentralized process by which the Senate currently sets its agenda, evaluations of the procedure likely will vary according to the observer's own political values. The system will seem admirable to those who believe that government should react quickly to expressions of social need, but it might seem harmful and pernicious to those who feel that the public sector already is too large and that government intervention in society has expanded beyond reasonable boundaries. The contemporary Senate could be characterized either as a highly responsive forum for the promotion of needed reforms, or as a hyperactive, government busybody, giving recognition to every dramatic or newsworthy appeal, no matter how weak the justification for action might be.

Agreement never could be reached on global assessments of the Senate's role in the American political system, but both conservatives and liberals might agree that the system is markedly haphazard and unsystematic. The open and competitive system of agenda setting being employed in the Senate encourages members and their staffs to search constantly for information about social problems and possible solutions. Once a general subject, like energy or poverty, becomes a prominent topic on the discretionary agenda, however, proposals begin to appear that either address problems whose dimensions are virtually uncharted or for which no feasible solutions are in sight. Some would argue that the Senate is justified in enacting legislation in situations of this kind, if only to insure that the problem becomes recognized as a responsibility of government. As Arrow has argued in a recent analysis of organizational problem solving:

> Once an item has arrived on the agenda, it is difficult not to treat it in a somewhat rational manner, if this is at all possible, and almost any considered solution may be better than neglect. I hasten to add that this generalization has its exception; there are problems for which there are no satisfactory solutions; placing such an item on the agenda may create a demand for a solution, which will of necessity be unsatisfactory.
>
> Thus there is some justification for the principle of ''salutary neglect,'' but on the whole this exception is not likely to be real. A unsatisfactory solution may be what is needed to provoke the needed information gathering to produce a better one, while neglect is never productive.[30]

Many Senators undoubtedly would agree with Arrow. They would blame shortcomings in the programs enacted at the end of legislative surges on administrators who do not sympathize with the fundamental purposes of the legislation, or who show too little imagination in working out the details of implementation. Much of the disillusionment felt by the public with social legislation enacted in the 1960s, however, results from unsuccessful efforts to implement poorly conceived or unmanageable human service programs. In selecting new agenda items, political leaders should not ignore the possible costs in damaged government credibility and increased public mistrust and cynicism that may result from badly designed programs in areas where the knowledge base is weak or practically nonexistent.

The agenda of any legislative body inevitably will include questionable, ill-conceived proposals that do not merit passage. If the legislative process is working efficiently, weak proposals will be discovered and rejected during hearings and floor debates, even though they address problems thought by a majority of the members to be in need of solution by government. The Senate should never allow its agenda to become closed to all controversial new ideas. Junior members should have ample opportunity to promote new departures in policy or to bring new problems to the attention of the leadership.

The major problem facing the Senate in the 1970s, however, is not how to open its agenda to fresh new ideas. The U.S. Senate now probably is the most accessible and responsive legislative body in the Western World. Individual Senators are more autonomous and have more talented aides than legislators in any other country. After years of debate over the seniority system and loud complaints about the veto power being exercised by conservative southern Senators, the Senate has slowly been transformed into a sensitive register of social and political change. The period of apprenticeship once required of junior Senators no longer is imposed. Power in the Senate has steadily been decentralized during the past 15 years. The Senate's current weakness lies not in an unwillingness to take up serious social problems or search for new solutions, but in its seeming inability to set clear policy priorities and to carry out a more coherent form of central legislative clearance.

Critics of the operation of the Senate would point to the aimless emergence of agenda items that become popular because of the chance appearance of an effective advocate, the development of a dramatic crisis, or a newsworthy change in a familiar social indicator. Programs often are debated that would not receive attention if taken entirely on their own merits, but they are brought up mainly because the Senate has become engaged with issues of this general type. Other proposals on different topics, whose cases for inclusion on the Senate's agenda might be stronger, do not yet have a sponsor who is able to capture the attention of fellow Senators. Items burst onto the discretionary agenda because of the work of individual political entrepreneurs.

No central agency in the Senate currently is engaged in systematically scanning the social horizon in search of emerging social problems that might require legislative scrutiny. The Senate's leadership seldom tries to select important problems that should be studied by several committees, so that informed proposals could be formulated. Agenda items of all types are being promoted by individual Senators and committees, but the majority leadership, acting on behalf of the party that controls the Senate, does not often try to choose issues that should be at the center of national debate. Nor does it encourage the relevant committee staffs and Senate staff support agencies—such as GAO, OTA, CRS, or CBO—to open investigations of them. The Senate is expected to respond to presidential initiatives, but the majority leadership does little on its own to shape the Senate's agenda.

A PROPOSAL FOR REFORM

If the Senate's leadership wishes to gain greater control over the discretionary portions of its legislative agenda, only a small increase in new staff will be required. The Senate already has access to all the information and analytical capacity needed to do an effective job of agenda setting. In fact, until more coherent direction is given to the deliberations of the Senate, it will be difficult to employ efficiently the extensive staff now available within the Congress and in private, nonprofit policy research agencies in Washington and throughout the country. If policy analysts and staff members were assured that a number of broad program areas—such as income maintenance or energy conservation—had authoritatively been selected as items of prime importance to the Senate for the next few years, the quality of staff work, and the depth of analysis and understanding within the Senate almost inevitably would improve. If it were widely understood that certain issues were going to receive serious attention in the Senate, the energies of hundreds of groups and agencies throughout the government system automatically would be channeled in those directions. The Senate's shifting legislative agenda already acts as a principal source of cues for lobbyists, policy researchers, ambitious Senators, agency chiefs, and journalists. If the majority party wished to achieve greater coordination among all these elements, it could do so without gaining explicit power over their activities and without creating a huge new bureaucratic structure. All that is required is greater effort by party leaders to establish their own legislative priorities.

Within the Senate the organizational foundations for greater control over the legislative agenda exist already in the party policy committees. These committees have been in place for 30 years, making reform possible without a fundamental change in the Senate's organization. They also are instruments of partisan control. Since the determination of the questions to be debated is one of the most important benefits of gaining majority status, the policy committees are the most appropriate arenas for control of the agenda. The committees are small and manageable. They also are composed mostly of party leaders and already are charged with formal responsibility for scheduling the issues for consideration on the floor. All these characteristics make the policy committees natural forums for debate over program priorities.

If the policy committees are to be employed more effectively to control the agenda, their precise makeup and the way in which their numbers are selected must carefully be reviewed. If they are to be effective instruments of central legislative clearance, the committees must speak with the authority of extraordinary majorities of their respective party conferences. Policy committee staff members should be engaged mainly in coordinating the activities of substantive committees and the general legislative support agencies. Conflict between policy committee staffs and substantive committee staffs should be avoided, as much as possible. The policy committees should serve as executive comittees for the party conferences and should include representatives from all the principal factions in the party coalitions.

The policy committee for the majority party, supplied with a strengthened staff and backed by a clear majority of the party conference, could serve several important functions. Most important, the committee could designate each year a small set of issues or programs as top priority items for Senate debate and action. Only a small number of issues would be chosen in this manner. The discretionary agenda always is crowded in the Senate; room always should remain for issues to emerge that are not included on the list of party priorities. Some of the items chosen for emphasis might be concrete proposals that already had been the subject of hearings and were ready for action on the Senate floor. The list also should include, however, general issues, such as programs of energy conservation or metropolitan planning, that are just beginning to attract interest and are in need of investigation by Senate committees. Several substantive committees might be called upon to begin hearings on these issues and the policy committee might even commission research and analysis from executive departments, legislative support agencies, universities, or private firms outside the Senate.

A list of priorities of this kind emanating from the majority party leadership would attract wide notice and inevitabily would stimulate activity and interest throughout the government. Instead of making haphazard responses to pressures from outside the Senate or from individual activists within the Congress, the party leaders could take the initiative and provide comprehensive guidance to policymakers in all sectors of the government system, at least in the range of issues where party consensus exists.

The legislative agenda necessarily must be developed on a partisan basis in the Senate, with the majority party setting the pace and selecting the principal topics for debate. The minority party cannot control the committees or manage the sequence of issues arising on the floor, but its influence would be magnified greatly if the minority leadership could obtain agreement from its party members on a limited number of general problems upon which it would seek to develop legislation. Much of what the minority eventually proposed either might be defeated or might appear as amendments to legislation proposed by the majority, but, if staff work could be concentrated on a selected group of issues over several years, a ready-made party platform would emerge for use in future elections. Also, debate in the Senate would be much better informed.

Ambitious Senators anxious to build national reputations by promoting new legislative proposals would still have opportunities for maneuver in a more centralized system of agenda setting, but now the policy committees would become additional new objects of their activism. When several proposals were competing for consideration by the Senate, the policy committees would became natural forums for debate among their proponents. Deliberations of this kind might prompt Senators to consider the broad trade-offs among different policy areas that seldom are addressed under the present, more decentralized system. More vigorous intervention by the policy committees might also send back to substantive committees the kind of poorly designed programs with shaky justifications that often appear toward the end of surges of activity in a policy area. No system would be able to stop the Senate from debating a bill that had the support of a large majority of its members, but more active leadership in agenda setting should make it necessary for proponents of new proposals to make more powerful supporting arguments. Simply by asking more questions, the policy committees could contribute to a significant improvement in the level of policy analysis and debate in the Senate.

CONCLUSION

The job of creating stronger, more active party leadership in the Senate would not be a simple or uncontroversial task. Opposition undoubtedly would come from many groups and individuals both inside and outside the Congress. More centralized agenda setting would require the alteration of many informal rules and customs, set up new lines of influence and communication and directly affect the power of many Senators. Organizational changes never come easily, but recent events, such as the early successes of the congressional budget reform, suggest that the Senate may be prepared to transform itself, especially if procedural changes promise to increase the influence of the legislative branch within the national policymaking system.

Today the Senate seems prepared to make rule changes that were completely unfeasible even a decade ago. The balance of political power has been shifting steadily—especially within the Democratic majority—so that the parties are more ideologically homogenous. During the past 25 years southern politics has been transformed by the enfranchisement of black voters, rapid urbanization and the rise of authentic two-party competition. As the number of conservative southern Democrats has been reduced, the number of liberal Democrats from states outside the South has been increasing, beginning with the many liberal victories in the 1958 election and the reelection of all of them six years later in the Democratic landslide of 1964. As these new liberals have moved into the Senate, many rules have been changed in order to allow junior members greater influence, more access to subcommittee chairmanships, and increased staff. The period of apprenticeship, formerly expected of first termers, gradually has disappeared, allowing newly elected Senators to plunge immediately into the legislative process. All these tendencies toward a more decentralized, activist legislative system further were encouraged by the shift in the majority party leadership from the closely held power of Lyndon Johnson to the more consensual leadership of Mike Mansfield.[31]

All signs point to the need at this time in the Senate's history for a reassertion of power by the majority leadership. The mandate for this new legislative system must be founded on the consent of the party conference. Legislative priorities must emerge from open debate that involves all members of the party. Reformers must avoid placing disabling obstacles in the paths of individual Senators bent on promoting new solutions or urging attention to problems that have been ignored by the leadership. Changes in the role of the policy committees and the procedures for agenda setting should not eliminate all activity by junior Senators or independent committee chairmen. The goal of reform should not be the creation of an all-powerful leadership, but rather to strike a new balance between the Senate's remarkable responsiveness to social problems, complaints, and trends and the need for greater programmatic coherence.

The social problems of the next two decades will require more consistent responses from government, more analysis in depth, and greater awareness of the broader implications of governmental programs. The helter-skelter activism of the past decade has served to raise many new issues long blocked from national debate. The Senate has made a major contribution during the past two decades by providing access to newly forming interest groups and steering the government into policy areas never seriously considered in the past. The needs of the next two decades require the Senate's leadership to gain greater control over its agenda and to generate more of its own policy initiatives. This demanding task of institutional reform must be carried out successfully if the legislative branch of American government is to realize its full potential as a modern expression of representative democracy.

9.8 Different Kinds of Policies Get Handled Differently: Policy Process Differences*

Randall B. Ripley and Grace A. Franklin

Ripley and Franklin promote a sophisticated interpretation of congressional policymaking by arguing that different kinds of policy gets handled in different ways. They contend that policy relationships in a given area vary by type of issue. The significance of this is to place in perspective certain models of policymaking. For example, the subgovernment model (that policy is thrashed out in a tripartite subsystem comprised of congressional subcommittees, relevant bureaus, and affected publics) is applicable only for distributive and structural policies. Other kinds of policies are made in different ways.

The basic notion behind our categorizations is that each type of policy generates and is therefore surrounded by its own distinctive set of political relationships. These relationships in turn help to determine substantive, concrete outcomes when policy decisions emerge. Table 9.8.1 summarizes the characteristics of the political relationships surrounding policymaking for each type of policy. The main features of the political relationships that we are concerned with in Table 9.8.1 are the identity of the primary actors, the basic nature of the interaction among those actors, the stability of their interaction, the visibility of the policy decisions to individuals not immediately involved or concerned, and the relative influence of different actors.

We have excluded competitive regulatory policy from Table 9.8.1 because it is a type of policy that is rarely formulated and legitimated; rather, competitive regulatory policy is concerned primarily with issues of implementation. Responsibility for competitive regulatory policy is almost totally delegated to bureaucratic agencies, regulatory commissions, or courts for implementation. It focuses on decisions about individual cases, and the actors involved are limited to relevant bureaucratic, judicial, or quasi-judicial agencies, the individuals competing for benefits being awarded, and occasional members of Congress who have a

* From Randall B. Ripley and Grace A. Franklin, *Congress, the Bureaucracy, and Public Policy,* rev. ed. (Homewood, Ill.: Dorsey Press, 1980), pp. 20–28. Copyright © 1980, The Dorsey Press. Reprinted by permission.

specific interest in the outcome. We have included a discussion of competitive regulatory policy in the sections immediately following to contrast it with the other types of policy, but because this book focuses on the formulation and legitimation of policymaking, we have not included competitive regulatory policy in the analysis.

DOMESTIC POLICY

Distributive Policy

Distributive policies and programs are aimed at promoting private activities that are said to be desirable to society as a whole and, at least in theory, would not or could not be undertaken otherwise. Such policies and programs provide subsidies for those private activites and thus convey tangible government benefits to the individuals, groups, and corporations subsidized. (A subsidy is a payment designed to induce desired behavior.) Many government policies turn out to be subsidies, even if they do not seem to be subsidies at first glance. Decisions about subsidies are typically made with only short-run consequences considered. The decisions are not considered in light of each other; rather they are disaggregated. Thus there appear to be only winners and no losers.

The case of characters (usually individuals or groups that comprise a subgovernment) involved in distributive decisions in a particular field (such as agricultural price supports, water resources, or subsidies for health research) is fairly stable over time, and their interactions are marked by low visibility and a high degree of cooperation and mutually rewarding logrolling. The congressional subcommittee generally makes the final decisions after receiving input from the other actors. The recipients of distributive subsidies are not aware of each other, and there is no sense of competing for limited resources—anyone can potentially be a recipient, and resources are treated as unlimited. Distributive decisions embody the federal pork barrel in its fullest sense, giving many people a bite of the federal pie. Distributive decisions, both within a field and between different substantive fields, are made individually, without consideration for their interrelation or overall impact—they are decentralized and uncoordinated.

Examples of distributive policies include direct cash payments for purchase of agricultural commodities; grants for scientific research in universities and private laboratories; grants to localities for airport construction, hospital construction, sewage facilities, and mass transit facilities; promoting home ownership through tax provisions allowing deductions for interest on home mortages and local property taxes; and issuing low-cost permits for grazing on public lands.

Competitive Regulatory Policy

Competitive regulatory policies and programs are aimed at limiting the provision of specific goods and services to only one or a few designated deliverers who are chosen from a larger number of competing potential deliverers. Some of the potential deliverers who want the business win; some lose. Some decisions allocate scarce resources that simply cannot be divided, such as television channels or radio frequencies. Some decisions maintain limited rather than unlimited competition in the provision of goods and services by allowing only certain potential deliverers to provide them and excluding other potential deliverers. Some decisions are aimed at regulating the quality of services delivered through choosing the deliverer periodically and imposing standards of performance. If those standards are not met, a new deliverer can be chosen. This type of policy is a hybrid, which subsidizes the winning competitors and also tries to regulate some aspects of service delivery in the public interest. Examples of competitive regulatory policies include the granting and review of licenses to operate television and radio stations; authorizing specific airlines to operate specified routes; and authorizing specific trucking companies to haul specified commodities over specified routes.

TABLE 9.8.1 POLITICAL RELATIONSHIPS FOR POLICYMAKING

POLICY TYPE	PRIMARY ACTORS	RELATIONSHIP AMONG ACTORS	STABILITY OF RELATIONSHIP	VISIBILITY OF DECISION
Distributive	Congressional subcommittees and committees; Executive Branch bureaus; small interest groups	Logrolling (everyone gains)	Stable	Low
Protective regulatory	Congressional subcommittees and committees; full House and Senate; Executive Branch agencies; trade associations	Bargaining; compromise	Unstable	Moderate
Redistributive	President and his appointees; committees and/or Congress; largest interest groups (peak associations); "liberals, conservatives"	Ideological and class conflict	Stable	High
Structural	Congressional subcommittees and committees; Executive Branch bureaus; small interest groups	Logrolling (everyone gains)	Low	Stable
Strategic	Executive Branch agencies; President	Bargaining; compromise	Unstable	Low until publicized; then low to high
Crisis	President and advisers	Cooperation	Unstable	Low until publicized; then generally high

Decisions on basic overall policy in this area are rare. Most decisions are delegated to bureaus, regulatory commissions, and courts. The influence of the competitors is high and over time most of them can be expected to get some benefits. Thus in application at the general level the policy resembles one of subsidy, especially for the largest competitors that can enter many specific competitions. For example, a major airline will not win every route from the Civil Aeronautics Board for which it competes but it will win enough routes over time to enhance its profitability. Congressional influence on individual decisions is present but usually in the form of intervention from specific Senators and Representatives.

PROTECTIVE REGULATORY POLICY

Protective regulatory policies and programs are designed to protect the public by setting the conditions under which various private activities can be undertaken. Conditions that are thought to be harmful (air pollution, false advertising) are prohibited; conditions that are thought to be helpful (the publication of interest rates on loans) are required.

Protective regulatory policies are not as disaggregatable as distributive decisions because they establish a general rule of law and require that behavior among a certain segment of the population conform to the law. The actors (coalitions of members of the full House and Senate, executive branch agencies, and representatives of trade associations) involved in protective regulatory decisions are much less stable than in the distributive arena, partially because of constantly shifting substantive issues. The ultimate decisions get made on the floor of the House and Senate.

Examples of federal protective regulatory policies include the requirement that banks,

INFLUENCE OF				
PRESIDENT, PRESIDENCY, AND CENTRALIZED BUREAUCRACY	BUREAUS	CONGRESS AS A WHOLE	CONGRESSIONAL SUBCOMMITTEES	PRIVATE SECTOR
Low	High	Low (supports subcommittees)	High	High (subsidized groups)
Moderately high	Moderate	Moderately high	Moderate	Moderately high (regulated interests)
High	Moderately low	High	Moderately low	High ("peak associations" representing clusters of interest groups)
Low	High	Low (supports subcommittees)	High	High (subsidized groups and corporations)
High	Low	High (often responsive to executive)	Low	Moderate (interest groups, corporations)
High	Low	Low	Low	Low

stores, and other grantors of credit disclose true interest rates; prohibitions of unfair business practices, unfair labor practices, and business combinations that lessen competition; limits on the conditions under which strip mining can be undertaken and requirements for the postmining restoration of land; the prohibition of harmful food additives; and high taxation to reduce the consumption of scarce commodities such as gasoline.

REDISTRIBUTIVE POLICY

Redistributive policies and programs are intended to manipulate the allocation of wealth, property rights, or some other value among social classes or racial groups in society. The redistributive feature enters because a number of actors perceive there are "winners" and "losers" in policies and that policies transfer some value to one group *at the expense* of another group. Thus the more well off sometimes perceive themselves to be losers in relation to a program that seeks to confer some benefits on the less well off. Whites sometimes perceive themselves to be losers in relation to a policy or a program that confers special benefits on minority groups.

Redistribution runs in several directions. Some programs redistribute items of value from the less well off to the more well off or from minorities to whites, but usually such programs are not perceived as redistributive. They do not generate the hot political controversy that is associated with redistributive attempts in the other direction. Thus the politics of redistribution almost always involves situations in which the intended beneficiaries are the relatively disadvantaged in society.

Since redistributive policy involves a conscious attempt to manipulate the allocation of wealth, property, rights, or some other value among broad classes or groups in society, the actors perceive that there will be distinct winners and losers. The stakes are thought to be high and this fact means that the policymaking process will be marked by a high degree of visibility and conflict. The coalitions that form over any redistributive issue may change in composition depending on the issue (integrated schools, open housing, public welfare programs) but they can generally be identified as a proponent (''liberal'') group and an opponent (''conservative'') group. Their debate on the issue at hand is cast in ideological terms. Whether redistributive policy will emerge from the coalitions' conflicting viewpoints depends on the presence of strong presidential leadership and the willingness of participants to retreat from ideological stances and adopt compromises. The principal political consideration among the participants during the process is who gets what at the expense of whom.

Examples of redistributive policy include setting progressive personal income tax rates so that more affluent people pay a higher percentage of their incomes in taxes than do less affluent people; requirements that housing, public accommodations and facilities, and public education be available to all, without racial discrimination; requirements of affirmative action in hiring by federal contractors to increase the employment of women and minorities; the provision of employment and training programs, food stamps, or special legal services for the disadvantaged; and government-sponsored health insurance to help the elderly meet the costs of medical care.

FOREIGN AND DEFENSE POLICY

Policy typologies in nondomestic issue areas are less clear-cut than in domestic areas. Lowi (1967: 324–325)* suggests that there are three distinctive patterns of politics in foreign policy. The first is crisis foreign policy. In this situation the perception of a threat to the national security cuts across normal channels of decisions, and an elite of formal officeholders within the executive branch makes the decisions with a minimum of conflict. In the absence of a crisis, there is time for ''normal'' patterns and concerns to emerge. Institutions become involved and interactions occur over a number of questions. Foreign policy then is basically either distributive or regulatory, with much the same sets of characteristics as domestic distributive or regulatory policy types.

In the area of defense policy, which has both domestic and foreign policy aspects, Huntington (1961) has identified two types—strategic and structural defense policy. Strategic defense policy is oriented toward foreign policy and international politics, and it involves the units and use of military force, their strength, and their deployment. Structural defense policy focuses on domestic politics and involves decisions about the procurement, allocation, and organization of personnel, money, and materiel that constitute the military forces. Structural decisions are made primarily within the context of strategic decisions and are made to implement those decisions.

We have drawn on both Lowi and Huntington in developing our ideas about the three categories of foreign and defense policy: structural, strategic, and crisis.

STRUCTURAL POLICY

Structural policies and programs aim primarily at procuring, deploying, and organizing military personnel and materiel, presumably within the confines and guidelines of previously determined strategic decisions. Since the federal government has no competitors in providing defense, the element of total subsidy for the enterprise is a given. But the details of that subsidy can vary greatly. Thus, as indicated in Table 9.8.1, structural policies are closely related to distributive policies. The process is characterized by the presence of subgovernments, by decentralized decision making, by nonconflictual relationships among the actors, and by decisions that treat internal resources as unlimited and separa-

* Reference list in Endnotes.

ble. Policy decisions emerge from the formal legislative process (bill introduction, committee hearings, passage by the House and Senate). Although Congress is generally responding to executive branch requests rather than initiating policy in this area, it nonetheless has final decision power.

Examples of structural policies include specific defense procurement decisions for individual weapons systems; the placement, expansion, contraction, and closing of military bases and other facilities in the United States; the retention, expansion, or contraction of reserve military forces; and the creation and retention of programs that send surplus farm commodities overseas.

STRATEGIC POLICY

Strategic policies and programs are designed to assert and implement the basic military and foreign policy stance of the United States toward other nations. Policy planning and proposals resulting from that planning stem primarily from Executive Branch activities. A number of Executive Branch agencies compete, bargain, and sometimes engage in conflict during policy development. Decisions are made by these agencies, with the final approval of the President. Public debate and congressional involvement usually occur after the formal decisions are announced. Congress may get involved in several ways—committees or individuals may lobby executive branch agencies for particular decisions, Congress may respond to an executive branch request for legislation to implement a decision already made, or Congress may protest and alter an action already completed. Congress does not make strategic decisions by itself; thus the influence of Congress as a whole can be high, but that potential influence is often used to respond supportively to Executive Branch initiatives.

Examples of strategic policies include decisions about the basic mix of military forces (for example, the ratio of ground-based missiles to submarine-based missiles to manned bombers); foreign trade (tariffs and quotas for specific goods and nations); sales of U.S. arms to foreign nations; foreign aid; immigration; and the level and location of U.S. troops overseas (both in general and in relation to specific "trouble spots").

CRISIS POLICY

Crisis policies are short-run responses to immediate problems that are perceived to be serious, that have burst on the policymakers with little or no warning, and that demand immediate action. The occurrence of crisis situations is unpredictable and tied to external (nondomestic) events. The principal actors are elite officeholders who work cooperatively together with a minimum of publicized conflict. Visibility of the decision-making process is also low, except to the extent that press releases and press conferences inform the public. The involvement of Congress is informal and limited and is usually made in the mode of consultation with key individuals. The full body may get involved formally, usually after the crisis, to make the action legitimate or to forbid similar exercises of executive power in the future.

Examples of crisis policies include decisions about the U.S. response to the Japanese attack on Pearl Harbor in 1941; the impending French collapse in Indochina in 1954; the Soviet Union's placement of missiles in Cuba in 1962; the North Korean seizure of a U.S. Navy ship in 1968; and the Cambodian seizure of a U.S. merchant ship in 1975.

9.9 Policy Consequences*

David R. Mayhew

In this second selection from Mayhew's important book, congressional policymaking is treated as a dependent variable. According to Mayhew, "assembly coherence" (certain characteristics of policymaking) is necessitated by the organizational features of Congress and by the electoral connection.

Now, if these are the impulsions behind legislating and overseeing, what are the effects? What seems to happen is that congressional policymaking activities produce a number of specifiable and predictable policy effects. Taken together these effects display what might be called an "assembly coherence"—an overall policy pattern that one might expect any set of assemblies constructed like the U.S. Congress to generate.[1]

One effect is *delay*—or, more properly, since the eye of the beholder creates it, a widespread perception of delay. Not too much should be made of this, but it is fair to say that over the years Congress has often lagged behind public opinion in enacting major legislation.[2] Thus a perceived "inaction" was the major source of dissatisfaction with Congress in a survey of a generally dissatisfied public in 1963.[3] Or the delay may exist in the eyes of elites; President Kennedy's tax cut proposal of 1963 and President Johnson's tax increase proposal of 1967, both set forth for the purpose of fiscal management, each took a year to wend its way through a Democratic Congress.[4] Recurrent perceptions of congressional delay on nonparticularized matters should cause little surprise. Mobilization may be halfhearted; there are so many other things to do; some issues may be uncomfortable to vote on at all; a live issue may be better than a live program; the effects are not important anyway.

A second effect is *particularism*—that is, a strong tendency to wrap policies in packages that are salable as particularized benefits. Not only do Congressmen aggressively seek out opportunities to supply such benefits (little or no "pressure" is needed), they tend in framing laws to give a particularistic cast to matters that do not obviously require it. The only benefits intrinsically worth anything, after all, are ones that can be packaged.[5] Thus in time of recession Congressmen reach for "accelerated public works" bills listing projects in the various districts; Presidents prefer more general fiscal effects. In the education field a Congressional favorite is the "impacted areas" program with its ostentatious grants to targeted school districts; again, Presidents prefer ventures of more diffuse impact. Presidents are capable of closing a hundred veterans' hospitals like a shot in the interest of "efficiency"; Congressmen combine to keep them open. The handling of revenue policy is particularistic; in Manley's exhaustive treatment of congressional tax processes there is hardly any mention of an interest in fiscal effects (though of course the members must worry about how it *looks* to vote for a tax cut or tax increase). Rather the concern is with distributive effects. The highly talented staff of the Joint Committee on Internal Revenue Taxation, serving both Senate Finance and House Ways and Means, is in the business of "explicating . . . how individuals and groups will be affected

---

* From David R. Mayhew, *Congress: The Electoral Connection* (New Haven, Conn.: Yale University Press, 1974), pp. 125–32.

by changes in the Internal Revenue code."[6] Across policy areas generally the programmatic mainstay of Congressmen is the categorical grant. In fact the categorical grant is for modern Democratic Congresses what rivers and harbors and the tariff were for pre-New Deal Republican Congresses. It supplies goods in small manipulable packets. "Congressmen . . . like categorical programs because of the opportunities they afford to interfere in administration and thus to secure special treatment, or at least the appearance of it, for constituents among whom . . . state and local as well as federal agencies sometimes figure prominently."[7] The quest for the particular impels Congressmen to take a vigorous interest in the organization of the federal bureaucucracy. Thus, for example, the Corps of Army Engineers, structured to undertake discrete district projects, must be guarded from Presidents who would submerge it in a quest for "planning."[8]

A third effect is the *servicing of the organized*.[9] This takes two familiar forms. First there is a deference toward nationally organized groups with enough widespread local clout to inspire favorable roll-call positions on selected issues among a majority of members. Thus, under four Presidents in a row—Harding through Roosevelt—Congress passed veterans' bonus bills, the Presidents vetoed them, and the House voted decisively to override the vetoes.[10] In recent years the National Rifle Association has weighed in against gun control legislation.[11] Second, there is deference toward groups with disposable electoral resources whose representatives keep a close watch on congressional maneuvers. Clientelism at the committee level is the result, with its manifestations across a wide range of policy areas. Agriculture is an obvious example.[12] Clientelism, like particularism, gives form to the federal bureaucracy. Congressmen protect clientele systems—alliances of agencies, Hill committees, and clienteles—against the incursions of Presidents and Cabinet Secretaries.[13]

A fourth effect is *symbolism*. The term needs explication. It is probably best to say that a purely symbolic congressional act is one expressing an attitude but prescribing no policy effects. An example would be a resolution deploring communism or poverty. But the term *symbolic* can also usefully be applied where Congress prescribes policy effects but does not act (in legislating or overseeing or both) so as to achieve them. No doubt the main cause of prescription–achievement gaps is the intractability of human affairs. But there is a special reason why a legislative body arranged like the U.S. Congress can be expected to engage in symbolic action by this second, impure construction of the term. The reason, of course, is that in a large class of legislative undertakings the electoral payment is for positions rather than for effects.

CHAPTER

10 Congress: Change, Issues, and the Future

A concluding discussion of Congress inevitably raises a number of important and interesting polemics: What have been the consequences of recent reforms and changes? Are they desirable? What are the major ethical problems Congress now faces and what might be done about them? What does the future portend for the Congress? What might be the nature of future congresses? Will they be materially different? Readings in this last section present essays by prominent congressional scholars that address these major questions.

10.1 Congress the Peculiar Institution*

Samuel C. Patterson

Despite the recent decade of change and transformation, there is an essential congressional character that, because of its uniqueness, seems to pass the test of time. The following brief excerpt from a major essay by Samuel C. Patterson speculates about Henry Clay's recognition of this essential character in a Congress much changed from the one within which he served.

THE REINCARNATION OF HENRY CLAY

Henry Clay was America's most remarkable congressional politician. Just after the turn of the 19th century he served in the Kentucky legislature, which twice sent him to the U.S. Senate. Then he was elected to the 12th Congress as a member of the House of Representatives. As a freshman Congressman, he was elected Speaker, and he served as Speaker off and on between 1811 and 1825. His leadership contributed importantly to the development of the House as an autonomous and politically unified policymaking body. After his House service, he was a presidential candidate in 1824, 1832, and 1844, and a U.S. Senator from Kentucky from 1831 to 1842 and from 1849 to 1852.

Clay was a Congressman and Senator during the years when Congress was becoming an imposing and powerful national legislative body. Although what we might call the "modern" Congress was not fully developed until after the 1880s, the institution came to be, in many fundamental ways, much as it is today during the period of Clay's service.[1]

If Henry Clay were alive today, and he were to serve again in the House and Senate to which he was chosen so many times in the 19th century, he would find much that was very familiar. He would certainly recognize where he was, and perhaps after some initial shock he surely would be reasonably comfortable in the modern congressional envelope. Of course, things have changed. Congress has a much larger membership. There were only 186 members of the House that Clay first entered as member and Speaker; there were only 52 Senators in the 1830s. Members and committees have vastly more staff help. A far greater array of policy decisions is required of Congress nowadays than before the Civil War. There is a fancy electronic gadget for voting in the House. The party memberships are less coherent, and the committee system is much more complex. Many more Congressmen are professionals now, in contrast to the relative amateurism of the pre-Civil War Congresses. The scale of things has grown; but the fundamental character of the institution has not changed so very much.

Congress is an extraordinarily stable institution. Many changes have occurred in the party leaderships, the committee systems, and the norms of the Congress, but the intrinsic internal order of the institution has shown enormous continuity. Although relationships between Congress and the executive branch were altered as the country came to be an urban, industrial society with a pivotal role in international affairs, Congress, unlike the legislative

---

* From Samuel C. Patterson, "The Semi-Sovereign Congress," in *The New American Political Systems,* ed. by Anthony King (Washington, D.C.: American Enterprise Institute, 1977), pp. 131–33, 176–77.

bodies of many other industrial nations, continues to be a highly autonomous institution. Certainly since the mid-19th century Congress has been embedded in its environment; this feature and its responsiveness as it performs its constituent function have become profoundly institutionalized. It has been said that the United States is a modern country with an antique political system, and in a sense that is true.[2] American governing institutions emerged in a particular way in the 19th century, and many of their present-day core features are readily traceable to earlier times. That is why Henry Clay, if he were a Congressman today, would surely find that Congress had not become unrecognizable. Institutions simply do not change very much, which is why they are called institutions.

Keeping that in mind is helpful to understanding the Congress of the 1970s. Congress has never experienced a "revolutionary" change. Congress is very stable. Stable institutions change as they adapt themselves to changes in the world around them. Thus, congressional changes are most appropriately viewed as the adaptations through which a very stable system maintains itself. Accordingly, reforms of Congress, relatively small in magnitude, are consequential largely in the ways in which they maintain the existing congressional structure. A marked transformation of a political institution like the Congress is not impossible, but it simply has not occurred in the whiggish context of American political history. As a result, it is the stability of Congress, and not changes in it, that is the most remarkable in the long term. Perhaps, therefore, we should distinguish between adaptive and transformative institutional change; changes in Congress are all adaptive.

CONCLUSION

It is an open question whether Henry Clay would find the Congress of the 1970s an improvement over the Congress in which he served. But there is reason to believe that he would be impressed. While retaining its basic shape and form, Congress has adapted itself in many important ways to the demands of a changing society. Thirty years ago, the architect of the Legislative Reorganization Act of 1946 wrote:

> Congress lacks adequate information and inspection facilities. Its internal structure is dispersive and duplicating. It is a body without a head. Leadership is scattered among the chairmen of 81 little legislatures who compete with each other for jurisdiction and power. Its supervision of executive performance is superficial. Much of its time is consumed by petty local and private matters which divert its attention from national policy-making. Elected by the people to protect the public interest, it yields too often to the importunities of lobbyists for special-interest groups. It lacks machinery for developing coherent legislative programs and for promoting party responsibility and accountability. Its posts of power are held on the basis of political age, regardless of ability or agreement with party policies. And its members are overworked and underpaid—the forgotten men of social security.[3]

Congress has acquired impressive staffs and information processing facilities; improvements have been made in its system of committees; oversight of the executive branch has expanded measurably; because of the growth in the scope and immediacy of national policy issues and the professionalization of its membership, far less of its time is spent on merely parochial issues; mainly on account of its extensive and expert staffs, it is substantially more impervious to special-interest pressure; seniority is no longer an automatic guarantee of committee power; and certainly its members are not underpaid (a 1977 increase raised members' pay to $57,500 a year).

Congress has great political power and an enormous capacity to frustrate the legislative ambitions of the President, as President Jimmy Carter discovered in the course of his first year in the White House. It tasted sovereignty during the exhilarating days of 1973 when it nearly removed a President, Richard Nixon, from office, and surely would have had he not resigned. We do not have congressional government in the United States in the sense that an omnipotent Congress makes all the laws, which the President and the executive branch merely enforce. Such a simplistic system never existed. But Congress is far more formidable as a political body today than it was in the more quiescent days of the 1950s and early 1960s. Congress is semisovereign.

It remains, nevertheless, a peculiar institution. The electoral connections of its members are highly individual and localized. Although its membership has become more ideologically homogeneous, and accordingly somewhat more partisan, its party leadership remains relatively weak. Its internal power structure continues to be highly dispersed, with legislative influence over policy decisions scattered over a large number of members manning its many subcommittees and conducting business in a remarkably open and public manner. It jealously guards its independence, enlarges the scope of its legislative activities, strengthens its capacity to scrutinize the executive, and demands a greater role in realms of policy previously left largely to the President. Its aggregate decision making is ''individualistic'' in the sense that party or committee influence on members' voting is not compelling. In short, Congress is an unusually democratic legislative institution. This makes it a very frustrating policymaking body for those politicians and intellectuals who have the ''received truth.'' And its democratic character makes it often seem painfully slow and incompetent to its attentive constituents. Its own internal dynamic, along with these external frustrations and annoyances, brings about cyclical pressures for reform. So it surely will be true that the Congress of the 1980s will not be very different from the Congress of the 1970s—but, equally, it will not be the same.

10.2 The Impact of Recent Reforms*

William J. Keefe

In this brief excerpt from a major text on Congress, a leading student of legislative life speculates about the impact of recent reforms and encourages more study of the policy consequences of institutional change.

Change in political institutions always leaves tracks. The problem for the analyst is that years may be required to distinguish which way they are headed, and sometimes the direction never becomes clear. The rash of changes in Congress is a case in point. We are still a long way from knowing exactly what kind of Congress these changes, taken together, have produced. Their lasting power, moreover, remains to be seen. But if allowance is made for generality, certain broad observations about the thrust of these reforms can be made.

The upheavals involving the seniority system, coupled with the revival of the caucus, have brought an end to government by standing committee chairmen—the dominant pattern from the Presidency of Roosevelt to that of Johnson. A chairman who leans noticeably toward autocracy will encounter difficulty surviving in the new Congress. In essence, the

---

* William J. Keefe, *Congress and the American People* (Englewood Cliffs, N.J.: Prentice-Hall, 1980) pp. 157–60. Copyright © 1980. Reprinted by permission of Prentice-Hall, Inc., Englewood Cliffs, N.J.

committee chairmanship is a new office, sharply reduced in independent authority, and reduced as well in its attractiveness for the occupant.

The decline in the authority of committee chairmen has been accompanied by a diffusion of power among numerous members, improving their opportunities for influencing legislative decisions. The increase in the number, independence, and importance of subcommittees has been spectacular. Concretely, these changes have pushed up the value of subcommittee chairmanships. At the same time, the proliferation of leadership positions and the antimonopoly stipulations concerning their distribution have produced a dramatic change in the opportunity structure of Congress. It now takes new members less time to gather power in their own right; for those in the majority party, a subcommittee chairmanship (in many committees) is not much farther than around the corner. Overall, the fragmentation of power has contributed to a condition under which individual members have greater opportunities to do what they want to do, free to ride all manner of hobbyhorses, relatively insulated from leadership controls. Perhaps at no time in the history of Congress have the individual preferences of members counted for as much as they do now.

In spite of the rediscovery of the caucus as an instrument of party, party management has become much more difficult in both houses. The eclipse of party machines, the decline of party loyalty in the electorate, the fierce independence and antiparty posturings of many candidates—all converge to drain vitality from the congressional parties. For most members, the element of party has rusted out in their electoral connection. Their incumbent status (with its awesome advantages) is likely to prove much more important to their reelection than their party affiliation or their record of support for party leaders, including the President. What counts, members know, is pleasing the voters by developing an "appropriate" image, addressing matters of high moment to them, responding to the claims of key interest groups, concentrating on local and state matters, and taking care of constituent problems with government.

Organizational change in Congress has also weakened the parties. The emergence of subcommittee government means that leaders have more bases to touch, more independent power centers with which to reckon, more interests to be accommodated, more "one-on-one" games to play. Finally, the pervasive openness of Congress undoubtedly diminishes the opportunities for party leaders to press hard on members, hoping to bring them into line. When exposed to too much light, party controls wither.

In certain respects, Congress has become a more independent institution, better able to fend for itself, better able to resist the pressures and blandishments of the President and the bureaucracy. Its growing independence results in part from the sharp growth in professional staff and from the creation of two new research arms, the Office of Technology Assessment and the Congressional Budget Office. In addition, it can call on the experts of the Congressional Research Service of the Library of Congress and on those of the General Accounting Office. Congress now has more experts responsible to it and to its members than could have been imagined just a few years ago, a resource that lessens its reliance on the experts of the executive branch.

But probably of greater significance is simply the spirit of independence within Congress. Most members manage to get elected on their own, forming their own electoral organizations, raising their own campaign money, and creating their own personal followings. Their success as solitary political entrepreneurs has habituated them to the need to guard their own careers. To enhance their independence, they have shaped a Congress in which old hands count for less and in which even the newest members must be taken seriously. For members who are more concerned with their reelection than with majority-building, this is the best of all worlds.

Their freedom, of course, creates problems in the system. The independence of Congress has added to the tensions between the branches.

Congressional responses to presidential initiatives have become more unpredictable. There are fewer incentives for members to go along with the leadership, and party has become a less reliable link for bridging the separation of powers. The result is that it has become measurably more difficult to put together the firm majorities necessary to make decisions and to adopt new policies. Immobilization occurs all too commonly.

Of related interest is the question of whether the independence that Congress has achieved from the chief executive has been matched by a comparable distancing between Congress and interest groups. The overwhelming impression among observers is that it has not. Probably at no time has Congress been whipsawed so frequently by single-interest, nonclass, high-intensity groups, arrayed on such passionate issues as gun control, abortion, conservation, nuclear power, equality, school prayer, and a thin slice of domestically volatile foreign policy questions. Emerging in one context after another, these issues crowd the congressional agenda and inflame the debate. The independence that Congress and its members have won from the chief executive and from the parties has been diminished by a new vulnerability to narrow pressure groups that regard anything less than complete accord with their positions as betrayal, or worse yet, as reason to carry on the fight where it hurts, among the voters in the next campaign. Weary of the "rectitude" issues and the "new politics" encirclement, it is no wonder that some members, not only elderly ones, slip out between the wagons, headed back home to stay.

Democratization of the congressional system was a major objective of the reform movement. Proceeding along two dimensions, it led to opening up congressional workings to public view and to a redistribution of power among members and units. As a result of various "sunshine" provisions adopted in the 1970s, secrecy has been virtually eliminated—in committees and caucuses and in voting. The broad consequence of openness has been to change the way members do business, putting them "on the record" much more often than in the past and presumably increasing their responsiveness and accountability to the public. At the same time, openness has increased the risks for members, at least as many perceive it, and added to the explanations (concerning positions, votes, and even personal finances) which they must make to those who pay attention and ask questions. It appears probable that the new openness has made members more likely to succumb to conspicuous displays of public pressure. Similarly, it may contribute to the success of interest groups in wringing larger accommodations out of Congress.

The redistribution of power brought about by alterations in the position of committee chairmen and in committee–subcommittee relations has pushed Congress toward extreme decentralization, offset only to the extent that party leaders, skillfully drawing on limited resources, can convince members to fall into line. The changes made in the name of democratization have contributed significantly to the further devolution of power in Congress.

The lasting importance of the changes made in Congress over the last decade remains to be seen. The immediate consequences, however, stand out, and are familiar by now. What is not clear is whether these changes have led to significantly different policy outcomes. That is the main question, and it is also the one on which there is the least systematic evidence. Investigation of the consequences of congressional reform for the political system, particularly in terms of public policy, ought to carry high priority for students of politics.

10.3 The Two Congresses and How They Are Changing*

Roger H. Davidson

In this essay, Davidson lists major sources of congressional change and presents several conclusions concerning their consequences. He distinguishes between two Congresses—(1) the institution, with its focus on legislation, and (2) the individuals, driven by a desire to represent constituents and gain reelection.

The U.S. Congress has a persistent image problem. The other branches of government have nothing quite comparable to the comic-strip figure of Senator Snort, the overblown and incompetent windbag. Pundits and humorists find Congress an inexhaustible source of new material. Seemingly, the public shares this disdain toward the institution. Since the mid-1960s, public approval of congressional performance has been notoriously low, surging upward only briefly at the time of President Nixon's 1974 resignation. In a recent nationwide opinion survey, nearly twice as many citizens gave Congress a negative rating as gave it positive marks.[1]

The view of Congress held by serious commentators—seasoned journalists, scholars, and commentators—is often scarcely more flattering than the public image. The currently fashionable textbook portrait of Congress, for example, is of a collection of politicians obsessed by reelection fears and surrounding themselves with staff and facilities for constituency errand-running (not a wholly erroneous picture, to be sure, but a caricature nonetheless). Legislators themselves often contribute to their shabby image by portraying themselves to their constituents as gallant warriors against the dragons back on Capitol Hill; as political scientist Richard F. Fenno, Jr., notes, they "run *for* Congress by running *against* Congress."[2]

Fenno's observation is a reminder that the U.S. Congress has a uniquely dual character: It is both a "deliberative assembly of one nation" and a "congress of ambassadors"—to use Edmund Burke's words to describe a most un-Burkean institution. It is not extravagant to observe that there is not one Congress, but two. They are analytically and even physically distinct, yet they are inextricably bound together. What affects one sooner or later affects the workings of the other.

One of these two entities is Congress as an institution. It is Congress the lawmaking and policy-determining body. It is Congress acting as a collegial body, performing its constitutional duties and debating legislative issues. Of course, as a large institution with a demanding workload, Congress functions more often in subgroups than as a single body. Yet its many work groups—there are now hundreds of them—are attending to public business, and the outcomes, whatever form they take, affect the public as a whole.

Yet there is a second Congress, every bit as important as the Congress of the textbooks. This is the Congress of 535 (actually 540) individual Senators and Representatives. They possess diverse backgrounds and follow varied paths to win office. Their electoral fortunes depend not upon what Congress produces as an institution but upon the support and goodwill of voters hundreds or thousands of miles away—

---

* From an updated version of Roger H. Davidson, "The Two Congresses and How They Are Changing," Paper prepared for Conference on "The Role of the Legislative in Western Democracies," Surrey, England, June 1979. Reprinted by permission of Roger H. Davidson.

voters whom they share with none of their colleagues on Capitol Hill. Journalist Richard Rovere once described members of Congress as tribesmen in an extraterritorial jungle whose chief concern while in Washington was what was going on around the council fires back home.

The dual character of Congress, though underscored by recent developments, is in fact dictated by the Constitution. Congress was intended as a lawmaking body, and it is no accident that the writers of the Constitution enumerated the powers of government, as understood in the 18th century, in that portion (Article I) devoted to the legislative branch. At the same time the House of Representatives was bound by frequent elections to popular needs and opinions. The Senate, although not originally conceived as a representative body, has become so in the 20th century.

The dichotomy between institutional and individual activities surfaces in legislators' role orientations and daily schedules. Like most of us, Senators and Representatives suffer from a scarcity of time in which to accomplish what is expected of them. No problem plagues the two houses more than balancing constituency work with legislative work (that is, committee and floor deliberations). Despite scheduling innovations for partitioning Washington and consituency work, Tuesday–Thursday Capitol Hill schedules persist. Legislators themselves acknowledge the primacy of the twin roles of legislator and constituency servant, though assigning different weights to these roles and budgeting their time differently to cope with them.

Citizens, for their part, view the Congress in Washington through different lenses than they do their own Senators and Representatives. Congress as an institution is perceived mainly as a legislative body. It is evaluated largely on the basis of citizens' generalized attitudes about policies and the state of the Union: Do people like the way things are going, or do they not? By contrast, citizens view their own representatives as agents of local interests, evaluating them on the basis of such factors as their ability to serve the district materially, their communication with constituents, and their "home style."

Significantly, citizens profess to be far happier with the performance of their individual legislators than with the performance of Congress as a whole. This is the source of the observation that Americans love their Congressmen but denigrate their Congress and explains why incumbents can be overwhelmingly returned to office while Congress itself remains low in the public's esteem.[3]

Notwithstanding a reputation for inertia, Congress—in both its manifestations—is now dramatically altered. The changes have rendered obsolete much of what scholars and journalists used to write about the House and Senate. They have touched virtually every nook and cranny on Capitol Hill—membership, structures, procedures, folkways, and staffs. Some changes resulted from pressures built up over many years; others occurred suddenly and almost casually. Some have been well chronicled by journalists and scholars; others are little known and even less well understood.

In cataloging the major forces for change and analyzing their consequences, it is useful to continue the metaphor of the two Congresses. What forces have impacted upon the Congress-as-institution? What forces have affected Congress-as-career-entrepreneurs? What innovations have these forces produced, and what new generation of problems have these innovations created?

CONGRESS-AS-INSTITUTION

If ours is an antiparliamentary age, it is surely because of profound and ever-shifting challenges emanating from the larger economic, social, and political environment. These may take the form of pressing national problems, rising public expectations, fast-moving events, competing institutions, or simply a burgeoning agenda. Like most of the world's legislative bodies, the U.S. Congress faces a prolonged crisis of adaptation to this larger environment. On this point most analysts are agreed, although they differ over the exact causes and outlines of the crisis. Whatever its origins, the crisis is acutely felt on Capitol Hill and stretches legislative structures and procedures to their limits, and sometimes beyond. Contributing to this state of affairs are several salient features in Congress's external environment.

Forces for Change

First, the government and Congress in turn continue to be asked to resolve all manner of problems. House and Senate workloads, in absolute terms, are staggering. In recent sessions, approximately 5,000 measures have been introduced in the Senate and nearly 20,000 in the House. Even if measures decline in number in the future, review of ongoing programs is a continuing, time-consuming challenge.

Second, relative to these policy demands, resources for resolving them in politically attractive ways have probably contracted. The United States is undergoing a painful transition from a growth-oriented society with cheap resources to a steady-state society of ever-more-costly resources. Rather than distributing benefits, politicians find themselves having to assign costs. In political scientists' terminology, this represents a shift from distributive to redistributive politics—an uncomfortable predicament for politicians, and comparatively novel for those in America.

Third, contemporary problems do not come in familiar packages or admit of traditional solutions. Many of them transcend traditional categories and jurisdictions, not to mention the two-year legislative timetable. President Carter's 1977 energy package embraced some 113 separate pieces of legislation, referred to half a dozen committees in each house. What is true of energy is equally true of other broad-gauged issues. The 1,806 health bills introduced in the House during the first five months of 1977, for example, were referred to no less than 18 of the 22 standing committees.

Fourth, challenges from the executive establishment cause acute stresses on Capitol Hill. On the one hand, legislators have grown accustomed to White House leadership and grumble when it is not forthcoming; on the other hand, they chafe under vigorous leadership, sensing a threat to legislative prerogatives. The Nixon period represented a high-water mark in the constitutional struggle between White House and Capitol Hill, with presidential incursions in impoundment, executive privilege, the war powers, dismantling of federal programs, and even abuse of the pocket veto. Although the pendulum swung toward Capitol Hill in the post-Watergate years, President Reagan's ability to put his budget and tax proposals on a fast legislative track shows vividly that presidential leadership, backed by skill and grassroots support, can turn the institution around in short order.

A final impetus for change—external in the sense that it emanates from electoral decisions—is the nation's shifting partisan and factional structure. Within both parties, regional variations have become muted while other voices have sought to be heard. Partisan and ideological ties—never compelling in the American system—have been gradually diluted. Interest groups are flooding into the vacuum left by the political parties' decline—not just the few traditionally powerful lobbies but rather a bewildering and shifting profusion of groups organized around all manner of issues and programs.

Institutional Innovations

In the wake of these shifts in its external environment, Congress has adopted a variety of innovations. Several of these are noteworthy: workload adjustments; committee and subcommittee proliferation; a framework for budgetary discipline; "democratization" of the two houses in reaction to the seniority system; and the growth of staff bureaucracies.

Workload Adjustments

From all accounts, the House and Senate are working more diligently than ever before. Within the past decade Congress has gone to virtually a year-long schedule. In the 20 years ending in 1976, House and Senate committee and subcommittee meetings doubled in number;

in the same period, the number of recorded floor votes tripled in the Senate and increased sixfold in the House. The average Senator or Representative puts in an 11-hour day when in the nation's Capital, according to surveys made in 1977.[4]

Congress has adapted to its burgeoning workload by manipulating its structure: concentrating on fewer but more complex issues, delegating many decisions to executive branch agents, and shifting its own role to one of monitor, vetoer, and overseer. Although introduced measures are more numerous and more wordy than ever before, fewer of them are reported by committees, considered in the House and Senate chambers, or passed into law.[5] Typically, legislation delegates vast powers but directs executives to report and recommend, oftentimes subjecting their actions to a legislative veto of one or both chambers or even a committee. Since 1932, nearly 200 laws containing some 270 separate legislative veto provisions have gone on the books. More than half of these date from the 1970s.[6]

Relying upon executive agents carries its own costs. To recover power they sense is slipping away, legislators grasp for new instruments of control. In the wake of the Watergate and Vietnam crises, and propelled by an anti-government mood, legislators of all persuasions proclaim their fealty to the concept of oversight. Predictably, cries of congressional "meddling" are heard from the White House, and some of the more ambitious oversight techniques have proven to be cumbersome and time-consuming.

Sometimes, as in the 1973 War Powers Resolution or the Budget and Impoundment Control Act of 1974, Congress seeks to recapture power but ends up giving formal recognition to *de facto* shifts toward the executive. As seen in President Reagan's use of the budget process, shrewd chief executives can turn these innovations to their own purposes.

WORK GROUP PROLIFERATION

Perhaps the most significant organizational phenomenon on Capitol Hill has been the profusion of work groups. In the 97th Congress there were 149 committees and subcommittees in the House (actually, the number constantly changes), with the average member serving on nearly six of them. Since 1977, the Senate has succeeded in paring its 175 subcommittees to 105. This has been achieved by coupling consolidation with limits on the number of subcommittee assignments and chairmanships each Senator can hold, thus assuring a more equitable distribution of committee posts.[7] The average number of assignments per Senator was cut from approximately 18 (4 committees and 14 subcommittees) to approximately 10 (3 committees and 7 subcommittees).

Still, Congress boasts an impressive number of work groups, and no one familiar with the ways of the Hill expects the number to decline drastically. Senators and Representatives are spread very thinly. Virtually any day the houses are in session, a large majority of legislators face meeting conflicts. Members are tempted to committee-hop, quorums are hard to maintain, and deliberation suffers. Committee specialization and apprenticeship norms have been diluted, casting doubt on the committees' continued ability to give in-depth consideration to detailed measures that come before them.

Jurisdictional competition among committees is the order of the day, resulting in member complaints about the need for tighter scheduling and coordination. Attractive issues often cause an unseemly scramble for advantage—sometimes breaking into open conflict, more frequently simply escalating decision-making costs by necessitating complicated informal agreements or awkward partitioning of issues.

THE "DEMOCRATIZATION" OF CONGRESS

Democracy is in full flower in the House and Senate. Formal positions of power still remain, as do inequalities of influence. But the Senate boasts nothing to match its bipartisan conservative "inner club" of the 1950s, which so vexed the tiny band of liberal Democrats. Over on the House side, the old committee barons have been replaced by a horde of committee and subcommittee baronets. Decision-making processes have been opened up and are no longer monopolized by the committees having jurisdiction on a given subject.

The war over the "seniority system" was fully recounted both in academic studies and in the mass media.[8] One attribute of seniority was that it recorded past electoral triumphs, rewarding a party's centers of strength as they existed in an earlier generation. When a party's factional balance shifted, the seniority system distorted its leadership ranks, causing a generational gap between leaders and backbenchers. Such a gap—in region, district type, ideology, and even age—lay at the heart of the Democrats' seniority struggles. By the late 1960s, internal contradictions within the congressional party were too glaring to continue and were resolved, inevitably, in favor of youth and liberalism. In the House, the revolts were spasmodic and occasionally bloody, punctuated by a series of intracommittee revolts against recalcitrant chairmen, dispersion of power into the subcommittees (1971 and 1973), and, finally, overthrow of several unpopular committee chairmen (1975). Since then no committee chairmen have been removed by the caucus, although several subcommittee chairmanships have been contested in committee caucuses—a clue, perhaps, to the current locus of power within the committee system.

In the Senate the transformation was more peaceful, hastened by caucus and chamber rules that dispersed desirable committee assignments, not to mention the permissive leadership of Majority Leader Mike Mansfield (1961–1976).

Republicans experienced similar tensions, although they were more generational than ideological. For the GOP, however, seniority was never the burning issue it was among Democrats. Because of the GOP's prolonged minority status, its seniority posts were simply less valuable than those of the Democrats. Moreover, lacking the incentive of chairmanships, senior GOP members were more willing to retire, producing more rapid generational turnover.

Reforms have not really eliminated seniority. As H. Douglas Price has remarked, "seniority, like monarchy, may be preserved by being deprived of most of its power."[9] The benefits of seniority have simply been extended to far more members. At the latest count, all Republican Senators and a majority of Democratic Representatives were committee or subcommittee chairmen. Thus, there are more seniority leaders in the House and Senate than ever before. If Woodrow Wilson were around to revise his classic book, *Congressional Government,* he would no doubt be led to observe that "Congressional government is subcommittee government."

The Growth of Staff Bureaucracies

To help cope with escalating workloads, proliferating work groups, and executive branch challenges, Congress has created an extensive staff apparatus. No visitor to the Hill these days can fail to be impressed by the hoardes of people who work there. More than 13,000 staff aides now work for members and committees, and some 25,000 more in congressional support agencies like the Congressional Research Service, the General Accounting Office, the Office of Technology Assessment, and the Congressional Budget Office.[10] Simply housing them is a major, unsolved logistical problem.

The Capitol Hill bureaucracy has grown in ways betraying the character of Congress as a decentralized, nonhierarchical institution. Congress has begotten not one bureaucracy but many, clustered about centers of power, in one sense defining those centers. Efforts to impose a common framework on the staff apparatus have thus far been stoutly resisted.

The Future Agenda

Post-World War II shifts in congressional organization and procedures—shifts that came to a head in the early 1970s—reinforced the historic decentralization in the House and Senate. Congressional history is a struggle of the general versus the particular, in which the particular seems the most powerful force. This particularism—so characteristic of Congress from its beginnings, and with rare exceptions ever since—is underscored by recent developments.

These changes have made the House and Senate more democratic bodies, and they have given members more channels for participating. What the past generation of reform has not solved, however, is how to orchestrate the work of the separate, semi-autonomous work groups into something resembling a coherent whole. Indeed, the advent of subcommittee government compounds the dilemmas of congressional leadership. The next generation of reform politics will have to direct its energies to unifying what the last generation of reforms has dispersed.

Two related problems of coordination will form the pivots for tomorrow's innovative efforts. These are strengthening the central leadership and realigning the committee system.

Congressional leadership embodies a paradox. Today's leaders are stronger on paper than any of their recent predecessors, and it is hard to imagine a group of leaders more skilled in employing their powers. Yet congressional leadership is extremely precarious, perhaps more so than at any time since the overthrow of Speaker Cannon in 1910.

The Speaker of the House, if a Democrat, has significant powers conferred by the Democratic Caucus. He chairs the Democratic Steering and Policy Committee and appoints nearly half of its members. He now nominates all Democratic members of the Committee on Rules, subject to ratification by the Caucus. For the first time since the days of Speaker Cannon, the Rules Committee serves as a leadership arm in regulating access to the House floor.[11]

The Speaker also exercises crucial new powers under the House rules. He may now make joint, split, or sequential referrals of bills to two or more committees with jurisdictional claims —options that are invoked hundreds of times each session. In sequential referrals, he may also lay down time limits upon the committees' deliberations. He is also empowered to create ad hoc legislative committees to handle bills claimed by two or more committees. Lacking the power to create a new committee with appropriate jurisdiction, Speaker O'Neill created an ad hoc body in 1977 to process the Carter energy package and coordinate the standing committees' deliberations. He selected its members from among loyalists, placed a deadline on the standing committees' work, and controlled floor deliberation through a carefully constructed "rule" governing floor debate. Yet the ad hoc committee was, as its name implies, a temporary expedient, cumbersome and not to be invoked every time coordination is required.

Over in the Senate, although leadership trends have been less clear, there are signs of new vigor. That tireless mechanic of Senate procedure, Senator Robert Byrd (D–W.Va.), employed his mastery of procedures and meticulous attention to detail to direct floor procedure. New limits on amendments after cloture has been invoked should give the Majority Leader and the presiding officer potent weapons in combating dilatory tactics. His successor, Senator Baker, has set off in new directions, stressing close coordination among committee leaders and envisioning tighter control over floor debate through such proposals as televised sessions.

Still, central leadership is suspect, and for the time being decentralizing forces predominate. The next few years will see the reform battle lines forming around leadership prerogatives.

Because a majority of members in both houses now have immediate stakes in preserving the present decentralized structure, efforts to centralize leadership will be hazardous. Moreover, party discipline is tenuous. Every legislator, it seems, is intent upon forging a unique voting record; blocs of members cluster less around the parties than around special-purpose caucuses—to exchange information, develop legislative stands, and even operate Whip systems. According to a recent estimate, nearly 70 of these groups are in operation.[12]

Leaders, for their part, seem not to know which way to turn. Oftentimes they seem reluctant to accept new prerogatives, preferring to rely on informal powers. Yet, they sense that, although publicly held responsible for congressional performance, they lack the power to coordinate or schedule the legislative program. That is why virtually every leader since House Speaker Sam Rayburn (1940–47; 1949–53; 1955–61) has supported reforms that promised to increase their leverage upon the legislative process.

Committee Revitalization

Reorganization efforts have thus far failed to recast House or Senate committees to dovetail with contemporary categories of public problems. A wide-ranging House committee realignment proposed by a House select committee in 1974 fell victim to intense lobbying by committee leaders who opposed curbs on their jurisdictions and by allied lobbyists who feared that structural shifts would unwire their mutually beneficial alliances. The reorganization plan was defeated by a reverse-lobbying process, in which committee members and staffs, seeking to preserve their positions, mobilized support from groups that had previously benefited from committee decisions.[13] An effort to revive committee reorganization three years later was struck down summarily, partly because of the same forces. A new committee reorganization effort was launched in 1979, though by the narrowest of floor votes and with a severely limited mandate. Its one structural proposal—an energy committee—was defeated by a coalition of committee leaders bent on protecting their turf.

The Senate was reasonably successful when a 1977 realignment package was adopted, with modifications. This realignment left jurisdictional lines pretty much untouched, concentrating instead on consolidating several obsolete committees. The scheme was accepted because, by limiting assignments and leadership posts, it succeeded in spreading the workload more equitably among the Senate's more junior members.

Committee-system modernization is politically the roughest reorganization challenge. It severely upsets the institution's internal balance, for it threatens not only members' committee careers but also their mutually supportive relationships with potent outside clientele groups.

And yet, Senators and Representatives profess to be profoundly dissatisfied with the present committee system. In a survey of 101 House and Senate members conducted during the 93d Congress, a foreign-policy commission discovered that 81 percent of the legislators were dissatisfied with "committee jurisdictions and the way they are defined in Congress." Only 1 percent of the legislators were "very satisfied" with the jurisdictional situation, while 13 percent were "very dissatisfied."[14] In a House study conducted in 1977, committee structure was the most frequently mentioned "obstacle" preventing the House from doing its job. "Scheduling" and "institutional inertia" were next in line.[15] In short, legislators are fully aware of the committee system's disarray, although as yet they have not brought themselves to pay the price for remedying the problem. Meanwhile, costs of operating under the present structure are escalating.

Dramatic evidence of the committee system's vulnerability occurred during President Reagan's first months in office. Rather than choosing the lengthy, laborious path of pushing proposals through the authorizing committees, Reagan and his advisers cleverly focused on the budget process as a short-cut way of shifting spending priorities. Time was short, they reasoned, and committees would be unwilling to curtail programs they had developed and nurtured. Committees were thus given spending ceilings and told to conform; and when the painful process yielded results somewhat short of the Administration's goals, a new budget resolution was prepared and pushed through. Both the process and the product unsettled many lawmakers on both sides of the aisle—especially more senior members with an investment in committee specialization. The budget mechanism may never be used in this way again. But the experience bared the weaknesses of the committee structure, and one can hardly blame the President and his advisers for seeking another way out.

For an institution reputed to be slow and tradition-bound, Congress has attempted a surprisingly large number of major reorganization efforts in the past generation. There have been two joint committee investigations (1945, 1965), three major committee reform efforts (1973–74 and 1979–80 in the House, 1976–77 in the Senate), two administrative review bodies (one for each house), and a major budgetary reform. Still, the agenda of innovations is lengthy, and pressures for further institutional innovation are going to persist. This is the most eloquent testimony to the continuing nature of Congress' crisis of adaptation.

CONGRESS-AS-CAREER-ENTREPRENEURS

A second set of pressures for a change emanates from individual members of Congress—their careers, activities, and goals. Senators and Representatives make their own claims upon the institution—claims that must in some measure be satisfied if Congress is to attract talented men and women, provide a workplace where this talent can be utilized, and command loyalty from its members.

Individual legislators harbor a variety of goals.[16] All members, or virtually all of them, want to be reelected; some members have no other interest. But men and women—even politicians—do not live by reelection alone. They seek opportunities to contribute, to shape public policy, to see their ideas become reality, to influence others, and to work in dignity and sanity. In a body of 535 politicians (540, actually), this jostling of individual goals and careers inevitably causes friction. No less than the institution itself, these individual careers are beset by stresses and strains.

First, of all the factors affecting today's politicians in the United States, the most conspicuous is the long-term ebbing of political party organizations and loyalties. In only a minority of areas do party organizations still serve as sponsors and anchors for political careers. Nor do voters rely as heavily as they once did upon party labels to guide their choices. Hence, politicians are thrust into the role of individual entrepreneurs, relying upon their own resources for building and nurturing supportive constituencies. This yields an electoral politics comprising a series of cottage industries—a situation strikingly parallel to the fragmentation of interest groups, in which the traditional array of broad-purpose groups is dissolving into a fluid system of narrow-purpose groupings.

Second, congressional careerism is apparently subsiding. Historically, the trend has been toward longer careers—a trend that reached its peak in the post-World War II era. Since the late 1960s, in fact, careerism seems to be on the wane. This phenomenon is not caused primarily by competition at the polls.

Third, rising constituency demands have inundated individual legislators and their staffs. The average state now numbers some 4 million people, the average House district more than half a million. Educational levels have risen; communications and transportation are easier. Public opinion surveys show unmistakably that voters expect legislators to "bring home the bacon" in terms of federal services and to communicate frequently with the home folks. In 1980, the House Post Office logged 150 million pieces of incoming mail—five times the 1970 figure. Surveys suggest that future constituency demands will not diminish.

Finally, citizens' traditional ambivalence toward politicians turned into overt cynicism in the 1970s. Politicians of all persuasions felt a backlash from the Vietnam War, the Watergate scandal, and the perceived ineffectiveness of government domestic and foreign policies. A number of congressional careers were halted by scandal—perhaps because a "new morality" spotlighted practices that previously might have escaped censure.

"The Incumbency Party"

At first glance, Senators' and Representatives' careers would seem to be thriving. Certainly incumbents generally do well at the polls. Since World War II, an average of 91 percent of all incumbent Representatives and 73 percent of incumbent Senators running for reelection have been successful.[17] In 1978, 95 percent of the House members and 68 percent of the Senators who contested in the general elections were returned to office.

Partisan swings are less pronounced than they once were. What is more, electoral competition has been relatively low, although recently there is a slight trend toward more competition, especially in Senate races. In any given election year, only about 15 percent of the congressional races are "marginal"—that is, won by a margin of 55 percent or less. Little wonder, then, that political observers remark that it is not the Democratic party or the Republican party, but rather the "incumbency party," that controls Congress.

In an era of weak political parties, incumbency itself—with its attendant visibility and opportunities for *ombudsman* service—is a potent factor (though not the only factor) in the electoral picture. A 1977 survey found that 15 percent of all citizens (or members of their families) had requested help from a member of Congress. By better than a two-to-one margin (69 percent to 31 percent), the citizens were satisfied with the service they had received.[18] No less than two thirds of all respondents claimed to have received some communication from their member of Congress. Half could correctly identify his or her name. And, as we have noted, citizens see their own representatives in far rosier hues than they do the Congress as a whole.

American legislators, especially House members, have always been expected to run errands for constituents. Yet in an era of limited government, there were few errands to run. At the turn of the century, for example, constituency mail was pretty much confined to rural mail routes, Spanish War pensions, free seed, and very occasionally a legislative matter. A single clerk sufficed to handle correspondence.

As Capitol Hill observers whose memories go back to the early 1960s can attest, this constituency service role has been transformed quantitatively and qualitatively. Senators and Representatives now head veritable cottage industries for communicating with voters—not merely responding to constituents' requests, but generating these requests through newsletters, targeted mailings, and free telephone access. Staff and office allowances have grown, district offices have proliferated, and recesses are now called "district work periods." This apparatus extends the legislators' ability to reach their constituents, and it provides badly needed *ombudsman* services for citizens who find coping with the federal bureaucracy a bewildering prospect.

Several years ago, the monetary value of this apparatus to the average Representative was placed at $567,000 annually—all provided by taxpayers.[19] This included $388,000 in staff salaries and office space, $143,000 in communication (mostly franked mail) and travel, and $36,000 in miscellaneous benefits. The biennial advantage for an incumbent would thus exceed $1 million—and the figure would be even higher for a Senator. Not included in this accounting are such ancillary services as reduced rates for radio and television recording studios and use of such informational resources as the Congressional Research Service.

Role Conflicts

Which came first, the congressional apparatus for performing constituency service functions or the public's expectation that such functions should be performed? I believe it can be plausibly argued that legislators are reacting to what they interpret as strongly held and legitimate voter expectations. There is no question that voters expect accessibility and material service, and that, in part, a large number of legislators evidence antipathy toward constituency chores—even while acknowledging they are essential aspects of the job, and ones that yield handsome dividends at the polls.

Indeed, legislative and constituency role conflicts are now at dangerously high levels because of heavy demands in both areas. Senators long ago relegated the bulk of their legislative work to staff aides; in the House the transition has been more recent and, for many, not without a sense of loss. Even in the early 1960s, many Representatives did their own research and preparation for committee meetings and floor debates. According to a 1965 study, the average House member devoted virtually one day a week to "legislative research and reading"; another 2.7 hours a week was spent writing speeches and articles.[20]

Today's Representatives probably spend as much time in the chamber and in committee as did their predecessors of two decades ago—given the burgeoning committee meetings and floor votes. Qualitatively, however, legislative duties are quite differently performed. According to a 1977 survey, the average Representative reportedly spent 12 minutes a day preparing legislation or speeches and another 11 minutes reading.[21] With such schedules, reliance upon staff aides is essential.

Legislators are beset by these conflicting demands, and many of them want to spend more time on legislation than they do. In the 1977 survey, 154 House members were asked to identify the differences between what others expected them to do and what they thought they should be doing. The most frequently mentioned problem, mentioned by fully half of the members, was that "constituent demands detract from other functions." A second complaint, cited by 36 percent of the legislators, was that "scheduling problems and time pressures detract from the work of the House."[22]

Role conflict is not the only factor impinging upon the congressional career. The seeming intractability of public problems and the difficulty of gaining credit for domestic policy achievements have tempered the rewards of public life. So has the post-Watergate antigovernment sentiment. The press and the public have adopted a moralistic stance toward government and its agents who are often regarded as guilty until proven otherwise. Stung by criticism, Congress has enacted stricter rules over campaign finance, financial disclosure, and ethics. However desirable, the new codes exact a price in legislators' morale and self-regard. Reactions in both houses have been embittered—accounting for the House's rejection of a reform package late in 1977 and the Senate's controversial delay of outside income limits in 1979. Several members have cited the codes in explaining their retirement from public life.

DECLINING CAREERISM?

Whatever the reason, many Senators and Representatives evidence weariness and alienation from their jobs. In a survey of House members in the mid-1960s, a generally high level of satisfaction with the institution's performance was discovered—an attitude characterized as "a vote of aye—with reservations."[23] A survey conducted a decade later yielded not even such measured optimism. That study, which focused on foreign policy, uncovered widespread discontent among members of both houses. Dissatisfaction was expressed by four fifths of the legislators and extended to all groups and factions of Capitol Hill.[24] In the 1977 survey of the House members, only 16 percent of the Representatives thought the House was "very effective" in performing its principal functions.[25]

Some might argue that testimony from retired legislators is suspect as rationalization; but comments from thoughtful, respected ex-members, many of whom departed in mid-career, are too numerous to ignore. James W. Symington (D–Mo., 1969–77) said leaving Congress is "a release from a kind of bondage." Thomas Rees (D–Calif., 1965–77) exulted that he no longer had "to listen to some hysterical person who calls me about an issue that I care nothing about."[26] Otis G. Pike

(D–N.Y., 1961–79) said he retired because he was ''tired of wasting time on drivel.''

Nor are these isolated sentiments of disgruntled legislators. During the past decade, the long-term rise in congressional careerism has been halted. When the 97th Congress convened in 1981, of the 535 members of the House and Senate, three quarters were first elected after 1970 and nearly two thirds since Richard M. Nixon resigned as President in 1974.

This was more a result of voluntary retirements than of voter discontent. In 1978, for instance, the total House turnover was 14 percent (62 members). But three quarters of these were voluntary retirements (38 members, or 9 percent). Only 24 retirements were involuntary, the result of defeat at the polls—5 in primaries and 19 in general elections. Thus, the *electoral* turnover was only 5.5 percent. The Senate is more hazardous. In 1978, its turnover rate was 20 percent, less than half of which was voluntary. And, considering that only a third of the Senate seats are contested in any given election year, the actual turnover rate was much higher. In surprising numbers (for modern times), legislators are choosing to retire from Congress or seek other jobs.

Congressional retirements are by no means a bad thing. In fact, turnover during the 1950s and 1960s was uncommonly low; and in the absence of meaningful competition in many states and a large majority of House districts, voluntary retirement may be the chief avenue for achieving turnover. Nonetheless, the number of voluntary retirements suggests that congressional life may not be as satisfying as it once was. Indeed, with other careers becoming relatively more attractive, with leadership within Congress more easily and rapidly attained, with congressional life betraying new stresses and strains, tomorrow's critics could conceivably be talking about a problem no one would have taken seriously a few years ago: how to keep Senators' or Representatives' jobs attractive enough to draw talented individuals and command these individuals' loyalty once they are there.

The heightened demands thrust upon the two Congresses may well lie beyond the reach of normal men and women. Reflecting on the multiplicity of presidential duties, Woodrow Wilson once remarked that the United States might be forced to pick its leaders from among ''wise and prudent athletes''—a small class of people. The same might now be said of Senators and Representatives. And if the job specifications exceed reasonable dimensions, will reasonable human beings volunteer for the jobs?

CONCLUSIONS

Congress is essentially a reactive institution. For better or worse, it mirrors the nation's political life—its values, standards, and organizing principles. Today's Congress is little different: it is open, representative, egalitarian, and fragmented. It lacks consensus and leadership, and there is less of the ideological or partisan commitment of earlier eras.

The members of Congress are by and large—and contrary to popular beliefs—a diligent, even harried, group of men and women. Although it has its share of *poseurs* and philanderers, Congress is populated mainly by earnest individuals who are so busy casting floor votes and keeping appointments that they have little time left for expertise or reflection. There pervades an atmosphere of frantic frustration: Members are busier than ever, but the complexity of their tasks and the fullness of their schedules militates against meaningful involvement in any given issue. Members are torn by conflicting expectations from the Washington community and the home communities that form their electoral bases.

In the 1960s, critics worried about the representative character of Congress. Long careers and low turnover seemed to heighten the insular, small-town atmosphere of the Hill; newly active ethnic and racial groupings were ill represented; because of the seniority system, leaders were especially unrepresentative; decision making was all too often done in closed circles and behind closed doors. Few commentators would now fault Congress on these counts.

Capitol Hill is a far more open, democratic place than it was a decade or so ago. The transformation of Congress is not unlike that which took place in the political parties during the same time period.

No doubt Congress reflects the atomization of political life in the United States. This era is likely to prevail until the pressure of adaptive challenges becomes too strong to resist, or the galvanizing force of an issue or a political movement once again changes the face of the American political landscape.

10.4 Congressional Ethics—Trouble on the Hill*

Robert S. Getz

The modern Congress has been plagued by several recent scandals involving ethical problems. In this essay, original to this publication, a long-time student of congressional ethics studies some recent scandals, analyzing them in terms of causes and institutional response. He concludes with a somewhat favorable assessment of the ethical character of Congress and an appreciation for the difficulties inherent in efforts to impose more stringent ethical standards there.

The congressional bribery scandal of 1980–81, popularly known as ''Abscam,'' hit Congress at the end of a 10-year reform effort designed to increase ethical standards and improve the institution's image. If the vast majority of the legislators muttered under their breath, ''We can't win for losing,'' one could hardly blame them.

In February 1980, it was announced that the FBI had engaged in a massive and highly secret undercover operation, ''Abscam,'' in which agents—posing as businessmen and wealthy Arab sheiks—had implicated six members of the House and one Senator in criminal wrongdoing involving bribes in return for promises of legislative favors or influence peddling. In each instance the accused were eventually convicted in federal court.

On October 2, 1980, the House expelled Michael (''Ozzie'') Meyers (D–Pa.), the first of the legislators to be convicted; John W. Jenrette, Jr. (D–S.C.) resigned after his conviction to avoid a similar fate. Both ran for reelection and were defeated. The voters eliminated the need for House action in three other cases by denying one member renomination and defeating two others during the 1980 general election. The sixth, Raymond F. Lederer (D–Pa.), was reelected, but his subsequent conviction led to his resignation.

The one senator charged, Harrison A. Williams, Jr. (D–N.J.), was not up for reelection in 1980. He was convicted in the spring of 1981 but has not resigned at the time of this writing.

Perhaps the two most widely publicized cases of congressional indiscretion during the 1970s were ''Koreagate''—the Tongsun Park affair—and the Wayne L. Hays (D–Ohio) ''affair of the heart'' with an employee, Elizabeth Ray.

---

* Specifically written for this volume. The major portion of this essay is from Robert S. Getz and Frank Feigert, *The Process and Politics of American Government* (Boston: Allyn & Bacon, 1982), chapter 10.

In June 1976 the Justice Department announced it was gathering evidence concerning a mysterious South Korean businessman, Tongsun Park, who was alleged to be behind the distribution of $500,000 to $1 million in cash and gifts to more than 26 past or present members of Congress and other officials. Park's alleged mission was to promote a "favorable legislative climate" for South Korea in Washington.

A federal grand jury had indicted Park on conspiracy, bribery, offering of illegal gratuities, and mail fraud, and the jury named former Representative Richard T. Hanna (D–Calif, 1963–74) as an unindicted coconspirator. Park and Hanna were alleged to have worked together in a scheme to get large commissions from sales of U.S. rice to South Korea and to use large portions of the money in an "influence purchasing effort" centered on the U.S. Congress during the period from 1967 through 1975. The indictment also contained a list of 25 present or former members of Congress (5 Senators and 20 Representatives) who had received money from Park, mainly in the form of campaign contributions. Most of those listed had acknowledged the receipt of these funds during the preceding months as press attention focused on Koreagate. The investigation fizzled, and the House probe ended in 1978 with the "reprimand" of three members.

Park eventually was granted immunity in return for his testimony, and all charges against him were dismissed in 1979. Hanna pleaded guilty to conspiracy and served a little more than a year in jail. The only other trials resulting from "Koreagate" led to the acquittal of one former member, and perjury charges against another ex-legislator were dropped.

A *Congressional Quarterly* survey of the 1973–75 period turned up few recorded votes that affected Korea, and most of these were "pro-Korean" by a substantial margin, reflecting the votes of many legislators who were not alleged to have had contacts with Park. And the 25 members listed did not vote the pro-Korean position consistently.[1]

The most famous congressional "affair of the heart" took place in 1976. Shock waves went through Congress when it was revealed that Wayne L. Hays, chairman of the powerful House Administration Committee, had kept a mistress on the public payroll. The lady in question, Elizabeth Ray, blew the whistle, and her charges were followed by the claims of a number of other women that accommodating their bosses' sexual demands was the price for job advancement. A threatened House investigation forced Hays' resignation, and the Administration Committee was stripped of its authority over congressional office allowances and other perquisites.

THE IMAGE PROBLEM

While stories of indiscretion make interesting reading, the misdeeds of some should not be taken as a condemnation of all legislators. Between 1941 and the spring of 1981 approximately 50 members of Congress have been indicted on criminal charges, and all but 11 pleaded guilty or were convicted.[2] This number represents only a small percentage of the individuals who have served in Congress over the 40-year period. However, while cases of criminal activity are few in number, they are highly publicized. And, in fairness, it must be said that Congress' image problem stems in part from the tendency of many people to lump all 535 members of Congress together, forgetting that the overwhelming majority of them perform their public service in an honest way.

Two other factors, however, can be blamed on the members. First is the well-documented reluctance of legislators to investigate and punish their colleagues. The House Committee on Standards of Official Conduct and the Senate Ethics Committee charged with this responsibility were created in 1965 and 1968, respectively, but had a history of pre-1979 avoidance of cases that was consistent with Congress' historical preference for gathering around offenders to shield them from embarrassment, to rely on and defer to the judicial system in criminal cases, and to allow the voters to determine whether or not an offender should be returned to office. When Congress has acted, it usually has been responding to public pressure generated by the exposure of wrongdoing by the media. And part of Congress' reluctance to take the lead in this area has been the knowledge that the publicity given to the actions of a few members casts doubt on the integrity of all the members. Fortunately, there is evidence that the committees now are taking a more active approach.

Congressional reluctance generated a great deal of public attention and anger in 1979 over the Senate's handling of charges against Herman E. Talmadge (D–Ga.), the seventh most senior member. He was a close friend of many Senators, held a number of powerful committee posts, and had undergone treatment for alcoholism. He was charged with irregularities in his campaign and office expense accounts, and with failure to disclose cash and other gifts that, it was alleged, allowed him to live on only $21 a week in pocket money.

The Talmadge case generated a considerable amount of sympathy for him from fellow Senators, who began to express unhappiness with the burdensome bookkeeping requirements and behavioral prohibitions of financial disclosure rules and the codes of conduct that some felt had little to do with enforcing ethical conduct.

The hearing was long and drawn out, and the Ethics Committee recommended that Talmadge be "denounced" rather than be "censored," the more formal manner of punishment. The Senate did "denounce" Talmadge, but some observers characterized the debate as a testimonial dinner for the Georgian, and others contended that he had received "a slap on the wrist."

Congress' quick response to the Abscam indictments may signal that the days of foot-dragging may be over, at least in the case of those incidents that involve well-publicized charges of criminal activity.

Second and perhaps most important for Congress' image are the constant questions that are raised about the use of the legal advantages of office, such as the franking privilege, expense accounts, and foreign travel. There also is considerable criticism about large campaign contributions and outside income derived from speaking and writing fees or service on boards of directors. While these activities are not illegal, they often raise questions about ethics, particularly when the sources of contributions and outside income are typically special-interest groups who are concerned with legislation before Congress.

THE BAD OLD DAYS

One of the ironies of Congress' image problem is that contemporary standards of ethics are considerably higher than the standards of the 19th century. At the beginning of that century there was little understanding about the responsibilities of public office, perhaps because the functions of government were so few and the possibility of a conflict of interest (a situation in which an official's conduct of his office conflicts with his private economic affairs) were so rare. The well-known 1833 letter from Senator Daniel Webster to Nicholas Biddle, president of the United States Bank, is an excellent example of this point:

> Sir,
>
> Since I have arrived here [Congress], I have had an application to be concerned, professionally, against the Bank, which I have declined, of course, although I believe my retainer has not been renewed, or refreshed as usual. If it be wished that my relation to the Bank should be continued, it may be well to send me the usual retainers.[3]

Webster had been offered money to work against the interests of the bank in his capacity as a Senator and was reminding Biddle that he had failed to send him his usual fee for serving as a "lobbyist" for the bank. By contemporary standards this would be no less than the solicitation of a bribe; however, it was an acceptable practice in Webster's time.

The low state of morality among elected and appointed officials in the period 1853–72 and the public indignation it aroused led to the passage of six of the eight conflict-of-interest statutes that preceded the major code revisions of 1962. The revisions were brought about by a number of scandals and the overdue realization on the part of the public that the growth of government activity had put to rest the notion that government and private life were neatly separated.[4]

HIGH COSTS, PRIVILEGE, AND POWER

Questions and concerns about congressional ethics can not be separated from the high cost of serving in office, the opportunities to make large financial gains, and the power wielded by the members over decisions that have a tremendous impact upon the private sector.

Members of Congress created a small storm of protest in 1977 when they did not reject a presidential recommendation to give themselves a $12,900 raise as part of a pay increase for members of all three branches. Their new salary of $57,500 is supplemented by annual cost-of-living increases that they can reject. Some of the fringe benefits include cheap health and life insurance, a retirement plan, a tax break if they maintain two residences (one in or around Washington and one back home), and a $7,000 personal expense account. In addition, contacts made in the course of a Washington career can lead to lucrative jobs later in life. The earnings of members average an increase of more than 30 percent when they leave office.

On the other hand, the extra expenses of office include nonreimbursed travel expenses over the travel allowance, maintaining two residences, entertaining constituents, and being expected to make contributions to numerous organizations. Of course, some members, particularly Senators, have large independent incomes; but for others, the congressional pay scale may leave them living well, but also well above their means. Many lawmakers turn to speaking engagements and to writing to supplement their incomes, and some claim this is the only way they can make ends meet. But large fees for these activities, paid by groups with vested interests in congressional decisions, can lead to ethical problems.

In 1977, the *Washington Post* published data from a survey of the personal financial situation of Senators. Some, particularly first-termers, were having a hard time making ends meet. Gary Hart (D–Colo.), for example, needed over $20,000 from speaking engagements and $5,000 from a constituents' fund (prohibited after 1977) to stay even. Under the new code, members without stock or real estate investments could be hard put. As Hart said:

> You're always sending flowers for a funeral, or wedding presents, or bar mitzvah gifts for the kids of somebody who worked on the campaign. It's nickels here and dimes here and there, but you end up spending a couple of thousand a year on it.[5]

In contrast to Hart's position, the survey's most significant point was the ability of Senators to make great improvements in their financial positions while serving in the Senate. Being in Congress, and in the Senate in particular, in the past has provided the opportunity to earn big fees that could be reinvested, and to raise and convert to personal use excess campaign contributions (now outlawed). While new provisions have eliminated certain opportunities, members of Congress serve on committees that make important economic decisions, and they appear to be in a position to make good use of the information they acquire through one source or another. The new code notwithstanding, Congress probably will remain a "land of opportunity."

Creating "friends" in high places is part of the political game, and lobbyists for special interests seek the sympathetic ear of members, particularly those on the committees that are considering bills vital to the interests of the particular organizations they represent. Lobbyists often court the favor of the legislators by providing free transportation on company planes or free vacations at resorts or hunting lodges. Of course, campaign contributions play a major role in the attempts to influence legislative outcomes.

Two dated, but still classic, examples occurred in 1974. The oil, real estate, securities, banking, public utilities, and trucking industries contributed over $100,000 to the campaigns of 14 members of the House Ways and Means Committee, the body most concerned with tax legislation. This represented about 20 percent of the Congressmen's campaign funds. Each of the industries had an interest in some specific tax bill before the committee. And maritime unions donated more than $330,000 to the 141 members of Congress who backed an oil import bill requiring 30 percent of all imported oil to be shipped in American tankers with American crews. Many of the recipients faced easy election contests. A number of safe candidates ranked among the 10 largest recipients of business, professional, and labor donations.

The "wine, women, song, and campaign contributions" approach of Tongsun Park and the occasional sex scandal on the Hill also are products, in part, of the environment of prestige and power in Washington. The point being made here is that people who have power are pursued and sometimes are the pursuers. People, men or women, are attracted to those in power, and abuse of office is not confined to members of either sex. Capitol Hill is a "heady," temptation-filled environment. Perhaps it is a testimony to the integrity of most of those who serve in Congress that there is not a greater incidence of financial or sexual corruption.

RULES OF CONDUCT

In March and April of 1977, the House and Senate adopted tough new ethics codes that were pushed by the respective floor leaders. House Speaker Thomas P. O'Neill, Jr. (D–Mass.) had promised the adoption of the code as a followup to the congressional pay raise. He told his colleagues, "The issue before us is not unofficial office accounts, honorariums, outside income, earned or unearned. The issue is credibility, restoring public confidence in this Congress."[6] On the Senate side, Majority Leader Robert C. Byrd (D–W. Va.) fought for passage of the code because of "the necessity of the times" and the "climate created by the errant actions of a minority of public officials," which demanded that the Senate take action to restore the public's confidence in Congress.[7]

The 1978 Ethics in Government Act codified the public financial disclosure requirements imposed by the new codes and it imposed a disclosure upon top executive branch and judicial branch employees. While one version of the bill called for criminal penalties for knowing and willful violations, this was dropped in favor of civil penalties on the grounds that a criminal charge, even if later disproven, could ruin a politician's career.

CONFLICT OF INTEREST AND THE REPRESENTATIVE FUNCTION

Prior to the establishment of the new codes, both houses had codes of ethics on the books which read like the Ten Commandments. They included such general admonitions as avoiding activities that conflict with official duties and giving a full day's labor for a full day's pay. Legislators are also covered by some provisions of the conflict-of-interest statutes, which prohibit their receiving compensation for services rendered in relation to matters affecting the government and their practice of law before the U.S. Court of Claims (claims against the government).

Some critics have argued that Congress used a double standard by applying some portions of the code to the executive branch and not to itself. For example, executive officials cannot act in an official capacity on matters in which they have a private interest. But the application of this particular provision would ignore the nature of the representative function that makes the members the intermediaries for their constituents in dealing with Executive agencies and in furthering their interests in particular legislation. Members of Congress consider and act upon measures that influence all sectors of the economy; and this factor coupled with their own financial interests makes it difficult for them to avoid all possible or actual conflicts between their legislative duties and their private interests. And members often have a ''community of interest'' with the constituents by their participation in a predominant economic enterprise of the district or state. For example, a legislator may have agricultural interests that would be directly affected by a bill, but a decision not to take part in deliberation and voting on the bill probably would conflict with the duty to represent a predominantly agricultural constituency.

Congress' major pre-1977 response to its ethical problems came in the form of disclosure rules requiring the filing of an annual public statement disclosing personal finances. The Senate version provided very little information to the public. Senators had to file public reports that only listed the source and amount of any gift of more than $50 (cash or value) and each honorarium of $300 or more. They were required to file a detailed report on their income, assets, and debts, and a copy of their income tax returns with the Comptroller General. But these reports were secret and would only be turned over to the Ethics Committee if requested in the course of an investigation. Representatives, on the other hand, filed annual reports open to public inspection listing sources of income. The theory behind disclosure was that the public could judge whether or not a Representative's financial situation might create conflicts of interest. But, the regulation's high threshold of $5,000—a Representative did not have to report most income or investments of a value of less than $5,000 or exact dollar amounts above that figure—and the lack of detailed information on amounts of money or extent of holdings created real loopholes.

The concept behind disclosure is that, while it does not bar any particular type of financial activity, the public nature of disclosure provides the people with the opportunity to judge whether or not a legislator may have been improperly influenced in his official behavior because of personal monetary interests. In turn, it gives the lawmakers an opportunity to point to the public record in an effort to combat insinuations or explicit accusations of conflict of interest. On the other hand, some members of Congress consider the disclosure rules to be an invasion of privacy.

Codes of ethics, conflict-of-interest statutes, and disclosure notwithstanding, Congress was still faced with a long list of practices that lent themselves to unethical behavior or the appearance of unethical behavior and led to a climate of public distrust.

The New Ethics Codes

The 1977 codes eliminated or reduced the potential impact of a number of questionable practices. Unofficial office accounts, financed by constituent and/or group contributions, have been eliminated, and foreign travel by defeated or retiring—''lame-duck''—members has been restricted. The acceptance of gifts totaling more than $100 from anyone with an interest in legislation is prohibited. Senate rules virtually prohibit the practice of law, and the earned income limit in the House has forced most Representatives to abandon their legal work. Finally, the codes provide for extensive financial disclosure of sources and amounts of income, holdings, gifts—including transportation, lodging, and food—real and personal property, debts, and business transactions. For the Senate, meaningful public disclosure is a dramatic change from the former rule.

The 1976 Federal Election Campaign Act limited to $25,000 annually what a member of Congress can earn from ''honoraria''—money received from speaking engagements or writing articles—unless the excess is to cover expenses or is donated to charity. The House uses a $750 ceiling for each ''honorarium,'' and the Senate uses $2,000.

Loopholes and Problems

A number of problems remain and will continue to tarnish Congress' image unless remedial action is taken. The disclosure rules require a listing of the ''category of value'' owned by the member, spouse, and dependents. A category represents a "range" of value such as "between $15,001 and $50,000," "between $100,001 and $250,000," and "over $250,000" for *unearned income*—interest, dividends, royalties, capital gains, etc.—rather than as compensation for services performed. The categories for real and personal property are similar. However, the top category in the House is "over $250,000," while in the more affluent Senate, categories top off at "over $5 million."

A classic example of the "categories of value" problem is that of Representative Fred Richmond (D–N.Y.). He did all that the law required when he reported his 1978 holdings in a particular concern as "over $250,000." However, the stock market value at that time was about $16.5 million, or $16.25 million more than he had to disclose.[8]

The most controversial part of the codes is the limitation (effective January 1, 1979) of "outside" earned income to 15 percent of official salary, which at the $57,500 figures amounted to $8,625 per year. "Earned" income refers to money made through honoraria—the days of the speaking gravy train are over—or professional practice, legal or otherwise. The limit does not apply to "unearned" income—such as dividends from stocks and bonds—or income from a family-controlled business. Speaker O'Neill had argued that the outside-income provision was the "heart and soul" of the package, but he acknowledged that it would require sacrifices by many members.

In March 1979, the Senate placed a four-year delay on the implementation of the earned income limitation. The action was a sudden move that took place with only six Senators on the floor and five minutes of debate. Some members were outraged, and a second vote took place on March 31, 1979. The attempt to reimpose the limit, sponsored by Gary Hart (D–Colo.), was rejected 44–54. Ted Stevens (R–Alaska) said that the limits made Senators "financial eunuchs" and compromised their independence. On the other side, the president of Common Cause called the action "the Senate's version of 'take the money and run and the public be damned.' "[9]

With reference to honoraria, groups are targeting their payments, concentrating on those members in a position to help them with their concerns. For example, in 1979 banking and credit union groups made honoraria payments of $37,700 to seven members of the Senate Banking Committee and $47,145 to 27 members of the House Banking Committee. Both bodies considered legislation making major changes in how the nation's banks and savings and loan institutions are allowed to conduct their business.[10]

While the problem of excessive campaign funding can only be met by spending limitations—struck down by the Supreme Court in 1976—or the proposed public financing of congressional campaigns, the institution and the people were the losers when Congress failed to come to grips with the conflict-of-interest situations created by "unearned" income from investments. The ethical question concerning stockholdings is the propriety of the members' having a financial interest in companies that can profit from the actions of their committees and subcommittees. For example, a member serving on a committee dealing with energy who has substantial holdings in oil company stocks may be faced with having to decide between the public interest and personal financial interests.

The problem is a real one. In 1979, no less than six members of the Senate Finance Committee, the body that writes key energy tax legislation, had oil holdings. The chairman, Russell D. Long (D–La.), owned $1.2 million worth of oil and gas property and earned $100,000 from these sources in 1978. In the House, 18 of the 43 members of the Agricultural Committee owned farms or other farm interest, and the Senate Agricultural Committee included three members with farm holdings. The chairman, Herman E. Talmadge (D–Ga.), owned a 1,388-acre farm valued at between $1 million and $2 million.[11]

Community of interest with constituents, the pre-office financial situation of the members, and the logic of assigning people to committees where their prior experience can be put to use make some conflict of interest inevitable. Nor is it suggested that we should only elect princes or paupers. But the long history of conflict between investments and committee assignments calls into question the motivations behind important decisions. It would not be unreasonable to require that a member sell holdings that conflict with committee assignments. At the very least, the codes should prohibit members of Congress from making investments while in office that create conflict-of-interest situations. Investments can create a direct relationship between legislators and special interests and make their attitudes one and the same. The end result can affect us because the connection may determine winners and losers in the legislative struggle. These post-election actions are avoidable and should not be tolerated.

CAN WE LEGISLATE MORALITY?

Can Congress enact laws that would have prevented the Abscam scandal? The answer is probably not. As one member of the House Committee on Standards of Official Conduct put it, "I don't know what kind of code we could pass to deal with this. The allegations here are simply plain old violations of the law." And Senator Lowell P. Weicker, Jr. (R–Conn.) asked, "If the allegations are true, would they [the members implicated]—under any code—have reported the money?"[12]

What Congress should do is make disclosure regulations more meaningful by requiring the reporting of the actual dollar value of investments, prohibit the acquisition of investments that create a conflict of interest with committee assignments, and perhaps ban a member from receiving honoraria from groups with a direct and obvious interest in present or future activities of the committees the member serves on.

Of course, public financing of congressional campaigns would eliminate a great deal of the clout of special interests. But it is unrealistic to expect incumbents, with their campaign fundraising advantage, to guarantee themselves a well-financed opponent in every race.

While Congress bears a responsibility for enacting and enforcing a reasonable set of ethical standards, the internal rules and laws can not cover every contingency. Senator Adlai E. Stevenson (D–Ill.), who headed the Ethics Committee, said, "Every time you try to legislate morality by prohibiting certain forms of misconduct, you end up by implication permitting everything you don't prohibit."[13] A vigilant press, an alert public, political opponents who avail themselves of the information provided by public disclosure, and constituencies that will not tolerate major violations of public trust share with Congress the role of creating and maintaining a high standard of ethics.

Questions of ethics are woven into the entire legislative process. But the recent reforms, if further strengthened, may lead to a public realization that Cabell Phillips of the *New York Times* was correct when, in 1967, he said:

> Congress is neither as doltish as the cartoonists portray it nor as noble as it portrays itself. While it has its quota of knaves and fools it has a fair share of knights. And sandwiched between these upper and nether crusts is a broad and representative slice of upper-middle-class America.[14]

Glossary: Learning Your Way Around*

Congress, like any work environment, has its own vocabulary. The following glossary presents a lexicon of some commonly used congressional terms. Familiarity with them is essential for an appreciation of the congressional environment.

ACT: The term for legislation which has passed both houses of Congress and has been signed by the President or passed over his veto, thus becoming law. Also used technically for a bill that has been passed by one House and engrossed. (*See* Engrossed Bill).

ADJOURNMENT SINE DIE: Adjournment without definitely fixing a day for reconvening; literally "adjournment without a day." Usually used to connote the final adjournment of a session of Congress. A new session usually begins on January 3 and can continue until noon, January 3, of the following year.

ADJOURNMENT TO A DAY CERTAIN: Adjournment under a motion or resolution which fixes the next time of meeting. Neither House can adjourn for more than three days without the concurrence of the other. A session of Congress is not ended by adjournment to a day certain.

AMENDMENT: Proposal of a member to alter the language or stipulations in a bill or act. It is usually printed, debated, and voted upon in the same manner as a bill.

APPEAL: A Senator's challenge of a ruling or decision made by the presiding officer of the Senate. The Senator appeals to members of the chamber to override the decision. If carried by a majority vote, the appeal nullifies the chair's ruling. Although rarely used, the same procedure is available in the House to appeal rulings made by the Speaker and the Chairman of the Committee of the Whole.

APPROPRIATION BILL: Grants the actual moneys usually approved by authorization bills, but not necessarily the total amount permissible under the authorization bill. An appropriation bill originates in the House, and normally is not acted on until its authorization measure is enacted. General appropriations bills are supposed to be enacted by the seventh day after Labor Day before the start of the fiscal year to which they apply. (*See* Continuing Appropriations.) In addition to general appropriation bills, there are two specialized types.

AUTHORIZATION BILL: Authorizes a program, specifies its general aim and conduct, and, unless "open-ended," puts a ceiling on moneys that can be used to finance it. Usually enacted before appropriation bill is passed. (*See* Contract Authorizations.)

BILLS: Most legislative proposals before Congress are in the form of bills, and are designated as HR (House of Representatives) or S (Senate) according to the house in which they originate and by a number assigned in the order in which they were introduced, from the beginning of each two-year congressional term. *Public bills* deal with general questions, and become *public laws* if approved by Congress and signed by the President. *Private bills* deal with individual matters such as claims against the govern-

* "Learning Your Way Around," *For New Employees of the United States House of Representatives*, 96th Congress, 2d session, pp. 71–88. Reprinted from the public domain.

ment, immigration and naturalization cases, land titles, etc., and become *private laws* if approved and signed.

The introduction of a bill, and its referral to an appropriate committee for action, follows the process given in "How Our Laws Are Made" (House Document No. 95–259). (*See also* Concurrent Resolution, Joint Resolution, Resolution.)

BILLS INTRODUCED: Any number of members may join in introducing a single bill. Many bills in reality are committee bills and are introduced under the name of the chairman of the committee or subcommittee as a formality. All appropriation bills fall into this category, as do many other bills, particularly those dealing with complicated, technical subjects. A committee frequently holds hearings on a number of related bills, and may agree on one of them or an entirely new bill. (*See* Clean Bill *and* By Request.)

BUDGET: The document sent to Congress by the President in January of each year estimating government revenue and expenditures for the ensuing fiscal year and recommending appropriations in detail. The President's budget message forms the basis for congressional hearings and legislation on the year's appropriations.

BY REQUEST: A phrase used when a Senator or Representative introduces a bill at the request of an executive branch agency or private organization but does not necessarily endorse the legislation.

CALENDAR: An agenda or list of pending business before committees or either chamber. The House uses five legislative calendars. (*See* Consent, Discharge, House, Private, *and* Union Calendars.)

In the Senate, all legislative matters reported from committee are placed on a single calendar. They are listed in order, but may be called up irregularly by the Majority Leader either by motion, or by obtaining the unanimous consent of the Senate. Frequently the Minority Leader is consulted to assure unanimous consent. Only cloture can limit debate on bills thus called up. (*See* Call of the Calendar.)

The Senate also uses one nonlegislative calendar for treaties, etc. (*See* Executive Calendar.)

CALENDAR WEDNESDAY: In the House on Wednesdays, committees may be called in the order in which they appear in Rule X of the House Manual, for the purpose of bringing up any of their bills from the House or the Union Calendars, except bills which are privileged. General debate is limited to two hours. Bills called up from the Union Calendar are considered in Committee of the Whole. Calendar Wednesday is not observed during the last two weeks of a session, and may be dispensed with at other times by a two-thirds vote.

CALL OF THE CALENDAR: Senate bills which are not brought up for debate by a motion or a unanimous consent agreement are brought before the Senate for action when the calendar listing them in order is "called." Bills considered in this fashion are usually noncontroversial, and debate is limited to five minutes for each Senator on a bill or on amendments to it.

CAUCUS: An organization of members of the House or Senate. The organizations may be officially recognized, as are the majority (Democratic) and minority (Republican) caucuses, or they may be unofficial groups of members having shared legislative interests.

CHAMBER: Meeting place for the total membership of either the House or the Senate, as distinguished from the respective committee rooms.

CLEAN BILL: Frequently after a committee has finished a major revision of a bill, one of the committee members, usually the chairman, will assemble the changes plus what is left of the original bill into a new measure and introduce it as a "clean bill." The new measure, which carries a new number, is then sent to the floor for consideration.

CLERK OF THE HOUSE: Chief administrative officer of the House of Representatives. (*See* Secretary of the Senate.)

CLOTURE: The process by which a filibuster can be ended in the Senate, other than by unanimous consent. A motion for cloture can apply to any measure before the Senate, including a proposal to change the chamber's rules. It requires 16 Senators' signatures for introduction and the votes of three fifths of the entire Senate membership (60 if there are no vacancies), except that to end a filibuster against a proposal to amend the Standing Rules of the Senate a two-thirds vote of Senators present and voting is required. It is put to a roll-call vote one hour after the Senate meets on the second day following introduction of the motion. If voted, cloture limits each Senator to one hour of debate.

COMMITTEE: A subdivision of the House or Senate which prepares legislation for action by the respective house, or makes investigations as directed by the respective house. There are several types of committees. (See standing and select or special committee.) Most standing committees are divided into subcommittees, which study legislation, hold hearings, and report their recommendations to the full committee.

Only the full committee can report legislation for action by the House or Senate.

COMMITTEE OF THE WHOLE: The working title of what is formally "The Committee of the Whole House [of Representatives] on the State of the Union." Unlike other committees, it has no fixed membership. It is comprised of any 100 or more House members who participate—on the floor of the chamber—in debating or altering legislation before the body. Such measures, however, must first have passed through the regular committees and be placed on the calendar.

Technically, the Committee of the Whole considers only bills directly or indirectly appropriating money, authorizing appropriations, or involving taxes or charges on the public. Actually, the Committee of the Whole often considers other types of legislation. Because the Committee of the Whole need number only 100 Representatives, a quorum is more readily attained, and business is expedited.

When the full House resolves itself into the Committee of the Whole, it supplants the Speaker with a "chairman." The measure is debated or amended, with votes on amendments as needed. When the committee completes its action on the measure, it dissolves itself by "rising." The Speaker returns, and the full House hears the chairman of the Committee of the Whole report that group's recommendations. The full House then acts upon the recommendations.

At this time members may demand a roll-call vote on any amendment adopted in the Committee of the Whole.

CONCURRENT RESOLUTION: A concurrent resolution, designated H. Con. Res. or S. Con. Res., must be passed by both houses but does not require the signature of the President and does not have the force of law. Concurrent resolutions generally are used to make or amend rules applicable to both houses or to express the sentiment of the two houses. A concurrent resolution, for example, is used to fix the time for adjournment of a Congress.

CONFERENCE: A meeting between the representatives of the House and Senate to reconcile differences between the two houses over provisions of a bill. Members of the Conference Committee are appointed by the Speaker and the President of the Senate and are called "managers" for their respective house. A majority of the managers for each house must reach agreement on the provisions of the bill (often a compromise between versions approved by the House and Senate) before it can be sent up for floor action in the form of a "conference report." There it cannot be amended and if not approved by both houses, the bill goes back to conference. Elaborate rules govern the conduct of the conferences. All bills which are passed by House and Senate in slightly different form need not be sent to conference; either chamber may "concur" in the other's amendments. (*See* Custody of the Papers.)

CONGRESS: This term refers to the legislative branch of our national government. The Congress is composed of the House of Representatives and the Senate. The term *Congress* may also refer to the two-year long cycle of legislative meetings beginning on January 3 of each odd numbered year.

CONGRESSIONAL RECORD: The daily, printed account of proceedings in both House and Senate chambers, with debate, statements, and the like reported verbatim. (Members of Congress may edit and revise remarks made on the floor.) Committee activities are not covered, except that their reports to the parent body are noted. Highlights of legislative and committee action are embodied in a Digest section of the *Record,* and members of Congress are entitled to include material on items of general interest in an appendix known as "Extension of Remarks."

CONGRESSIONAL TERMS OF OFFICE: Begin on January 3 of the year following the general election and terminate in two years for the House and six years for the Senate.

CONSENT CALENDAR: Members of the House may place on the Consent Calendar any bill appearing on the Union or House Calendar which is considered to be noncontroversial. Bills on the Consent Calendar are normally called on the first and third Mondays of each month. On the first occasion when a bill is called in this manner, consideration may be blocked by the objection of any member. On the second time, if there are three objections, the bill is stricken from the Consent Calendar. If less than three members object, the bill is given immediate consideration.

A bill on the Consent Calendar may be postponed in another way. A member may ask that the measure be passed over "without prejudice." In that case, no objection is recorded against the bill, and its status on the Consent Calendar remains unchanged.

A bill stricken from the Consent Calendar remains on the Union or House Calendar.

CONTINUING APPROPRIATIONS: When a fiscal year begins and Congress has not yet enacted all the regular appropriation bills for that year, it passes a joint resolution "continuing appropriations" at rates generally based on the previous year's appropriations for government agencies not yet funded.

CONTRACT AUTHORIZATIONS: Found in both authorization and appropriation bills, these authorizations are stopgap provisions which permit the federal government to let contracts or obligate itself for future payments from funds not yet appropriated. The assumption is that funds will be available for payment when contracted debts come due.

CORRECTING THE RECORD: Rules prohibit members from changing their votes after the result has been announced. But frequently, hours, days, or months after a vote has been taken, a member announces that he was "incorrectly recorded." In the Senate, a request to change one's vote almost always receives unanimous consent. In the House, members are prohibited from changing their votes if tallied by the electronic voting system. If taken by roll call, a vote may be changed if consent is granted. Errors in the text of the *Record* may be corrected by unanimous consent.

CUSTODY OF THE PAPERS: To reconcile differences between the House and Senate versions of a bill, a conference may be arranged. The House with "custody of the paper"—the engrossed bill, engrossed amendments, messages of transmittal—is the only body empowered to request the conference. That body then has the advantage of acting last on the conference report when it is submitted.

DILATORY MOTION: A motion, usually made upon a technical point, for the purpose of killing time and preventing action on a bill. The rules outlaw dilatory motions, but enforcement is largely within the discretion of the presiding officer.

DISCHARGE A COMMITTEE: Relieve a committee from jurisdiction over a measure before it.

In the House, if a committee does not report a bill within 30 days after the bill was referred to it, any member may file a discharge motion. This motion, treated as a petition, needs the signatures of 218 members (a majority of the House).

If a resolution to consider a bill (see rule) is held up in the Rules Committee for more than seven legislative days, any member may enter a motion to discharge the committee. The motion is handled like any other discharge petition in the House.

Occasionally, to expedite noncontroversial legislative business, a committee is discharged upon unanimous consent of the House, and a petition is not required. (For Senate procedure, *see* Discharge Resolution.)

DISCHARGE CALENDAR: The House calendar to which motions to discharge committees are referred when the necessary 218 signatures have been obtained.

DISCHARGE MOTION: In the House, a motion to discharge a committee from considering a bill. If passed by a majority, the bill is brought to the floor for consideration without being reported by the committee. Alternatively, a discharge petition requires signatures of 218 House members.

DISCHARGE RESOLUTION: In the Senate, a special motion any Senator may introduce to relieve a committee from consideration of a bill before it. The resolution can be called up on motion for approval or disapproval, in the same manner as other matters of Senate business. (For House procedure, *see* Discharge a Committee.)

DIVISION VOTE: Same as standing vote. (See below.)

ENACTING CLAUSE: Key phrase in bills saying, "Be it enacted by the Senate and House of Representatives. . . ." A successful motion to strike the enacting clause from legislation kills the measure.

ENGROSSED BILL: The final copy of a bill as passed by one House, with the text as amended by floor action and certified to by the Clerk of the House or the Secretary of the Senate.

ENROLLED BILL: The final copy of a bill which has been passed in identical form by both houses. It is certified to by an officer of the house of origin (House Clerk or Senate Secretary) and then sent on for signatures of the House Speaker, the Senate President, and the President of the United States. An enrolled bill is printed on parchment.

EXECUTIVE CALENDAR: An additional, nonlegislative calendar, in the Senate, on which presidential documents such as treaties and nominations are listed.

EXECUTIVE DOCUMENT: A document, usually a treaty, sent to the Senate by the President for consideration or approval. These are identified for each session of Congress as Executive A, 97th Congress, 1st Session; Executive B, etc. They are referred to committee in the same manner as other measures. Unlike legislative documents, however, treaties do not die at the end of a Congress, but reamin "live" proposals until acted on by the Senate or withdrawn by the President.

EXECUTIVE SESSION: Meeting of a Senate or a House committee (or, occasionally, of the entire membership) which only the group's members are privileged to attend. Frequently witnesses appear before committees meeting in executive session, and other members of Congress may be invited, but the public and press are not allowed to attend.

EXPENDITURES: The actual spending of money as distinguished from the appropriation of it. Expenditures are made by the disbursing officers of the Administration; appropriations are made only by Congress. The two are rarely identical: in any fiscal year expenditures may represent money appropriated one, two, or more years previously.

FILIBUSTER: A time-delaying tactic used by a minority in an effort to prevent a vote on a bill. The most common method is unlimited debate, but other forms of parliamentary maneuvering may be used. The stricter rules in the House make filibusters more difficult, but they may be attempted through various delaying tactics.

FISCAL YEAR: Financial operations of the government are carried out in a 12-month fiscal year, beginning on October 1 and ending on September 30. The fiscal year carries the date of the calendar year in which it ends.

FLOOR: The chamber in which the House or the Senate meets.

FLOOR MANAGER: A member, usually representing sponsors of a bill, who attempts to steer it through debate and revision to a final vote in the chamber. Floor managers are frequently chairmen or ranking members of the committee that reported the bill. Managers are responsible for apportioning the time granted supporters of the bill for debating it. The Minority Leader or the ranking minority member of the committee often apportions time for the opposition.

FRANK: The facsimile signature of a member of Congress used on envelopes in lieu of stamps for official outgoing mail.

GERMANE: Pertaining to the subject matter of the measure at hand. All House amendments must be germane to the bill. The Senate requires that amendments be germane only when they are proposed to general appropriation bills, bills being considered under cloture, or, often, when proceeding under an agreement to limit debate.

GRANTS-IN-AID: Payments by the federal government which aid the recipient state, local government, or individual in administering specified programs, services, or activities.

HEARINGS: Committee sessions for hearing witnesses. At hearings on legislation, witnesses usually include specialists, government officials and spokesmen for persons affected by the bills under study. Subpoena power may be used to summon reluctant witnesses. The public and press may attend "open" hearings, but are barred from "closed" or "executive" hearings.

HOPPER: Box on House Clerk's desk where bills are deposited on introduction.

HOUSE: The House of Representatives, as distinct from the Senate, although each body is a "house" of Congress.

HOUSE CALENDAR: Listing of public bills, other than appropriations or revenue measures, awaiting action by the House of Representatives.

IMMUNITY: Constitutional privilege protecting members of Congress from judicial actions concerning their legislative duties.

JOINT COMMITTEE: A committee composed of a specified number of members of both House and Senate. Usually a joint committee is investigative in nature. There are a few standing joint committees, such as the Joint Economic Committee and the Joint Committee on Taxation.

JOINT RESOLUTION: A joint resolution, designated H.J. Res. or S.J. Res., requires the approval of both houses and the signature of the President, just as a bill does, and has the force of law if approved. There is no real difference between a bill and a joint resolution. The latter is generally used in dealing with limited matters, such as a single appropriation for a specific purpose.

Joint resolutions also are used to propose amendments to the Constitution. They do not require presidential signature, but become a part of the Constitution when three fourths of the states have ratified them.

JOURNAL: The official record of the proceedings of the House and Senate. The Journal records the actions taken in each chamber, but unlike the *Congressional Record,* it does not include the verbatim report of speeches, debate, etc.

LAW: An act of Congress which has been signed by the President, or passed over his veto by the Congress. Laws are listed numerically by Congress; for example, the Civil Rights Act of 1964 (H.R. 7152) became Public Law 88–352 during the 88th Congress.

LEGISLATIVE DAY: The "day" extending from the time either house meets after an adjournment until the time it next adjourns. Because the House normally adjourns from day to day, legislative days and calendar days usually coincide. But in the Senate, a legislative day may, and frequently does, extend over several calendar days. (*See* Recess.)

LOBBY: Any group seeking to influence the passage or defeat of legislation. Originally the term referred to persons frequenting the lobbies or corridors of legislative chambers in order to speak to lawmakers.

The right to attempt to influence legislation is based on the First Amendment to the Constitution which says Congress shall make no law abridging the right of the people "to petition the government for a redress of grievances."

MAJORITY LEADER: Chief strategist and floor spokesman for the party in nominal control in either chamber. He is elected by his party colleagues.

MAJORITY WHIP: In effect, the assistant Majority Leader, in the House or Senate. His job is to help marshal majority forces in support of party strategy.

MANUAL: The official handbook in each house prescribing its organization, procedures, and operations in detail. The *House Manual* contains rules, orders, laws and resolutions affecting House business; the *Senate Manual* is the equivalent for that chamber. Both volumes contain previous codes under which Congress functioned and from which it continues to derive precedents. Committee powers are outlined. The rules set forth in the manuals may be changed by elaborate chamber actions also specified by the manuals.

MARKING UP A BILL: Going through a measure, usually in committee, taking it section by section, revising language, penciling in new phrases, etc. If the bill is extensively revised, the new version may be introduced as a separate bill, with a new number. (*See* Clean Bill.)

MEMORIAL: A request for congressional opposition or an objection from an organization or citizens' group to particular legislation or government practice under the purview of Congress. All communications, both supporting and opposing legislation, from state legislatures are embodied in memorials which are referred to appropriate committees.

MINORITY LEADER: Floor leader for the minority party. (*See* Majority Leader.)

MINORITY WHIP: Performs duties of Whip for the minority party. (*See* Majority Whip.)

MORNING HOUR: The time set aside at the beginning of each legislative day for the consideration of regular routine business. The "hour" is of indefinite duration in the House, where it is rarely used. In the Senate it is the first two hours of a session following an adjournment, but it can be terminated earlier if the morning business has been completed. This business includes such matters as messages from the President, communications from the heads of departments, messages from the House, the presentation of petitions and memorials, reports of standing and select committees, and the introduction of bills and resolutions.

During the first hour of the morning hour in the Senate, no motion to proceed to the consideration of any bill on the calendar is in order except by unanimous consent. During the second hour, motions can be made but must be decided without debate. Senate committees may meet while the Senate is in the morning hour.

MOTION: Request by a member of Congress for any one of a wide array of parliamentary actions. He "moves" for a certain procedure, or the consideration of a measure or a vote, etc. The precedence of motions, and whether they are debatable, is set forth in the House and Senate Manuals.

NOMINATIONS: Appointments to office by the Executive Branch of the government, subject to Senate confirmation.

NOTICE QUORUM CALL: In the Committee of the Whole House a notice quorum call may be made by the chairman when the point of order is made that a quorum is not present. If 100 members, which constitute a quorum in the Committee of the Whole House, appear within the specified time period, the notice quorum call is not recorded. If 100 members fail to appear, a regular quorum call, which is recorded, is made. (*See* Quorum.)

OMNIBUS CLAIMS BILL: See Private Calendar.

ONE-MINUTE SPEECHES: Addresses by House members at the beginning of a legislative day. The speeches may cover any subject, but are limited strictly to one minute's duration. By unanimous consent, members may also be recognized to address the House for longer periods after completion of all legislative business for the day. Senators, by unanimous consent, are permitted to make speeches of a predetermined length during "morning hour."

OVERRIDE A VETO: If the President disapproves a bill and sends it back to Congress with his objections, Congress may override his veto by a two-thirds vote in each chamber. The Constitution requires a yea-and-nay roll call. The question put to each house is: "Shall the bill pass, the objections of the President to the contrary notwithstanding?" (*See also* Pocket Veto *and* Veto.)

PAIR: Historically, a gentleman's agreement between two lawmakers on opposite sides to withhold their votes on roll calls so the absence of one from Congress will not affect the outcome of a recorded vote.

In the House, "live" and "general" pairs are used. When a vote is taken, the names of members paired are printed in the *Congressional Record* with a record of the vote. A "live" pair indicates how a member would have voted; a "general" pair gives no such indication.

PARLIAMENTARIAN: The officer charged with advising the presiding officer regarding questions of procedure.

PETITION: A request or plea sent to one or both chambers from an organization or private citizen's group asking support of particular legislation or favorable consideration of a matter not yet receiving congressional attention. Petitions are referred to appropriate committees for appropriate action. (*See* Memorial.)

POCKET VETO: The act of the President in withholding his approval of a bill after Congress has adjourned—either for the year or for a specified period. However, the U.S. District Court of Appeals for the District of Columbia on August 14, 1974, upheld a congressional challenge to a pocket veto used by President Richard Nixon during a six-day congressional recess in 1970, declaring that it was an improper use of the pocket veto power. When Congress is in session, a bill becomes law without the President's signature if he does not act upon it within 10 days, excluding Sundays, from the time he gets it. But if Congress adjourns within that 10-day period, the bill is killed without the President's formal veto.

POINT OF ORDER: An objection raised by a Member of Congress that the House is departing from rules governing its conduct of business. The objector cites the rule violated, the chair sustaining his objection if correctly made. Order is restored by the chair's suspending proceedings until it conforms to the prescribed "order of business." Members sometimes raise a "point of no order"—when there is noise and disorderly conduct in the chamber.

PRESIDENT OF THE SENATE: Presiding officer of the Senate, normally the Vice President of the United States. In his absence, a President *pro tempore* (president for the time being) presides.

PRESIDENT PRO TEMPORE: The chief officer of the Senate in the absence of the Vice President. He is elected by his fellow Senators. The recent practice has been to elect to the office the Senator of the majority party with longest continuous service.

PREVIOUS QUESTION: In this sense, a "question" is an "issue" before the House for a vote and the issue is "previous" when some other topic has superseded it in the attention of the chamber. A motion for the previous question, when carried, has the effect of cutting off all debate and forcing a vote on the subject originally at hand. If, however, the previous question is moved and carried before there has been any debate on the subject at hand and the subject is debatable, then 40 minutes of debate is allowed before the vote. The previous question is sometimes moved in order to prevent amendments from being introduced and voted on. The motion for the previous question is a debate-limiting device and is not in order in the Senate.

PRIVATE CALENDAR: Private House bills dealing with individual matters such as claims against the government, immigration, land titles, etc., are put on this calendar. Two members may block consideration of a private bill in the chamber. If blocked, it is then recommitted to committee. An "omnibus claims bill" is several private bills considered as one. As with any bill, no part of an omnibus claims bill may be deleted without a vote. When a private bill goes to the floor in this form, it can be defeated only by a majority of those present. The private calendar can be called on the first and third Tuesdays of each month.

PRIVILEGE: Privilege relates to the rights of members of Congress and to the relative priority of the motions and actions they may make in their respective chambers. The two are distinct. "Privileged questions" concern legislative business. "Questions of privilege" concern legislators themselves. (*See below.*)

PRIVILEGED QUESTIONS: The order in which bills, motions, and other legislative measures may be considered by Congress is governed by strict priorities. For instance, a motion to recommit can be superseded by a motion to table, and a vote would be forced on the latter motion only. A motion to adjourn, however, would take precedence over this one, and is thus considered of the "highest privilege."

PRO FORMA AMENDMENT: *See* Strike out the Last Word.

QUESTIONS OF PRIVILEGE: These are matters affecting members of Congress individually or collectively.

Questions affecting the rights, safety, dignity and integrity of proceedings of the House or Senate as a whole are questions of privilege of the House or Senate, as the case may be.

Questions of "personal privilege" relate to individual members of Congress. A member's rising to a question of personal privilege is given precedence over almost all other proceedings. An annotation in the House rules points out that the privilege of the member rests primarily on the Constitution, which gives him a conditional immunity from arrest and an unconditional freedom to speak in the House.

QUORUM: The number of members whose presence is necessary for the transaction of business. In the Senate and House, it is a majority of the membership (when there are no vacancies, this is 51 in the Senate and 218 in the House). A quorum is 100 in the Committee of the Whole House. If a point of order is made that a quorum is not present, the only business in order is either a motion to adjourn or a motion to direct the Sergeant at Arms to request the attendance of absentees or a quorum call indicating the presence of a sufficient number of members.

READINGS OF BILLS: Traditional parliamentary law required bills to be read three times before they were passed. This custom is of little modern significance except in rare instances. Normally the bill is considered to have its first reading when it is introduced and printed, by title, in the *Congressional*

Record. Its second reading comes when floor consideration begins and may be an actual reading of the bill. The third reading (usually by title) takes place when action has been completed on amendments.

RECESS: Distinguished from adjournment, a recess does not end a legislative day and therefore does not interfere with unfinished business. The rules in each house set forth certain matters to be taken up and disposed of at the beginning of each legislative day. The House usually adjourns from day to day. The Senate often recesses.

RECOMMIT TO COMMITTEE: A simple motion, made on the floor after deliberation on a bill, to return it to the committee which reported it. If approved, recommittal usually is considered a death blow to the bill. A motion to recommit may include instructions to the committee to report the bill again with specific amendments or by a certain date. Or the instructions may be to make a particular study, with no definite deadline for final action.

RECONSIDER A VOTE: A motion to reconsider the vote by which an action was taken has, until it is disposed of, the effect of suspending the action. In the Senate the motion can be made only by a member who voted on the prevailing side of the original question, or by a member who did not vote at all. In the House it can be made only by a member on the prevailing side.

A common practice after close votes in the Senate is a motion to reconsider, followed by a motion to table the motion to reconsider. On this motion to table, Senators vote as they voted on the original question, to enable the motion to table to prevail. The matter is then finally closed and further motions to reconsider are not entertained. In the House, as a routine precaution, a motion to reconsider usually is made every time a measure is passed. Such a motion almost always is tabled immediately.

Motions to reconsider must be entered in the Senate within the next two days of actual session after the original vote has been taken. In the House, they must be entered either on the same day or on the next succeeding day the House is in session.

RECORDED VOTE: A vote upon which each member's stand is individually made known. In the Senate, this is accomplished through a rollcall of the entire membership, to which each Senator on the floor must answer "yea," "nay," or, if he does not wish to vote, "present." Since January 1973, the House has used an electronic voting system both for yeas and nays and other recorded votes. (*See* Teller Vote.)

The Constitution requires yea-and-nay votes on the question of overriding a veto. In other cases, a recorded vote can be obtained by the demand of one fifth of the members present.

REPORT: Both a verb and a noun, as a congressional term. A committee which has been examining a bill referred to it "reports" its findings and recommendations to the whole body when the committee returns the measure. The process is called "reporting" a bill.

A "report" is the document setting forth the committee's explanation of its action. House and Senate reports are numbered separately and are designated S. Rept. or H. Rept. Conference reports are numbered and designated in the same way as regular committee reports.

Most reports favor a bill's passage. Adverse reports are occasionally submitted, but more often, when a committee disapproves a bill, it simply fails to report it at all. When a committee report is not unanimous, the dissenting committeemen may file a statement of their views, called minority views and referred to as a minority report. Sometimes a bill is reported without recommendation.

RESCISSION: An item in an appropriation bill rescinding, or cancelling, funds previously appropriated but not spent. Also, the repeal of a previous appropriation by the President to cut spending, if approved by Congress under procedures in the Budget and Impoundment Control Act of 1974.

RESOLUTION: A simple resolution, designated H. Res. or S. Res., deals with matters entirely within the prerogatives of one house or the other. It requires neither passage by the other chamber nor approval by the President, and does not have the force of law. Most resolutions deal with the rules of one house. They also are used to express the sentiments of a single house, as condolences to the family of a deceased member or to give "advice" on foreign policy or other executive branch business. (*See also* Concurrent *and* Joint Resolutions.)

RIDER: A provision, usually not germane, which its sponsor hopes to have approved more easily by tacking it on to other legislation. Riders become law if the bills in which they are included become law. Riders providing for legislation in appropriation bills are outstanding examples, though technically they are banned. The House, unlike the Senate, has a strict germaneness rule; thus riders are usually Senate devices.

RULE: The term has two specific congressional meanings. A rule may be a standing order governing the conduct of House or Senate business and listed in the chamber's book of rules. The rules deal with duties of officers, order of business, admission to the floor, voting procedures, etc.

In the House, a rule also may be a decision made by its Rules Committee about the handling of a particular bill on the floor. The committee may determine under which standing rule a bill shall be considered, or it may provide a "special rule" in the form of a resolution. If the resolution is adopted by the House, the temporary rule becomes as valid as any standing rule.

A special rule sets the time limit on general debate. It may also waive points of order against provisions of the bill in question or against specified amendments intended to be proposed to the bill. It may even forbid all amendments or all amendments except, in some cases, those proposed by the legislative committee which handled the bill. In this instance it is known as a "closed" or "gag" rule as opposed to an "open" rule which puts no limitation on floor amendments. (*See* Suspend the Rules.)

SECRETARY OF THE SENATE: Chief administrative office of the Senate, responsible for direction of duties of Senate employees, education of pages, administration of oaths, receipt of registration of lobbyists, and other activities necessary for the continuing operation of the Senate.

SELECT OR SPECIAL COMMITTEE: A committee set up for a special purpose and a limited time by resolution of either House or Senate. Most special committees are investigative in nature.

SENATORIAL COURTESY: Sometimes referred to as "the courtesy of the Senate," it is a general practice without written rule applied to consideration of executive nominations. In practice, generally it means nominations from a state are not to be confirmed unless they have been approved by the Senators of the President's party of that state, with other Senators following their lead in the attitude they take toward such nominations.

SERGEANT AT ARMS: The officer charged with maintaining order in the chamber, under the direction of the Speaker or presiding officer.

SESSION OF CONGRESS: Each Congress is composed of two sessions. A new session of Congress begins each January 3 at noon and continues until adjourned "sine die." (See adjournment sine die.)

SINE DIE: *See* Adjournment sine die.

SLIP LAWS: The first official publication of a bill that has been enacted into law. Each is published separately in unbound, single-sheet or pamphlet form. Slip laws usually become available two to three days after the date of presidential approval.

SPEAKER: The presiding officer of the House of Representatives, elected by its members.

SPECIAL SESSION: A session of Congress which takes place after Congress has adjourned sine die. Special sessions are convened by the President of the United States under his constitutional powers.

STAND: A lawmaker's position, for or against, on a given issue or vote. He can make known his stand on a rollcall vote by answering "yea" or "nay," by "pairing" for or against, or by "announcing" his position to the House or Senate. (*See* Pair, *and* Recorded Vote, above. *See also* Teller Vote, below.)

STANDING COMMITTEES: A group permanently provided for by House and Senate rules. The standing committees of the House were last reorganized by the Committee Reorganization Act of 1974. Senate committees were reorganized in the Legislative Reorganization Act of 1946 and by a special resolution in 1977.

STANDING VOTE: A nonrecorded vote used in both House and Senate. A standing vote, also called a division vote, is taken as follows: Members in favor of a proposal stand and are counted by the presiding officer; then members opposed stand and are counted. There is no record of how individual members voted. In the House, the presiding officer announces the number for and against. In the Senate, usually only the result is announced.

STATUTES-AT-LARGE: A chronological arrangement of the laws enacted in each session of Congress. Though indexed, the laws are not arranged by subject matter nor is there an indication of how they affect previous law. (See U.S. Code.)

STRIKE FROM THE RECORD: Remarks made on the House floor may offend some member, who moves that the offending words be "taken down" for the Speaker's cognizance, and then expunged from the verbatim report carried in the *Congressional Record*.

STRIKE OUT THE LAST WORD: A motion by which House members are entitled to speak for a fixed time on a measure then being debated by the chamber. A member gains recognition from the chair by moving to strike out the last word of the amendment or section of the bill then under consideration. The motion is pro forma, and customarily requires no vote.

SUBSTITUTE: A motion, an amendment, or an entire bill introduced in place of pending business. Passage of a substitute measure kills the original measure by supplanting it. A substitute may be amended.

SUPPLEMENTAL APPROPRIATIONS: An appropriation to cover the difference between an agency's regular appropriation and the amount deemed necessary for it to operate for the full fiscal year.

SUSPEND THE RULES: Often a time-saving procedure for passing bills in the House. The wording of the motion, which may be made by any member recognized by the Speaker, is: "I move to suspend the rules and pass the bill . . . ." A favorable vote by two thirds of those present is required for passage. Debate is limited to 40 minutes and no amendments from the floor are permitted. If a two-thirds favorable vote is not attained, the bill may be considered later under regular procedures. The suspension procedure is in order on the first and third Mondays and Tuesdays of each month.

TABLE A BILL: The motion to "lay on the table" is not debatable in either house, and is usually a method of making a final, adverse disposition of a matter. In the Senate, however, different language is sometimes used. The motion is worded to let a bill "lie on the table," perhaps for subsequent "picking up." This motion is more flexible, merely keeping the bill pending for later action, if desired.

TELLER VOTE: In the House, members file past tellers and are counted as for or against a measure, but they are not recorded individually. The teller vote is not used in the Senate. In the House, tellers are ordered upon demand of one fifth of a quorum. This is 44 in the House, 20 in the Committee of the Whole.

The House also has a recorded teller vote procedure, introduced in 1971 (now largely supplanted by electronic voting), under which the individual votes of members are made public just as they would be on a yea-and-nay vote. (*See* Recorded Vote.)

TREATIES: Executive Branch proposals which must be submitted to the Senate for approval by two thirds of the Senators present. Before acting on such foreign policy matters, Senators usually send them to committee for scrutiny. Treaties are read three times and debated in the chamber much as are legislative proposals, but are rarely amended. After approval by the Senate, they are ratified by the President.

UNANIMOUS CONSENT: *See* Without Objection.

UNION CALENDAR: Bills that directly or indirectly appropriate money or raise revenue are placed on this House calendar chronologically according to the date reported from committee.

U.S. CODE: A consolidation and codification of the general and permanent laws of the United States arranged by subject under 50 titles, the first six dealing with general or political subjects, and the other 44 alphabetically arranged from agriculture to war and national defense. The code is now revised every six years and a supplement is published after each session of Congress.

VETO: Disapproval by the President of a bill or joint resolution, other than one proposing an amendment to the Constitution. When Congress is in session, the President must veto a bill within 10 days, excluding Sundays, after he has received it; otherwise it becomes law with or without his signature. When the President vetoes a bill, he returns it to the House of its origin with a message stating his objections. The veto then becomes a question of high privilege. (*See* Override a Veto.)

When Congress has adjourned, the President may pocket veto a bill by failing to sign it. (*See* Pocket Veto.)

VOICE VOTE: In either House or Senate, members answer "aye" or "no" in chorus and the presiding officer decides the result. The term also is used loosely to indicate action by unanimous consent or without objection.

WHIP: See Majority Whip.

WITHOUT OBJECTION: Used in lieu of a vote on noncontroversial measures. If no member voices an objection, motions, amendments or bills are thus passed in either the House or the Senate. (*See* Illustration G.1 on p. 496.)

ILLUSTRATION G1 EXAMPLE OF A SENATE UNANIMOUS CONSENT RESOLUTION

The Senate, being less structured and more informal than the House, has no counterpart to the House Rules Committee which sets the terms of floor debate in the House. Although Senate rules permit unlimited debate (filibustering) and nongermane amendments, the time and terms of debate in the Senate are frequently agreed to informally through a unanimous consent rule of which the following is an example.

S. 1360 (ORDER NO. 310)

2.—*Ordered,* That when the Senate proceeds to the consideration of S. 1360 (Order No. 310), a bill to establish an Advisory Committee on Timber Sales Procedure appointed by the Secretary of Agriculture for the purposes of studying, and making recommendations with respect to, procedures by which timber is sold by the Forest Service, and to restore stability to the Forest Service timber sales program and provide an opportunity for congressional review, DEBATE on any amendment in the first degree shall be limited to 1 hour, to be equally divided and controlled by the mover of such and the manager of the bill, debate on any amendment in the second degree shall be limited to 30 minutes, to be equally divided and controlled by the mover of such and the manager of the bill, and debate on any debatable motion, appeal, or point of order which is submitted or on which the Chair entertains debate shall be limited to 20 minutes, to be equally divided and controlled by the mover of such and the manager of the bill: *Provided,* That in the event the manager of the bill is in favor of any such amendment or motion, the time in opposition thereto shall be controlled by the minority leader or his designee: *Provided further,* That no amendment that is not germane to the provisions of the said bill shall be received.

Ordered further, That on the question of FINAL PASSAGE of the said bill, debate shall be limited to 3 hours, to be equally divided and controlled, respectively, by the Senator from Idaho (Mr. Church) and the Senator from Oregon (Mr. Hatfield): *Provided,* That the said Senators, or any one of them, may, from the time under their control on the passage of the said bill, allot additional time to any Senator during the consideration of any amendment, debatable motion, appeal, or point of order. (July 28, 1977.)

Endnotes

1.1

1. U.S. Congress, Joint Committee on the Organization of the Congress, *Hearings,* part 3 (Washington, D.C.: Government Printing Office, 1945), pp. 670–71.
2. Two useful examples are Aaron Wildavsky, *The Politics of the Budgetary Process* (Boston: Little, Brown, 1964); and Samuel Huntington, *The Common Defense* (New York: Columbia University Press, 1961), esp. pp. 123–46.
3. Ralph K. Huitt, "What Can We Do About Congress?" *Milwaukee Journal,* part 5 (December 13, 1964), p. 1.
4. See Ralph K. Huitt, "Congressional Reorganization: The Next Chapter." Paper presented at the annual meeting of the American Political Science Association, Chicago, Illinois, September 8–12, 1964.
5. Ernest S. Griffith, *Congress: Its Contemporary Role* (New York: New York University Press, 1951), p. 7.
6. James Burnham, *Congress and the American Tradition* (Chicago: Henry Regnery, 1959), p. 276.
7. Ibid., pp. 277–78.
8. Willmoore Kendall, *The Conservative Affirmation* (Chicago: Henry Regnery, 1963), pp. 15, 30–31, 85.
9. Maj. Gen. Thomas A. Lane (USA, Ret.), in U.S. Congress, Joint Committee on the Organization of the Congress, *Hearings,* part 7 (Washington: Government Printing Office, 1965), p. 1090. Referred to hereafter as *Joint Committee Hearings* (1965).
10. Lane, *Joint Committee Hearings* (1965).
11. *Saturday Evening Post* (March 21, 1964), p. 10. See also the remarks of Senator Clark in *Joint Committee Hearings,* part 1 (1965), pp. 18–19.
12. Burnham, *Congress and the American Tradition,* p. 349.
13. Griffith, *Congress,* p. 3. See also Kendall, *The Conservative Affirmation,* pp. 41ff.
14. Ralph K. Huitt, "Congressional Organization in the Field of Money and Credit" in Commission on Money and Credit, *Fiscal and Debt Management Policies* (Englewood Cliffs, N.J.: Prentice-Hall, 1963), p. 494. For a discussion of the "defensive advantages" that minorities exercise in the congressional system, see David B. Truman, *The Governmental Process* (New York: Alfred A. Knopf, 1951), chapters 11 and 12.
15. See the discussion of numerical and concurrent majorities in Burnham, *Congress and the American Tradition,* chapters 24–25.
16. In a forthcoming analysis, John S. Saloma III distinguishes between "Presidential–Constitutionalists" and "Whigs," the latter of whom advocate strong congressional leadership and weak executives. See his "Congressional Performance: Evaluation and Implications for Reform" (in preparation). For an analysis that is vintage Whiggism, see Alfred de Grazia's *Republic in Crisis* (New York: Federal Legal Press, 1965).
17. Burnham, *Congress and the American Tradition,* p. 350.
18. *Wesberry* v. *Sanders,* 376 U.S. 1 (1964). In the wake of this decision, House Judiciary Committee Chairman Emanuel Celler (D–N.Y.) sponsored a bill (H.R. 5505) during the 89th Congress that would require congressional districts to deviate no more than 15 percent (greater or less) from the average size in a given state. The bill also specifies that districts be of "contiguous territory, in as compact form as practicable."
19. See Andrew Hacker, "The Voice of 90 Million Americans," *The New York Times Magazine* (March 4, 1962).
20. See Martin Shapiro, *Law and Politics on the Supreme Court* (New York: Free Press of Glencoe, 1964), pp. 50–75.
21. Some ideologues (from both right and left) have urged a polarization of our two parties into a Liberal and a Conservative party. Such a development would most probably be dysfunctional for conservatives favoring the literary theory of Congress since polarization would reduce the legislative "braking" function of dispersed, decentralized parties.
22. A dissenter here is Samuel P. Huntington, who argues that centralized congressional leadership would revivify Congress. For reasons that will become apparent in the following sections, this development might actually have the opposite effect. See Huntington, "Congressional Responses to the Twentieth Century," in *The Congress and America's Future,* ed. David B. Truman. (Englewood Cliffs, N.J.: Prentice-Hall, 1965).
23. *Federalist,* 70.
24. Leonard D. White, *The Federalists* (New York: Macmillan, 1956), p. 510. "Statist" methods and democratic objectives find their convergence in Herbert Croly, *The Promise of American Life,* ed. Arthur M. Schlesinger, Jr. (Cambridge, Mass.: Harvard University Press, 1965).
25. Richard Bolling, *House Out of Order* (New York: E. P.

Dutton & Co., 1965), p. 27. On the Jeffersonian strategy, see James M. Burns, *The Deadlock of Democracy* (Englewood Cliffs, N.J.: Prentice-Hall, 1963), chapter 2. A thorough historical review is provided in Wilfred Binkley, *The President and Congress* (New York: Alfred A. Knopf, 1947).

26. Edward S. Corwin, *The President, Office, and Powers,* 4th ed. (New York: New York University Press, 1957), p. 272.
27. Clinton Rossiter, *The American Presidency* (New York: New American Library), p. 151. See also Richard Neustadt, *Presidential Power: The Politics of Leadership* (New York: John Wiley & Sons, 1960).
28. "Strength to Govern Well," *Washington Post* (July 4, 1963), p. A19.
29. Walter Lippmann, *The Public Philosophy* (Boston: Little, Brown, 1954), pp. 54–57.
30. The case is put in two of Burns' books, *Congress on Trial* (New York: Harper & Brothers, 1949), and *Deadlock of Democracy* (Englewood Cliffs, N.J.: Prentice-Hall, 1963).
31. December 17, 1962. Reprinted in *Congressional Quarterly Weekly Report* (December 21, 1962), p. 2278.
32. Burns, *Deadlock,* p. 337. For a remarkably similar analysis, see Burnham, *Congress and the American Tradition* p. 327.
33. Woodrow Wilson, *Constitutional Government in the United States* (New York: Columbia University Press, 1908), p. 68. See also Corwin, chapter 1.
34. Burns, *Congress on Trial,* p. 59.
35. Joseph S. Clark, *Congress: The Sapless Branch* (New York: Harper & Row, 1964), p. 30.
36. *Ibid.,* p. 235.
37. Lippmann, *The Public Philosophy,* p. 30.
38. Chet Holifield (D–Calif.) in *Joint Committee Hearings,* part 2 (1965), p. 185.
39. Lippmann, *The Public Philosophy,* p. 30. For a description of these congressional roles in military policy making, see Samuel P. Huntington, *The Common Defense,* pp. 123–146.
40. Joseph P. Harris, *Congressional Control of Administration* (Washington, D.C.: Brookings Institution, 1964), p. 295. Also see Walter Lippmann in *Newsweek* (January 20, 1964), pp. 18–19.
41. See, for example, Robert Dahl, *Congress and Foreign Policy* (New York: Harcourt, Brace & Co., 1950), p. 143.
42. Clark, *Congress,* p. 109. See also Holifield in *Joint Committee Hearings* (1965).
43. For an exposition of the Fulbright viewpoint, see James A. Robinson, *Congress and Foreign Policy-Making* (Homewood, Ill: Dorsey Press, 1962), pp. 13 and 212–214.
44. American Political Science Association, Committee on Political Parties, *Toward a More Responsible Two-Party System* (New York: Rinehart & Co., 1950), p. 1.
45. Burns, *Congress on Trial,* pp. 142–43.
46. A discussion of theories of the political party is found in Samuel Eldersveld, *Political Parties: A Behavioral Analysis* (Chicago: Rand-McNally, 1964).
47. *Toward a More Responsible Two-Party System,* pp. 15ff.
48. Burns, *Congress on Trial,* p. 110.
49. *Toward a More Responsible Two-Party System,* p. 57 (italics in the original).
50. Bolling, *House Out of Order,* p. 242.
51. *Toward a More Responsible Two-Party System,* pp. 88–89.
52. *Toward a More Responsible Two-Party System,* pp. 57–64. See also Burns, *Deadlock,* pp. 327–332; and Bolling, *House Out of Order,* pp. 239ff.

2.1

1. The wording of the questions used in this analysis can be found in the codebook for the 1978 election study available from the Inter-University Consortium for Political and Social Research (ICPSR, 1979). Since both the sample and the survey instrument were designed primarily to study House races, the data are not ideal for the purpose of comparing Senate and House voting. Some questions asked about House candidates were not repeated for the Senate candidates. In addition, the number of respondents in states with Senate races is less than optimal and these respondents are concentrated in a relatively small number of heavily populated states. Nevertheless, these limitations do not seriously jeopardize the validity of the findings reported in this article.
2. The correlation (tau) between ideological proximity and perceived ideological distance was .26 for Senate incumbents and .15 for House incumbents.
3. Two recent studies of campaign spending in congressional elections have concluded that higher spending by challengers significantly improves their performance while spending by incumbents has little effect (Glantz, Abramowitz, and Burkart, 1977; Jacobson, 1978).

2.2

1. Donald E. Stokes and Warren E. Miller, "Party Government and the Saliency of Congress," chapter 11 in Angus Campbell et al., *Elections and the Political Order* (New York: John Wiley & Sons, 1966), p. 205. The same may not be true among, say, mayors.
2. *Ibid.,* p. 204. The likelihood is that Senators are also better known than their challengers, but that the gap is not so wide as it is on the House side. There is no hard evidence on the point.
3. In Clapp's interview study, "Conversations with more than 50 House members uncovered only one who seemed to place little emphasis on strategies designed to increase communications with the voter." The exception was an innocent freshman. Charles L. Clapp (see #4 for particulars).
4. A statement by one of Clapp's Congressmen: "The best speech is a nonpolitical speech. I think a commencement speech is the best of all. X says he has never lost a precinct in a town where he has made a commencement speech." See Charles L. Clapp, *The Congressman: His Work as He Sees It* (Washington, D.C.: Brookings Institution. 1963), p. 96.
5. These and the following figures on member activity are from Donald C. Tachenon and Morris K. Udall, *The Job of the Congressman* (Indianapolis: Bobbs Merrill, 1966), pp. 283–288.
6. Another Clapp Congressman: "I was looking at my TV film today—I have done one every week since I have

been here—and who was behind me but Congressman X. I'll swear he had never done a TV show before in his life but he only won by a few hundred votes last time. Now he has a weekly television show. If he had done that before he wouldn't have had any trouble.'' Clapp, *The Congressman,* p. 92.

7. On questionnaires generally see Walter Wilcox, ''The Congressional Poll—and Non-Poll,'' in eds. Edward C. Dreyer and Walter A. Rosenbaum, *Political Opinion and Electoral Behavior* (Belmont, Calif.: Wadsworth, 1966), pp. 390–400.
8. Ellen Szita, Ralph Nader Congress Project profile on George E. Shipley (D., Ill.) (Washington, D.C.: G. Rossman, 1972), p. 12. The Congressman is also a certified diver. ''When Shipley is home in his district and a drowning occurs, he is sometimes asked to dive down for the body. 'It gets in the papers and actually, it's pretty good publicity for me,' he admitted.'' p. 3. Whether this should be classified under ''casework'' rather than ''advertising'' is difficult to say. (Congress Project profiles referred to in future footnotes will be called ''Nader profiles'' for short. For all of them the more complete citation is the one given here.)
9. Lenore Cooley, Nader profile on Diggs, p. 2.
10. Anne Zandman and Arthur Magida, Nader profile on Flood, p. 2.
11. Norman C. Miller, ''Yes, You are Getting More Politico Mail. And It Will Get Worse,'' *The Wall Street Journal,* March 6, 1973, p. 1.
12. Monthly data compiled by Albert Cover.
13. After serving his two terms, the late President Eisenhower had this conclusion: ''There is nothing a Congressman likes better than to get his name in the headlines and for it to be published all over the United States.'' From a 1961 speech quoted in *The New York Times,* June 20, 1971.
14. In practice the one might call out the Army and suspend the Constitution.
15. These have some of the properties of what Lowi calls ''distributive'' benefits. Theodore J. Lowi, ''American Business, Public Policy, Case-Studies, and Political Theory,'' *World Politics* 16 (1964), p. 690.
16. On casework generally see Kenneth G. Olson, ''The Service Function of the United States Congress,'' in American Enterprise Institute, *Congress: The First Branch of Government* (Washington, D.C.: American Enterprise Institute for Public Policy Research, 1966), pp. 337–74.
17. Sometimes without justification. Thus this comment by a Republican member of the House Public Works Committee: ''The announcements for projects are an important part of this. . . . And the folks back home are funny about this—if your name is associated with it, you get all the credit whether you got it through or not.'' James T. Murphy, ''Partisanship and the House Public Works Committee,'' Paper presented to the annual convention of the American Political Science Association, 1968, p. 10.
18. ''They've got to *see* something; it's the bread and butter issues that count—the dams, the post offices and the other public buildings, the highways. They want to know what you've been doing.'' A comment by a Democratic member of the House Public Works Committee. *Ibid.*
19. The classic account is in E. E. Schattschneider, *Politics, Pressures, and the Tariff* (New York: Prentice-Hall, 1935).
20. ''Israeli Schools and Hospitals Seek Funds in Foreign-Aid Bill,'' *The New York Times,* October 4, 1971, p. 10.
21. Richard F. Fenno, Jr., *Congressmen in Committees* (Boston: Little, Brown, 1973), p. 40. Cf. this statement on initiative in the French Third Republic: ''Most deputies ardently championed the cause of interest groups in their district without waiting to be asked.'' Bernard E. Brown, ''Pressure Politics in France,'' *Journal of Politics* 18 (1956), p. 718.
22. For a discussion of the politics of tax loopholes, see Stanley S. Surrey, ''The Congress and the Tax Lobbyist—How Special Tax Provisions Get Enacted,'' *Harvard Law Review* 70 (1957), pp. 1145–82.
23. A possible example of a transaction of this sort: During passage of the 1966 ''Christmas tree'' tax bill, Sen. Vance Hartke (D–Ind.) won inclusion of an amendment giving a tax credit to a California aluminum firm with a plant in the Virgin Islands. George Lardner, Jr., ''The Day Congress Played Santa,'' *The Washington Post,* December 10, 1966, p. 10. Whether Hartke was getting campaign funds from the firm is not wholly clear, but Lardner's account allows the inference that he was.
24. Thus this comment of a Senate aide, ''The world's greatest publicity organ is still the human mouth. . . . When you get somebody $25.00 from the Social Security Administration, he talks to his friends and neighbors about it. After a while the story grows until you've single-handedly obtained $2,500 for a constituent who was on the brink of starvation.'' Donald R. Matthews, *U.S. Senators and Their World* (Chapel Hill: University of North Carolina Press, 1960). p. 226.
25. For some examples of particularistically oriented Congressmen, see the Nader profiles by Sven Holmes on James A. Haley (D–Fla.), Newton Koltz on Joseph P. Addabbo (D–N.Y.), Alex Berlow on Kenneth J. Gray (D–Ill.), and Sarah Glazer on John Young (D–Tex.). For a fascinating picture of the things House members were expected to do half a century ago, see Joe Martin, *My First Fifty Years in Politics* (New York: McGraw-Hill, 1960), pp. 55–59.
26. Michael Barone, Grant Ujifusa, and Douglas Matthews, *The Almanac of American Politics* (Boston: Gambit, 1972), pp. 479–80.
27. Any teacher of American politics has had students ask about Senators running for the Presidency (Goldwater, McGovern, McCarthy, any of the Kennedys), ''But what bills has he passed?'' There is no unembarrassing answer.
28. Fenno, *Congressmen in Committees,* pp. 242–55.
29. In the terminology of Stokes, statements may be on either ''position issues'' or ''valence issues.'' Donald E. Stokes, ''Spatial Models of Party Competition,'' chapter 9 in Campbell, et al., *Elections and the Political Order,* pp. 170–74.
30. Clapp, *The Congressman,* p. 108. A difficult borderline question here is whether introduction of bills in Congress should be counted under position taking or credit claiming. On balance probably under the former. Yet another Clapp congressman addresses the point: ''I in-

troduce about sixty bills a year, about 120 a Congress. I try to introduce bills that illustrate, by and large, my ideas—legislative, economic, and social. I do like being able to say when I get cornered, 'Yes, boys, I introduced a bill to try to do that in 1954.' To me it is the perfect answer." *Ibid.*, p. 141. But voters probably give claims like this about the value they deserve.

31. On floor speeches generally see Matthews, *U.S. Senators,* p. 247. On statements celebrating holidays cherished by ethnic groups, Hearings on the Organization of Congress before the Joint Committee on the Organization of the Congress, 89th Congress, 1st session, 1965, p. 1127; and Arlen J. Large, "And Now Let's Toast Nicolaus Copernicus, the Famous German," *The Wall Street Journal,* March 12, 1973, p. 1.
32. Sometimes members of the Senate ostentatiously line up as "cosponsors" of measures—an activity that may attract more attention than roll-call voting itself. Thus in early 1973, seventy-six senators backed a provision to block trade concessions to the U.S.S.R. until the Soviet government allowed Jews to emigrate without paying high exit fees. " 'Why did so many people sign the amendment?' a northern Senator asked rhetorically. 'Because there is no political advantage in not signing. If you do sign, you don't offend anyone. If you don't sign, you might offend some Jews in your state.' " David E. Rosenbaum, "Firm Congress Stand on Jews in Soviet Is Traced to Efforts by Those in U.S.," *The New York Times,* April 6, 1973, p. 14.
33. ". . . an utterly hopeless proposal and for that reason an ideal campaign issue." V. O. Key, Jr., *Southern Politics* (New York: Alfred A. Knopf, 1949), p. 232.
34. Instructions on how to do this are given in Tacheron and Udall, *Job of the Congressman,* pp. 73–74.
35. William Lazarus, Nader profile on Edward R. Roybal (D–Cal.), p. 1.
36. On obfuscation in congressional position taking see Raymond A. Bauer, Ithiel de Sola Pool, and Lewis A. Dexter, *American Business and Public Policy* (New York: Atherton, 1964), pp. 431–32.
37. "Elaborate indexes of politicians and their records were kept at Washington and in most of the states, and professions of sympathy were matched with deeds. The voters were constantly apprised of the doings of their representatives." Peter H. Odegard, *Pressure Politics: The Story of the Anti-Saloon League* (New York: Columbia University Press, 1928), p. 21.
38. On Farm Bureau dealings with congressmen in the 1920s see Orville M. Kile, *The Farm Bureau through Three Decades* (Baltimore: Waverly Press, 1948), chapter 7.
39. V. O. Key, Jr., "The Veterans and the House of Representatives: A Study of a Pressure Group and Electoral Mortality," *Journal of Politics* 5 (1943), pp. 27–40.
40. "The American Medical Association: Power, Purpose, and Politics in Organized Medicine," 63 *Yale Law Journal* (1954), pp. 1011–18. See also Richard Harris, *A Sacred Trust* (New York: New American Library, 1966).
41. On the NRA generally, see Stanford N. Sesser, "The Gun: Kingpin of 'Gun Lobby' Has a Million Members, Much Clout in Congress," *The Wall Street Journal,* May 24, 1972, p. 1. On the defeat of Sen. Joseph Tydings (D–Md.) in 1970: "Tydings himself tended to blame the gun lobby, which in turn was quite willing to take the credit. 'Nobody in his right mind is going to take on that issue again [i.e., gun control],' one Tydings strategist admitted." John F. Bibby and Roger H. Davidson, *On Capitol Hill: Studies in the Legislative Process* (Hinsdale, Ill.: Dryden Press, 1972), p. 50.
42. A cautious politician will not be sure of an issue until it has been tested in a campaign. Polling evidence is suggestive, but it can never be conclusive.
43. David Prios, *Who Makes the Laws?* (Cambridge, Mass.: Schenkman, 1972), p. 29. Magnuson was chairman of the Senate Commerce Committee. "Onto the old Magnuson, interested in fishing, shipping, and Boeing Aircraft, and running a rather sleepy committee, was grafted a new one: the champion of the consumer, the national legislative leader, and the patron of an energetic and innovative legislative staff." *Ibid.* p. 78.
44. Marjorie Hunter, "Hollings Fight on Hunger Is Stirring the South," *The New York Times,* March 8, 1969, p. 14. The local reaction was favorable. "Already Senator Herman E. Talmadge, Democrat of Georgia, has indicated he will begin a hunger crusade in his own state. Other Senators have hinted that they may do the same."
45. Robert Griffith, *The Politics of Fear: Joseph R. McCarthy and the Senate* (New York: Hayden, 1970), p. 29. Richard Rovere's conclusion: "McCarthy took up the Communist menace in 1950 not with any expectation that it would make him a sovereign of the assemblies, but with the single hope that it would help him hold his job in 1952." Richard Rovere, *Senator Joe McCarthy* (Cleveland: World, 1961), p. 120.
46. Robert A. Schoenberger, "Campaign Strategy and Party Loyalty: The Electoral Relevance of Candidate Decision-Making in the 1964 Congressional Elections," *American Political Science Review* 63 (1969), pp. 515–20.
47. Robert S. Erikson, "The Electoral Impact of Congressional Roll Call Voting," *American Political Science Review* 65 (1971), p. 1023.
48. Griffith, *The Politics of Fear,* pp. 122–31. The defeat of Sen. Millard Tydings (D–Md.) was attributed to resources (money, endorsements, volunteer work) conferred or mobilized by McCarthy. "And if Tydings can be defeated, then who was safe? Even the most conservative and entrenched Democrats began to fear for their seats, and in the months that followed, the legend of McCarthy's political power grew." *Ibid.*, p. 123.
49. Paul H. Douglas, *In the Fullness of Time* (New York: Harcourt Brace Jovanovich, 1972).
50. Barone, et al., *Almanac of American Politics,* p. 53. Maillaird was given a safer district in the 1972 line drawing.
51. On member freedom, see Bauer, et al., *American Business and Public Policy,* pp. 406–07.
52. Linda M. Kupferstein, Nader profile on William A. Barrett (D–Pa.), p. 1. This profile gives a very useful account of a machine Congressman's activities.
53. One commentator on New York detects "a tendency for the media to promote what may be termed 'press release politicians.' " A result is that "younger members tend to gravitate towards House committees that have high rhetorical and perhaps symbolic importance, like Foreign Affairs and Government Operations, rather than those with bread-and-butter payoffs." Donald Haider, "The New York City Congressional Delegation," *City Almanac* (published bimonthly by the

Center for New York City Affairs of the New School for Social Research), vol. 7, no. 6, April 1973, p. 11.

54. Leo M. Snowiss, "Congressional Recruitment and Representation," *American Political Science Review* 60 (1966), pp. 627–39.
55. The term is from Joseph A. Schlesinger, *Ambition and Politics: Political Careers in the United States* (Chicago: Rand McNally, 1966), p. 10.
56. *Ibid.*, p. 92; Matthews, *U.S. Senators*, p. 55. In the years 1953–72 three House members were appointed to the Senate, and 85 gave up their seats to run for the Senate. Thrity-five of the latter made it, giving a success rate of 41 percent.
57. Thus upstate New York Republicans moving to the Senate commonly shift to the left. For a good example of the advertising and position-taking strategies that can go along with turning a House member into a Senator, see the account on Sen. Robert P. Griffin (R–Mich.) in James M. Perry, *The New Politics* (New York: Clarkson N. Potter, 1968), chapter 4.
58. Fenno, *Congressmen in Committees*, pp. 141–42.
59. "Thurmond Image Seen as Changing," *The New York Times*, October 17, 1971, p. 46.

3.1

REFERENCES

Asher, H. B. "Committees and the Norm of Specialization." *Annals of the American Academy of Political and Social Science* 411 (January 1974): 63–74.

Corson, J. J., and R. S. Paul. *Men Near the Top*. Baltimore: Johns Hopkins University Press, 1966.

Davidson, R. H. "Congress and the Executive: The Race for Representation," in *Congress: The First Branch of Government*. Edited by A. De Grazia. Garden City, N.Y.: Doubleday. 1967.

Fenno, R. F., Jr. *The President's Cabinet*. New York: Vintage, 1959.

———. *Congressmen in Committees*. Boston: Little, Brown, 1973.

———. *Home Style: House Members in Their Districts*. Boston: Little, Brown, 1978.

Foss, P. O. *Politics and Grass*. Seattle: University of Washington Press, 1960.

Heclo, H. *A Government of Strangers: Executive Politics in Washington*. Washington, D.C.: Brookings Institution, 1977.

Huntington, S. P. "Congressional Responses to the Twentieth Century." In *Congress and America's Future*. 2d ed. Edited by D. B. Truman. Englewood Cliffs, N.J.: Prentice-Hall, 1973.

Kilpatrick, F. P., M. C. Cummings, and M. K. Jennings. *The Image of the Federal Service*. Washington, D.C.: Brookings Institution, 1963.

Lowi, T. J. "How the Farmers Get What They Want." In *Legislative Politics U.S.A.* 3d ed. Edited by T. J. Lowi and R. B. Ripley. Boston: Little, Brown, 1973.

Mayhew, D. R. *Congress: The Electoral Connection*. New Haven, Conn.: Yale University Press, 1974.

Neustadt, R. E. "Politicians and Bureaucrats." In *Congress and America's Future*. 2d ed. Edited by D. B. Truman. Englewood Cliffs, N.J.: Prentice-Hall, 1973.

Polsby, N. W. "Institutionalization in the House of Representatives." *American Political Science Review* 62 (March 1968): 144–68.

Price, H. D. "The Congressional Career—Then and Now." In *Congressional Behavior*. Edited by N. W. Polsby. New York: Random House, 1971.

Ripley, R. B. *Power in the Senate*. New York: St. Martin's Press, 1969.

Stanley, D. T. *The Higher Civil Service*. Washington, D.C.: Brookings Institution, 1964.

Stanley, D. T., D. E. Mann, and J. W. Doig. *Men Who Govern*. Washington, D.C.: Brookings Institution, 1967.

Wilensky, H. L. *Organizational Intelligence*. New York: Basic Books, 1967.

Witmer, T. R. "The Aging of the House." *Political Science Quarterly* 79 (December 1964): 526–41.

3.2

1. Although the question has not been studied systematically or in great detail, this conclusion seems to be fair on the basis of a number of case studies. See, for instance, Richard F. Fenno, Jr., *The Power of the Purse* (Boston: Little, Brown, 1966, pp. 646 ff.; Gilbert Y. Steimer, *The Congressional Conference Committee* (Urbana: University of Illinois Press, 1954); James M. Landis, "The Legislative History of the Securities Act of 1933." *George Washington Law Review* 28 (1959–60): 19–29: or the following recent comment by Senator Lee Metcalf (formerly a member of the House Ways and Means Committee): "No matter what the Finance Committee does or the Senate does, when we come back from conference with the House we have given in to Wilbur Mills. He runs both committees" (*Washington Post*, January 14, 1969).
2. Nelson W. Polsby, Miriam Gallaher, and Barry Spencer Rundquist. "The Growth of the Seniority System in the U.S. House of Representatives," *American Political Science Review* (in press; to appear in September 1969), goes into the history of seniority more fully. See also Michael Abram and Joseph Cooper, "The Rise of Seniority in the House of Representatives," *Polity* 1 (Fall 1968): 52–85.
3. Nelson W. Polsby, "Two Strategies of Influence: Choosing a Majority Leader, 1962." in *New Perspectives on the House of Representatives*, ed. R. L. Peabody and N. W. Polsby (Chicago: Rand McNally, 1963), p. 211.
4. Different points of view on the nature of the Senate are expressed by William S. White, *The Citadel* (New York: Harper & Row, 1956); Donald Matthews, *U.S. Senators and Their World* (Chapel Hill: University of North Carolina Press, 1960); Joseph S. Clark, *et al.*, *The Senate Establishment* (New York: Hill and Wang, 1963); and Ralph K. Huitt and Robert L. Peabody, *Congress: Two Decades of Analysis* (New York: Harper & Row, 1969), especially pp. 159–208.
5. A more familiar view of Senate specialization may be found in Matthews. *U.S. Senators*.

3.4

1. While the discussion here focuses on Congressional district offices, the study is based on research conducted

during 1974 in Los Angeles County, California, and which included the district office operations of all 91 federal, state, and local office holders who were maintaining legislative field offices in Los Angeles County that year. Thus, the sample here includes 20 House offices plus two Senate offices, along with 69 state and local offices. In many ways the district office activities of, for example, Los Angeles City Councilmen or California State Assemblymen (both of whom have generous staff resources) are indistinguishable from those of L.A.-based Congressmen. That is especially true when all share the same constituency. Accordingly, some of the data to be presented here as well as some of the discussion applies to legislative district offices in general, irrespective of level of government. During the research, some 130 political aides were interviewed. The interviews, which generally involved the aide in charge of each district operation, averaged 70 minutes in length and followed elaborate printed formats. In a few cases, incumbents were also interviewed. (These data were supplemented in 1976 by interviews with district aides to Colorado Congressmen.) All interviewees were promised anonymity; therefore, quotes, anecdotes, and data are attributed to office types rather than specific individuals.

2. There has been relatively little research done on Congressional activities outside of Washington, D.C. The major work, of course, is Richard F. Fenno, Jr., *Home Style: House Members in Their Districts* (Boston: Little, Brown, 1978). See also John D. Cranor and Joseph W. Westphal, "Congressional District Offices, Federal Programs, and Electoral Benefits," paper presented at the 1978 Meeting of the Midwest Political Science Association, April 20–22, 1978; Jamie R. Wolf, "A Congressman's Day at the District Office," *The Washington Monthly,* April 1974, pp. 45–57; "House Members Use District Offices in Increasing Number, Many Different Ways," *Staff* 8 (94th Congress); "Senate Use of State Offices Shows Highly Varied Pattern," *Staff* 4 (94th Congress). *Staff,* a publication very useful in these matters, was published until March 1979 by the now defunct House Commission on Information and Facilities. A number of the back issues of *Staff* are reproduced in the *Final Report of the House Commission on Information and Facilities,* 95th Congress, 1st Session, House Document No. 95–22, December 1976. See also the author's Ph.D. dissertation, from which this paper is drawn: "Political Staffing: A View from the District," UCLA, 1975.

3. Steven H. Schiff, "Congressional Office Management, with Emphasis on the Assignment of Staff to District Offices," Paper presented at the American Political Science Association Convention, Washington, D.C., September 2, 1979.

4. A number of district offices use part-time employees—typists who come in once a week, caseworkers who work one or two days a week, lawyers and PR specialists on call for when their expertise is needed. If these people were to be carried on the payroll they would count as one of the 18 allowable employees. The solution is to rotate part-timers on and off the payroll at irregular intervals but to utilize their services regularly and as needed. In one House office I visited, a political science professor worked full-time during the summers and academic breaks and was available as a consultant year round. He was actually paid whenever "holes" in the payroll were available—regardless of whether or not they coincided with the periods he worked. In another congressional office the top aide that I interviewed, as well as the press aide, were off the payroll—for three months—in order to campaign. Their combined salaries of some $5,000 per month were being reallocated to various part-time workers to compensate them for work already done and work that would be expected in 1975. Of the 435 Representatives, 107 appeared to be using this payroll shuffle technique. They were culled from the House payroll reports as employing 21 or more clerks in a six-month period during fiscal year 1974 *and* having one or more persons who rotate on and off the payroll. The House payrolls (and other office expenditures) can be found in *Report of the Clerk of the House,* published twice annually. The practice of shuffling the payroll is perfectly legal, but it involves a serious complication. If a staffer were to be injured or taken ill or die while working in a Congressional office—but not carried on the payroll at that particular time—he or she would be ineligible for the various disability compensations, death gratuities, survivor premiums, and other benefits normally available. A lesser problem is the fact that the payroll shuffling itself can involve a considerable number of manhours—and becomes an added management burden for offices that follow the practice.

5. W. C. Love, Jr., "The Congressman as Educator," Unpublished master's thesis, MIT, August 1966. Also see John S. Saloma III, *Congress and the New Politics* (Boston: Little, Brown, 1969), pp. 174–77.

6. Saloma, *Congress and the New Politics,* p. 185.

7. For an excellent discussion of this matter and of Congressional casework in general, see John R. Johannes, "Congressional Caseworkers: Attitudes, Orientations, and Operations," Paper delivered at the 1978 annual meeting of the Midwest Political Science Association Meeting, Chicago, April 20–22, 1978, pp. 20–23.

8. John R. Johannes, "Casework as a Technique of Congressional Oversight of the Executive," paper presented at the 1978 Annual Meeting of the American Political Science Association, New York City, August 31–September 3, 1978.

9. Saloma, *Congress and the New Politics,* p. 192. Charles L. Clapp, *The Congressman: His Work as He Sees It* (Garden City, N.Y.: Anchor Books, 1963) pp. 74, 84, 94. Michael Walter advised in his political how-to-do-it book: "One last thing: the records kept in the office—mailing lists, financial reports, correspondence—are very important, necessary if political activity is to be sustained for any length of time or renewed after some temporary setback. Someone should look after them, and activists should insist that they are in fact looked after by people they know and trust." Michael Walters, *Political Action* (Chicago: Quadrangle Books, 1971), p. 47.

10. David Mayhew, *Congress: The Electoral Connection* (New Haven, Conn.: Yale University Press, 1974), p. 5.

11. Larry Light, "Crack Outreach Programs No Longer Ensure Re-election," *Congressional Quarterly Weekly Report,* February 14, 1981, pp. 316–18.

12. U.S. Congress, Joint Committee on the Organization of Congress, Hearings Pursuant to S. Con. Res. 2, (May 24, 1965), p. 264.

13. Morriss P. Fiorina, *Congress: Keystone of the Washington Establishment* (New Haven, Conn.: Yale University Press, 1977).

3.5

1. Decentralization of operations generally involves the assignment of staff to handle casework, and in some instances federal projects and press work, in state offices. See, for example, the discussion in the Commission study, "Constituent Services." In addition, some Senators are increasing the number of state (field) offices. Space limitations on Capitol Hill and decentralization of federal agencies are factors influencing these changes. One result may be that managerial problems of coordination and overview of office operations will become more dificult.
2. The degree of "integration" varies. There are cases of committee staff performing noncommittee work, but the thrust in most instances is to regularize personnel policies.
3. Other Commission studies deal with salaries and conditions of employment, uniformity of or various congressional employee groups.
4. The October 1976 pay raise for federal government employees resulted in increased clerk-hire allowances for Senators; the range in now $449,063 to $902,301.

4.1

1. On the Rules Committee, which sets the House agenda, the majority party enjoys a two-to-one edge, while on the committees responsible for raising and spending federal revenues—Ways and Means, Appropriations, and Budget—the majority party holds at least 60 percent of the seats. Republicans were outraged in 1981 when Democrats continued to hold 65 percent of the Ways and Means seats.
2. The one exception is the Rules Committee, whose Democratic members are appointed by the Speaker. Also on Rules, unlike other committees, Democrats' tenure need not be respected by the Speaker.
3. Democrats call their full membership the Caucus, while Republicans refer to theirs as the Conference. House Republicans have an intermediate step, with the Executive Committee's work being reviewed by the full Committee on Committees before referral to the Conference.
4. The House Appropriations Committee is an exception to this practice. The Democratic Caucus approves nominees to chair the subcommittees of this one committee.

REFERENCES

Bullock, Charles S., III. "Initial Committee Assignments of the 92nd Congress." Paper presented at the annual meeting of the Southwest Political Science Association, Dallas, Texas, 1973.

______. "House Committee Assignments." In *The Congressional System*. 2d ed. Edited by Leroy N. Rieselbach. North Scituate, Mass.: Duxbury, 1979, pp. 58–86.

Shepsle, Kenneth A. *The Giant Jigsaw Puzzle*. Chicago: University of Chicago Press, 1978.

Wolanin, Thomas R. "Committee Seniority and the Choice of House Subcommittee Chairmen: 80th–91st Congresses." *Journal of Politics* 36 (August 1974): 687–702.

4.2

1. Walter Bagehot discussed the dignified and efficient parts of English government in *The English Constitution* (World's Classics ed., London: Oxford University Press, 1928).

4.3

1. An excellent discussion of this problem will be found in: Robert Samberg, "Conceptualization and Measurement of Political System Output," unpublished manuscript (University of Rochester: Rochester, 1971).

5.4

1. The unanimous consent procedure expedites business on the floor but it is always subject to blockage by a single member of the Senate. The membership usually follows the majority leader in his procedural program; occasionally, however, a Senator deems his own position more important and objects.
2. An extreme partisan statement by Mr. Underwood of Alabama when he was leader of the Senate and when the Senate was considering passage of the Panama bill in the 63d Congress, might be noted in this connection:

   > I have served from one Democratic Administration to another. I have never scratched a party ticket; I have always endeavored to live up to and sustain my party's platform. . . . The Democratic Party, not I, wrote this provision as to free tolls in its platform. I believe this plank of the platform is right. . . . Believing it is right, there is but one position that I can take, and that is to sustain the position of my party as expressed in its convention and in its platform.

3. The leaders are also in charge of seeing when and what resolutions relative to *sine die* adjournment are to be called up and agreed to, for example: resolutions informing the President of the United States that Congress is ready to adjourn, resolutions congratulating the President of the Senate and President pro tempore for the manner in which they presided over the Senate during the year, and resolutions to authorize the Vice President or President pro tempore to sign duly enrolled bills, and to make certain authorized appointments during adjournments.

   In the case of the three-day adjournment or an adjournment for a longer period of time with the consent of the House, the leader is responsible either for making such a motion or submitting such a resolution for accomplishing that end, but he must also take many factors into consideration before taking such action. He must be aware of any legislation needing immediate enactment, how far along the Senate is in enacting its legislative program for the year, and the sentiments of the other members of the Senate.

In the case of adjournment for several days, it falls upon the leader to insure that necessary orders are obtained in advance—including orders to authorize the Secretary of the Senate to receive messages from the President of the United States or the House of Representatives, or to authorize the appropriate presiding officer of the Senate to sign duly enrolled bills during the adjournment.

5.5

1. Senate Republican Conference Rules, February 9, 1971, 2.
2. As assistant to the floor leader, the party Whip has responsibilities in several areas, including: (1) the scheduling and management of legislation; (2) keeping his party advised about proposed action on legislation; (3) securing party unity to insure that the legislative program is carried out; (4) remaining informed about national and international problems and the status of bills in standing committees; (5) dealing with all procedural questions on the floor; and (6) offering various technical motions relative to the organization of the Senate at the beginning of each new Congress. Since 1941, for example, the majority party Whip has announced the hour of meeting for the Senate. See Floyd M. Riddick, "Majority and Minority Leaders of the Senate." Senate Document 95–24 (Washington, D.C.: U.S. Government Printing Office, 1977).
3. Personal interview, Mr. Cecil Holland, administrative assistant to Sen. Robert Griffin. Washington, D.C., April 1972.
4. Marvin E. Stromer, "The Making of a Political Leader," (1969), 49.
5. Personal interview, Senator Thomas Kuchel. April 1970. Washington, D.C.
6. Personal interview, Senator Robert Griffin, Washington, D.C., April 1972.
7. *Congressional Record* (May 12, 1936), p. 7046.
8. Stromer, "Political Leader," p. 46.
9. Personal Interview, Sen. Leverett Saltonstall, November 1969, Boston, Mass.
10. David B. Truman, *The Congressional Party,* 1959, chapter 8.
11. *The New York Times,* March 29, 1934, p. 22.
12. Personal interview, Sen. Robert Griffin. Washington, D.C., April 1972.
13. Press release (1–77), Office of U.S. Senator Alan Cranston, January 5, 1977, p. 1.
14. Personal interview. Sen. Ted Stevens. Washington, D.C., February 1977.
15. It was reported, for example, that "the choice of Senator Humphrey for Democratic whip was intended to give the party's advanced liberal wing a greater voice in the leadership councils." See *The New York Times,* December 2, 1960, p. 24. Geography, too, may play a role in the selection of party whips. In 1956, Sen. George Smathers (D–Fla.) thought of seeking the whip position but stated that since a southerner, Lyndon Johnson of Texas, already held the floor leader's post, a geographic division in the leadership was desirable. See *The New York Times,* November 13, 1956, p. 1. For further discussion of the geographic aspects of Whip selection see Rowland Evans and Robert Novak, "Lyndon B. Johnson: The Exercise of Power" (1966), pp. 41–44.

5.6

REFERENCES

Davidson, R. H. "Congressional Committees: The Toughest Customers." *Policy Analysis* 2 (Spring 1976): 299–323.

Dreyfus, D. A. "The Limitation of Policy Research in Congressional Decision-making." *Policy Studies Journal* 4 (Spring 1976): 269–274.

Fenno, R. F. *Congressmen in Committees,* Boston: Little, Brown, 1973.

Havemann, J. "Congress Tries to Break Ground Zero in Evaluating Federal Programs." *National Journal,* May 22, 1976, pp. 706–13.

Jones, C. O. "Why Congress Can't Do Policy Analysis (or words to that effect)." *Policy Analysis* 2 (Spring 1976): 251–64.

———. "Somebody Must be Trusted: An Essay on Leadership of the U.S. Congress." In *Congress in Change: Evolution and Reform.* Edited by N. J. Ornstein. New York: Praeger Publishers, 1975.

———. *Party and Policy-Making: The House Republican Policy Committee.* New Brunswick, N.J.: Rutgers University Press, 1964.

Ripley, R. B. "Congressional Party Leadership and the Impact of Congress on Foreign Policy," in vol. 5 of Appendices to Report of the Commission on the Organization of the Government for the Conduct of Foreign Policy. Washington, D.C.: Government Printing Office, 1975.

———. "Congressional Party Leaders and Standing Committees." *Review of Politics* 36 (July 1974): 394–400.

Schick, A. "The Supply and Demand for Analysis on Capitol Hill." *Policy Analysis* 2 (Spring/1976): 215–34.

Stewart, J. G. "Central Policy Organs in Congress." In *Congress Against the President.* Edited by H. C. Mansfield. New York: Academy of Political Science, 1975.

5.7

1. John Dewey, *The Public and Its Problems* (New York: Holt, 1927), p. 149.
2. Alexis de Tocqueville, *Democracy in America* (New York: Alfred A. Knopf, 1945), p. 249.
3. T. V. Smith, *The Democratic Way of Life* (Chicago: University of Chicago Press, 1926), p. 185.
4. *Ibid.,* p. 191.
5. *Ibid.,* pp. 189–190.
6. Lindsay Rogers, *The American Senate* (New York: Alfred A. Knopf, 1926), p. ix.
7. Nelson W. Polsby, "Strengthening Congress in National Policymaking," in *Congressional Behavior,* ed. Nelson W. Polsby (New York: Random House, 1971), p. 7.
8. T. V. Smith, *The Legislative Way of Life* (Chicago: University of Chicago Press, 1940), p. 16.

9. "Will Reform Change Congress," in *The Role of Congress II* (New York: Time, Inc., 1975).
10. Rogers, *The American Senate,* p. 254.
11. *Ibid.,* p. 255.
12. Woodrow Wilson, *Congressional Government* (Boston: Houghton Mifflin, 1885), pp. 213–14.
13. Randall B. Ripley, *Power in the Senate* (New York: St. Martin's Press), p. 24.
14. Robert L. Peabody, *Leadership in Congress* (Boston: Little, Brown, 1976), p. 336.

5.8

1. On committee assignments, see Nicholas A. Masters, "Committee Assignments in the House of Representatives," *American Political Science Review* 55 (June 1961): 345–57. On the impact of seniority, see Barbara Hinckley, *The Seniority System in Congress* (Bloomington, Ind., 1971).
2. For the data supporting this example, see Randall B. Ripley, *Power in the Senate* (New York, 1969), pp. 62–63, 71–72.
3. See Richard F. Fenno, Jr., *Congressmen in Committees* (Boston, 1973), for a comparison of six House committees on many points, including partisanship. For additional detail on partisanship in the committees mentioned in the text see Frank Munger and Richard F. Fenno, Jr., *National Politics and Federal Aid to Education* (Syracuse, New York, 1962) on Education and Labor; John F. Manley, *The Politics of Finance* (Boston, 1970) on Ways and Means; and Richard F. Fenno, Jr., *The Power of the Purse* (Boston, 1966) on Appropriations.
4. On the impact of majority and minority status on congressional parties and party leaders, see Charles O. Jones, *The Minority Party in Congress* (Boston, 1970); and Randall B. Ripley, *Majority Party Leadership in Congress* (Boston, 1969).
5. The term *subgovernments* to describe this phenomenon comes from Douglass Cater, *Power in Washington* (New York, 1964). The term *whirlpools* for the same phenomenon comes from Ernest S. Griffith, *Congress: Its Contemporary Role* (New York, 1961).
6. For an analysis of the Republican Policy Committee in the early 1960s, see Charles O. Jones, *Party and Policy-Making* (New Brunswick, N.J., 1964).
7. This pattern is described in Ripley, *Power in the Senate*.

5.9

1. Among some of the better-known studies of the revolt are: Charles R. Atkinson, *The Committee on Rules and the Overthrow of Speaker Cannon* (New York: Columbia University Press, 1911); William Rea Gwinn, *Uncle Joe Cannon, Archfoe of Insurgency: A History of the Rise and Fall of Cannonism* (New York: Bookman Associates, 1957); Kenneth W. Hechler, *Insurgency: Personalities and Politics of the Taft Era* (New York: Columbia University Press, 1940), chapter 3; and James Holt, *Congressional Insurgents and the Party System, 1909–1916* (Cambridge Mass.: Harvard University Press, 1967), chapter 2. An effort to parallel the revolt against Cannon with the 1961 Rules Committee fight may be found in Charles O. Jones, "Joseph G. Cannon and Howard W. Smith: An Essay on the Limits of Leadership in the House of Representatives," *Journal of Politics* 30 (August 1968): 617–46.
2. Nelson W. Polsby, "The Institutionalization of the U.S. House of Representatives," *American Political Science Review* 62 (March 1968): 144–68; and Nelson W. Polsby, Miriam Gallaher, and Barry Spencer Rundquist, "The Growth of the Seniority System in the U.S. House of Representatives," *American Political Science Review* 63 (September 1969): 787–807.
3. Certainly not all of the authors listed here would agree totally with my characterization of the House, but their studies provide sufficient data to enable one to gain this portrait. In addition to the Polsby articles cited above, some of the recent books and articles which have tried to assess the contemporary House within an institutionalized context are: Michael Abram and Joseph Cooper, "The Rise of Seniority in the House of Representatives," *Polity* 1 (Fall 1968): 52–85; Roger H. Davidson, *The Role of the Congressman* (New York: Pegasus, 1969), esp. chapter 2; Samuel P. Huntington, "Congressional Responses to the Twentieth Century," in *The Congress and America's Future,* ed. David B. Truman (Englewood Cliffs, N.J.: Prentice-Hall, 1965), pp. 5–31; Charles O. Jones, *Every Second Year: Congressional Behavior and the Two-Year Term* (Washington, D.C.: Brookings Institution, 1967); Charles O. Jones, *The Minority Party in Congress* (Boston: Little, Brown, 1970); Randall B. Ripley, *Party Leaders in the House of Representatives* (Washington, D.C.: Brookings Institution, 1967); Randall B. Ripley, *Majority Party Leadership in Congress* (Boston: Little, Brown, 1969); Barbara Hinckley, *Stability and Change in Congress* (New York: Harper & Row, 1971); Robert L. Peabody, "Party Leadership Change in the United States House of Representatives," *American Political Science Review* 61 (September 1967): 675–693; and T. Richard Wittmer, "The Aging of the House," *Political Science Quarterly* 79 (December 1964): 526–41; and the articles by H. Douglas Price and Morris P. Fiorina, David W. Rohde, and Peter Wissel, in *Congress in Change: Evolution and Reform,* ed. Norman J. Ornstein (New York: Praeger Publishers, 1975), pp. 2–57.
4. Hinckley, *Stability and Change in Congress,* p. 121. She also deals with this subject in greater detail in "Congressional Leadership Selection and Support: A Comparative Analysis," *Journal of Politics* 32 (May 1970): 268–87, esp. pp. 275–78.
5. Peabody, "Party Leadership Change," pp. 687–688.
6. Robert L. Peabody, *Leadership in Congress: Stability, Succession, and Change* (Boston: Little, Brown, 1976), p. 443. Peabody also indicates that the implication of his earlier research that party differences were less important than status differences has been changed. He now sees the party identity factor in leadership change as "considerable" (p. 291).
7. The existence of party-related voting patterns is generally acknowledged. How much of the variations in the patterns is attributable to party factors is the debatable issue. Compare two entries in the debate: Cleo H.

Cherryholmes and Michael J. Shapiro, *Representatives and Roll Calls* (Indianapolis, Ind.: Bobbs-Merrill, 1969), pp. 106–10, on the importance of party influence; and Aage R. Clausen, *How Congressmen Decide: A Policy Focus* (New York: St. Martin's Press, 1973), pp. 91–100, for a caveat.

8. David R. Mayhew, *Party Loyalty among Congressmen: The Difference between Democrats and Republicans, 1947–1962* (Cambridge: Harvard University Press, 1966), pp. 148–60. Two nonacademic books make a similar argument: Dean Acheson, *A Democrat Looks at His Party* (New York: Harper and Brothers, 1955); and Milton Viorst, *Fall from Grace: The Republican Party and the Puritan Ethic,* rev. ed. (New York: Simon and Schuster, 1971), esp. chapter 5 on "The Lost Constituencies."

9. Joseph A. Schlesinger, "Political Careers and Party Leadership," in *Political Leadership in Industrialized Societies: Studies in Comparative Analysis,* ed. Lewis J. Edinger (New York: John Wiley & Sons, 1967), pp. 266–93, esp. pp. 280–84.

10. Wendell Bell, Richard J. Hill, and Charles R. Wright, *Public Leadership* (San Francisco: Chandler Publishing Co., 1961), p. 6.

11. William Loughton Smith of South Carolina was the initial chairman of Ways and Means as a standing committee. He was replaced in the Third Session of that Congress by Robert Goodloe Harper, also of South Carolina. Harper is the first party floor leader mentioned by DeAlva Stanwood Alexander in his chapter on floor leaders in *History and Procedure of the House of Representatives* (Boston: Houghton, Mifflin, 1916), p. 107. For an assessment of how and when the various leadership posts came into being in the House, see Garrison Nelson, "Leadership Position-Holding in the United States House of Representatives," *Capitol Studies* 4 (Fall 1976): 11–36.

12. Ripley indicates the presence of both positional leaders in his description of majority leadership patterns between 1861 and 1911. See his *Party Leaders,* p. 84. Thaddeus Stevens of Pennsylvania, Chairman of Ways and Means (1861–1865) was the first to chair the Appropriations Committee. Henry L. Dawes of Massachusetts chaired both Appropriations (1869–1871) and Ways and Means (1871–1875). In the years from 1880 through 1911 when the House Rules Committee functioned under the chairmanship of the Speaker, 24 of the other 38 committee assignments held by the two other majority members were from Ways and Means (17) and Appropriations (7).

13. Chang-Wei-Chiu, *The Speaker of the House of Representatives Since 1896* (New York: Columbia University Press, 1928), pp. 318–20. See also *The New York Times,* January 19, 1911, p. 1.

14. Prior to 1863, there were 13 multiballot speakership floor contests: the 3d (1793–1795); 6th (1799–1801); 9th (1805–1807); 11th (1809–1811); Second Session of the 16th (1820–1821); 17th (1821–1823); 19th (1825–1827); Second Session of the 23d (1834–1835); 26th (1839–1841); 30th (1847–1849); 31st (1849–1851); 34th (1855–1857); and the 36th (1859–1861) Congresses. See the *House Journals* for the relevant years and various issues of *Niles' Weekly Register* (Baltimore).

15. The only exception involved Frederick Gillett of Massachusetts, who was renominated by the Republican caucus in 1923 to be its candidate for Speaker, but it took nine ballots before he was able to gain the votes of 20 Republican members who cast their earlier ballots for Henry A. Cooper of Wisconsin and Martin B. Madden of Illinois. *House Journal,* 68th Congress, First Session, pp. 5–11.

16. Ripley, *Party Leaders,* p. 28. James R. Mann of Illinois was the first to be designated "Chairman of the Minority Conference," in the *Congressional Directory,* 62d Congress, 1st Session (May 1911), p. 190.

17. Randall B. Ripley, "The Party Whip Organizations in the United States House of Representatives," *American Political Science Review* 58 (September 1964): 561–76. Ripley, using Edward T. Taylor's *A History of the Committee on Appropriations,* House Document 299, 77th Congress, First Session (1941), p. 51, argues the case for Reed's appointment of Tawney in 1897.

18. Ripley, *Party Leaders,* p. 33. See also *The New York Times,* March 12, 1919, p. 1.

19. Ripley, *Party Leaders,* pp. 36–38.

20. The Democratic Caucus for the 94th Congress voted down a proposal to make the whip post an elective one, 138–32, *Congressional Quarterly Weekly Report* 33 (December 7, 1974), p. 3247. The organizing caucus for the 95th Congress "shouted down" the proposal without a vote, see the *Boston Globe* (December 9, 1976), p. 20.

21. See "Tawney Republican Leader," in *The New York Times,* December 3, 1905, p. 3. An early comment on Tawney's aggressive role may be found in "House Chiefs in Panic at Tawney's War Howl," *New York Times,* December 18, 1905, p. 9.

22. A list of the leaders selected for this study may be found in Garrison Nelson, "Appendix: Roster of Leaders of the United States House of Representatives, 1789–1976," *Capitol Studies* 4 (Fall 1976): 25–36.

23. Frederick A. C. Muhlenberg served as Speaker for both the Federalist First Congress (1789–1791) and the Democratic–Republican Third Congress (1793–1795); see William Henry Smith, *Speakers of the House of Representatives of the United States* (Baltimore: Simon J. Gaeng, 1928), p. 20. The other two leaders to serve under differing party majorities were John W. Taylor and Louis McLane, who served as Speaker and Ways and Means chairman respectively as National Republicans in the 19th Congress (1825–1827) after holding the same posts during the Democratic–Republican majorities earlier.

24. On Albert's election in 1962, see Nelson W. Polsby, "Two Strategies of Influence: Choosing a Majority Leader, 1962," in *New Perspectives on the House of Representatives,* ed. Robert L. Peabody and Nelson W. Polsby, 2d ed. (Chicago: Rand McNally, 1969), pp. 325–58. Specific references to Albert's service as Whip are made on pp. 335 and 342. Hale Boggs' victory is described in Larry L. King, "The Road to Power in Congress," *Harper's Magazine* 252 (June 1971): 39–63, esp. pp. 48 and 62 on the "leadership ladder." See also John F. Bibby and Roger H. Davidson, *On Capitol Hill: Studies in the Legislative Process,* 2d ed. (Hinsdale, Ill.: Dryden Press, 1972), pp. 124–44. O'Neill's position as Whip was mentioned in all of the news accounts covering his contests for leader and in these accounts, the pattern of ordered succession was

often described, see *The New York Times,* November 11, 1972, p. 20, and the editorial, "Potential Speaker," *New York Times,* November 24, 1972, p. 36. See also Peabody, *Leadership in Congress,* chapter 8.

25. Following the Democratic defeat in the 1946 congressional elections, Sam Rayburn purportedly intended to leave the House leadership to John McCormack. Opposition to McCormack from a number of southern members was strong enough to dissuade Rayburn and he reluctantly accepted the nomination as Minority Leader. He then appointed McCormack to be Whip. *New York Times,* January 3, 1947, pp. 1 and 4; and January 8, 1947, p. 14.
26. These terms come from Joseph A. Schlesinger, *Ambition and Politics: Political Careers in the United States* (Chicago: Rand McNally, 1966), p. 90 for *penultimate office,* and p. 46 for *career office*. There have been only three Republican Whips since 1933: Harry Englebright of California, 1933–1943; Leslie Arends of Illinois, 1943–1974; and Robert Michel of Illinois, 1975–present.
27. Hinckley, "Congressional Leadership," pp. 275–77.
28. O'Neill was nominated without a contest, but McFall finished fourth in a four-man field and was eliminated on the first ballot. See "House Democrats Elect Leaders, Slow Reforms," *Congressional Quarterly Weekly Report* 34 (December 11, 1976): 3291–95. The eventual winner, Jim Wright of Texas, defeated Philip Burton on the third ballot, 148–147.
29. In both the 1959 Martin–Halleck and 1965 Halleck–Ford contests, commentators noted the presence of style considerations and the absence of philosophical ones. See Charles O. Jones, *Party and Policy-Making: The House Republican Policy Committee* (New Brunswick, N.J.: Rutgers University Press, 1964), pp. 37–38; and Robert L. Peabody, *The Ford–Halleck Minority Leadership Contest* (New York: McGraw-Hill, 1966), p. 32
30. Caucus nominations in the Democratic party were contested in 1871, 1873, 1875, 1876, 1877, 1879, 1883, 1891, 1897, and 1899. See various editions of *The New York Times* and *The Washington Post*.
31. Caucus nominations in the Republican party were contested in 1881, 1883, 1885, and 1889.
32. Peabody, "Party Leadership Change," pp. 676–78.
33. Polsby, "The Institutionalization of the House," pp. 145–53.
34. *The New York Times,* February 28, 1925, p. 1. Longworth defeated Martin Madden of Illinois, 140–85 on the first ballot. Madden had been one of the two Republican candidates challenging speaker Gillet's reelection on the floor during the previous Congress.
35. *Congressional Quarterly Weekly Report* 31 (December 5, 1973): 3171.
36. Ripley asserts that "Chairmen of various party committees (for example, Committee on Committees, Steering Committee, Policy Committee) or of the party caucus or conference have *occasionally* been prominent figures in the majority party in the House," in *Majority Party Leadership in Congress,* pp. 3–4 (emphasis added). Jones states, "Although they have existed on occasion in both parties, until the 1960s policy or steering committees were not heavily relied on by the minority party," in *The Minority Party in Congress,* p. 38.
37. Rainey defeated John McDuffie of Alabama, who had served as Whip under Garner. The vote was decided on the first ballot: Rainey's 166 to McDuffie's 112. *New York Times,* March 3, 1933, p. 1. A fuller account of this contest may be found in Robert A. Waller, "The Selection of Henry T. Rainey as Speaker of the House," *Capitol Studies* 2 (Spring 1973): 37–47.
38. Albert defeated John Conyers of Michigan, 220–20. *Congressional Quarterly Weekly Report* 29 (January 22, 1971): 176.
39. The final tally on the second ballot was Boggs, 140; Udall, 88; and Sisk, 17; in *Congressional Quarterly Weekly Report* 29 (January 22, 1971): 176.
40. The most serious threat to Byrns came from Sam Rayburn, but Rayburn withdrew after Pennsylvania announced for Byrns. C. Dwight Dorough, *Mr. Sam* (New York: Random House, 1962), p. 253. See also *New York Times,* December 13, 1934, p. 17.
41. Both cases involved Philip P. Barbour of Virginia. He defeated Speaker John W. Taylor in 1821 and was later defeated for reelection as Speaker by Henry Clay two years later. See *Niles' Weekly Register* 21 (December 8, 1821): 234; and 25 (December 6, 1923): 22, respectively. One unusual case which does not technically qualify for this category occurred in 1834 when John Bell, a Whig, was elected to preside over the 2d Session of the Democratically controlled 23d Congress when the Democrats could not agree on a candidate. In the next Congress, the united Democrats elected James K. Polk over Bell. See *Niles' Weekly Register* 46 (June 7, 1834): 248; and *Niles' Weekly Register* 49 (December 12, 1835): p. 248 for the two contests.
42. This contest has been described earlier, see note 15, *supra*. See also Paul D. Hasbrouck, *Party Government in the House of Representatives* (New York: Macmillan, 1927), p. 19; and *New York Times,* December 6, 1923, pp. 1–2.
43. This may be seen in the decline of multiballot floor contests and the fact that the mean percentage of votes received by the top two Speakership candidates since 1865 in 58 regular and two special Speakership elections has been 98.86 percent. The lowest percentage was 93.4 in the 55th Congress (1899). The first ballot percentage in 1923 was 94.4 for Gillett and Garrett combined.
44. This information is derived from the accounts of two newspapers, *The New York Times* and *The Washington Post*. The first contest reported by the *Post* occurred in 1879. A number of caucus nominations were simply reported with no mention of the number of members present or the votes cast. When this happened, I recorded it as "no reported contest" and assumed that the nomination had met with no opposition.
45. Randall was defeated by Carlisle, 106–52; Samuel Cox received 30 votes. *New York Times,* December 3, 1883, p. 1.
46. Woodrow Wilson, *Congressional Government* (New York: Meridian Books, 1956), pp. 82–83. This book was originally published in Boston by Houghton, Mifflin in 1885.
47. *Congressional Quarterly Weekly Report* 27 (January 3, 1969): 2. Wilbur Mills received four votes.
48. Albert defeated Conyers by 202–25 in the 93d Congress. *Congressional Quarterly Weekly Report* 31 (January 6, 1973): 5. Conyers' opposition to Albert in

1971 was due to the Speaker's lack of support for an effort to strip three Mississippi members of their seniority. In 1973 he tried for support beyond the Black Congressional Caucus.

49. *New York Times,* February 28, 1919, p. 1.
50. Snell's nomination was made unanimous on the eighth ballot. His tally over Tilson on the seventh ballot was 96–64. *New York Times,* December 1, 1931, pp. 1 and 4.
51. Accounts of the Halleck–Martin contest may be found in Martin's own book, *My First Fifty Years in Politics* (New York: McGraw-Hill, 1960), pp. 12–19; and in Charles O. Jones, *Party and Policy-Making,* pp. 33–42. The Ford–Halleck struggle is covered by Robert L. Peabody in *The Ford–Halleck Minority Leadership Contest,* and in "Political Parties: House Republican Leadership," in *American Political Institutions and Public Policy: Five Contemporary Studies* ed. Allan P. Sindler (Boston: Little, Brown, 1969), pp. 181–229.
52. Noble E. Cunningham, Jr., *The Jeffersonian Republicans in Power: Party Operations, 1801–1890* (Chapel Hill: University of North Carolina Press, 1963), p. 88. Macon was a candidate for Speaker in the 11th Congress and lost to Varnum on the second ballot, 45–65. *Annuals of Congress,* 11th Congress, First Session, p. 56. Macon's relationship with Randolph is described by Cunningham on pp. 77, 86–88, and 230.
53. Muhlenberg was apparently not a contestant in the Second Congress. According to a letter from Elbridge Gerry to his wife, the two leading candidates were Jonathan Trumbull of Connecticut, who had lost to Muhlenberg in the previous Congress, and John Laurence of New York. The letter was dated October 24, 1791, and may be found in the Russell W. Knight Collection of Elbridge Gerry Papers in the Massachusetts Historical Society. Special thanks are extended to Prof. Patrick J. Furlong of the Department of History of Indiana University at South Bend for this reference.
54. Wood withdrew a week before the balloting amidst speculation that he was trying to arrange an appointment to the chairmanship of Ways and Means, which was not forthcoming. *New York Times,* December 1, 1875, p. 1. A fuller account of the 1875 election may be found in Albert V. House, "The Speakership Contest of 1875: Democratic Response to Power," *Journal of American History* 52 (September 1965): 252–74.
55. *The New York Times,* March 3, 1871, p. 1.
56. Knutson was described as a "Cannon pupil" at the time of the 1919 Whip contest. *New York Times,* March 12, 1919, p. 1. Four years later he voted for the leading insurgent candidate in the caucus, Henry A. Cooper of Wisconsin. *New York Times,* December 2, 1923, p. 1. The Republican Committee on Committees gave the post to Albert Vestal of Indiana. See the *Washington Post,* December 13, 1923, p. 5.
57. Richard E. Welch, Jr., *Theodore Sedgwick, Federalist: A Political Portrait* (Middletown, Conn.: Wesleyan University Press, 1965), p. 211n.
58. John Randolph in 1807, Ezekiel Bacon in 1812, William Lowndes in 1819, George McDuffie in 1831, Thomas Bayly in 1851, and J. Glancy Jones in 1858. Both Bacon and Jones were removed between sessions of a Congress. Serious questions existed about their fitness for floor leadership. Alexander, *History and Precedure of the House,* pp. 124–25.
59. Two chairmen of Ways and Means, William R. Morrison in 1877 and William Springer in 1893, one chairman of Appropriations, William S. Holman in 1893, and one Whip, Oscar Underwood in 1901, were removed from their appointive posts.
60. Waller, "The Selection of Henry T. Rainey," p. 45.
61. Ripley reports that Priest "decides not to continue as whip in 1955 because he had become Chairman of the Committee on Interstate and Foreign Commerce," in "Party Whip Organizations," eds. Peabody and Polsby, *New Perspectives,* 2d ed., p. 208n.
62. See Arthur Krock, "Rep. Ford's Defeat," *New York Times,* January 17, 1965, p. IV-13. Arends defeated Frelinghuysen 70–59. *New York Times,* January 15, 1965, p. 1.
63. These figures are based upon a recomputation of Table 10, "Violations of Seniority by Speaker, 1881–1910," in Polsby, Gallaher, and Rundquist, "The Growth of the Seniority System," p. 799.
64. Peabody, "Party Leadership Change," p. 688. Joe Martin certainly felt that the size of the 1958 defeat had cost him the minority leadership; see his book, *My First Fifty Years in Politics,* pp. 4–5.
65. The two Republican minority contests occurred in 1883 and 1885.
66. The four Democratic minority contests occurred in 1871, 1873, 1897, and 1899. The last contest took six ballots before James D. Richardson of Tennessee defeated David DeArmond of Missouri, 90–47. *New York Times,* December 3, 1899, p. 2.
67. James R. Mann was elected majority leader by the caucus after his defeat for the speakership nomination. He refused the post and Frank Mondell of Wyoming was elected. *The New York Times,* March 12, 1919, p. 1.
68. *New York Times,* March 5, 1867, p. 1.
69. *House Journal,* 38th Congress, First Session, p. 11.
70. Peabody, "Party Leadership Change," p. 687.
71. A case in point is that of "Tip" O'Neill, whose widespread popularity made his move from appointed Whip to elected floor leader without opposition. Peabody reports that Congressman Sam Gibbons of Florida, who had hoped to challenge O'Neill, told him, " 'Tip, I can tell you something that nobody else in this room can. You haven't got an enemy in the place.' " *Leadership in Congress,* p. 258.
72. David B. Truman, *The Congressional Party: A Case Study* (New York: John Wiley & Sons, 1959), pp. 205–208. A recent study suggests that the "middleman" role is adopted following the selection as leader rather than being a reason for the selection itself. See William E. Sullivan, "Criteria for Selecting Party Leadership in Congress: An Empirical Test," *American Politics Quarterly* 3 (January 1975): 25–44.
73. Hinckley, "Congressional Leadership," pp. 281–84.
74. Peabody, "Party Leadership Change," pp. 681–86. The fullest presentation of this typology may be found in *Leadership in Congress,* pp. 266–94.
75. Randall was renominated in 1877 with 75 percent of the votes on the first ballot (*New York Tribune,* October 15,

1877, p. 1); and in 1879 with 53 percent on the first ballot (*Washington Post,* March 18, 1879, p. 1).

76. Keifer defeated George D. Robinson of Massachusetts, 44–15. *New York Times,* December 2, 1883, p. 1. Six years later Reed received 85 votes of 166 cast in a second-ballot victory. *Washington Post,* December 1, 1889, p. 1. Cannon received 162 votes of 187 cast on the first ballot in 1909. *New York Times,* March 14, 1909, p. 1.
77. During the second period the number of committees increased from 38 in 1863 to 61 by 1905, the highest figure ever recorded for the House. See Lauros G. McConachie, *Congressional Committees* (New York: Thomas Y. Crowell, 1898), pp. 349–58, and various issues of the *Congressional Directory.* As a measure of the care with which committees were selected, the Speakers in the 25 Congresses from 1857–1907 averaged 42.2 days in making their final committee appointments. *Hinds Precedents of the House of Representatives of the United States* (Washington, D.C.: U.S. Government Printing Office, 1907), vol 4, p. 891.
78. The Democratic caucus in 1975 ended the chairmanship career of Representatives Wright Patman of Banking and Currency, W. R. Poage of Agriculture, and F. Edward Hebert of Armed Services. Two subcommittee chairmanships were also voided. *Congressional Quarterly Weekly Report* 33 (January 18, 1975): 114–18; (January 25, 1975): 210–12; and (February 1, 1975), p. 275. The most recent victim was Robert L. Sikes, who was stripped of his chairmanship of the Military Construction Subcommittee on January 26, 1977. *Congressional Quarterly Weekly Report* 35 (January 29, 1977): 159.
79. Peabody, "Party Leadership Change," pp. 692–93.
80. Keifer had become a serious embarrassment to many of his fellow House Republicans because of his intemperate attacks on the press and reports of nepotism in the staffing of his office. *New York Times,* March 7, 1883, p. 1. On the eve of the vote for Speaker of the 48th Congress he rebuffed suggestions that he not run for the Republican nomination. He won the caucus nomination, but only 59 of the Congress' 118 Republicans attended, and 15 of them voted against him. *New York Times,* December 2, 1883, p. 1.
81. Congresses in this category include: the 39th (1865–1867, 43d (1873–1875), 54th (1895–1897), 59th (1905–1907), 66th (1919–1921), 67th (1921–1933), 69th (1925–1927), 71st (1929–1931), 80th (1947–1949), and the 83d (1953–1955).

6.1

1. *Constitution, Jefferson's Manual, and Rules of the House of Representatives,* 94th Congress, 2d Session, House Document No. 94–663, pp. 121–22.
2. U.S. Congress, Senate, *Congressional Record,* January 26, 1977, 123, S 1538–S 1541. Majority Leader Robert C. Byrd requested and received the unanimous consent of the Senate to bypass the committee stage and place the measure directly on the calendar for immediate floor consideration. For important bills, this is an unusual procedure.
3. The *Los Angeles Times,* February 7, 1977, p. 5.
4. U.S. Congress, House, *Congressional Record,* March 9, 1976, 122, H1779.
5. The formal rules of the House are contained in *Constitution, Jefferson's Manual, and Rules of the House of Representatives,* 94th Congress, 2d Sess., House Document No. 94–663. The Senate's formal rules are in *Senate Manual,* 95th Congress, 1st Session, Senate Document No. 95–1.
6. Lewis Deschler, *Deschler's Procedure, A Summary of the Modern Precedents and Practices of the U.S. House of Representatives, 86th–94th Congress* (Washington, D.C.: Government Printing Office, 1974); and Floyd M. Riddick, *Senate Procedure, Precedents and Practices* (Washington, D.C.: Government Printing Office, 1974).
7. Donald Matthews, *U.S. Senators and Their World* (Chapel Hill: University of North Carolina Press, 1960), chapter 5. Several of the folkways described by Matthews have undergone considerable change. For example, the norm of "apprenticeship," specifying that new members should be seen and not heard, has all but disappeared in both chambers.

6.2

1. *Senate Journal,* April 23, 1789. The original rule provided: When a bill or other message shall be sent from the Senate to the House of Representatives, it shall be carried by the Secretary, who shall make one obeisance to the chair on entering the door of the House of Representatives, and another on delivering it at the table into the hands of the Speaker. After he shall have delivered it, he shall make an obeisance to the Speaker, and repeat it as he retires from the House.
2. When the Speaker and/or the Vice President are unable to sign duly enrolled bills or joint resolutions, they may be signed by the authorized presiding officers of the two bodies.
3. Article 1, Section 7, provides that: "Every bill which shall have passed the House of Representatives and the Senate, shall, before it become a law, be presented to the President of the United States; if he approve he shall sign it, but if not he shall return it, with his objections to that house in which it shall have originated, who shall enter the objections at large on their Journal, and proceed to reconsider it. If after such reconsideration two thirds of that house shall agree to pass the bill, it shall be sent, together with the objections, to the other house, by which is shall likewise be reconsidered, and if approved by two thirds of that house, it shall become a law. But in all such cases the votes of both houses shall be determined by yeas and nays, and the names of the persons voting for and against the bill shall be entered on the Journal of each house respectively. If any bill shall not be returned by the President within ten days (Sundays excepted) after it shall have been presented to him, the Same shall be a law, in like manner as if he had signed it, unless the Congress by their adjournment prevent its return, in which case it shall not be a law."
4. In the computation of the 10 days, the day on which the bill is presented to the President, like Sundays, is excluded.

6.3

1. For example, see *Congressional Quarterly Almanac, 1978* (Washington, D.C.: Congressional Quarterly Press, 1979).
2. For detailed examination of the vast complex of government publications available, see guides, including: Joe Morehead, *Introduction to United States Public Documents,* 2d ed. (Littleton, Colo.: Libraries Unlimited, 1978); Vladimir M. Palic, *Government Publications: A Guide to Bibliographic Tools* (New York: Pergamon Press, 1977); Laurence F. Schmeckebier and Roy B. Eastin, *Government Publications and their Use,* 2d rev. ed. (Washington, D.C.: Brookings Institution, 1969).

6.4

1. Richard F. Fenno, Jr., *The Power of the Purse: Appropriations Politics in Congress* (Boston: Little, Brown, 1966), pp. 616–78; John A. Ferejohn, *Pork Barrel Politics: Rivers and Harbors Legislation, 1947–1968* (Stanford, Calif.: Stanford University Press, 1974), pp. 116–26; John F. Manley, *The Politics of Finance: The House Committee on Ways and Means* (Boston: Little, Brown, 1970), pp. 269–370; David J. Vogler, "Patterns of One-House Dominance in Congressional Conference Committees," *Midwest Journal of Political Science* 14 (1970): 303–20; David J. Vogler, *The Third House: Conference Committees in the United States Congress* (Evanston, Ill.: Northwestern University Press, 1971).
2. The evidence is consistent, even though different writers use different definitions of "winning." Fenno used differences in dollars at the bureau level and declared a victory for the chamber whose version was closest to final conference version; Manley used various measures including expected total revenue gain or loss; and Vogler used the codings of Congressional Quarterly. See also Gilbert Y. Steiner, *The Congressional Conference Committee: Seventieth to Eightieth Congresses* (Urbana: University of Illinois Press, 1951) for an alternative set of results which show the House predominates in conference.
3. Fenno, *Power of the Purse* pp. 661–70.
4. Manley, *Politics of Finance,* pp. 272–79.
5. Vogler, "Patterns of One-House Dominance," p. 309.
6. Arnold Kanter, "Congress and the Defense Budget: 1960–1970," *American Political Science Review* 66 (March 1972): 129–43.
7. In the present study, 136 conferences in the 92d Congress were identified and separately coded four times, twice at one-month intervals by the senior author, and once each by two graduate students who were purposely kept unaware of the main hypothesis of this study. If the conference bill was closer overall to the House bill, that conference outcome was coded a House victory; if the conference bill was closer to the Senate bill, it was coded a Senate victory; and if the conference bill was equally close to the House and Senate bills, it was coded a draw. "Closeness," however, is a subjective judgment. This is problematic, but is somewhat less so if the subjective judgments of different coders agree. For the 92d Congress, the reliability of the coding was very high. Intracoder reliability was 95 percent; intercoder reliability averaged 83 percent. On only three bills were there major disagreements (i.e., one coder coding a House victory, another a Senate victory, or vice versa). These three were declared unclassifiable. All other disagreements involved one coder coding a draw while another coded a House or Senate victory.
8. Fenno, *Power of the Purse,* pp. 668–69.
9. Ada C. McCown, *The Congressional Conference Committee* (1927; rpt. New York: AMS Press, 1967), pp. 61–64.
10. Fenno, *Power of the Purse,* pp. 667–70.
11. Manley, *Politics of Finance,* p. 274. See also Bertram M. Gross, *The Legislative Struggle: A Study in Social Combat* (New York: McGraw-Hill, 1953), pp. 317–27.
12. Vogler, "Patterns of One-House Dominance," p. 319.
13. Ferejohn, *Pork Barrel Politics,* p. 118fn.
14. See especially, Fenno, *Power of the Purse,* pp. 649–52; and Lewis A. Froman, Jr., *The Congressional Process: Strategies, Rules, and Procedures* (Boston: Little, Brown, 1967), pp. 5–15.
15. Fenno, *The Power of the Purse,* p. 678.
16. Froman, *The Congressional Process,* pp. 155–58, and Ferejohn, *Pork Barrel Politics,* pp. 118–19.
17. Note further that of the 30 conferences which resulted in a draw, 21 percent (N=95) were on bills that originated in the House and 26 percent (N=38) were on Senate bills.
18. Vogler, "Patterns of One-House Dominance," p. 309.
19. Ibid.
20. This confirms Fenno's hypothesis that it is a characteristic of the Senate that explains conference outcomes; Fenno, *The Power of the Purse,* p. 666. The invariance of the legislative sequence on appropriations bills, however, prohibited him from examining this particular characteristic of the Senate. Manley faced the same problem in his study of tax social security tariff legislation.
21. Ferejohn, *Pork Barrel Politics,* p. 123.
22. *Ibid.,* p. 119.

7.1

1. Barbara Deckard, "State Party Delegations in the U.S. House of Representatives: A Comparative Study of Group Cohesion," *Journal of Politics* 34 (1972).
2. C. Clapp, *The Congressman: His Work as He Sees It* (Garden City, N.Y.: Anchor Books, 1963), p. 141.
3. Donald Matthews, *U.S. Senators and Their World* (Chapel Hill: University of North Carolina Press, 1960), p. 246.
4. Charles J. Zinn, *How Our Laws Are Made,* revision by E. F. Willett (Washington, D.C.: U.S. Government Printing Office, 1978), p. 16.
5. *Ibid.*
6. Arthur G. Stevens, Jr., Arthur H. Miller, and Thomas E. Mann, "Mobilization of Liberal Strength in the House, 1955–1970: The Democratic Study Group," *American Political Science Review* 68 (1974).
7. Mark F. Ferber, "The Formation of the Democratic Study Group," in *Congressional Behavior* ed. N. W. Polsby (New York: Random House, 1971), pp. 249–69.
8. Stevens, et al., "Mobilization."

9. Clapp, *The Congressman,* pp. 188–89.
10. Malcolm E. Jewell and Samuel C. Patterson, *The Legislative Process in the United States,* 3d ed. (New York: Random House, 1977), p. 289.
11. Lester W. Milbrath, "Lobbying as a Communications Process," *Public Opinion Quarterly* 19 (1955–56): 32–53; *The Washington Lobbyists* (Chicago: Rand McNally, 1963).
12. Donald G. Tacheron and Morris K. Udall, *The Job of the Congressman* (Indianapolis, Ind.: Bobbs-Merrill, 1966), pp. 140–43.
13. Raymond A. Bauer, Itiel de Sola Pool and Lewis A. Dexter, *American Business and Public Policy* (New York: Atherton, 1963), p. 351. Also see Lewis A. Dexter, *How Organizations are Represented in Washington* (Indianapolis, Ind.: Bobbs-Merrill, 1969), p. 73.
14. Holbert N. Carroll, *The House of Representatives and Foreign Affairs* (Pittsburgh: University of Pittsburgh Press, 1966), pp. 27–29.
15. John S. Saloma, III, *Congress and the New Politics* (Boston: Little, Brown, 1969), p. 214.
16. Clapp, *The Congressman,* p. 126.
17. John W. Kingdon, *Congressmen's Voting Decisions* (New York: Harper & Row, 1973), p. 227.
18. *Ibid.*
19. Donald R. Matthews and James A. Stimson, *Yeas and Nays* (New York: John Wiley & Sons, 1975), pp. 102–10.
20. Charles R. Dechert, "Availability of Information for Congressional Operations," in *Congress: The First Branch of Government,* p. 173.
21. Tacheron and Udall, *The Job,* p. 125.
22. Saloma, *Congress and the New Politics,* p. 218.
23. Kingdon, *Congressmen's Voting,* pp. 223–25.
24. Edward Schneier, "The Intelligence of Congress: Information and Public Policy Patterns," *Annals of the American Academy of Political and Social Science* 388 (1970): 16.

7.2

1. Two of the most recent studies are Gary Orfield, *Congressional Power: Congress and Social Change* (New York: Harcourt Brace Jovanovich, 1975), and Randall B. Ripley and Grace A. Franklin, *Congress, The Bureaucracy, and Public Policy* (Homewood, Ill.: Dorsey Press, 1976).
2. Probably the most extensively studied aspects are committees and roll-call voting. On the former topic, see Richard F. Fenno, *Congressmen in Committees* (Boston: Little Brown, 1973); and David Price, *Who Makes the Laws?* (Cambridge, Mass.: Schenkman 1972). On the latter, see John W. Kingdon, *Congressmen's Voting Decisions* (New York: Harper & Row, 1973): and Aage R. Clausen, *How Congressmen Decide* (New York: St. Martin's Press, 1973).
3. Probably the most extensive treatment was Kenneth Kofmehl, *Professional Staffs of Congress* (West Lafayette, Ind.: Purdue University Press, 1962). Among the more recent studies are Norman Ornstein, "Information, Resources and Legislative Decision-Making: Some Comparative Perspectives on the U.S. Congress," Unpublished Ph.D. dissertation, University of Michigan, 1972; Samuel C. Patterson, "The Professional Staffs of Congressional Committees," *Administrative Science Quarterly* 15 (March 1970): 22–37; and various works by Harrison W. Fox and Susan Webb Hammond, including "Congressional Staffs and Congressional Change," paper delivered at the 1973 annual meeting of the American Political Science Association.
4. In addition to the authors of this paper, a third participant in this project was Robert L. Peabody. A report of the general findings of this project may be found in Norman Orstein, Robert Peabody, and David Rohde, "The Changing Senate: From the 1950's to the 1970's," in eds. Larry Dodd and Bruce Oppenheimer, *The Congress Reappraised* (New York: Praeger Publishers, 1977).
5. For example, in the 93d Congress (1973–1975) the Senate faced 1,138 roll-call votes, the most of any Congress. In addition, they made hundreds of other decisions which did not involve record votes.
6. These elements are, of course, not ultimate values. For example, Fenno cites a variety of Member goals which may be served by committee service (Fenno, *Congressmen in Committees,* chapter I). The elements are, however, attributes which are linked to involvement and, as such, are adequate for distinguishing among reasons for activity.

7.3

1. Julius Turner, *Party and Constituency: Pressures on Congress,* rev. ed., revised by Edward V. Schneider, Jr. (Baltimore: Johns Hopkins University Press, 1970), p. 34.
2. Donald R. Matthews and James A. Stimson, *Yeas and Nays: Normal Decision-Making in the U.S. House of Representatives* (New York: Wiley-Interscience, 1975).
3. Aage R. Clausen, *How Congressmen Decide: A Policy Focus* (New York: St. Martin's Press, 1973), p. 14.
4. John W. Kingdon, *Congressmen's Voting Decisions* (New York: Harper & Row, 1973), p. 230. Also see the second edition of this work, 1981.
5. Lewis Dexter, *The Sociology and Politics of Congress* (Chicago: Rand McNally, 1969), p. 159. Also see Lewis Anthony Dexter, "The Job of the Congressman," in *Readings on Congress,* ed. R. E. Wolfinger (Englewood Cliffs, N.J.: Prentice-Hall, 1971), p. 81.
6. Kingdon, *Congressmen's Voting,* p. 22.
7. Kovenock discovered that information inputs coming directly from members of the House were three times as great as from other sources. See Kovenock, as quoted in John S. Saloma, III, *Congress and the New Politics* (Boston: Little, Brown, 1969), p. 218. Bauer, Pool, and Dexter note that "Congressmen develop an implicit roster of fellow Congressmen whose judgement they respect, whose viewpoint they normally share, and to whom they can turn for guidance on particular topics of the colleague's competence." See Raymond A. Bauer, Ithiel de Sola Pool, and Lewis Anthony Dexter, *American Business and Public Policy* (New York: Atherton Press, 1963), p. 437.
8. Kingdon, *Congressmen's Voting,* p. 227.
9. Davidson, Kovenock, and O'Leary found that "the most frequently mentioned problems were associated

with the complexity of decision-making: the lack of information.'' The problem of deficient information for decision-making was cited by 62 percent of their sample—the most frequently mentioned complaint. See Roger H. Davidson, David M. Kovenock, and Michael D. O'Leary, *Congress in Crisis: Politics and Congressional Reform* (Belmont, Calif.: Wadsworth, 1966), pp. 75–78.

10. Turner, *Party and Constituency,* p. 34.
11. Clausen, *How Congressmen Decide,* p. 14.
12. Roger H. Davidson, *The Role of the Congressman* (New York: Pegasus, 1969), p. 117.
13. See the following for historical and analytical reviews of legislative behavior research: Heinz Eulau and Katherine Hinckley, ''Legislative Institutions and Processes,'' in *Political Science Annual, 1966* ed. J. A. Robinson (Indianapolis, Ind.: Bobbs-Merrill, 1966), pp. 85–181; Norman Meller, ''Legislative Behavior Research,'' *Western Political Quarterly* 13 (1960): 131–53; Norman Meller, ''Legislative Behavior Research Revisited: A Review of Five Years' Publications,'' *Western Political Quarterly* 18 (1965): 776–93; Norman Meller, ''Legislative Behavior Research,'' in *Approaches to the Study of Political Science,* ed. M. Haas and H. S. Kariel (Scranton, Pa.: Chandler, 1970), pp. 239–66; Robert L. Peabody, ''Research on Congress: A Coming of Age,'' in *Congress: Two Decades of Analysis* ed. R. K. Huitt and R. L. Peabody (New York: Harper & Row, 1969), pp. 3–73; and John C. Wahlke, ''Behavioral Analyses of Representative Bodies,'' in *Essays on the Behavioral Study of Politics,* ed. A. Ranney (Urbana: University of Illinois Press, 1962), pp. 173–90.
14. Peabody, ''Research on Congress,'' p. 70.
15. Meller, ''Legislative Behavior,'' p. 251.
16. Theodore J. Lowi, ''American Business, Public Policy, Case Studies, and Political Theory,'' *World Politics* 16 (1964): 677–715; T. J. Lowi, ''Distribution, Regulation, Redistribution: The Functions of Government,'' in *Public Policies and Their Politics* ed. R. Ripley (New York: W. W. Norton, 1966), pp. 27–40; T. J. Lowi, ''Four Systems of Policy, Politics, and Choice,'' *Public Administration Review* 32 (1972): 298–301.
17. Randall B. Ripley and Grace A. Franklin, *Congress, the Bureaucracy, and Public Policy,* rev. ed. (Homewood, Ill.: Dorsey Press, 1980).
18. John M. Bacheller, ''Lobbyists and the Legislative Process: The Impact of Environmental Constraints,'' *American Political Science Review* 71 (1977): 252–63.
19. Michael T. Hayes, ''The Semi-Sovereign Pressure Groups,'' *Journal of Politics* 37 (1978): 136–61.
20. Charles O. Jones, ''Speculative Augmentation in Federal Air Pollution Policy-Making,'' *Journal of Politics* 36 (1974): 438–64.
21. David E. Price, ''Policy-Making in Congressional Committees: The Impact of Environmental Factors,'' *American Political Science Review* 72 (1978): 548–74.
22. James Q. Wilson, *Political Organizations* (New York: Basic Books, 1973), and *American Government: Institutions and Policies* (Lexington, Mass.: D.C. Heath, 1980).
23. For a complete report of the results of the research, see David C. Kozak, *Contexts of Congressional Decision Behavior,* unpublished Ph.D. dissertation, University of Pittsburgh, 1979.
24. Price, ''Policy-Making,'' p. 572.
25. Kingdon, *Congressmen's Voting,* pp. 292–93.
26. James D. Thompson, *Organizations in Action* (New York: McGraw-Hill, 1967), p. 134.
27. Fredrick N. Cleaveland, ''Legislating for Urban Areas: An Overview,'' in *Congress and Urban Problems* ed. F. N. Cleaveland (Washington, D.C.: Brookings Institution, 1969), pp. 356–57.
28. *Ibid.,* p. 357.
29. The position that cue-taking is best viewed as an extension of ideological voting, or a means to it, is presented by John W. Kingdon, ''Models of Legislative Voting,'' *Journal of Politics* 36 (1977): 563–95; and Helmut Norpoth, ''Explaining Party Cohesion in Congress: The Case of Shared Policy Attitudes,'' *American Political Science Review* 70 (1976): pp. 1156–71.
30. Roland Young, *The American Congress* (New York: Harper & Row, 1958), p. viii.

7.4

1. The University of Michigan-based Inter-University Consortium for Political and Social Research has put on computer tapes all congressional roll calls up to the present time and made the tapes available free or at nominal cost to hundreds of colleges and universities in the United States and abroad. All roll-call votes can be found in the *Congressional Quarterly Weekly Report.*
2. Cf. John Kingdon, *Congressmen's Voting Decisions,* 2d ed. (New York: Harper & Row, 1981), p. 314. Lobby ratings may be found in *CQ,* and in Michael Barone, Grant Ujifusa, and Douglas Matthews, *The Almanac of American Politics, 1980* (New York: E. P. Dutton, 1979).
3. William R. Shaffer, *Party and Ideology in the United States Congress* (Lanham, Md.: University Press of America, 1980).
4. *Congressional Quarterly Weekly Report,* January 26, 1980, pp. 193–98; cf. Jerrold E. Schneider, *Ideological Coalitions in Congress* (Westport, Conn.: Greenwood Press, 1979). For definitions of ''progressive,'' ''liberal'', and ''conservative,'' see pp. 147–148, 159–60, 165, and 200–203, of Schneider.
5. *Congressional Quarterly Weekly Report,* January 19, 1980, pp. 145–49.
6. *Ibid.,* January 12, 1980, pp. 91–102.
7. Duncan MacRae, Jr., *Issues and Parties in Legislative Voting: Methods of Statistical Analysis* (New York: Harper & Row, 1970).
8. Aage R. Clausen, ''Subjectivity and Objectivity in Dimensional Analysis: Illustrations from Congressional Voting,'' *Mathematical Applications in Political Science,* VII, ed. James F. Herndon and Joseph L. Bernd (Charlottesville: University of Virginia Press, 1974), p. 17.
9. *Ibid.*
10. A study by John Hoadley, ''The Dimensions of Congressional Voting, 1971–1978: Some Preliminary Considerations,'' paper presented at the annual meeting of the Midwest Political Science Association, Chicago, April 1980, using multidimensional scaling, produced the same finding of unidimensionality as in Schneider, *Ideological Coalitions.* Hoadley's scatterplot array of

the Senators dimensionally is remarkably intuitive from a contextual standpoint.

11. Cf. Aage Clausen, *How Congressmen Decide: A Policy Focus* (New York: St. Martin's Press, 1973); David B. Truman, *The Congressional Party: A Case Study* (New York: John Wiley & Sons, 1959); Schneider, *Ideological Coalitions.*
12. Joseph A. Pechman, ed., *Setting National Priorities: The 1982 Budget* (Washington D.C.: Brookings Institution, 1981). This is part of a series continuous since 1970.
13. Clifton Daniel, "Aiken Admits 'Sins' in Farewell," *The New York Times,* December 12, 1974, p. 40.
14. Cf. Walter J. Oleszek, *Congressional Procedures and the Policy Process* (Washington D.C.: Congressional Quarterly Press, 1978), pp. 105–31, 151–80.
15. Kingdon, *Congressmen's Voting;* David Kozak, *The Context of Congressional Decision Behavior,* (Nashville: University of Tennessee Press, forthcoming); Schneider, *Ideological Coalitions;* and Hoadley, "The Dimensions of Congressional Voting."
16. Heinz Eulau, review of John E. Jackson, *Constituencies and Leaders in Congress: Their Effects on Senate Voting Behavior,* in the *American Journal of Sociology* 81, no. 4 (January 1976): 953–55.
17. Aage Clausen and Carl Van Horn, "How to Analyse Too Many Roll Calls," paper presented to the Conference on Mathematical Models of Congress, Aspen, Colorado, June 16–23, 1974, p. 21.
18. Cf. *Congressional Quarterly Weekly Report,* January 12, 1980, p. 93.
19. On the norms associated with votes on conference reports, see James MacGregor Burns, *Edward Kennedy and the Camelot Legacy* (New York: W. W. Norton, 1976), p. 141.
20. Herbert Weisberg, *Dimensional Analysis of Legislative Roll Calls,* unpublished Ph.D. dissertation, University of Michigan, 1968, p. 38ff.
21. Barbara Deckard (Sinclair), "Political Upheaval and Congressional Voting—The Effects of the 1960s on Voting Patterns in the House of Representatives," paper delivered at the Midwest Political Science Association, 1975, pp. 2–3.
22. Cf. Paul F. Lazrsfeld, "Evidence and Inference in Social Research," in *Evidence and Inference,* ed. Daniel Lerner (Glencoe, Ill.: Free Press, 1958), pp. 107–17.
23. Duncan MacRae, Jr., *Dimensions of Congressional Voting: A Statistical Study of the House of Representatives in the Eighty-First Congress* (Berkeley: University of California Publications in Sociology, 1958).
24. Leslie Kish, "Some Statistical Problems in Research Design," in *The Quantitative Analysis of Social Problems,* ed. Edward R. Tufte (Reading, Mass.: Addison-Wesley, 1970), p. 392.
25. Weisberg, *Dimensional Analysis,* pp. 41ff.
26. MacRae, *Issues and Parties,* pp. 175–290.
27. Where these tabulations cannot be published by edict of editors, they should be automatically available on call to interested scholars.

8.1

1. The data for the open-ended congressional evaluation questions in the 1977 survey were obtained from U.S. House of Representatives (1977). We have recoded these data into the categories utilized in coding the 1968 data in order to facilitate comparisons and sharpen patterns of congressional evaluations. A description of the recoding scheme is available from the authors.

REFERENCES

Fenno, Richard F., Jr. "If, as Ralph Nader Says, Congress Is 'The Broken Branch,' How Come We Love Our Congressmen So Much?" In *Congress in Change: Evolution and Reform.* Edited by Norman J. Ornstein. New York: Praeger Publishers, pp. 277–87.

Fiorina, Morris P. *Congress: Keystone of the Washington Establishment.* New Haven, Conn.: Yale University Press, 1977.

Frankfurter, Felix. *The Public and Its Government.* New Haven, Conn.: Yale University Press, 1930.

Harris, Louis & Associates. Study no. 1900. Contracted by Roger H. Davidson, under a grant from the Committee on Governmental and Legal Services, Social Science Research Council, 1968.

Lipset, Seymour M. *Political Man.* New York: Anchor Books, 1963.

Mitchell, William C. "The Ambivalent Social Status of the American Politician." *Western Political Quarterly* 12 (September 1959): 683–98.

Rosenberg, Morris. "The Meaning of Politics in Mass Society." *Public Opinion Quarterly* 15 (Spring 1951): 5–15.

———. "Some Determinants of Political Apathy." *Public Opinion Quarterly* 18 (Winter 1954): 349–66.

U.S. House of Representatives, Commission on Administrative Review. *Final Report: Survey Materials.* H. Doc. 95–272 (95th Congress, 1st session, 1977), vol. 2, pp. 817–19.

8.2.

1. Daniel Berman, *A Bill Becomes a Law* (New York: Macmillan, 1962). See also Eugene Eidenburg and Roy D. Morey, *An Act of Congress* (New York: W. W. Norton, 1969). In describing the enactment of the Elementary and Secondary Education Act of 1965, the authors describe in detail floor action on crucial amendments raised by opponents.
2. Woodrow Wilson, *Congressional Government* (New York: World, 1956), pp. 57–98.
3. Leroy Rieselbach, *Congressional Politics* (New York: McGraw-Hill, 1973), p. 237.
4. Richard Fenno, *Congressmen in Committees* (Boston: Little, Brown, 1973), p. 237.
5. Lester Milbrath, *The Washington Lobbyists* (Chicago: Rand McNally, 1963), pp. 209–52, 328–54.
6. See, for example, Theodore Lowi, "American Business, Public Policy, Case Studies, and Political Theory," *World Politics* 16 (July 1964): 677–715. More recently, Lowi has proposed a refined version of this argument; see Lowi, "Four Systems of Policy, Politics and Choice," *Public Administration Review* 32 (July/August 1972): 298–310. Also see Robert Salisbury, "The Analysis of Public Policy: A Search for Theories and Roles," in *Political Science and Public Policy,* ed., Austin Ranney (Chicago: Markham, 1968).
7. Raymond Bauer, Ithiel de Sola Pool, and Lewis A.

Dexter. *American Business and Public Policy* (New York: Aldine Publishing, 1963), pp. 444–58.

8. Fenno, *Congressmen in Committees,* p. 45.
9. Grant McConnell, *Private Power and American Democracy* (New York: Alfred A. Knopf, 1966), pp. 298–335.
10. McConnell, *Private Power and American Democracy,* pp. 196–245, 298–335. Also see J. David Greenstone, *Labor in American Politics* (New York: Random House, 1969), pp. 39–89, and Milbrath, *Washington Lobbyists*.
11. E. E. Schattschneider makes essentially the same argument in *The Semi-Sovereign People* (New York: Holt, Rinehart & Winston, 1960).
12. The organizational memberships of those who did not respond were similar to those who did.
13. *Congressional Record, 91st Congress,* vol. 116, pp. H2970–H2991, H7337–H7365, H12432–H12436.
14. *Congressional Quarterly Almanac,* 1970 (Washington, D.C.: Congressional Quarterly Press, 1971).
15. This method of measuring respondents interests could conceivably generate measurement error, since the interests of some lobbyists may fall in more than one category. To investigate the possibility of this sort of error, responses to the question were examined. Eighty-eight percent of the respondents answering the open-ended question answered exclusively with subject areas defined as falling within only one category. Thus, the activities of lobbyists appear to be rather specialized, and the amount of error introduced by this method of measurement should be small.
16. *New York Times Index, 1968* (New York: The New York Times, 1969). Statements made by a candidate in response to questions posed by the *New York Times* were excluded from the tabulation of campaign issues because they were responses to questions from a specific organization rather than attempts to inform the public of his position initiated by the candidate. Thus, they may not represent areas emphasized in the campaign. In addition, because they were initiated by the *Times,* responses in these areas are particularly unlikely to represent the issues covered by the media nationally.
17. Although questions were asked in the same form in both the interviews and the questionnaire, those from the interviews allowed open-ended responses, while those from the questionnaire were closed. Responses from the interviews were coded twice, independently. See Appendix A.
18. Milbrath, *Washington Lobbyists,* calls these techniques "direct" and "indirect."
19. See Appendix A for the exact wording of the questions. Responses taken exclusively from the mail questionnaire. Lobbyists were also questioned as to differences between the houses of Congress during the interviews. No significant differences were found in focus of activity or techniques used.
20. Nonmass groups were distinguished from mass groups on the basis of whether the memberships of the groups studied were individuals or organizations.
21. Responses taken exclusively from the mail questionnaire.
22. Of course committee recruitment as well as leadership patterns affect integration as well. See Richard Fenno, "The House Appropriations Committee as a Political System," *American Political Science Review* 56 (June 1962): 310–24; and *idem,* "The House of Representatives and Federal Aid to Education," in *New Perspectives on the House of Representatives,* ed. Robert L. Peabody and Nelson Polsby, 2d ed. (Chicago: Rand McNally, 1969), pp. 283–323.
23. Warren Miller and Donald Stokes, "Constituency Influence in Congress," *The American Political Science Review* 57 (March 1963): 45–56.

8.3

1. U.S. Congress, Senate, Committee on Government Operations and the Special Committee on National Emergencies and Delegated Emergency Powers, *The National Emergencies Act (Public Law 94–412), Source Book: Legislative History, Texts, and Other Documents,* Committee Print, 94th Congress, 2d session, November 1976, p. 5.
2. 10 *USC* 3750 and 20 *USC* 241–1.
3. 10 *USC* 4501, 4502, 9501, and 9502.
4. PL 94–412, 90 *Stat.* 1255; 50 *USC* 1601.
5. 90 *Stat.* 1257, sec. 201 (5) (*d*).
6. PL 93–148, 87 *Stat.* 555; 50 *USC* Supp. V (1975) 1541.
7. *Ibid.,* at sec. 3; *ibid.,* sec. 1543.
8. U.S. Congress, House, Committee on Foreign Affairs, *War Powers Resolution of 1973,* House Report No. 93–287, 93d Congress, 1st session, June 15, 1963 [sic] [1973], pp. 6–7.
9. Harvey G. Zeidenstein and Hibbert R. Roberts, "The War Powers Resolution, Institutionalized Checks and Balances, and Public Policy," Paper presented at the Southern Political Science Association Convention, Nashville, Tenn., November 6–8, 1975, pp. 103–105.
10. *New York Times,* May 16, 1975, p. 15.
11. PL 93–250, 88 *Stat.* 11; 31 *USC* 16.
12. PL 92–403, 86 *Stat.* 619; 1 *USC* Supp. V (1975) 112b.
13. PL 94–412, 90 *Stat.* 1257, at sec. 301; 50 *USC* 1631.
14. *Ibid.,* at sec. 401; *ibid.,* sec. 1641.
15. PL 93–148, 87 *Stat.* 555, at sec. 4; 50 *USC* Supp. V (1975) 1544.
16. *Ibid.,* at sec. 4; *ibid.,* sec. 1544.
17. PL 93–559, 88 *Stat.* 1804; 22 *USC* 2422.
18. U.S. Congress, Senate, Sen. Harold Hughes interpreting the intent of his amendment, 93d Congress, 2d session, October 2, 1974, *Congressional Record,* vol. 120, part 25, p. 33490.
19. Mitchell Rogovin, special counsel to the Director of CIA, to A. Searle Field, staff director of the House Select Committee on Intelligence, January 6, 1976, in U.S. Congress, House, *Intelligence Agencies and Activities: Risks and Control of Foreign Intelligence, Hearings before the Select Committee on Intelligence,* Part 5, 94th Congress, 1st session, November and December 1975, p. 2020. This committee, chaired by Representative Otis Pike, investigated the CIA.
20. Rogovin to Field, *ibid.,* p. 2016.
21. U.S. Congress, Senate, Committee on Government Operations, *Oversight of U.S. Government Intelligence Functions, Hearings before the Senate Committee on Government Operations,* 94th Congress, 2d session, January and February 1976, p. 130. Hereafter cited as Senate hearings, *Oversight of Intelligence*.

22. *Ibid.*
23. U.S. Congress, Senate, 94th Congress, 2d session, vol. 122 *Congressional Record,* No. 74, S 7563–S 7565 (daily ed., May 19, 1976). Hereafter cited as Senate Res. 400 with appropriate section number.
24. Senate Res. 400, sec 11 (*a*).
25. Senate Res. 400, sec. 3 (*a*) and (*b*).
26. Senate Res. 400, sec. 8.
27. U.S. Congress, Senate, *Annual Report to the Senate of the Select Committee on Intelligence, United States Senate,* Senate Report No. 95–217, 95th Congress, 1st session, May 18, 1977, p. 18.
28. U.S., Congress, House, 95th Congress, 1st session, vol. 123 *Congressional Record,* No. 119 H, 7104–H 7106 (daily ed., July 14, 1977). Hereafter cited as House Res. 658, with appropriate section number. Note that this resolution amended the *Rules of the House of Representatives* by adding Rule XLVII, Permanent Select Committee on Intelligence.
29. Senate Res. 400, sec. 8 (*b*).
30. House Res. 658, sec. 7 (*b*) (7).
31. *Ibid.,* and Senate Res. 400, sec. 8(*b*).
32. U.S. Congress, House, 95th Congress, 1st session, vol. 123 *Congressional Record,* No. 119 H, 7115 (daily ed., July 14, 1977).
33. *Ibid.,* H 7119.
34. PL 93–344, 88 *Stat.* 297; 31 *USC* 1301.
35. PL 94–412, 90 *Stat.* 1255; 50 *USC* 1621.
36. PL 93–148, 87 *Stat.* 555 at sec. 5(*c*); 50 *USC* Supp. V (1975) 1545 (*c*).
37. PL 94–412, 90 *Stat.* 1255; 50 *USC* 1622 for National Emergencies Act. PL 93–148, 87 *Stat.* 555 at sec. 7; 50 *USC* Supp. V 1975) 1547 for War Powers Resolution.
38. PL 93–559, 88 *Stat.* 1814; 22 *USC* 2776.
39. *Congressional Quarterly Almanac 1975* (Washington, D.C.: Congressional Quarterly, Inc.), p. 353.
40. *Congressional Quarterly Almanac 1975* (Washington, D.C.: Congressional Quarterly, Inc.), pp. 358–359, and *Congressional Quarterly Weekly Report,* vol, 35, Sept. 3, 1977, pp. 1857–1863.
41. PL 93–344, 88 *Stat.* 332; 31 *USC* 1400.
42. *Ibid.,* at 337 in the *Statutes* and 1407 in the *U.S. Code.*
43. PL 93–148, *87 Stat.* 555 at sec. 5 (*b*); 50 *USC* Supp. V (1975) 1545(*b*).
44. *Ibid.* at sec. 6 in the *Statutes* and 1546 in the *U.S. Code.*
45. *Ibid.,* at sec. 5 in the *Statutes* and 1545 in the *U.S. Code.*
46. *PL 93–344, 88 Stat.* 332; 31 *USC* 1402.
47. PL 94–412, 90 *Stat.* 1255; 50 *USC* 1601.
48. *Congressional Quarterly Almanac 1976* (Washington, D.C.: Congressional Quarterly Press), p. 522.
49. PL 94–412, 90 *Stat.* 1258; 50 *USC* 1651.

9.1

1. *Panama Refining Co.* v. *Ryan,* 293 U.S. 388 (1935); *Schechter Corp.* v. *United States,* 295 U.S. 495, 553 (1935).
2. *Wayman* v. *Southard,* 10 Wheat. 1, 46 (1825). Congress may also legislate contingently, leaving to others the task of ascertaining the facts which bring its declared policy into operation—e.g., *Brig Aurora* v. *United States,* 11 U.S. (7 Cr.) 382, 386 (1813). See Louis Fisher, *President and Congress* (1972), pp. 55–84.
3. Robert E. Cushman, *The Independent Regulatory Commissions* (1941), p. 429.
4. For example, *Field* v. *Clark,* 143 U.S. 649, 692 (1891), and *Hampton & Co.* v. *United States,* 276 U.S. 394, 406 (1928).
5. *Amalgamated Meat Cutters & Butcher Work* v. *Connally,* 337 F. Supp. 737, 750 (D.D.C. 1971). The 1970 Act (84 Stat. 799) was extended by 84 Stat. 1468, 85 Stat. 13, and 85 Stat. 38, before being fundamentally rewritten by an act of December 22, 1971 (85 Stat. 743) which provided for more specific standards, procedural safeguards, and judicial review.
6. *California Bankers Assn.* v. *Shultz,* 416 U.S. 21, 90–93 (1974) (Justice Douglas and Brennan dissenting).
7. *Algonquin Sng., Inc.* v. *Federal Energy Admin.,* 518 F.2d 1051, 1060 (D.C. Cir. 1975).
8. *Commonwealth of Massachusetts* v. *Simon,* Civil Action No. 74–0129, and *Algonquin Sng., Inc.* v. *Simon,* Civil Action No. 75–0130 (D.D.C. 1975), reprinted at 518 F.2d 1064 (1975).
9. *Algonquin Sng., Inc.* v. *Federal Energy Admin.,* 518 F.2d 1051, 1056, 1061 (D.C. Cir. 1975).
10. *FEA* v. *Algonquin Sng. Inc.,* 49 L Ed 2d 49, 57 (1976).
11. Theodore J. Lowi, *The End of Liberalism* (New York: W. W. Norton, 1969), p. 298.
12. Locke's Appeal, 72 Pa. St. 491, 498–499 (1873).
13. E.g., *Buttfield* v. *Stranahan,* 192 U.S. 470, 496 (1904); *Union Bridge Co.* v. *United States,* 294 U.S. 364, 386 (1907); *Monongahela Bridge Co.* v. *United States,* 216 U.S. 177 (1910); and *United States* v. *Grimaud,* 220 U.S. 506, 516 (1911).
14. Kenneth Culp Davis, *Discretionary Justice* (1969) and his article, "A New Approach to Delegation," *U. Chi. L. Rev.* 36 (1968): 713.
15. *Eisenberg* v. *Corning,* 179 F. 2d 275 (D.C. Cir. 1949).
16. *Feliciano* v. *United States,* 297 F. Supp. 1356, 1358 (D. Puerto Rico 1969), aff'd, 422 F. 2d 943 cert. denied, 400 U.S. 823 (1970).
17. For the development of defense reprograming, see Louis Fisher, *Presidential Spending Power* 80–98 (1975).
18. As an example, see sec. 741 of the Defense Appropriations Act for fiscal year 1977, Public Law 94–419, 90 Stat. 1298.
19. H. Rep. 1363, 93d Congress, 2d session 27 (1974).
20. General Accounting Office, "LTV Aerospace Corp.," B–183851 (October 1, 1975), at 21–22.
21. 3 Dall. 378.
22. *Hinds' Precedents,* IV, § 3483.
23. *Ibid.,* II, §§1593–94.
24. H. Rep. 120, 76th Congress, 1st session, 6 (1939). See *Currin* v. *Wallace,* 306 U.S. 1 (1939).
25. *Buckley* v. *Valeo,* 46 L. Ed. 2d 659, 839 (1976).
26. For the debate and vote, see 122 *Congressional Record* H 10666–10719 (daily ed. September 21, 1976).
27. Several cases are currently pending before the courts which raise the question of the constitutionality of the legislative veto: *Clark* v. *Valco* (C.A.D.C. No. 76–1825), concerning congressional veto of regulations issued by the Federal Election Commission, and *Atkins* v.

United States (Ct. Cl. No. 41–76), involving congressional veto of Federal salaries (2 U.S.C. 359).

28. Louis Fisher, *President and Congress,* (1972), pp. 1–27.
29. Woodrow Wilson, *Congressional Government* (1887), p. 297.
30. Assistance could be provided by the Congressional Research Service, which, upon request by any committee or member, will prepare a memorandum with respect to one or more legislative measures "upon which hearings by any committee of the Congress have been announced, which memorandum shall contain a statement of the purpose and effect of each such measure, a description of other relevant measures of similar purpose or effect previously introduced in the Congress, and a recitation of all action taken theretofore by or within the Congress with respect to each such other measure." 2 U.S.C. 166(*d*) (7).

9.3

1. I use the abverb *usually* because oversight can be performed in a terribly destructive manner if Congress does not exercise a minimum level of self-restraint. The prime example is the McCarthy "investigation" of government personnel practices in the 1950s.
2. There are certainly benefits to be gained from reviewing a program in a persistent yet unsystematic manner. However, the major payoff from either sporadic or regular unsystematic oversight probably comes from the anticipation by the administrators that the overseers just might uncover something embarrassing.
3. See especially Scher (1963), Ogul (1976), and Bibby (1968, 1974).
4. The data are presented in Appendix G of the report, pp. 267–275. The percentage of all hearing and meeting days devoted to oversight, in what must be a typographical error, is erroneously presented as 1.1 percent (p. 268) rather than 11 percent in that report. (The raw numbers show 231 days devoted to oversight out of a total of 2,095 days.)
5. The hearings or meetings of formal Joint Committees and those held jointly by House and Senate Committees were also exluded from the analysis. Hearings or meetings of party committees (e.g., steering, policy, and personnel committees) were not included in the data set.
6. I have not yet had the time to analyze these data fully, but one would certainly want to look at such factors as increasing staff resources, larger numbers of liberal Democrats, and changing patterns in committee and subcommittee chairmanships for explanations of the pattern presented in the table.
7. Split partisan control might also be very important as a contextual factor influencing the relationship between other variables and oversight, but one would require data from a period in which the same party controlled the two institutions in order to establish this. Relevant data for the 87th to 90th and the 95th Congresses are now being processed.
8. It is food for thought that on the plane of general activity, staff increases were quite pronounced in the Senate committees between 1973 and 1975, yet overall committee hearings and meetings days actually dropped.
9. Staff has been on the increase for quite some time, although not quite at the recent rate. A longer time frame for the analysis will provide some additional evidence from which to infer the ways in which these variables operate in the Congress.
10. The assumption here is that the larger the number of subcommittees, the more dispersed power is likely to be. This assumption is probably a reasonable one in most cases but there are some potential pitfalls. For example, in a committee with many subcommittees the chairman and a small clique might control the key subcommittees which have jurisdiction over the crucial programs within the committee's jurisdiction.
11. The oversight activity indicator was coded as oversight = 1, other = 0.
12. The percentages for the 92d and 93d Congresses were 35.5 percent and 29.0 percent, respectively.
13. The House Government Operations Committee, I should note as supplementary evidence, was below the average of oversight units in its oversight efforts, although not as low as in the Senate.

REFERENCES

Bibby, J. F. "Oversight—Congress' Neglected Function: Will Watergate Make a Difference?" Paper presented at the 1974 Meeting of the Western Political Science Association.

———. "Congress' Neglected Function," in *Republican Papers.* Edited by M. Laird. New York: Praeger Publishers, 1968, pp. 477–88.

Harris, J. *Congressional Control of Administration.* Washington, D.C.: Brookings Institution, 1964.

Ogul, M. *Congress Oversees the Bureaucracy.* Pittsburgh: University of Pittsburgh Press, 1976.

Ornstein, N. J. "Causes and Consequences of Congressional Change: Subcommittee Reforms in the House of Representatives, 1970–73," in *Congress in Change: Evolution and Reform,* edited by N. J. Ornstein. New York: Praeger Publishers, 1975.

Scher, S. "Conditions for legislative control." *Journal of Politics,* August, 1963, pp. 526–661.

Schick, A. "Evaluating Evaluation: A Congressional Perspective," *Legislative Oversight and Program Evaluation.* Washington, D.C.: Government Printing Office, 1976, pp. 341–54.

Singer, J. W. "Labor and Congress–New Isn't Necessarily Better," *National Journal* (March 1978), pp. 351–53.

U.S. Congress, Commission on the Operation of the Senate Interim Report of the Commission on the Operation of the Senate, Senate Document, 94th Congress, 2d session, 1976.

U.S. Congress, House Select Committee on Committees (Bolling Committee), Committee Reform Amendments of 1974, Report to Accompany House Resolution 988, 93d Congress, 2d session, 1974, House Report 93–916, part II.

U.S. Congress, Senate Temporary Select Committee to Study the Senate Committee System (1976) The Senate Committee System, Committee Print, 94th Congress, 2d session, 1976.

9.4

1. *Washington Post,* January 21, 1974, p. A-20.
2. Quoted in David E. Price, *Who Makes the Laws? Creativity and Power in Senate Committees* (Cambridge, Mass., 1972), p. 1.
3. David Brinkley, "Foreword," in *Congress Needs Help,* Philip Donham and Robert J. Fahey (New York, 1966), p. vi.
4. Quoted in Roger H. Davidson, "Congress and the American Political System," in *Legislatures in Developmental Perspective,* eds. Allan Kornberg and Lloyd D. Musolf (Durham, N.C., 1970), p. 139.
5. James A. Robinson, "Staffing the Legislature," in Kornberg and Musolf, pp. 373, 377.
6. Charles R. Adrian, et al., *American Government 73/74 Encyclopedia* (Guilford, Conn., 1973), p. 175. For the now Classic argument that Congress does not and should not initiate, see Samuel P. Huntington, "Congressional Responses to the Twentieth Century," in *The Congress and America's Future,* 2d ed.; ed. David B. Truman (Englewood Cliffs, N.J., 1973), pp. 6–38.
7. Alan Rosenthal, "The Effectiveness of Congress," in *The Performance of American Government: Checks and Minuses,* ed. Gerald M. Pomper et al. (New York, 1972), pp. 118–19.
8. Quoted in Price, *Who Makes the Laws?* p. 1.
9. U.S. Congress, House Select Committee on Committees, "Toward a House of Worse Repute or How to Be a Rubber Stamp With Honor," *Committee Organization in the House,* 93d Congress, 1st session, 1973, p. 781.
10. See, for example, Ralph K. Huitt, "Congress: The Durable Partner," in *Congress: Two Decades of Analysis,* eds. Huitt and Robert L. Peabody (New York: Harper & Row, 1969), pp. 109–29; Dale Vinyard, *Congress* (New York, 1968), pp. 19–20; John S. Saloma, III, *Congress and the New Politics* (Boston, 1969), pp. 93–97; John F. Bibby and Roger H. Davidson, *On Capitol Hill: Studies in the Legislative Process,* 2d ed. (Hinsdale, Ill., 1972), pp. 3–6, and Nelson W. Polsby, "Policy Analysis and Congress," *Public Policy* 18 (Fall 1969), 61–74.
11. Lawrence H. Chamberlain, *The President, Congress and Legislation* (New York, 1946), pp. 453–54.
12. Nonetheless, several writers have tried, producing estimates of congressional initiatives ranging from 20 to 80 percent of all laws and 20 to 95 percent of all bills. See Chamberlain, *The President,* p. 450; Brinkley, "Foreword," p. iv; Charles E. Lindbloom, *The Policy-Making Process* (Englewood Cliffs, N.J., 1968), p. 86; Robert Bendiner, *Obstacle Course on Capitol Hill* (New York, 1964), p. 31; and Daniel M. Berman, *In Congress Assembled* (New York, 1964), p. 70.
13. Stephen K. Bailey, *Congress Makes a Law: The Story Behind the Employment Act of 1946* (New York, 1950), p. 236. Many writers fall into what Price calls the "zero-sum fallacy" in trying to classify initiatives too neatly as presidential or congressional (*Who Makes the Laws?* p. 296).
14. For a partial list see John R. Johannes, "Congress and the Initiation of Legislation," *Public Policy* 20 (Spring 1972): 282, note 7. See also Price, *Who Makes the Laws?;* Robert L. Peabody, et al., *To Enact a Law: Congress and Campaign Financing* (New York, 1972); Mark V. Nadel, *The Politics of Consumer Protection* (Indianapolis, 1971); Alan K. McAdams, *Power and Politics in Labor Legislation* (New York, 1964); and Ernest A. Chaples, Jr., "Congress Gets New Ideas from Outside Experts," in *To Be a Congressman: The Promise and the Power,* eds. Sven Groennings and Jonathan P. Hawley (Washington, D.C., 1973), pp. 169–83. For an analysis of congressional influence and initiative based on some of these and many more case studies, see Ronald Moe and Steven Teel, "Congress as Policy-Maker: A Necessary Reappraisal," *Political Science Quarterly* 85 (September 1970): 443–70.
15. See Harold Wolman, *The Politics of Federal Housing* (New York, 1971), pp. 73, 80; and Price, *Who Makes the Laws?* pp. 206–07. For an elaboration on these forms of initiation, see John R. Johannes, *Policy Innovation in Congress* (Morristown, N.J., 1972), pp. 5–16, 27–28.
16. James L. Sundquist, *Politics and Policy: The Eisenhower, Kennedy, and Johnson Years* (Washington, D.C., 1969). Bertram Gross goes to the extreme: "I know of no cases whatsoever outside of some foreign legislation [sic] where important innovations ever took place without congressional initiative preceding executive action." *Committee Organization in the House,* p. 334.
17. Sundquist, *Politics and Policy,* pp. 195–200; Price, *Who Makes the Laws?* p. 201; and J. W. Anderson, *Eisenhower, Brownell and the Congress: The Tangled Origins of the Civil Rights Act of 1956–57* (University: University of Alabama Press, 1964).
18. John R. Johannes, "Study and Recommend: Statutory Reporting Requirements as a Technique of Legislative Initiation," paper presented to the annual meeting of the American Political Science Association, Chicago, September 1974.
19. John R. Johannes, "Where Does the Buck Stop?—Congress, President, and the Responsibility for Legislative Initiation," *Western Political Quarterly* 25 (September 1972): 396–415.
20. For examples, see M. Kent Jennings, "Legislative Politics and Water Pollution Control, 1956–61," in *Congress and Urban Problems,* ed. Frederick N. Cleaveland, et al., (Washington, D.C., 1969), pp. 72–109; Randall B. Ripley, "Congress and Clean Air: The Issue of Enforcement," in Cleaveland, *Congress and Urban Problems,* pp. 224–78; and Price, *Who Makes the Laws?* pp. 99, 218–19, 231.
21. For an example of a crisis, as well as one showing how Senators can generate outside interest, see Richard Harris, *The Real Voice* (New York, 1964).
22. Sundquist, *Politics and Policy,* p. 509; Cleaveland, "Legislating for Urban Areas: An Overview," in Cleaveland, *Congress and Urban Problems,* pp. 352–53; Price, *Who Makes the Laws?;* and Chaples, "Congress Gets New Ideas."
23. See Randall B. Ripley, *Power in the Senate* (New York, 1969), pp. 170–84; Polsby, "Policy Analysis and Congress."

24. See Roger H. Davidson, *The Role of the Congressman* (New York: Pegasus, 1969), chapters 3–4.
25. Price, *Who Makes the Laws?*, p. 172.
26. Nadel, *Politics of Consumer Protection,* pp. 36–37.
27. For examples of the differences of opinion, see Cleaveland, "Overview," p. 352; Price, *Who Makes the Laws?* pp. 310–14; Nadel, *Politics of Consumer Protection,* p. 152; Chaples, "Congress Gets New Ideas"; and Johnannes, *Policy Innovation in Congress,* p. 17.
28. Richard F. Fenno, Jr., *Congressmen in Committees* (Boston, 1973), pp. 278–79.
29. Bibby and Davidson, *On Capitol Hill,* pp. 186–91.
30. Price, *Who Makes the Laws?,* pp. 196, 330–31. More generally, see Samuel C. Patterson, "Congressional Committee Professional Staffing: Capabilities and Constraints," in eds. Kornberg and Musolf, pp. 390–428; and the collection of working papers and testimony in *Committee Organization in the House,* pp. 186–221, 659–91.
31. Harrison W. Fox and Susan Webb Hammond, "Congressional Staffs and Congressional Change," paper presented to the annual meeting of the American Political Science Association, New Orleans, September 1973, esp. pp. 7, 10–13, 27–34.
32. Currin V. Shields, ed., *Considerations on Representative Government* (Indianapolis, 1958), p. 76.
33. Willmoore Kendall, "The Two Majorities," *Midwest Journal of Political Science* 4 (November 1960): 317–45; Saloma, *Congress and the New Politics,* chapter 3.
34. Joseph Cooper and David W. Brady, "Organization Theory and Congressional Structure," paper presented to the annual meeting of the American Political Science Association, New Orleans, September 1973, pp. 34–36.
35. For a discussion of several models for organizing power, see Saloma, *Congress and the New Politics,* chapter 2.

9.5

1. Passage of revenue bills follows the same general procedure as appropriation bills, except that revenue measures are reported by the Ways and Means Committee in the House and by the Finance Committee in the Senate.

9.6

REFERENCES

Arnold, R. Douglas. *Congress and the Bureaucracy.* New Haven, Conn.: Yale University Press, 1979.

Bailey, Stephen K. *Congress Makes a Law.* New York: Columbia University Press, 1950.

Berman, Daniel M. *A Bill Becomes a Law.* New York: Macmillan, 1966.

Eidenberg, Eugene, and Roy Morey. *An Act of Congress.* New York: W. W. Norton, 1969.

Ippolito, Dennis S. *The Budget and National Politics.* San Francisco: W. H. Freeman, 1978.

Jones, Charles O., and Dieter Matthes. "Policy Formation." *Encyclopedia of Policy Studies.* New York: Marcel Dekker, 1982.

LeLoup, Lance T. *The Fiscal Congress: Legislative Control of the Budget.* Westport, Conn.: Greenwood Press, 1980.

Mansfield, Harvey C., ed. *Congress Against the President.* New York: Praeger Publishers, 1975.

Neustadt, Richard E. *Presidential Power.* New York: John Wiley & Sons, 1960.

Peabody, Robert L., et al. *To Enact a Law: Congress and Campaign Financing.* New York: Praeger Publishers, 1972.

Price, David E. *Who Makes the Laws?* Cambridge, Mass.: Schenkman, 1972.

Ranney, Austin, ed. *Political Science and Public Policy.* Chicago: Markham, 1968.

Redman, Eric. *The Dance of Legislation.* New York: Simon & Schuster, 1973.

Ripley, Randall B., and Grace A. Franklin. *Congress, the Bureaucracy, and Public Policy.* Homewood, Ill.: Dorsey Press, 1980.

Schick, Allen. *Congress and Money.* Washington, D.C.: The Urban Institute, 1980.

Sundquist, James L. *Politics and Policy: The Eisenhower, Kennedy, and Johnson Years.* Washington, D.C.: Brookings Institution, 1968.

9.7

1. Raymond A. Bauer, Ithiel de Sola Pool, and Lewis Anthony Dexter, *American Business and Public Policy: The Politics of Foreign Trade* (New York: Atherton Press, 1963), p. 405.
2. Recent writing by political scientists about the political agenda begins with two articles by Peter Bachrach and Morton Baratz, "Two Faces of Power," *American Political Science Review,* December 1962, pp. 947–952; and "Decisions and Nondecisions: An Analytical Framework," *American Political Science Review,* September 1963, pp. 632–642. For a contrary review, see Raymond E. Wolfinger, "Nondecisions and the Study of Local Politics." *American Political Science Review,* December 1971, pp. 1063–80, 1102–11. For a review of the controversy, see Frederick W. Frey, "Comment: On Issues and Non-Issues in the Study of Power," *American Political Science Review,* December 1971, pp. 1081–1101. More recent books and papers include Roger W. Cobb and Charles D. Elder, *Participation in American Politics: The Dynamics of Agenda Building* (Baltimore: Johns Hopkins University Press, 1975); Matthew A. Crenson. *The Unpolitics of Air Pollution* (Baltimore: The Johns Hopkins Press, 1971); Donald A. Schon, *Beyond the Stable State: Public and Private Learning in a Changing Society* (London: Maurice Temple Smith, 1971); David Braybrooke, *Traffic Congestion Goes Through the Issue-Machine* (London: Routledge & Kegan Paul. 1974); Anthony Downs, "Up and Down with Ecology—the 'Issue-Attention Cycle'," *The Public Interest,* Summer 1973, pp. 38–50; J. Clarence Davies, III, "How Does the Agenda Get Set?" resources for the Future Conference Paper, Washington, D.C., January 22, 1974; Stuart H. Rakoff and Guenther F. Schaefer, "Politics, Policy, and Political Science," *Politics and Society,* November

1970; Raymond A. Bauer and Kenneth J. Gergen, eds, *The Study of Policy Formation* (New York: Free Press, 1968); Nelson W. Polsby, "Policy Initiation in the American Political System." in ed. Irving Louis Horowitz, *The Use and Abuse of Social Science,* (New Brunswick, N.J.: Transaction, Inc., 1971); and William Solesbury, "Issues and Innovations in Environmental Policy in Britain, West Germany, and California," *Policy Analysis,* Winter 1976, pp. 1–38.

3. For a good description of the demanding pressures of life in the Senate, see James Boyd, "A Senator's Day," in *Inside the System,* eds. Charles Peters and Timothy Adams (New York: Praeger Publishers, 1970).
4. For descriptions of the interlocking system of subgovernments that guide the formulation of policy in Washington, see J. Leiper Freeman, *The Political Process* (New York: Random House, 1965); Grant McConnell, *Private Power and American Democracy* (New York: Alfred A. Knopf, 1966); and Douglas Cater, *Power in Washington* (New York: Random House, 1964).
5. For insightful commentary on the importance of this factor in encouraging members of Congress to engage in promotional activity, see David E. Price, "Policy-Making in Congressional Committees: The Impact of Environmental Factors."
6. For a similar description of the way information is collected in the Senate, see Allen Schick, "The Supply and Demand for Analysis on Capitol Hill," *Policy Analysis,* Spring 1976.
7. The description of the debate and passage of traffic safety legislation in this section draws directly from David E. Price, "Who Makes the Laws? The Legislative Roles of three Senate Committees," Ph.D. dissertation, Yale University, 1969, pp. 82–107; and Elizabeth B. Drew, "The Politics of Auto Safety," *Atlantic Monthly* (October 1966).
8. New York: Grossman, 1965.
9. For a description, and a slashing attack, on this community, see Nader's chapter on "The Traffic Safety Establishment," in *Unsafe at Any Speed.* Also see Ronald G. Havelock, *Highway Safety Research Communication: Is There a System?* (Ann Arbor, Mich.: Institute for Social Research, The University of Michigan, 1973).
10. Data for the death rate per 100 million miles driven was obtained from the publication *Accident Facts,* published annually by the National Safety Council. The data for the technical literature—defined as articles, monographs or books intended for experts or professionals in the field rather than the general public—came from *The International Bibliography of Highway Safety Research* (Ann Arbor, Mich.: Highway Safety Research Institute, The University of Michigan, 1973). The data on *The New York Times* is the number of column inches on the subject appearing in the *New York Times Index.*
11. For an excellent description of these aspects of the controversy, see Thomas Whiteside, *The Investigation of Ralph Nader* (New York: Pocket Books, 1972).
12. *The Congressional Quarterly Almanac,* 1970, p. 69A.
13. "Does America Need the Occupational Safety and Health Act?" *Journal of American Society of Safety Engineers,* February 1969, p. 8.
14. For a description of the many professional associations with an interest in the safety field, see Bertram D. Dinman, "IMA is not Alone," *Journal of Occupational Medicine,* April 1966, pp. 183–87.
15. Mark V. Nadel, *The Politics of Consumer Protection* (Indianapolis: Bobbs-Merrill, 1971), pp. 36–41.
16. "Analysis of the 1969 Occupational Safety and Health Bill," *Journal of the American Society of Safety Engineers,* December 1969, p. 28.
17. For a good review of recent history in the area, see C. L. Christenson and W. H. Andrews, "Coal Mine Injury Rates in Two Eras of Federal Control," *Journal of Economic Issues,* March 1973, pp. 61–82.
18. Two excellent articles giving details on coal mine safety are Rand Guffey, "Enforcing of New Law Bogs Down Stirring Uproar in Coalfields," *The Wall Street Journal,* June 25, 1970, p. 1; and Bob Harwood, "Bitter Miners Assert the 'Black Lung' Law Is Filled with Loopholes," *The Wall Street Journal,* September 24, 1971, p. 1.
19. The state of the art is described in Thomas Lindley Ehrich, "Broad Research Is Launched into Removing Some of the Deadly Hazards of Coal Mining," *The Wall Street Journal,* June 15, 1971, p. 30; John V. Conti, "Coal Mine Study Shows Record Can Be Improved When Firms Really Try," *The Wall Street Journal,* January 18, 1973, p. 1; W. H. Andrews and C. L. Christenson, "Some Economic Factors Affecting Safety in Underground Bituminous Coal Mines," *Southern Economic Journal,* January 1974, pp. 364–76; and "Coal: Where Management and Labor Share the Blame," *Business Week,* November 2, 1974, pp. 76–77.
20. Data on coverage in the *New York Times* is collected in the same manner as in Figure 9.7.2—see footnote 10—but data for the technical literature were collected from *Index Medicus* and *The Engineering Index,* and data for death rates were collected from *The Yearbook of Labor Statistics* (U.S. Department of Labor).
21. See C. L. Christenson and W. H. Andrews, "Coal Mine Injury Rates in Two Eras of Federal Control."
22. Data for this figure were collected from the same sources employed for Figure 9.7.3—see footnote 20.
23. "A Message from the President," *Journal of the American Society of Safety Engineers,* April 1968, p. 9.
24. For a follow-up story on the inadequate—in fact, virtually nonexistent enforcement of the bill, see Ben A. Franklin, "The Dam Builders, Congressional Pets," *New York Times,* July 4, 1976, D4.
25. Many examples of this shifting basis for debate can be found in the period from 1974 to the present. A recent one is: James W. Singer, "NEW OSHA Task Force—New Political Payoff or False Alarm," *National Journal,* July 10, 1976, pp. 973–75.
26. Matthew A. Crenson. *The Un-Politics of Air Pollution* (Baltimore: Johns Hopkins University Press, 1971), p. 172.
27. For a thoughtful analysis of the importance of different kinds of problems in affecting the political agenda, see Albert O. Hirschman, "Policy-Making and Policy Analysis in Latin America—A Return Journey," *Policy Sciences* (forthcoming).
28. Nelson J. Polsby, "Goodbye to the Inner Club," in ed. Norman J. Ornstein, *Congress in Change, Evolution and Reform* (New York: Praeger Publishers, 1975), p. 215.
29. (New York: Random House, 1980). Matthews' book

covers the years 1947–1957, the decade prior to the rapid growth of liberal strength in the elections from 1958 through 1968.

30. Kenneth J. Arrow, *The Limits of Organization* (New York: W.W. Norton, 1974), pp. 47–48.
31. This interpretation of recent developments in the Senate comes directly from David W. Rohde, Norman J. Ornstein, and Robert L. Peabody, "Political Change and Legislative Norms in the United States Senate," paper delivered at the 1974 annual meeting of the American Political Science Association, August, 1974. Also see Nelson J. Polsby, "Goodbye to the Inner Club."

9.8

REFERENCES

Huntington, S. P. *The Common Defense*. New York: Columbia University Press, 1961.

Lowi, T. J. "Making Democracy Safe for the World: National Politics and Foreign Policy." In *Domestic Sources of Foreign Policy*. Edited by J. N. Rosenau. New York: Free Press, 1967.

9.9

1. In recent years the study of policy effects has effloresced among analysts writing in a number of different scholarly traditions. The range of writings on policies substantially shaped by Congress includes the following: James T. Bonnen, "The Distribution of Benefits from Cotton Price Supports," in *Problems in Public Expenditure Analysis,* ed. Samuel B. Chase (Washington, D.C.: Brookings Institution, 1968); on urban renewal: Theodore J. Lowi, *The End of Liberalism* (New York: W. W. Norton, 1969), chapter 9; Richard Urban and Richard Mancke, "Federal Regulation of Whisky Labelling: From the Repeal of Prohibition to the Present," *Journal of Law and Economics* 15 (1972): 411–26; Richard S. Smerne, Alvin Rabushka, and Helen A. Scott, "Serving the Elderly—An Illustration of the Niskanen Effect," *Public Choice* 13 (1972): 81–90; A. Bruce Johnson, "Federal Aid and Area Redevelopment," *Journal of Law and Economics* 14 (1971): 245–84; James W. Davis, Jr., and Kenneth M. Dolbeare, "Selective Service and Military Manpower: Induction and Deferment Policies in the 1960's" chapter 5 in *Political Science and Public Policy,* ed. Austin Ranney (Chicago: Markham, 1968); Yale Brozen, "The Effect of Statutory Minimum Wage Increases on Teen-Age Employment," *Journal of Law and Economics* 12 (1969): 109–22; on national policies generally: Charles L. Schultze, et al., Setting National Priorities, the 1973 Budget (Washington, D.C.: Brookings, 1972), chapter 15. There is an analysis of the attention (or rather the lack of it) that Congress gave to impact at the time it considered a policy decision in Aaron Wildavsky, "The Politics of ABM," *Commentary,* November 1969, pp. 55–63.
2. Thus, for example, this critique: "The people of this country . . . are, as it seems to me, thoroughly tired of the stagnation of business and the general inaction of Congress. They are disgusted to see year after year go by and great measures affecting the business and political interests of the country accumulation at the doors of Congress and never reach the stage of action." The author was Henry Cabot Lodge in 1889. Quoted in George B. Galloway, *History of the House of Representatives* (New York: Thomas Y. Crowell, 1961), p. 133.
3. Roger H. Davidson, David M. Kovenock, and Michael K. O'Leary, *Congress in Crisis* (Belmont, Calif.: Wadsworth, 1966), pp. 56–59.
4. See G. L. Bach, *Making Monetary and Fiscal Policy* (Washington, D.C.: Brookings Institution, 1971), pp. 118, 155.
5. The only theories of legislative logrolling that make any sense are the ones that impose information costs on observers. Thus Barry on the "pork barrel": "[I]t is perhaps easy to guess that logrolling under conditions of imperfect information will tend to produce over-investment in projects which yield specific benefits to determinate groups, because such benefits are highly visible to the beneficiaries whereas costs are not so visible to the general taxpayer." Brian Barry, *Political Argument,* (London: Routledge and Kegan Paul, 1965), p. 318.
6. John F. Manley, *The Politics of Finance: The House Committee on Ways and Means* (Boston: Little, Brown, 1970), p. 309. Coleman makes the relevant point that Keynesian macroeconomics is after all an "organic-type theory" not built by aggregating individual preferences. "The fact that Keynes' goal is a benevolent one, supposedly beneficial to the people, has often obscured the fact that its perspective is that of the state, and that there is no microeconomic substructure through which individual pursuit of their interests leads to a Keynesian policy." "Individual Interests and Collective Action," pp. 53–54.
7. Edward C. Banfield, "Revenue Sharing in Theory and Practice," *The Public Interest,* Spring 1971, pp. 41–42.
8. On struggles over the corps under Roosevelt and Truman, see Arthur Maass, *Muddy Waters: The Army Engineers and the Nation's Rivers* (Cambridge, Mass.: Harvard University Press, 1951), chapters 3, 5. Particularism is no doubt universal. It is hard to top this example drawn from the experience of the Italian parliament of the late 19th century: "The deputies, in fact, look upon themselves as agents to procure favors for their constituents, and a striking illustration of the extent to which this is carried is furnished by the difficulty the government found when it managed the railroads in running fast express trains, on account of the interference of the members of the chamber, who insisted that all the trains passing through their districts should stop at way stations." A. L. Lowell, *Governments and Parties in Continental Europe* (Boston: Houghton Mifflin, 1896), I: 220.
9. Sets of voters who are organized for political action should not be confused with sets of voters who have intense preferences. Whether the latter become the former depends upon whether there are incentives to organize and stay organized. One specific pattern is that

producers have better incentives than consumers. On the general point, see Mancur Olson, Jr., *The Logic of Collective Action* (Cambridge, Mass.: Harvard University Press, 1965), pp. 125–31; and Barry, *Political Argument*, p. 273.

10. E. E. Schattschneider, *Party Government* (New York: Rinehart, 1959), p. 194. In the 1930s, 1931 and 1936 were the only years in which the fiscal effects of tax and spending activities of American governments (at all levels) were clearly countercyclical. In both cases the Keynesian instruments were apparently veterans' bonus bills passed over presidential vetoes (Hoover's and Roosevelt's). See E. Cary Brown, "Fiscal Policies in the Thirties: A Reappraisal," *American Economic Review* 46 (1956): 483.
11. "It is difficult to imagine any other issue on which Congress has been less responsive to public sentiment for a longer period of time." Hazel Erskine, "The Polls: Gun Control," *Public Opinion Quarterly* 36 (1972): 456.
12. There is an analysis of agricultural clientelism in Lowi, *The End of Liberalism*, pp. 102–15. A clientele system less developed in Congress than in some European parliaments is the one in education. With the nationalization of educational financing it seems likely that the two congressional houses will sooner or later create independent education committees (separate from labor) whose members will service education groups in bipartisan fashion.
13. The best analysis of the impact of Congressmen's electoral needs on the organization of the Executive Branch is in Harold Seidman, *Politics, Position, and Power: The Dynamics of Federal Organization* (New York: Oxford University Press, 1970): chapters 2, 5.

10.1

1. For a concise analysis of the emergence of Congress as an institution, see Randall B. Ripley, *Congress: Process and Policy* (New York: W. W. Norton, 1975), pp. 27–57; and Malcolm E. Jewell and Samuel C. Patterson, *The Legislative Process in the United States*, 3d ed. (New York: Random House, 1977), pp. 30–59.
2. Samuel P. Huntington, *Political Order in Changing Societies* (New Haven: Yale University Press, 1968), pp. 93–139.
3. George B. Galloway, *Congress at the Crossroads* (New York: Thomas Y. Crowell, 1946), p. 334.

10.3

1. Associated Press/NBC News Poll 66, April 1981.
2. Richard F. Fenno, Jr., *Home Style: House Members in their Districts* (Boston: Little, Brown, 1978), p. 168.
3. Glenn R. Parker and Roger H. Davidson, "Why Do Americans Love Their Congressmen So Much More than Their Congress?" *Legislative Studies Quarterly* 4 (February 1979): 53–61.
4. U.S. House of Representatives, Commission on Administrative Review, *Administrative Reorganization and Legislative Management* H. Doc. 95–232 (95th Congress, 1st session, 1977), vol. 2, pp. 20–22; Allen Schick, "Complex Policymaking in the United States Senate," U.S. Senate, Commission on the Operation of the Senate, *Policy Analysis on Major Issues*, Committee Print (94th Congress, 2d session, 1977), p. 6.
5. Schick, "Complex Policymaking," p. 7.
6. Clark F. Norton, *Congressional Approval and Disapproval Resolutions, 1975–1980* (Congressional Research Service, March 19, 1981), mimeographed.
7. See U.S. Senate, Committee on Rules and Administration, *Committee Systems Reorganization of 1977*, S. Rept. 95–2 (95th Congress, 1st session).
8. Two reliable accounts of aspects of the change are: Norman J. Ornstein, "Causes and Consequences of Congressional Change: Subcommittee Reforms in the House of Representatives, 1970–73," in ed. Norman J. Ornstein, *Congress in Change* (New York: Praeger Publishers, 1975), pp. 88–114; and David W. Rhode, "Committee Reform in the House of Representatives and the Subcommittee Bill of Rights," *Annals of the American Academy of Political and Social Sciences* 411 (January 1974): 39–47.
9. H. Douglas Price, "Congress and the Evolution of Legislative 'Professionalism'," in Ornstein, *Congress in Change*, p. 19.
10. Harrison W. Fox, Jr., and Susan Webb Hammond, *Congressional Staffs* (New York: Free Press, 1977), pp. 168, 171.
11. See Spark M. Matsunaga and Ping Chen, *Rulemakers of the House* (Urbana: University of Illinois Press, 1976), pp. 52–54, 60ff.
12. Daniel F. Mulhollan and Arthur G. Stevens, "Congressional Liaison and the Rise of Informal Groups in Congress," paper presented at the annual meeting of the Western Political Science Association, March 1979.
13. Roger H. Davidson and Walter J. Oleszek, *Congress Against Itself* (Bloomington: Indiana University Press, 1977).
14. Commission on the Organization of the Government for the Conduct of Foreign Policy, *Report*, Appendix vol. 5 (Washington: Government Printing Office, 1975), Appendix M.
15. U.S. House of Representatives, Commission on Administrative Review, *Report*, H. Doc. 95–272 (95th Congress, 1st session, 1977), vol. 2, pp. 868–69.
16. Richard F. Fenno, Jr., *Congressmen in Committees* (Boston: Little, Brown, 1973), chapter 1.
17. *Congressional Quarterly Weekly Report* 3 (April 5, 1980): 908.
18. U.S. House of Representatives, Commission on Administrative Review, *Final Report*, vol. 2, pp. 814–16, 830–31.
19. Rhodes Cook, "Midterm Elections: Past Trends Indicate Small Democratic Loss," *Congressional Quarterly Weekly Report* 38 (March 15, 1978): 755.
20. From research completed by John S. Saloma, III, and reported in Donald G. Tacheron and Morris K. Udall, *The Job of the Congressman* (Indianapolis, Ind.: Bobbs-Merrill, 1966), pp. 280–81.
21. U.S. House of Representatives, Commission on Administrative Review, *Administrative Reorganization and Legislative Management*, vol. 2, p. 18.
22. U.S. House of Representatives, Commission on Administrative Review, *Final Report*, vol. 2, pp. 875–76.
23. Roger H. Davidson, David M. Kovenock, and Michael

K. O'Leary, *Congress in Crisis* (Belmont, Calif.: Wadsworth, 1966), p. 76.
24. Davidson and Oleszak, *Congress Against Itself.*
25. U.S. House of Representatives, Commission on Administrative Review, *Final Report,* vol. 2, p. 869.
26. Ann Cooper, "Ex-Members of Congress: Some Go Home, Many Don't," *Congressional Quarterly Weekly Report* 35 (September 17, 1977): 1970–71.

10.4

1. The most convenient coverage of Koreagate is found in the *Congressional Quarterly Weekly Reports* for 1977 and 1978.
2. See *Congressional Quarterly Weekly Report* 38 (February 9, 1980): 340–42 for the pre-Abscam cases.
3. Charles McGrane, ed., *The Correspondence of Nicholas Biddle* (Boston: Houghton Mifflin, 1919), p. 218.
4. For a review of the codes, see Robert S. Getz, *Congressional Ethics: The Conflict of Interest Issue* (New York: Van Nostrand Reinhold, 1967), chapter 2.
5. T. R. Reid, "The Rich Man's Club," *Washington Post,* March 14, 1977, pp. A1–A4.
6. Quoted in *Congressional Quarterly Weekly Report* 35 (March 5, 1977): 388; see pp. 387–91 for details of the House code.
7. Quoted in *Congressional Quarterly Weekly Report* 35 (April 2, 1977): 591; see pp. 596–99 for details of Senate code.
8. For a comprehensive review of disclosure, see *Congressional Quarterly Weekly Report* 37 (September 1, 1979): 1823–92. The Richmond example is from p. 1830.
9. *Congressional Quarterly Weekly Report* 37 (March 10, 1979): 399.
10. *Congressional Quarterly Weekly Report* 38 (August 23, 1980): 2466.
11. *Congressional Quarterly Weekly Report* 37 (September 1, 1979): 1824–25.
12. Quoted in *Congressional Quarterly Weekly Report* 38 (February 9, 1980): 330.
13. *Ibid.,* p. 331.
14. Quoted by Larry L. King, "Dear Congressman: Is Doddism Dead?" *New York Times Magazine,* April 16, 1967, p. 26.